HOUGHTON MIFFLIN

Math Steps

Teacher Edition
LEVEL 1

Contents

HOUGHTON MIFFLIN

Boston • Atlanta • Dallas • Denver • Geneva, Illinois • Palo Alto • Princeton

Grateful acknowledgment is given for the contributions of

Student Book

Rosemary Theresa Barry
Karen R. Boyle
Barbara Brozman
Gary S. Bush
John E. Cassidy
Dorothy Kirk

Sharon Ann Kovalcik
Bernice Kubek
Donna Marie Kvasnok
Ann Cherney Markunas
Joanne Marie Mascha
Kathleen Mary Ogrin

Judith Ostrowski
Jeanette Mishic Polomsky
Patricia Stenger
Annabelle L. Higgins Svete

Teacher Book
Contributing Writers

Dr. Judy Curran Buck
Assistant Professor of Mathematics
Plymouth State College
Plymouth, New Hampshire

Dr. Richard Evans
Professor of Mathematics
Plymouth State College
Plymouth, New Hampshire

Dr. Mary K. Porter
Professor of Mathematics
St. Mary's College
Notre Dame, Indiana

Dr. Anne M. Raymond
Assistant Professor of Mathematics
Keene State College
Keene, New Hampshire

Stuart P. Robertson, Jr.
Education Consultant
Pelham, New Hampshire

Dr. David Rock
Associate Professor,
Mathematics Education
University of Mississippi
Oxford, Mississippi

Michelle Lynn Rock
Elementary Teacher
Oxford School District
Oxford, Mississippi

Dr. Jean M. Shaw
Professor of Elementary Education
University of Mississippi
Oxford, Mississippi

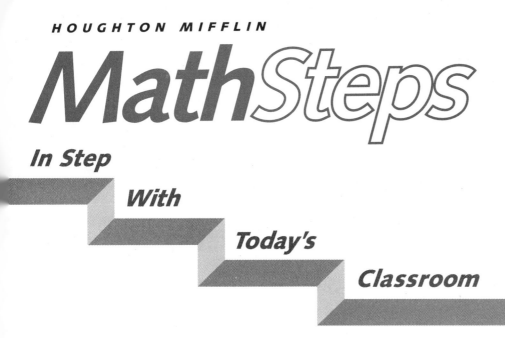

HOUGHTON MIFFLIN

MathSteps

In Step With Today's Classroom

What is *MathSteps* ?

 MathSteps is a Kindergarten through Middle grades mathematics program that *explicitly teaches* all the essential content covered at your grade level.

 MathSteps is the one program *designed* to focus specifically on the development of skills and sub-skills, so that all students can be successful.

 MathSteps is the *highly systematic,* step-by-step instructional plan that's easier for students to follow—and easier to implement efficiently and effectively in any classroom.

 MathSteps is the comprehensive program that even offers a fully integrated, *easily managed* Tutorial for intervention and remediation.

MathSteps is the *right step* for teachers and students alike, to improve skills mastery, build confidence in mathematics, and rise to higher standards of success.

What does *MathSteps* offer?

 MathSteps uses an explicit instructional approach that clearly develops the mathematical content. Operations, thinking skills, problem solving, estimation, data, statistics, geometry, and probability are emphasized appropriately at all grade levels.

 MathSteps' instructional philosophy is incorporated into Workbook texts that provide a consistent, easy-to-use format.

 MathSteps follows a simple structure, supporting a natural teaching and learning style with:

- Clear, unambiguous teaching models that begin each lesson, helping teachers convey procedures and rules.

- Carefully selected exercises that provide practice of new learning and lead students toward mastery of skills.

- Two Problem Solving lessons in every unit that teach a systematic problem solving plan.

- Frequent "Quick Checks" that provide ongoing assessment opportunities and integrate fully with the Tutorial kit.

HOUGHTON MIFFLIN

MathSteps

What is the *MathSteps* Skills Tutorial?

 The Skills Tutorial is an individualized diagnostic and prescriptive program designed to help all students master computational skills. It is a total package that includes all the materials you need for pre- and post-testing, instructional practice, and record keeping.

 The Skills Tutorial is organized by grade level, by strand, and by skill, with a:

- Teaching Card for each skill

- Practice Sheet for each skill

- Comprehensive Teacher Manual

- Diagnostic Computation Test

For your convenience, the entire **Skills Tutorial** is available on CD-ROM.

MathSteps :

What every student needs!

Lesson Support Contents

Unit 1 • Geometry

📖 Teaching Strategies: Your In-Service Handbook

Lesson Support

Annotated Student Book

The annotated Student Book for Unit 1 may be found on pages 1–26.

Unit 2 • Numbers through 10 and Data

Annotated Student Book

The annotated Student Book for Unit 2 may be found on pages 31–64.

Unit 3 • Addition Facts through 6

Annotated Student Book

The annotated Student Book for Unit 3 may be found on pages 65–92.

Unit 4 • Subtracting from 6 or Less

Annotated Student Book

The annotated Student Book for Unit 4 may be found on pages 93–112.

Unit 5 • Addition and Subtraction Facts through 6

Annotated Student Book

The annotated Student Book for Unit 5 may be found on pages 113–134.

Unit 6 • Addition and Subtraction Facts through 10

Teaching Strategies: Your In-Service Handbook

Lesson Support

Annotated Student Book

The annotated Student Book for Unit 6 may be found on pages 135–164.

Unit 7 • Place Value through 99

Teaching Strategies: Your In-Service Handbook

Lesson Support

Annotated Student Book

The annotated Student Book for Unit 7 may be found on pages 165–198.

Unit 8 • Time and Money

Annotated Student Book

The annotated Student Book for Unit 8 may be found on pages 199–226.

Unit 9 • 2-Digit Addition and Subtraction

Teaching Strategies: Your In-Service Handbook

Lesson Support

Annotated Student Book

The annotated Student Book for Unit 9 may be found on pages 227–250.

Unit 10 • Fractions and Measurements

Annotated Student Book

The annotated Student Book for Unit 10 may be found on pages 251–278.

Unit 11 • Addition and Subtraction Facts through 20

Lesson
Support

Geometry

Vocabulary

- above
- after
- before
- behind
- below
- between
- circle
- cone
- corner
- cube
- cylinder
- face
- far
- in front of
- left
- near
- next to
- pattern
- pyramid
- rectangle
- rectangular prism
- right
- same shape
- same size
- side
- sphere
- square
- symmetry
- triangle

Unit Objectives

1A Identify, classify, and sort plane and solid figures by common attributes

1B Compare the size, shape, and position of geometric figures

1C Determine location by using a picture; use Find a Pattern and other strategies to solve problems

About This Unit

The support pages that follow provide more information on prerequisite skills, methods for teaching skills and concepts, daily routines, tips on classroom management and materials, and useful dialogue techniques.

Assessments
Use Beginning of the Year Inventory for entry-level assessment.

Ongoing Evaluation Quick Checks, Reteach Worksheets, the Skills Tutorial Inventories and the Midyear Test help ensure that children are progressing adequately to meet the standards.

Summative Evaluation Use Test Preps, Unit Review (p. T25), Cumulative Review (p. T26), and Reteach Worksheets to assure that children have achieved the standards for the unit.

Diagnosing Errors The Quick Checks highlight common errors and provide remediation. See also the **Teaching Strategies Handbook** pp. T16–T19, where short discussions labeled Common Misconceptions appear as needed with the strategies for key concepts.

Homework and Family Involvement
Home Note In the Student Book, the Dear Family Home Note provides objectives, vocabulary, and a sample skill discussion for family participation. (**Teaching Strategies Handbook** pages also provide homework and family involvement tips.)

Education Place Refer families to Houghton Mifflin's EduPlace Web site at http://www.eduplace.com; for resources and activities for students at http://www.eduplace.com/math; and additional resources and activities at http://www.eduplace.com/parents.

Helping Your Children Learn Math This book has activities for children ages 5–13 and tips for getting involved in children's mathematics education. (Houghton Mifflin, 1994)

Lessons	Student Pages	Teacher Pages	Resources	State or Local	
				Objectives	Assessment
1.1 Solids	3–4	**T20**	Unit 1 Pretest		
1.2 Relating Solids to Plane Figures	5–6	**T20**			
1.3 Plane Figures	7–8	**T21**	Reteach 1, 2, 3; Extension 1, 2, 3; Teaching Resource 1		
1.4 Position of Figures	9–10	**T21**			
1.5 Sides and Corners	11–12	**T22**			
1.6 Same Size and Same Shape	13–14	**T22**	Reteach 4, 5, 6; Teaching Resource 2		
1.7 Problem Solving Strategy: Find a Pattern	15–16	**T23**			
1.8 Symmetry	17–18	**T23**	Reteach 7		
1.9 Problem Solving Application: Use a Picture	19–20	**T24**			
1.10 Follow Directions	21–22	**T24**	Unit 1 Posttest; Reteach 8		

Teaching Strategies

Math Background — Geometry

Geometry, the spatial side of mathematics, concerns figures and their relationships. As children work with two- and three-dimensional figures, such as circles, triangles, squares, rectangles, spheres, cones, and cubes, they'll build a vocabulary that identifies and describes objects in their world. Many of the solids and planes in this unit will be familiar to them.

Geometry also helps children develop strong reasoning skills. When children compare figures, focus on their attributes (size; number of surfaces, sides, or corners), and make groups of shapes, they are building vital thinking skills. Work in geometry also provides opportunities for children to use positional vocabulary words such as *beside, between, near,* and *far* and to develop skills in working with patterns.

A Positive Start

Geometry is an exciting topic for the beginning of Level 1. Children have handled three-dimensional objects all of their lives and many children can already identify common shapes. You can easily extend their knowledge and engage their attention through visual and tactile learning. With your guidance, they'll make relevant connections to geometry in the world. You'll get them off to a great start and foster your own self-confidence in teaching mathematics.

Linking Past and Future Learning

The chart shows key concepts for this unit that children learned in kindergarten—and what they'll learn next year. Knowing the scope of the unit's basic skills and concepts can help you focus your instruction.

Concept/Skills	Last Year	This Year	Next Year
Solid and Plane Figures	Identify solid and plane figures	Identify, describe, compare, and sort solid and plane figures	Identify, describe, and classify solid and plane figures; identify and describe congruent and symmetrical figures
Positions	Use positional terms to describe the location of objects	Identify the position of figures	Identify ordinal numbers first through twentieth
Geometric Patterns	Recognize patterns and identify the next object in sequence	Identify the next geometric figure in sequence in color, shape, and size patterns	Identify number patterns

Methods and Management

This unit relies on many types of materials to make the content meaningful. Gather your materials ahead of time. Also, you'll work on vocabulary as you go along, so skim the pages to see what words you and the children will be using.

Teaching Strategy: Solid and Plane Figures

Geometry is inherently visual, and drawing and tracing figures provides children with a multisensory approach as they explore plane and solid geometric figures. Counting the number of sides and corners helps children to identify the plane figure. Demonstrate with drawings and cutout figures to show where these attributes are. Then let children point to or trace them with their hands.

- Help children focus on properties, or attributes, of figures. Model your thinking as you present figures by saying, *Here's a square. Let's see, four sides— 1, 2, 3, 4, and they're all the same length. Four corners, too—1, 2 3, 4.*

▶ *Then Ask: What is the name for this figure? How many sides does it have? Does this figure have any corners? How many? What is it called?*

- Let children handle solids, and describe and classify them. Have children point out classroom examples such as a filing cabinet, building blocks, paperweights, or a globe.

▶ *Vocabulary Development* As you introduce the names of figures and show examples, let children repeat the names, in unison and individually. You may also want to write and display the figure names, so that children will be exposed to them on a regular basis.

▶ *Common Misconceptions* Many children may confuse squares with other rectangles because all have four sides and square corners. Be sure that the rectangular models you present have a pair of sides that are distinctly longer than the other two sides.

Teaching Strategy: Positions

Words and phrases such as *next to, above, between,* and *far away from* are essential in everyday life. When teaching geometry, it's easy and natural to use these positional words.

- Give each child a cube and a paper triangle. Say: *Put the cube on top of your head,* below *your chair seat,* beside *the triangle.* Vary the game by letting one child place the cube while a partner tells where the cube is in relation to the triangle.

- Place three or more solid figures in a line, and establish that the line begins at the children's left. After children name the figures, ask which figure is *between, next to, before,* or *after* others.

Warming Up Once you have introduced the names of figures, start each lesson by showing examples and letting children say the names in unison.

Collecting Materials Collect as many real-world examples of geometric figures as you can. Use them for identifying and sorting, as well as demonstrating that geometry is all around us. Children's family members may be able to send examples, too.

Good Routine As you finish using materials, delegate children to help put them away. Though it may be easier to do it yourself, remember that you are establishing a routine of caring for materials and assuming responsibility.

Diverse Learning Place shapes in a bag or box and let children search with their hands for the one you designate. Encourage children to talk about the shapes they are seeing and feeling.

Getting Physical Tape outlines of large plane figures to the floor, and let children walk around them, counting sides or corners as they do so.

Sorting and Classifying Give children a variety of plane and solid figures. Ask them to sort them and tell the rule they used for sorting.

Extra Practice Any spare minute can be used to reinforce positional vocabulary. As children line up, let them tell who's *next to* them, which classmates they're *between*, who's on their *right* or *left*, or who's *near* them.

Good Routine Post your daily schedule, and ask children to describe events with positional words: *What comes* after *math time? What do we do right* before *lunch? What activity is* last *in the day?*

More Positions Ask three or four children to line up, and let classmates describe their positions using several pertinent words or phrases.

Figure Search Post paper figures around the room and play "I Spy." Give clues such as the following: *I spy a figure in the* back *of the room. It's* up high, *to the* left *of a red one. Which one is it?*

Kids in Patterns Use children to model patterns—for example, one sitting, one standing, one sitting, one standing. Or have 6–8 children hold large paper shapes and line up; then, let classmates extend the pattern.

Pacing Tip Try to keep children's attention by moving at a brisk pace, by offering lots of positive reinforcement for paying attention, and by using a variety of materials.

Quick Check Every once in a while, let children do a quick "thumbs up" or "thumbs down" to respond to each other's answers. This will provide a reason to pay attention to each response.

▶ *Common Misconceptions* Often several positional words may fit a situation, so encourage multiple responses with questions such as, *Are there other ways to tell about the position of the circle?*

▶ *Vocabulary Development* You may want to make word cards for the most important positional words from the unit. Not all children will be able to read them at this point, but use the cards as you and the children demonstrate and use positions to locate objects.

Teaching Strategy: Geometric Patterns

Start with simple repeating patterns. Be sure to give children opportunities to describe, extend, and explain the patterns they see and make.

- Start with patterns that repeat two elements: ABABAB. Using figures such as cone, cube, cone, cube, create a pattern stem of at least two repetitions; then, ask children what is likely to come next. Let them arrange two-dimensional cutouts and then extend and tell about the patterns.

Vary the patterns you present by changing the orientation of the shapes or figures.

▶ *Ask: What figure will come next? Why do you think so?*

▶ *Common Misconceptions* Children may mistake an ABAB pattern for one that is ABAABA. Help them identify which part it is that repeats and say the shape names: *Circle, square, circle, square, circle square—What would come next?* Having a child draw a line under the repeating part may help.

Opportunities to Assess

Observation

Use this first unit to get to know the children better. By observing them, listening to their responses, looking at their papers, and observing their work habits you can identify and make notes of those who are eager to respond, those who need to build self-confidence, and those whose attention must be focused.

Homework

Ask children to bring in examples of the shapes or patterns you are studying. Use the objects for "show and tell" sessions, or display them on a sharing table, perhaps arranged in categories with child-made labels.

 ### Family Involvement

The Dear Family note in the Student Book provides information on this unit to families. You may need to arrange additional opportunities for families to participate in the unit—providing materials, making visuals, and working with children at home in recognizing and naming geometric figures.

Teacher/Student Dialogue

How to Extend Responses

As you engage children in discussion of geometric figures, often you can start with questions that invite several answers. See what children say, and then help them extend and focus their responses.

Teacher: (*Displays a red triangle, cut from paper*) Here's another figure. What can you tell about it?

Student: *It's red.*

Teacher: Yes. What else can you say about it? Children?

Students: (*Several respond*) *A triangle! It's a triangle!*

Teacher: How do you know it's a triangle? Kim.

Student: *It looks like this. (Makes a triangular shape with hands.)*

Teacher: Okay, Kim. Come show us. Trace around the triangle and tell us what you are tracing. Here's one . . . (*Guides student*)

Student: *Side. Here's a side. And here's a side.*

Teacher: It has three sides. It has corners, too. Bill, show us the corners.

Student: (*Complies and leads more counting*)

Teacher: So, everyone, can you tell me all the things we know about this triangle? (*Helps children reiterate and then places a circle cutout next to the triangle. After soliciting information about the position of the circle, the teacher pursues more information about the circle's properties.*)

Questioning Techniques

You can complement children's verbal responses by asking them to touch and point. Here are some additional tried and true questioning techniques:

- Begin with a question that has many good answers.

- When you repeat or reword a child's response, it not only acknowledges the answer in a positive way, but it can also presents the information again, providing reinforcement for all the children. But avoid too much repeating—children will tune you out.

- Phrases such as *What else, Tell me more,* and *What other things* let children know that many responses may be appropriate to describe a figure.

What to do

When

At the beginning of the unit, start a list of geometric figures from everyday life. Post the list, and as the unit proceeds, encourage children to dictate additions to it. Include examples of patterns with figures and shapes, too.

What to do

Every Day

Begin or end with a two-minute review of vocabulary and concepts. This will help keep ideas alive and let children use the growing list of words from the unit.

LESSON 1
PAGES 3–4

OBJECTIVE
Identify spheres, cylinders, cubes, rectangular prisms, cones, and pyramids; sort solids and explain sorting rules

PREREQUISITES
Concepts
• Understand the concept of same and different

Skills
• To recognize same and different
• To sort

VOCABULARY
pyramid, sphere, rectangular prism, cone, cube, cylinder

MATERIALS
box

Solids

Presenting the Lesson
Introduce the Skill Draw a square on the chalkboard. Show children a box. Ask questions about each figure to guide children to see the 2-dimensionality of the square and the 3-dimensionality of the box. For example: *Can you see how long the square is? the box? Can you see how wide the square is? the box? Can you see how deep the square is? the box?* Have children look at the figures at the top of page 3. Read the names of each.

Check Understanding Ask, *How is a rectangular prism like a cube? How is it different?* (Answers will vary. Possible answer: Alike: both have straight edges; Different: prism has different length edges, cube has all of the same length edges.)

Guided Practice
Complete exercise 1 with the class. Then discuss the solids at the top of page 4. Discuss how children can sort them. Guide children to see that some solids have curves and some do not.

Independent Practice
Have children complete the remaining exercises on pages 3 and 4 independently.

Closing the Lesson Ask, *Which solids can roll?* (sphere, cylinder, cone) *Which can not?* (pyramid, rectangular prism, cube)

LESSON 2
PAGES 5–6

OBJECTIVE
Identify plane figures as faces of solids

PREREQUISITES
Concepts
• Understand concepts of 2-dimensional and 3-dimensional figures

Skills
• To recognize and identify solid figures
• To recognize plane figures

VOCABULARY
face

MATERIALS
boxes, cans

Relating Solids to Plane Figures

Presenting the Lesson
Introduce the Skill Bring in or have volunteers bring in empty solid containers such as boxes or cans. Have children experiment by tracing different faces of the solids. Guide children to see that they can trace the flat faces of the figures, but not the curved sides.

Check Understanding Ask, *Can you trace the face of a sphere ?* (No) *Why or why not?* (Answers will vary. Possible answer: It has no faces.)

Guided Practice
Have children do exercises 1 and 5. Check that they understand the figure must match the shaded face of the solid.

Independent Practice
Have children complete the remaining exercises on pages 5 and 6 independently.

Closing the Lesson Ask, *If you want to draw a circle, which solid would you trace?* (a cone)

LESSON 3
PAGES 7–8

OBJECTIVE
Identify, describe, and compare triangles, circles, squares, and rectangles

PREREQUISITES
Concepts
• Understand concepts of 2-dimensional and 2-dimensional shapes
• Understand the concept of attributes

Skills
• To recognize sides and corners
• To recognize same and different

VOCABULARY
triangle, square, rectangle, circle

MATERIALS
triangle, square, rectangle, and square cut outs, box

Copymasters
Reteach 1–3, pp. 71–73
Extension 1–3, pp. 163–165
Teaching Resource 1, (Shapes) p. 199

Plane Figures

Presenting the Lesson
Introduce the Skill   Place cut outs of triangles, rectangles, squares, and circles in a box. Use Teaching Resource 1 for figures. Demonstrate how to pick out a figure, hide it, and describe it. Have children guess the figure. Then have volunteers take turns picking out and describing figures for the rest of the class to guess. Let children use the pictures at the top of page 7 to identify and describe the figures.

Check Understanding   Ask, *How is a square like a triangle? How is it different?* (Answers will vary. Possible answer: Alike: Both have straight sides and corners; Different: A square has 4 sides and a triangle has 3 sides.)

Guided Practice
Work together with the class as they color the figures on page 7. Check that they know which color to make each figure. Have children compare their pictures before going on to page 8.

Independent Practice
Have children complete the exercises on page 8 independently. Use the Quick Check for assessment.

Closing the Lesson   Ask, *How are all triangles alike? How can they be different?* (They all have 3 sides; they can be different sizes.)

LESSON 4
PAGES 9–10

OBJECTIVE
Identify the position of figures

PREREQUISITES
Concepts
• Understand the concept of plane figures and position

Skills
• Identify circles, squares, rectangles, and triangles

VOCABULARY
before, after, between

Position of Figures

Presenting the Lesson
Introduce the Skill   Line up 5 children in the front of the room. Give position clues about a child and have classmates guess the name. If they are correct they can take that person's place. Give clues such as: *I am thinking of the child who is after John, but before Pam.* Then read the examples on page 9 together with the class.

Check Understanding   Ask, *How would you describe the position of the square at the top of page 9?* (Answers will vary. Possible answer: It is between the two triangles.)

Guided Practice
Have children complete exercises 1 and 2. Check that they first identify the two figures they are working with, then identify the one in the correct position.

Independent Practice
Have children complete the remaining exercises independently.

Closing the Lesson   Ask, *If you are first in a line can anyone be before you? After you?* (No; Yes)

LESSON 5
PAGES 11–12

OBJECTIVE
Identify the number of sides and corners of a plane figure

PREREQUISITES
Concepts
• Understand the concept of numbers
• Understand the concept of plane figures

Skills
• Count and write 0 through 6
• Recognize plane figures

VOCABULARY
sides, corners

MATERIALS
masking tape

Sides and Corners

Presenting the Lesson
Introduce the Skill   Use masking tape to make a large rectangle on the floor in the middle or front of the room. Have a volunteer walk around the perimeter. Have the class count aloud as the child reaches each corner. Guide children to discover that the figure has 4 sides and 4 corners.

Check Understanding   Ask, *How many corners does a circle have?* (0) *How many sides?* (0)

Guided Practice
Have children complete exercises 1 and 2. Check that they realize each figure has the same number of corners as sides.

Independent Practice
Have children complete the remaining exercises on 11 and 12 independently.

Closing the Lesson   Ask, *Do all plane figures with 4 sides and 4 corners look alike?* (No) *Why or why not?* (Answers will vary. Possible answer: Their sides can be different sizes or in different positions as in exercises 4 and 8.)

LESSON 6
PAGES 13–14

OBJECTIVE
Identify plane figures that are the same size and same shape

PREREQUISITES
Concepts
• Understand the concepts of same and different
• Understand the concept of plane figures

SKILLS
• Recognize same and different
• Recognize and identify plane figures and their properties

VOCABULARY
same size, same shape

MATERIALS
box of various-sized crayons, pencils, chalk

Copymasters
Reteach 4–6, pp. 74–76
Teaching Resource 2, (Shapes) p. 200

Same Size and Same Shape

Presenting the Lesson
Introduce the Skill   Have volunteers look through a box filled with various-sized crayons, pencils, and chalk. Challenge them to find two items in the box that are the same shape, then two items that are the same size, and finally two items that are the same size and shape. Teaching Resource 2 has a collection of figures that can be used for comparing.

Check Understanding   Hold up a square. Then hold up a piece of paper with the same size square drawn on it. Ask, *How can I check if these squares are the same size and shape?* (Answers will vary. Possible answer: Trace the square onto the piece of paper and see if the sides and corners match.)

Guided Practice
Have children complete exercise 1. Check that they understand that although both choices are the same shape, only one is the same size and same shape.

Independent Practice
Have children complete the remaining exercises on pages 13 and 14 independently. Use the Quick Check for Assessment.

Closing the Lesson   Ask, *Can a circle and a triangle be the same size and same shape?* (No)

LESSON 7
PAGES 15–16

OBJECTIVE
Use the Find a Pattern strategy to solve problems

PREREQUISITES
Concepts
• Understand the concept of order

Skills
• Recognize plane figures

VOCABULARY
pattern

Problem Solving Strategy: Find a Pattern

Presenting the Lesson
Introduce the Strategy Tell children that they will find patterns to solve problems.

Model the Four-Step Problem Solving Process Work together with the class to solve the problem at the top of page 15.

• **Understand** Ask, *What do I need to find out to solve this problem?* (which figure most likely comes next.)

• **Decide** Ask, *What can I do to solve this problem?* (I can look for a pattern by looking at how the triangles are arranged. I see the pattern small big big small big big.)

• **Solve** Ask, *What is the solution to this problem?* (The next triangle in the pattern will most likely be small.)

• **Look back** Ask, *How can I check my answer?* (Answers will vary. Possible answer: Say each kind of triangle aloud and see if the answer fits the pattern you say.)

Check Understanding Ask, *How can you show the same pattern as the triangles using colors?* (Answers will vary. Possible answers: red, blue, red, blue, red, blue.)

Guided Practice
Have children solve problem 1. Check that they understand that the pattern is based on size.

Independent Practice
Have children complete the remaining exercises independently.

Closing the Lesson Ask, *What pattern can you draw that uses shape and size?*
(Possible answer: green triangle, red circle, white circle, green triangle, red circle, white circle)

LESSON 8
PAGES 17–18

OBJECTIVE
Identify pictures that show mirror images; determine and draw lines of symmetry

PREREQUISITES

Concepts
• Understand concept of same and matching

Skills
• Recognize same size and shape

VOCABULARY
symmetry

MATERIALS
blank paper, scissors

Copymasters
Reteach 7, p. 77

Symmetry

Presenting the Lesson
Introduce the Skill Give children white sheets of paper. Have them draw a rectangle on the paper and cut it out. Then have children fold the rectangle in half lengthwise and open it up. Ask, *Are both sides of the fold the same?* (Yes) *How else can you fold your rectangle so that both parts of the fold match?* (From top to bottom)

Check Understanding Hold up a drawing of a circle with a line down the middle. Ask, *If I fold this circle on the line will both sides of the line match?* (Yes)

Guided Practice
Have children complete exercise 1. Check that they were able to recognize when parts do not match. Then have them do exercise 5. Explain that a line that makes two parts match is a line of symmetry. Check that they understand that a line going across this shape would not be a line of symmetry.

Independent Practice
Have children complete the remaining exercises on pages 17 and 18 independently.

Closing the Lesson Ask, *Which figure has many lines of symmetry?* (Circle)

LESSON 9
PAGES 19–20

OBJECTIVE
Solve problems by using a picture to determine location

PREREQUISITES
Concepts
• Understand the concept of position

Skills
• Identify objects that are near, far, below, above, behind, in front of, next to, left and right

VOCABULARY
above, behind, below, far, in front of, left, near, next to, right

Problem Solving Application: Use a Picture

Presenting the Lesson
Introduce the Focus of the Lesson   Point out to children that in this lesson they will use pictures to solve problems.

Model the Four-Step Problem Solving Process   Work together with the class to solve problem 1:

• **Understand** Ask, *What do I need to do to solve this problem?* (Find the tree that is far from the Old Mac's sign and draw an X on it.)

• **Decide** Ask, *What can I do to solve this problem?* (I can look for trees and decide which one is far from the sign.)

• **Solve** Ask, *How do I solve the problem?* (I draw the X on the small tree at the top because it is farther from the sign than the other tree.)

• **Look back** Ask, *How can I check if my answer makes sense?* (Answers will vary. Possible answer: Compare the two trees and check that the one I drew the X on is further than the other from the sign.)

Guided Practice
Have children complete problem 5. Discuss how they arrived at their answer before having them work on their own. Check that they understand the position words.

Independent Practice
Have children complete the remaining exercises on pages 19 and 20 independently.

Closing the Lesson   Ask, *How could you use a picture to show someone where our school is?* (Possible answer: Draw the school and places that are near it.)

LESSON 10
PAGES 21–22

OBJECTIVE
Follow directions to identify location on a grid

PREREQUISITES
Concepts
• Understand the concept of direction

Skills
• Recognize direction words up, right
• Count to 5

VOCABULARY
up, right

MATERIALS
Copymasters
Reteach 8, p. 78

Follow Directions

Presenting the Lesson
Introduce the Skill   Practice using the words *right* and *up* to give children direction commands. Play "Simon Says" with directions such as "Simon says take two steps to the right and one step up toward me." Then draw a 3 x 3 grid on the chalkboard and demonstrate how to find points on the grid using the same directions.

Check Understanding   Point to the place that is right 1 space and up 1 space. Ask, *What directions would you give to get to this point?* (right 1 space, up 1 space)

Guided Practice
Have children complete exercises 1 and 5. Check that they understand that they must start at 0 each time they begin a new set of directions.

Independent Practice
Have children complete the remaining exercises independently.

Closing the Lesson   Ask, *Which direction do you always begin with when finding points on a grid?* (right)

UNIT 1 REVIEW
Pages 23–24

Item Analysis

Items	Unit Obj.
1–2	1A
3–4	1A
5–6	1B
7–8	1A
9–12	1B
13–14	1C

Answers to Unit 1 review items can be found on pages 23 and 24 of the Teacher's Annotated Edition.

Administering the Review
These pages review concepts and skills taught in this unit. Make sure children understand all direction lines. You may wish to do the first example in each section cooperatively to ensure understanding.

Scoring Chart

Number Correct	14	13	12	11	10	9	8	7	6	5	4	3	2	1
Score	100	93	86	79	71	64	57	50	43	36	29	21	14	7

After the Review
• The Item Analysis chart on the left shows the Unit 1 objective covered by each test item. This chart can help you determine which objectives need review or extra practice.

• For additional assessment, use the Posttest for Unit 1, Copymasters, pp. 13–14.

UNIT 1 CUMULATIVE REVIEW

Pages 25–26

Item Analysis

Items	Unit Obj.
1–3	1A
4	1B
5	1A
6–7	1B
8–9	1C

Answers to Cumulative Review items can be found on pages 25 and 26 of the Teacher's Annotated Edition.

Administering the Review

These pages review concepts and skills from the unit as well as providing practice with standardized test formats. Children should mark their answers directly on the test pages.

Test-Taking Tip Remind children to listen to the entire question before they mark their answer.

Exercises 1–9 This test is administered orally. Before reading each question, ask children to find the correct item number and then listen carefully. Read each question twice, and pause between items to give children time to find and mark their answers.

ex. 1. *Which item is the same shape as the ice cream cone? Mark the space under your answer.*

ex. 2. *Which figure matches the shaded face? Mark the space under your answer.*

ex. 3. *Which figure is a circle? Mark the space under your answer.*

ex. 4. *Which item shows the square before the circle? Mark the space under your answer.*

ex. 5. *Which figure has 3 sides? Mark the space under your answer.*

ex. 6. *Which figure is the same size and shape? Mark the space under your answer.*

ex. 7. *Which figure shows a line of symmetry? Mark the space under your answer.*

ex. 8. *Which picture shows the baseball to the left of the bat? Mark the space under your answer.*

ex. 9. *Which figure most likely comes next? Mark the space under your answer.*

Test-Taking Tip Remind children to look back to check that they marked the answer they wanted to choose.

Scoring Chart

Number Correct	9	8	7	6	5	4	3	2	1
Score	100	89	78	67	56	44	33	22	11

After the Review

The Item Analysis chart on the left shows the unit objective covered by each test item. This chart can help you determine which objectives need review or extra practice.

Teacher Notes

Numbers through 10 and Data

Vocabulary

- bar graph
- between
- cent
- decide
- equal to
- fewer
- greater than
- greatest
- just after
- just before
- least
- less than
- look back
- more
- number line
- number words
- order
- penny
- picture graph
- solve
- tally marks
- understand
- zero through ten

Unit Objectives

2A Compare groups and use the terms *more* and *fewer* to describe them

2B Count 0 through 10 objects and write the numbers

2C Count pennies and write the values to 10¢

2D Order numbers 0 through 10

2E Use the symbols $<$ (is less than), $>$ (is greater than), and $=$ (is equal to) in comparing numbers

2F Solve problems by using a graph; use Draw a Picture and other strategies to solve problems

About This Unit

The support pages that follow provide more information on prerequisite skills, methods for teaching skills and concepts, daily routines, tips on classroom management and materials, and useful dialogue techniques.

Assessments

Use Beginning of the Year Inventory for entry-level assessment.

Ongoing Evaluation Quick Checks, Reteach Worksheets, the Skills Tutorial Inventories and the Midyear Test help ensure that children are progressing adequately to meet the standards.

Summative Evaluation Use Test Preps, Unit Review (p. T42), Cumulative Review (p. T43), Reteach Worksheets, and the Skills Tutorial Inventory, Strand P1, Skills 1–3 to assure that children have achieved the standards for the unit.

Diagnosing Errors The Quick Checks highlight common errors and provide remediation. See also the **Teaching Strategies Handbook** pp. T30–T33, where short discussions labeled Common Misconceptions appear as needed with the strategies for key concepts.

Homework and Family Involvement

Home Note In the Student Book, the Dear Family Home Note provides objectives, vocabulary, and a sample skill discussion for family participation. (**Teaching Strategies Handbook** pages also provide homework and family involvement tips.)

Education Place Refer families to Houghton Mifflin's EduPlace Web site at http://www.eduplace.com; for resources and activities for students at http://www.eduplace.com/math; and additional resources and activities at http://www.eduplace.com/parents.

Helping Your Children Learn Math This book has activities for children ages 5–13 and tips for getting involved in children's mathematics education. (Houghton Mifflin, 1994)

Lessons	Student Pages	Teacher Pages	Resources	State or Local	
				Objectives	Assessment
2.1 More and Fewer	29–30	**T34**	Unit 2 Pretest		
2.2 Problem Solving Strategy: Draw a	31–32	**T34**			
2.3 Counting and Writing 0 through 3	33–34	**T35**	Teaching Resource 3		
2.4 Counting and Writing 4 through 6	35–36	**T35**	Reteach 9; Teaching Resource 3 Skills Tutorial: Strand P1, Skill 1, Skill 2		
2.5 Counting and Writing 7 and 8	37–38	**T36**	Teaching Resource 3		
2.6 Counting and Writing 9 and 10	39–40	**T36**	Teaching Resource 3		
2.7 Number Recognition through 10	41–42	**T37**	Reteach 10, 11; Extension 4, 5; Teaching Resource 5; Skills Tutorial: Strand P1, Skill 3		
2.8 Counting Pennies	43–44	**T37**	Teaching Resource 11		
2.9 Order	45–46	**T38**	Teaching Resource 18		
2.10 Greater, Greatest	47–48	**T38**	Reteach 12, 13, 14		
2.11 Lesser, Least	49–50	**T39**			
2.12 Comparing Numbers: Using > and <	51–52	**T39**	Teaching Resource 4		
2.13 Comparing Numbers: Using >, <, and =	53–54	**T40**	Reteach 15, 16, 17; Teaching Resource 4		
2.14 Tallying	55–56	**T40**	Reteach 18		
2.15 Making Graphs	57–58	**T41**	Reteach 19		
2.16 Problem Solving Application: Use a Graph	59–60	**T41**	Unit 2 Posttest; Extension 6		

Teaching Strategies

Math Background	Numbers through 10 and Data

You're about to start another foundational mathematics chapter. You'll work with children to picture and write the numbers 0–10, and to break numbers into parts. Discuss familiar instances in which numbers are used—money, clocks, television channels, schedules, or game scores, for example.

In this unit, you'll help children build algebraic reasoning skills as they begin to use the >, <, and = signs. Children also learn about graphs. They'll use tally marks to represent data, make and interpret graphs, and solve problems based on graphs.

With symbols and graphs, children are representing ideas, and they must learn the meanings behind the symbols. Through this process, they are building important ideas for future reasoning.

A Positive Start

Even though the content in this unit is very basic, you'll want to plan carefully to reach all of your students. When they gain a solid understanding of numbers and some simple mathematical symbols, they are better prepared for the rest of this school year and for the future. This important foundation will give them confidence in their ability to succeed in mathematics. Their willingness to try will be boosted, and their pleasure—and yours—in the learning process will be a great asset.

Linking Past and Future Learning

The chart shows key concepts for this unit—what children learned last year and what they will encounter next year—to provide a scope for your instructional planning.

Concept/Skills	Last Year	This year	Next year
Recognizing, Representing, and Writing Numbers	Count groups of objects through 10; identify and write the numbers 0 through 10	Recognize number words; represent numbers through 10 using objects; write the numbers 0 through 10	Recognize number words through 19; represent numbers through 100 using words, models, and expanded form; write numbers through 1000
Comparing and Ordering Numbers	Compare groups of objects through 10 using *more, fewer, most, fewest*; order numbers through 10	Compare groups of objects through 10 using *more, fewer*; compare numbers through 10 using words and symbols; use the terms *just before, just after,* and *between* to order numbers	Compare numbers using the symbols >, <, =, and ≠; order numbers through 100
Making and Interpreting Graphs	Make a bar graph and picture graph; use a bar graph to solve problems	Make and interpret picture graphs and bar graphs; compare and use data from graphs to solve problems	Make and interpret bar graphs; Use a bar graph to solve addition and subtraction problems

Methods and Management

Children need many different models to develop their concepts of numbers, number relationships, and graphs. They must associate physical representations, such as counters and pictures, with symbols. To maximize learning for all children, keep them actively involved. Some useful strategies follow.

Teaching Strategy: Recognizing and Writing Numbers

Allow for plenty of practice in rote counting. When counting objects, have children attach a number name to each object. Encourage moving or pointing to objects as they are counted.

- Show that the number of objects in a group stays the same even when the objects are rearranged. Repeat with other numbers of objects to 10.

1   2   3   1   2   3

- Demonstrate these combinations: 2 boys and 3 girls, 5 boys, or 4 girls and 1 boy. Point out that each group of children makes up the number 5.

▶ *Ask: How can we make 6?* Invite many responses. Write on the board the numeral and the word form for every number the class explores.

▶ *Common Misconceptions* "Zero means nothing, so why do we write it?" This question may arise, and you'll want to explain that the 0 symbol is needed to indicate *none.* Write a list of numerals to represent numbers of objects and demonstrate how leaving a blank or space in the list, instead of writing 0, could be confusing.

Teaching Strategy: Comparing and Ordering Numbers

Which number represents a *greater* amount? Which number is *less than* the other? Use the symbols <, >, and =. Connect the symbols to objects first, so that symbols are meaningful.

- Have children take turns removing two handfuls of counters or small blocks from a bag and count the two groups.

▶ *Ask: Which has more, the greater amount? Which group has fewer? Or do they have equal numbers? How can you tell?* Record the children's decision on the board (8 > 4, for example). Then demonstrate showing symbols first and corresponding objects.

- Have children create 3 or 4 groups of counters and then arrange the groups in order from least to greatest.

▶ *Common Misconceptions* Children may confuse the < and > signs. Show them how the greater opening of each sign is closest to the greater number, and the smaller part of each sign points toward the lesser number.

Teacher Tips

Managing Materials Ask children and families to help you collect small objects to use as counters—plastic lids, paper clips, small stones, acorns, or craft sticks, for example. Have a few helpers pre-package sets of 10 counters in plastic bags so they'll be ready for children to use in class activities.

Daily Routine Lead children in counting so that the order of numbers sounds natural and right to them. Count as you start the day, as you begin each math lesson, and as children line up. Write large clear numerals as models. Have children follow along, making numerals in the air and then writing them on paper.

Books on Counting A wide variety of number books are available, so try to read one each day, and make books available in your reading corner.

Make Your Own Involve children in making individual and group number books. They can draw pictures, attach stickers, use a stamp pad and stamps, or even make numbers of holes with a paper punch. Have them write numerals near each number representation.

Write, Write, Write Provide many opportunities to write numerals. Children who have trouble might trace over large, clear numerals that you provide, or trace numerals in a thin layer of sand or cornmeal in a tray.

Real-Life Comparisons Have children suggest examples of number comparisons in the classroom. You might have equal numbers of wastebaskets and filing cabinets, a greater number of windows than doors, and a lesser number of teachers than children.

Draw and Compare Ask partners to draw 3–10 objects on paper and then count each other's objects and compare their numbers. Children write expressions for the comparisons and post them below their drawings.

Collaboration Make several sets of number cards for 0–10. Mix them up. Make sets of cards for >, <, =. Provide partners with a stack of cards and one set of symbols. Each partner draws a card and together they decide on the correct comparative symbol for the numbers. Play continues until all cards are used.

Counting by 5's Building rote knowledge of "the fives" will help as children later count nickels, tell time, and interpret tally marks.

Quick Check Write on the board, at random, 3 or 4 numbers and corresponding groups of tally marks. Let children show how to match the numbers and tallies.

Words of Experience Remember that not every child will fully comprehend the > and < symbols the first time around. Continue to work on the symbols, as well as the ideas they represent, and your patience will pay off.

Vocabulary As children interpret and solve problems based on graphs, *greater, lesser, equal,* and other comparative words come into play again. Emphasize the words as you use them, and be sure that each child has opportunities to use them.

Teaching Strategy: Making and Interpreting Graphs

As you help children gather data and display it with tally marks and graphs, provide opportunities for the children to talk about what the symbols and graphic forms mean.

- Make a simple picture graph of data. Photocopy an outline picture of an object for each child. Have children color the picture with their favorite color (within a 4-color range that you choose). Create a bulletin board graph so that children can post their pictures within color categories.

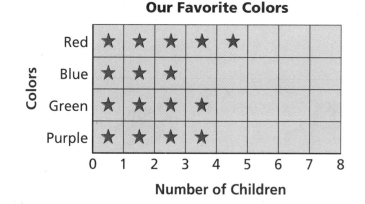

Our Favorite Colors

▶ *Ask: What does our graph show? How many of you chose red? Are any colors equal in number? Which color has the greatest number?* Interpret the graph together. You might leave the labels until last and ask, *What's the name of this category? What's a good title for our graph?*

▶ *Common Misconceptions* When children collect data using tallies, they may not understand why there is a cross mark for the fifth tally. Draw 8 tallies with and without the cross marks and ask which representation is easier and quicker to count.

Opportunities to Assess

Keeping Track

Save samples of each child's work from this time of year, such as their drawings of groups of objects and their written work on numerals and symbols. Later in the year, you and family members can compare the samples with the child's current work—and doubtless, you'll see a lot of progress.

Family Involvement

Comparing numbers is a topic in which home support is a bonus. Ask children to make "more and fewer" pictures of items in their homes and then use symbols to represent the comparisons. Family members can help count items and write number labels, such as 1 < 6 (1 sofa < 6 beds).

Teacher/Student Dialogue

How to Enliven a Lesson

Add some action to a lesson about numbers, to vary your routine or to refocus children's attention.

Teacher: Let's exercise and count. *(Writes the numbers 1–4 on the board)* Josie, pick an exercise for us; something easy.

Student: *We can run in place.*

Teacher: Good one. Lets' do it! Four sets, and remember to count 1, 2, 3, 4, 1, 2, 3, 4. *(Leads the group running in place and counting)*

Student: *Let's do arm circles!*

Teacher: Sets of 6. One arm first. *(Demonstrates)* Count with me!

Students: *1, 2, 3, 4, 5, 6, 1, 2, . . .*

Teacher: Now the other arm, 2 sets of 8. What will this sound like? Everybody?

Students: *1, 2, 3, 4, 5, 6, 7, 8.*

Teacher: Great, let's go! *(Finishes sets)* Have a seat and let's breathe slowly, two long, deep breaths.

What to do

When

Children often do not fully comprehend the > and < symbols the first few times they are taught. Some children cannot remember which is which when one symbol is shown without the other. Assure frustrated children that they will surely "get it." Post various visuals for the symbols—with labels and with corresponding numbers—and refer to them often.

What to do

Every Day

"It's Number Time!" Have children bring to school each day a number they saw outside of school, such as street numbers, phone numbers, numbers on packages, prices in stores, and so on.

For Better Participation

Don't fight it! When children are restless and inattentive, recognize it and *do something!* Make a short mental or written list of actions to take when children's attention wanders. A moment to wiggle or stretch, a chant with exercises, clapping, or even a two-minute water break may pay big dividends in better participation by the children. Children may make good suggestions. Once you've initiated an action, decide quickly what to do next, and use children's suggestions then or later, even another day.

Unit 2   Numbers through 10 and Data

LESSON 1
PAGES 29–30

OBJECTIVE
Compare groups using the terms *more* and *fewer*

PREREQUISITES
Concepts
• One-to-one correspondence
Skills
• To match objects to show one-to-one correspondence

VOCABULARY
more, fewer

More and Fewer

Presenting the Lesson
Introduce the Skill   Play musical chairs with the children. Have them tell a sentence that compares the number of children and chairs at the end of each round. For example, *There are more children than chairs;* or, *There are fewer chairs than children.*

Check Understanding   *How can you tell if there are more objects in one group than another?* (Answers will vary. Possible answer: I can compare the groups and see which has objects left over.)

Guided Practice
Complete exercises 1 and 5 with the class. Have children do exercise 2. Have children compare their answers to exercise 2 and tell how they knew which group to ring.

Independent Practice
Have children complete the remaining exercises on pages 29 and 30 independently.

Closing the Lesson   *How can we tell if we have more desks than children?* Have volunteers act out their answers. (Answers may vary. Possible answer: Match each child to 1 desk. See if we have desks or children left over.)

LESSON 2
PAGES 31–32

OBJECTIVE
Use the Draw a Picture strategy to solve problems involving more and fewer

PREREQUISITES
Concepts
• Understand more and fewer

VOCABULARY
understand, decide, solve, look back

Problem Solving Strategy: Draw a Picture

Presenting the Lesson
Introduce the Strategy   Have children draw pictures with more and fewer. For example: *Draw more circles than squares.* Have children share and compare pictures. Then use page 31 to model the problem solving process. Read the problem and discuss each step.

• **Understand** *What do I need to do to solve the problem?* (I need to give Martina more balloons than Alex.)

• **Decide** *What can I do to solve this problem?* (I can draw strings from the balloons to Martina and Alex.)

• **Solve** *How can I use my drawing to solve the problem?* (Count the balloons each child has.)

• **Look back** *Does my answer make sense? Is there another way to solve the problem?* (Yes; Martina could have 5 balloons and Alex 1.)

Guided Practice
Have children complete the model problem on page 31. Check that they understand how they draw and trace numbers that show more balloons for Martina than for Alex.

Independent Practice
Have children complete problems 1 and 2 on page 32 independently.

Closing the Lesson   Ask, *Do all problems have just one right answer? How can you tell?* (Possible answer: No; We found different right answers.)

LESSON 3

PAGES 33–34

OBJECTIVE
Recognize and count groups of 0, 1, 2, and 3 and write the numerals

PREREQUISITES
Concepts
• Understand groups

Skills
• Count one object for each number

VOCABULARY
zero, one, two, three

MATERIALS
Copymaster
Teaching Resource 3, (Writing Grids) p. 201

Counting and Writing 0 through 3

Presenting the Lesson
Introduce the Skill Write the numbers 0, 1, 2, and 3 across the chalkboard. Call six children up to the front of the room. Challenge them to arrange themselves so that the correct number of children are standing in front of each number. Discuss results with the class. Teaching Resource 3 provides practice for writing numbers.

Check Understanding Ask, *How many different ways can you show two?* (Answers will vary. Possible answers: write the number 2, write the word *two*, show 2 objects)

Guided Practice
Have students complete rows 1–4 and exercises 5 and 7. Check that they understand how to decide which number to write and how many to draw.

Independent Practice
Have children complete the remaining exercises independently.

Closing the Lesson *Which number means none?* (zero) *Which number means a single thing?* (1) *Which number means a pair?* (2)

LESSON 4

PAGES 35–36

OBJECTIVE
Recognize and count groups of 4, 5, and 6 and write the numerals

PREREQUISITES
Concepts
• Understand numbers and groups

Skills
• Count and write 0 through 3

VOCABULARY
four, five, six

MATERIALS
counters

Copymasters
Reteach 9, p. 79
Teaching Resource 3, (Writing Grids) p. 201

Skills Tutorial
Strand P1: Skill 1 Practice 1–6, Skill 2 Practice 1–6

Counting and Writing 4 through 6

Presenting the Lesson
Introduce the Skill Provide children with counters or other small objects. Have them experiment to show as many combinations as they can using 4 counters, then 5, then 6. For example, some children might show 4 as 2 red and 2 blue; others can show it as 1 red and 3 blue, etc. Have children share and compare combinations.

Check Understanding Ask, *How can you use counters to show how to count to six?* (Answers may vary. Possible answer: I can count from 1 to 6 and put down a counter for each number I say.)

Guided Practice
Have children complete rows 1-3. Check that they write each number correctly.

Independent Practice
Have children complete the exercises on page 36 independently. Use the Quick Check for assessment.

Closing the Lesson *If you wanted to give an apple to each of your six friends, what number shows how many apples you would need?* (6)

LESSON 5
PAGES 37–38

OBJECTIVE
Recognize and count groups of 7 and 8 and write the numerals

PREREQUISITES
Concepts
• Understand numbers and groups from 0 through 6

Skills
• Count and write 0 through 6

VOCABULARY
seven, eight, number word

MATERIALS
Copymaster
Teaching Resource 3, (Writing Grids) p. 201

Counting and Writing 7 and 8

Presenting the Lesson
Introduce the Skill   Tell children you want 7 children to stand in the front of the room. Have volunteers call up different combinations of boys and girls that will equal 7. Repeat with 8 children. Teaching Resource 3 provides practice for writing numbers.

Check Understanding   Have children draw pictures to show 8 in as many different ways as they can. Share and compare pictures. (Answers will vary. possible answers: 8; eight; pictures of eight objects)

Guided Practice
Discuss the number words and numerals on page 37. Have children complete rows 1 and 2. Check that they write each number correctly.

Independent Practice
Have children complete the remaining exercises on pages 37 and 38 independently.

Closing the Lesson   Say, *Hold up 7 fingers. Hold up 8 fingers.* (Answers will vary. Possible answers: for 7: 4 and 3; 5 and 2; for 8: 4 and 4; 5 and 3)

LESSON 6
PAGES 39–40

OBJECTIVE
Recognize and count groups of 9 and 10 and write the numerals

PREREQUISITES
Concepts
• Understand numbers and groups from 0 through 8

Skills
• Count and write 0 through 8

VOCABULARY
nine, ten

MATERIALS
Copymaster
Teaching Resource 3, (Writing Grids) p. 201

Counting and Writing 9 and 10

Presenting the Lesson
Introduce the Skill   Write the number 9 on one side of the chalkboard and 10 on the other. Have volunteers come up and draw the correct number of circles under each number as the class counts each circle aloud as it is drawn. Teaching Resource 3 provides practice for writing numbers.

Check Understanding   Ask, *If there are ten children in a room and there are more boys than girls, how many boys could there be?* (Possible answers: 6, 7, 8, 9, or 10)

Guided Practice
Discuss the number words and numerals on page 39. Have children complete rows 1 and 2. Check that they write each number correctly.

Independent Practice
Have children complete the remaining exercises on pages 39 and 40 independently.

Closing the Lesson   *If you want to hold up 9 fingers, do you have to hold up all of the fingers on at least one hand?* (Yes, because if you don't you won't have enough fingers held up.)

LESSON 7
PAGES 41–42

OBJECTIVE
Recognize numerals and draw objects for 0 through 10

PREREQUISITES
Concepts
• Understand numbers and groups from 0 through 10

Skills
• Count and write 0 through 10

MATERIALS
index cards, counters

Copymasters
Reteach 10–11, pp. 80–81
Extension 4–5, pp. 166–167
Teaching Resource 5, (Number Word Cards) p. 203

Skills Tutorial
Strand P1: Skill 3 Practice 1–6

Number Recognition through 10

Presenting the Lesson
Introduce the Skill Show numbers from 0 through 10 one at a time on index cards. Have children show the number of counters for each number you hold up. Children can make number word cards using Teaching Resource 5.

Check Understanding Ask, *How can you use the number 10 in a sentence about school?* (Answers may vary. Possible answers: I read my book in school for 10 minutes; I answered 10 questions in math.)

Guided Practice
Have children complete exercise 1. Check that they drew the correct number of balls.

Independent Practice
Have children complete the remaining exercises on pages 41 and 42 on their own. Use the Quick Check for assessment.

Closing the Lesson *How can you check if you drew the correct number of balls next to the number 9?* (Answers may vary. Possible answer: I can count each ball by writing a number under each from 1 to 9.)

LESSON 8
PAGES 43–44

OBJECTIVE
Identify the value of a penny as 1 cent

PREREQUISITES
Concepts
• Understand numbers and groups from 1–10
• Understand the ¢ sign

Skills
• Count and write numbers from 1 to 10

VOCABULARY
penny, cent

MATERIALS
play coins: pennies, box

Copymasters
Teaching Resource 11, (Coins and Rulers) p. 209

Counting Pennies

Presenting the Lesson
Introduce the Skill Put 6 pennies in a box. Shake the box. Have children guess how many pennies. Then have a volunteer count the pennies to check their guess. Show children two different ways to write the amount: 6¢ and 6 cents. Repeat with different numbers. Teaching Resource 11 can be used for a collection of pennies.

Check Understanding *If I have 4 cents in my pocket, how many pennies do I have?* (4)

Guided Practice
Have children complete exercise 1 on page 43 and exercise 4 on page 44. Check that they understand that they can ring the correct number of coins more than one way. Have volunteers show the different ways they can ring 8 pennies to show 8 cents.

Independent Practice
Have children complete the remaining exercises on pages 43 and 44 independently.

Closing the Lesson *If you have 6 pennies, can you buy a pencil that costs 8 cents? Why or why not?* (No, 6 pennies is only 6 cents. 8 cents is more than 6 cents.)

LESSON 9
PAGES 45–46

OBJECTIVE
Identify missing numbers in a sequence; use the terms *just before*, *just after*, and *between*; count backward

PREREQUISITES
Concepts
- Understand order

Skills
- Count from 0 to 10

VOCABULARY
between, just after, just before, order, number line

MATERIALS
index cards

Copymaster
Teaching Resource 18, (Number Lines to 12) p. 216

Order

Presenting the Lesson
Introduce the Skill   Put index cards with the numbers 1 to 10 on the chalk tray in mixed up order. Have volunteers arrange the cards in correct order. Have a volunteer identify the index card with the number just before 5, just after 3, and between 3 and 5. (4) Then turn to page 45 and show children that the number line shows the same order. Teaching Resource 18 can be used to provide practice with number lines.

Check Understanding   *How can you use the words "just after" in a sentence with the number 8?* (Answers may vary. Possible answer: Eight is just after 7.)

Guided Practice
Have children complete exercise 1, the first item for exercises 7, 8, 9, and exercise 10. Discuss how they arrived at each answer before having them work on their own. Encourage children to use the number line.

Independent Practice
Have children complete the remaining exercises on pages 45 and 46 independently.

Closing the Lesson   *Which is greater, the number just after 4 or just before it?* (just after)

LESSON 10
PAGES 47–48

OBJECTIVE
Compare numbers using the terms *greater* and *greatest*

PREREQUISITES
Concepts
- Understand order
- Understand numbers from 0–10

Skills
- Count and write numbers from 0–10
- Order numbers from 0–10

VOCABULARY
greater, greater than, greatest

MATERIALS
counters

Copymasters
Reteach 12–14, pp. 82–84

Greater, Greatest

Presenting the Lesson
Introduce the Skill   Write the numbers 6 and 8 on the board. Have children make sets of each using counters or drawings on the board, then tell which set has the greater number of counters. Compare other numbers using the same procedure. Then have children look at the number line on page 47. Have them identify another number that is greater than 4. Then have children look at the number line on page 48. Have them identify the greatest number on the number line.

Check Understanding   *How can you use a number line to tell which of two numbers is greater?* (Find both numbers on the number line. The one to the right is greater.)

Guided Practice
Have children complete exercise 1 on page 47 and exercise 19 on page 48. Check that they understand the difference between *greater* and *greatest*. *When do you use the word* greatest *to compare numbers?* (when you are comparing more than 2 numbers) *When do you use the word* greater? (when you are comparing 2 numbers)

Independent Practice
Have children complete the remaining exercises independently. Use the Quick Check for assessment.

Closing the Lesson   *What are three numbers greater than 2?* (Answers will vary. Possible answers: 5, 6, 7) *Of those numbers, which is the greatest?* (7)

LESSON 11
PAGES 49–50

OBJECTIVE
Compare numbers using the terms *lesser* and *least*

PREREQUISITES
Concepts
• Understand order
• Understand numbers from 0–10

Skills
• Count and write numbers from 0–10
• Order numbers from 0–10

VOCABULARY
lesser, less than, least

MATERIALS
counters

Lesser, Least

Presenting the Lesson
Introduce the Skill   Repeat the same activity as you did in Lesson 10, but focus on having children identify the lesser and least numbers.

Check Understanding   *How can you use a number line to tell which of two numbers is less?* (Find both numbers on the number line. The one to the left is less.)

Guided Practice
Have children complete exercise 1 on page 49 and 19 on page 50. Check that they understand the difference between less and least. Ask: *When do you use the word* least *to compare numbers?* (when you are comparing more than 2 numbers) *When do you use the word* less? (when you are comparing 2 numbers)

Independent Practice
Have children complete the remaining exercises independently.

Closing the Lesson   Ask, *How is finding the lesser number like finding the greater? How is it different?* (Answers will vary.)

LESSON 12
PAGES 51–52

OBJECTIVE
Compare numbers using the symbols > and <

PREREQUISITES
Concepts
• Understand order
• Understand numbers from 0–10

Skills
• Compare and order numbers from 0–10

VOCABULARY
greater than, less than

MATERIALS
Copymasters
Teaching Resource 4, (Digit and Symbol Cards) p. 202

Comparing Numbers Using > and <

Presenting the Lesson
Introduce the Skill   Draw the symbols > and < on the chalkboard. Label them on top as "greater than" and "less than." Demonstrate how to compare and write true sentences. For example: Show 5 circles above the numeral 5 on one side of the > and 4 circles above the numeral 4 on the other. Challenge volunteers to do the same with other quantities. Teaching Resource 4 can be used to make digit and symbol cards for comparing numbers. Have children look at the examples on page 51 that show < and >. Suggest they refer to these examples if they forget what each symbol means.

Check Understanding   Write 4 > 2 on the chalkboard. *What must I do if I switch the positions of 4 and 2? Why?* (Change the sign to <, because if you don't you will have 2 > 4 which is incorrect.)

Guided Practice
Have children complete exercises 1 and 10. Check that they understand what the symbols mean.

Independent Practice
Have children complete the remaining exercises independently.

Closing the Lesson Write the following on the chalkboard: □ < □. *What two numbers can I write in the boxes to make this sentence true?* (Answers vary. Possible answers: 4, 5)

LESSON SUPPORT

LESSON 13
PAGES 53–54

OBJECTIVE
Compare numbers using the symbols <, > and =

PREREQUISITES
Concepts
• Understand order
• Understand numbers from 0–10

Skills
• Compare and order numbers from 0–10 using < and >.

VOCABULARY
less than, greater than, equal to

MATERIALS
Copymasters
Reteach 15–17, pp. 85–87
Teaching Resource 4, (Digit and Symbol Cards) p. 202

Comparing Numbers Using >, <, and =

Presenting the Lesson
Introduce the Skill Draw and label the symbols >, < and = on the chalkboard. Demonstrate how to write numbers on each side of the symbols to make a true number sentence. (Show 4 > 2; 8 < 9; and 5 = 5, for example). Challenge volunteers to replace numbers with other numbers and still keep each sentence true. Have children look at the examples on page 53. Suggest they refer to these examples if they forget what each symbol means.

Check Understanding Write 8 > □ ; 8 < □ ; 8 = □ *What numbers can I write in the boxes to make each sentence true?* (Answers may vary. Possible answers: 7, 9, 8)

Guided Practice
Have children complete the exercises 1 and 16. Check that they understand when to write an equal sign.

Independent Practice
Have children complete the remaining exercises on pages 53 and 54 independently.

Closing the Lesson *How can you use < to make a true sentence with the numbers 5 and 8?* (5 < 8) *How can you use > with the same numbers?* (8 > 5)

LESSON 14
PAGES 55–56

OBJECTIVE
Represent and compare data using tally marks

PREREQUISITES
Concepts
• Understand one-to-one correspondence
• Understand more
• Understand numbers from 0–10

Skills
• Count and write numbers from 0–10
• Compare numbers and quantities from 0 to 10

VOCABULARY
tally marks

MATERIALS
play money: pennies

Copymasters
Reteach 18, p. 88

Tallying

Presenting the Lesson
Introduce the Skill Draw a chart on the chalkboard:

Girls	
Boys	

Have a volunteer choose 10 children and call out whether each is a girl or boy. As the word is called out, show a tally mark in the chart. When you reach 5, show how to mark the fifth tally as a diagonal line.

Check Understanding Ask, *Why do you think we mark off the fifth tally as a diagonal line?* (It makes it easier to count the total number of tallies without making a mistake.)

Guided Practice
Have children complete exercise 1. Demonstrate how to count on from 5 for the total. Have them work in pairs. Have pairs toss their coins and record the results in the chart on page 55. Check that children used tally marks correctly. Share and compare results.

Independent Practice
Have children complete the exercises on page 56 independently.

Closing the Lesson Ask, *Why are there 10 tally marks in all in Sergio's chart?* (Because that's how many times he tossed his coin. Each tally stands for one toss.)

LESSON 15
PAGES 57–58

OBJECTIVE
Represent and compare data using picture graphs and bar graphs

PREREQUISITES
Concepts
• Understand data
• Understand numbers 1–10

Skills
• Count and write numbers from 0–10
• Compare numbers and quantities from 0 to 10

VOCABULARY
bar graph, picture graph

MATERIALS
play money: pennies

Copymasters
Reteach 19, p. 89

Making Graphs

Presenting the Lesson
Introduce the Skill   Draw a graph on the board like the one on page 57. Toss a coin 5 times. Have volunteers record the results on the graph. Discuss the results.

Check Understanding   *What do you think the pictures at the bottom of the graph on page 57 mean?* (They tell whether the coin landed on heads or tails.) *What do the numbers on the side mean?* (They tell how many times the coin landed on each side.)

Guided Practice
Have children work in pairs to complete exercise 1. Check that they have counted correctly. Have children share and compare their results.

Independent Practice
Have children complete exercise 2 on page 57 and page 58 independently.

Closing the Lesson   *How many boxes in the first column of your graph did you fill in? Why?* (5; because there were 5 apples in the set of apples)

LESSON 16
PAGES 59–60

OBJECTIVE
Solve problems by using data from picture graphs and bar graphs

PREREQUISITES
Concepts
• Understand data
• Understand one-to-one correspondence
• Understand numbers from 0–10

Skills
• Count and write numbers and quantities from 0–10
• Compare numbers and quantities from 0 to 10

MATERIALS
Copymasters
Extension 6, p. 168

Problem Solving Application: Use a Graph

Presenting the Lesson
Introduce the Focus of the Lesson   Explain to children that in this lesson they will learn how to use a graph to solve problems.

Model the Four-Step Problem Solving Process   Work through the first problem.

• **Understand** Read the title and labels on the graph. Discuss the information the graph contains. (It shows how many children voted for each kind of animal.) Read the first question. *What are you being asked to find out?* (how many children voted for the cat)

• **Decide** *How might you answer this question?* (Look in the column that shows the picture of a cat on the graph and count the number of votes in that column.)

• **Solve** Count the votes together with the class. (8)

• **Look back** *How can you check the answer?* (Answers may vary. Possible answer: Look on the graph to see at which number the pictures in the cat column stops.)

Guided Practice
Have children do problem 1 on page 59 and problem 5 on page 60.

Independent Practice
Have children complete the remaining exercises on pages 59 and 60 independently.

Closing the Lesson   *In the Favorite Sports graph, do you need to count the votes for each sport to tell which was the favorite? Why or why not?* (No, you can just look and see which column is the highest: Soccer)

UNIT 2 REVIEW
Pages 61–62

Item Analysis

Items	Unit Obj.
1–4	2A
5, 6	2B
7, 8	2C
9, 10	2D
11–13	2E
14	2F

Answers to Unit 2 review items can be found on pages 61 and 62 of the Teacher's Annotated Edition.

Administering the Review

These pages review concepts and skills taught in this unit. Make sure children understand all direction lines. You may wish to do the first example in each section cooperatively to ensure understanding.

Scoring Chart

Number Correct	14	13	12	11	10	9	8	7	6	5	4	3	2	1
Score	100	93	86	79	71	64	57	50	43	36	29	21	14	7

After the Review

• The Item Analysis chart on the left shows the Unit 2 objective covered by each test item. This chart can help you determine which objectives need review or extra practice.

• For additional assessment, use the Posttest for Unit 2, Copymasters, pp. 17–18.

Item Analysis

Items	Unit Obj.
1, 2	1B
3, 4	1C
5, 6	2A
7	2B
8	2E

Answers to Cumulative Review items can be found on pages 63 and 64 of the Teacher's Annotated Edition.

Administering the Review

These pages review concepts and skills from the unit as well as providing practice with standardized test formats. Children should mark their answers directly on the test pages.

Test-Taking Tip Remind children to listen to the entire question before looking at all of the choices.

Exercises 1–8 This test is administered orally. Before reading each question, ask children to find the correct item number and then listen carefully. Read each question twice, and pause between items to give children time to find and mark their answers.

ex. 1. *Which item shows the triangle before the square? Mark the space under your answer.*
ex. 2. *Which item shows the circle before the triangle? Mark the space under your answer.*
ex. 3. *Which figure most likely comes next? Mark the space under your answer.*
ex. 4. *Which picture shows the hat to the right of the glove? Mark the space under your answer.*
ex. 5. *Which group shows more baseballs than the group at the beginning of the row? Mark the space under your answer.*
ex. 6. *Which group shows fewer footballs than the group at the beginning of the row? Mark the space under your answer.*
ex. 7. *Which group has this number of triangles? Mark the space under your answer.*
ex. 8. *Which is true? Mark the space under your answer.*

Test-Taking Tip Remind children to look at every choice before marking the one they think is correct.

Scoring Chart

Number Correct	8	7	6	5	4	3	2	1
Score	100	88	75	63	50	38	25	13

After the Review

The Item Analysis chart on the left shows the unit objective covered by each test item. This chart can help you determine which objectives need review or extra practice.

Unit 3 Planner

Addition Facts through 6

Vocabulary

- add
- addition sentence
- equals
- fact
- nickel
- number sentence
- order property
- plus
- sum

Unit Objectives

3A Add all facts that make 6 or less in vertical or horizontal form

3B Count and add money to 6¢ using a nickel or pennies

3C Solve addition problems using a picture; use Write a Number Sentence and other strategies to solve problems

About This Unit

The support pages that follow provide more information on prerequisite skills, methods for teaching skills and concepts, daily routines, tips on classroom management and materials, and useful dialogue techniques.

Assessments
Use Beginning of the Year Inventory for entry-level assessment.

Ongoing Evaluation Quick Checks, Reteach Worksheets, the Skills Tutorial Inventories and the Midyear Test help ensure that children are progressing adequately to meet the standards.

Summative Evaluation Use Test Preps, Unit Review (p. T55), Cumulative Review (p. T56), Reteach Worksheets, and the Skills Tutorial Inventory, Strand P2, Skill 1 to assure that children have achieved the standards for the unit.

Diagnosing Errors The Quick Checks highlight common errors and provide remediation. See also the **Teaching Strategies Handbook** pp. T46–T49, where short discussions labeled Common Misconceptions appear as needed with the strategies for key concepts.

Homework and Family Involvement
Home Note In the Student Book, the Dear Family Home Note provides objectives, vocabulary, and a sample skill discussion for family participation. (**Teaching Strategies Handbook** pages also provide homework and family involvement tips.)

Education Place Refer families to Houghton Mifflin's EduPlace Web site at http://www.eduplace.com; for resources and activities for students at http://www.eduplace.com/math; and additional resources and activities at http://www.eduplace.com/parents.

Helping Your Children Learn Math This book has activities for children ages 5–13 and tips for getting involved in children's mathematics education. (Houghton Mifflin, 1994)

| Lessons | Student Pages | Teacher Pages | Resources | State or Local | |
				Objectives	Assessment
3.1 Stories with Sums through 6	67–68	**T50**	Unit 3 Pretest		
3.2 Sums through 6	69–70	**T50**			
3.3 Problem Solving Strategy: Write a Number Sentence	71–72	**T51**			
3.4 Adding 1 More	73–74	**T51**	Reteach 20, 21, 22		
3.5 Vertical Form	75–76	**T52**			
3.6 Adding 0	77–78	**T52**			
3.7 Order Property	79–82	**T53**	Reteach 23, 24; Skills Tutorial: Strand P2; Skill 1		
3.8 Penny, Nickel	83–84	**T53**	Reteach 25; Teaching Resource 11		
3.9 Problem Solving Application: Use a Picture	85–86	**T54**	Extension 7		
3.10 Missing Addends	87–88	**T54**	Unit 3 Posttest; Reteach 26		

Teaching Strategies

Math Background — Addition Facts through 6

Addition—combining numbers—is a basic part of mathematics. It is the foundation of subtraction, multiplication, and division; consequently, children's understanding of addition is vital for their competence in the operations. By the end of the school year, you'll want all of your children to have committed to memory the addition facts with sums to 20.

In this unit you will help children explore what addition means. Addition includes working with parts and finding a whole, and with increases. You'll begin work on extending the part-part-whole idea to finding missing addends. Children will write and solve number sentences for problem situations

Many situations in children's lives require addition, such as figuring out how much to pay for two or more items, adding game scores, or finding out how many objects there are when two or more groups are combined. Present numerous real-life examples to children, and ask them about instances in which they use addition.

A Positive Start

By now, you've probably observed that encouraging active involvement and building understanding pay big dividends in the children's achievement and confidence levels. So continue to plan varied ways to engage children by giving them a balance between working with concrete representations of ideas and with symbols. During this unit, note the activities that are especially effective in helping children learn. You'll be able to use variations of these activities later in the year as you teach more advanced concepts, and you'll be building your teaching repertoire for the future.

Linking Past and Future Learning

Your meaningful work in this unit continues to set the stage for the skills expected of children at the next levels. Use the chart to help you focus your instruction.

Concept/Skills	Last Year	This Year	Next Year
Meaning of Addition	Introduce the joining and part-part-whole meanings of addition	Recognize the difference between the joining and part-part-whole meanings of addition	Use the meanings of addition to understand and solve story problems
Writing Number Sentences to Solve Addition Problems	Use a picture to complete number sentences by finding and writing the addends and sum	Use pictures to write number sentences including + and = symbols	Use a word problem to write number sentences including + and = symbols
Strategies for Addition	Use pictures and the Act It Out strategy to solve addition problems	Use the strategies adding 1, adding 0, and the order property to solve addition problems	Use the order and grouping properties as strategies to solve addition problems

Teaching Strategies

Before you begin the unit, think of situations and examples of addition that the children might find interesting. Plan experiences to appeal to children's visual, auditory, and tactile or kinesthetic abilities.

Teaching Strategy: Meaning of Addition

Present ideas in real contexts. Talk with children about situations in their lives when they need to add.

- Model addition as joining by asking 2 children to stand and say that 3 more will join them. Ask children to predict how many children there will be. Then have those 3 stand and count to verify the total.

- Show addition as an increase. Model starting with 4 children, *increase* that number by 1, and ask for the sum. Add another child and ask children to describe what happens.

- Model part-part-whole relationships. Have children use blocks or counters and follow along.

▶ *Ask: Part of my counters are red, part are blue—2 reds, 1 blue: How many counters are there?* Record $2 + 1 = 3$.

▶ *Then Ask: I have 5 counters—some red and some green—so how many of each color might I have?* Let children show various combinations. Record the children's work as they verify it. Then read aloud their combinations. Introduce 5 and 0 and 0 and 5 if no one suggests them.

▶ *Vocabulary Development* Words such as *add, sum, total,* and *plus* are important in this unit. Emphasize them when you write addition sentences on the board. Explain that the *plus sign* (+) is used to show that you are adding. You may also want to use the term *addends* for the numbers added.

▶ *Common Misconceptions* As they use counters and pictures that represent addition, children may not realize that they are to join two groups and find the total number. Rather, they may simply count each group. Help them see that they should count *all* items—or find out how many altogether.

Teaching Strategy: Writing Number Sentences

Give each child 6 counters and present several problems like the one that follows.

▶ *Say: Jody has 3 tacos on her plate. She's really hungry so her brother gives her one of his. How many tacos does Jody have now?* Let children model the problem and tell the answer. Then have them help you write the number sentence ($3 + 1 = 4$) and tell why it fits the problem.

▶ *Vocabulary Development* *Number sentence* is a key vocabulary term, and it's one that the children will continue to use in mathematics. Share with the children that an addition number sentence tells a complete thought about what happens to two numbers that are added.

Teacher Tips

Materials Let children make their own background pictures for number stories. Ask each to draw a scene (landscape, playground, city block, etc.) and then use counters on this background for telling and acting out addition stories.

Spin and Add Make a spinner with numbers 0–6. Spin a number to be the sum and ask children to use counters to find different number sentences to produce that sum. *Will there be more ways to make a sum of 5 than a sum of 3?* Pose the question and let children explain their answers.

Money Models Use pennies and number sentence cards ($3 + 2 = \_\_, 4 + 0 = \_\_, 2 + 1 = \_\_$, and so on) to model various addition problems. Let children tell stories to match the number sentences and then use pennies to find the sums.

Quick Idea Draw two groups of objects next to each other. Write the corresponding horizontal number sentences below the drawing. Then draw the same two groupings, but with one below the other. Ask, Is the same number shown in each drawing? Write the corresponding vertical number sentence and point out that the sentences show the same amount.

$$1 + 4 = 5 \quad \text{and} \quad \begin{array}{r} 1 \\ +4 \\ \hline 5 \end{array}$$

Add 1 or Add 0 Make some cards that say "add 1" or "add 0." Let volunteers name a number from 0 through 5. Then turn over a card, announce what it says, and have the class tell the sum as quickly as possible. Pause during the game to review the strategies for adding 1 and 0.

Practice Pairs Assign pairs of children to work together using fact cards for adding to 6. Provide counters for figuring sums, but encourage children to tell the sums without using counters if they can. Partners can check each other, or you might use cards with sums on the back.

Group Project Have children write an addition sentence on paper and then draw a picture to match. Staple their pages together for a class addition book.

Parts of a Sentence Write a number sentence such as 3 + 2 = 5 on the board. Around it write *plus, sum,* and *equals.* Help children read and identify each part.

Teaching Strategy: Strategies for Addition

Addition patterns, the zero property, and the commutative or order property are introduced in this unit.

- Write 0–6 in order.

▶ ***Ask:*** *What's 1 more than 3? What's 0 and 1 more? What's 5 plus 1 more?* Ask until a pattern becomes clear: 1 more gives the next counting number.

- Have 2 children stand then call for 0 more.

▶ ***Ask:*** *What happens? What is the sum?* Point out that the number stays the same. Repeat this, guiding children to tell you how to solve any addition problem with zero: Any number plus zero is that same number.

- Use this strategy to show the order property.

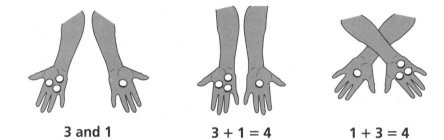

3 and 1   **3 + 1 = 4**   **1 + 3 = 4**

▶ ***Common Misconceptions*** Ask, *What are some ways to find sums for addition facts?* With this question, you can find out what strategies children are using and check their understanding of addition concepts. At the same time, children can learn about others' thinking.

Opportunities to Assess

 Observation

Assign children to groups of three. Give each group a number sentence such as 4 + 1 = ___. Have the children assume roles to act out a story to fit the sentence, write the sentence on the board, and tell the answer to the problem. Observe each group as they report to the class. Did children seem to understand the work? Did they confidently present their problems?

Family Involvement

As the unit progresses, have children regularly find things to add at home, add them, and then show the addition fact to family members. In the classroom, ask children what items they added. Make a list in a prominent place.

Teacher/Student Dialogue

How to Summarize the Unit

Toward the end of a unit, use a discussion to help children recall and summarize what they have learned.

Teacher: What have we been working so hard on lately? Joy, what's one thing?

Student: *We have been adding, like 2 + 2.*

Teacher: Yes, and everyone, what's the sum of 2 plus 2?

Students: *4*

Teacher: When we add, what does it mean? Joel?

Student: *Well, you put them together. Take numbers and you see how many all together.*

Teacher: That's good. Sometimes you put parts together, too. What's another idea about addition? Everybody, think of something, and I'll try to give everyone a chance.

Student: *Zero and 6 is 6.*

Teacher: Zero plus 6 *is* 6! What happens when you add a zero to another number? 3 plus 0?

Students: *Zero doesn't make it bigger. It's 3. It's the same.*

Teacher: Did someone say adding zero makes it stay the same? I'll write 0 + 3 and 4 + 0 and 0 + 1, and let's see the sums.

Questioning Techniques

Starting with an open-ended question, you'll invite any pertinent response. If after several answers you don't get important points from the children, then ask questions for specifics.

If you call a child's name and then ask a question, sometimes the attention of the other children wanders. Pose a question first, invite everyone to think about it, and then call on an individual.

Math Myth

Some people believe that children should start immediately to memorize facts. But research shows that when children have good concepts of what operations like addition mean and when they have practiced strategies to make finding sums easier, they memorize facts more easily and retain them longer. So the time you spend now developing confidence and understanding will result in better achievement.

Special Needs

You may have children who still need work on representing numbers, writing numerals, and counting accurately. Without support, they make many errors and can't do addition very well. Get help *now*. Enlist the help of peer tutors, helpers from a higher grade, parents, or others. With time, encouragement, and individual attention, all children can make progress.

Unit 3   Addition Facts Through 6

LESSON 1
PAGES 67–68

OBJECTIVE
Understand the joining and part-part-whole meanings of addition; act out addition stories

PREREQUISITES
Concepts
• Understand the concept of numbers 0–6

Skills
• Recognize numbers 0–6
• Count from 0 through 10

MATERIALS
counters

Stories with Sums through 6

Presenting the Lesson
Introduce the Skill   Have children use their counters to act out the following story as you tell it. Invite 6 children to act it out in front of the class.

Three children walked to the back of the room. (Pause to allow children to walk or use counters.) Then three more children joined them. *Ask, How many children are in the back of the room?*

Check Understanding   Have 3 children stand. Then have 2 more stand. Ask, *Who can tell a story about what just happened?* (Possible answer: 3 children stood up. Then 2 more stood up. Now 5 children are standing.)

Guided Practice
Have children complete exercise 1 as you read the story. Check that they use counters correctly on their student book pages as they act it out and write the sum.

Independent Practice
Have children complete the remaining exercises independently as you read the stories to the class.

Closing the Lesson   Bring 4 children to the front of the room. Invite a volunteer to tell a story about the 4 children and have children act it out.

LESSON 2
PAGES 69–70

OBJECTIVE
Recognize the plus and equal signs and the term *sum*; find sums through 6

PREREQUISITES
Concepts
• Understand the concept of numbers 0–6

Skills
• Recognize numbers 0–6
• Count sets of 0 through 6

VOCABULARY
number sentence, plus, equals

MATERIALS
counters

Sums through 6

Presenting the Lesson
Introduce the Skill   Have children use counters to act out the addition picture at the top of page 69. Then call on a volunteer to say the number sentence the counters show and give the sum. Write the problem as a number sentence on the chalkboard. ($1 + 1 = 2$). Discuss the meaning of the $+$ and $=$ signs and the word "sum."

Check Understanding   Hold up 3 fingers on one hand and 2 fingers on the other. Ask, *What number sentence tells how many in all?* Have a volunteer write the number sentence on the chalkboard.

Guided Practice
Help children complete exercise 1 on page 69 and exercise 7 on page 70. Check that they can use pictures to help add correctly.

Independent Practice
Have children complete pages 69–70 independently.

Closing the Lesson   Write on the board: $\square + \square = 5$. Have a volunteer write two numbers in the boxes.

LESSON 3
PAGES 71–72

OBJECTIVE
Use the Write a Number Sentence strategy to solve addition problems through 6

PREREQUISITES
Concepts
• Understand number sentences
• Understand the joining meaning of addition

Skills
• Add through sums of 6

Problem Solving Strategy: Write a Number Sentence

Presenting the Lesson
Introduce the Strategy Explain to children that in this lesson they will learn to write number sentences to help them solve story problems.

Model the Four-Step Problem Solving Process Work through the model problem on page 71 with the class.

• **Understand** *Look at the picture story. As you look at the picture, you need to look for the math ideas.*

• **Decide** *What is happening? I can write a number sentence to help me solve the problem.*

• **Solve** *What number sentence describes the picture story?* (1 + 1 = 2)

• **Look back** *Does the number sentence match the picture? How can you tell?* (Yes. I can count the birds and compare that number with my sum.)

Guided Practice
Have children complete problem 1 by going through each step in the problem solving process. Check that they understand the process.

Independent Practice
Have children complete exercises 2–9 independently.

Closing the Lesson *How does writing a number sentence help you solve problems?* (Possible answer: It helps me see the numbers I am working with and then I can decide what to do.)

LESSON 4
PAGES 73–74

OBJECTIVE
Understand the increasing meaning of addition

PREREQUISITES
Concepts
• Understand the meaning of addition

Skills
• Add, sums through 6

VOCABULARY
add, more

MATERIALS
classroom objects

Copymasters
Reteach 20–22, pp. 90–92

Adding 1 More

Presenting the Lesson
Introduce the Skill Show different numbers of objects such as 3 books, 2 pieces of chalk, etc. Ask children to tell how many you would have if you added 1 more. Then add 1 more and count the total number of objects.

Check Understanding *How can counting help you add 1 more?* (The answer is always the next number when you count.)

Guided Practice
Read the example on top together with children. Check that they understand which numbers to put in each box and why.

Independent Practice
Have children complete exercises 1 through 10 on their own. Use the Quick Check for assessment.

Closing the Lesson *What happens when you add 1 more to a number?* (The number goes up by 1.)

LESSON 5
PAGES 75–76

OBJECTIVE
Recognize the vertical form of addition

PREREQUISITES
Concepts
• Understand the meaning of addition

Skills
• Add, sums through 6

VOCABULARY
sum

MATERIALS
counters

Vertical Form

Presenting the Lesson
Introduce the Skill Distribute counters. Write 3 + 1 = 4 on the chalkboard. Have children place their counters horizontally to show the number sentence: • • •   •

Then ask children to move one counter below the three and ask if the total number changes: • • •

•

Show how to write the number sentence vertically and ask if the sum changes.

Check Understanding *How can you write 0 + 3 = 3 differently?*

Guided Practice
Discuss the example with children. Then have them complete exercise 1. Check responses.

Independent Practice
Have children complete the remaining exercises on pages 75 and 76 independently. Then discuss the problem solving question.

Closing the Lesson *How is adding vertically the same as adding across? How is it different?* (same sum, different set up)

LESSON 6
PAGES 77–78

OBJECTIVE
Solve addition facts with an addend of zero

PREREQUISITES
Concepts
• Understand the meaning of zero
• Understand the meaning of addition

Skills
• Recognize zero sets
• Add vertically and horizontally

Adding 0

Presenting the Lesson
Introduce the Skill Practice oral problems involving the concept of adding 0. For example, say, *If we have zero children in the front of the room and we need five, how many more do we need?* Write the number sentences to show the problem, then act out the problems to show the number sentences are correct.

Check Understanding *What can you add to 6 to get a sum of 6?* (zero)

Guided Practice
Have children do exercise 1. Check that they understand how to identify sets of zero. In exercise 7, make sure children understand where they should draw their pictures to match the number sentence. In exercises 13 and 16, check that children write a number sentence that matches the picture shown.

Independent Practice
Have children complete the remaining exercises on their own.

Closing the Lesson *What happens when you add zero to a number?* (The sum is the same as the number.)

LESSON 7
PAGES 79–82

OBJECTIVE
Understand the order property of addition

PREREQUISITES
Concepts
• Understand the meaning of addition

Skills
• Recognize number combinations through 6
• Add, sums through 6

VOCABULARY
order property
fact

MATERIALS
Copymasters
Reteach 23–24, pp. 93–94

Skills Tutorial
Strand P2: Skill 1 Practice 1–7

Order Property

Presenting the Lesson
Introduce the Skill Have 3 children stand in the front of the room and 1 in the back. Then have the child in the back join the 3 in front. Have a volunteer tell what happened and write the number sentence on the board: 3 + 1 = 4. Repeat with the same children, but this time have 1 in front and 3 in the back. Have children tell what happened and write the number sentence: 1 + 3 = 4. *What did we do that was different?* (different order) *What was the same?* (same number of children in all)

Check Understanding *What fact does 4 + 1 = 5 help you know?* (1 + 4 = 5)

Guided Practice
Discuss the exercises at the top of the page. Guide children as they do exercise 1 on page 79 and exercise 7 on page 80. Check that they realize that one addition fact can help them know the answer to another fact without having to do the addition twice. Make sure children follow exercise 14 in order on page 81 and understand the directions for exercise 29 on page 82.

Independent Practice
Have children complete the remaining exercises on their own. Use the Quick Check for assessment.

Closing the Lesson *What happens if you change the order of two numbers you are adding?* (The sum stays the same.)

LESSON 8
PAGES 83–84

OBJECTIVE
Identify and know the value of a penny as 1 cent and a nickel as 5 cents; add money using the cent symbol

PREREQUISITES
Concepts
• Understand the meaning of addition
• Understand the ¢ sign

Skills
• Add, sums through 6
• Recognize combinations through 6

VOCABULARY
penny, nickel, cent, cents

MATERIALS
play coins: pennies, nickels

Copymasters
Reteach 25, p. 95
Teaching Resource 11, (Coins and Rulers) p. 209

Penny, Nickel

Presenting the Lesson
Introduce the Skill Have children use play money to act out simple problems such as: *Maria had 3 pennies and her mother gave her 1 more. How many pennies did she have in all?* Ask volunteers to describe how they solved the problems. Teaching Resource 11 can be used for a collection of coins.

Check Understanding Ask, *How many pennies are the same value as a nickel?* (5)

Guided Practice
Have children do exercise 1 on page 83 and 9 on page 84. Check answers and have children explain how they arrived at each.

Independent Practice
Have children complete the remaining exercises independently.

Closing the Lesson *What are 2 different ways to make 6¢?* (6 pennies or 1 nickel and 1 penny)

LESSON 9
PAGES 85–86

OBJECTIVE
Solve addition problems by using a picture

PREREQUISITES
Concepts
• Understand the joining meaning of addition

Skills
• Write number sentences
• Add, sums through 6

MATERIALS
Copymasters
Extension 7, p. 169

Problem Solving Application: Use a Picture

Presenting the Lesson
Introduce the Focus of the Lesson   Draw children's attention to the picture at the top of the page. Ask children to describe what they see.

• **Understand** *What are you being asked to do?* (tell a story that matches the picture)

• **Decide** *How can you come up with a story that goes with the picture?* (Look at the items in the picture. How many of them are there? What are they doing? What action is shown?)

• **Solve** Tell a story that matches the picture. Make sure it tells about the action taking place and the total number of objects shown. (Possible answer: 4 cars are parked in the parking lot. Then 1 more car drives in. Now there are 5 cars in the parking lot.)

• **Look back** *Does the story match the picture?* (Yes; The numbers of each group and the total match the numbers in the picture.)

Guided Practice
Discuss the model problem on page 85. Have children explain how the numbers are related to the picture. Discuss the process for solving the exercise. Check that children's stories are accurate.

Independent Practice
Have children complete the remaining exercises and share stories and solutions with the class when finished.

Closing the Lesson   Ask, *How did you know which facts matched the pictures?* (Possible answer: I counted the number in each picture.)

LESSON 10
PAGES 87–88

OBJECTIVE
Find the missing addend

PREREQUISITES
Concepts
• Understand the concept of addition
• Understand the concept of number sentences

Skills
• Add, sums through 6
• Recognize combinations through 6

MATERIALS
box, counters

Copymasters
Reteach 26, p. 96

Missing Addends

Presenting the Lesson
Introduce the Skill   Play "Guess How Many." Show children a box with 3 counters in it. Have children count and record the number of counters. Then hide the box and secretly put in 1 counter. Show children the box again. Have them count the total. Say, *Guess how many counters I put in.* Have children discuss how they can check their answers. Repeat with other number combinations.

Check Understanding   Show 3 fingers. *How many more fingers do I need to make 5?* (2)

Guided Practice
Have children complete the exercises in rows 1 and 3. Discuss how they found their answers and how they can check if they are correct.

Independent Practice
Have children complete the remaining exercises independently.

Closing the Lesson   Ask, *How can you tell what number to add to 3 in order to make 5?* (Possible answer: I can count on 2 more numbers to get to 5.)

UNIT 3 REVIEW
Pages 89–90

Item Analysis

Items	Unit Obj.
1–9	3A
10–13	3B
14–19	3C

Answers to Unit 3 review items can be found on pages 89 and 90 of the Teacher's Annotated Edition.

Administering the Review

These pages review concepts and skills taught in this unit. Make sure children understand all direction lines. You may wish to do the first example in each section cooperatively to ensure understanding.

Scoring Chart

Number Correct	19	18	17	16	15	14	13	12	11	10
Score	100	95	89	84	79	74	68	63	58	53

Number Correct	9	8	7	6	5	4	3	2	1
Score	47	42	37	32	26	21	16	11	5

After the Review

• The Item Analysis chart on the left shows the Unit 3 objective covered by each test item. This chart can help you determine which objectives need review or extra practice.

• For additional assessment, use the Posttest for Unit 3, Copymasters, pp. 21–22.

UNIT 3 CUMULATIVE REVIEW

Pages 91–92

Item Analysis

Items	Unit Obj.
1	1B
2, 3	1C
4	2A
5	2B
6	2E
7–10	3A

Answers to Cumulative Review items can be found on pages 91 and 92 of the Teacher's Annotated Edition.

Administering the Review

These pages review concepts and skills from the unit as well as providing practice with standardized test formats. Children should write their answers directly on the test pages.

Test-Taking Tip Remind children to listen to the entire question before looking at all of the choices.

Exercises 1–6 This test is administered orally. Before reading each question, ask children to find the correct locator and then listen carefully. Read each question twice, and pause between items to give children time to find and mark their answers.

ex. 1. *Which picture shows the triangle between the circles? Mark the space under your answer.*

ex. 2. *Which shape most likely comes next in the pattern of figures at the beginning of the row? Mark the space under your answer.*

ex. 3. *Which picture shows the dog on the left side of the cat? Mark the space under your answer.*

ex. 4. *Which group has more items than the group at the beginning of the row? Mark the space under your answer.*

ex. 5. *How many hats are in the picture at the beginning of the row? Mark the space under your answer.*

ex. 6. *Which symbol belongs in the circle to make the sentence true? Mark the space under your answer.*

Exercises 7–10 Tell children that they will complete the rest of the test independently.

Test-Taking Tip Remind children to make sure they filled in the circle under the answers they think are correct.

Number Correct	10	9	8	7	6	5	4	3	2	1
Score	100	90	80	70	60	50	40	30	20	10

Scoring Chart

After the Review

The Item Analysis chart on the left shows the unit objective covered by each test item. This chart can help you determine which objectives need review or extra practice.

Teacher Notes

Subtracting from 6 or Less

Vocabulary

- difference
- minus
- subtract
- subtraction sentence
- take away

Unit Objectives

4A Subtract from numbers through 6 in vertical or horizontal form

4B Subtract money through 6¢

4C Solve subtraction problems using a picture; use Write a Number Sentence and other strategies to solve problems

About This Unit

The support pages that follow provide more information on prerequisite skills, methods for teaching skills and concepts, daily routines, tips on classroom management and materials, and useful dialogue techniques.

Assessments
Use Beginning of the Year Inventory for entry-level assessment.

Ongoing Evaluation Quick Checks, Reteach Worksheets, the Skills Tutorial Inventories and the Midyear Test help ensure that children are progressing adequately to meet the standards.

Summative Evaluation Use Test Preps, Unit Review (p. T68), Cumulative Review (p. T69), Reteach Worksheets, and the Skills Tutorial Inventory, Strand P3, Skill 1 to assure that children have achieved the standards for the unit.

Diagnosing Errors The Quick Checks highlight common errors and provide remediation. See also the **Teaching Strategies Handbook** pp. T60–T63, where short discussions labeled Common Misconceptions appear as needed with the strategies for key concepts.

Homework and Family Involvement
Home Note In the Student Book, the Dear Family Home Note provides objectives, vocabulary, and a sample skill discussion for family participation. (**Teaching Strategies Handbook** pages also provide homework and family involvement tips.)

Education Place Refer families to Houghton Mifflin's EduPlace Web site at http://www.eduplace.com; for resources and activities for students at http://www.eduplace.com/math; and additional resources and activities at http://www.eduplace.com/parents.

Helping Your Children Learn Math This book has activities for children ages 5–13 and tips for getting involved in children's mathematics education. (Houghton Mifflin, 1994)

Lessons		Student Pages	Teacher Pages	Resources	State or Local	
					Objectives	Assessment
4.1	Subtraction Stories through 6	95–96	**T64**	Unit 4 Pretest		
4.2	Taking Away from 6 or Less	97–98	**T64**			
4.3	Vertical Form	99–100	**T65**	Reteach 27, 28; Skills Tutorial: Strand P3, Skill 1		
4.4	How Many More? How Many Fewer?	101–102	**T65**			
4.5	Problem Solving Strategy: Write a Number Sentence	103–104	**T66,**			
4.6	Subtracting from 6 or Less	105–106	**T66**			
4.7	Problem Solving Application: Use a Picture	107–108	**T67**	Extension 8		
4.8	Subtracting Money	109–110	**T67**	Unit 4 Posttest; Reteach 29, 30, 31, Teaching Resource 11		

Teaching Strategies

Math Background	Subtracting from 6 or Less

Subtraction has several meanings, and you'll help children understand two of them—take away and comparisons. "Take away" situations are familiar to children, occurring when we spend money or when we want to find "How many are left," for example. Comparison situations answer "How many more?" and "How many fewer?" A sample comparison situation would be: *Kenny eats 4 carrot sticks. Melanie eats 6. How many more did Melanie eat than Kenny?*

In this unit, children can work with counters, classroom materials, pictures, and pennies to learn about subtraction. They will use problem solving situations and write number sentences to fit them, thus supplementing their previous work with algebraic ideas.

A Positive Start

Like addition, subtraction is an important math topic, and it's your job to help children build understandings and skills. Plan well for this unit. You'll be preparing children for their work in later units and in Level 2. A variety of experiences are essential, especially activities that vividly illustrate the meaning of subtraction. Be sure to provide time for children to practice what they are learning. For yourself, spend time reflecting on what you've accomplished lesson to lesson, and what you'll do differently next time. Praise yourself as abundantly as you praise your students.

Linking Past and Present Learning

The chart shows a selection a key concepts for the unit and how they have relate to what children learned in Kindergarten and what they'll learn in Level 2. Use it to help you focus your instruction.

Concept/Skills	Last Year	This Year	Next Year
Meanings of Subtraction	Introduce the take away meaning of subtraction	Introduce the comparison meaning of subtraction; recognize the difference between the take away and comparison meanings of subtraction	Use the meanings of subtraction to understand and solve story problems
Writing Number Sentences for Subtraction Problems	Use a picture to complete number sentences by finding and writing the difference	Use pictures to write number sentences including − and = symbols	Use a word problem to write number sentences including − and = symbols

Teaching Strategies

Some children will more quickly understand the ideas in this unit than other children. Plan so that you'll have things for them to do as you work with others who need assistance.

Teaching Strategy: Meanings of Subtraction

Introduce take-away subtraction. Have 5 children stand, and then ask 2 to leave the group. Demonstrate symbolically on the board.

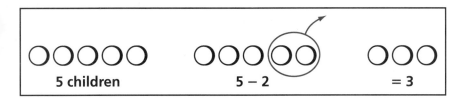

5 children   5 − 2   = 3

▶ **Ask:** *What has happened? How many are left?*
Count the students who are left. Finish the number sentence. Point out the minus sign. Model more take-away situations and use both horizontal and vertical formats to record the work.

- Introduce comparison subtraction. Call for two groups of children—3 in one group and 5 in the other.

▶ **Ask:** *Which group has more? How many more? How can we find out?*
Children may suggest matching the children, putting them in one-to-one correspondence. The number of children without partners tells "how many more."

▶ **Common Misconceptions** Comparison subtraction, asking, "How many more?" may result in addition because of the word *more.* Help children by modeling two unequal groups, matching items one-to-one, and pointing out the "extras." The number of extras tells how many more.

Teaching Strategy: Writing Number Sentences

It's a tried and true approach to "work in reverse" to deepen understanding. In this unit, children write subtraction number sentences to fit situations—and they tell stories to match subtraction sentences.

- Tell a subtraction story and let children tell you why they think it is subtraction. Help them write a number sentence for the story.

- Write 4 − 1 = __ and encourage children to tell a variety of stories that fit the number sentence.

▶ **Ask:** *What's the answer to 4 − 4? What's a story for 4 − 4? What's the answer to 5 − 0? What's a story for 5 − 0? What is special about a subtraction sentence with a zero?* These questions will help children to generate appropriate stories, and also think about the role of 0 in subtraction.

▶ **Vocabulary Development** Be sure that children have opportunities to use the words *minus, subtract, subtraction,* and *number sentence* during the unit. Occasionally write subtraction sentences, asking children to identify the parts as well as the difference.

Patience Pays Be aware that subtraction, which requires a reverse in thinking from addition, may be harder for some children than addition. Offer lots of experiences to help children build their subtraction skills.

Time Saver When children work well together, they can save you time. Team more confident children with less confident children for subtraction practice. The more confident child can check the answers as well as help show her or his partner what to do.

Real-World Children can "spend" pennies in a classroom store and see how many are left. You might want to let children start playing in the store just two at a time, and then increase the number as children learn to talk in quiet voices and take turns.

Materials Many children will need counters or other concrete materials to help them learn subtraction. Encourage them to use their minds and write answers that they know, but let them use counters for a problem they're stuck on.

▶ *Common Misconceptions* If children write plus signs instead of minus signs, or if they add instead of subtract, have them highlight the signs in problems before they solve them.

Teaching Strategy: Practicing Subtraction

Vary the ways in which children practice subtraction. Plan discussions and oral work as well as pencil-and-paper practice.

- Let children handle pennies, "spend" some, and see how many are left.

- Let partners take turns writing problems. One can copy problems you write on the board, and the partner can write the answer. Partners may also check each other's work.

▶ *Ask: Who can help me solve this problem? I've been shopping. I have 2¢ left. How many pennies did I start with?*
This question is not easy, but it invites many answers. Suggest an answer such as *I had 6 pennies and I spent 4* (6 − 4) or *I didn't spend any pennies* (2 − 0). Then record children's suggestions. You'll have an impressive array of subtraction problems with the answer 2.

▶ *Common Misconceptions* As children work with pictures and cross out the number that's being subtracted, they may record this number rather than the number that is left. Watch for this error and emphasize what the problem asks: *How many are left?*

▶ *Vocabulary Development* Discuss subtraction terms to see how children interpret the vocabulary words. Ask, *What does subtraction mean? What does the minus sign tell us to do?*

Opportunities to Assess

Observation

Have individuals self-evaluate their work from the unit. Ask them to share some things that were easy for them and some that were more difficult. Ask, *What were some things that helped you learn? What things were not so much fun?* Note their ideas to guide your planning for future units.

Family Involvement

Send home with children a list of 3 to 5 subtraction facts (perhaps 5 − 3, 4 − 0, 6 − 1, and 2 − 2). Ask that family members let the child show what the facts mean, find the differences, and tell a few more facts that they know.

Teacher/Student Dialogue

How to Talk about a Picture

Display a large, interesting picture, or draw a simple one on the board. Use the picture to stimulate conversation and cover subtraction ideas.

Teacher: We haven't looked at this picture before. What do you see? Bobby?

Student: *It's in a store. That guy is selling fruit.*

Student: *The woman wants to buy something.*

Teacher: Let's look at the fruit. What kinds are there, Pippa?

Student: *Bananas, some grapes, and one apple.*

Teacher: Count the bananas with me. *(Points and leads counting)*

Students: *1, 2, 3, 4, 5.*

Teacher: Five bananas. How many more bananas than apples? Janie?

Student: *One apple!*

Teacher: Right, Janie, 1; but how many *more* bananas than apples?

Student: *Umm . . .*

Teacher: Let's draw. Just one apple. Five bananas. Are there enough to match?

Student: *Oh! There's 4 extra bananas!*

Teacher: Good thinking, Janie. Let's write the number sentence. *(Writes 5 − 1 = 4, and then presents subtraction problems that include pennies)*

Questioning Techniques

Look around your classroom for props that could be used in a dialogue about subtraction. The teacher in the example used a picture that was intended to be part of her social studies program, but it worked well with mathematics.

A picture can provide opportunities for talking about numbers of people, objects, and money, and addition and subtraction. At times, you may wish to supplement a picture with a drawing, to demonstrate a concept in detail, such as rearranging items in one-to-one correspondence so that children can see how many more.

Finally, notice that you can guide children away from a misinterpretation to a correct response. When a child makes an error, build on it, and guide the child to correct herself or himself.

What to do

When

When children can't offer subtraction stories, act out a "silent story," asking them to watch carefully. Show 3 pencils and then put 1 away. Look puzzled and gesture a question with your hands. Children will probably be able to tell you about the story and help in writing the number sentence 3 − 1 = 2.

What to do

Every Day

Reinforce children's rote counting skills by counting to 10 and back to 1. If most of the children do this confidently, practice counting on, starting with a number other than 1, such as 5, 6, 7, 8, 9, 10, for example.

Unit 4   Subtracting from 6 or Less

LESSON 1
PAGES 95–96

OBJECTIVE
Understand the take away and comparison meanings of subtraction; act out subtraction stories

PREREQUISITES
Concepts
• Understand the meaning of subtraction

Skills
• Recognize numbers 0–6
• Count from 0 through 6

MATERIALS
counters, mats

Subtraction Stories through 6

Presenting the Lesson
Introduce the Skill   Have children use their counters and mats to act out the following story as you tell it and invite 6 children to act it out.

Six children walk into the room. (Pause to allow children to walk in and others to use counters.) *Then four of them walk back out. How many children are left?*

Check Understanding   Have 4 boys and 2 girls stand in the front of the room. *Who can tell a story that compares the number of boys to girls?* (There are 4 boys and 2 girls. There are 2 more boys than girls.)

Guided Practice
Have children complete exercise 1 as you read the story. Check that they use counters correctly as they act it out and write the difference. Continue reading the stories for exercises 2–7 as children complete the lesson.

Closing the Lesson   Have children tell a subtraction story about 5 birds in a tree. (Answers will vary. Possible answer: 5 birds are in a tree. 3 fly away. Now there are 2 birds left.)

LESSON 2
PAGES 97–98

OBJECTIVE
Recognize the minus sign and the term *difference*; find differences through 6

PREREQUISITES
Concepts
• Understand the meaning of subtraction

Skills
• Recognize numbers 0–6
• Count sets of 0 through 6

VOCABULARY
take away, minus, difference

MATERIALS
counters

Taking Away from 6 or Less

Presenting the Lesson
Introduce the Skill   Have children use counters to act out the subtraction picture at the top of page 97. Then call on a volunteer to say the number sentence the counters show and give the answer. Write the problem as a number sentence on the board. ($4 - 1 = 3$) Discuss the meaning of the $-$ sign and the word *difference*.

Check Understanding   Hold up 5 fingers on one hand. Then put down 1. *What number sentence tells how many are left up?* ($5 - 1 = 4$)

Guided Practice
Have children complete exercises 1 and 5. Check that they understand which number in the number sentences tells them how many to cross out.

Independent Practice
Have children complete pages 97–98 independently.

Closing the Lesson   Have children draw pictures that go with the number sentence $3 - 1 = 2$. (Children's pictures should show 3 items with 1 crossed out.)

LESSON 3
PAGES 99–100

OBJECTIVE
Recognize the vertical form of subtraction

PREREQUISITES
Concepts
• Understand meaning of subtraction

Skills
• Subtract through 6

VOCABULARY
subtraction sentence

MATERIALS
counters

Copymasters
Reteach 27–28, pp. 97–98

Skills Tutorial
Strand P3: Skill 1 Practice 1–3

Vertical Form

Presenting the Lesson
Introduce the Skill   Distribute counters. Write $3 - 1 = 2$ on the board. Have children place their counters horizontally on their desks. Then take 1 away to show the difference. Then ask children to place counters vertically and take one away. Show how to write the number sentence vertically and ask if the difference changes.

Check Understanding   *How do you know how many turtles to cross out in exercise 1?*

Guided Practice
Have children complete exercises 1 and 11.

Independent Practice
Have children complete the remaining exercises on pages 99 and 100 independently. Use the Quick Check for assessment.

Closing the Lesson   *How is writing subtraction sentences vertically the same as writing them across?* (The number after the minus sign tells me how many to subtract, same difference) *How is it different?* (Numbers are in different places, no = .)

LESSON 4
PAGES 101–102

OBJECTIVE
Subtract to compare groups

PREREQUISITES
Concepts
• Understand the meaning of subtraction
• Understand the terms *more* and *fewer*

Skills
• Subtract from 6 or less

VOCABULARY
more, fewer

MATERIALS
classroom objects

How Many More? How Many Fewer?

Presenting the Lesson
Introduce the Skill   Show different pairs of objects such as 3 erasers and 2 pieces of chalk. Ask children to tell how they can tell how many more erasers there are than pieces of chalk. Demonstrate how to write a number sentence to show the comparison: $3 - 2 = 1$. Repeat with other objects to show fewer.

Check Understanding   *How can we find out how many more (or fewer) boys there are than girls in our class?* (Answers will vary. Possible answer: Match one boy with one girl until there are only boys or girls left over. Count how many are left.)

Guided Practice
Have children complete exercises 1 and 7. Check that they understand how to use the picture to tell how many more or how many fewer.

Independent Practice
Have children complete the remaining exercises independently.

Closing the Lesson   *How did you find out how many more circles there are than triangles in exercise 11?* (Answers will vary. Possible answer: I counted the circles and triangles.)

LESSON 5
PAGES 103–104

OBJECTIVE
Use the Write a Number Sentence strategy to solve subtraction problems

PREREQUISITES
Concepts
- Understand number sentences
- Understand the meaning of subtraction

Skills
- Subtract through 6

Problem Solving Strategy: Write a Number Sentence

Presenting the Lesson
Introduce the Strategy   Explain to children that in this lesson they will learn to write subtraction number sentences to describe pictures.

Model the Four-Step Problem Solving Process   Work through the model problem on page 103 with the class.

- **Understand** *What are you being asked to do?* (I am being asked to write a number sentence for the picture.)

- **Decide** *Does the picture show addition or subtraction?* (Subtraction)

- **Solve** Invite children to trace over the cued number sentence.

- **Look back** *Does your number sentence match the picture?* (One ball is not crossed out. My number sentence matches.)

Guided Practice
Check that children understand the problem solving process before moving on to problems 1–9.

Independent Practice
Have children complete problems 1–9 independently.

Closing the Lesson   *How did you know how many pictures to cross out in exercise 9?* (I looked at the second number — the number being taken away in the number sentence.)

LESSON 6
PAGES 105–106

OBJECTIVE
Solve subtraction facts through 6 in vertical and horizontal form

PREREQUISITES
Concepts
- Understand the meaning of subtraction

Skills
- Recognize numbers 0–6
- Recognize vertical form

VOCABULARY
subtract

Subtracting from 6 or Less

Presenting the Lesson
Introduce the Skill   Have volunteers practice writing number sentences on the board as you give oral problems such as: *I had 5 light bulbs.* (Wait for the child to write 5.) *I broke 1.* (Pause) *How many do I have left?*

Check Understanding   *What number sentence can you write to show 5 take away 4?* ($5 - 4 = 1$)

Guided Practice
Have children then do exercises 1 and 9. Check that they understand how to use pictures to find the difference.

Independent Practice
Have children complete the remaining exercises on their own.

Closing the Lesson   *What happens when you subtract zero from a number?* (The difference is the same as the number.)

LESSON 7

PAGES 107–108

OBJECTIVE
Solve subtraction problems by using a picture

PREREQUISITES

Concepts
• Understand the meaning of subtraction

Skills
• Write number sentences
• Subtract through 6

MATERIALS

Copymasters
Extension 8, p. 170

Problem Solving Application: Use a Picture

Presenting the Lesson

Introduce the Focus of the Lesson   Explain to children that in this lesson they will tell stories about pictures and then use the pictures to choose the number sentence that matches.

Model the Four-Step Problem Solving Process   Work through the first problem on page 107.

• **Understand** Ask, *What does the first picture show?* (6 tops) *What does the second picture show?* (3 tops spinning away, and 3 tops left)

• **Decide** Ask, *How can you decide which number sentence matches the pictures?* (Find the number sentence that shows 3 being taken away from 6.)

• **Solve** Ring the top number sentence.

• **Look back** Check to see if the pictures show 6 things, then 3 taken away and 3 left. *Does your answer make sense?*

Guided Practice

Check that children understand the problem solving process.

Independent Practice

Have children complete the remaining problems and share stories and solutions with the class when finished.

Closing the Lesson   Invite children to share their picture stories from problem 7.

LESSON 8

PAGES 109–110

OBJECTIVE
Solve subtraction facts with pennies and nickels

PREREQUISITES

Concepts
• Understand the meaning of subtraction
• Understand the ¢ sign

Skills
• Subtract through 6
• Recognize money amounts through 6 cents

MATERIALS
play coins: pennies, nickels

Copymasters
Reteach 29–31, pp. 99–101
Teaching Resource 11, (Coins and Rulers) p. 209

Subtracting Money

Presenting the Lesson

Introduce the Skill   Have children use coins to act out simple problems such as: *Rosa has 4 cents. She spends 1 cent. How much does she have now?* Ask volunteers to describe how they solved the problems.

Check Understanding   Draw 3 pennies on the board. Cross out 2. *Who can tell a story to match the picture?* (Stories may tell about having 3 cents, spending 2 cents, and having 1 cent left.)

Guided Practice

Have children do exercise 1 and explain how they arrived at their answer.

Independent Practice

Have children complete the remaining exercises independently. Use the Quick Check for assessment.

Closing the Lesson   Draw 4 pennies with 1 crossed out. Ask, *What number sentence goes with the picture?* (4¢ − 1¢ = 3¢)

UNIT 4 REVIEW
Page 111

Item Analysis

Items	Unit Obj.
1–6	4A
7–8	4B
9–11	4C

Answers to Unit 4 review items can be found on page 111 of the Teacher's Annotated Edition.

Administering the Review

These pages review concepts and skills taught in this unit. Make sure children understand all direction lines. You may wish to do the first example in each section cooperatively to ensure understanding.

Scoring Chart

Number Correct	11	10	9	8	7	6	5	4	3	2	1
Score	100	91	82	73	64	55	45	36	27	18	9

After the Review

• The Item Analysis chart on the left shows the Unit 4 objective covered by each test item. This chart can help you determine which objectives need review or extra practice.

• For additional assessment, use the Posttest for Unit 4, Copymasters, p. 24.

UNIT 4 CUMULATIVE REVIEW

Page 112

Item Analysis

Items	Unit Obj.
1–2	1C
3	2B
4	2E
5	3A
6	4A

Answers to Cumulative Review items can be found on page 112 of the Teacher's Annotated Edition.

Administering the Review

These pages review concepts and skills from the unit as well as providing practice with standardized test formats. Children should mark their answers directly on the test pages.

Test-Taking Tip Remind children to listen to the entire question before looking at all of the choices.

Exercises 1–6 This test is administered orally. Before reading each question, ask children to find the correct item number and then listen carefully. Read each question twice, and pause between items to give children time to find and mark their answers.

ex. 1. *Which picture shows a car on the right side of the plane? Mark the space under your answer.*
ex. 2. *Which figure most likely comes next? Mark the space under your answer.*
ex. 3. *How many mittens are in the picture? Mark the space under your answer.*
ex. 4. *Which symbol belongs in the circle to make the sentence true? Mark the space under your answer.*
ex. 5. *How much is 4 + 2? Mark the space under your answer.*
ex. 6. *How much is 5 minus 1? Mark the space under your answer.*

Scoring Chart

Number Correct	6	5	4	3	2	1
Score	100	83	67	50	33	17

After the Review

The Item Analysis chart on the left shows the unit objective covered by each test item. This chart can help you determine which objectives need review or extra practice.

Addition and Subtraction Facts through 6

Vocabulary

- fact family
- related facts

Unit Objectives

5A Solve all addition and subtraction facts through 6

5B Write fact families through 6

5C Solve problems by choosing to add or subtract; use Draw a Picture and other strategies to solve problems

About This Unit

The support pages that follow provide more information on prerequisite skills, methods for teaching skills and concepts, daily routines, tips on classroom management and materials, and useful dialogue techniques.

Assessments

Use Beginning of the Year Inventory for entry-level assessment.

Ongoing Evaluation Quick Checks, Reteach Worksheets, the Skills Tutorial Inventories and the Midyear Test help ensure that children are progressing adequately to meet the standards.

Summative Evaluation Use Test Preps, Unit Review (p. T81), Cumulative Review (p. T82), and Reteach Worksheets, to assure that children have achieved the standards for the unit.

Diagnosing Errors The Quick Checks highlight common errors and provide remediation. See also the **Teaching Strategies Handbook** pp. T72–T75, where short discussions labeled Common Misconceptions appear as needed with the strategies for key concepts.

Homework and Family Involvement

Home Note In the Student Book, the Dear Family Home Note provides objectives, vocabulary, and a sample skill discussion for family participation. (**Teaching Strategies Handbook** pages also provide homework and family involvement tips.)

Education Place Refer families to Houghton Mifflin's EduPlace Web site at http://www.eduplace.com; for resources and activities for students at http://www.eduplace.com/math; and additional resources and activities at http://www.eduplace.com/parents.

Helping Your Children Learn Math This book has activities for children ages 5–13 and tips for getting involved in children's mathematics education. (Houghton Mifflin, 1994)

Lessons	Student Pages	Teacher Pages	Resources	State or Local	
				Objectives	**Assessment**
5.1 Related Facts through 4	115–116	**T76**	Unit 5 Pretest		
5.2 Fact Families through 4	117–118	**T76**			
5.3 Writing Fact Families through 4	119–120	**T77**	Reteach 32, 33, 34		
5.4 Problem Solving Strategy: Draw a Picture	121–122	**T77**	Extension 9		
5.5 Related Facts through 6	123–124	**T78**			
5.6 Fact Families for 5 and 6	125–126	**T78**			
5.7 Making True Sentences	127–128	**T79**	Reteach 35, 36, 37		
5.8 Problem Solving Application: Choose the Operation	129–130	**T79**			
5.9 Adding and Subtracting Money	131–132	**T80**	Unit 5 Posttest; Reteach 38; Extension 10; Teaching Resource 11		

Teaching Strategies

Math Background	Addition and Subtraction Facts through 6

Children's formal work with addition and subtraction began just a few weeks ago. In this unit, children continue their work with both addition and subtraction to understand the relationship between the two operations. They consider problem situations and decide which operation to use.

Related facts, such as $4 + 1 = 5$, $1 + 4 = 5$, $5 - 1 = 4$, and $5 - 4 = 1$, are called fact families, and they illustrate the inverse relationship of addition and subtraction. Children will need meaningful work and a lot of practice to help them fully comprehend these concepts. You've already provided time for children to practice basic facts. Your plans for this unit should also include varied opportunities for them to deepen their skills competence in addition and subtraction.

A Positive Start

Review with children a few situations in which they use addition and subtraction, and ways in which their family members use these operations. Discuss the importance of knowing when to add, or join things, and knowing when to subtract, or separate things.

Ask children whether they have noticed that older children and adults know many addition and subtraction facts "by heart"; they don't have to think very long about the answers. Explain that their ability comes from applying and practicing skills over time. Assure children that they, too, will learn facts "by heart," and that adding and subtracting will get easier.

Linking Past and Future Learning

Which addition and subtraction facts have children already learned? How far will they advance at the next level? The chart below provides a quick scope of a selection of basic skills and concepts in this unit to help you focus your instruction.

Concept/Skills	Last Year	This Year	Next Year
Related Addition and Subtraction Facts.	Use pictures to solve addition and subtraction facts	Solve related addition and subtraction facts and fact families through 6 using pictures	Write the related fact and fact families through 14 given an addition sentence
Addition and Subtraction Problems	Use pictures to solve addition and subtraction problems	Choose whether to add or subtract when solving simple addition and subtraction problems through 6	Choose whether to add or subtract when solving addition and subtraction problems through 14

Methods and Management

Children need daily routines that establish a sense of structure. But like anyone else, they appreciate variety. As you plan your lessons, look for opportunities to enliven the expected and routine with the unexpected. You can refine your creative and resourceful ideas as you learn from children what works and as you gain confidence and experience.

Teaching Strategy: Related Facts Through 6

As you start teaching related addition and subtraction facts, review the commutative property with children. Model related facts using a part-part-whole mat. Try some of these ideas:

- Write an expression, such as 2 + 3, on the board. Ask children to show 2 fingers on one hand and 3 on the other, and then tell you how many fingers they are showing in all. Ask them to reverse their hands, showing 3 and 2. Ask, *What's the sum?* Point out that the sum is still 5. Repeat with another example. Help children generalize about reversing the order of addends.

▶ *Show This:*

2 + 1

▶ *Ask:* How many shapes are there altogether?
Reverse the order of the shapes and write 1 + 2 = 3. Remove 1 shape.

▶ *Then Ask:* How many are left? What if we remove 2 shapes?
Let children record number sentences as you work.

- Write the number sentence 5 − 1 = 4. Ask, *What are three more related facts?* If children hesitate, prompt them to use all 3 numbers, but with different arrangements and signs. Help them find 2 addition sentences and 2 subtraction sentences.

▶ *Vocabulary Development* Related facts and fact families are important ideas, but they don't lend themselves well to formal definitions for students at this level. You'll teach the meanings through examples and experiences rather than direct discussion.

▶ *Common Misconceptions* When children write 3 + 1 = 4 and 1 + 3 = 4, some are likely to write 3 − 1 = 4 or 1 − 3 = 4 as related facts. This may indicate that they don't really understand how the numbers are related. Take the time to go back to illustrate with counters. Show that 3 and 1 are indeed 4, but removing 1 from 3 doesn't leave 4.

Teacher Tips

Acting Out Facts Have 2 children stand and 1 more join them. Write 2 + 1 = 3. Now reverse the order and have 1 child stand and 2 join her. Ask, *What if 1 child leaves?* Write and act out 3 − 1 = 2.

0 and 1 Strategies Review strategies for adding 0 and 1: Zero plus any number is that same number—nothing is added. And adding 1 is finding the next counting number.

Practice Options Let small groups work with number cards and +, −, and = signs to arrange related number sentences. Or let one child suggest a basic fact, then have others write a related fact.

Fact Match Give children fact cards and cards with addition and subtraction pictures. Ask children to match the fact cards with the picture cards and tell the sum or difference.

Different Operations To help children clarify the difference between addition and subtraction stories, tell similar stories with the same numbers: *4 children are playing; 1 more comes; how many children now? 4 children are playing; 1 leaves; how many children now?* Let children write number sentences and see that, like the stories, the answers are different too.

Stories for Sentences Write a number sentence and let children tell many different stories to fit it.

Jot It Down Reflect on your lessons soon after you've taught. Think about what worked and what you'd like to improve. Jot down notes in a folder to refer to next year, or attach them to the pages in your teacher's book.

Facts Activity Have children write the numbers 0 through 6 and record an addition or subtraction fact for each number. When they've finished, let them write on the board and point out the many different facts for each number.

Thumbs Up or Down Write several number sentences on the board. Make them mostly true, but include a few that are incorrect. Ask the class to show thumbs up or thumbs down to judge the whether the sentences are correct. Volunteers can correct sentences that need it.

Zero Children who think that adding always results in a greater number and subtraction always results in a lesser number may make errors on problems with 0. Show with counters that adding or subtracting 0 does not affect a number.

Teaching Strategy: Solving Addition and Subtraction Problems

Present addition and subtraction situations with both objects and coins. Children can choose the operation to use by listening to the structure of each problem situation. Use situations like these:

- *You have 5 pennies. You spend 3 pennies. How many pennies are left?*

- *4 cars are in the lot. 1 more drives in. How many cars are there?*

- *Paul reads 3 books. Kerry reads 6 books. Who read more books? How many more?*

▶ *Ask:* *What helps you know whether to add or subtract?*
Listen carefully to children's thinking processes. Clarify that joining groups is often addition, while separating or comparing is usually subtraction.

▶ *Special Support* As you tell stories for addition and subtraction, encourage children who are learning English to try to focus in on the number words. Have them write down the numbers they hear, then go back and repeat the words that indicate whether to use a + or − sign, helping children to complete their sentences.

▶ *Vocabulary Development* As children discuss and model problems, use and reinforce words such as *join, separate, how many more, how many fewer, how many are left, earn,* and *spend* as important in deciding whether to add or subtract.

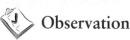
Opportunities to Assess

Observation

Walk around the classroom regularly. Make your observations seem like a natural part of teaching rather than a testing situation.

Homework

Use pictures as a way of assessing children's understanding of addition and subtraction. Have children fold a paper in half and write an addition fact on one half. Instruct them to write a related subtraction fact on the other side. At home, they can draw a picture for each number sentence. Encourage children to add any words they wish to their drawings.

 ### Family Involvement

The Dear Family note in the Student Book provides information on the math topics and vocabulary in this unit. Solicit from families ideas for learning and practicing addition and subtraction. This may reveal perceptions about how mathematics "should" be taught, and at the same time, provide some excellent activities. Open and frequent communication with family members often yields support and enthusiasm for your work.

👥 Teacher/Student Dialogue

How to Connect Addition and Subtraction to Daily Life

When you build a discussion around the ways in which people use math in daily activities, children see how applicable math skills are to the "real world."

Teacher: Guess what I did last night? I put up some pictures and did some more chores around my house. I had 4 pictures to hang. After I hung 1, the phone rang. How many pictures were left?
Student: *5, 5!*

Teacher: Stevie, how did you know that?
Student: *Well, 4 and 1 more . . . umm . . . no.*

Teacher: There were 4 in all, and I only hung one.
Student: *Um, 3.*

Teacher: That's it, Stevie. How did you know to subtract?
Student: *Well, you didn't hang them all.*

Teacher: And so 4 minus 1 leaves 3. *(Writes 4 − 1 = 3)* I'll tell some more of my story later. You tell me some ways you can add and subtract at home. Raise your hand. Anita?
Student: *Well, we opened 2 cans of soup and 1 more can of peas.*
Student: *That's 3.*
Student: *I've got one!*
Students: *Me too! Teacher, me!*

Teacher: We want to hear them all. One at a time. Rosie, yours first, then Kofi's, then Roberta's.
Student: *I had 6 pancakes and I ate them all. How many are left?*

Teacher: Wow! Everyone, is that a subtraction story or an addition story? *(The children respond and offer other suggestions that they identify as addition or subtraction.)*

New Teacher Note

You may need to spend more time and effort in helping children with subtraction than with addition. Addition is like going forward with numbers; for some children, subtraction is like going in reverse. It is harder conceptually. Over time, you'll collect techniques that work for these children, but the most important strategy is to keep trying, with patience.

What to do

Every Day

Pose a "Problem of the Day." Have children tell you whether it's addition or subtraction and how they know. Write the number sentence, and related facts to the one that fits the problem.

Questioning Techniques

Notice how the teacher started with a common situation but didn't dwell on it. The teacher let the children take turns offering examples. To focus the discussion on mathematics, ask questions about the operation and write number sentences to match the children's stories.

Follow up a dialogue such as this one by having children draw pictures of a favorite addition or subtraction story. Children can write the number sentences, or even related facts, for their drawings. Those who want to write words to tell their stories might do so, using invented or conventional spelling.

Unit 5   Addition and Subtraction Facts through 6

LESSON 1
PAGES 115–116

OBJECTIVE
Solve related addition and subtraction facts through 4

PREREQUISITES
Concepts
• Understand the numbers 0–4
• Understand addition and subtraction

Skills
• Add, sums through 4
• Subtract from 4 or less

VOCABULARY
related fact

MATERIALS
counters

Related Facts through 4

Presenting the Lesson

Introduce the Skill   Write 2 + 1 on the chalkboard. Have children use counters, for example 2 red counters and 1 white counter, to act out the number sentence. Write the sum on the chalkboard. (2 + 1 = 3) *What did we just do with the white counter?* (added it). *How can we undo what we just did?* (take it away)

Have children take away the white counter. *What number sentence shows what we just did?* (3 − 1 = 2).

Check Understanding   *How are addition and subtraction related?*

Guided Practice

Have children complete exercises 1 and 7. Check that they notice that one exercise is addition and the other is subtraction.

Independent Practice

Have children complete the remaining exercises independently.

Closing the Lesson   *3 birds are in a tree. 1 more bird comes. Now there are 4. Who can tell a related subtraction story?*

LESSON 2
PAGES 117–118

OBJECTIVE
Complete fact families through 4

PREREQUISITES
Concepts
• Understand the inverse relationship between addition and subtraction

Skills
• Add, sums through 4
• Subtract from 4 or less

VOCABULARY
fact family

MATERIALS
2 counters per group

Fact Families through 4

Presenting the Lesson

Introduce the Skill   Give groups 2 counters each. Have children experiment with the counters to act out and record as many number sentences as they can using both counters. List the various number sentences on the chalkboard. (2 + 0 = 2; 0 + 2 = 2; 2 − 0 = 2; 2 − 2 = 0; 1 + 1 = 2; 2 − 1 = 1)

Check Understanding   Ask, *Is there any number sentence you can act out with just one counter?* (Yes, 1 + 0 = 1; 0 + 1 = 1; 1 − 0 = 1; 1 − 1 = 0)

Guided Practice

Have children complete exercise 1. Check that they understand that the subtraction facts are made up of the sum minus each addend in the addition facts.

Independent Practice

Have children complete the remaining exercises independently.

Closing the Lesson   *Can you make a fact family with the numbers 1, 2, 4? Why or why not?* (No, none of the numbers is the sum or difference of the other two.)

LESSON 3
PAGES 119–120

OBJECTIVE
Write number sentences for fact families through 4

PREREQUISITES
Concepts
• Understand the inverse relationship between addition and subtraction

Skills
• Add sums through 4
• Subtract differences from 4 or less
• Solve related number sentences

MATERIALS
self-adhesive squares

Copymasters
Reteach 32–34, pp. 102–104

Writing Fact Families through 4

Presenting the Lesson
Introduce the Skill   Draw the following on the chalkboard:

$$\square + \square = \square$$
$$\square - \square = \square.$$

Write the numbers 1, 3, 4 on self-adhesive squares. Have volunteers come up to the board and stick the numbers in the boxes as many ways as they can to make true number sentences.

Check Understanding   *How are 1, 3, and 4 related?* (4 is the sum of 1 and 3; 3 is the difference between 4 and 1; 1 is the difference between 4 and 3.)

Guided Practice
Have children complete exercise 1. Check that they write the correct addition and subtraction sentences.

Independent Practice
Have children complete the remaining exercises independently. Use the Quick Check for assessment.

Closing the Lesson   *What is the family of facts for 3 and 0?* ($3 + 0 = 3$; $0 + 3 = 3$; $3 - 0 = 3$; $3 - 3 = 0$)

LESSON 4
PAGES 121–122

OBJECTIVE
Use the Draw a Picture strategy to solve addition and subtraction problems

PREREQUISITES
Concepts
• Understand addition and subtraction
• Understand number sentences

Skills
• Add and subtract through 6

MATERIALS
Copymasters
Extension 9, p. 171

Problem Solving Strategy: Draw a Picture

Presenting the Lesson
Introduce the Strategy   Explain to children that in this lesson they will learn to draw a picture to solve problems.

Model the Four-Step Problem Solving Process   Work through the problem on page 121 with the class.

• **Understand** *Think about whether you will add or subtract while reading the problem.*

• **Decide** *What strategy can you use to solve the problem?* (Draw a picture.)

• **Solve** *What picture will match the problem?* (Draw 4 circles, cross out 3. Count the circles that are left.)

• **Look back** *How can you check your answer?* (See if the number sentence that shows the problem matches the picture.)

Guided Practice
Have children complete the model problem. Check that they drew pictures that represented the problem and solved the problem correctly.

Independent Practice
Have children complete the remaining problems independently.

Closing the Lesson   *How can you check that your answer to problem 2 is correct?* (Check that $3 - 1 = 2$. It does.)

LESSON 5
PAGES 123–124

OBJECTIVE
Solve related addition and subtraction facts through 6

PREREQUISITES
Concepts
- Understand the numbers 0–6
- Understand addition and subtraction

Skills
- Add, sums through 6
- Subtract from 6 or less

Related Facts through 6

Presenting the Lesson
Introduce the Skill   Write $3 + 1 = 4$ on the chalkboard. Ask a volunteer to write a related subtraction sentence. ($4 - 1 = 3$). Then write $5 + 1 = 6$. Have a volunteer write a related subtraction sentence. ($6 - 1 = 5$)

Check Understanding   *How do you write a related subtraction sentence for 5 + 1 = 6?* (I wrote the sum as the first number, and subtracted the second number in the addition sentence.)

Guided Practice
Have children complete exercise 1.

Independent Practice
Have children complete the remaining exercises independently.

Closing the Lesson   *4 frogs are in a pond. 2 more frogs go into the pond. Now there are 6. Who can tell a related subtraction story?* (6 frogs in a pond. 2 jump away. Now there are 4.)

LESSON 6
PAGES 125–126

OBJECTIVE
Complete fact families for 5 and 6

PREREQUISITES
Concepts
- Understand the inverse relationship between addition and subtraction

Skills
- Add, sums through 6
- Subtract from 6 or less

MATERIALS

Fact Families for 5 and 6

Presenting the Lesson
Introduce the Skill   Write a fact family for 5 on the board. Then start another fact family for 5 and have a volunteer complete it.

Check Understanding   *How are the numbers 1, 4, and 5 related?* (5 is the sum of 1 + 4; 1 is the difference between 5 and 4; 4 is the difference between 5 and 1.)

Guided Practice
Have children complete exercise 1. Check that they understand that the subtraction facts are made up of the sum minus each addend in the addition facts.

Independent Practice
Have children complete the remaining exercises independently.

Closing the Lesson   Write the following on the chalkboard: 1, 2, 3, 5. *Which 3 numbers can you use to make a fact family?* (1, 2, 3 or 5, 3, 2)

LESSON 7
PAGES 127–128

OBJECTIVE
Choose the operation necessary to make number sentences true

PREREQUISITES
Concepts
• Understand the inverse relationship between addition and subtraction

Skills
• Add, sums through 6
• Subtract from 6 or less

MATERIALS
counters
Copymasters
Reteach 35–37, pp. 105–107

Making True Sentences

Presenting the Lesson
Introduce the Skill   Give each group 6 counters. Do several problems following this procedure. *Place 3 counters on your mat. Will I need to add or subtract to have 5 counters?* (Add) Have children act out with counters to show 3 + 2.

Check Understanding   *I had 4 counters. Now I have 2. Did I add or subtract?* (Subtract)

Guided Practice
Have children complete the model exercise.

Independent Practice
Have children complete the remaining exercises independently. Use the Quick Check for assessment.

Closing the Lesson   Have partners make up their own number sentence with a missing sign and exchange and solve them.

LESSON 8
PAGES 129–130

OBJECTIVE
Solve problems by choosing to add or subtract

PREREQUISITES
Concepts
• Understand addition and subtraction

Skills
• Write number sentences
• Add and subtract through 6

Problem Solving Application: Choose the Operation

Presenting the Lesson
Introduce the Focus of the Lesson   Explain to children that in this lesson they will decide whether they need to add or subtract to solve problems.

Model the Four-Step Problem Solving Process   Work through the first problem on page 129.

• **Understand** *What does the problem tell?* (4 cats and 2 walk away) *What do you need to find out?* (How many cats are left)

• **Decide** *Will you need to add or subtract? Why?* (Subtract, because the cats are being taken away.)

• **Solve** *Which number sentence will you ring?* (4 − 2 = 2)

• **Look back** *How can you check that your answer makes sense?* (Possible answer: Draw a picture and check that the picture matches the number sentence.)

Guided Practice
Have children complete problems 2, and 5. Discuss the process for solving them.

Independent Practice
Have children complete the remaining problems independently.

Closing the Lesson   *How did you decide which operation to use in problem 8?* (Answers will vary. Possible answer: I know that some of the cats are left.)

LESSON 9
PAGES 131–132

OBJECTIVE
Solve addition and subtraction problems with money amounts to 6¢

PREREQUISITES
Concepts
- Understand adding and subtracting money
- Understand the ¢ sign

Skills
- Add and subtract numbers through 6
- Recognize money amounts through 6 cents

MATERIALS
play coins: pennies, nickels
Copymasters
Reteach 38, p. 108
Extension 10, p. 172
Teaching Resource 11, (Coins and Rulers) p. 209

Adding and Subtracting Money

Presenting the Lesson

Introduce the Skill Have children use play money to act out simple addition and subtraction money problems such as: "Rosa had 4 cents. She spent 1 cent. How much does she have now?" or "Juan has 1 cent and finds 3 cents more. How much does he have now?" Ask volunteers to use coins to demonstrate how they solved the problems. Then discuss the model problems on pages 131 and 132. Teaching Resource 11 provides a collection of pennies for children to use.

Check Understanding *If I have money and spend some, do I add or subtract to find out how much I have left?* (Subtract)

Guided Practice

Have children do exercises 1 and 7. Check answers and have children explain how they arrived at each.

Independent Practice

Have children complete the remaining exercises independently.

Closing the Lesson *How is adding and subtracting money like adding and subtracting numbers? How is it different?* (Same: sums and differences; Different: Money uses a cent sign in the answer.)

UNIT 5 REVIEW

Page 133

Item Analysis

Items	Unit Obj.
4–5	5A
6–7	5B
8–11	5C

Answers to Unit 5 review items can be found on page 133 of the Teacher's Annotated Edition.

Administering the Review

These pages review concepts and skills taught in this unit. Make sure children understand all direction lines. You may wish to do the first example in each section cooperatively to ensure understanding.

Scoring Chart

Number Correct	11	10	9	8	7	6	5	4	3	2	1
Score	100	91	82	73	64	55	45	36	27	18	9

After the Review

• The Item Analysis chart on the left shows the Unit 5 objective covered by each test item. This chart can help you determine which objectives need review or extra practice.

• For additional assessment, use the Posttest for Unit 5, Copymasters, p. 260.

UNIT 5 CUMULATIVE REVIEW

Page 134

Item Analysis

Items	Unit Obj.
1	2B
2	2E
3	5B
4	5C
5–6	5A

Answer to Cumulative Review items can be found on page 134 of the Teacher's Annotated Edition.

Administering the Review

These pages review concepts and skills from the unit as well as providing practice with standardized test formats. Children should mark their answers directly on the test pages.

Test-Taking Tip Remind children to listen to the entire question before looking at all of the choices.

Exercises 1–4 This test is administered orally. Before reading each question, ask children to find the correct item number and then listen carefully. Read each question twice, and pause between items to give children time to find and mark their answers.

ex. 1. *How many crayons are in the picture? Mark the space under your answer.*
ex. 2. *Which symbol belongs in the circle to make the sentence true? Mark the space under your answer.*
ex. 3. *Which number sentence is missing from the fact family? Mark the space under your answer.*
ex. 4. *Which number sentence solves the story problem? Mark the space under your answer. There are 3 balls. 2 balls roll away. How many are left?*

Exercises 5–6 Tell children they will complete the rest of the test on their own.

Test-Taking Tip Remind children to look back to check that they marked the choice they wanted.

Scoring Chart

Number Correct	6	5	4	3	2	1
Score	100	83	67	50	33	17

After the Review

The Item Analysis chart on the left shows the unit objective covered by each test item. This chart can help you determine which objectives need review or extra practice.

Teacher Notes

Addition and Subtraction Facts through 10

Vocabulary

- dime
- grouping property
- three addends

Unit Objectives

6A Add and subtract facts through 10

6B Write fact families through 10

6C Add three 1-digit numbers through 10

6D Identify missing addends in facts through 10

6E Count and add money through 10¢ using a dime or nickels and pennies

6F Solve problems using data from a table; use Conjecture and Verify and other strategies to solve problems

About This Unit

The support pages that follow provide more information on prerequisite skills, methods for teaching skills and concepts, daily routines, tips on classroom management and materials, and useful dialogue techniques.

Assessments
Use Beginning of the Year Inventory for entry-level assessment.

Ongoing Evaluation Quick Checks, Reteach Worksheets, the Skills Tutorial Inventories and the Midyear Test help ensure that children are progressing adequately to meet the standards.

Summative Evaluation Use Test Preps, Unit Review (p. T96), Cumulative Review (p. T97), Reteach Worksheets, and the Skills Tutorial Inventory, Strand P2, Skills 2 and 4, and Strand P3, Skill 2 to assure that children have achieved the standards for the unit.

Diagnosing Errors The Quick Checks highlight common errors and provide remediation. See also the **Teaching Strategies Handbook** pp. T86–T89, where short discussions labeled Common Misconceptions appear as needed with the strategies for key concepts.

Homework and Family Involvement
Home Note In the Student Book, the Dear Family Home Note provides objectives, vocabulary, and a sample skill discussion for family participation. (**Teaching Strategies Handbook** pages also provide homework and family involvement tips.)

Education Place Refer families to Houghton Mifflin's EduPlace Web site at http://www.eduplace.com; for resources and activities for students at http://www.eduplace.com/math; and additional resources and activities at http://www.eduplace.com/parents.

Helping Your Children Learn Math This book has activities for children ages 5–13 and tips for getting involved in children's mathematics education. (Houghton Mifflin, 1994)

Lessons	Student Pages	Teacher Pages	Resources	State or Local	
				Objectives	Assessment
6.1 Related Facts through 8	137–138	**T90**	Unit 6 Pretest; Extension 11		
6.2 Fact Families for 7 and 8	139–140	**T90**			
6.3 Related Facts through 10	159–160	**T95**	Reteach 39, 40; Skills Tutorial: Strand P2, Skill 2; Strand P3, Skill 2; Extension 12, 13		
6.4 Fact Families for 9 and 10	143–144	**T91**			
6.5 Three Addends through 7	145–146	**T92**			
6.6 Three Addends through 10	147–148	**T92**	Reteach 41, 42; Skills Tutorial: Strand P2, Skill 4		
6.7 Missing Addends	149–150	**T93**			
6.8 Function Tables	151–152	**T93**			
6.9 Problem Solving Application: Use a Table	153–154	**T94**			
6.10 Pennies, Nickels, and Dimes	155–156	**T94**	Reteach 43, 44, 45; Teaching Resource 11		
6.11 Adding and Subtracting Money	157–158	**T95**	Reteach 46; Teaching Resource 11		
6.12 Problem Solving Strategy: Conjecture and Verify	159–160	**T95**	Unit 6 Posttest		

Teaching Strategies

Math Background | Addition and Subtraction Facts through 10

Children work with addition and subtraction facts, related facts, and fact families through 10. Children learn to add three numbers in horizontal and vertical forms. They add three groups of pennies, and trade pennies for nickels and dimes. The content in this unit is broad and challenging.

Children's problem solving and reasoning abilities are also extended. They work with function tables and the rules that determine numbers in the tables. For example, if the rule is "subtract 2," then 2 becomes 0, 3 becomes 1, and 10 becomes 8. They also use the *Use a Table* and *Conjecture and Verify* ("guess and check") strategies to solve problems. When they make conjectures, for example, they make quick predictions of sums or differences, and then complete the operation and test their predictions to verify them.

A Positive Start

All of the skills in this unit are related to real–life examples as people shop, read, and select information from tables by combining numbers and finding differences. When children understand and can picture ideas, then they are prepared for the important tasks of committing facts to memory and solving problems confidently. Use your creative ideas for connecting these skills to the real world, and enjoy and share your sense of satisfaction as children make progress.

Linking Past and Present Learning

What preparation for facts did children learn last year? What will be expected of them next year? Use the scope below to help you plan and direct your instruction for the unit.

Concept/Skills	Last Year	This Year	Next Year
Solving Addition and Subtraction Facts	Use pictures to solve addition and subtraction facts	Solve related addition and subtraction facts and fact families through 10 using pictures	Given an addition sentence, write the related fact and fact families through 20
Function Tables	Identify and write numbers through 10; complete addition and subtraction facts	Complete the table using addition and subtraction	Complete the table using addition and subtraction; complete the rule

Methods and Management

Involve children in many multisensory ways to help them with the unit's increasingly complex material. Besides the ideas suggested here, take clues from the children to gain more ways to help them learn.

Teaching Strategy: Addition and Subtraction Facts

Vary experiences to help children understand addition and subtraction situations. This will be a good foundation for memorizing the facts.

▶ *Show This:*

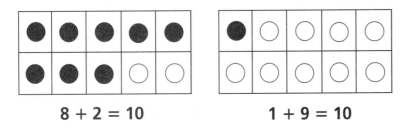

$$8 + 2 = 10 \qquad 1 + 9 = 10$$

Help children see that when the ten–frames are filled, there are 10. Use two-color counters to model facts and record sums.

Demonstrate how to make and use triangular flash cards to show related facts.

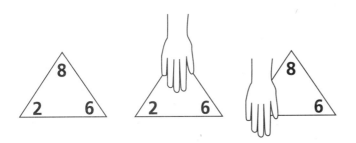

Cover the sum and ask for the sum. Cover an addend and ask for the missing addend or the difference.

Introduce three addends. Establish that the first two addends are added, followed by adding the third addend for the sum. Record number sentences for each example.

Use "targets" like these for finding addends. Let children drop 2 counters or small sponge pieces on a target, and then drop a third piece and find the sum.

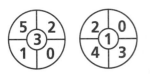

▶ *Vocabulary Development* Children may have trouble with the term *addend*, hearing "add in," or not understanding why numbers that are subtracted are not called "subtractends." Praise questions that show creative thinking, and use these questions as an opportunity to clarify and redefine unit vocabulary.

Teacher Tips

Fact Families For groups of 5 children, make 6 large signs: 3 with numbers for a fact family, and $+$, $-$, and $=$ signs. Let the children arrange and rearrange themselves, each holding a sign, to show related facts such as $5 + 4 = 9$, $4 + 5 = 9$, $9 - 5 = 4$, and $9 - 4 = 5$.

Partner Practice Provide time for children to work with partners practicing basic facts with triangular or traditional flashcards. They should quickly say and check as many answers as possible, but use counters to work out the ones they don't know.

Daily Routine Present one or two missing addend situations each day. As children suggest what the answers are, check by saying, *We want 5 + something to equal 9. Does it sound right to say 5 + 4 = 9?*

Time Saver Ask family members to help you provide dot cards for pairs of numbers. Hold a card horizontally, write the addition fact to match, then turn the domino around for a related fact. Then hold it vertically and write the same fact in vertical form. You can also show related subtraction facts.

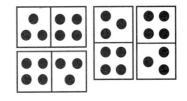

Review Polish children's skills working with $<$, $>$, and $=$. Recall what each symbol means, and let children fill in the blank for problems such as

$$1 + 5 \_\_ 6 - 3.$$

Pacing Allow time for several demonstrations for functions. Draw a function machine in which numbers go in and out, changing based on a rule. Write a rule, such as + 1, state a number to go in. Ask students what number will come out. Repeat with different numbers. Then challenge children to state the rule. You can draw "machines" in a sequence, or give children pairs of numbers (3, 5; 6, 8; 8, 10, for example) and ask them to figure out what rule the machine used.

Partner Work Provide pennies, nickels, and dimes, or similar play money, and let children work with partners. State rules such as "add 1 penny," and let children show numbers of pennies that follow the rule. Children can make trades when possible—5 pennies for a nickel or 2 nickels for a dime—talking through the trades as they work.

Home Support Family members may be willing to help create the classroom "store" and make posters showing trades with pennies, nickels, and dimes to help children remember equivalent values for these coins.

Good Routine Build confidence by including easier concepts in your reviews. When you begin a concept, start with easier and more obvious situations. For conjecture and verify situations, for example: *You have a dime; you want a two-cent item; do you have enough money? You want to buy things that cost 4¢ and 3¢; you have 2 pennies. Can you buy the items?*

▶ *Common Misconceptions:* When children ignore operation signs and use addition in all exercises, ask them to circle the minus signs, complete all subtraction exercises first, and finally complete exercises for addition.

Teaching Strategy: Function Tables

Children's work with patterns and their prior knowledge of addition and subtraction are brought together as they explore function tables. Using rules, such as "add 1" or "subtract 2," children find the missing value.

- Draw a robot-like character and write a rule for it such as "add 1." Explain that the robot *always* follows its rule. Ask, *If you "input" 6, what would the robot's "output" be?* Complete several examples and then change to a subtraction rule.

- Make cards that say "add 1," "increase by 2," "make it 1 more," "subtract 0," "take away 2," and so on. Let volunteers show the class a number card (from 0 – 10) with a rule card, and ask for the result. Then use a rule card and the numbers cards to fill in a function table.

▶ *Ask: If the rule is add 0, what's the shortcut? Is it an adding or a subtracting rule when 5 becomes 3 and 8 becomes 6? How can you tell?*
After children respond, use other numbers and fill in function tables.

▶ *Vocabulary Development* Words such as *function* and *rule* are best taught in context rather than through direct discussion. Use the words often yourself, but be less concerned that children are able to use them.

▶ *Common Misconceptions* Children may not efficiently find values from tables or they may guess at the values because they do not know how to look for them. Guide them with words and gestures to help read across or down a table and to find values below category names or to the right of names.

Opportunities to Assess

 Observation

You'll learn a lot about each child as he or she completes this short performance assessment task. Give each child in a group a fact card, ask the child to read it aloud and use counters to model the answer. Children can tell their answers, then you might also ask them to tell a story to match their completed fact. Mark results on a checklist.

 Homework

Have children take home several triangular flash cards each afternoon with the request that they show a family member how the cards work and use the cards to practice addition and subtraction facts.

👥 Teacher/Student Dialogue

A Quick Review

What facts do children recall? What was hard for them; what was easy? As children review concepts through discussion, listen to their reasoning processes. This is a chance to sort out which lessons and strategies were effective in helping children learn. Take notes about children's accomplishments and challenges, and record for yourself what worked well.

Teacher: We've been working on lots of things. Let's name some of them. I'll write them and we'll talk about them.

Students: *5 plus 5 makes 10! Lots of adding and subtracting. We used tables. Money. We added nickels and dimes.*

Teacher: (*Quickly writes*) Let's talk about adding and subtracting. We worked with facts through 10. What was hard for you? Raise your hands.

Students: *Well, 9. What was the rule for. . . adding big numbers?*

Teacher: Let's take adding and subtracting with 8 and 9. What helped you work with them. Sandra?

Student: *When I use counters I can see what to do.*

Teacher: What helped you find the answers to working with 8 and 9, Adan?

Students: *I took home the flash cards, and my uncle helped me and we said them over and over.*

Teacher: Now, what was easier that you learned?

Student: *It's easy with 2 plus 2 and 2 minus 2.*

Teacher: What about 2 minus 2, and 5 minus 5 and 9 minus 9? (*Writes these on the board*)

Students: *Zero. That makes 0.*

Teacher: And what about another thing with zero?

Students: *If you subtract zero, you get the same number. (Writes 4 − 0, 10 − 0 and children tell the answers) Add zero and it stays the same, too.*

Teacher: Give us some examples of that too. (*The children comply, and the teacher probes for more easy topics from the unit.*)

Questioning Techniques

Two techniques to use occasionally: repeating a response so that the child can think about whether what he or she said is what was meant; and quickly writing responses on the board. Too much repeating will cause children to "tune out." Too much writing will slow down your teaching. But by showing the math during a discussion, children have a longer opportunity to absorb meaning. A visual explanation lasts longer that an oral one, and can be surveyed and reconsidered by the children.

What to do

When

When children who are learning English hesitate to speak to the class, call on them to write answers on the board or show answers with counters or coins. Build their confidence starting with answers you think they know. Throughout your teaching, make a point of assuring any and all children that making a mistake is okay, that it is part of learning math.

What to do

Every Day

Begin your math lesson with several orally presented facts and have children write answers for them. State two problems and have children write the answers quickly. Then write the facts on the board and have children check to verify their answers. Repeat the process with additional sets of problems.

Unit 6　Addition and Subtraction Facts through 10

LESSON 1

PAGES 137–138

OBJECTIVE
Solve related addition and subtraction facts through 8

PREREQUISITES
Concepts
- Understand numbers 0–8
- Understand addition and subtraction

Skills
- Add, sums through 8
- Subtract from 8 or less

MATERIALS
Copymasters
Extension 11, p. 173

Related Facts through 8

Presenting the Lesson

Introduce the Skill　Have children connect what they learned about related facts through 6 to related facts through 8. Complete the exercise at the top of page 137 together.

Check Understanding　*How are 5 + 3 and 8 − 3 related?* (Answers will vary. Possible answers: The sum of 5 + 3 is the first number in the related subtraction sentence 8 − 3. They are opposites.)

Guided Practice

Have children complete exercise 1 on page 137. Check that they are aware that one fact is addition and the other is the opposite, subtraction.

Independent Practice

Have children complete the remaining exercises independently.

Closing the Lesson　*5 ducks are at the pond. 3 more ducks join them. Now there are 8. Who can tell a related subtraction story?* (Answers will vary. Possible answer: There are 8 ducks at the pond. 3 swim away. Now there are 5.)

LESSON 2

PAGES 139–140

OBJECTIVE
Complete fact families for 7 and 8

PREREQUISITES
Concepts
- Understand the inverse relationship between addition and subtraction

Skills
- Add, sums through 8
- Subtract from 8 or less

Fact Families for 7 and 8

Presenting the Lesson

Introduce the Skill　Have a volunteer write the fact family for 5 + 1 on the chalkboard. Then erase a number at a time from each fact and replace it with a number of the fact family for 7 + 1. Guide children to see how the relationships are the same, but the numbers are different.

Check Understanding　Ask, *How are the addition facts in a fact family the same? How are they different?* (Same numbers and sum; different order)

Guided Practice

Have children complete exercise 1. Check that they understand that the subtraction facts are made up of the sum minus each number in the addition facts. Guide children as they complete exercise 4.

Independent Practice

Have children complete pages 139 and 140 independently.

Closing the Lesson　Ask, *How are the subtraction facts in a fact family the same? How are they different?* (Same: They use the same numbers. Different: Difference in one is the number being subtracted in the other.)

LESSON 3
PAGES 141–142

OBJECTIVE
Solve related addition and subtraction facts through 10

PREREQUISITES
Concepts
• Understand numbers 0–10
• Understand addition and subtraction

Skills
• Add, sums through 10
• Subtract from 10 or less

MATERIALS
Copymasters
Reteach 39–40, pp. 109–110
Extension 12–13, pp. 174–175

Skills Tutorial
Strand P2: Skill 2 Practice 1–5;
Strand P3: Skill 2 Practice 1–4

Related Facts through 10

Presenting the Lesson
Introduce the Skill   Continue having children observe the relationships between facts they have studied and new facts. Write $7 + 1 = 8$ on the chalkboard. Ask a volunteer to write a related subtraction sentence next to it. ($8 - 1 = 7$). Then write $8 + 1 = 9$. Have a volunteer write a related subtraction sentence. ($9 - 1 = 8$) Guide children to see the pattern.

Check Understanding $3 + 4 = 7$. *What is a related subtraction fact?* ($7 - 3 = 4$ or $7 - 4 = 3$)

Guided Practice
Have children complete the exercises in row 1 on page 141 and problem 6 on page 142. Check that children understand how the facts are related in row 1 and how the picture, problem, and number sentences are related.

Independent Practice
Have children complete the remaining exercises independently. Use the Quick Check for assessment.

Closing the Lesson   Ask volunteers to make up story problems for other children to solve.

LESSON 4
PAGES 143–144

OBJECTIVE
Complete fact families for 9 and 10

PREREQUISITES
Concepts
• Understand the inverse relationship between addition and subtraction

Skills
• Add, sums through 10
• Subtract from 10 or less

Fact Families for 9 and 10

Presenting the Lesson
Introduce the Skill   Write $3 + 7 =$ on the chalkboard. Challenge volunteers to write the 3 other facts in this family. Ask children to explain how the four facts are related.

Check Understanding   Ask, *What fact family for 10 has only two related facts in the family?* ($5 + 5 = 10$; $10 - 5 = 5$)

Guided Practice
Have children complete exercise 1. Check that they understand that the subtraction facts are made up of the sum minus each of the two addends in the addition facts.

Independent Practice
Have children complete pages 139 and 140 independently.

Closing the Lesson   *What is a fact family?* (a group of related addition and subtraction facts that all use the same numbers)

LESSON 5
PAGES 145–146

OBJECTIVE
Add three addends with sums through 7

PREREQUISITES
Concepts
• Understand grouping in addition

Skills
• Add, sums through 7

MATERIALS
counters

Three Addends through 7

Presenting the Lesson

Introduce the Skill   Have children use counters to model 3 + 2 + 1. Have them group the counters in different ways to see that they get the same sum. Repeat using different numbers such as 2 + 2 + 3 and 2 + 1 + 4.

Check Understanding   *Does it matter which two numbers you add first?* (No)

Guided Practice

Have children complete exercise 1 on page 145 and exercise 9 on page 146. Check that they group first, then add. Make sure children see the relationship between the illustrations and the number sentences.

Independent Practice

Have children complete the remaining exercises independently.

Closing the Lesson   *What are two different ways you can group the numbers to add 3 + 2 + 1?* ((3 + 2) + 1 = 5 + 1 = 6 and 3 + (2 + 1) = 3 + 3 = 6))

LESSON 6
PAGES 147–148

OBJECTIVE
Add three addends with sums through 10

PREREQUISITES
Concepts
• Understand grouping in addition

Skills
• Add, sums through 10

VOCABULARY
three addends

MATERIALS
counters

Copymasters
Reteach 41–42, pp. 111–112

Skills Tutorial
Strand P2: Skill 4 Practice 1–4

Three Addends through 10

Presenting the Lesson

Introduce the Skill   Guide children to see the relationship between this lesson and Lesson 5. Have them use counters to act out problems with three addends with sums of 8, 9, and 10 as they did with sums through 7 in Lesson 5.

Check Understanding   *How would you group to add 4 + 2 + 1? Why?* (Answers will vary. Possible answer: group 2 + 1 first because it is easier to add than 4 + 2)

Guided Practice

Have children complete exercises 1 and 9. Check that they get the same sum for both ways of grouping and that they understand how the number sentences represent the pictures in each exercise.

Independent Practice

Have children complete pages 147–148 independently. Use the Quick Check for assessment.

Closing the Lesson   *How can you change 5 + 4 = 9 to three addends with the same sum?* (Answers will vary. Possible answer: 3 + 2 + 4 = 9)

LESSON 7
PAGES 149–150

OBJECTIVE
Find the missing addend in number sentences through 10

PREREQUISITES
Concepts
• Understand addition
• Understand number sentences

Skills
• Add, sums through 10
• Recognize combinations through 10

MATERIALS
box, counters

Missing Addends

Presenting the Lesson
Introduce the Skill   Play "Guess How Many" as you did in Unit 3, Lesson 10, but with sums through 10. For example, show 6 counters in a box. Have children count and record the number of counters. Then hide the box and secretly put in 3 more counters. Show children the box again. Have them count the total. Say, *Guess how many counters I put in.* Have children guess, then check their answers by writing a number sentence: *Does 6 + 3 = 9?* (yes) Ask children to explain how they found the right answer.

Check Understanding   Show 7 fingers. *How many more fingers do I need to make 10?* (3)

Guided Practice
Have children complete the exercise 1 on page 149 and exercise 5 on page 150. Discuss how they found their answers. They can check the picture or check by writing a number sentence: Does 3 + 3 = 6? (yes); Does 3 + 1 = 4? (yes)

Independent Practice
Have children complete the remaining exercises independently.

Closing the Lesson   *How can you tell what number to add to 6 in order to make 8?* (Answers will vary. Possible answer: I count 2 more numbers from 6 to get to 8.)

LESSON 8
PAGES 151–152

OBJECTIVE
Complete addition and subtraction function tables through 10

PREREQUISITES
Concepts
• Understand the concepts of addition and subtraction

Skills
• Add and subtract through 10

MATERIALS
counters

Function Tables

Presenting the Lesson
Introduce the Skill   Have children pretend they are in/out function machines. Have 4 volunteers hold 1, 2, 3, and 4 counters. Then say, *I am going to put 2 counters in each machine. Guess how many will come out?* For example: *Jenna has 3 counters. I will put in 2. How many will come out?* (Act out putting in 2 and showing that 5 come out.) Do the same with each machine. Then repeat by taking away a specific number of counters from each machine to show subtraction function machines. Then complete exercise 1 on page 151 together with children.

Check Understanding   Ask, *What part of function table 1 stays the same? What part changes?* (The number you add stays the same; the numbers in the columns change.)

Guided Practice
Have children complete problems 1 and 4 on page 151 and problem 10 on page 152. Check that they understand that they must follow the rule to find the missing numbers in the Out row of function table 10. Be sure they see how the table is set up differently, but functions the same, in problem 10.

Independent Practice
Have children complete the remaining problems independently.

Closing the Lesson   Draw a function table with only the In row filled in with numbers 1–4. Have children think of a rule, then fill in the Out row.

LESSON 9
PAGES 153–154

OBJECTIVE
Solve problems using data from a table

PREREQUISITES
Concepts
• Understand data and tables

Skills
• Read data from a table

Problem Solving Application: Use a Table

Presenting the Lesson

Introduce the Focus of the Lesson   Explain to children that in this lesson they will solve problems by using a table.

Model the Four-Step Problem Solving Process   Work through the first problem on page 153.

• **Understand** Ask, *What do you need to find out to solve this problem?* (How many children like oranges.)

• **Decide** Ask, *How can you solve this problem?* (I can look in the table, find the orange and see the number of children that go with oranges.)

• **Solve** Ask, *According to the table, how many children like oranges?* (9)

• **Look back** Ask, *How can you check that your answer is correct?* (Answers will vary. Possible answer: I can look back in the table and see if there is a 9 that goes with oranges.)

Guided Practice

Have children fill in problem 1. Check that they understand how to read the data in the table.

Independent Practice

Have children complete the remaining problems on pages 153 and 154 independently. Make sure children understand that they need to read the table in order to solve problems 8 and 9.

Closing the Lesson   *How did you decide which coins to ring in problem 9?* (Answers will vary. Possible answer: I used the table to see that the dog costs 5¢, then marked that much money.)

LESSON 10
PAGES 155–156

OBJECTIVE
Identify values of coin combinations including pennies, nickels, and dimes

PREREQUISITES
Concepts
• Understand combining coins
• Understand the ¢ sign

Skills
• Identify the value of a penny and nickel and combinations

MATERIALS
play coins: pennies, nickels, dimes

Copymasters
Reteach 43–45, pp. 113–115
Teaching Resource 11, (Coins and Rulers) p. 209

Pennies, Nickels, and Dimes

Presenting the Lesson

Introduce the Skill   Review the value of a penny and nickel as shown at the top of page 155. Introduce the value of a dime. Have children use play money to experiment with using different coin combinations to make various money amounts. Teaching Resource 11 may be used for a collection of coins.

Check Understanding   *Which coin or coins could I use to buy a pencil for 5 cents?* (a nickel or 5 pennies)

Guided Practice

Have children do exercise 1 on page 155. Check answers and have children explain how they arrived at each.

Independent Practice

Have children complete the remaining exercises independently. Use the Quick Check for assessment.

Closing the Lesson   *Would you rather have 1 dime or 8 pennies? Why?* (Answers will vary. Possible answer: 1 dime because it is worth more than 8 pennies)

LESSON 11
PAGES 157–158

OBJECTIVE
Add and subtract money
amounts through 10¢

PREREQUISITES
Concepts
• Understand the concepts of
adding and subtracting money
• Understand the ¢ sign

Skills
• Add and subtract numbers
through 10
• Recognize money amounts
through 10 cents
• Identify the value of a penny,
nickel, dime

MATERIALS
play coins: pennies, nickels, dimes

Copymasters
Reteach 46, p. 116
Teaching Resource 11, (Coins
and Rulers) p. 209

Adding and Subtracting Money

Presenting the Lesson
Introduce the Skill   Have children use play money to act out simple addition and
subtraction money problems such as: "Leroy has 10 cents. He spends a nickel. How
much does he have now?" or "Janell has a nickel and finds 3 cents more. How much
does she have now?" Ask volunteers to use coins to demonstrate how they solved
the problems.

Check Understanding   *If I have 3 pennies in one pocket and a nickel in the other,
how can I find out how much money I have in all?* (add the money amounts:
3¢ + 5¢ = 8¢)

Guided Practice
Have children do exercises 1, 7, and 12. Check that children count the money amount
before they subtract in exercise 12.

Independent Practice
Have children complete the remaining exercises independently.

Closing the Lesson   Ask, *If you have 7 cents, how much more money do you need
to have the same value as a dime? How do you know?* (3 cents, because a dime is 10
cents and 7 + 3 = 10 or 10 − 7 = 3)

LESSON 12
PAGES 159–160

OBJECTIVE
Use the Conjecture and Verify
strategy to solve problems with
money

PREREQUISITES
Concepts
• Understand money
• Understand greater and less

Skills
• Compare money amounts
• Find the value of a combina-
tion of coins

Problem Solving Strategy: Conjecture and Verify

Presenting the Lesson
Introduce the Stategy   Explain to children that in this lesson they will solve problems by guessing and then checking their answers.

Model the Four-Step Problem Solving Process   Work through the sample problem on page 159.

• **Understand** *What do you need to find out?* (If I have enough money to buy the ball)

• **Decide** *What strategy can you use?* (I can guess how much I have, then check to see if
it is enough.)

• **Solve** Invite children to look at the coins to guess if there is enough money. Have
them count to check.

• **Look back** *How much more money would you need to buy the ball?*

Guided Practice
Have children complete problem 1. Check that they use guess and check to solve it.

Independent Practice
Have children complete the remaining problems independently.

Closing the Lesson   *If you have the same amount of money as the price of the
item, do you have enough?* (Yes)

UNIT 6 REVIEW
Page 161–162

Item Analysis

Items	Unit Obj.
1–2	6B
3–12	6A
13–17	6C
18–20	6D
21–23	6E
24–26	6F

Answers to Unit 6 review items can be found on pages 161–162 of the Teacher's Annotated Edition.

Administering the Review

These pages review concepts and skills taught in this unit. Make sure children understand all direction lines. You may wish to do the first example in each section cooperatively to ensure understanding.

Scoring Chart

Number Correct	26	25	24	23	22	21	20	19	18	17	16	15	14
Score	100	96	92	88	85	81	77	73	69	65	62	58	54

Number Correct	13	12	11	10	9	8	7	6	5	4	3	2	1
Score	50	46	42	39	35	31	27	23	19	15	12	8	4

After the Review

• The Item Analysis chart on the left shows the Unit 6 objective covered by each test item. This chart can help you determine which objectives need review or extra practice.

• For additional assessment, use the Posttest for Unit 6 , Copymasters, pp. 29–30.

Item Analysis

Items	Unit Obj.
1–2	1C
3	2E
4–6	5C, 6A
7	6B
8–13	6A

Answers to Cumulative Review items can be found on pages 163–164 of the Teacher's Annotated Edition.

Administering the Review

These pages review concepts and skills from the unit as well as providing practice with standardized test formats. Children should mark their answers directly on the test pages.

Test-Taking Tip Remind children to listen to the entire question before looking at all of the choices.

Exercises 1–7 This test is administered orally. Before reading each question, ask children to find the correct item number and then listen carefully. Read each question twice, and pause between items to give children time to find and mark their answers.

ex. 1. *Which shape most likely comes next? Mark the space under your answer.*
ex. 2. *Which picture shows the ball above the basket? Mark the space under your answer.*
ex. 3. *Which symbol makes the sentence true? Mark the space under your answer.*
ex. 4. *Which number sentence solves the problem? Mark the space under your answer. There are 3 cats. 7 more join them. How many in all?*
ex. 5. *Which number sentence solves the problem? Mark the space under your answer. There are 6 mice. 2 run away. How many are left?*
ex. 6. *Which number sentence solves the problem? Mark the space under your answer. There are 2 birds. 2 fly away. How many are left?*
ex. 7. *Which fact is related to the fact in the beginning of the row? Mark the space under your answer.*

Exercises 8–13 Tell children they will complete the rest of the test on their own.

Test-Taking Tip Remind children to check that they used the correct operations throughout the test.

Scoring Chart

Number Correct	13	12	11	10	9	8	7	6	5	4	3	2	1
Score	100	92	85	77	69	62	54	46	38	31	23	15	8

After the Review

The Item Analysis chart on the left shows the unit objective covered by each test item. This chart can help you determine which objectives need review or extra practice.

Place Value through 99

Vocabulary

- number words
- ones
- ordinal number
- skip-count
- tens

Unit Objectives

7A Count, read, order, and write numbers through 100

7B Count and write numbers through 99 as tens and ones

7C Identify one more than, one less than, ten more than, and ten less than a given number

7D Skip-count by 2's, 5's, and 10's

7E Use the >, <, and = symbols to compare 2-digit numbers

7F Use the ordinal numbers *first* through *seventh* to identify the position of an object

7G Solve problems using estimation; use Find a Pattern and other strategies to solve problems

About This Unit

The support pages that follow provide more information on prerequisite skills, methods for teaching skills and concepts, daily routines, tips on classroom management and materials, and useful dialogue techniques.

Assessments

Use Beginning of the Year Inventory for entry-level assessment.

Ongoing Evaluation Quick Checks, Reteach Worksheets, the Skills Tutorial Inventories and the Midyear Test help ensure that children are progressing adequately to meet the standards.

Summative Evaluation Use Test Preps, Unit Review (p. T112), Cumulative Review (p. T113), Reteach Worksheets, and the Skills Tutorial Inventory, Strand P1, Skills 4, 5, 6, and 9 to assure that children have achieved the standards for the unit.

Diagnosing Errors The Quick Checks highlight common errors and provide remediation. See also the **Teaching Strategies Handbook** pp. T100–T103, where short discussions labeled Common Misconceptions appear as needed with the strategies for key concepts.

Homework and Family Involvement

Home Note In the Student Book, the Dear Family Home Note provides objectives, vocabulary, and a sample skill discussion for family participation. (**Teaching Strategies Handbook** pages also provide homework and family involvement tips.)

Education Place Refer families to Houghton Mifflin's EduPlace Web site at http://www.eduplace.com; for resources and activities for students at http://www.eduplace.com/math; and additional resources and activities at http://www.eduplace.com/parents.

Helping Your Children Learn Math This book has activities for children ages 5–13 and tips for getting involved in children's mathematics education. (Houghton Mifflin, 1994)

Lessons	Student Pages	Teacher Pages	Resources	State or Local	
				Objectives	Assessment
7.1 Place Value through 15	167–168	**T104**	Unit 7 Pretest		
7.2 Place Value through 19	169–170	**T104**	Teaching Resource 6, 8		
7.3 Tens through 90	171–172	**T105**	Reteach 47, 48; Teaching Resource 7; Skills Tutorial: Strand P1, Skills 4, 5		
7.4 Place Value to 50	173–174	**T105**	Teaching Resource 7		
7.5 Place Value to 80	175–176	**T106**	Teaching Resource 7		
7.6 Place Value through 99	177–178	**T106**	Reteach 49, 50; Teaching Resource 7, 9; Skills Tutorial: Strand P1, Skills 6, 9		
7.7 Comparing Numbers: Using >, <, and =	179–180	**T107**	Teaching Resource 7		
7.8 Counting through 19	181–182	**T107**	Teaching Resource 6		
7.9 Counting through 50	183–184	**T108**	Reteach 51, 52, 53; Teaching Resource 10		
7.10 Counting through 100	185–186	**T108**	Extension 14, 15; Teaching Resource 9, 10		
7.11 Counting by 10's	187	**T109**	Teaching Resource 10		
7.12 Counting by 2's and 5's	188	**T109**	Reteach 54, 55, 56; Teaching Resource 10		
7.13 Problem Solving Application: Use a Picture	189–190	**T110**			
7.14 Ordinal Numbers	191–192	**T110**	Reteach 57		
7.15 Problem Solving Strategy: Find a Pattern	193–194	**T111**	Unit 7 Posttest		

Teaching Strategies

Math Background | Place Value through 99

Level 1 students began the year using numbers through 10, but now it's time to extend their learning to interpreting and using numbers through 99. Two-digit numbers are everywhere, and most children have seen and used them to tell ages of older people, determine how many children are in the class, read the calendar, and find prices under $1.00. This unit includes practice in reading and writing numbers, comparing and ordering them, and using ordinal numbers. Skip-counting by 2's, 5's, and 10's lets children count quickly, read time in five-minute intervals, count nickels and dimes, and assimilate important guide numbers for counting with greater numbers.

The unit also features work with some interesting and valuable problem solving strategies—using pictures and finding patterns. Applying their understanding of what 10 objects look like and what place value means, children estimate greater numbers of objects and then find groups of 10 to verify their answers.

This unit is built around place-value concepts. The place-value system groups numbers, therefore making it possible to write very great numbers with relatively few digits. The place-value system is also additive; we add the values in each place for a total value. Thus Level 1 students learn that a number like 35 means 3 tens and 5 ones, or 30 and 5, or 30 + 5.

A Positive Start

Place value lays the foundation for future work with greater numbers and also for understanding decimals. Children need to picture numbers and understand their values rather than simply learning them by rote. The ideas and models you develop for this unit may serve you your entire teaching career. Collect images, prepare number lines and hundreds charts on poster board, and enlist the creative ideas of other teachers.

Linking Present and Future Learning

Not only will you help children achieve this year's goals, but by looking ahead, you can prepare them well for the next level. Use the chart to see what children learned last year and what they'll learn in Level 2.

Concept/Skills	Last Year	This Year	Next Year
Identifying Tens and Ones	Identify tens and more in numbers to 30	Identify tens and ones in numbers to 99	Identify hundreds, tens, and ones in numbers to 1000
Counting, Comparing, and Writing Numbers	Count, write, and compare numbers to 30	Count, compare, and write numbers through 99	Order, compare, and write numbers through 1000
Use the Find a Pattern Strategy to Solve Problems	Identify the next number in a repeating number pattern	Identify 1 more than and 1 less than a given number and 10 more and 10 less than a number on a hundred chart	Identify the next most likely number in number patterns

Methods and Management

Gather numerous objects for counting and work with children to see what numbers such as 34 and 79 look like. Plan different ways for children to handle the materials and relate them to place-value charts, number lines, and hundred charts.

Teaching Strategy: Identifying Tens and Ones

Begin by writing the numbers 1 through 10 and asking children what's special about 10. Point out that it has two digits and sets a pattern for other two-digit numbers. Have children handle groups of 12 and 16 counters, gathering 10 in a group, and then seeing 1 group and 2 counters; 1 group and 6 counters.

- Explain that each "teen" number means 10 and another number less than 10. *Fifteen* means 10 and 5. Lead children in saying number words for 10 through 19 and then writing them.

- Provide counters and show children how to count and group or bundle counters when they reach 10 or a multiple of ten.

▶ *Ask:* Can you make a group of 10 yet? No? Let's keep counting: 17, 18, 19, 20. Can you make a group of 10 now?
   Have children make another group, then write 20 and discuss the idea that 20 means 2 groups of 10 and 0 ones.

▶ *Show This:*

Tens	Ones

Have children suggest numbers for tens and ones and then tell the number. Demonstrate the number with counters.

▶ *Vocabulary Development* Develop the meaning of *tens* and *ones* with models and pictures. Help children build the habit of displaying tens to the left and ones to the right, as numbers are written and read.

▶ *Common Misconceptions* It's easy to see why children confuse numbers like 58 and 85; they have the same digits. Models, place-value charts, and explanations show them how different the numbers are, that the order of the digits is crucial.

Teaching Strategy: Counting, Comparing, and Writing Numbers

Learning greater numbers is exciting, and some children like to "go wild" with numbers, expressing their enthusiasm. When you solicit examples, give a range so that children don't jump too far ahead.

- Use two-digit number cards. Choose one and have children read it, then count on from that number.

- Introduce number lines for a series of numbers, such as 10–20, 30–50, and 60–90. Use adding machine tape to make a number line to stretch across the room. Write multiples of 10 in one color, and write 5 and numbers ending in 5 in another. Have children locate numbers, tell if the numbers are greater or less than a given number, and tell their place values.

Teacher Tips

Visual Aids Use these simple visual organizers and have children show 15, 11, and 18 with counters, 10 on the frame and the rest to the side. Ask children to tell the number of tens and ones for each number.

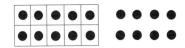

Help from Home Ask family members to participate by giving them specific tasks. For example, suggest that they work with the children to make a chart that shows the place values of numbers from 11 through 19, including visual examples and the words clearly printed. Charts can be used in class or kept at home for math support.

More Materials Work with each child to make a tens and ones workmat out of paper folded once and then labeled on each side of the fold. Use bundled and loose straws or craft sticks to represent tens and ones.

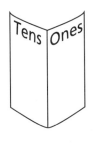

Materials Table-top number lines and hundred charts for each pair of children are invaluable aids. They're easier to see than a large copy at the front of the room, and having them available encourages participation. When these materials are laminated, children can rub off their marks for easy reuse.

Before, Between, After Identify a number and have children use a number line to locate the numbers before and after it. Now name two numbers and have children find what number or numbers are between them. Pose similar questions and see if the children can answer them without referring to the number line.

Ordinal Numbers Present and review ordinal numbers for days of the week, such as *the first day is Sunday, the second day is Monday,* and so on. As children line up, ask the *third* child to wave, the *fifth* child to squat, the *seventh* child to stand with hands on hips, and so on.

Finding Patterns As you start work with the hundred chart, let children tell what they notice about it. Point out that in rows, the ones increase from left to right, and in columns, the tens increase from top to bottom.

Visual Support Use the over-head projector to briefly show 40 to 60 paper clips. Place a paper over the clips so they're no longer in view, then let children tell how many they think are there and why. Remove the paper and slide 10 clips together so children can see a benchmark. Cover the display again, let children conjecture. Finally, arrange the clips by tens and ones to show the actual number.

▶ *Vocabulary Development* *Greater, less, greatest, least, order, before, between, after* and *ordinal numbers* are words that you'll use frequently in the unit. Display the words on a bulletin board and let each child write at least one number sentence to post beside each term.

▶ *Common Misconceptions* The > and < symbols are easy to confuse when children are still learning meanings of two-digit numbers. Use plenty of pictures and hands-on materials to build the concepts. Review that the *wider* part of the > sign is next to the *greater* number.

Teaching Strategy: Patterns and Problem Solving

Prepare children for making conjectures and for finding patterns in the hundred chart.

- Choose a number on the hundred chart and ask children to model the number with place-value materials and write it in a place-value chart. Ask children to show one more and one fewer than the number, locating these numbers on the chart, and modeling them.

▶ *Ask:* *What does 10 more or 10 fewer look like? What is the name for 10 more? How many tens are there; how many ones? Where is it on the chart?* Help children explore changing ones and tens, and explaining their reasoning.

▶ *Common Misconceptions* Children may not know where to start in making conjectures about numbers of items. If they are confused or seem to guess wildly, show them 10 items or let them circle 10 items on a page. Use this as a benchmark for making conjectures.

▶ *Vocabulary Development* Review *pattern* as children work with the hundred chart or number line, showing how patterns repeat.

Opportunities to Assess

Observation

Work with small groups for a performance assessment. Give each child a different two-digit number on a card to model with place value materials. Have children say their numbers and tell how many tens and ones the numbers have. Then ask for 10 more and 1 less than the number. These tasks will quickly show you who understand the main ideas and who needs more practice.

Family Involvement

Ask children to find at least three different samples of two-digit numbers at home. They might look for labels on food containers, find examples in newspapers and magazines, or note numbers on calendars. Request that they write the numbers and bring them to school to share.

Teacher/Student Dialogue

How to Help Children Lead

As we teach, we learn. By putting ideas into words, and by showing a concept step by step, learning takes place. Let children lead and support one another.

Teacher: I have some number cards here and we can see the hundred chart and number line. You can take turns being the teacher and use these things to ask a question of the class. Sandy, it looks like you are ready. Come up lead us.

Student: *(Shows the 48 card)* What number does this say? Manolito?

Student: *48, and it's 4 tens and 8 ones.*

Teacher: Thanks, boys. Manolito, you told two things about the number; very good. Now Lina, you be the teacher, and let's use 48 again. Ask us about numbers greater than or less than 48.

Student: *Well, tell me 1 more than 48.*

Students: *49! 49!*

Teacher: Good job, Lina. You spoke clearly. Now pick someone else to be the teacher and use the hundred chart.

Student: *(Complies and Steven comes up)* Read me these everybody. *(Points to the 50's row in the chart and praises classmates as they count)*

Students: 50, 51, 52, 53, 54 . . .

Teacher: Very nice, Steven; you helped us count quickly. Everybody, that was so good that I need to hear you count backward on that row too. *(Points to 60 and leads children in counting backwards)*

Questioning Techniques

Stay in control of the situation when children act as teachers. To maintain their interest, move the conversation along and allow turns for as many children as possible. Keep your praise brief and specific. Use these tips:

- Props help children ask questions and are a visual stimulus for those who answer.

- More than 1 question about a number leads children in different directions.

- Prompt children as they ask questions to lead to different aspects of the topic.

- Interject your own questions, as appropriate, to focus and guide the children.

What to do

When

If children confuse the "teen numbers" whose names are in a different pattern than other two-digit numbers, tell them that the number words mean "ten and a number," but we say them backward. Show them that *thirteen*, for example, means 10 and 3.

What to do

Every Day

Have two children stand and hold large number cards. Have the class say the number that's formed and tell its place value. Count on from the number, then tell the number 1 greater and 10 greater and the number 1 less and 10 less. Finally have the children reverse places and use the new number that's formed to repeat the steps.

Unit 7   Place Value through 99

LESSON 1
PAGES 167–168

OBJECTIVE
Count and write the number of tens and ones through 15; read and write the numerals 10 through 15

PREREQUISITES
Concepts
• Understand place value
• Understand number and quantity

Skills
• Count, read, and write numbers and quantities from 0–10

VOCABULARY
tens, ones

MATERIALS
variety of items to count such as crayons, chalk, counters

Place Value through 15

Presenting the Lesson
Introduce the Skill   Have children experiment with a variety of objects to see, count, and show what 1 group of ten looks like. They can make bundles of 10 crayons, 10 sticks, or 10 counters. Then discuss the model problem on page 167 to show children what 1 ten looks like in picture form.

Check Understanding   *How are the groups of ten we found alike? How are they different?* (Each group has the same number of items, but the items are different.)

Guided Practice
Have children complete the model exercise and exercise 1. Check that they count tens and ones accurately.

Independent Practice
Have children complete the remaining exercises independently.

Closing the Lesson   *Which digit in a number tells how many tens?* (the digit in the next to last place)

LESSON 2
PAGES 169–170

OBJECTIVE
Count and write the number of tens and ones through 19; read and write the numerals 16 through 19

PREREQUISITES
Concepts
• Understand place value
• Understand number and quantity

Skills
• Count, read, and write numbers and quantities from 0–15

MATERIALS
number cards 10–19
place-value sticks

Copymasters
Teaching Resource 6 (Number Cards 10–20), 8 (Place-value Table), pp. 204, 206

Place Value through 19

Presenting the Lesson
Introduce the Skill   Review the numbers 10–15. Use the place-value table on Teaching Resource 8. Have volunteers take turns showing how many place-value sticks belong in each pocket for the numbers 10–15. Have them predict and show how many for 16–19. Then have them do the same using the number cards for 10–19 on Teaching Resource 6.

Check Understanding   *How are the numbers 10–19 alike? Different?* (Same number of tens; different number of ones)

Guided Practice
Have children complete exercise 1. Check that they understand the 10 that is added means 1 ten.

Independent Practice
Have children complete the remaining exercises independently.

Closing the Lesson   *If you have a box of 10 crayons and 7 more crayons, how many crayons do you have?* (17)

LESSON 3
PAGES 171–172

OBJECTIVE
Count and write the number of
tens through 90; read the number words ten through ninety

PREREQUISITES
Concepts
• Understand ten
• Understand place value

Skills
• Identify tens and ones
• Count quantities of ten

VOCABULARY
number word

MATERIALS
counters, place-value sticks

Copymasters
Reteach 47–48, pp. 117–118
Teaching Resource 7, (Place-
value Models) p. 205

Skills Tutorial
Strand P1: Skill 4 Practice 1–4,
Skill 5 Practice 1–7

Tens through 90

Presenting the Lesson
Introduce the Skill   Have children experiment with making groups of ten. Give each group of children a pile of counters or place-value sticks and have them make as many bundles of ten as they can. Tell children to give back any counters or sticks that are left over after they make their bundles. Have each group count their bundles and tell how many sticks or counters they have. Use Teaching Resource 7 for place-value sticks and bundles.

Check Understanding   *If I have 40 sticks, how many bundles of ten do I have?* (4)

Guided Practice
Have children complete exercises 1 and 6. Check that they understand why they must write a 0 in the ones column.

Independent Practice
Have children complete the remaining exercises independently. Use the Quick Check for assessment.

Closing the Lesson   *What pattern do you see in the number words?* (Answers will vary. Possible answer: Sixty through ninety all have the word for the number of tens in the name.)

LESSON 4
PAGES 173–174

OBJECTIVE
Count and write the number
of tens and ones and numerals
to 50

PREREQUISITES
Concepts
• Understand tens
• Understand place value

Skills
• Identify tens and ones
• Identify tens through 90

MATERIALS
place value models

Copymasters
Teaching Resource 7,(Place-
value Models) p. 205

Place Value to 50

Presenting the Lesson
Introduce the Skill   Demonstrate and have children practice using place-value models to show numbers to 50. Have children then work in pairs. Have one partner show a number using the models and the other tell the number. Partners then switch roles and repeat.

Check Understanding   *Can you have a number that does not have any tens? If so, give an example. If not tell why.* (Yes; 0–9)

Guided Practice
Have children complete exercise 1. Check that they understand that 20 stands for the digit 2 in 24.

Independent Practice
Have children complete the remaining exercises independently.

Closing the Lesson   *Name a number that has more ones than tens.* (Answers will vary. Possible answer: 35)

LESSON 5
PAGES 175–176

OBJECTIVE
Count and write the number of tens and ones and numerals to 80

PREREQUISITES
Concepts
• Understand tens
• Understand place value

Skills
• Identify tens and ones
• Identify tens through 90

MATERIALS
place-value models

Copymasters
Teaching Resource 7, (Place-value Models) p. 205

Place Value to 80

Presenting the Lesson
Introduce the Skill   Have children continue practicing using place-value models to show numbers to 80 as they did in the previous lesson with numbers to 50.

Check Understanding   *Which has a greater value in the number 68, the 6 or 8? Why?* (6, because it stands for 60. The 8 stands for 8. 60 is greater than 8.)

Guided Practice
Have children complete exercises 1 and 4. Check that they understand that the digit 5 in 53 stands for 50.

Independent Practice
Have children complete the remaining exercises independently.

Closing the Lesson   *How many 2-digit numbers have a 7 in the tens place?* (10; 70 through 79)

LESSON 6
PAGES 177–178

OBJECTIVE
Count and write the number of tens and ones and numerals through 99

PREREQUISITES
Concepts
• Understand tens
• Understand place value

Skills
• Identify tens and ones
• Identify tens through 90

MATERIALS
place-value models

Copymasters
Reteach 49–50, pp. 119–120
Teaching Resource 7 (Place-value Models), 9 (Hundred-square Grid), pp. 205, 207

Skills Tutorial
Strand P1: Skill 6 Practice 1–9, Skill 9 Practice 1–7

Place Value through 99

Presenting the Lesson
Introduce the Skill   Have children continue practicing using place-value models to show numbers to 99 as they did in the previous lesson with numbers to 80.

Check Understanding   *Which numbers between 1 and 99 have the same number of tens as ones?* (11, 22, 33, 44, 55, 66, 77, 88.)

Guided Practice
Have children complete exercises 1 and 4. Check that they understand the 8 in 82 means 80 or 8 tens.

Independent Practice
Have children complete the remaining exercises independently. Use the Quick Check for assessment.

Closing the Lesson   *Which number has a 4 in the ones place and a 9 in the tens place?* (94)

LESSON 7
PAGES 179–180

OBJECTIVE
Compare numbers though 99 using the symbols >, <, and =

PREREQUISITES
Concepts
• Understand greater, greatest, less, least
• Understand place value

Skills
• Identify tens and ones
• Use >, <, and =
• Read, write numbers 1–99

MATERIALS
place value sticks

Copymasters
Teaching Resource 7, (Place-value Models) p. 205

Comparing Numbers: Using >, <, and =

Presenting the Lesson
Introduce the Skill   Have children use place-value sticks to model 18 and 15. Have them show 18 above 15 and line up the tens and ones of each number. *How do the tens compare?* (They are the same.) *How do the ones compare* (18 has more than 15.) *Which number is greater? Which is less?* (18 is greater than 15; 15 is less than 18.) Review the same process in pictorial form with the top problem on page 179.

Check Understanding   *How can you use sticks to compare 12 and 17?* (Model the numbers. Compare the tens. If they are the same, then compare the ones.)

Guided Practice
Have children complete exercises 1, 5, 9, 13, and 17. Check that they understand how to compare three numbers.

Independent Practice
Have children complete the remaining exercises independently.

Closing the Lesson   *If two 2-digit numbers do not have the same number of tens, should you compare the ones to see which is greater? Why or why not?* (No, because the number with more tens is always greater.)

LESSON 8
PAGES 181–182

OBJECTIVE
Count and write numbers through 19 in order

PREREQUISITES
Concepts
• Understand order

Skills
• Count and write numbers through 10.

MATERIALS
nineteen index cards numbered 1–19

Copymasters
Teaching Resource 6, (Number Cards 10–20) p. 204

Counting through 19

Presenting the Lesson
Introduce the Skill   Give out index cards 1 through 5 to five children. Teaching Resource 6 has number cards 10 through 20. Have children arrange themselves in order, then display their numbers on the chalk tray. Repeat with five more numbers at a time until they have arranged the numbers in order from 1 through 19. Then compare the numbers on the tray to the number lines on pages 181 and 182.

Check Understanding   *If you want to name a number greater than 6, will you go to the right or left of 6 on the number line?* (Right)

Guided Practice
Have children complete exercises 1 and 6–8. Check that they understand how to write numbers in order.

Independent Practice
Have children complete the remaining problems independently.

Closing the Lesson   *Which numbers come between 11 and 18?* (12, 13, 14, 15, 16, 17)

LESSON 9
PAGES 183–184

OBJECTIVE
Count and write numbers through 50 in order; count and write by tens to 50

PREREQUISITES
Concepts
• Understand order

Skills
• Count and write numbers through 19

MATERIALS
hundred chart cut in half (to 50) per child

Copymasters
Reteach 51–53, pp. 121–123
Teaching Resource 10, (Hundred Chart) p. 208

Counting through 50

Presenting the Lesson
Introduce the Skill   Distribute copies of numbers 1–50 of the Hundred Chart on Teaching Resource 10. Work together with children to read numbers, count, and identify number patterns on the chart.

Check Understanding   *How does the number line help you find the numbers just before or just after a given number?* (The number line helps me see the order)

Guided Practice
Have children complete exercises 1–3. Check that they remember the meaning of *after, between,* and *before.*

Independent Practice
Have children complete the remaining problems independently. Use the Quick Check for assessment.

Closing the Lesson   *Does the number 38 come after or before 40?* (Before)

LESSON 10
PAGES 185–186

OBJECTIVE
Count and write numbers through 100 in order

PREREQUISITES
Concepts
• Understand order

Skills
• Count and write numbers through 50

Copymasters
Extension 14–15, pp. 176–177
Teaching Resource 9 (Hundred-square Grid), 10 (Hundred Chart), pp. 207, 208

Counting through 100

Presenting the Lesson
Introduce the Skill   Have children practice counting from various starting points to a specific ending point. For example, start at 47 and count to 62. Have the class count together, then call on individual volunteers to do the same. Allow children to use the number lines on pages 185 and 186 as references if they need them.

Check Understanding   *Do any 2-digit numbers with 8 tens come after number 89? Before? If so, what are they?* (No; Yes: 88, 87, 86, 85, 84, 83, 82, 81, 80)

Guided Practice
Have children complete exercises 1–3 . Check that they understand how to use the number line to help them.

Independent Practice
Have children complete the remaining problems independently.

Closing the Lesson   *If you can write the numbers 0 through 9, can you write the numbers 10 through 100? Why or why not?* (Yes; all of the numbers are made up of the digits 0 through 9.)

LESSON 11
PAGE 187

OBJECTIVE
Skip-count by 10's to 100

PREREQUISITES
Concepts
• Understand counting

Skills
• Count by 1's from 1 to 100
• Count and write the number of tens through 100

VOCABULARY
skip-count

MATERIALS
Copymasters
Teaching Resource 10, (Hundred Chart), p. 208

Counting by 10's

Presenting the Lesson
Introduce the Skill   Have children practice skip-counting orally from 10 through 100 using the Hundred Chart on Teaching Resource 10 to refer to as needed. *Which column will we read down to skip-count by tens?* (the last one)

Check Understanding   *How are the numbers alike? How are they different?* (Alike: All 0's in the ones. Different: number of tens)

Guided Practice
Have children do the first rows in exercise 1. Check that they can write the numbers and realize they are actually counting the number of rabbits by 10's.

Independent Practice
Have children complete the remaining exercises independently.

Closing the Lesson   *What pattern do you see in the numbers when you skip count by 10's?* (The number of tens increased by 1 for each number.)

LESSON 12
PAGE 188

OBJECTIVE
Skip-count by 2's and 5's

PREREQUISITES
Concepts
• Understand counting

Skills
• Count by 1's from 1 to 100

Copymasters
Reteach 54–56, pp. 124–126
Teaching Resource 10, (Hundred Chart) p. 208

Counting by 2's and 5's

Presenting the Lesson
Introduce the Skill   Have children practice skip-counting orally by 2's and by 5's using the Hundred Chart on Teaching Resource 10 to refer to as needed.

Check Understanding   *What pattern do you see in the ones place when you count by 5's?* (All numbers end in 0 or 5.)

Guided Practice
Have children complete exercises 1 and 3. Check that they realize that they are counting the number of hearts by 2's and the number of starfish arms by 5's.

Independent Practice
Have children complete the remaining exercises independently. Use the Quick Check for assessment.

Closing the Lesson   Have a group of children hold up 1 hand each and have volunteers count by 5's to tell how many fingers in all. Then count eyes or ears by counting by 2's.

LESSON 13
PAGES 189–190

OBJECTIVE
Solve problems by using a picture to estimate

PREREQUISITES
Concepts
• Understand estimation

Skills
• Count by tens

Problem Solving Application: Use a Picture

Presenting the Lesson
Introduce the Focus of the Lesson Explain to children that in this lesson they will use a picture to help solve problems.

Model the Four Step Problem Solving Process Work through the first problem on page 189.

• **Understand** *What do you know? What do you need to find out?* (You know the top box has 10 stars. You want to know which of the two boxes below has 50 stars.)

• **Decide** *How can you solve this problem.* (I can use the picture of ten stars to estimate how many stars are in each of the other boxes.)

• **Solve** *Based on the picture, which box looks like it has about 50 stars?* (gray box)

• **Look back** *How can you check that your answer is correct?* (Ring groups of 10 in each box and see which has 5 groups of ten or 50.)

Guided Practice
Once children complete problem 1, check their guesses.

Independent Practice
Have children complete page 190.

Closing the Lesson *Did you have to know the exact number of dots in each box to solve problem 2? Why or why not?* (No, because I just needed to know which box had a little more than 60 dots.)

LESSON 14
PAGES 191–192

OBJECTIVE
Recognize ordinal positions first through seventh

PREREQUISITES
Concepts
• Understand position

Skills
• Count in order from 1–7

VOCABULARY
ordinal number

MATERIALS
Copymasters
Reteach 57, p. 127

Ordinal Numbers

Presenting the Lesson
Introduce the Skill Have 7 children stand in line in the front of the room. Have volunteers identify who is first, second, third, etc. Then give directions using ordinal numbers for students to follow, such as "Stand in line so that Jan is first and Dan is sixth."

Check Understanding *If you are seventh in line and you are last, how many people are in line?* (seven)

Guided Practice
Have children complete exercises 1 and 8. Check that they can identify ordinal positions. Point out that children should count from left to right.

Independent Practice
Have children complete the remaining exercises independently.

Closing the Lesson Have children draw 7 boxes and color in the 1st, 3rd, and 5th boxes. Check drawings.

LESSON 15
PAGES 193–194

OBJECTIVE
Use the Find a Pattern strategy to solve problems

PREREQUISITES
Concepts
• Understand patterns

Skills
• Count by 1's, 2's, 5's, and 10's

Problem Solving Strategy: Find a Pattern

Presenting the Lesson

Introduce the Strategy   Explain to children that in this lesson they will find patterns to solve problems.

Model the Four-Step Problem Solving Process   Work through the model problem on page 193.

• **Understand** *As you read, ask yourself questions.*

• **Decide** *How can you find the number? Can you see a pattern?*

• **Solve** *What is the next number in the pattern on the chart?* (65)

• **Look back** *What other strategy could you use to solve the problem?*

Guided Practice

Once children complete the model problem, ask them to describe the pattern they see.

Independent Practice

Have children complete problems 1–8.

Closing the Lesson   *What strategy did you use to solve exercises 5–8? How might finding a pattern help?* (I used the Finding a Pattern strategy and it helped because the numbers could be found on the chart.)

UNIT 7 REVIEW
Page 195–196

Item Analysis

Items	Unit Obj.
1–2	7A
3–6	7B
7–10	7C
11–13	7D
14–15	7E
16	7F
17–18	7G

Answers to Unit 7 review items can be found on pages 195–196 of the Teacher's Annotated Edition.

Administering the Review

These pages review concepts and skills taught in this unit. Make sure children understand all direction lines. You may wish to do the first example in each section cooperatively to ensure understanding.

Scoring Chart

Number Correct	18	17	16	15	14	13	12	11	10	9	8	7	6	5	4	3	2	1
Score	100	94	89	83	78	72	67	61	56	50	44	39	33	28	22	17	11	6

After the Review

• The Item Analysis chart on the left shows the Unit 7 objective covered by each test item. This chart can help you determine which objectives need review or extra practice.

• For additional assessment, use the Posttest for Unit 7, Copymasters, pp. 33–34.

Item Analysis

Items	Unit Obj.
1	5C
2	6B
3	7A
4	7B
5–7	7D
8	7E
9	7F
10	7C
11	7G
12–13	6A

Answers to Cumulative Review items can be found on pages 197–198 of the Teacher's Annotated Edition.

Administering the Review

These pages review concepts and skills from the unit as well as providing practice with standardized test formats. Children should mark their answers directly on the test pages.

Test-Taking Tip Remind children to listen to the entire question before looking at all of the choices.

Exercises 1–11 This test is administered orally. Before reading each question, ask children to find the correct item number and then listen carefully. Read each question twice, and pause between items to give children time to find and mark their answers.

ex. 1. There are 6 ants. 4 ants run away. How many are left? Which number sentence will solve the problem? Mark the space next to your answer.

ex. 2. Which number sentence is missing from the fact family? Mark the space next to your answer.

ex. 3. Count by 1's. Which number comes next? Mark the space under your answer.

ex. 4. Which table shows how many tens and ones are in the 2-digit number? Mark the space under your answer.

ex. 5. Count by 2's. Which number comes next? Mark the space under your answer.

ex. 6. Count by 5's. Which number comes next? Mark the space under your answer.

ex. 7. Count by 10's. Which number is missing? Mark the space under your answer.

ex. 8. Which symbol belongs in the circle? Mark the space under your answer.

ex. 9. Which is the 3rd figure? Mark the space under your answer.

ex. 10. Which number is 10 more than 28? Mark the space under your answer.

ex. 11. Use the part of the hundred chart shown to help tell which number comes next in the pattern. Mark the space under your answer.

Exercises 12–13 Tell children they will complete the rest of the test independently.

Test-Taking Tip Remind children to check that they filled in an answer for every question.

Scoring Chart

Number Correct	13	12	11	10	9	8	7	6	5	4	3	2	1
Score	100	92	85	77	69	62	54	46	38	31	23	15	8

After the Review

The Item Analysis chart on the left shows the unit objective covered by each test item. This chart can help you determine which objectives need review or extra practice.

Time and Money

Vocabulary

- calendar
- digital clock
- elapsed time
- half hour
- hour
- hour hand
- minute
- minute hand
- o'clock
- quarter
- telling time

Unit Objectives

8A Tell and write the time to the hour and half hour and compare time related to events

8B Demonstrate understanding of the calendar including days of the week, months of the year

8C Count and give the value of a collection of coins up to 99¢

8D Solve problems by using a table; use Conjecture and Verify and other strategies to solve problems

About This Unit

The support pages that follow provide more information on prerequisite skills, methods for teaching skills and concepts, daily routines, tips on classroom management and materials, and useful dialogue techniques.

Assessments

Use Beginning of the Year Inventory for entry-level assessment.

Ongoing Evaluation Quick Checks, Reteach Worksheets, the Skills Tutorial Inventories and the Midyear Test help ensure that children are progressing adequately to meet the standards.

Summative Evaluation Use Test Preps, Unit Review (p. T127), Cumulative Review (p. T128), and Reteach Worksheets to assure that children have achieved the standards for the unit.

Diagnosing Errors The Quick Checks highlight common errors and provide remediation. See also the **Teaching Strategies Handbook** pp. T116–T119, where short discussions labeled Common Misconceptions appear as needed with the strategies for key concepts.

Homework and Family Involvement

Home Note In the Student Book, the Dear Family Home Note provides objectives, vocabulary, and a sample skill discussion for family participation. (**Teaching Strategies Handbook** pages also provide homework and family involvement tips.)

Education Place Refer families to Houghton Mifflin's EduPlace Web site at http://www.eduplace.com; for resources and activities for students at http://www.eduplace.com/math; and additional resources and activities at http://www.eduplace.com/parents.

Helping Your Children Learn Math This book has activities for children ages 5–13 and tips for getting involved in children's mathematics education. (Houghton Mifflin, 1994)

Lessons	Student Pages	Teacher Pages	Resources	State or Local	
				Objectives	Assessment
8.1 Ordering Events	201	**T120**	Unit 8 Pretest		
8.2 Comparing Time	202	**T120**			
8.3 Hour	203–204	**T121**	Reteach 58, 59, 60 Teaching Resource 12		
8.4 Half Hour	205–206	**T121**	Teaching Resource 13		
8.5 Digital Clocks	207	**T122**	Extension 16; Teaching Resource 12		
8.6 Elapsed Time	208	**T122**	Reteach 61, 62, 63		
8.7 Problem Solving Application: Use a Table	209–210	**T123**			
8.8 Calendar	211–212	**T123**	Teaching Resource 15		
8.9 Counting Nickels and Pennies	213–214	**T124**			
8.10 Counting Dimes, Nickels, and Pennies	215–216	**T124**	Reteach 64, 65, 66; Teaching Resource 11		
8.11 Find the Amount	217–218	**T125**	Reteach 67; Teaching Resource 11		
8.12 Quarter	219–220	**T125**	Reteach 68		
8.13 Problem Solving Strategy: Conjecture and Verify	221–222	**T126**	Unit 8 Posttest		

Teaching Strategies

Math Background — Time and Money

Time and money concepts affect people's lives every day. People consult clocks and watches as they keep appointments, prepare recipes, catch buses, and get to lunch on time. Most people handle money each day, selecting coins for purchases, checking change, and paying bills. Learning about time and money contributes to children's mathematical literacy and understanding of the world.

In this unit, children work with a variety of time concepts: ordering and comparing time periods; building concepts of hours, half-hours, and minutes; and telling time on the hour and half-hour. They solve simple elapsed-time problems such as this one: *If an event begins at 5:00 and ends at 6:30, how much time has passed?* Finally, children become familiar with calendars as time-keeping devices.

Children's work with money builds on their knowledge of the values of pennies, nickels and dimes; it extends to using quarters, counting several coins to determine their total value, and making exchanges (for example, 20¢ could be 2 dimes, 20 pennies, 1 dime and 2 nickels, or other combinations). Problem solving with money challenges children to find totals of several prices and make conjectures about what they could purchase with given amounts of money.

A Positive Start
Time and money are such relevant topics to children's lives that it's easy to involve them in role-playing situations and in handling model clocks and coins. Most children need lots of practice, so provide varied opportunities for building time and money skills and concepts.

Linking Past and Present Learning

Look at the goals for some of the key concepts in this unit and see how they relate to what children learned last year and what they'll encounter next year. This can help you plan and direct your instruction.

Concept/Skills	Last Year	This Year	Next Year
Using Clocks and Calendars	Tell time to the hour; identify seasons of the year	Tell time to the hour and half hour; use a calendar to name the days of the week and months of the year	Tell time in 5-minute intervals; tell time using terms quarter past and quarter to
Counting Coins to 99¢	Identify and count pennies, nickels, and dimes	Identify the quarter; find the value of a collection of coins including pennies, nickels, dimes, and quarters	Add money amounts using 2-digit addition; subtract money amounts to make change
Problem Solving with Time	Identify activities that occur in the morning, afternoon, and evening	Read a schedule to solve problems	Read a schedule to solve elapsed time problems

Methods and Management

To find out children's prior knowledge, let them tell what they already know about time and money. Start the unit by having children discuss ways in which they use time and money in everyday life.

Teaching Strategy: Using Clocks and Calendars

Incorporate these concepts into your classroom routine. Discuss what events come first and last in the day, what events precede and follow others, and which events take about an hour or half-hour.

- Play "Which Takes a Longer Time?" offering pairs of events (washing your hands or washing a load of clothes; making a pizza or eating the pizza). Let children make up questions for others and judge their answers.

▶ *Ask: What events take about an hour? A half-hour? A minute?*
  Make lists as children give responses. Use a model clock to show how the hands move for an hour, a half-hour, and a minute.

▶ *Ask: How many times can you write your name in a minute?*
  Pose questions such as this, and have children make conjectures about the numbers. Then, have children perform the tasks and find the actual numbers.

- Show a paper "digital clock," and have children name various times and set the corresponding time. Have another child set an analog clock to match.

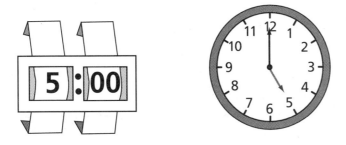

▶ *Vocabulary Development* Throughout the unit, you'll be deepening children's understanding of the concepts of *hour, half-hour, minute, longer time,* and *shorter time*. Encourage them to offer examples and relate times to real life.

▶ *Common Misconceptions* Children may mistake the clock's hour and minute hands, so tape words onto the hands of your model clock. For *half past*, show the hour hand *between* two hours on the clock.

Teaching Strategy: Counting Coins to 99¢

Review coin names and values. Lead children in counting aloud numbers of pennies, nickels, and dimes as you write the numbers on the board.

- Provide coin-combination cards and cent-value cards for children to match. Code the answers on the back for self-checking.

▶ *Ask: What are some ways that you could pay for an item that costs 30¢?*
  Let children model the value with coins, record their answers, and explain how they know their coin combinations represent 30¢.

Teacher Tips

Counting Aloud Start setting the stage now for counting coins and understanding money amounts. Lead children in counting aloud by 5's and 10's. Stop at various points, and have children count on by 1's, for example, 5, 10, 15, 20; 21, 22, 23, 24 . . .

Pacing Several times during the unit, stop what you are doing a few minutes before the hour or half-hour. Ask children to look at the classroom clock, predict the upcoming time, and watch the hands reach the hour or half-hour.

Clock Collage Provide catalog pages, and let children clip pictures of clocks and watches. Have them glue their pictures to paper and write the ending to "Clocks and watches help us . . ."

When Is a Minute Up? To build children's understanding of the concept of a minute, ask them to put their heads down and close their eyes, then raise their heads and open their eyes when they think a minute has passed. Tell children when a half minute and minute are up. Let them discuss how they judged the minute and whether or not it seemed like a long time.

Calendar Time Cut three successive months from an old calendar. Show children how the pages fit together. If the first month ends on Friday, the second month will begin on Saturday. Help children notice that the number of days in the months varies.

Good Routine Write a daily schedule for children to see. As you begin and end activities, draw their attention to the clock and schedule.

More Counting Aloud Review counting by 5's and 10's and then counting on: 10, 20, 30, 40; 41, 42, 43 . . . Introduce counting by 25's: *25, 50, 75, a dollar.*

Writing Prices Review the cent sign, and show children how to write it. Let them draw pictures of items and write prices on them. Children can then exchange pictures and select coins to match the prices.

Management Organize this partner activity. Ask partners to choose four coins each and then compare their values: *Which has the greatest value? The least? Or are the coins the same value?* Vary the number of coins that pairs use.

Money Chart Post a chart showing the following equivalencies:

Penny	1¢
Nickel	5¢
Dime	10¢
Quarter	25¢

Reasoning Support Show 3–4 coins briefly; then, move them out of sight. Let a child tell what the coins were. Next, ask everyone to make a quick conjecture about the total value of the coins and write it down. Finally, show the coins again, letting children count them in order from greatest to least value. Repeat the process, this time asking children to explain their reasoning when they make their conjecture.

▶ *Vocabulary Development* As you review *penny, nickel,* and *dime* and introduce *quarter,* let children handle real coins and arrange plastic ones. Talk about the coins' colors, sizes, and values. Discuss the people and symbols shown on each coin, and show children where to find the cent value.

▶ *Common Misconceptions* Children may count groups of coins inaccurately because they're unsure of coin values or because they cannot count well by 5's or 10's. Review coin values on a chart with pictures and coin values. Have children practice counting by 5's and 10's on a hundred chart.

Teaching Strategy: Problem Solving with Time

Problem solving with time involves figuring elapsed time and using information from simple schedules.

• Introduce a *schedule* by showing an example. Invite children to list and discuss examples from their personal schedules or routines.

▶ *Ask:* Where are you at 10:00 in the morning? Suppose a half-hour has passed, where would you be then? Would you be there after two hours? What time is that?

• Use model clocks to show how the hands move as a half-hour and an hour pass. Invite children to tell what they might be doing at various times.

▶ *Common Misconceptions* Some children may not understand the basic format for a schedule, which is the listing of an event paired with a time. Let classmates demonstrate various examples, explaining how to locate the needed information.

Opportunities to Assess

 Observation

Make notes concerning children's progress as the unit proceeds. Identify children who might help others and those who need more practice. Focus on specific problems that children might need help with. For example, a child who is unsure of individual coin values won't be able to determine the value of several coins, so offer extra support on how much each coin is worth before combining coins.

Family Involvement

Request that families help children read clocks and identify and count coins. These real-life opportunities to practice math are not time consuming, and regular practice is beneficial.

Teacher/Student Dialogue

How to Lead an "Act It Out" Situation

Acting out situations with time and money adds "real world" to classroom discussions, and can build children's ability to express their ideas.

Teacher: We've been working with time and money. Today let's work in groups and act out some things. Jeremy, Carmelita, and Joseph, you act out something about waking up in the morning. Here's a clock to use because you have to show us something about the time. Let's practice first and then we'll do it again, okay?

Students: (Jeremy pretends to sleep) *It's time to get up, Jeremy, It's time for the alarm.*

Student: *Ring, ring, ring! It's 6:00!* (Jeremy yawns)

Student: *Just look, the long hand is on 12, and the short hand is on 6. Get up now!* (Jeremy complains that it's too early and then gets up)

Teacher: We liked your skit. You showed us about the hour hand and minute hand. Let's tell two more things we liked. Michelle, then Jamie.

Student: *It was funny.*

Student: *They used the clock, and he still wouldn't get up.*

Teacher: Now let's have another group show us how to buy a ticket and catch the train.
(*The skits continue, and the teacher asks for a few specific comments or compliments after each one. The lesson ends with a summary of things that were learned.*)

Questioning Techniques

When children give skits, it's important to keep things moving along. Specific directions about content help children plan what to say. Only brief comments between skits are necessary. Use props to stimulate dialogue and make the content more intelligible. Give a summary to help the children recap what they have learned.

When

Some children need more practice, while others are "whizzes" at working with time and money. Let confident children help their classmates. They may be able to provide support and simple explanations for their peers. Also, challenge children who know the content to write or draw word problems or invent simple games for the rest of the class.

What to do

Every Day

Start the day with time or money questions. Have children read the times on three clocks you have drawn on the board, or figure elapsed time from two clocks. Ask them to find the value of three or four coins, or consider two groups of coins and tell which would buy more. Spend a few extra minutes on the calendar, asking children to tell the date of the second Monday, how many Thursdays there are, or what day of the week the 12th is.

Unit 8   Time and Money

LESSON 1
PAGE 201

OBJECTIVE
Order a sequence of events

PREREQUISITES
Concepts
• Understand the concept of time
• Understand the concept of order

Skills
• Identify before and after

MATERIALS
old comic strips

Ordering Events

Presenting the Lesson
Introduce the Skill   Have children cut out panels of simple comic strips, then mix up the panels, then put them back in correct time order.

Check Understanding   *What is something you do before school? After school?* (Answers will vary. Possible answers: eat breakfast; eat supper)

Guided Practice
Have children complete exercise 1. Check that they understand the order of the three events shown.

Independent Practice
Have children complete the remaining exercises independently.

Closing the Lesson   *Do you study before or after you take a spelling test?* (before)

LESSON 2
PAGE 202

OBJECTIVE
Determine whether an event takes minutes or hours

PREREQUISITES
Concepts
• Understand the concept of time

Skills
• Identify shorter and longer

VOCABULARY
hour
minute

Comparing Time

Presenting the Lesson
Introduce the Skill   Discuss the events shown at the top of page 202. Have children tell what activities they do that take hours and what activities they do that take minutes. Guide them to understand that hours means a longer time than minutes. Have volunteers describe events that take hours and others that take minutes.

Check Understanding   Ask, *Does it take longer to cook a pizza or eat a grape?* (cook a pizza)

Guided Practice
Have children complete exercise 1. Check that they understand the difference between hours and minutes.

Independent Practice
Have children complete the rest of the page independently.

Closing the Lesson   Say, *Name something that takes a shorter time to do than paint a room.* (Answers will vary. Possible answer: comb my hair)

LESSON 3
PAGES 203–204

OBJECTIVE
Tell and write time to the hour

PREREQUISITES
Concepts
• Understand the concepts of time and hours

Skills
• Read and write numbers to 12

VOCABULARY
o'clock

MATERIALS
analog clock with moveable hands

Copymasters
Reteach 58–60, pp. 128–130
Teaching Resource 12, (Clock) p. 210

Hour

Presenting the Lesson
Introduce the Skill   Distribute copies of clocks from Teaching Resource 12 and have children practice showing different hours. Then show times on your clock and have children read the hour.

Check Understanding   Say, *Explain how to show 4 o'clock.* (Put the small hand on the 4 and big hand on the 12.)

Guided Practice
Have children complete exercise 1. Check that they look at which number the hour hand is pointing to in order to write the correct time.

Independent Practice
Have children complete the remaining exercises independently. Use the Quick Check for assessment.

Closing the Lesson   Ask, *How are the clocks on this page alike? How are they different?* (Possible answer: All the big hands point to the 12; the small hands point to different numbers.)

LESSON 4
PAGES 205–206

OBJECTIVE
Tell and write time to the half hour

PREREQUISITES
Concepts
• Understand the concepts of time, hours, and minutes

Skills
• Tell and write time to the hour

VOCABULARY
hour hand
minute hand

MATERIALS
analog clock with moveable hands

Copymasters
Teaching Resource 13, (Cut-out Clocks) p. 211

Half Hour

Presenting the Lesson
Introduce the Skill   Use an analog clock to demonstrate how the hour hand moves when the minute hand moves toward the 6. Explain that when the time is on the half hour the hour hand moves halfway past the hour. Use clocks from Teaching Resource 13 to have children practice showing half-hour times. Check that they show the hour hand halfway past the hour and the minute hand on 6. Review hour times.

Check Understanding   Ask, *What two numbers will the hour hand be between at 9:30?* (9 and 10)

Guided Practice
Have children complete exercise 1. Check that they understand how to read the hour hand when the time is half past the hour.

Independent Practice
Have children complete the remaining exercises independently.

Closing the Lesson   Say, *Explain how to show 6:30 on a clock.* (Show the hour hand between 6 and 7; show the minute hand on 6.)

LESSON 5
PAGE 207

OBJECTIVE
Tell time on both digital and analog clocks

PREREQUISITES
Concepts
• Understand concept of time, hours, and minutes

Skills
• Read time to the hour and half hour on analog clocks

VOCABULARY
digital clock

MATERIALS
digital clock

Copymasters
Extension 16, p. 178
Teaching Resource 12, (Clock) p. 210

Digital Clocks

Presenting the Lesson
Introduce the Skill   Show a digital clock set to 1:30. Have children show the time on an analog clock using Teaching Resource 12. Repeat with other times on the hour and half hour.

Check Understanding   Ask, *What number is always on a digital clock when it is half past the hour?* (30)

Guided Practice
Have children complete exercise 1. Check that they remember that *:00* means o'clock.

Independent Practice
Have children complete the remaining exercises independently.

Closing the Lesson   Ask, *What do the numbers to the left of the colon on a digital clock tell?* (the hour) *What do the numbers to the right tell?* (the number of minutes past the hour)

LESSON 6
PAGE 208

OBJECTIVE
Understand elapsed time

PREREQUISITES
Concepts
• Understand concept of time, hours, and minutes

Skills
• Tell time to the hour and half hour

VOCABULARY
elapsed time

MATERIALS
analog clock with moveable hands, timer

Copymasters
Reteach 61–63, pp. 131–133

Elapsed Time

Presenting the Lesson
Introduce the Skill   Demonstrate how time passes using an analog clock. Show children what the clock looks like at 3:00, and then what it looks like 1 hour later. Have children describe the difference. (The hour hand is now on 4 instead of 3.) You may want to set a timer to go off every hour in your class. Each time the timer goes off, have children notice how the clock hands on the classroom clock have changed and discuss what they have done in the hour that has elapsed.

Check Understanding   Say, *Suppose it is 2:00.* Ask, *What time will it be in 1 hour?* (3:00)

Guided Practice
Have children complete exercise 1. Check that they label each time correctly and understand that the total elapsed time is from the first clock to the third.

Independent Practice
Have children complete the remaining exercises independently. Use the Quick Check for assessment.

Closing the Lesson   Ask, *How much time elapses from 6:00 to 7:00?* (1 hour)

LESSON 7
PAGES 209–210

OBJECTIVE
Solve problems related to time by using a table

PREREQUISITES
Concepts
• Understand the concept of time

Skills
• Subtract through 10
• Read data from a table

Problem Solving Application: Use a Table

Presenting the Lesson
Introduce the Focus of the Lesson   Tell children they are going to use a table to solve problems.

Model the Four-Step Problem Solving Process   Work together to solve problem 1.

• **Understand** *What are you being asked to find out?* (what time math starts)

• **Decide** *How can you find out when math starts?* (Find math in the table, then look at the time shown next to it.)

• **Solve** Invite children to look at the table to find out when math starts. Have them trace over the answer in exercise 1.

• **Look back** Ask, *How can you check your answer?* (Possible answer: Look up 10:00 in the table and see if that is when math begins.)

Guided Practice
Check that children understand how to read the tables.

Independent Practice
Have children complete the remaining problems independently.

Closing the Lesson   *How did the tables help you solve the problems?* (Answers will vary. Possible answer: I used the information in the tables to help solve the problems.)

LESSON 8
PAGES 211–212

OBJECTIVE
Use a calendar to understand days of the week and months of the year

PREREQUISITES
Concepts
• Understand the concept of time

Skills
• Read numbers
• Identify ordinal numbers

VOCABULARY
calendar

MATERIALS
calendar page from current month

Copymasters
Teaching Resource 15, (Calendar) p. 213

Calendar

Presenting the Lesson
Introduce the Skill   Look at the calendar on the top of the page with children. Have volunteers read the month and days of the week. Work together to read the calendar by identifying specific days. Ask questions such as: *Which day of the week is the 22nd? What date is the last Thursday?*

Check Understanding   Ask, *What date is two weeks after the 10th?* (24th)

Guided Practice
Have children complete exercise 1. Check that they understand how to read the names of the days of the week.

Independent Practice
Have children complete the remaining exercises independently. Make sure a calendar page from the current month is displayed in your classroom so that children can successfully complete exercise 5. For further practice, Teaching Resource 15 provides a blank calendar for children to fill in.

Closing the Lesson   Have volunteers recite the days of the week and months of the year.

LESSON 9
PAGES 213–214

OBJECTIVE
Count by 5's and 1's to identify the value of collections of nickels and pennies

PREREQUISITES
Concepts
• Understand the value of nickels and pennies

Skills
• Count by 5's

Counting Nickels and Pennies

Presenting the Lesson
Introduce the Skill   Review counting by 5's by having children stand up and hold up their hands. Have volunteers count by 5's to count how many fingers.

Check Understanding   Ask, *Which coin do you count by 5's? Why?* (nickel, because it has a value of 5 cents so you could count nickels by 5's to find out a total amount)

Guided Practice
Have children complete problems 1 and 7. Check that they understand how to count nickels by 5's and then count on pennies by 1's to find the amounts.

Independent Practice
Have children complete the remaining exercises independently.

Closing the Lesson   Ask, *What is the greatest number of nickels you could have if you had 23 cents?* (4)

LESSON 10
PAGES 215–216

OBJECTIVE
Count by 10's, 5's, and 1's to identify the value of collections of dimes, nickels, and pennies

PREREQUISITES
Concepts
• Understand the value of dimes, nickels, and pennies

Skills
• Count by 5's and 10's

MATERIALS
play coins

Copymasters
Reteach 64–66, pp. 134–136
Teaching Resource 11, (Coins and Rulers) p. 209

Counting Dimes, Nickels, and Pennies

Presenting the Lesson
Introduce the Skill   Review counting by 5's and 10's. Have children count by 10's, 10's and 1's, and 10's and 5's using play coins. Encourage them to see the relationship between counting dimes, nickels, and pennies and counting nickels and pennies as they did in Lesson 9. Teaching Resource 11 has a collection of coins to use for counting.

Check Understanding   Ask, *When I count amounts that have different coins, which coins do I count first? Why?* (the coins with the greater value because it is easier to count on by 1's.)

Guided Practice
Have children complete problems 1, 3, and 5. Check that they understand how to first count dimes by 10's and then count on pennies by 1's or nickels by 5's.

Independent Practice
Have children complete the remaining exercises independently. Use the Quick Check for assessment.

Closing the Lesson   Ask, *How can I make 40 cents using both dimes and nickels?* (Answers will vary. Possible answer: 3 dimes, 2 nickels) *Using only dimes?* (4 dimes)

LESSON 11
PAGES 217–218

OBJECTIVE
Find the value of collections of coins including dimes, nickels, and pennies

PREREQUISITES
Concepts
• Understand the value of dimes, nickels, and pennies

Skills
• Count by 5's and 10's
• Count dimes, nickels, and pennies

MATERIALS
play coins: pennies, nickels, dimes

Copymasters
Reteach 67, p. 137
Teaching Resource 11, (Coins and Rulers) p. 209

Find the Amount

Presenting the Lesson
Introduce the Skill Have children use dimes, nickels, and pennies to practice counting out various money amounts.

Check Understanding *If I have a dime, a nickel, and a penny, in what order should I count the amount?* (greatest to least: dime, nickel, penny) *How much do I have?* (16 cents)

Guided Practice
Have children do exercise 1. Check that they understand that it helps to count the coins from greatest to least value.

Independent Practice
Have children complete the remaining exercises independently.

Closing the Lesson Ask, *If you have 2 dimes, what coins do you need to make 23 cents?* (3 pennies)

LESSON 12
PAGES 219–220

OBJECTIVE
Find different combinations of coins that equal a quarter; count coins and write the amount

PREREQUISITES
Concepts
• Understand the value of dimes, nickels, and pennies

Skills
• Count by 5's and 10's
• Count dimes, nickels, and pennies

VOCABULARY
quarter

MATERIALS
play coins

Copymasters
Reteach 68, p. 138

Quarter

Presenting the Lesson
Introduce the Skill Have children look at the first exercise on page 219. Have them use coins to show that 2 dimes and 1 nickel make 25 cents.

Check Understanding Ask, *Could you buy a whistle that costs 30 cents with a quarter? Why or why not?* (No, because a quarter is only worth 25 cents.)

Guided Practice
Allow children to use coins to find other ways to make 25 cents as they complete the chart in exercise 1. Check that they understand they are to record the number of each type of coin they used to make an amount equivalent to 25 cents in each column.

Independent Practice
Have children complete the remaining exercises independently.

Closing the Lesson Ask, *How much would you have if you had one of each coin?* (41 cents)

LESSON 13
PAGES 221–222

OBJECTIVE
Use the Conjecture and Verify strategy to solve money-related problems

PREREQUISITES
Concepts
• Understand the concepts of money and addition

Skills
• Compare money amounts
• Add money amounts

Problem Solving Strategy: Conjecture and Verify

Presenting the Lesson
Introduce the Strategy   Explain to children that in this lesson they will solve problems by guessing and checking.

Model the Four-Step Problem Solving Process   Work through the sample problem on page 221.

• **Understand** *What do you need to find out to solve this problem?* (which stamps Emily buys)

• **Decide** Ask, *What strategy can you use?* (I can try picking two stamps, then check to see if their cost adds up to 5 cents.)

• **Solve** Help children to see that with this strategy, if the first guess is incorrect, you can guess again until you think you found the correct answer. Use the first and second guess shown on the page to help children understand. (2¢ + 3¢ = 5¢. They are the two stamps Emily bought.)

• **Look back** Reread the problem. Ask, *Does your answer make sense? Why?* (Possible answer: I can check that I added the amounts correctly. 2¢ + 3¢ = 5¢. My answer makes sense.)

Guided Practice
Have children complete problem 1. Check that they can use guess and check to solve the problem.

Independent Practice
Have children complete the remaining problems independently.

Closing the Lesson   Have children use the stamps in problem 6 to make up a new problem. Have them share and compare their problems and solutions.

UNIT 8 REVIEW
Pages 223–224

Item Analysis

Items	Unit Obj.
1–5	8A
6–7	8B
8–11	8C
12–15	8D

Answers to Unit 8 review items can be found on pages 223–224 of the Teacher's Annotated Edition.

Administering the Review
These pages review concepts and skills taught in this unit. Make sure children understand all direction lines. You may wish to do the first example in each section cooperatively to ensure understanding.

Scoring Chart

Number Correct	15	14	13	12	11	10	9	8	7	6	5	4	3	2	1
Score	100	93	87	80	73	67	60	53	47	40	33	27	20	13	7

After the Review
• The Item Analysis chart on the left shows the Unit 8 objective covered by each test item. This chart can help you determine which objectives need review or extra practice.

• For additional assessment, use the Posttest for Unit 8, Copymasters, pp. 37–38.

UNIT 8 CUMULATIVE REVIEW

Pages 225–226

Item Analysis

Items	Unit Obj.
1	7A
2	7B
3	7D
4	7E
5	7F
6	6A
7	7G
8–10	8A
11	8C

Answers to Cumulative Review items can be found on pages 225–226 of the Teacher's Annotated Edition.

Administering the Review

These pages review concepts and skills from the unit as well as providing practice with standardized test formats. Children should mark their answers directly on the test pages.

Test-Taking Tip Remind children to listen to the entire question before looking at all of the choices.

Exercises 1–11 This test is administered orally. Before reading each question, ask children to find the correct item number and then listen carefully. Read each question twice, and pause between items to give children time to find and mark their answers.

ex. 1. *Which number is missing? Mark the space under your answer.*
ex. 2. *Which tells how many tens and ones are in the 2-digit number? Mark the space under your answer.*
ex. 3. *Count by 5's. Which number is missing? Mark the space under your answer.*
ex. 4. *Which symbol belongs in the circle? Mark the space under your answer.*
ex. 5. *Which is the fifth letter? Mark the space under your answer.*
ex. 6. *Which number sentence solves the problem? Mark the space under your answer. There are 9 birds. One flies away. How many are left?*
ex. 7. *Which number comes next in the pattern? Mark the space under your answer.*
ex. 8. *Which time does the clock show? Mark the space under your answer.*
ex. 9. *Which picture shows an event that takes hours? Mark the space under your answer.*
ex. 10. *Look at the clocks. How long from start to finish? Mark the space under your answer.*
ex. 11. *Count the coins. How much money? Mark the space under your answer.*

Test-Taking Tip Remind children to read all of the choices before marking their answer.

Scoring Chart

Number Correct	11	10	9	8	7	6	5	4	3	2	1
Score	100	91	82	73	64	55	45	36	27	18	9

After the Review

The Item Analysis chart on the left shows the unit objective covered by each test item. This chart can help you determine which objectives need review or extra practice.

Teacher Notes

2-Digit Addition and Subtraction

Unit Objectives

9A Add 2-digit numbers without regrouping

9B Subtract 2-digit numbers without regrouping

9C Add and subtract 2-digit money amounts

9D Solve problems by choosing to add or subtract; use Make a Table and other strategies to solve problems

About This Unit

The support pages that follow provide more information on prerequisite skills, methods for teaching skills and concepts, daily routines, tips on classroom management and materials, and useful dialogue techniques.

Assessments

Use Beginning of the Year Inventory for entry-level assessment.

Ongoing Evaluation Quick Checks, Reteach Worksheets, the Skills Tutorial Inventories and the Midyear Test help ensure that children are progressing adequately to meet the standards.

Summative Evaluation Use Test Preps, Unit Review (p. T141), Cumulative Review (p. T142), Reteach Worksheets, and the Skills Tutorial Inventory, Strand P2, Skills 6–8, and Strand P3, Skills 4–6 to assure that children have achieved the standards for the unit.

Diagnosing Errors The Quick Checks highlight common errors and provide remediation. See also the **Teaching Strategies Handbook** pp. T132–T135, where short discussions labeled Common Misconceptions appear as needed with the strategies for key concepts.

Homework and Family Involvement

Home Note In the Student Book, the Dear Family Home Note provides objectives, vocabulary, and a sample skill discussion for family participation. (**Teaching Strategies Handbook** pages also provide homework and family involvement tips.)

Education Place Refer families to Houghton Mifflin's EduPlace Web site at http://www.eduplace.com; for resources and activities for students at http://www.eduplace.com/math; and additional resources and activities at http://www.eduplace.com/parents.

Helping Your Children Learn Math This book has activities for children ages 5–13 and tips for getting involved in children's mathematics education. (Houghton Mifflin, 1994)

Lessons	Student Pages	Teacher Pages	Resources	State or Local	
				Objectives	Assessment
9.1 Adding 1-Digit to 2-Digit	229–230	T136	Unit 9 Pretest; Skills Tutorial: Strand P2, Skill 6; Extension 17; Teaching Resource 7		
9.2 Adding 2-Digit to 2-Digit	231–232	T136	Skills Tutorial: Strand P2, Skills 7, 8; Teaching Resource 7		
9.3 Adding 2-Digit Numbers	233–234	T137	Reteach 69; Extension 18		
9.4 Subtracting 1-Digit from 2-Digit	235–236	T137	Skills Tutorial: Strand P3, Skill 4; Extension 19; Teaching Resource 7		
9.5 Subtracting 2-Digit from 2-Digit	237–238	T138	Skills Tutorial; Strand P3, Skills 5, 6; Teaching Resource 7		
9.6 Subtracting 2 Digit Numbers	239–240	T138	Reteach 70; Extension 20		
9.7 Adding and Subtracting Money	241–242	T139	Reteach 71		
9.8 Problem Solving Application: Choose the Operation	243–244	T139			
9.9 Problem Solving Strategy: Make a Table	245–246	T140	Unit 9 Posttest		

Teaching Strategies

Math Background | 2-Digit Addition and Subtraction

From their work with place value and adding and subtracting to 10, it's a natural progression for children to work with addition and subtraction of 2-digit numbers. They first learn about adding and subtracting a 1-digit and a 2-digit number, then move on to combining and separating situations where both numbers have two digits. No regrouping (often called "carrying" and "borrowing") is involved in the problems for this unit. For example, children learn to compute 16 + 2, 42 + 5, 44 − 23, and 39 − 11, but not 46 + 18 or 50 − 13.

Mental images of addition and subtraction situations help children develop their understanding of these operations. Handling materials bundled or grouped as tens and ones should precede using pictures and symbols. Dimes and pennies also help children to picture the meaning of tens and ones, and facilitate work with real-life situations.

A Positive Start
Heighten children's enthusiasm by telling a story to provide the context for a problem. Model addition and subtraction with materials as you talk about and demonstrate place value. It is helpful to also refer to now-familiar number lines and hundred charts as you work.

Linking Past and Future Learning

Use the chart to see prerequisite skills for some of the key topics in the unit, to plan your instruction and to prepare children for work at the next level.

Concept/Skills	Last Year	This Year	Next Year
Adding and Subtracting 2-Digit Numbers	Solve addition and subtraction facts to 10	Add and subtract 2-digit numbers without regrouping	Add and subtract 2-digit numbers with and without regrouping
Adding and Subtracting Money Amounts	Count pennies, nickels, and dimes; write the total value	Add and subtract 2-digit money amounts without regrouping	Add and subtract 2-digit money amounts with and without regrouping

Methods and Management

As in previous units, continue to model addition and subtraction, to talk about related situations, and to write symbols to represent these operations.

Teaching Strategy: Adding and Subtracting 2-Digit Numbers

Relate new ideas to simpler addition and subtraction and to place value.

- Review finding $5 + 4$, and let children tell stories to reflect the addition. Then, present $15 + 4$.

▶ *Show This:*

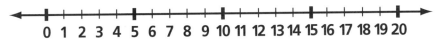

▶ **Ask:** *Where is 15 on a number line? What number is 4 more than 15?*
Verify by having children use 15 counters; then, add 4, and see how many counters there are in all. Repeat the process with $5 - 3$, $15 - 3$.

- Model how to line up numbers as tens and ones, labeling the columns so that they combine or separate similar things.

Tens	Ones		Tens	Ones
🥢🥢	⎮⎮⎮		2	3
🥢🥢🥢	⎮⎮⎮⎮	+	1	4
			3	7

▶ **Vocabulary Development** Review *tens* and *ones* as you write 2-digit numbers. As they record their work, ask children to identify *addends*, *sums*, and *differences* as well as the $+$, $-$, and $=$ signs.

▶ **Common Misconceptions** When working with 2-digit numbers, children may work only with ones or only with tens, forgetting the digits in the other place. Prompt them verbally. Also, have them model numbers with materials so they can see the magnitude of the numbers.

Teacher Tips

Materials Bind 10 craft sticks, straws, or toothpicks with rubber bands to represent tens. Use individual objects to represent ones. Let children help with binding materials so that they will be see that their bundles contain 10 ones.

Routines Continue practicing basic facts each week. Draw attention to doubles, such as $1 + 1$, $2 + 2$, $3 + 3$, $4 + 4$, and $5 + 5$, and point out patterns in the sums. (They are even numbers, or numbers we say when counting by 2's.) Show children how to use a double, such as $4 + 4$, to solve a doubles-plus-1 problem, such as $4 + 5$. (Find the sum of $4 + 4$; then, add 1. The sum is 9.)

Help from Home Some family members may be interested in providing stamps and stamp pads for this unit. Children can stamp images for addition and subtractions stories, based on numbers you suggest. (*Stamp 14 images and then stamp 4 more. How many images are there in all? Now stamp 23 times, cross out 12. How many are left?*)

Management Set up partner work with number sentences. Show $34 + 13 =$ _____ and $34 - 13 =$ _____. Let children work with partners to make up a story for each sentence. Pairs can share with others and compare answers.

Add the Coins Make rubbings of dimes. Tape different numbers of rubbings to index cards to represent different money amounts. Use index cards to make the operation cards for addition (+) and subtraction (−). Have children draw two coin cards and an operation card. Remind them to subtract the lesser number from the greater number. Have students record their work, including the ¢ sign.

Dimes and the Hundreds Chart Have a child choose a number of tens from a hundred chart while classmates select a number of dimes to match. Announce a number of dimes to add or subtract an ask a volunteer to show the answer on the hundred chart. Record examples on the board.

Which Buys More? Have a child choose two numbers to represent collections of dimes. Classmates determine the value in cents and decide which group of dimes would buy more or less: 20¢ < 50¢, for example. They write number sentences to find how much more or less: 50 − 20 = 30; 30¢ less.

Teaching Strategy: Adding and Subtracting Money Amounts

Review skip-counting by 10's. Then practice counting pennies and dimes.

- Show several dimes and pennies. Have children write the value of the dimes and the value of the pennies. Have them write a number sentence for the total value: 30¢ + 6¢ = 36¢, for example.

- Have children model 20¢ + 50¢ by placing 2 dimes in one row and 5 dimes in another row. Combine them, and write 20¢ + 50¢ = 70¢.

▶ *Ask:* *What if you want to buy something for 35¢? You have 4 dimes. Do you have enough money? How much money will you have left?*
Let children role-play situations like this, then work in pairs and pose similar questions to each other.

▶ *Common Misconceptions* Children may mistake dimes for pennies, thinking of each coin as representing 1¢, rather than 10¢. Review coin values and trading equivalent amounts, such as 1 dime can be traded for 10 pennies. Picture, word, and numeral cards can help.

| 4 dimes | 40¢ |

Opportunities to Assess

 Observation

Ask children to fold a piece of paper in half. Have them write 13 + 34 on one side and 44 − 12 on the other side, and then solve each problem. Children can tell a story to match each number sentence. Check children's work for accurate solutions and reasonable addition and subtraction stories.

 Family Involvement

Send home a table for family members to complete together. The table might feature postage stamps, coins, or furniture. On another occasion, send home a blank table and suggest that family members work with children to think of a table idea and fill it in. Let children share their results in class.

Teacher/Student Dialogue

Preparing Children for Symbolic Representation

Stories, objects, and pictures can help children better understand mathematical symbols.

Teacher: We want to work with 14 and 20. (*Writes on the board*) I need someone to tell a story. Then we'll decide if it's an addition story or a subtraction story. Raise your hand. Keiko?

Student: *There were 14 horses and 20 more came.*

Teacher: Yes, 14 and 20 more. Do we add or subtract? Everybody?

Students: *Addition! Add!*

Teacher: How did you know that? Hershel?

Student: *More came, so we need to add.*

Teacher: So we're combining, or putting them together. Good thinking, Hershel. Now, Laurie, count out 14 with these place-value blocks, Orlando, you get 20. How many tens and ones do you have, Laurie?

Student: *One ten and four ones.*

Teacher: Orlando, put your two tens with Laurie's. Is that addition or subtraction? Harold?

Students: *Addition.*

Teacher: How many ones are there now? How many tens? Tanya?

Students: *Three tens and 4 ones, 34!*

Teacher: That's right, Tanya, 34 in all. Now, Jorge, come up and write this on the board. (*Jorge records work on the board*) Who can retell our original story about the horses? Samuel? (*Samuel responds.*) Who can tell us a subtraction story? Marguerite? (*Children model the story, draw a picture, and finally record the symbols to match.*)

What to do

When

Some children ignore the + and − signs, using addition for every problem. Have them color the operation signs—green for addition and red for subtraction. Prompt them to use the green signal to *go ahead and add*, but to *stop, then subtract* when they see red.

What to do

Every Day

Offer a "problem of the day" that relates to children's classroom life. For example: *There are 23 children in the classroom. Then 12 leave for a special class. How many are left?*

Questioning Techniques

Vary your questions and the tasks you ask children to complete. Be sure that children speak loudly enough for all to hear and that they write legibly. You might work with them on the overhead projector for easy viewing. Here are additional tips:

- Words, models, pictures, symbols can all represent addition and subtraction. Use each kind of representation to help children internalize the processes.

- When analyzing different parts of a problem, maintain children's interest by involving a number of them in the discussion.

- Toward the end of the representational sequence, review the main idea.

Unit 9 2-Digit Addition and Subtraction

LESSON 1
PAGES 229–230

OBJECTIVE
Add 1-digit numbers to 2-digit numbers without regrouping using pictorial models

PREREQUISITES
Concepts
• Understand the concept of addition
• Understand place value

Skills
• Add 1-digit numbers

MATERIALS
place-value models

Copymasters
Extension 17, p. 179
Teaching Resource 7, (Place-value Models) p. 205

Adding 1-Digit to 2-Digit

Presenting the Lesson
Introduce the Skill   Review place-value concepts by asking volunteers to model 2-digit numbers with place-value materials or drawings. Have children use place-value models or copies of Teaching Resource 7 to model adding 1-digit numbers to 2-digit numbers. After each problem, ask volunteers to demonstrate and explain what they did.

Check Understanding   Have volunteers make up word problems to go with some of the addition problems.

Guided Practice
Have children complete exercises 1 and 5. Check that they understand how to use the pictorial model to help them add.

Independent Practice
Have children complete the remaining exercises independently.

Closing the Lesson   *What will happen if you add zero to a 2-digit number?* (The sum will be the same as the 2-digit number.)

LESSON 2
PAGES 231–232

OBJECTIVE
Add 2-digit numbers to 2-digit numbers without regrouping using pictorial models

PREREQUISITES
Concepts
• Understand the concept of addition
• Understand place value

Skills
• Add 1-digit numbers
• Add 1-digit numbers to 2-digit numbers

MATERIALS
place-value models

Copymasters
Teaching Resource 7, (Place-value Models) p. 205

Adding 2-Digit to 2-Digit

Presenting the Lesson
Introduce the Skill   Have children continue as they did for Lesson 1 using place-value models or copies of Teaching Resource 7 to model addition, this time adding 2-digit to 2-digit numbers. After each problem, ask volunteers to demonstrate and explain what they did.

Check Understanding   Have volunteers make up word problems to go with some of the addition problems.

Guided Practice
Have children complete exercises 1 and 6. Check that they understand how to use the pictorial model to help them add.

Independent Practice
Have children complete the remaining exercises independently.

Closing the Lesson   Ask, *How would you tell someone who did not know how to add 2-digit numbers what to do?* (Answers will vary. Possible answer: add the ones to the ones and the tens to the tens)

LESSON 3
PAGES 233–234

OBJECTIVE
Add 1- and 2-digit numbers to 2-digit numbers without regrouping

PREREQUISITES
Concepts
• Understand addition
• Understand place value

Skills
• Add 1-digit numbers
• Add 2-digit numbers to 2-digit numbers

MATERIALS
Copymasters
Reteach 69, p. 139
Extension 18, p. 180

Skills Tutorial
Strand P2: Skill 6 Practice 1–3, Skill 7 Practice 1–3, Skill 8 Practice 1–3

Adding 2-Digit Numbers

Presenting the Lesson
Introduce the Skill   Tell children that in this lesson they will no longer use pictures to help them add. Point out that the place-value chart will help them add the right places. Review addition facts to 9 before assigning the pages in this lesson.

Check Understanding   Check that all children know their addition facts to 10.

Guided Practice
Help children complete exercises 1, 5, and 9 on page 233 and exercise 21 on page 234. Make sure children understand they must add tens to tens and ones to ones.

Independent Practice
Have children complete the remaining exercises independently. Use the Quick Check for assessment.

Closing the Lesson   Have volunteers draw pictures to show a few exercises from this page.

LESSON 4
PAGES 235–236

OBJECTIVE
Subtract 1-digit numbers from 2-digit numbers without regrouping using pictorial models

PREREQUISITES
Concepts
• Understand subtraction
• Understand place value

Skills
• Subtract 1-digit numbers

MATERIALS
place-value models

Copymasters
Extension 19, p. 181
Teaching Resource 7, (Place-value Models) p. 205

Subtracting 1-Digit from 2-Digit

Presenting the Lesson
Introduce the Skill   Review subtraction facts to 10. Then, have children use place-value models or copies of Teaching Resource 7 to model subtracting 1-digit from 2-digit numbers. Be sure to give children numbers that will not require regrouping. After each problem, ask volunteers to demonstrate and explain what they did.

Check Understanding   Have volunteers make up word problems to go with some of the problems.

Guided Practice
Have children complete exercise 1 on page 235 and exercise 5 on page 236. Check that they understand how to use the pictorial model to help them subtract.

Independent Practice
Have children complete the remaining exercises independently.

Closing the Lesson   *What will happen if you subtract zero from a 2-digit number?* (The difference will be the same as the 2-digit number.)

LESSON 5
PAGES 237–238

OBJECTIVE
Subtract 2-digit numbers from 2-digit numbers without regrouping using pictorial models

PREREQUISITES
Concepts
• Understand subtraction
• Understand place value

Skills
• Subtract 1-digit numbers from 2-digit numbers

MATERIALS
place-value models

Copymasters
Teaching Resource 7, (Place-value Models) p. 205

Subtracting 2-Digit from 2-Digit

Presenting the Lesson
Introduce the Skill   Have children continue as they did for Lesson 4 using place-value models or copies of Teaching Resource 7 to model subtraction, this time subtracting 2-digit from 2-digit numbers. After each problem, ask volunteers to demonstrate and explain what they did.

Check Understanding   Have one partner give the other a subtraction problem to model and solve, then switch roles and repeat.

Guided Practice
Have children complete exercise 1 on page 237 and exercise 5 on page 238. Check that they understand how to use the pictorial model to help them subtract and are subtracting tens from tens and ones from ones.

Independent Practice
Have children complete the remaining exercises independently.

Closing the Lesson   Ask, *How would you tell someone who did not know how to subtract 2-digit numbers what to do?* (Answers will vary. Possible answer: subtract the ones from the ones and the tens from the tens.)

LESSON 6
PAGES 239–240

OBJECTIVE
Subtract 1- and 2-digit numbers from 2-digit numbers without regrouping

PREREQUISITES
Concepts
• Understand subtraction
• Understand place value

Skills
• Subtract 1-digit numbers
• Subtract 2-digit numbers

MATERIALS
Copymasters
Reteach 70, p. 140
Extension 20, p. 182

Skills Tutorial
Strand P3: Skill 4 Practice 1–5, Skill 5 Practice 1–4, Skill 6 Practice 1–5

Subtracting 2-Digit Numbers

Presenting the Lesson
Introduce the Skill   Tell children that in this lesson they will no longer use pictures to help them subtract, but that the place-value chart will guide them in subtracting correctly. Review subtraction facts through 9 before assigning the pages in this lesson.

Check Understanding   Check that all children know their subtraction facts through 9.

Guided Practice
Have children complete exercises 1 and 9 on page 239 and exercise 17 on page 240.

Independent Practice
Have children complete the remaining exercises independently. Use the Quick Check for assessment.

Closing the Lesson   Have volunteers draw pictures to show several exercises on these pages.

LESSON 7
PAGES 241–242

OBJECTIVE
Add and subtract money amounts without regrouping

PREREQUISITES
Concepts
• Understand the value of coins
• Understand addition and sub-traction situations

Skills
• Count by tens
• Add and subtract 2-digit num-bers without regrouping

MATERIALS
play coins

Copymasters
Reteach 71, p. 141

Adding and Subtracting Money

Presenting the Lesson
Introduce the Skill Have children act out money problems that don't require regrouping using play coins.

Check Understanding Have volunteers make up and solve a word problem where they must add money amounts and one where they must subtract.

Guided Practice
Discuss exercise 1 and solve it with the class. Then have children complete problems 5 and 9. Check that they pay attention to the signs and the place values of the digits.

Independent Practice
Have children complete the remaining exercises independently.

Closing the Lesson *How is adding and subtracting money like adding and sub-tracting numbers? How is it different?* (Answers will vary. Possible answer: same process, but money requires a ¢ sign in the answer)

LESSON 8
PAGES 243–244

OBJECTIVE
Solve problems by choosing to add or subtract

PREREQUISITES
Concepts
• Understand the concept of addition and subtraction

Skills
• Add and subtract 2-digit numbers

Problem Solving Application: Choose the Operation

Presenting the Lesson
Introduce the Focus of the Lesson Explain to children that in this lesson they will solve problems by choosing to add or subtract.

Model the Four-Step Problem Solving Process Work through the first problem on page 243.

• **Understand** *What do you need to find out to solve this problem?* (how many shells Pablo has in all)

• **Decide** *How can you decide whether to add or subtract?* (I know I am joining sets of shells, so I will add to find how many in all.)

• **Solve** *What's the solution?* (32 + 17 = 49. Pablo has 49 shells in all.)

• **Look back** *How can you check that your answer makes sense?* (Answers will vary. Possible answer: I can draw a picture to check my answer.)

Guided Practice
Have children complete problem 1. Check that they understand why addition is the correct operation for solving the problem.

Independent Practice
Have children complete the remaining problems on pages 243 and 244 independently.

Closing the Lesson *Draw a picture to match one of the problems on this page.*

LESSON 9
PAGES 245–246

OBJECTIVE
Use the Make a Table strategy to solve problems

PREREQUISITES
Concepts
• Understand the concept of skip counting

Skills
• Skip count by 2's and 5's
• Read data from a table

Problem Solving Strategy: Make a Table

Presenting the Lesson

Introduce the Strategy   Tell children they are going to use the Make a Table strategy to solve problems.

Model the Four-Step Problem Solving Process   Work together to solve the model problem.

• **Understand** *As you read the question, think about the math ideas.*

• **Decide** *What strategy can you use to solve the problem?*

• **Solve** *Fill the table to solve the problem.*

• **Look back** *How can you check that your answer makes sense?*

Guided Practice

Have children complete the model problem. Check that they understand how to complete and then read the table.

Independent Practice

Have children complete the table and problems 1–5 on page 246 independently.

Closing the Lesson   Ask, *How did you know how to complete the table?* (Answers will vary. Possible answer: I skip counted by 5's because there are 5 fingers on each hand.)

UNIT 9 REVIEW
Pages 247–248

Item Analysis

Items	Unit Obj.
1–8	9A
9–16	9B
17–20	9C
21–26	9D

Answers to Unit 9 review items can be found on pages 247–248 of the Teacher's Annotated Edition.

Administering the Review

These pages review concepts and skills taught in this unit. Make sure children understand all direction lines. You may wish to do the first example in each section cooperatively to ensure understanding.

Scoring Chart

Number Correct	26	25	24	23	22	21	20	19	18	17	16	15	14
Score	100	96	92	88	85	81	77	73	69	65	62	58	54

Number Correct	13	12	11	10	9	8	7	6	5	4	3	2	1
Score	50	46	42	38	35	31	27	23	19	15	12	8	4

After the Review

• The Item Analysis chart on the left shows the Unit 9 objective covered by each test item. This chart can help you determine which objectives need review or extra practice.

• For additional assessment, use the Posttest for Unit 9, Copymasters, pp. 41–42.

UNIT 9 CUMULATIVE REVIEW
Pages 249–250

Item Analysis

Items	Unit Obj.
1	6B
2	7A
3	7B
4	7D
5	7E
6	8A
7	8C
8–9	6A
10–11	9A
12–13	9B

Answer to Cumulative Review items can be found on pages 249–250 of the Teacher's Annotated Edition.

Administering the Review

These pages review concepts and skills from the unit as well as providing practice with standardized test formats. Children should mark their answers directly on the test pages.

Test-Taking Tip Remind children to listen to the entire question before looking at all of the choices.

Exercises 1–7 This test is administered orally. Before reading each question, ask children to find the correct item number and then listen carefully. Read each question twice, and pause between items to give children time to find and mark their answers.

ex. 1. *Which fact belongs in the same fact family as the numbers shown at the beginning of the row? Mark the space next to your answer.*
ex. 2. *Which number does the number word name? Mark the space under your answer.*
ex. 3. *Which shows the number? Mark the space under your answer.*
ex. 4. *Count by 2's. Which number is missing? Mark the space under your answer.*
ex. 5. *Which symbol belongs in the circle? Mark the space under your answer.*
ex. 6. *Which picture shows what happens first? Mark the space under your answer.*
ex. 7. *How much money is shown? Mark the space under your answer.*

Exercises 8–13 Tell children that they will complete the rest of the test on their own.

Test-Taking Tip Remind children to read check operation signs before marking their choices.

Scoring Chart

Number Correct	13	12	11	10	9	8	7	6	5	4	3	2	1
Score	100	92	85	77	69	62	54	46	38	31	23	15	8

After the Review

The Item Analysis chart on the left shows the unit objective covered by each test item. This chart can help you determine which objectives need review or extra practice.

Teacher Notes

Fractions and Measurement

Vocabulary

- centimeter
- equal parts
- fraction
- heavier
- holds less
- holds more
- inch
- lighter
- longer
- one fourth
- one half
- one third
- shorter

Unit Objectives

10A Identify and show equal parts of a region

10B Identify $\frac{1}{2}$, $\frac{1}{3}$, or $\frac{1}{4}$ of a region

10C Compare the length, weight, capacity, and volume of two or more objects

10D Measure length using a centimeter ruler

10E Measure length using an inch ruler

10F Solve problems by using a chart ; use Act It Out and other strategies to solve problems

About This Unit

The support pages that follow provide more information on prerequisite skills, methods for teaching skills and concepts, daily routines, tips on classroom management and materials, and useful dialogue techniques.

Assessments

Use Beginning of the Year Inventory for entry-level assessment.

Ongoing Evaluation Quick Checks, Reteach Worksheets, the Skills Tutorial Inventories and the Midyear Test help ensure that children are progressing adequately to meet the standards.

Summative Evaluation Use Test Preps, Unit Review (p. T156), Cumulative Review (p. T157), and Reteach Worksheets to assure that children have achieved the standards for the unit.

Diagnosing Errors The Quick Checks highlight common errors and provide remediation. See also the **Teaching Strategies Handbook** pp. T146–T149, where short discussions labeled Common Misconceptions appear as needed with the strategies for key concepts.

Homework and Family Involvement

Home Note In the Student Book, the Dear Family Home Note provides objectives, vocabulary, and a sample skill discussion for family participation. (**Teaching Strategies Handbook** pages also provide homework and family involvement tips.)

Education Place Refer families to Houghton Mifflin's EduPlace Web site at http://www.eduplace.com; for resources and activities for students at http://www.eduplace.com/math; and additional resources and activities at http://www.eduplace.com/parents.

Helping Your Children Learn Math This book has activities for children ages 5–13 and tips for getting involved in children's mathematics education. (Houghton Mifflin, 1994)

Lessons		Student Pages	Teacher Pages	Resources	State or Local	
					Objectives	Assessment
10.1	Equal Parts	253–254	**T150**	Unit 10 Pretest; Teaching Resource 17		
10.2	One Half	255–256	**T150**	Teaching Resource 17		
10.3	One Fourth	257–258	**T151**	Reteach 72, 73, 74; Teaching Resource 17		
10.4	One Half, One Third, and One Fourth	259–260	**T151**	Extension 21, 22; Teaching Resource 17		
10.5	Measuring Length	261–262	**T152**			
10.6	Problem Solving Application: Use a Chart	263–264	**T152**			
10.7	Inch	265–266	**T153**	Reteach 75, 76, 77; Extension 23, 24; Teaching Resource 11		
10.8	Centimeter	267–268	**T153**	Teaching Resource 11, 16		
10.9	Problem Solving Strategy: Act It Out	269–270	**T154**			
10.10	Comparing Weight	271–272	**T154**	Extension 25, 26		
10.11	Holds More, Holds Less	273–274	**T155**	Unit 10 Posttest; Reteach 78, 79, 80; Extension 27, 28, 29, 30		

Teaching Strategies

Math Background | Fractions and Measurement

When children share items among one, two, or three friends, they're typically concerned about equal parts or equal shares. In this unit, you can build on their prior experience as you present halves, thirds, and fourths and the symbols $\frac{1}{2}$, $\frac{1}{3}$, and $\frac{1}{4}$.

Measurement at this level focuses on length, weight, and capacity. Children compare objects, telling which is longest and shortest, heaviest and lightest, and which would hold the most and least. Vocabulary from previous units is important as are opportunities to handle objects and compare them directly. Children learn the basis for standard units—inches and centimeters—and learn to read simple rulers. Children also use nonstandard units, common objects, to measure. For example, children might conjecture how many

small scoops are needed to fill a container, and then use the scoops and count the actual number. This helps them understand the idea that measurement is a process in which people combine a *number* and a *unit*.

A Positive Start

You'll have many creative opportunities to involve children in the content of this unit. Children learn as they handle objects, talk about what they are doing, and associate symbols with concepts and experiences. Plan well so that your classroom experiences are organized and so that each child can participate.

↻ Linking Past and Future Learning

Your meaningful work in this unit continues to set the stage for children's full understanding of skills and concepts they'll encounter in the future. Use the chart below to help you plan and focus your instruction.

Concept/Skills	Last Year	This Year	Next Year
Halves, Thirds, and Fourths	Identify the whole that has been divided into 2 equal parts or halves	Identify and show one half, one third, and one fourth of a region	Identify, write, and compare fractions of a region from $\frac{1}{2}$ through $\frac{1}{12}$; identify, write, and compare fractions of a set
Length, Weight, and Capacity	Use nonstandard measurement to compare the length, weight, and capacity of objects	Measure length of objects to the nearest inch and centimeter; measure length using customary and metric units	Measure length using customary and metric units; use a referent to estimate weight and capacity

Methods and Management

You'll need many materials for this unit, but they needn't be fancy—paper, scissors, and classroom objects will help children learn. Arrange to borrow a simple balance if you do not have one in the classroom.

Teaching Strategy: Halves, Thirds, and Fourths

Fold and cut various paper shapes into halves. Demonstrate that if the parts match "exactly" then one part is *half*. Show shapes in which two parts are clearly not the same and point out that they are *not halves*.

Now show how halves are split in two equal parts to form fourths. Then introduce thirds last.

▶ *Ask:* What if you wanted to share a small pizza equally with a friend. What fraction would you each get? What if you share with two friends? Three friends?

Let children name fractions and draw their solutions on the board.

▶ *Show This:*

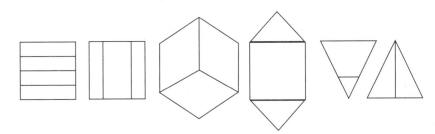

Have children identify figures that show halves, thirds, fourths.

▶ *Vocabulary Development* You'll use the word *fraction* constantly during the unit; emphasize that fractions tell how many *equal* parts are shown. Be sure that children use the terms *half, third*, and *fourth* to describe real objects and pictures. Also, point out the plural word form for each.

▶ *Common Misconceptions* Children may mistake $\frac{1}{2}$ for thirds, or 3, because they add the numbers 1 and 2 in the fraction. Review that $\frac{1}{2}$ means 1 of 2 equal parts. Similarly $\frac{1}{3}$ means 1 of 3 equal parts, and $\frac{1}{4}$ means 1 of 4 equal parts.

Teaching Strategy: Length, Weight, Capacity

The following activities can help you present comparisons and how to use nonstandard units to measure objects.

- Have groups of children arrange paper strips in order from longest to shortest. Guide them to place one end of each strip on a common baseline.

- Fill 3 or 4 paper bags with items of different weights—crushed newspaper, books, a stuffed animal, and several pairs of scissors. Let children lift the bags and place them in order from lightest to heaviest.

- Have children place two different objects in the pans of a balance. Model how to say, *The pencil weighs* about *2 crayons* or *The book weighs* between *15 and 16 crayons.*

Teacher Tips

Fold It! Provide paper squares, rectangles, equilateral triangles, circles, and hexagons for children to fold, then cut into halves, fourths, or thirds. Encourage them to show each other how the parts they make are equal and to name the fractions they are making.

"Show Me" Give each child 3 or 4 pictures with regions divided into halves, thirds, and fourths, and a few pictures that don't show equal parts. Say, *Show me all the halves* or *Show me pictures without equal parts.* Check by glancing around to see what children hold up.

Real World What foods can be cut into halves, thirds, and fourths? Invite children to list examples. Or let children draw pictures for a bulletin board display.

Tactile Reinforcement Cut drinking straws into various lengths and place them in a bag. Display one of the straws and then ask a child to reach into the bag without peeking and select a *longer* straw. The child can show the straw and confirm its length by placing it beside the original. Then ask another child to try to find a *shorter* straw, show it, and confirm its length.

Benchmarks Help children make chains of 5 or 10 paper clips and use these as nonstandard units for measuring length.

Words of Experience Let children use pourable solids such as dry rice or small beans to measure capacity. Work over a plastic tub or tray to minimize spills. Ask how many of a smaller container will fill a larger one, and let the children find the answer.

Materials Props help children understand ideas being discussed and promote interest in the topic under discussion. Student helpers can assist in distributing materials before you begin your lesson.

Good Routine Each day, have children bring to class a small object to display and then add a label to tell the approximate measure. A crayon may be about 4 inches long, a pencil may measure close to 12 centimeters in length, and so on.

Management Have children work in groups to make a measurement book. They can use narrow strips of colored paper to create different lengths. Then let them label each strip and glue the strips into a booklet.

- Display a medium-sized box or bowl and let children find classroom containers that would hold more, less, and about the same amount.

▶ *Ask: Which container holds more? Which will be heavier if you fill them both almost to the top with water?*

- Invite conjectures, then let children fill the containers and verify their predictions about weight.

▶ *Vocabulary Development* Prompt children to use *longer, shorter, heavier, lighter, holds more,* and *holds less* as well as the superlative forms of these words. Write the words on the board when you use them.

▶ *Common Misconceptions* Children may think that larger objects are always heavier than smaller ones. Provide some counterexamples: fill a small bag with crayons and a larger bag with foam pieces. Let the children lift the bags and place them on a balance, then make judgments.

Opportunities to Assess

Observation

Give each child 3 paper rectangles and ask that they show halves three different ways. As children work, walk around and ask them to explain how they know they have halves. Next, let them fold at least one of the rectangles to show fourths.

Family Involvement

Ask children to work with family members to find and draw examples of halves, thirds, or fourths at home. Back at school, let children share their drawings and then use rulers to measure and label lengths in several parts of their drawings.

Teacher/Student Dialogue

How to Teach Comparisons

Help children talk about different measurement attributes, how we use them, and tools for measuring each.

Teacher: We've been doing lots of things with measurement. What have we talked about? Raise your hands, and I'll call on you. *(Write key words as students respond)*

Students: *Length. How long it is . . . and longer and longest. . . and how many cubes fit inside. Does it hold more or less?*

Teacher: There's one more. What about weight. Kara?

Student: *That's how heavy it is.*

Teacher: Yes. Good. Now look at this. *(Shows a storage box)* What if I need to know how to measure length? *(Demonstrates)*

Students: *How long it is. Use a ruler.*

Teacher: Great. I was showing the length of the box. *(Points to "length" on the board)* So Cal, come up and measure. Which tool will you use?

Student: *(Selects an inch ruler and measures) It's about 4 inches.*

Teacher: That's right. Show again where to put the end of the ruler, right on the end of the box. Now if I want the capacity of the box, what does that mean? Sherry?

Student: *It holds stuff.*

Teacher: I'm listening. Tell me more.

Student: *How much it holds.*

What to do

When

If children don't match up the end or zero point of a ruler with the end of an object, review this procedure, reminding them to make the ends "even."

What to do

Every Day

Offer time at a center where children can work freely with materials to show fractions or practice measurement concepts. They might make clay shapes and cut them in fractions with plastic knives, show fractions on geoboards, cut longer and shorter strips of paper, order several strips of paper by length, or pour rice from one container to another and find the container that holds the most.

Questioning Techniques

For most objects, many measurement attributes apply. In the dialogue, the teacher discussed more than the box's length and made connections between the concept and the tool to use to measure.

Noting key words—*length, capacity,* and *weight*—on the board helps children see words for the ideas that being demonstrated. The list may prompt you to be sure to focus the conversation to include all the concepts.

Unit 10 Fractions and Measurement

LESSON 1
PAGES 253–254

OBJECTIVE
Identify and show equal parts of a region

PREREQUISITES
Concepts
• Understand the concept of equal

Skills
• Recognize equality

VOCABULARY
equal parts

MATERIALS
square sheets of paper

Copymasters
Teaching Resource 17, (Fractions) p. 215

Equal Parts

Presenting the Lesson

Introduce the Skill   Discuss the examples of equal parts at the top of page 253. Then cut up the nine figures from Teaching Resource 17 into cards. Make several copies of each. Place the pile of cards face down on a table. Have children take turns picking a card and telling how many equal parts.

Check Understanding   *How many times must I fold a square to make 2 equal parts?* (1 time) Demonstrate.

Guided Practice

Have children complete exercise 1 on page 253 and exercise 6 on page 254. Check that they understand that equal parts must be the same size and shape.

Independent Practice

Have children complete the remaining exercises independently.

Closing the Lesson   Have children fold a square twice to make 4 equal parts. Have them share and compare the squares.

LESSON 2
PAGES 255–256

OBJECTIVE
Identify and show one half of a region

PREREQUISITES
Concepts
• Understand the concept of equal parts

Skills
• Recognize 2 equal parts

VOCABULARY
one half

MATERIALS
fraction models

Copymasters
Teaching Resource 17, (Fractions) p. 215

One Half

Presenting the Lesson

Introduce the Skill   Use the same cards as you did in Lesson 1. Make some additional cards that show $\frac{1}{2}$ and some that show 2 unequal parts. This time spread the cards face down on a table and have children take turns picking 2 cards at a time trying to make pairs that both show one half.

Check Understanding   Ask, *How can you show 2 parts of a figure and not show $\frac{1}{2}$?* (make the parts unequal)

Guided Practice

Discuss the models at the top of page 255. Then help children complete exercise 1. Check that they understand how to show one half.

Independent Practice

Have children complete the remaining exercises independently.

Closing the Lesson   Draw a rectangle divided into 4 equal parts. Challenge volunteers to color one half.

LESSON 3
PAGES 257–258

OBJECTIVE
Identify and show one fourth of a region

PREREQUISITES
Concepts
• Understand the concept of equal parts

Skills
• Recognize 4 equal parts

VOCABULARY
one fourth

MATERIALS
fraction models
sheets of paper cut up into shapes: circles, squares, rectangles

Copymasters
Reteach 72–74, pp. 142–144
Teaching Resource 17, (Fractions) p. 215

One Fourth

Presenting the Lesson
Introduce the Skill   Use the same activity as you did in Lesson 2. This time make some additional cards that show $\frac{1}{4}$ and that show 4 unequal parts, and have children take turns picking 2 cards at a time trying to make pairs that show one fourth.

Check Understanding   *If you break a cracker into fourths, how many pieces will you have?* (4)

Guided Practice
Discuss the models at the top of page 257. Then have children complete exercise 1. Check that they understand how to show one fourth.

Independent Practice
Have children complete the remaining exercises independently. Use the Quick Check for assessment.

Closing the Lesson   Have children fold different figures such as rectangles, squares, and circles to show fourths.

LESSON 4
PAGES 259–260

OBJECTIVE
Identify and show one third of a region; review one half, one fourth, and one third of a region

PREREQUISITES
Concepts
• Understand the concept of equal parts

Skills
• Recognize $\frac{1}{2}$, $\frac{1}{4}$ of a region

VOCABULARY
fraction
one third

MATERIALS
fraction models

Copymasters
Extension 21–22, pp. 183–184
Teaching Resource 17, (Fractions) p. 215

One Third, One Half, and One Fourth

Presenting the Lesson
Introduce the Skill   Use the same activity as you did in Lessons 2 and 3. This time make some additional cards that show $\frac{1}{3}$ and have children take turns picking 2 cards at a time trying to make pairs that show one third.

Check Understanding   *If you color in $\frac{1}{3}$ of a circle, how many thirds are not colored in?* (2)

Guided Practice
Discuss the figures at the top of page 259. Check that they understand how to show one third before completing the page. For exercise 8, ask, *How many equal parts are shown?* (2) *How many parts are colored?* (1) *What fraction says that?* ($\frac{1}{2}$)

Independent Practice
Have children complete pages 259 and 260 independently.

Closing the Lesson   *If $\frac{1}{2}$ means 1 out of 2 equal parts, what do $\frac{1}{3}$ and $\frac{1}{4}$ mean?* (1 out of 3 equal parts and 1 out of 4 equal parts)

LESSON 5
PAGES 261–262

OBJECTIVE
Measure and compare lengths of objects using nonstandard units

PREREQUISITES
Concepts
• Understand the concept of length, longer, and shorter

Skills
• Count by 1's

VOCABULARY
longer
shorter

MATERIALS
various classroom objects
paper clips
chalkboard erasers

Measuring Length

Presenting the Lesson

Introduce the Skill   Have children compare lengths of pairs of classroom objects visually, identifying which is longer, shorter. Repeat using 3 objects and identifying longest and shortest.

Check Understanding   Have volunteers show how to measure the length of a desk using chalkboard erasers.

Guided Practice
Discuss how the desk at the top of page 261 was measured. Then guide children as they complete exercise 1. For exercise 7, check that they understand that they must place each eraser or paper clip end to end to measure correctly.

Independent Practice
Have children complete the remaining exercises on pages 261 and 262 independently.

Closing the Lesson   Have children draw a line they think is about 5 paper clips long. Have them check their drawings using small paper clips.

LESSON 6
PAGES 263–264

OBJECTIVE
Solve measurement problems by using a chart

PREREQUISITES
Concepts
• Understand the concepts of length, shorter, longer, shortest, longest

Skills
• Read data from a chart

Problem Solving Application: Use a Chart

Presenting the Lesson

Introduce the Focus of the Lesson   Tell children they are going to use a chart to solve problems about measurement.

Model the Four-Step Problem Solving Process   Work together to solve problem 1:

• **Understand** Ask, *What information is shown on the chart?* (the lengths of different objects) *What do you want to find out?* (which of the objects listed is the shortest)

• **Decide** Ask, *How can you solve this problem?* (look up the information in the chart, compare all the lengths and see which is the shortest)

• **Solve** Ask, *Which object on the chart is the shortest?* (the crayon)

• **Look back** Ask, *How can you check the answer?* (Look for the smallest measure on the chart, then look to see what object is next to it. The smallest measure is about 3 and it is next to the crayon. The answer is correct.)

Guided Practice
Have children complete problem 1. Check that they understand how to read the chart.

Independent Practice
Have children complete the remaining problems independently.

Closing the Lesson   *Would you need more paper clips or more erasers to measure your height? Why?* (more paper clips, because they are smaller)

LESSON 7
PAGES 265–266

OBJECTIVE
Measure objects to the
nearest inch

PREREQUISITES
Concepts
• Understand length

Skills
• Measure length
• Count by 1's

VOCABULARY
inch

MATERIALS
inch rulers

Copymasters
Reteach 75–77, pp. 145–147
Extension 23–24, pp. 185–186
Teaching Resource 11, (Coins
and Rulers) p. 209

Inch

Presenting the Lesson

Introduce the Skill   Have children go on a measurement scavenger hunt. Give partners inch rulers from Teaching Resource 11 and have them find objects in the classroom that measure about 2 inches, 3 inches, and 6 inches in length. Have pairs share and compare findings.

Check Understanding   Have children look at the inch blocks at the top of page 265. Ask, *How many blocks long is your ruler?* (12)

Guided Practice

Have children complete exercise 1. Check that they understand each block represents a 1-inch unit.

Independent Practice

Have children complete the remaining exercises independently. Use the Quick Check for assessment.

Closing the Lesson   Ask, *Where do you put the ruler to measure an object?*
(Line up the front end of the ruler with the front end of the object.)

LESSON 8
PAGES 267–268

OBJECTIVE
Measure objects to the nearest
centimeter

PREREQUISITES
Concepts
• Understand length

Skills
• Measure length
• Count by 1's

VOCABULARY
centimeter

MATERIALS
centimeter ruler

Copymasters
Teaching Resource 11, (Coins
and Rulers), 16, (Centimeter
Grid) pp. 209, 214

Centimeter

Presenting the Lesson

Introduce the Skill   Have children go on a measurement scavenger hunt as they did in Lesson 7. This time give partners centimeter rulers from Teaching Resource 11 and have them find objects in the classroom that measure about 6 centimeters, 10 centimeters, and 20 centimeters in length. Have pairs share and compare findings.

Check Understanding   Have children look at the centimeter blocks at the top of page 267. Ask, *How many blocks long is your centimeter ruler?* (20)

Guided Practice

Have children complete exercise 1. Check that they understand each block pictured beneath the pen is a 1-centimeter unit.

Independent Practice

Have children complete the remaining exercises independently.

Closing the Lesson   Ask, *How are inches and centimeters alike? Different?*
(Both measure length; inches are longer than centimeters.)

LESSON 9
PAGES 269–270

OBJECTIVE
Use the Act It Out strategy to solve measurement problems

PREREQUISITES
Concepts
• Understand the concept of length and height

Skills
• Use a centimeter tape measure to measure length and height

MATERIALS
centimeter tape measures, chalk

Problem Solving Strategy: Act It Out

Presenting the Lesson
Introduce the Strategy   Tell children they are going to use the Act It Out strategy to solve problems about measurement.

Model the Four-Step Problem Solving Process   Work together to solve the model problem on page 269.

• **Understand** *What are you being asked to find out?* (how tall I am)

• **Decide** *What strategy can you use?* (I will use a tape measure and chalk to measure myself.)

• **Solve** Model for children how you can stand against a wall and mark your height with chalk. Then measure your height from the floor to the mark with a tape measure. Then invite children to measure their own height and record their findings in the space provided on the page.

• **Look back** Ask, *Does your measurement seem reasonable? Why or why not?* Show children how they can look back at the tape measure and their measurements to see if their answers make sense.

Guided Practice
Have children complete problem 1. Check that they understand how to act out the solution using a tape measure.

Independent Practice
Have children complete the remaining problems on page 270 working with a partner.

Closing the Lesson   Ask, *What other strategy could you use to solve these problems?* (Answers will vary. Possible answer: Guess and Check.)

LESSON 10
PAGES 271–272

OBJECTIVE
Compare the weights of two objects using the terms *heavier* and *lighter*

PREREQUISITES
Concepts
• Understand weight

Skills
• Make comparisons

VOCABULARY
heavier
lighter

MATERIALS
various classroom objects, balance, paper clips, cubes, pennies

Copymasters
Extension 25–26, pp. 187–188

Comparing Weight

Presenting the Lesson
Introduce the Skill   Discuss the definitions of *heavier* and *lighter* at the top of page 271. Have children compare weights of various classroom objects by holding two objects in their hands and deciding which is heavier and which is lighter.

Check Understanding   Ask, *Which is heavier, a brick or a pillow?*

Guided Practice
Help children complete exercises 1 and 7. Check that they understand which objects are heavier and lighter and can correctly use a balance.

Independent Practice
Have children complete the remaining exercises independently. If you have a limited number of balances, children may need to work in groups to complete exercises 8–10.

Closing the Lesson   Ask, *Which measurement tool do you use to measure length? weight?* (ruler, scale)

LESSON 11
PAGES 273–274

OBJECTIVE
Use direct comparison and non-standard units to compare the capacities of two containers

PREREQUISITES
Concepts
• Understand capacity

Skills
• Make comparisons

VOCABULARY
holds more
holds less

MATERIALS
various empty containers
box, cubes

Copymasters
Reteach 78–80, pp. 148–150
Extension 27–30, pp. 189–192

Holds More, Holds Less

Presenting the Lesson
Introduce the Skill   Discuss the examples of containers that hold more and hold less on page 273. Have children compare capacity of various containers by directly visually comparing two containers and telling which holds more and which holds less. If possible, use water to fill each container, then empty each into a third container and measure which holds more.

Check Understanding   Say, *Give an example of a container that holds about the same amount as a glass.* (Answers will vary. Possible answer: a cup)

Guided Practice
Have children complete exercise 1. Check that they understand the concepts of holds more and holds less and can compare capacities of three containers at a time.

Independent Practice
Have children complete the remaining exercises independently. Use the Quick Check for assessment.

Closing the Lesson   Say, *Name something that holds more than a bath tub.* (Answers will vary. Possible answer: a pool)

UNIT 10 REVIEW
Pages 275–276

Item Analysis

Items	Unit Obj.
1	10A
2–4	10B
5	10E
6	10D
7–9	10C
10–12	10F

Answers to Unit 10 review items can be found on pages 275–276 of the Teacher's Annotated Edition.

Administering the Review

These pages review concepts and skills taught in this unit. Make sure children understand all direction lines. You may wish to do the first example in each section cooperatively to ensure understanding.

Scoring Chart

Number Correct	12	11	10	9	8	7	6	5	4	3	2	1
Score	100	92	83	75	67	58	50	42	33	25	17	8

After the Review

• The Item Analysis chart on the left shows the Unit 10 objective covered by each test item. This chart can help you determine which objectives need review or extra practice.

• For additional assessment, use the Posttest for Unit 10 , Copymasters, pp. 45–46.

UNIT 10 CUMULATIVE REVIEW
Pages 277–278

Item Analysis

Items	Unit Obj.
1	6A
2	6B
3	7B
4	7D
5	10B
6	10C
7	10D
8	10E
9–11	9A
12–14	9B

Answers to Cumulative Review items can be found on pages 277–278 of the Teacher's Annotated Edition.

Administering the Review
These pages review concepts and skills from the unit as well as providing practice with standardized test formats. Children should mark their answers directly on the test pages.

Test-Taking Tip Remind children to listen to the entire question before looking at all of the choices.

Exercises 1–9 This test is administered orally. Before reading each question, ask children to find the correct item number and then listen carefully. Read each question twice, and pause between items to give children time to find and mark their answers.

ex. 1. Which number sentence solves the problem? Mark the space under your answer. There are 9 eggs. 7 eggs break. How many eggs are left?
ex. 2. Which fact is not in the same family as the fact in the beginning of the row? Mark the space under your answer.
ex. 3. Which number is shown in the table? Mark the space under your answer.
ex. 4. Count by 10's. Which number is missing? Mark the space under your answer.
ex. 5. Which fraction of the circle is shaded? Mark the space under your answer .
ex. 6. Which holds the most? Mark the space under your answer.
ex. 7. How many centimeters long is the worm? Mark the space under your answer.
ex. 8. How many inches long is the crayon? Mark the space under your answer.

Exercises 9–14 You will complete the rest of the test on your own.

Test-Taking Tip Remind children to check operation signs before marking their choices.

Scoring Chart
After the Review

Number Correct	14	13	12	11	10	9	8	7	6	5	4	3	2	1
Score	100	93	86	79	71	64	57	50	43	36	29	21	14	7

The Item Analysis chart on the left shows the unit objective covered by each test item. This chart can help you determine which objectives need review or extra practice.

Addition and Subtraction Facts through 20

Unit Objectives

11A Solve addition and subtraction facts through 20

11B Represent equivalent forms of the same number using number expressions

11C Write fact families through 18

11D Solve problems by choosing to add or subtract; use Draw a Picture and other strategies to solve problems

About This Unit

The support pages that follow provide more information on prerequisite skills, methods for teaching skills and concepts, daily routines, tips on classroom management and materials, and useful dialogue techniques.

Assessments

Use Beginning of the Year Inventory for entry-level assessment.

Ongoing Evaluation Quick Checks, Reteach Worksheets, the Skills Tutorial Inventories and the Midyear Test help ensure that children are progressing adequately to meet the standards.

Summative Evaluation Use Test Preps, Unit Review (p. T170), Cumulative Review (p. T171), Reteach Worksheets, and the Skills Tutorial Inventory, Strand P2, Skill 3, and Strand P3, Skill 3 to assure that children have achieved the standards for the unit.

Diagnosing Errors The Quick Checks highlight common errors and provide remediation. See also the **Teaching Strategies Handbook** pp. T160–T163, where short discussions labeled Common Misconceptions appear as needed with the strategies for key concepts.

Homework and Family Involvement

Home Note In the Student Book, the Dear Family Home Note provides objectives, vocabulary, and a sample skill discussion for family participation. (**Teaching Strategies Handbook** pages also provide homework and family involvement tips.)

Education Place Refer families to Houghton Mifflin's EduPlace Web site at **http://www.eduplace.com**; for resources and activities for students at **http://www.eduplace.com/math**; and additional resources and activities at **http://www.eduplace.com/parents**.

Helping Your Children Learn Math This book has activities for children ages 5–13 and tips for getting involved in children's mathematics education. (Houghton Mifflin, 1994)

Lessons	Student Pages	Teacher Pages	Resources	State or Local	
				Objectives	Assessment
11.1 Related Facts through 12	281–284	**T164**	Unit 11 Pretest Extension 31		
11.2 Fact Families for 11 and 12	285	**T164**			
11.3 Names for Numbers through 12	286	**T165**	Reteach 81, 82, 83		
11.4 Related Facts through 16	287–290	**T165**	Extension 32		
11.5 Fact Families through 16	291	**T166**			
11.6 Names for Numbers through 16	292	**T166**	Reteach 84, 85, 86		
11.7 Related Facts through 18	293–296	**T167**	Skills Tutorial: Strand P2, Skill 3; Strand P3, Skill 3; Extension 33		
11.8 Fact Families through 18	297	**T167**			
11.9 Names for Numbers through 18	298	**T168**	Reteach 87, 88		
11.10 Problem Solving Application: Choose the Operation	299–300	**T168**			
11.11 Adding and Subtracting through 20	301–302	**T169**	Reteach 89		
12 Problem Solving Strategy: Draw a Picture	303–304	**T169**	Unit 11 Posttest		

Teaching Strategies

Math Background	Addition and Subtraction Facts through 20

In this final unit, children use their knowledge of addition and subtraction and apply it to facts with sums through 20. Because basic facts are also important in upper level mathematics, you'll spend more time on picturing and finding answers to facts, seeing how facts are related, and solving problems with addition and subtraction.

For most basic facts there are three related ones: 7 + 8 = 15 is part of a *fact family* that also includes 8 + 7 = 15, 15 − 7 = 8, and 15 − 8 = 7. When children realize and use this idea, the number of facts they must commit to memory is only one fourth of what it would be if facts were perceived as unrelated information. When 10 is added or subtracted, children's work with place value also helps them find the answer easily.

In previous units, you may have introduced *doubles*—adding a number to itself—which results in an even number. Doubles are easy for most children to learn, and knowledge of doubles can easily extend to *near doubles* (8 + 8 = 16, so 8 + 9 is 16 + 1 or 17). Using strategies or "shortcuts" such as these helps children reason mathematically, cuts down their work, and promotes feelings of confidence.

A Positive Start
The school year is almost finished, and you can see how much the children have learned. Keep your enthusiasm high to make this final unit productive. Remember that time spent planning will help you implement classroom activities confidently and smoothly—and will be useful to you next year too.

Linking Past and Future Learning

Look across the levels to see how these key skills and concepts evolve. Talk with teachers at higher levels to find out which skills are typically in need of practice or reteaching.

Concept/Skills	Last Year	This Year	Next Year
Solving Addition and Subtraction Facts	Use pictures to solve addition and subtraction facts	Solve addition and subtraction facts through 20	Solve addition and subtraction facts through 20; use the grouping property to add three addends
Working with Related Facts	Use pictures to solve addition and subtraction facts	Solve related addition and subtraction facts and fact families through 18 using pictures	Write the related fact given an addition or subtraction sentence; write fact families through 18
Solving Addition and Subtraction Problems	Use pictures to solve addition and subtraction problems	Choose whether to add or subtract when solving simple addition and subtraction problems through 20	Choose whether to add or subtract when solving addition and subtraction problems through 20

Methods and Management

Extend children's understanding of the meaning of addition and subtraction as they work with greater numbers. Help them think algebraically as they picture and write facts, using their knowledge to solve problems. Following are some suggestions.

Teaching Strategy: Solving Addition and Subtraction Facts

Introduce new facts a few at a time, for example, fact with sums to 12, 16, 18, and then 20. Show children how new facts build on ones they already know. Point out that $9 + 2$ is not much different from $8 + 2$.

- Use counters and part-part-whole mats to model addition. Talk through many sums for a number such as 12: $10 + 2$, $9 + 3$, $8 + 4$, $7 + 5$, and so on. Encourage children to discuss patterns they see in the addends.

- Use part-part-whole mats for subtraction. Start with a number as a whole, then show children how to separate counters to one part, see how many are left, moving them to the other part. Write facts in both horizontal and vertical formats.

- Use triangular flash cards to demonstrate fact families and missing addends.

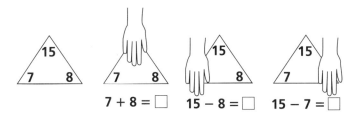

$7 + 8 = \square$ $15 - 8 = \square$ $15 - 7 = \square$

▶ **Ask:** *The sum is 15—what could the addends be? The difference is 7—what could the subtraction problem be?*
These questions have many good answers, so provide time for children to mention several. Record and discuss responses on the board.

▶ **Vocabulary Development** Create a bulletin board with boxes for *addend, addend,* and *sum* in both horizontal and vertical formats. Provide number cards for children to place in the boxes to show a different problem daily.

Teaching Strategy: Working with Related Facts

Committing facts to memory is much easier when facts are learned in families. When children know one fact, they can find three more related facts.

- Use part-part-whole diagrams or mats. Children can record related facts in this format and then write the number sentences.

Teacher Tips

Materials Sketch a series of triangular flash cards and addition and subtraction fact cards, and request that family members make sets for each child. Explain that when practicing, children should put in a separate pile the cards for which they cannot quickly say the answers, and then go back to these and work out the answers with counters.

Management Partners can use fact cards in a simple activity. Each gets 10 to 12 cards, shuffled. They simultaneously turn over cards as you call out *higher value,* or *lower value.* When values are the same, or their cards match, children can call back the amount.

Spin and Subtract Prepare a spinner with 12-20 and another with 5-10. Let pairs of children spin two numbers, subtract the lesser from the greater, and record the difference. If they disagree, have them use counters to work out the difference.

Extra Support Pair confident children with those who need help. They can help with rephrasing story situations, modeling with stories and pictures, and checking answers.

Money Problems Pose problems with "spending" and "earning" money through 20¢. Provide coins for children to model the situations and to trade coins of equal values as needed.

Notes for Next Year As you finish the year, make notes about things that worked well and those that could be improved upon.

Mark number cubes 5 through 10 on their faces. Have pairs of children toss the cubes, write an addition number sentence to match the numbers, and then record 3 more facts to complete the fact family.

On the Board Write several facts on the board. Have children take turns writing related facts.

Number Line Support Show children how a fact like $5 + 7 = 12$ can be shown with two "hops" on the number line. Then $12 - 7$ can be shown with the same hops—backward. Ask, *What are two more related facts?* Let children show them on the number line too.

Paper Clip Facts Attach paper clips to each end of a note card to show two addends. Have children record the two addends and sum, then reverse the card, see that the order of addends has reversed, and write the number sentence. Finally, review the total number of clips, cover one group of clips, and see how many are left. Write a subtraction sentence to match. Use the card and clips to cover each fact in the family.

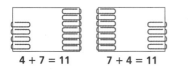

$4 + 7 = 11$	$7 + 4 = 11$

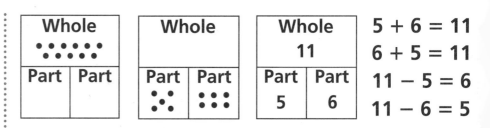

Whole ● ● ● ● ● ●		Whole		Whole 11		$5 + 6 = 11$
Part	Part	Part	Part	Part 5	Part 6	$6 + 5 = 11$
		⁘	⠋			$11 - 5 = 6$
						$11 - 6 = 5$

▶ *Ask:* Here's a triangular flashcard with 17, 9, and 8. What fact family goes with it?
Have children write the fact family, then check each others' papers.

Teaching Strategy: Solving Addition and Subtraction Problems

Present many opportunities for children to choose which operation to use, to draw pictures to represent problem situations, and to explain their thinking when they solve problems. Stress that addition involves combining, while subtraction involves separating or comparing.

- Give cards with different number sentences to groups of three children. Each group can draw or act out a situation to match the number sentence, and explain to the class how they knew whether to add or subtract.

▶ *Say* Some children are playing and some leave to go home How many are left? Is this addition or subtraction? How do you know?
Have children supply various numbers to fit the story and then write subtraction sentences.

▶ *Common Misconceptions* When children are unsure about whether to add or subtract, let them retell problem situations. Illustrate combining by moving groups together, and show subtraction by moving groups apart or comparing groups.

Opportunities to Assess

 Observation

Present a problem such as: *14 children were singing and 6 took a break. How many are still singing?* Have children draw a picture and write the number sentence for the story. Next, use 5 and 9, asking children to write or draw a picture for an addition situation. Look over the children's work observing their answers, their ability to write number sentences, and their ability to interpret or create stories for problem situations.

 Family Involvement

Ask that families practice basic facts for a few minutes each day. Offer to lend games or send home flashcards if these would be useful. Family members can help children keep track of progress. One new fact learned each day should be considered a success.

Teacher/Student Dialogue

How to Share Strategies

Midway through the unit, conduct a discussion in which children share strategies for learning basic facts. The way in which one child thinks about facts may help others solve and practice facts, and then commit them to memory.

Teacher: Let's talk about some things that have helped you learn your facts. Raise your hand if you can tell us a strategy—a way to figure it out. Tammy?

Student: *Well when I add 0, like 8 + 0, it's the same number, it's 8.*

Student: *And subtract 0, too.*

Teacher: Why does that happen? *(Writes 6 + 0)* When you add 0, why do you get the same number? Yes, Lorenzo.

Student: *It's the same number as you started with.*

Teacher: Now, why does that work? Tell me more.

Student: *You don't add anything*

Teacher: That's right. What about another strategy for facts. Liza, you showed me something about adding 9.

Student: *You add 10, then take away 1. If you have 7 + 9, well 7 + 10 is 17, so then you subtract 1. It's 16.*

Teacher: I'm going to write it. *(Writes Liza's example, then has another child try 5 + 9 and another 2 + 9.)* Good. Now everyone, try this one on paper using the strategy: 8 + 9. *(Walks around and checks)* How does it work?

Student: *Well, 8 + 10 is 18, then one less.*

Student: *Because 9 is 10 minus 1!*

Teacher: Janie, tell us in your words what Roberto and Billy said.

Student: *(Tries to explain. The conversation continues to other strategies including the use of facts within families.)*

What to do

When

If children seem puzzled about answers, give them a moment to think of responses. You may want to pose a question, wait 3 to 5 seconds, and then restate the question before calling on volunteers.

What to do

Every Day

Provide several minutes for children to work alone, with partners, or in small groups to commit facts to memory. Provide several choices for practice—traditional or triangular flashcards or games with spinners or number cubes. Some children may simply prefer to practice writing facts on paper.

Questioning Techniques

"Why?" and "how?" are extremely valuable questions, so ask them often. Children's answers to these questions reveal their thought processes. These questions also show children that mathematics is a subject in which logical reasoning is expected and valued.

Here are some additional tips to consider:

- An open-ended question can begin a discussion as you clarify what the topic is.

- Written examples give visual learners opportunities to focus on the content.

- For more clarity, ask a child to explain again in his or her own words.

Unit 11 Addition and Subtraction Facts through 20

LESSON 1
PAGES 281–284

OBJECTIVE
Solve related addition and subtraction facts through 12

PREREQUISITES
Concepts
• Understand numbers 0–12
• Understand addition and subtraction

Skills
• Add, sums through 10
• Subtract from 10 or less

MATERIALS
counters

Copymasters
Extension 31, p. 193

Related Facts through 12

Presenting the Lesson
Introduce the Skill   Have children connect what they learned about related facts through 10 to related facts through 12. Draw sets of objects on the board to illustrate facts for 11 and 12. Have children use counters to solve the facts and share their answers.

Check Understanding   Have children use counters to show that $9 + 2$ and $11 - 2$ are related.

Guided Practice
Have children complete exercise 1 on page 281 and exercise 7 on page 282. Check that they recognize how the two facts in each exercise are related.

Independent Practice
Have children complete the remaining exercises independently.

Closing the Lesson   Have volunteers make up story problems for related facts for 11 and 12.

LESSON 2
PAGE 285

OBJECTIVE
Complete fact families for 11 and 12

PREREQUISITES
Concepts
• Understand the inverse relationship between addition and subtraction
• Understand the order property of addition

Skills
• Add, sums through 12
• Subtract from 12 or less

Fact Families for 11 and 12

Presenting the Lesson
Introduce the Skill   Review fact families for 9 and 10. Explain that in this lesson children will study fact families for 11 and 12. Work together to complete exercise 1.

Check Understanding   *How are all of the facts in exercise 1 alike?* (They are all made up of the numbers 4, 7, and 11.)

Guided Practice
Have children complete exercise 1. Check that they understand how to use the addition facts to complete the subtraction facts in a family.

Independent Practice
Have children complete the remaining exercises on page 285 independently.

Closing the Lesson   *What fact family for 12 can be made with the numbers 6 and 12?* ($6 + 6 = 12$; $12 - 6 = 6$)

LESSON 3
PAGE 286

OBJECTIVE
Identify names for numbers through 12 using number expressions

PREREQUISITES
Concepts
• Understand numbers through 12

Skills
• Know facts through 12

MATERIALS
counters

Copymasters
Reteach 81–83, pp. 151–153

Names for Numbers through 12

Presenting the Lesson
Introduce the Skill   Give each group 10 counters. Challenge children to use counters to make as many different combinations of numbers as they can that equal 7. Then have them show as many facts as they can that equal a difference of 7. Repeat with other numbers to 12.

Check Understanding   Have volunteers identify a variety of number sentences for 6; for example, $3 + 3 = 6$; $7 - 1 = 6$.

Guided Practice
Have children complete exercise 1. Check that they understand why the 3 addends name 12.

Independent Practice
Have children complete the remaining exercises independently. Use the Quick Check for assessment.

Closing the Lesson   *Which number do 5 + 7, 8 + 4, and 6 + 6 all name?* (12)

LESSON 4
PAGES 287–290

OBJECTIVE
Solve related addition and subtraction facts through 16

PREREQUISITES
Concepts
• Understand numbers 0–16
• Understand addition and subtraction

Skills
• Add, sums through 12
• Subtract from 12 or less

MATERIALS
counters

Copymasters
Extension 32, p. 194

Related Facts through 16

Presenting the Lesson
Introduce the Skill   Review related facts through 12. Then complete exercise 1 together with the class.

Check Understanding   Have children use counters to show that $9 + 4$ and $13 - 4$ are related.

Guided Practice
Have children complete exercises 1 and 7. Check that they add and subtract accurately and that they understand how the two facts are related.

Independent Practice
Have children complete the remaining exercises independently.

Closing the Lesson   Write: There are ___ children. ___ more join them. How many children are there now? Have volunteers fill in the blanks so that the answers are 13, 14, 15, and 16.

LESSON 5
PAGE 291

OBJECTIVE
Complete fact families through 16

PREREQUISITES
Concepts
• Understand the inverse relationship between addition and subtraction
• Understand the order property of addition

Skills
• Add, sums through 16
• Subtract from 16 or less

Fact Families through 16

Presenting the Lesson

Introduce the Skill   Review fact families for 11 and 12. Explain that in this lesson children will study fact families for numbers through 16. Work together to complete exercise 1.

Check Understanding   *Which numbers from 13 to 16 will have doubles as addition facts?* (14 will have $7 + 7$; 16 will have $8 + 8$)

Guided Practice

Have children complete exercise 1. Check that they understand how to use the addition facts to complete the subtraction facts in a family.

Independent Practice

Have children complete the remaining exercises independently.

Closing the Lesson   *What fact family can you write with the numbers 5, 9, 14?* ($9 + 5 = 14$; $5 + 9 = 14$; $14 - 9 = 5$; $14 - 5 = 9$)

LESSON 6
PAGE 292

OBJECTIVE
Identify names for numbers through 16 using number expressions

PREREQUISITES
Concepts
• Understand numbers through 16

Skills
• Know number facts through 16

MATERIALS
Copymasters
Reteach 84–86, pp. 154–156

Names for Numbers through 16

Presenting the Lesson

Introduce the Skill   Review identifying names for numbers through 12. Explain that in this lesson children will identify names for numbers through 16.

Check Understanding   *How can you use a number expression to name your age?* (Answers will vary.)

Guided Practice

Have children complete exercise 1. Check that they understand why the 3 addends name 13.

Independent Practice

Have children complete the remaining exercises independently. Use the Quick Check for assessment.

Closing the Lesson   *How can you name the number 12 using a subtraction expression?* (Answers will vary. Possible answer: $14 - 2$)

LESSON 7
PAGES 293–296

OBJECTIVE
Solve related addition and subtraction facts through 18

PREREQUISITES
Concepts
• Understand numbers 0–18
• Understand addition and subtraction

Skills
• Add, sums through 16
• Subtract from 16 or less

MATERIALS
Copymasters
Extension 33, p. 195

Related Facts through 18

Presenting the Lesson
Introduce the Skill   Review related facts through 16. Explain that in this lesson children will learn fact families through 18. Complete exercise 1 together with the class.

Check Understanding   *Which subtraction facts do you know if you know that 9 + 7 = 16?* (16 − 7 = 9 and 16 − 9 = 7)

Guided Practice
Have children complete exercise 1 on page 293 and 7 on page 294. Check that they add and subtract accurately and that they understand the relationship between the two facts in each exercise.

Independent Practice
Have children complete the remaining exercises independently.

Closing the Lesson   Have children draw pictures to go with the number sentences 9 + 8 = 17; 9 + 9 = 18; 18 − 9 = 9.

LESSON 8
PAGE 297

OBJECTIVE
Complete fact families through 18

PREREQUISITES
Concepts
• Understand the inverse relationship between addition and subtraction
• Understand the order property of addition

Skills
• Add, sums through 18
• Subtract from 18 or less

Fact Families through 18

Presenting the Lesson
Introduce the Skill   Review some fact families through 16 including doubles facts such as 8 + 8 = 16. Explain that in this lesson children will study fact families through 18. Work together to complete exercise 1.

Check Understanding   Challenge volunteers to make up a word problem that can be solved using one of the facts in exercise 1.

Guided Practice
Have children complete exercise 1. Check that they understand the relationship among the three numbers in the facts and that they add and subtract accurately.

Independent Practice
Have children complete the remaining exercises on page 297 independently.

Closing the Lesson   *How many fact families did we learn for 17? 18?* (1, 1)

LESSON 9
PAGE 298

OBJECTIVE
Identify names for numbers through 18 using number expressions

PREREQUISITES
Concepts
• Understand numbers through 18

Skills
• Know number facts through 18

MATERIALS
Copymasters
Reteach 87–88, pp. 157–158

Skills Tutorial
Strand P2: Skill 3 Practice 1–5; Strand P3: Skill 3 Practice 1–4

Names for Numbers through 18

Presenting the Lesson
Introduce the Skill Review identifying names for numbers through 16. Explain that in this lesson children will identify names for numbers through 18.

Check Understanding *How can you name 15 using an expression with 3 addends?* (Answers will vary. Possible answer: 3 + 5 + 7)

Guided Practice
Have children complete exercise 1. Check that they understand how to add 4 addends.

Independent Practice
Have children complete the remaining exercises independently. Use the Quick Check for assessment.

Closing the Lesson Ask, *How can you name the number 18 using an expression with 4 addends?* (Answers will vary. Possible answer: 4 + 5 + 4 + 5)

LESSON 10
PAGES 299–300

OBJECTIVE
Solve problems by choosing to add or subtract

PREREQUISITES
Concepts
• Understand addition and subtraction

Skills
• Add and subtract basic facts through 18

Problem Solving Application: Choose the Operation

Presenting the Lesson
Introduce the Focus of the Lesson Explain to children that in this lesson they will solve problems by choosing to add or subtract.

Model the Four-Step Problem Solving Process Work through the problem 1 on page 299.

• **Understand** *What do you need to find out to solve this problem?* (How many erasers Anna had to start with.)

• **Decide** *How can you decide whether to add or subtract?* (I need to find the difference between the number she added and the total number to find how many she started with. Finding the difference means I have to subtract.)

• **Solve** *What's the solution?* (I subtract 6 from 13 and get 7. She started with 7 erasers.)

• **Look back** *How can you check that your answer makes sense?* (I know that 6 + 7 = 13. My answer makes sense.)

Guided Practice
Have children complete problem 1. Check that they understand why subtraction is the correct operation.

Independent Practice
Have children complete the remaining problems on pages 299 and 300 independently.

Closing the Lesson *Is there another way to solve exercise 4?* (Answers will vary.)

LESSON 11
PAGES 301–302

OBJECTIVE
Solve addition and subtraction facts through 20

PREREQUISITES
Concepts
• Understand addition and subtraction
• Understand number sentences

Skills
• Add and subtract, basic facts through 18

MATERIALS
counters

Copymasters
Reteach 89, p. 159

Adding and Subtracting through 20

Presenting the Lesson
Introduce the Skill　Give groups of children 20 counters each. Have them model the first four items of exercise 1 on page 301. Ask, *If 10 + 4 = 14, what is 14 − 10?* (4) *What is 13 − 10?* (3)

Check Understanding　*What do you add to 10 to get 12?* (2)

Guided Practice
Have children do exercise 1. Check that their answers are accurate. Talk about the pattern you see.

Independent Practice
Have children complete the remaining exercises independently.

Closing the Lesson　Have children look back at the subtraction exercises on page 301. *What do you think 20 − 11 will be?* (9)

LESSON 12
PAGES 303–304

OBJECTIVE
Use the Draw a Picture strategy to solve problems with facts through 20

PREREQUISITES
Concepts
• Understand addition and subtraction

Skills
• Add and subtract, facts through 20

Problem Solving Strategy: Draw a Picture

Presenting the Lesson
Introduce the Strategy　Explain to children that in this lesson they will learn to draw a picture to solve problems.

Model the Four-Step Problem Solving Process　Work through the model problem on page 303 with the class.

• **Understand** *What are you being asked to do?* (I need to find out how many children are in the line.)

• **Decide** *What strategy can you use to solve the problem?* (I can draw a picture to find out.)

• **Solve** Ask, *How many children does your picture show?* (Have children trace the picture and see that 11 children are shown.)

• **Look back** *How can you check that your answer is correct?* (Have children check by adding 3 + 8 = 11.)

Guided Practice
Have children complete the model problem. Check that they understand how the picture represents the problem.

Independent Practice
Have children complete the remaining problems independently.

Closing the Lesson　Ask, *What other strategy could you use to solve problem 3?* (Answers will vary. Possible answer: Write a number sentence.)

UNIT 11 REVIEW

Page 305–306

Item Analysis

Items	Unit Obj.
1–20	11A
21–22	11C
23–25	11B
26–28	11D

Answers to Unit 11 review items can be found on pages 305–306 of the Teacher's Annotated Edition.

Administering the Review

These pages review concepts and skills taught in this unit. Make sure children understand all direction lines. You may wish to do the first example in each section cooperatively to ensure understanding.

Scoring Chart

Number Correct	28	27	26	25	24	23	22	21	20	19	18	17	16	15
Score	100	96	93	89	86	82	79	75	71	68	64	61	57	54

Number Correct	14	13	12	11	10	9	8	7	6	5	4	3	2	1
Score	50	46	43	39	36	32	27	25	21	18	14	11	7	4

After the Review

• The Item Analysis chart on the left shows the Unit 11 objective covered by each test item. This chart can help you determine which objectives need review or extra practice.

• For additional assessment, use the Posttest for Unit 11, Copymasters, pp. 49–50.

UNIT 11 CUMULATIVE REVIEW
Pages 307–308

Item Analysis

Items	Unit Obj.
1	10B
2, 3	10C
4	10D
5	10E
6	11C
7	11D
8, 9	9A
10, 11	9B
12–15	11A

Answers to Cumulative Review items can be found on pages 307–308 of the Teacher's Annotated Edition.

Administering the Review

These pages review concepts and skills from the unit as well as providing practice with standardized test formats. Children should mark their answers directly on the test pages.

Test-Taking Tip Remind children to listen to the entire question before looking at all of the choices.

Exercises 1–7 This test is administered orally. Before reading each question, ask children to find the correct item number and then listen carefully. Read each question twice, and pause between items to give children time to find and mark their answers.

ex. 1. *Which fraction of the rectangle is shaded? Mark the space under your answer.*
ex. 2. *Which holds less than the container shown at the beginning of the row? Mark the space under your answer .*
ex. 3. *Which is heavier than the object shown at the beginning of the row? Mark the space under your answer.*
ex. 4. *How long is the paperclip? Mark the space under your answer.*
ex. 5. *How tall is the spool? Mark the space under your answer.*
ex. 6. *Which fact belongs in the same family as the fact shown at the beginning of the row? Mark the space next to your answer.*
ex. 7. *Which number sentence solves the problem? Mark the space under your answer. There are 15 coins on a table. 8 are heads. The rest are tails. How many are tails?*

Exercises 8–15 Tell children they will complete the rest of the test on their own.

Test-Taking Tip Remind children to check operation signs before marking their choices in exercises 8–15.

Number Correct	15	14	13	12	11	10	9	8	7	6	5	4	3	2	1
Score	100	93	87	80	73	67	60	53	47	40	33	27	20	13	7

Scoring Chart

After the Review

The Item Analysis chart on the left shows the unit objective covered by each test item. This chart can help you determine which objectives need review or extra practice.

Teacher Notes

HOUGHTON MIFFLIN

Math Steps

Contents

UNIT 1 • TABLE OF CONTENTS

Geometry

Dear Family,

During the next few weeks our math class will be learning about geometry – solid and plane figures.

You can expect to see homework that provides practice in identifying spheres, cylinders, cubes, rectangular prisms, cones, pyramids, triangles, circles, squares, and rectangles. You may wish to keep the following as a guide.

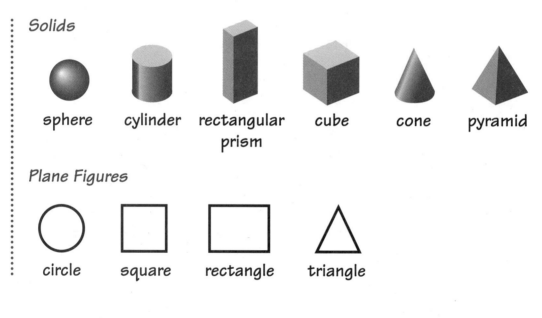

Recognizing shapes can help children solve spatial problems.

Sincerely,

Teacher Note: **Check Understanding** Ask, How is a rectangular prism like a cube? How is it different?

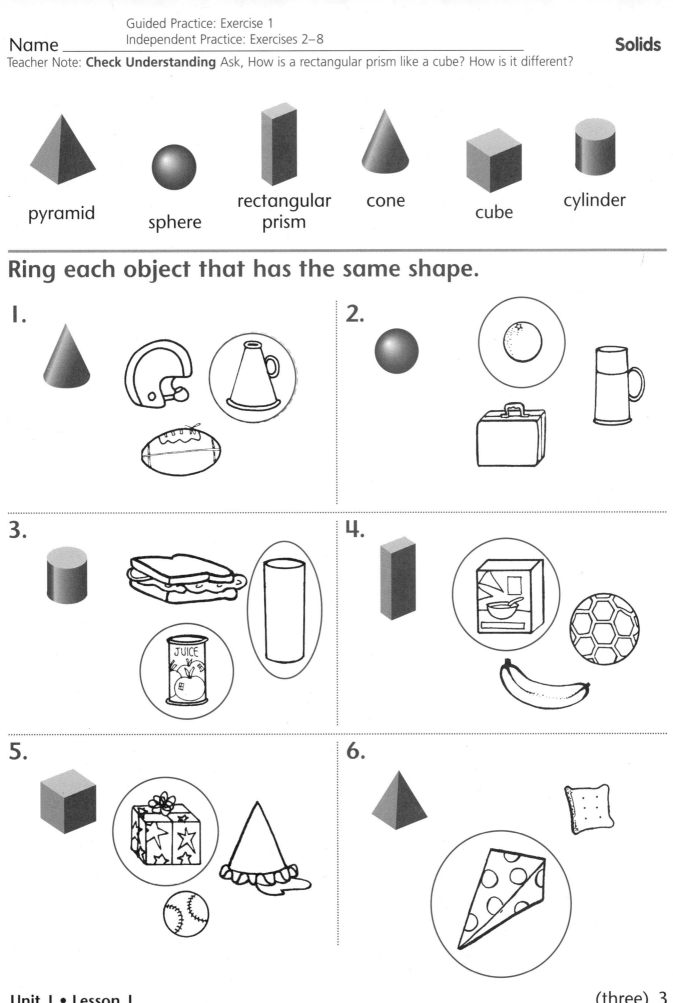

pyramid   sphere   rectangular prism   cone   cube   cylinder

Ring each object that has the same shape.

1.

2.

3.

4.

5.

6.

Unit 1 • Lesson 1

(three) 3

pyramid   sphere   rectangular   cone   cube   cylinder
                       prism

Look at the solids.
How can you sort them into two groups?
Draw to show your sort.

Answers may vary. Possible answer: curves and edges

7.

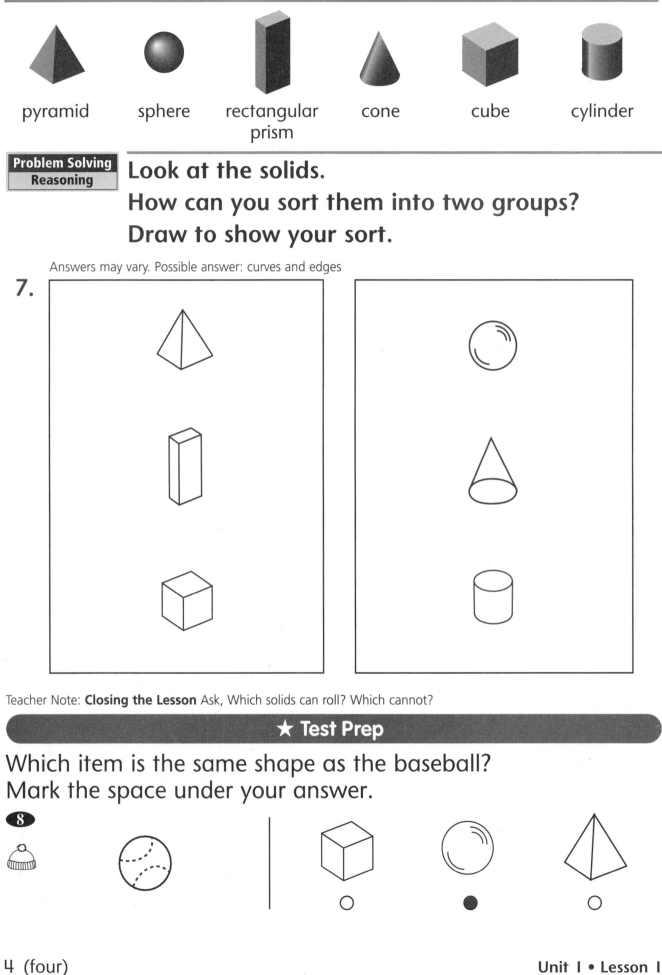

Teacher Note: **Closing the Lesson** Ask, Which solids can roll? Which cannot?

★ Test Prep

Which item is the same shape as the baseball?
Mark the space under your answer.

8

4 (four)

Unit I • Lesson I

Guided Practice: Exercises 1 and 5
Independent Practice: Exercises 2–4 and 6–9

Relating Solids to Plane Figures

Teacher Note: **Check Understanding** Ask, Can you trace the face of a sphere? Why or why not?

The **face** of this cone is a circle.

Look at the solid.
Ring the figure that matches the shaded face of each solid.

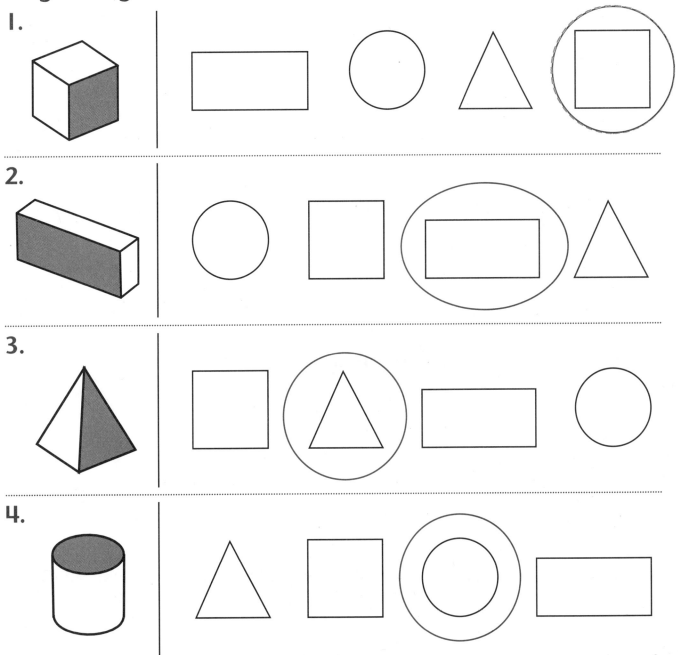

1.

2.

3.

4.

Look at the object.
Ring the figure that matches the shaded face.

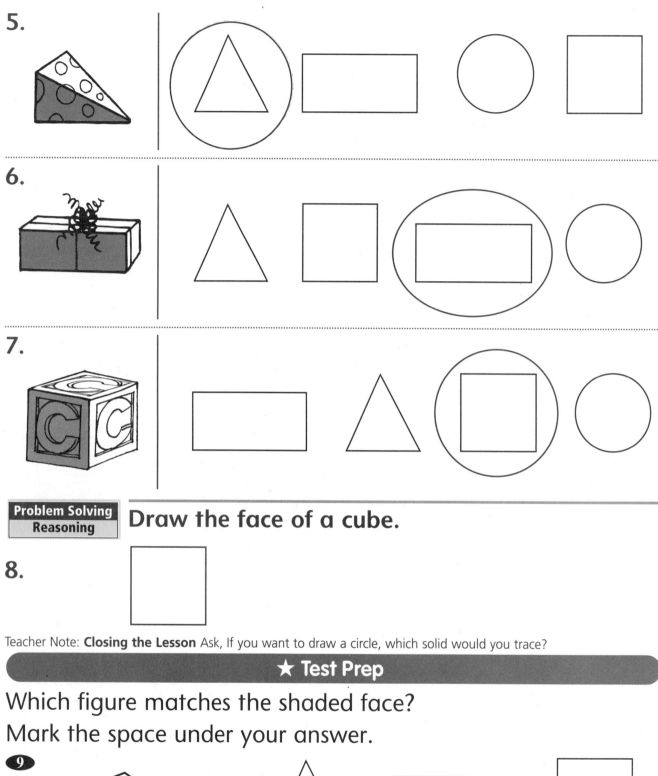

5.

6.

7.

| Problem Solving Reasoning |

Draw the face of a cube.

8.

Teacher Note: **Closing the Lesson** Ask, If you want to draw a circle, which solid would you trace?

★ Test Prep

Which figure matches the shaded face?
Mark the space under your answer.

9

6 (six)

Guided Practice: Model Exercise, Exercise 1
Independent Practice: Exercise 2

Plane Figures

Teacher Note: **Check Understanding** Ask, How is a square like a triangle? How is it different?

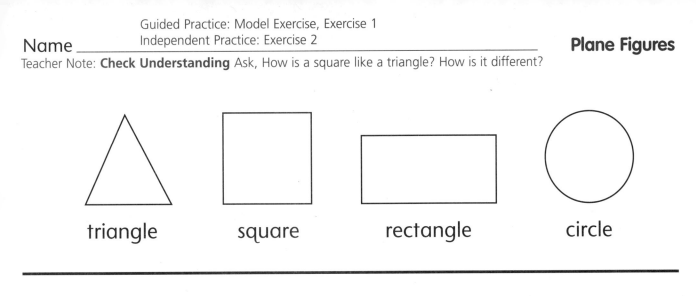

triangle   square   rectangle   circle

Color the triangles blue.
Color the squares red.
Color the rectangles green.
Color the circles yellow.

Unit 1 • Lesson 3

(seven) 7

Ring the triangles.

1.

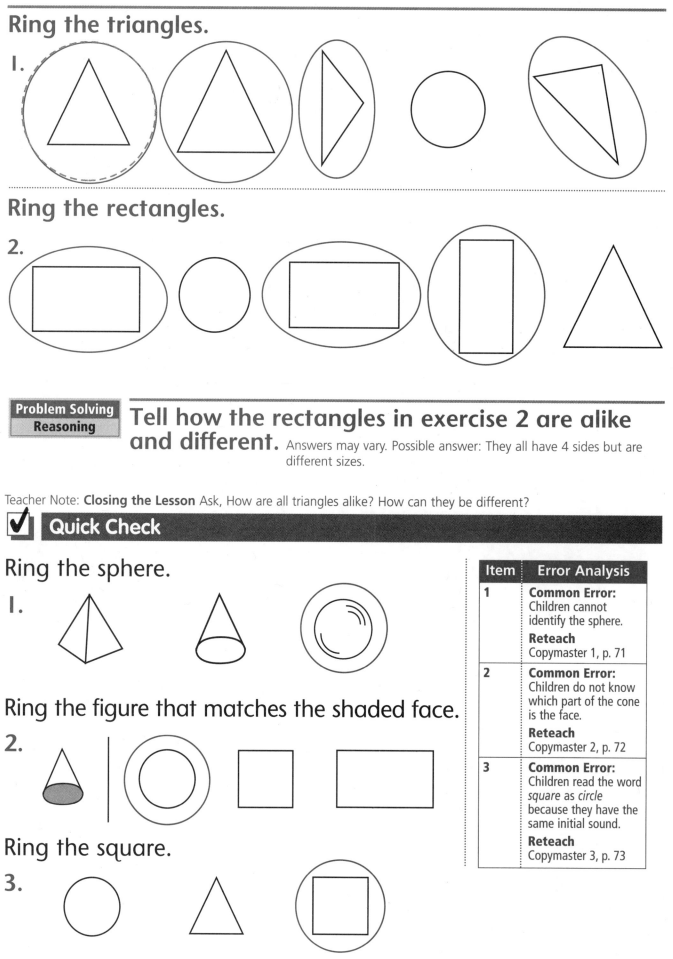

Ring the rectangles.

2.

Tell how the rectangles in exercise 2 are alike and different. Answers may vary. Possible answer: They all have 4 sides but are different sizes.

Teacher Note: **Closing the Lesson** Ask, How are all triangles alike? How can they be different?

✓ Quick Check

Ring the sphere.

1.

Ring the figure that matches the shaded face.

2.

Ring the square.

3.

Item	Error Analysis
1	**Common Error:** Children cannot identify the sphere. **Reteach** Copymaster 1, p. 71
2	**Common Error:** Children do not know which part of the cone is the face. **Reteach** Copymaster 2, p. 72
3	**Common Error:** Children read the word *square* as *circle* because they have the same initial sound. **Reteach** Copymaster 3, p. 73

Guided Practice: Exercises 1 and 2
Independent Practice: Exercises 3–9

Name

Position of Figures

Teacher Note: **Check Understanding** Ask, How would you describe the position of the square at the top of page 9?

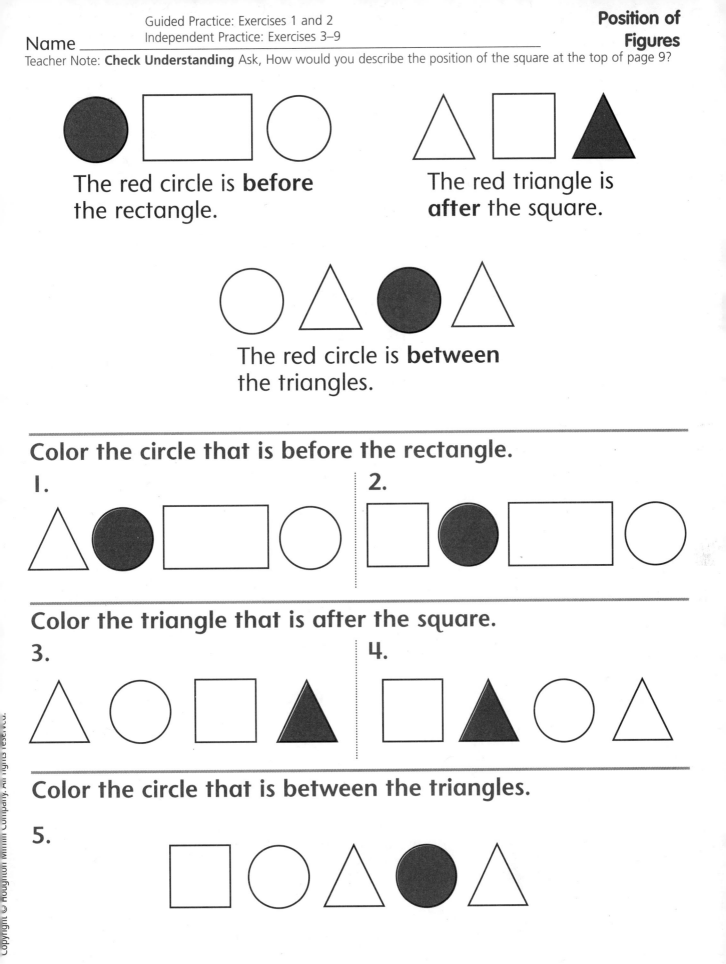

The red circle is **before** the rectangle.

The red triangle is **after** the square.

The red circle is **between** the triangles.

Color the circle that is before the rectangle.

1.

2.

Color the triangle that is after the square.

3.

4.

Color the circle that is between the triangles.

5.

Color the triangle that is after the circle.

6.

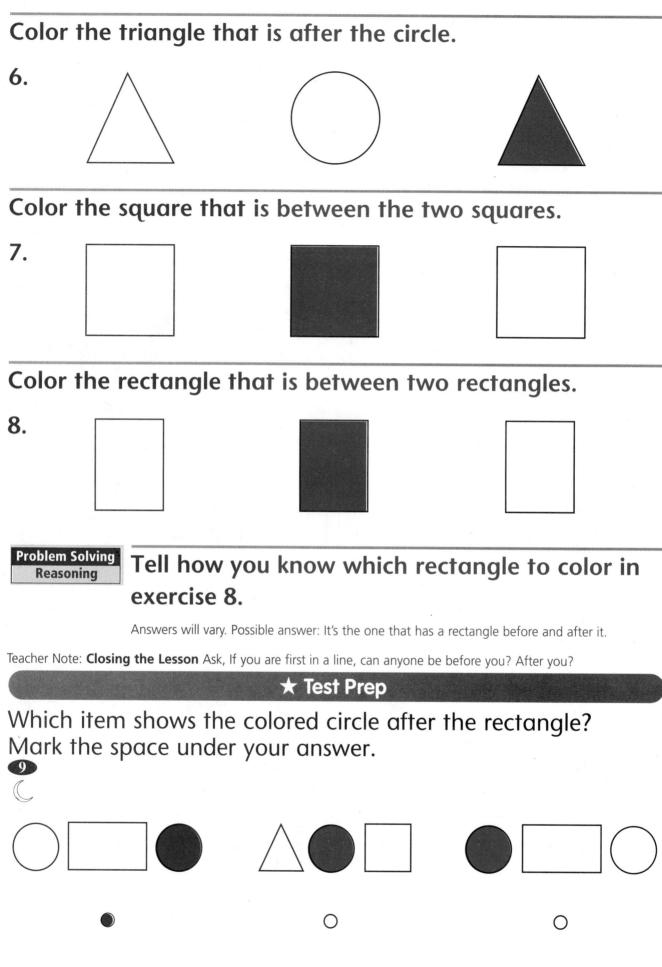

Color the square that is between the two squares.

7.

Color the rectangle that is between two rectangles.

8.

Problem Solving Reasoning

Tell how you know which rectangle to color in exercise 8.

Answers will vary. Possible answer: It's the one that has a rectangle before and after it.

Teacher Note: **Closing the Lesson** Ask, If you are first in a line, can anyone be before you? After you?

★ Test Prep

Which item shows the colored circle after the rectangle? Mark the space under your answer.

9

Teacher Note: **Check Understanding** Ask, How many corners does a circle have? How many sides?

Trace each side. Write how many sides and corners.

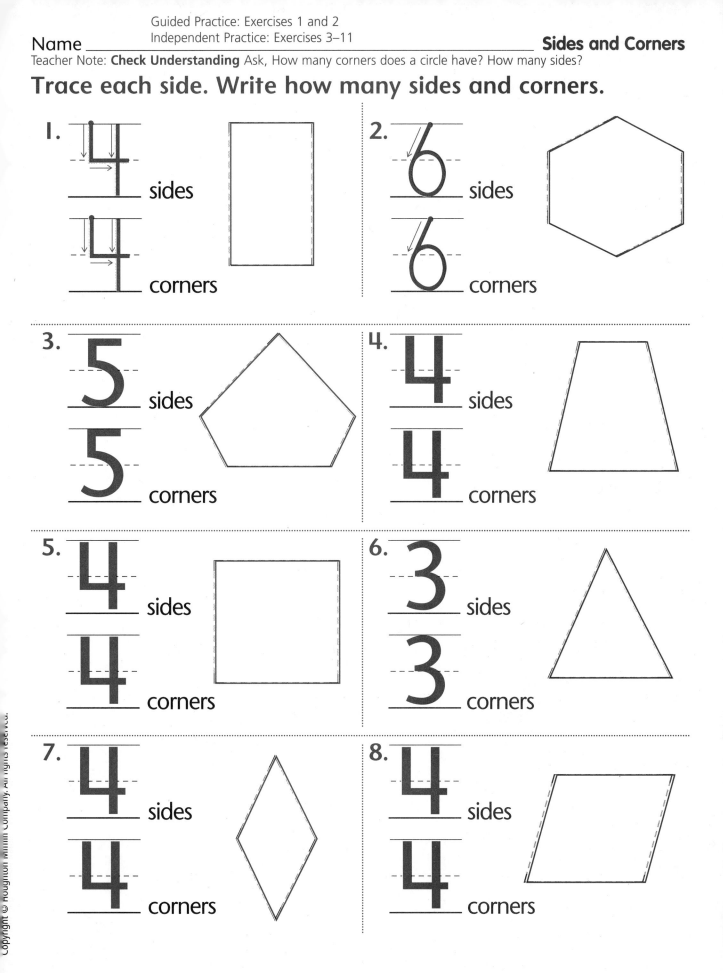

1. ___4___ sides
   ___4___ corners

2. ___6___ sides
   ___6___ corners

3. ___5___ sides
   ___5___ corners

4. ___4___ sides
   ___4___ corners

5. ___4___ sides
   ___4___ corners

6. ___3___ sides
   ___3___ corners

7. ___4___ sides
   ___4___ corners

8. ___4___ sides
   ___4___ corners

Look at the group of figures.
Think about sides and corners.
Draw a figure that belongs.
Draw a figure that does not belong.

Answers will vary but should reflect directions.

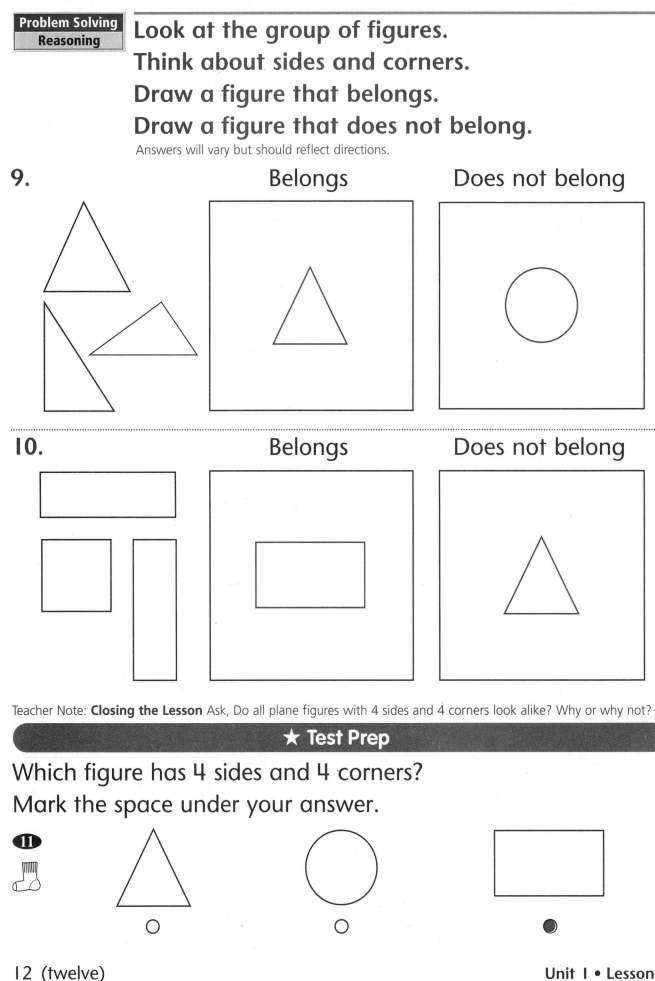

9.   Belongs   Does not belong

10.   Belongs   Does not belong

Teacher Note: **Closing the Lesson** Ask, Do all plane figures with 4 sides and 4 corners look alike? Why or why not?

★ **Test Prep**

Which figure has 4 sides and 4 corners?
Mark the space under your answer.

11

Name _____

Teacher Note: **Check Understanding** Hold up a square. Then hold up a piece of paper with the same size square drawn on it. Ask, How can I check if these squares are the same size and shape?

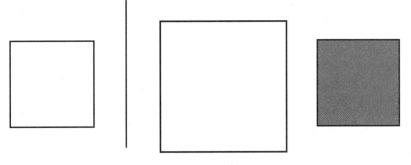

Color the figure that is the same size and same shape.

1.

2.

3.

Unit 1 • Lesson 6

(thirteen) 13

Color the figure that is the same size and shape.

4.

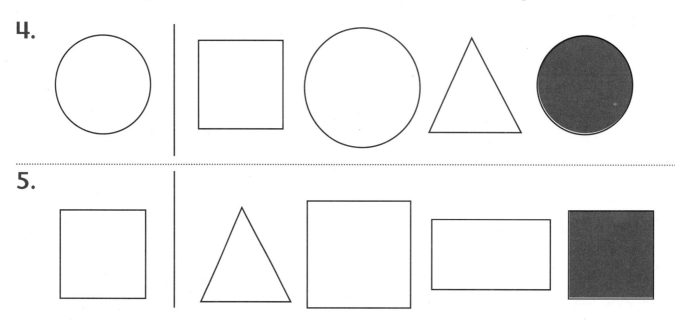

5.

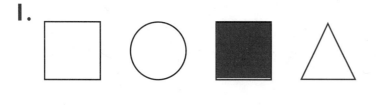

Teacher Note: **Closing the Lesson** Ask, Can a circle and a triangle be the same size and shape?

✓ Quick Check

Color the square that is after the circle.

1.

Write the number of corners.

2.

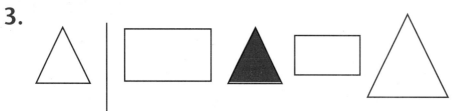

3 corners

Color the figure that is the same size and shape.

3.

Item	Error Analysis
1	**Common Error:** Children confuse after with before. **Reteach** Copymaster 4, p. 74
2	**Common Error:** Children do do not count sides and corners accurately. **Reteach** Copymaster 5, p. 75
3	**Common Error:** Children only look at the shape and ignore the size. **Reteach** Copymaster 6, p. 76

Unit 1 • Lesson 6

Problem

What figure most likely comes next?

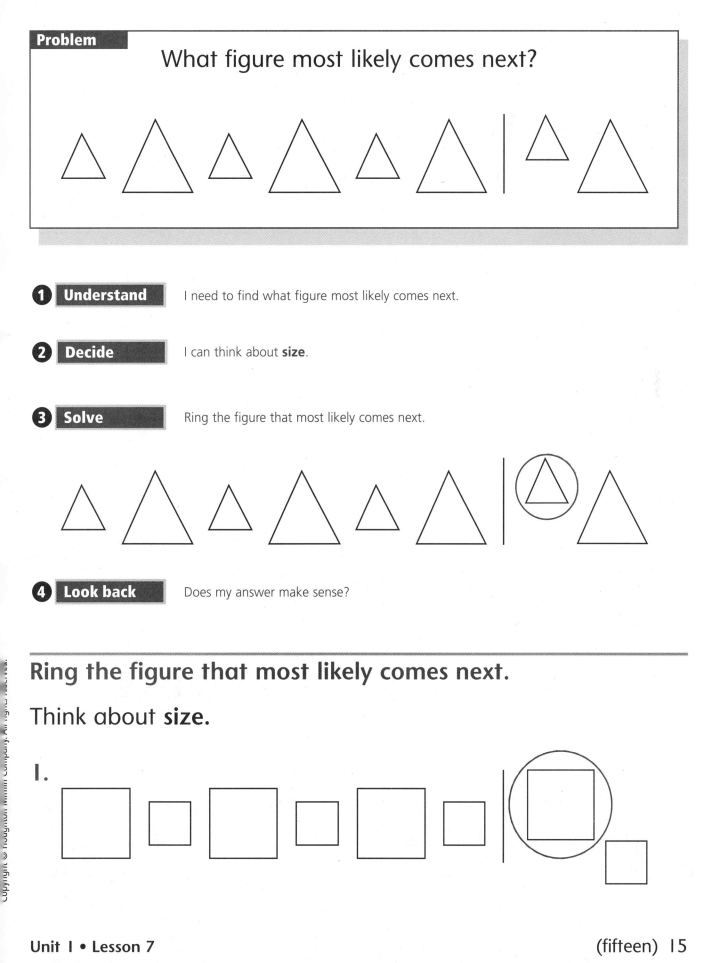

1 Understand   I need to find what figure most likely comes next.

2 Decide   I can think about **size**.

3 Solve   Ring the figure that most likely comes next.

4 Look back   Does my answer make sense?

Ring the figure that most likely comes next.

Think about **size.**

I.

Ring the figure that most likely comes next.

Think about **color**.

2.

Think about **shape**.

3.

Think about **size** and **color**.

4.

Think about **shape** and **size**.

5.

Think about **color** and **shape**.

6.

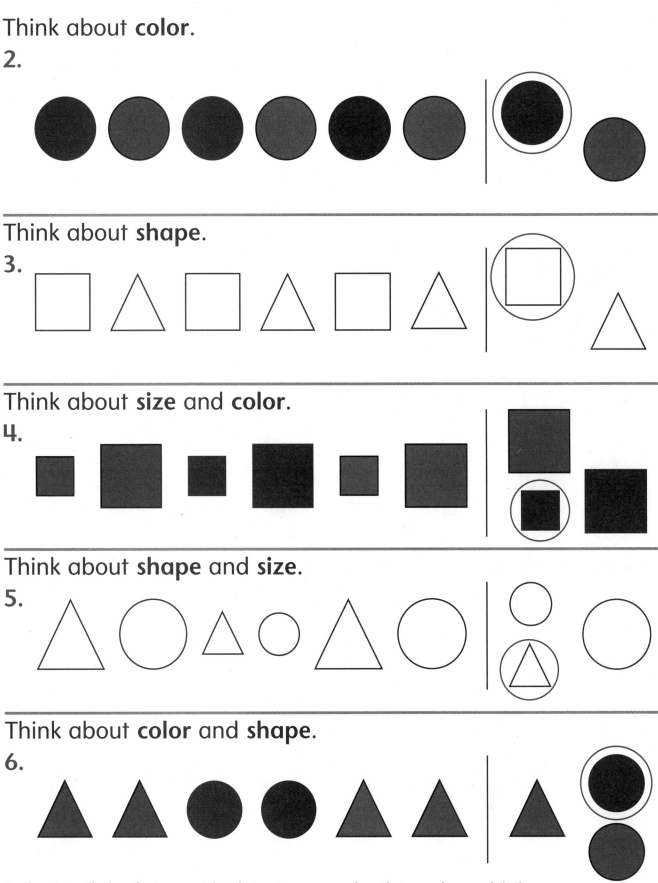

Teacher Note: **Closing the Lesson** Ask, What pattern can you draw that uses shape and size?

16 (sixteen)

Unit 1 • Lesson 7

Guided Practice: Exercises 1 and 5
Independent Practice: 2–4 and 6–12

Symmetry

Teacher Note: **Check Understanding** Hold up a drawing of a circle with a line down the middle. Ask, If I fold this circle on the line, will both sides of the circle match?

Both parts of
this heart match.

Ring the objects with matching parts.

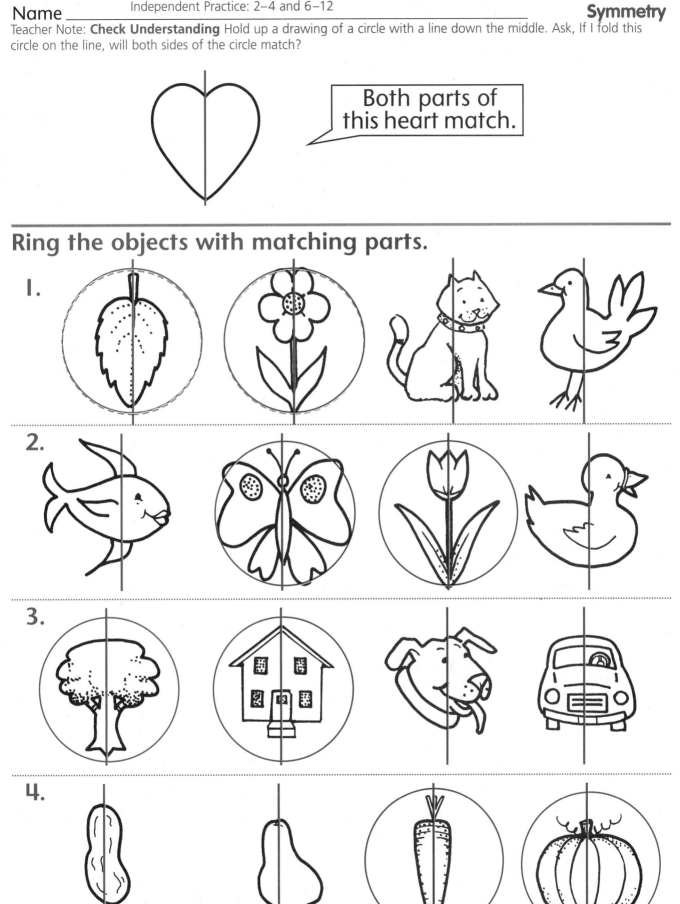

Draw a line to make two parts that match.

Answers for ex. 6 and 9 may vary.

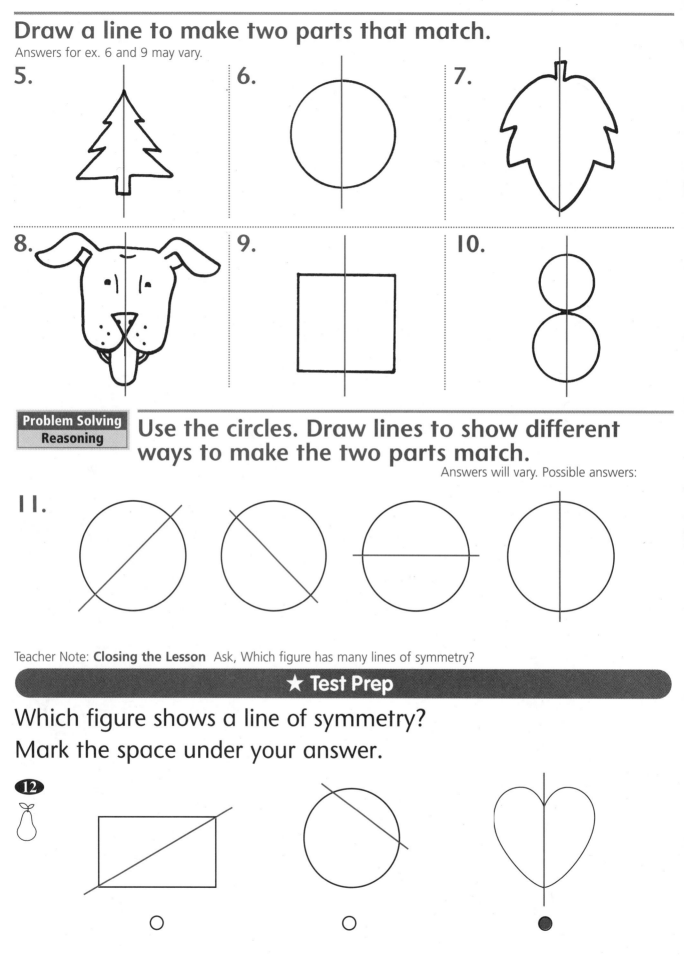

5.

6.

7.

8.

9.

10.

Problem Solving
Reasoning

Use the circles. Draw lines to show different ways to make the two parts match.

Answers will vary. Possible answers:

11.

Teacher Note: **Closing the Lesson** Ask, Which figure has many lines of symmetry?

★ Test Prep

Which figure shows a line of symmetry?

Mark the space under your answer.

12

○   ○   ●

18 (eighteen)

Unit 1 • Lesson 8

**Problem Solving Application:
Use a Picture**

Draw to complete the picture.

1. Draw an X on the  that is far from the sign.

2. Draw a next to the .

3. Draw a near the .

4. Draw a to the left of the .

Help locate each figure on the grid.

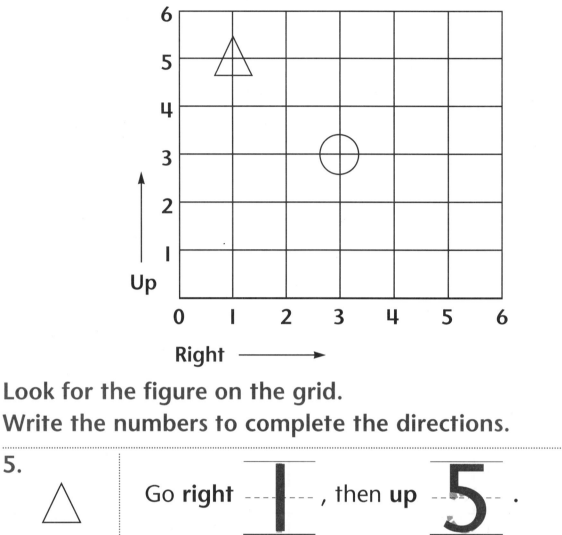

Look for the figure on the grid.

Write the numbers to complete the directions.

5.

△

Go **right** ——**1**——, then **up** ——**5**——.

6.

◯

Go **right** —**3**—, then **up** —**3**—.

Teacher Note: **Closing the Lesson** Ask, Which direction do you always begin with when finding points on a grid?

★ Test Prep

Which picture shows the coat below the hat?

Mark the space under your answer.

7

◯   ●   ◯

22 (twenty-two)   Unit 1 • Lesson 10

Name _____

Ring each object that has the same shape. (1A)

1.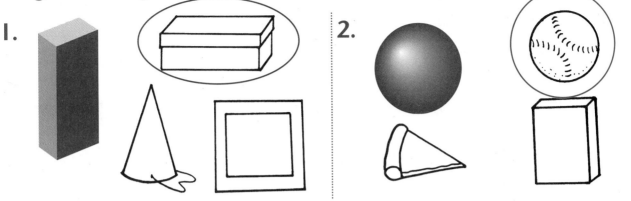

2.

Ring the figure that matches the shaded face of the solid.
(1A)

3.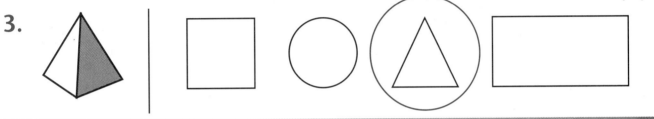

Ring the squares. (1A)

4.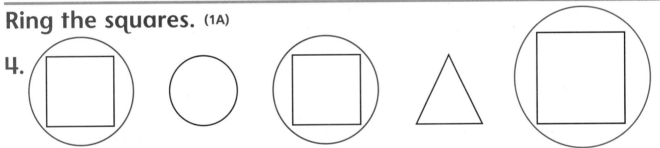

Ring the triangle that is after the square. (1B)

5. 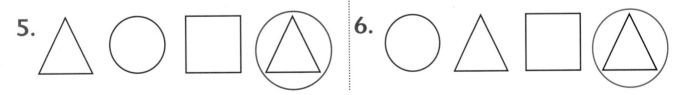 6.

Write how many sides and corners. (1A)

7. 3 ___ sides
   3 ___ corners

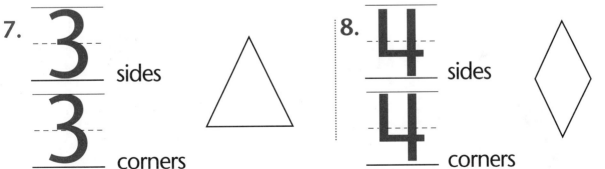

8. 4 ___ sides
   4 ___ corners

Ring the figure that is the same size and shape. (1B)

9.

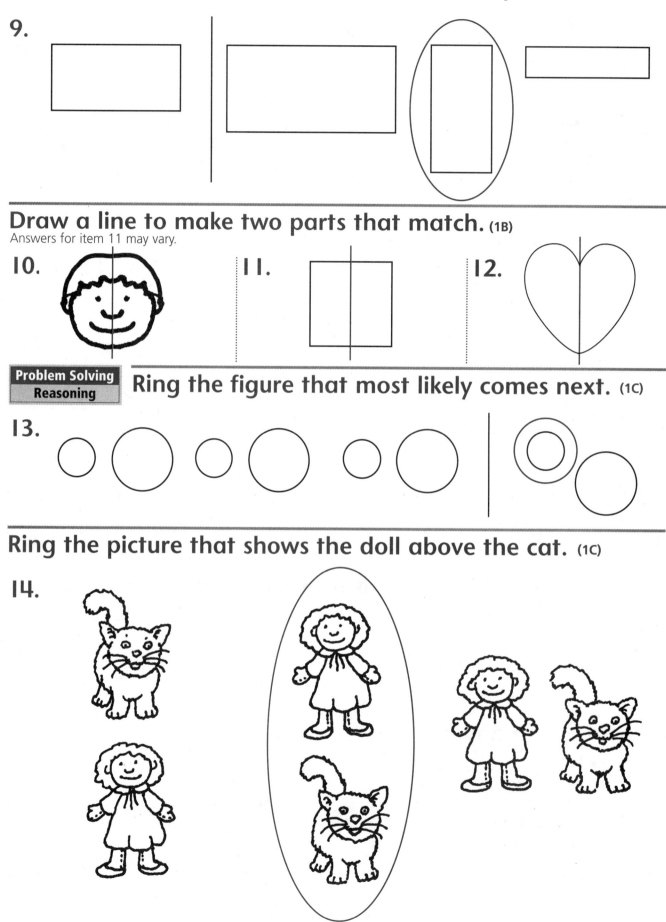

Draw a line to make two parts that match. (1B)

Answers for item 11 may vary.

10.   **11.**   **12.**

Problem Solving Reasoning

Ring the figure that most likely comes next. (1C)

13.

Ring the picture that shows the doll above the cat. (1C)

14.

24 (twenty-four)

Unit 1 • Review

Name _____

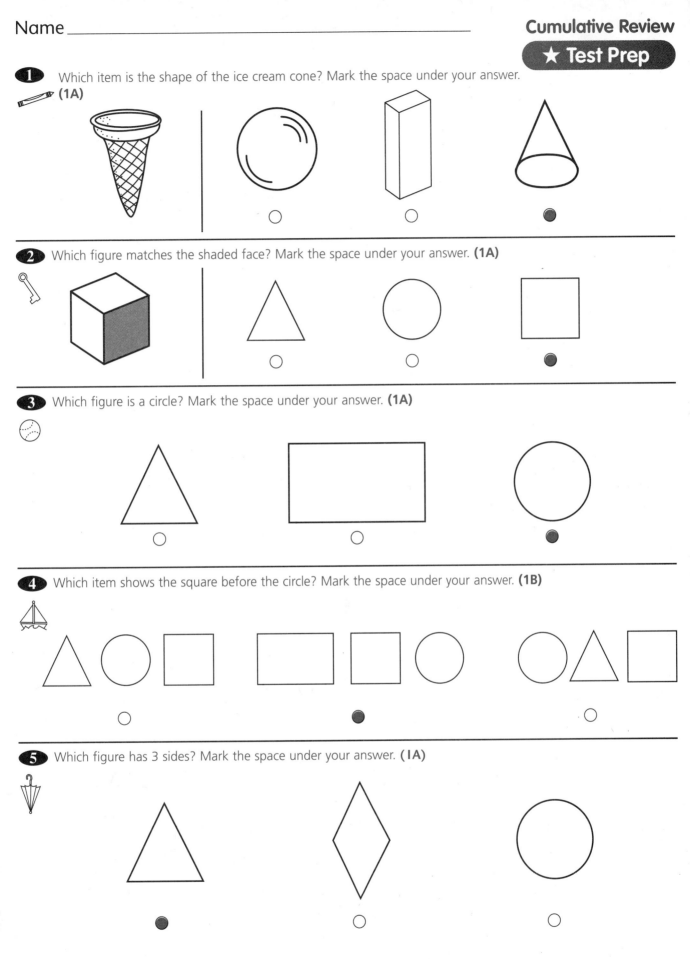

★ **Test Prep**

1 Which item is the shape of the ice cream cone? Mark the space under your answer.
(1A)

2 Which figure matches the shaded face? Mark the space under your answer. **(1A)**

3 Which figure is a circle? Mark the space under your answer. **(1A)**

4 Which item shows the square before the circle? Mark the space under your answer. **(1B)**

5 Which figure has 3 sides? Mark the space under your answer. **(1A)**

Unit I • Cumulative Review

6 Which figure is the same size and shape? Mark the space under your answer. **(1B)**

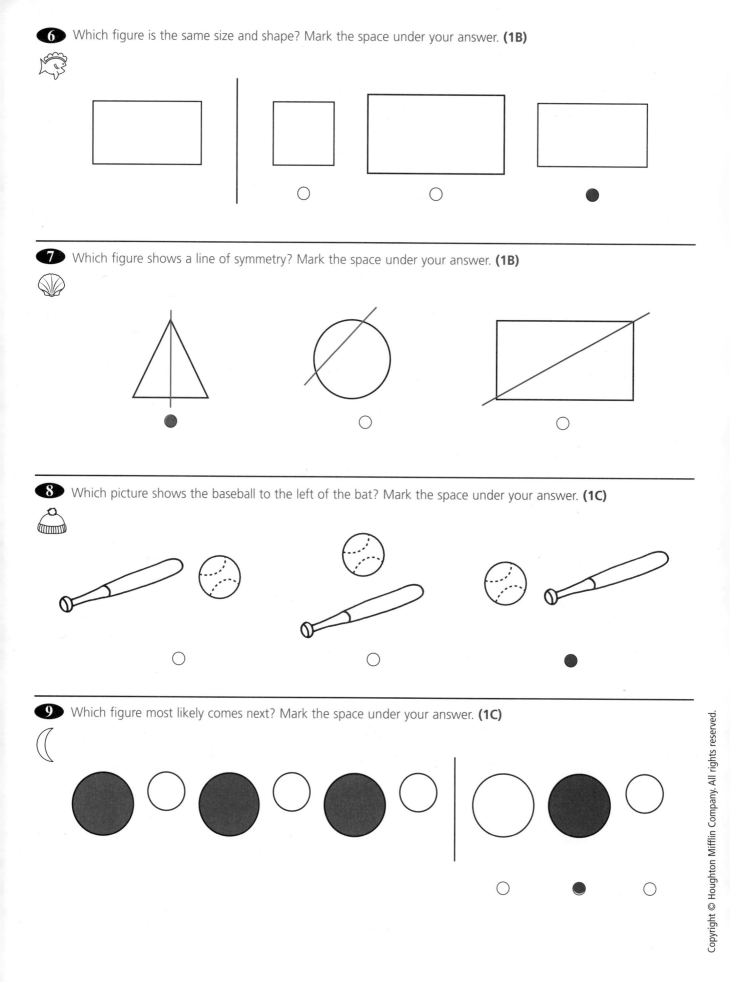

7 Which figure shows a line of symmetry? Mark the space under your answer. **(1B)**

8 Which picture shows the baseball to the left of the bat? Mark the space under your answer. **(1C)**

9 Which figure most likely comes next? Mark the space under your answer. **(1C)**

Unit I • Cumulative Review

UNIT 2 • TABLE OF CONTENTS

Numbers through 10 and Data

Dear Family,

During the next few weeks our math class will be counting groups and writing the numbers 0 through 10.

You can expect to see homework that provides practice in recognizing and comparing numbers.

As we learn to recognize and compare numbers using symbols, you may wish to keep the following as a guide.

Comparing Numbers using Symbols

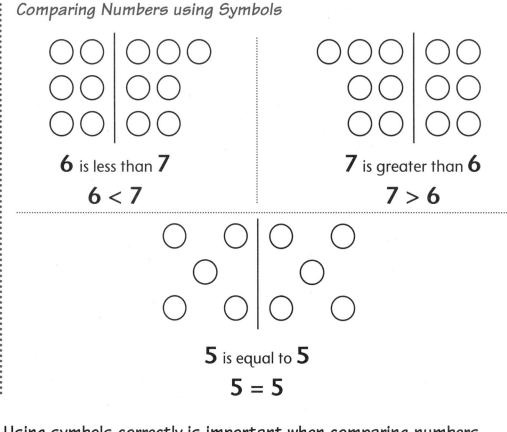

6 is less than **7**

6 < 7

7 is greater than **6**

7 > 6

5 is equal to **5**

5 = 5

Using symbols correctly is important when comparing numbers.

Sincerely,

Teacher Note: **Check Understanding** Ask, How can you tell if there are more objects in one group than another?

Match the objects.
Ring the group that has more.

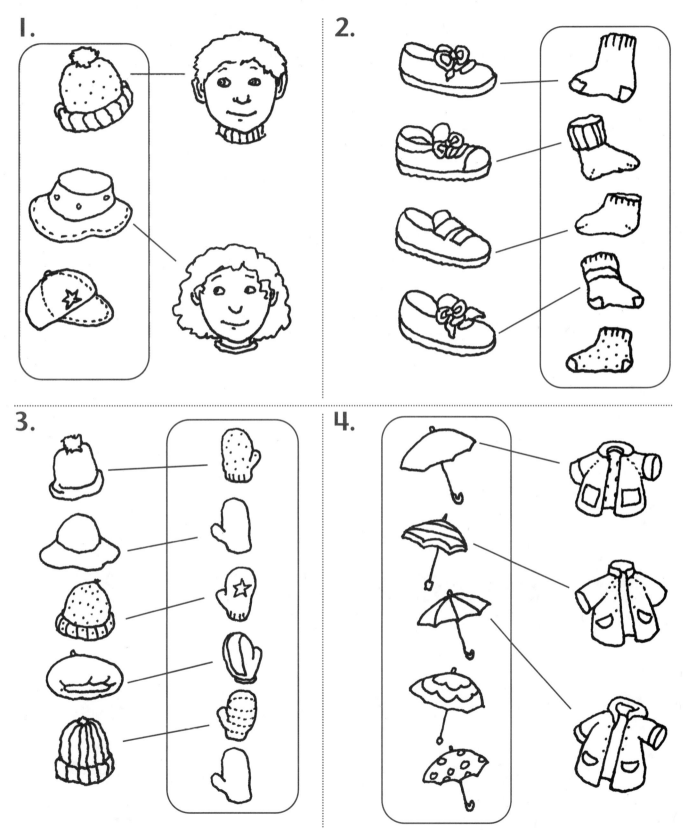

1.

2.

3.

4.

Match the objects.
Ring the group that has fewer.

5. 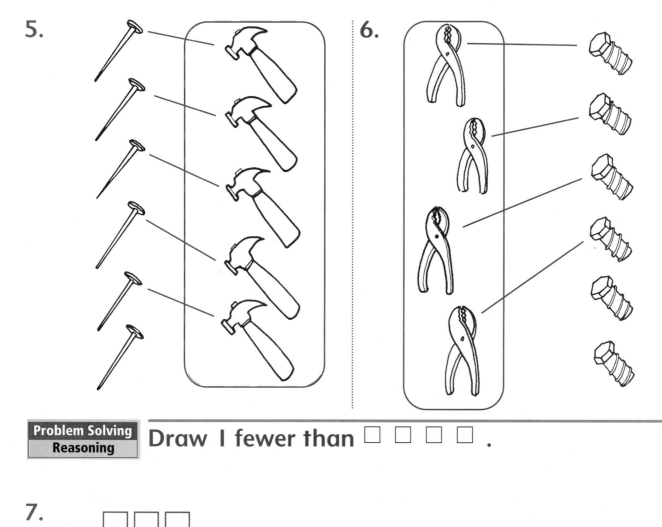 6.

Draw 1 fewer than ☐ ☐ ☐ ☐ .

7. ☐ ☐ ☐

Teacher Note: **Closing the Lesson** Ask, How can we tell if we have more desks than children? Have volunteers act out their answers.

★ Test Prep

Which group shows more stars?
Mark the space under your answer.

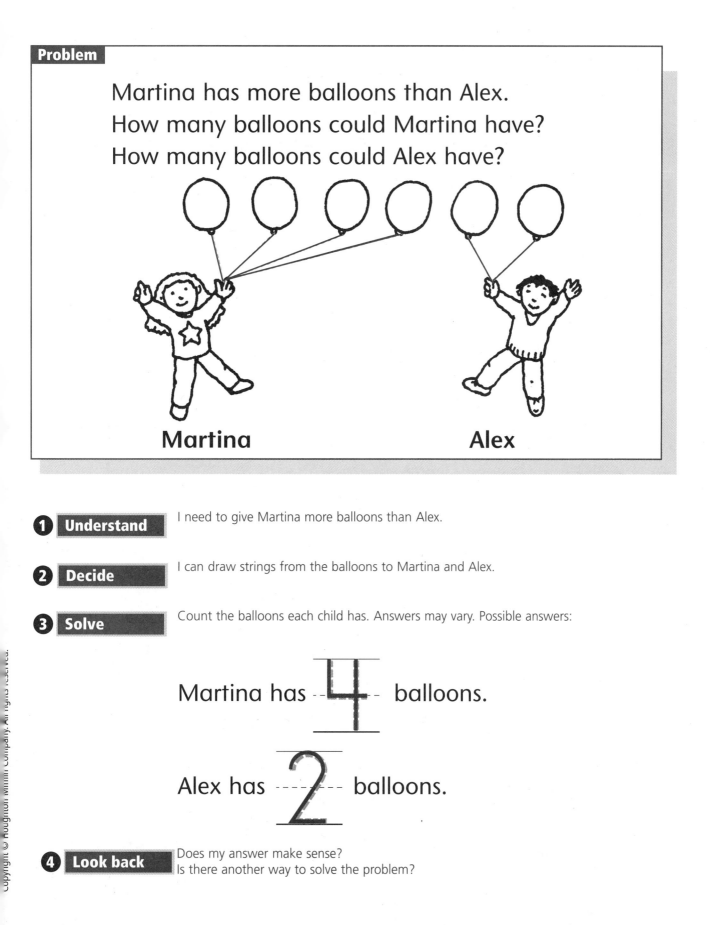

Problem

Martina has more balloons than Alex.
How many balloons could Martina have?
How many balloons could Alex have?

Martina   **Alex**

1 Understand   I need to give Martina more balloons than Alex.

2 Decide   I can draw strings from the balloons to Martina and Alex.

3 Solve   Count the balloons each child has. Answers may vary. Possible answers:

Martina has ⁻⁻4⁻⁻ balloons.

Alex has ⁻⁻⁻2⁻⁻ balloons.

4 Look back   Does my answer make sense?
Is there another way to solve the problem?

Draw to solve. Answers may vary. Possible answer shown.

1. Rita has fewer balloons than Max.

   How many balloons could Rita have? ----- 1

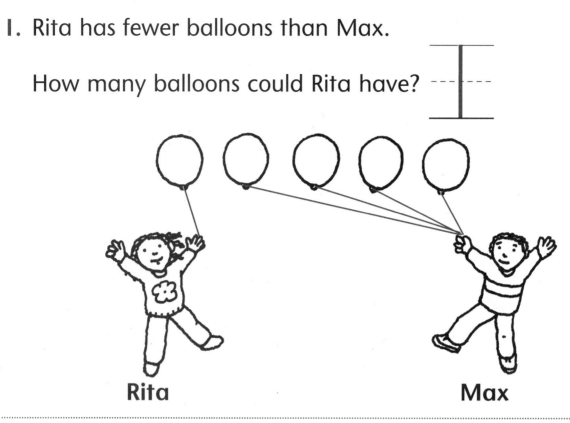

Rita   **Max**

Is there another answer?

Try it again. Answers may vary. Possible answer shown.

2. Rita has fewer balloons than Max.

   How many balloons could Rita have? ----- 2

Rita   **Max**

Closing the Lesson Ask, Do all problems have just one right answer? How can you tell?

Unit 2 • Lesson 2

Guided Practice: Rows 1–5, Exercise 7
Independent Practice: Exercises 6, 8, 9, and 10

**Counting and Writing
0 through 3**

Check Understanding Ask, How many different ways can you show two?

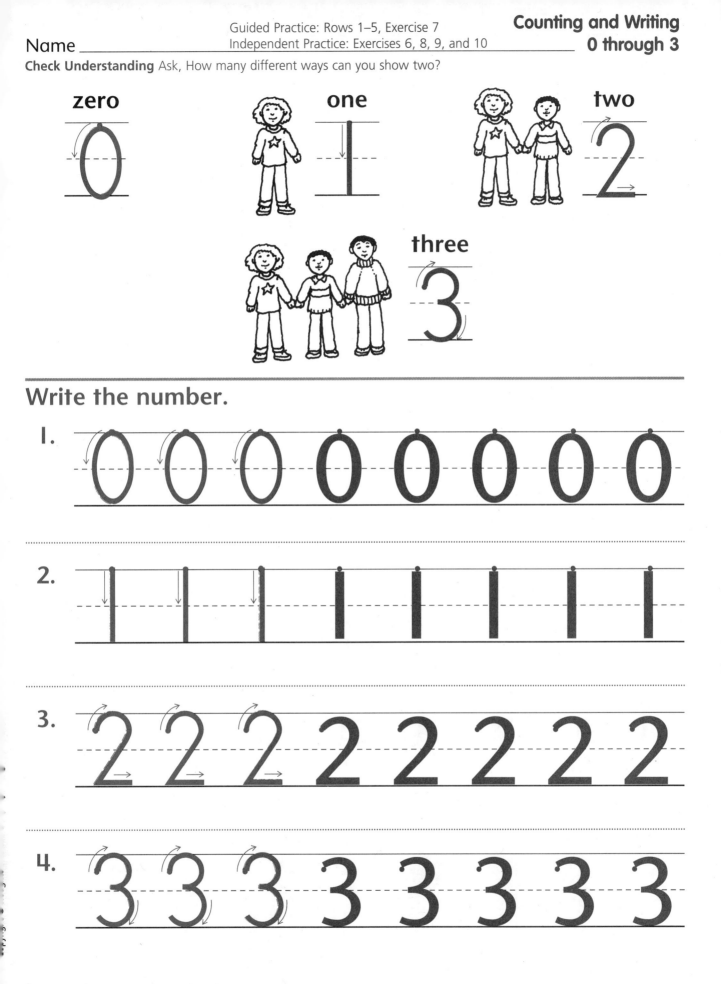

zero

one

two

three

Write the number.

1.

2.

3.

4.

Write how many.

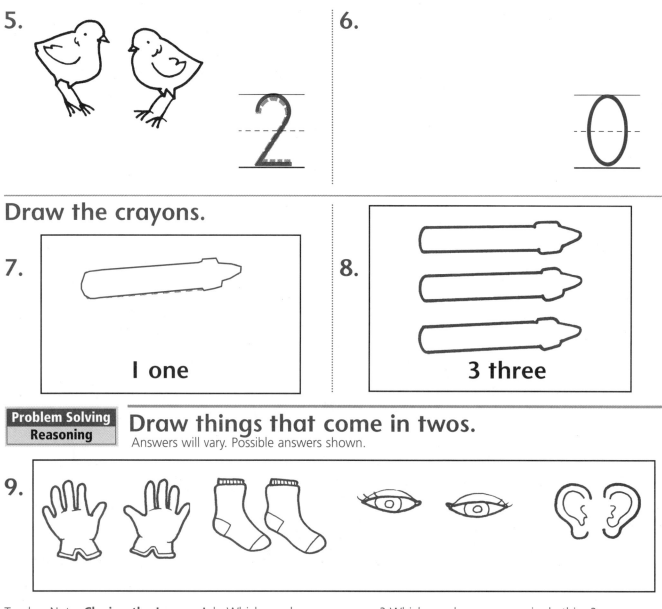

5.

6.

Draw the crayons.

7.

I one

8.

3 three

Problem Solving
Reasoning

Draw things that come in twos.
Answers will vary. Possible answers shown.

9.

Teacher Note: **Closing the Lesson** Ask, Which number means none? Which number means a single thing? Which number means a pair?

★ Test Prep

Which group has this number of flags?

Mark the space under your answer.

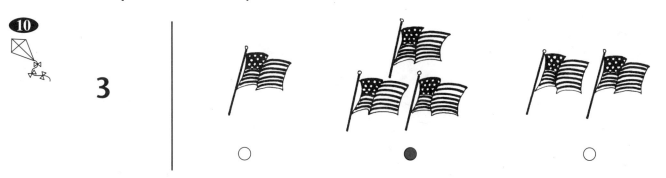

10.

3

Teacher Note: **Check Understanding** Ask, How can you use counters to show how to count to six?

four   **4**

five   **5**

six   **6**

Write the number.

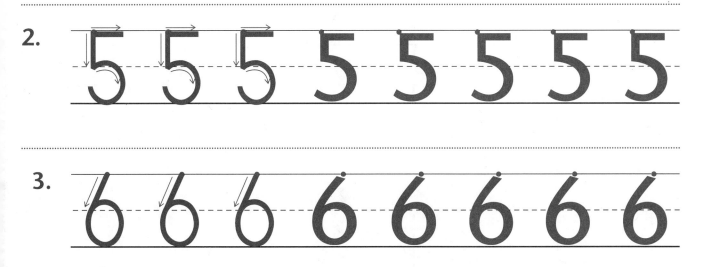

1. 4 4 4 4 4 4 4 4

2. 5 5 5 5 5 5 5 5

3. 6 6 6 6 6 6 6 6

Write how many.

4.

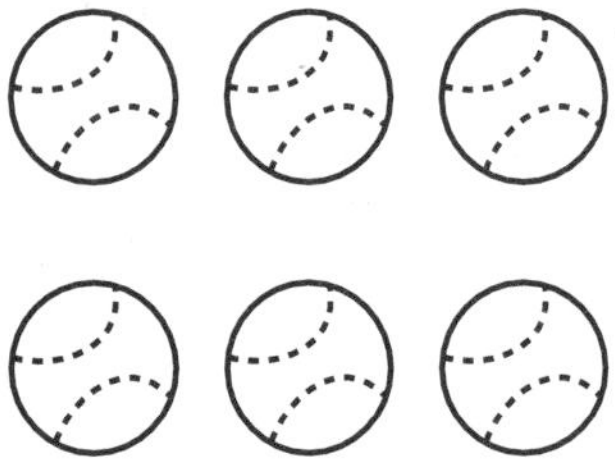

6

5.

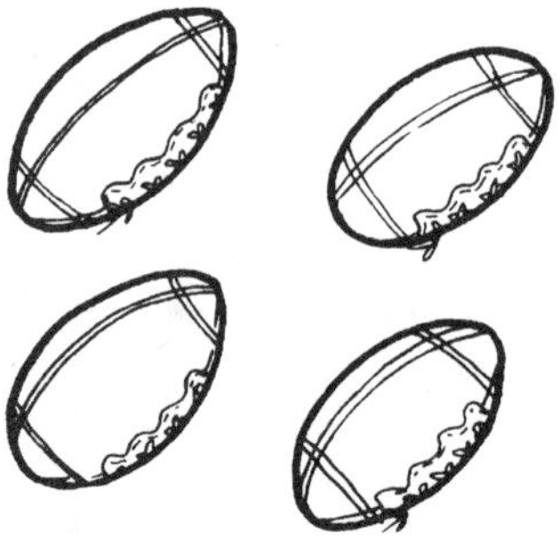

4

Write the number. Draw that number of balls. Ring the group that has fewer.

6.

5 five

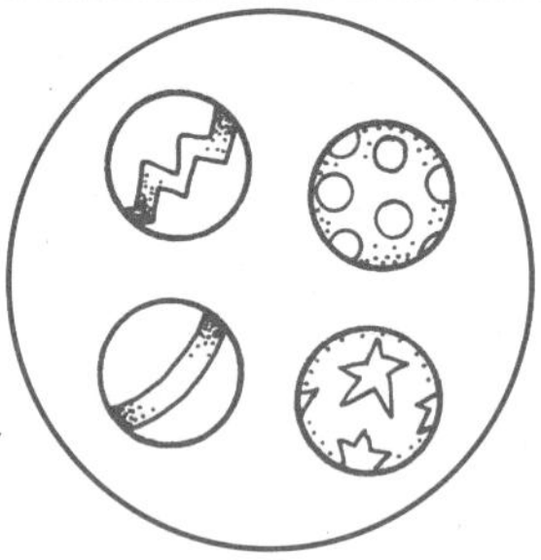

4 four

Teacher Note: **Closing the Lesson** Ask, If you wanted to give an apple to each of your six friends, what number shows how many apples you would need?

✔ Quick Check

Ring 1 more than ☐ ☐ ☐.

1.  ☐ ☐   ☐   (☐ ☐ ☐ ☐)

Write how many.

2.

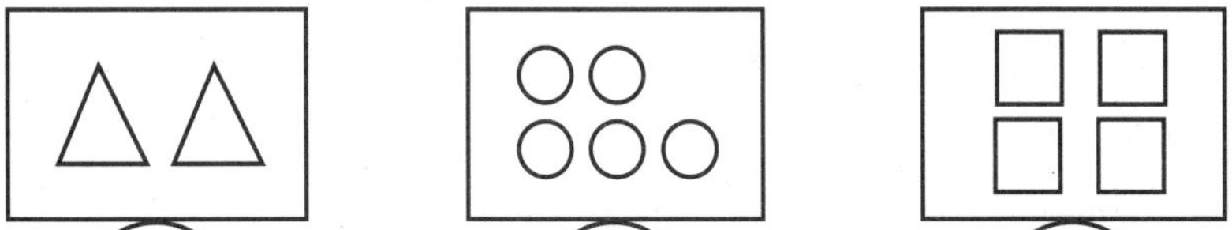

2

5

4

3.

3

0

4

Item	Error Analysis
1	**Common Error:** Children have difficulty with the concepts of more and fewer. **Reteach** Copymaster 9, p. 79
2, 3	**Common Error:** Children have difficulty writing the numbers 0–6. **Skills Tutorial** Strand P1, Skills 1, 2

Teacher Note: **Check Understanding** Have children draw pictures to show 8 in as many different ways as they can. Share and compare pictures.

seven

7

eight

8

Write the number.

1.

7 7 7 7 7 7 7 7 7 7

2.

8 8 8 8 8 8 8 8 8 8

Write how many.

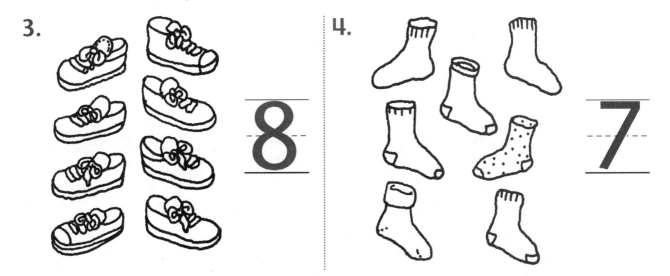

3.

8

4.

7

Unit 2 • Lesson 5

(thirty-seven) 37

Write how many.

5.

6.

_ _ _ _ _
7

_ _ _ _ _
8

Write the number. Draw that number of hats.
Ring the group that has more.

7.

_ _ _ _ _
7   seven

_ _ _ _ _
8   eight

Teacher Note: **Closing the Lesson** Say, Hold up 7 fingers. Hold up 8 fingers.

★ Test Prep

Which group has this number of hats?
Mark the space under your answer.

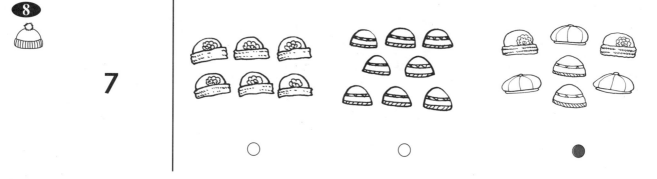

8

7

○   ○   ●

38 (thirty-eight)

Unit 2 • Lesson 5

Name _____

Teacher Note: **Check Understanding** Ask, If there are ten children in a room and there are more boys than girls, how many boys could there be?

nine

9

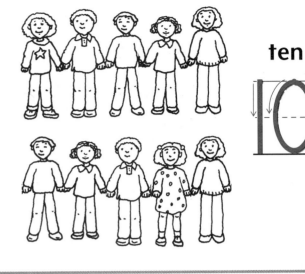

ten

10

Write the number.

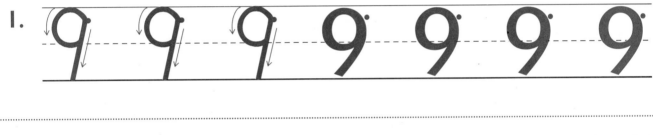

1. 9 9 9 9 9 9 9

2. 10 10 10 10 10 10

Write how many.

3. 9

4. 10

Unit 2 • Lesson 6

Write how many.

5.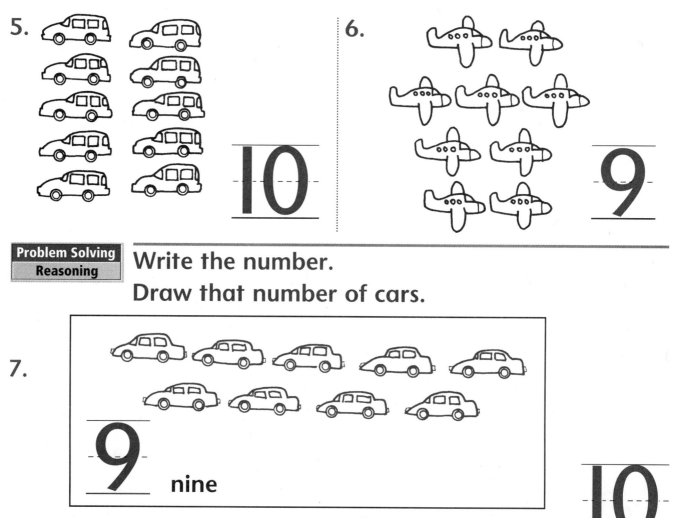

10

6.

9

Write the number.
Draw that number of cars.

7.

9 nine

What number is one more than 9? ___10___

Teacher Note: **Closing the Lesson** Ask, If you want to hold up 9 fingers, do you have to hold up all of the fingers on at least one hand?

★ Test Prep

Which group has this number of boats?
Mark the space under your answer.

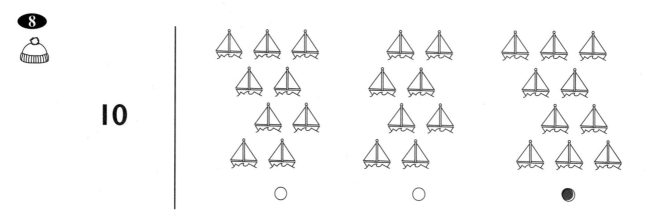

8

10

○   ○   ●

Guided Practice: Exercise 1
Independent Practice: Exercises 2–12

Teacher Note: **Check Understanding** Ask, How can you use the number 10 in a sentence about school?

Draw balls to match the number.

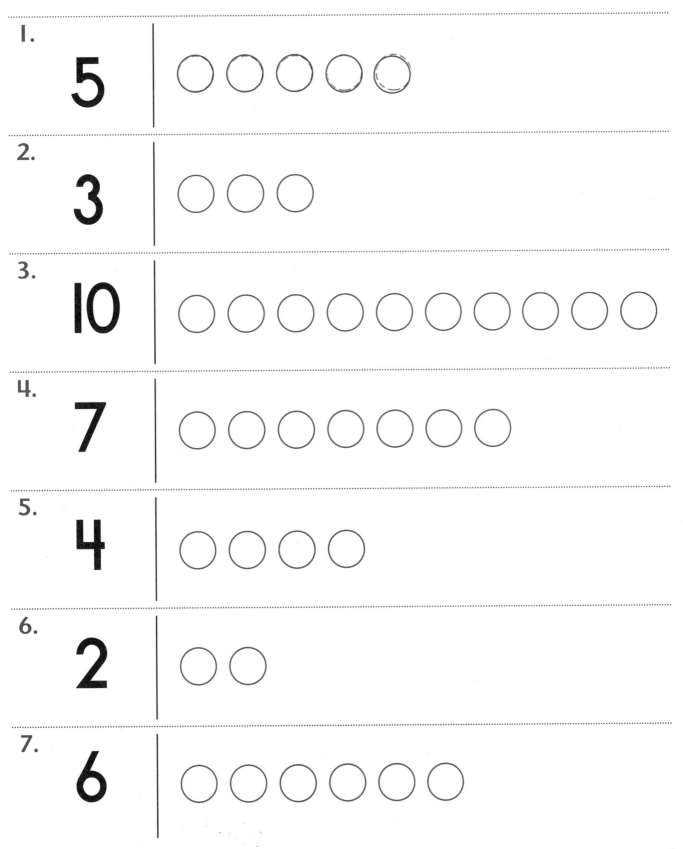

1. 5

2. 3

3. 10

4. 7

5. 4

6. 2

7. 6

Unit 2 • Lesson 7

Draw balls to match the number.

8.
9 ◯ ◯ ◯ ◯ ◯ ◯ ◯ ◯ ◯

9.
1 ◯

10.
8 ◯ ◯ ◯ ◯ ◯ ◯ ◯ ◯

Look at the picture.

11. How many 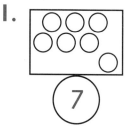? 2

12. How many ? 3

Teacher Note: **Closing the Lesson** Ask, How can you check if you drew the correct number of balls next to the number 9?

☑ **Quick Check**

Write how many.

1.

| ☆ ☆ ☆ |
| ☆ ☆ ☆ ☆ |

7   6   7

Item	Error Analysis
1	**Common Error:** Children have difficulty writing the numbers 6–10. **Skills Tutorial** Strand P1, Skill 3 **Reteach** Copymasters 10–11, pp. 80–81

Unit 2 • Lesson 7

Name

Teacher Note: **Check Understanding** Ask, If I have 4 cents in my pocket, how many pennies do I have?

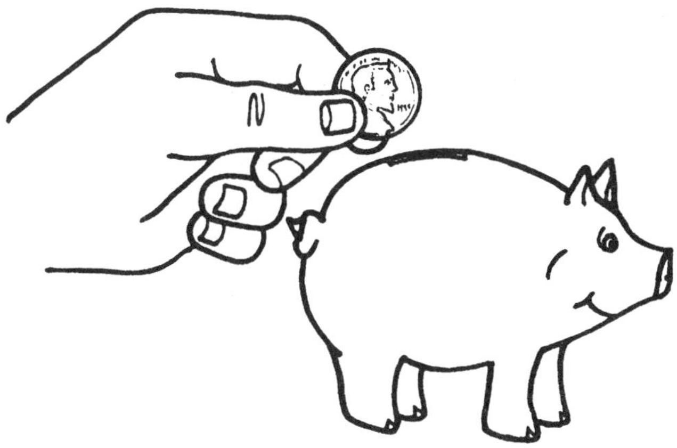

I penny　　**I penny**

I cent　　**I cent**
I ¢　　**I ¢**

Ring the pennies you need.

1. **8 ¢**

2. **10 ¢**

3. 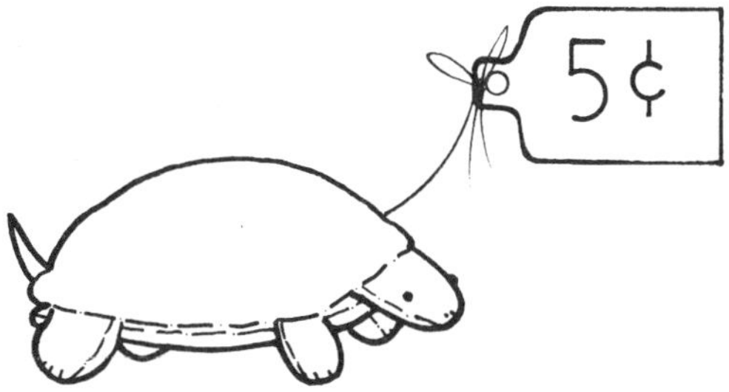 **5 ¢**

Unit 2 • Lesson 8

Write the amount.

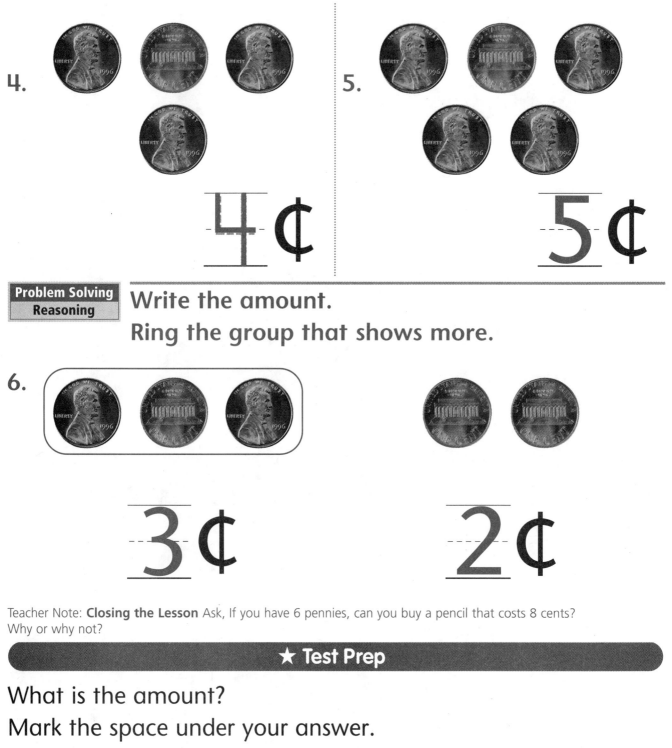

4. 4¢

5. 5¢

Write the amount.
Ring the group that shows more.

6. 3¢   2¢

Teacher Note: **Closing the Lesson** Ask, If you have 6 pennies, can you buy a pencil that costs 8 cents? Why or why not?

★ Test Prep

What is the amount?
Mark the space under your answer.

7.

3¢ ○   5¢ ○   4¢ ●

Guided Practice: Exercise 1; first item for exercises 7–9; exercise 10
Independent Practice: Exercises 2–6; second item for exercises 7–9; exercises 11–15

Teacher Note: **Check Understanding** Ask, How can you use the words "just after" in a sentence with the number 8?

```
← |   |   |   |   |   |   |   |   |   |   | →
  0   1   2   3   4   5   6   7   8   9  10
```

The number **4** is **just after 3**.

The number **4** is **just before 5**.

The number **4** is **between 3** and **5**.

Write the number.

1. Which number is between **4** and **6**? ☐ **5**

2. Which number is between **0** and **2**? ☐ **1**

3. Which number comes just after **8**? ☐ **9**

4. Which number comes just after **6**? ☐ **7**

5. Which number comes just before **1**? ☐ **0**

6. Which number comes just before **10**? ☐ **9**

Write the missing numbers.

7. Between

0, | 1 |, 2

4, | 5 |, 6

8. Just before

| 1 |, 2, 3

| 7 |, 8, 9

9. Just before and just after

| 2 |, 3, | 4 |

| 8 |, 9, | 10 |

Write the missing numbers.

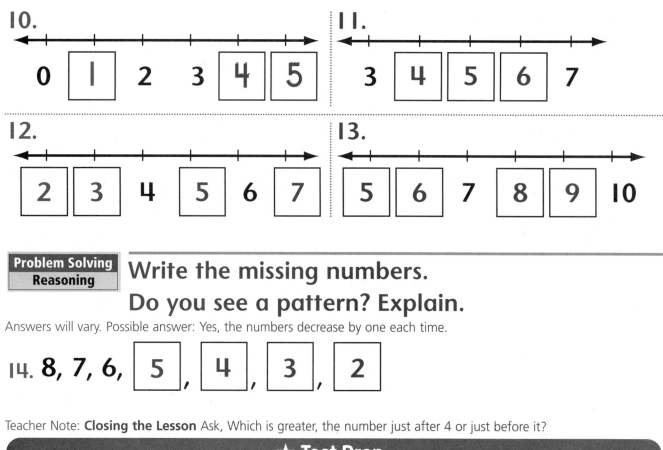

10.

0 | 1 | 2 3 | 4 | | 5 |

11.

3 | 4 | | 5 | | 6 | 7

12.

| 2 | | 3 | 4 | 5 | 6 | 7 |

13.

| 5 | | 6 | 7 | 8 | | 9 | 10

Problem Solving Reasoning

Write the missing numbers.
Do you see a pattern? Explain.

Answers will vary. Possible answer: Yes, the numbers decrease by one each time.

14. 8, 7, 6, | 5 |, | 4 |, | 3 |, | 2 |

Teacher Note: **Closing the Lesson** Ask, Which is greater, the number just after 4 or just before it?

★ Test Prep

Which number comes just after the number shown?
Mark the space under your answer.

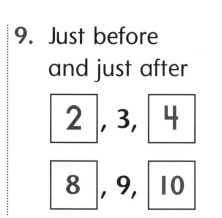

15

3 | 2   4   5

○   ●   ○

Name _____

Teacher Note: **Check Understanding** Ask, How can you use a number line to tell which of 2 numbers is greater?

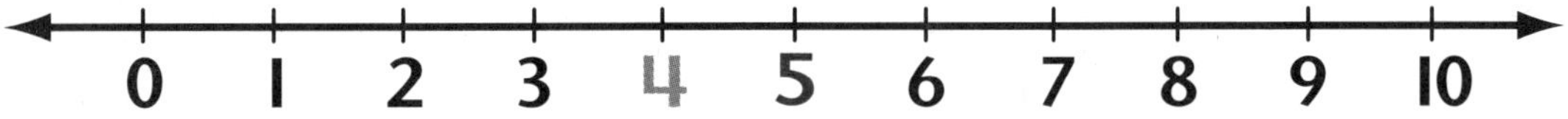

```
←——+——+——+——+——+——+——+——+——+——+——→
    0   1   2   3   4   5   6   7   8   9   10
```

5 is **greater than** 4.

Ring the greater number.

1. 2 ⑤

2. ③ 1

3. ⑨ 7

4. 2 ③

5. 1 ②

6. 8 ⑩

7. ⑦ 4

8. ② 0

9. ④ 0

10. ⑥ 1

11. 6 ⑦

12. ④ 2

13. ⑥ 4

14. 3 ⑥

15. ⑦ 5

16. 8 ⑨

17. ⑩ 7

18. 3 ⑤

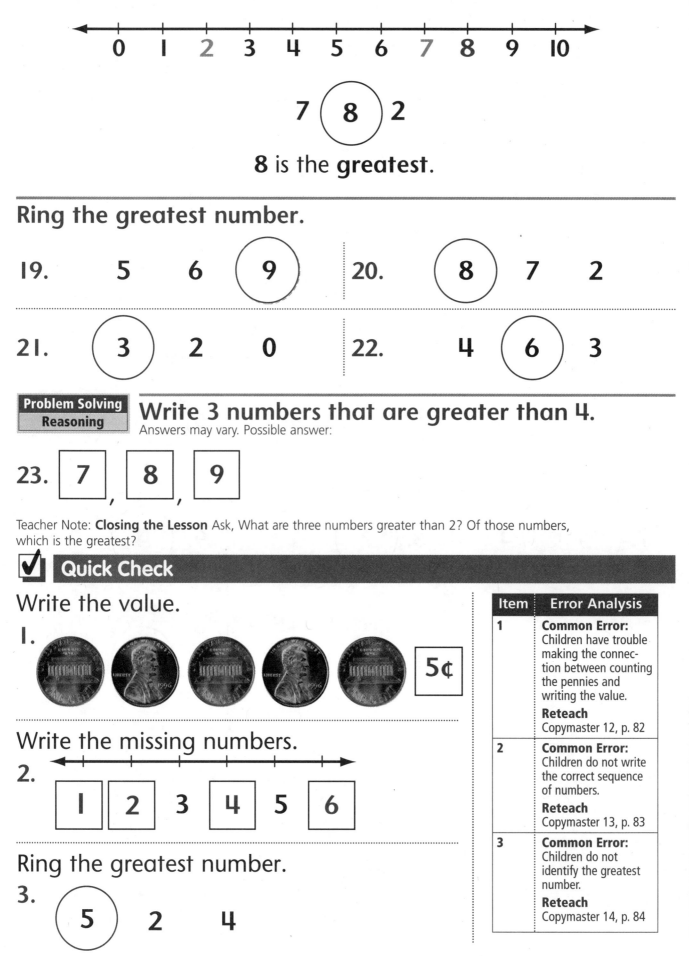

0 1 2 3 4 5 6 7 8 9 10

7 (8) 2

8 is the **greatest**.

Ring the greatest number.

19.   5   6   (9)   20.   (8)   7   2

21.   (3)   2   0   22.   4   (6)   3

Problem Solving Reasoning   **Write 3 numbers that are greater than 4.**
Answers may vary. Possible answer:

23. [7] , [8] , [9]

Teacher Note: **Closing the Lesson** Ask, What are three numbers greater than 2? Of those numbers, which is the greatest?

☑ **Quick Check**

Write the value.

1.   5¢

Write the missing numbers.

2.   [1] [2] 3 [4] 5 [6]

Ring the greatest number.

3.   (5)   2   4

Item	Error Analysis
1	**Common Error:** Children have trouble making the connection between counting the pennies and writing the value. **Reteach** Copymaster 12, p. 82
2	**Common Error:** Children do not write the correct sequence of numbers. **Reteach** Copymaster 13, p. 83
3	**Common Error:** Children do not identify the greatest number. **Reteach** Copymaster 14, p. 84

Name _____

Teacher Note: **Check Understanding** Ask, How can you use a number line to tell which of two numbers is lesser?

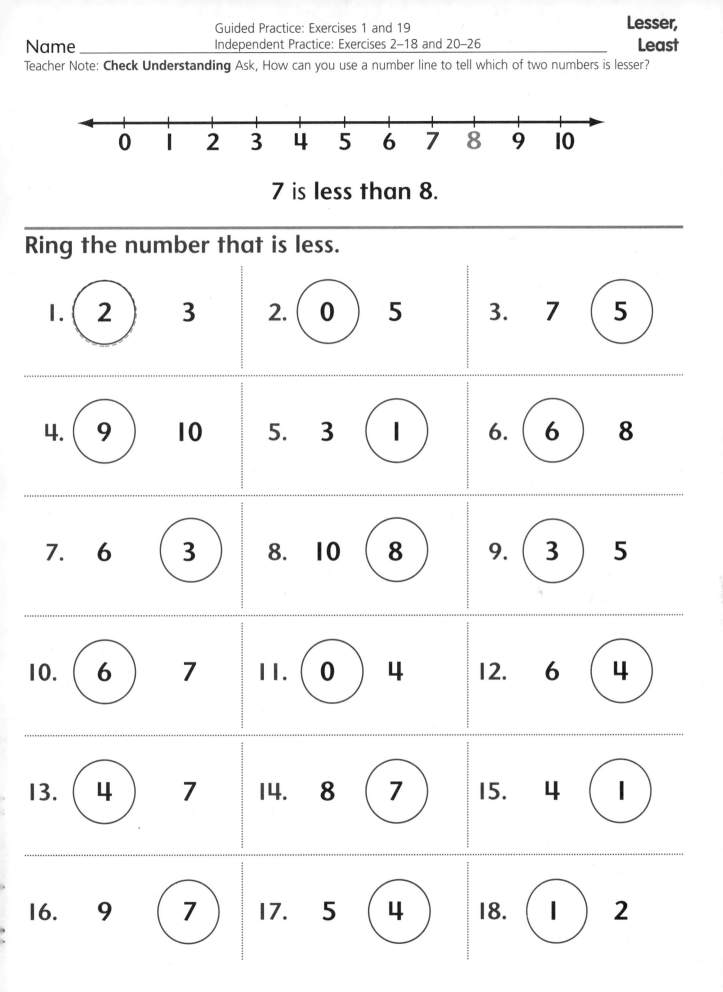

0   1   2   3   4   5   6   7   8   9   10

7 is **less than 8.**

Ring the number that is less.

1. **(2)**   3

2. **(0)**   5

3. 7   **(5)**

4. **(9)**   10

5. 3   **(1)**

6. **(6)**   8

7. 6   **(3)**

8. 10   **(8)**

9. **(3)**   5

10. **(6)**   7

11. **(0)**   4

12. 6   **(4)**

13. **(4)**   7

14. 8   **(7)**

15. 4   **(1)**

16. 9   **(7)**

17. 5   **(4)**

18. **(1)**   2

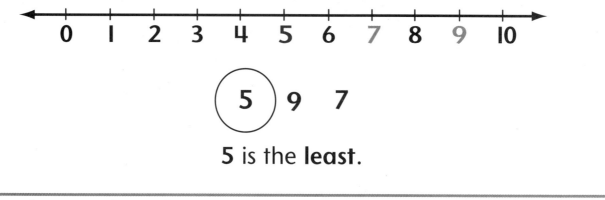

5 is the **least**.

Ring the number that is least.

19. **(6)** 7 9 | 20. **(0)** 3 1

21. 9 7 **(4)** | 22. 6 **(3)** 10

23. **(2)** 3 4 | 24. 6 **(1)** 5

 **Write 3 numbers that are less than 7.**
Answers may vary. Possible answer:

25. 5 , 4 , 3

Teacher Note: **Closing the Lesson** Ask, How is finding the lesser number like finding the greater? How is it different?

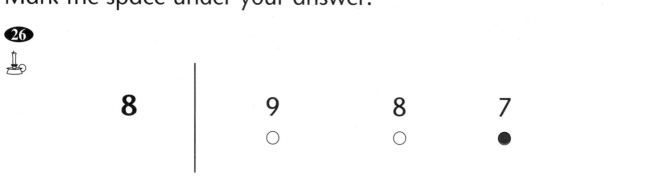

Which number is less than the number shown?
Mark the space under your answer.

26

8 | 9 8 7
○ ○ ●

Teacher Note: **Check Understanding** Write 4 > 2 on the board. Ask, What must I do if I switch the positions of 4 and 2? Why?

2 is greater than **1.**

2 > 1

4 is less than **5.**

4 < 5

Write < or > in the ◯ .

1.

3 ◯< 4

2.

1 ◯< 2

3.

5 ◯< 8

4.

7 ◯> 1

5.

4 ◯< 7

6.

6 ◯< 7

7.

3 ◯< 7

8.

2 ◯> 0

9.

5 ◯< 6

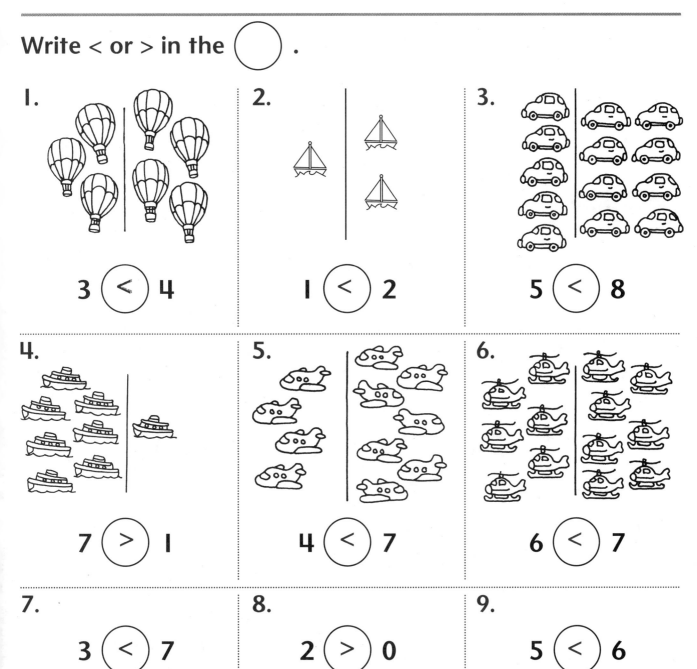

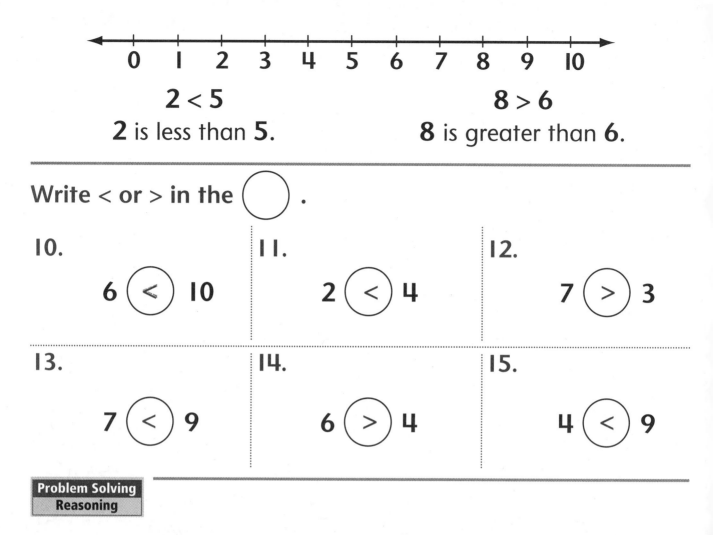

2 < 5
2 is less than **5**.

8 > 6
8 is greater than **6**.

Write < or > in the ◯ .

10.

6 ⟨<⟩ 10

11.

2 ⟨<⟩ 4

12.

7 ⟨>⟩ 3

13.

7 ⟨<⟩ 9

14.

6 ⟨>⟩ 4

15.

4 ⟨<⟩ 9

Problem Solving
Reasoning

16. How does the number line help you compare the numbers?

Answers will vary. Possible answer: If a number is to the left of another number on the number line, it is < that other number. If a number is to the right of another number on the number line, it is > than that other number.

Teacher Note: **Closing the Lesson** Write the following on the chalkboard: ☐ < ☐. Ask, What two numbers can I write in the boxes to make this sentence true?

★ **Test Prep**

Which is true?
Mark the space under your answer.

17

10 < 7
○

8 > 6
●

3 > 6
○

52 (fifty-two)

Unit 2 • Lesson 12

Name _____

**Comparing Numbers:
Using >, <, and =**

Teacher Note: **Check Understanding** Write 8 > ☐, 8 < ☐, and 8= ☐. Ask, What numbers can I write in the boxes to make each sentence true?

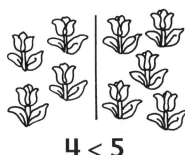

$4 < 5$

4 is less than **5**.

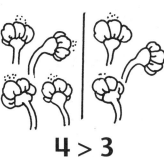

$4 > 3$

4 is greater than **3**.

$4 = 4$

4 is equal to **4**.

Write <, >, or = in the ◯ .

1.
$4 \enspace < \enspace 5$

2.
$2 \enspace < \enspace 3$

3.
$6 \enspace = \enspace 6$

4.
$5 \enspace > \enspace 2$

5.
$6 \enspace < \enspace 8$

6.
$8 \enspace > \enspace 3$

7.
$5 \enspace = \enspace 5$

8.
$1 \enspace < \enspace 2$

9.
$3 \enspace < \enspace 4$

10.
$6 \enspace > \enspace 4$

11.
$5 \enspace > \enspace 1$

12.
$8 \enspace = \enspace 8$

13.
$2 \enspace < \enspace 7$

14.
$3 \enspace > \enspace 2$

15.
$6 \enspace > \enspace 1$

Unit 2 • Lesson 13

(fifty-three) 53

Write <, >, or = in the ○ .

16.
9 ⟨>⟩ 8

17.
6 ⟨=⟩ 6

18.
7 ⟨<⟩ 9

19.
8 ⟨=⟩ 8

20.
3 ⟨<⟩ 4

21.
6 ⟨<⟩ 10

Problem Solving Reasoning

Write the number.
Answers may vary in exercise 22 and 24. Possible answers shown.

22.
[3] > 2

23.
[6] = 6

24.
[7] < 8

Teacher Note: **Closing the Lesson** Ask, How can you use < to make a true sentence with the numbers 5 and 8? How can you use > with the same numbers?

✔ **Quick Check**

Ring the number that is less.

1. 10 ⟨8⟩

2. 6 ⟨3⟩

Ring the number that is least.

3. 4 ⟨2⟩ 7

Item	Error Analysis
1–3	**Common Error:** Children ring the incorrect numbers. **Reteach** Copymaster 15, p. 85
4–7	**Common Error:** Children place the greater than and less than symbols incorrectly. **Reteach** Copymasters 16–17, pp. 86–87.

Write <, >, or = in the ○ .

4. 1 ⟨=⟩ 1

5. 7 ⟨>⟩ 6

6. 3 ⟨<⟩ 9

7. 2 ⟨<⟩ 4

54 (fifty-four)

Unit 2 • Lesson 13

Teacher Note: **Check Understanding** Ask, Why do you think we mark off the fifth tally as a diagonal line?

Tally marks can help you count.

1	2	3	4	5
one	two	three	four	five
		||	|||	||||	⧚

6	7	8	9	10
six	seven	eight	nine	ten
⧚		⧚ ||	⧚ |||	⧚ ||||	⧚ ⧚

Toss a penny 10 times.
Use tally marks to show your results.
Write the totals.

1.

	Tally	Total
Heads	Answers will vary. Possible answers: | | |	3
Tails	|||| / | | |	7

Sergio tosses a coin 10 times.
These are his results.

	Tally	Total
Heads 	|||| /		6
Tails 	||||	4

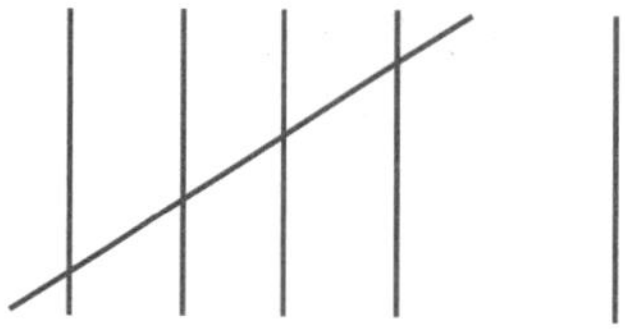

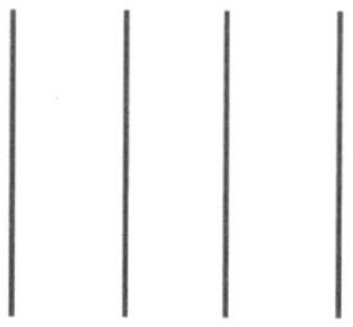

Use the chart.

2. Complete the chart.

3. How many times did Sergio toss heads?   6

4. How many times did Sergio toss tails?   4

5. Did Sergio toss more heads or tails? _____ **heads** _____

Teacher Note: **Closing the Lesson** Ask, Why are there 10 tally marks in all in Sergio's chart?

★ Test Prep

Which set of tally marks means 4?
Mark the space under your answer.

6

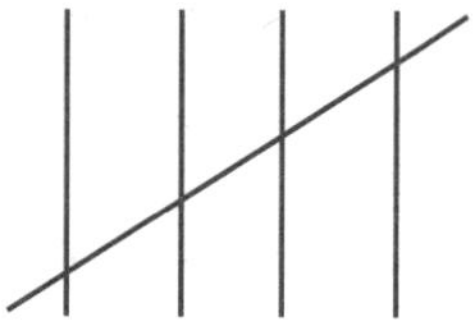

○   ○   ●

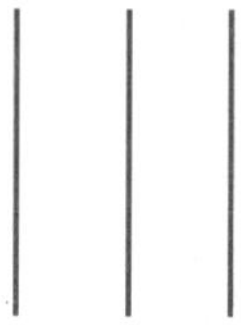

Name _____

Teacher Note: **Check Understanding** Ask, what do you think the pictures at the bottom of the graph on page 57 mean? What do the numbers on the side mean?

Spill 5 pennies out of a cup.
Sort them by heads and tails.
Place the pennies on the graph.
Trace to show heads and tails.

1.

Answers will vary. Possible answers shown.

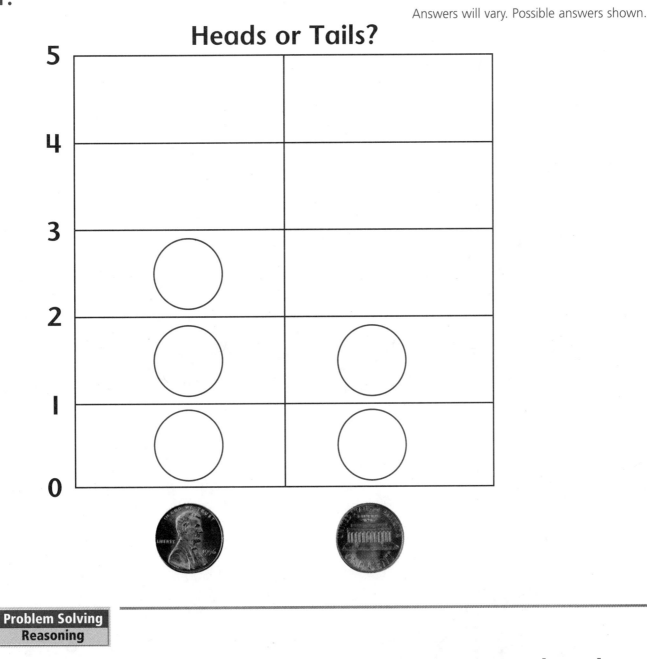

Heads or Tails?

Problem Solving
Reasoning

2. Which did you get more often, heads or tails? ___heads___

Unit 2 • Lesson 15

Write the number.

3.

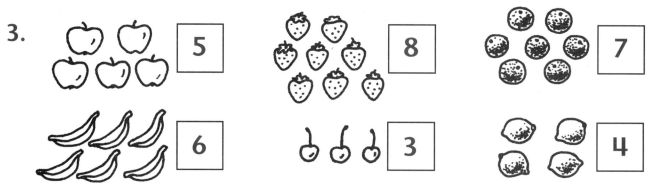

Fill in the graph.

4.

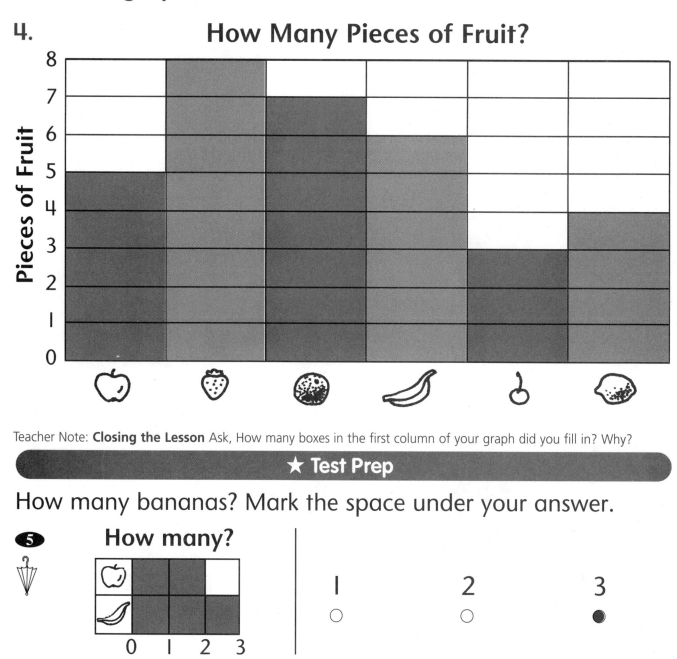

Teacher Note: **Closing the Lesson** Ask, How many boxes in the first column of your graph did you fill in? Why?

★ **Test Prep**

How many bananas? Mark the space under your answer.

Unit 2 • Lesson 15

Name _____

Problem Solving Application:
Use a Graph

Each child voted for an animal.

| Problem Solving Plan |
| 1. Understand 2. Decide 3. Solve 4. Look back |

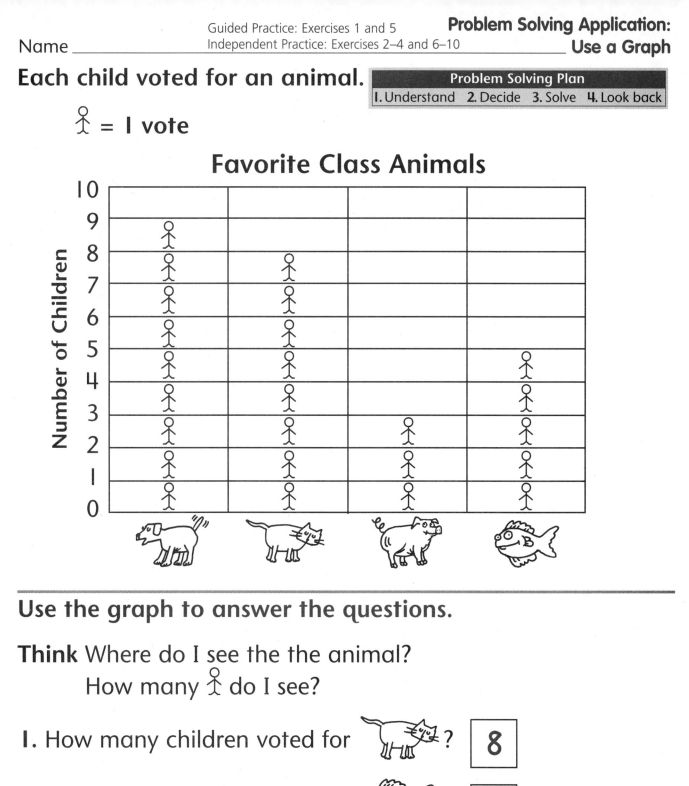

☃ = 1 vote

Favorite Class Animals

Use the graph to answer the questions.

Think Where do I see the the animal?
        How many ☃ do I see?

1. How many children voted for 🐱 ? **8**

2. How many children voted for 🐟 ? **5**

3. How many children voted for 🐶 ? **9**

4. How many children voted for 🐷 ? **3**

Unit 2 • Lesson 16

Each child voted for a favorite sport.

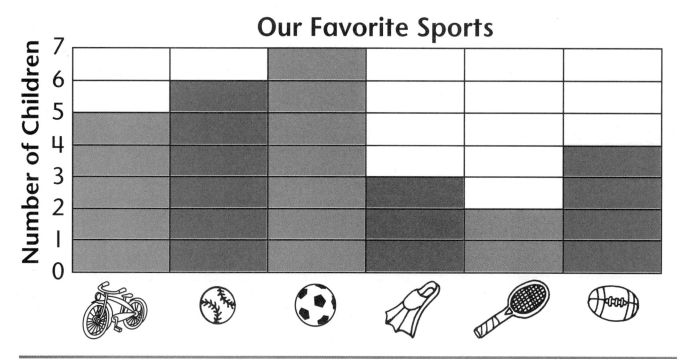

Our Favorite Sports

Use the graph to answer the questions.

Think Where is the object pictured?

At what number does the bar stop?

5. How many children like 🎾 ? ☐ **2**

6. How many children like ⚾ ? ☐ **6**

7. How many children like ⚽ ? ☐ **7**

8. How many children like 🚲 ? ☐ **5**

Teacher Note: **Closing the Lesson** Ask, In the Favorite Sports graph, do you need to count the votes for each sport to tell which was favorite? Why or why not?

Extend Your Thinking

Ring your answer.

9. Do more children like 🎾 than 🏈 ?   yes   (no)

10. Do more children like ⚾ than 🏊 ?   (yes)   no

Match the objects.
Ring the group that has more. (2A)

1.

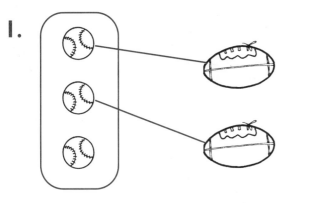

2.

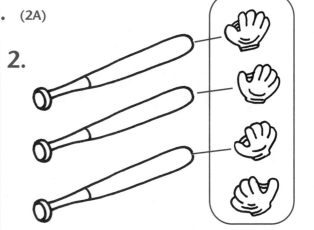

Match the objects.
Ring the group that has fewer. (2A)

3.   **4.**

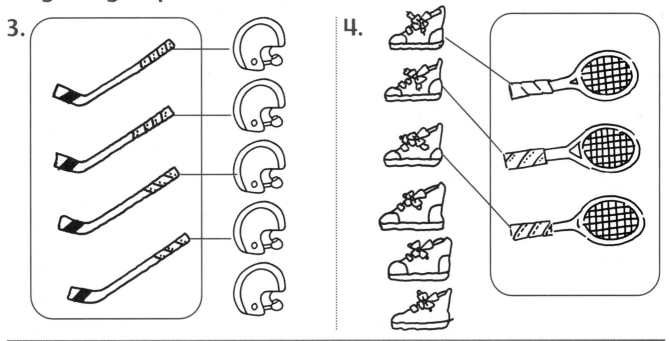

Write how many. (2B)

5.

5

6.

7

Write the amount. (2C)

7. 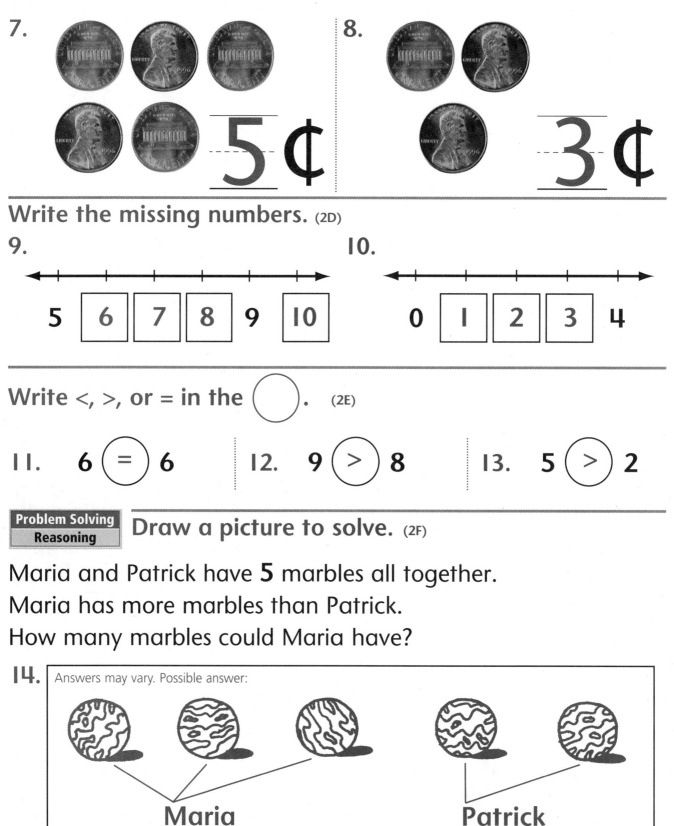 5¢

8. 3¢

Write the missing numbers. (2D)

9.

| 5 | 6 | 7 | 8 | 9 | 10 |

10.

| 0 | 1 | 2 | 3 | 4 |

Write <, >, or = in the ◯. (2E)

11.   6 (=) 6

12.   9 (>) 8

13.   5 (>) 2

Problem Solving Reasoning Draw a picture to solve. (2F)

Maria and Patrick have **5** marbles all together.
Maria has more marbles than Patrick.
How many marbles could Maria have?

14. Answers may vary. Possible answer:

Maria   Patrick

Maria has 3 marbles.

Name_____

★ **Test Prep**

1 Which item shows the triangle before the square? Mark the space under your answer. **(1A)**

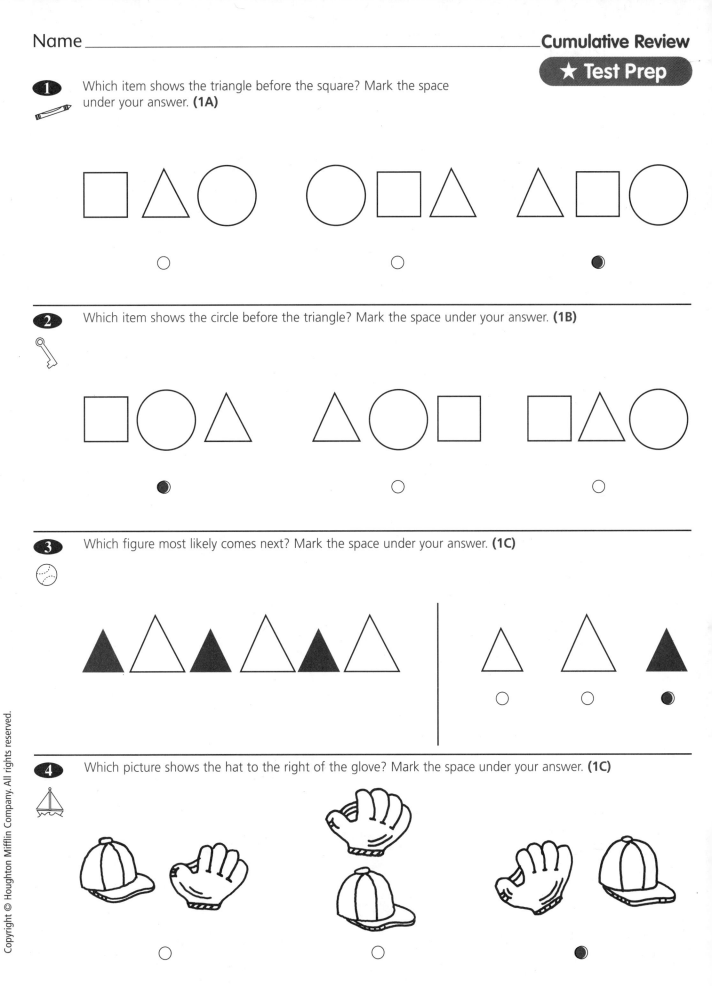

2 Which item shows the circle before the triangle? Mark the space under your answer. **(1B)**

3 Which figure most likely comes next? Mark the space under your answer. **(1C)**

4 Which picture shows the hat to the right of the glove? Mark the space under your answer. **(1C)**

Unit 2 • Cumulative Review

(sixty-three) 63

5 Which group shows more baseballs than the group at the beginning of the row? Mark the space under your answer. **(2A)**

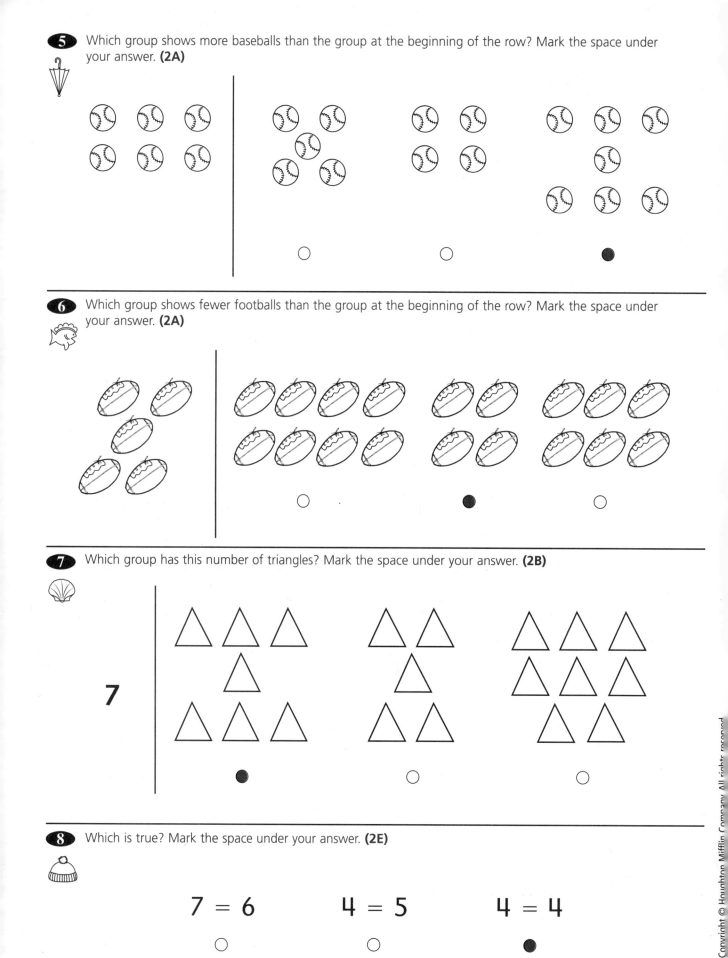

6 Which group shows fewer footballs than the group at the beginning of the row? Mark the space under your answer. **(2A)**

7 Which group has this number of triangles? Mark the space under your answer. **(2B)**

7

8 Which is true? Mark the space under your answer. **(2E)**

$7 = 6$ $4 = 5$ $4 = 4$

64 (sixty-four)

Unit 2 • Cumulative Review

UNIT 3 • TABLE OF CONTENTS

Addition Facts through 6

Dear Family,

During the next few weeks our math class will be learning addition facts with sums through 6.

You can expect to see homework that provides practice with these addition facts. You may wish to keep the following sample as a guide.

Sums through 6

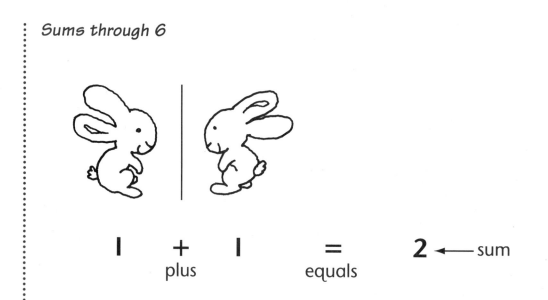

1 **+** 1 **=** **2** ←— sum
   plus   equals

Knowing that addition is joining two or more groups to find the whole or the sum will help children identify addition situations in their lives.

Sincerely,

Name _____
Guided Practice: Exercise 1
Independent Practice: Exercises 2–7

Teacher Note: **Check Understanding** Have 3 children stand. Then have 2 more stand. Ask, Who can tell a story about what just happened?

Listen.

Use counters to act out the story.

Write how many.

Read the following stories aloud. Have children act them out with counters and write the numbers below.
1. 2 boys go down the slide. 2 girls play in the sandbox. How many children are playing in all?
2. 1 girl goes down the slide. 3 boys play in the sandbox. How many children are playing in all?
3. 4 boys play in the sandbox. 2 girls are on the swings. How many children are playing in all?

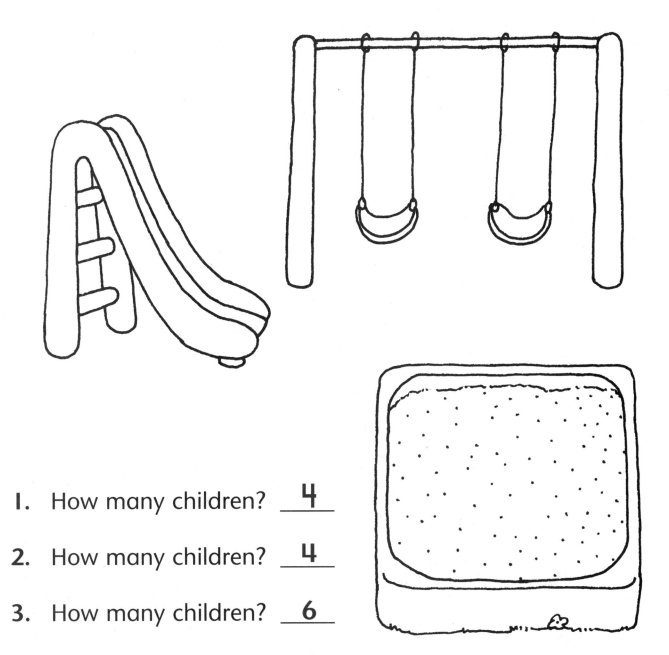

1. How many children? __4__

2. How many children? __4__

3. How many children? __6__

Listen.
Use counters to act out the story.
Write how many.

Read the following stories aloud. Have children act them out with counters and write the numbers below.
4. Max puts 3 apples in the box. Then he puts 2 more apples in the box. How many apples are in the box now?
5. Jan puts 2 bananas in the bowl. Max puts 2 more bananas in the bowl. How many bananas are in the bowl now?
6. Max puts 1 banana in the box. Jan puts 1 banana in the bowl. How many bananas do they put in altogether?

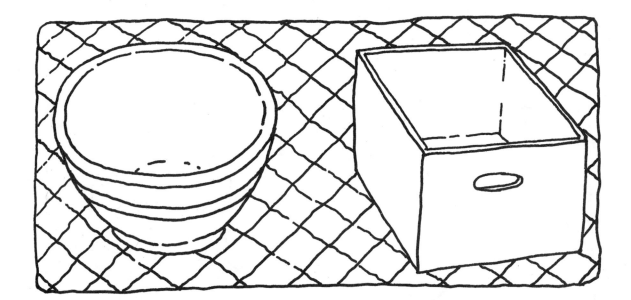

4. How many 🍎 ? __5__

5. How many 🍌 ? __4__

6. How many 🍌 ? __2__

Teacher Note: **Closing the Lesson** Bring 4 children to the front of the room. Invite a volunteer to tell a story about the 4 children and have children act it out.

★ Test Prep

Listen. Mark the space under your answer.

7 3 people walk into a room. Then 3 more people come in. How many people are in the room now?

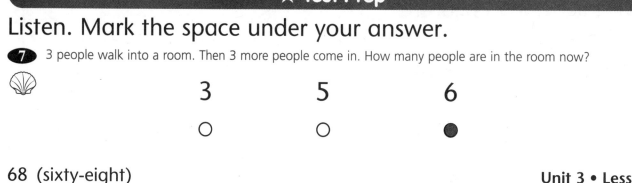

3	5	6
○	○	●

68 (sixty-eight)

Unit 3 • Lesson 1

Teacher Note: **Check Understanding** Hold up 3 fingers on one hand and 2 fingers on the other. Ask, What number sentence tells how many in all? Have a volunteer write the number sentence on the chalkboard.

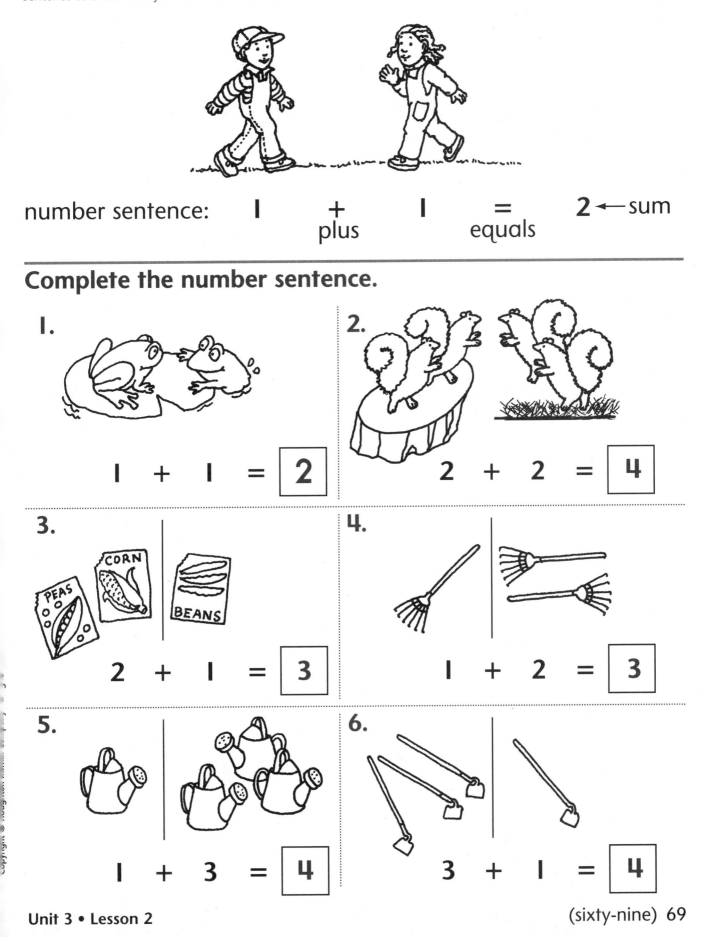

number sentence: 1   +   1   =   2 ← sum
                       plus   equals

Complete the number sentence.

1.

1   +   1   =   **2**

2.

2   +   2   =   **4**

3.

2   +   1   =   **3**

4.

1   +   2   =   **3**

5.

1   +   3   =   **4**

6.

3   +   1   =   **4**

Complete the number sentence.

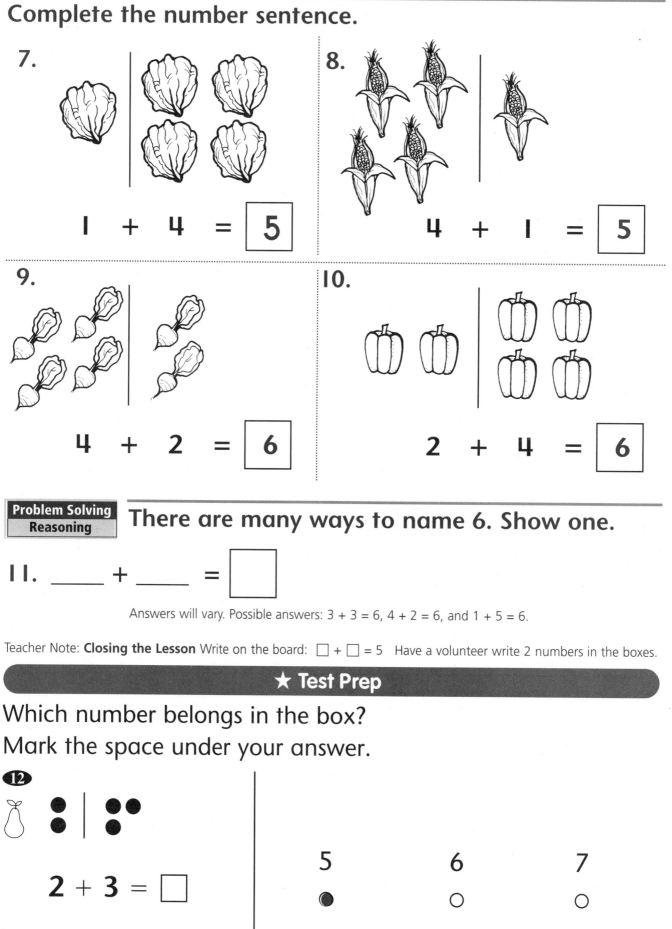

7.

$$1 \quad + \quad 4 \quad = \quad \boxed{5}$$

8.

$$4 \quad + \quad 1 \quad = \quad \boxed{5}$$

9.

$$4 \quad + \quad 2 \quad = \quad \boxed{6}$$

10.

$$2 \quad + \quad 4 \quad = \quad \boxed{6}$$

| Problem Solving |
| Reasoning |

There are many ways to name 6. Show one.

11. ____ + ____ = $\boxed{}$

Answers will vary. Possible answers: 3 + 3 = 6, 4 + 2 = 6, and 1 + 5 = 6.

Teacher Note: **Closing the Lesson** Write on the board: $\square + \square = 5$ Have a volunteer write 2 numbers in the boxes.

★ Test Prep

Which number belongs in the box?
Mark the space under your answer.

12

$$2 + 3 = \boxed{}$$

5 ●   6 ○   7 ○

Problem

1 Understand Say, Look at the picture story. As you look at the picture, you need to look for the math ideas.

2 Decide Say, What is happening? I can write a number sentence to help me solve the problem.

3 Solve Ask, What number sentence describes the picture story?

$$1 + 1 = 2$$

4 Look back Ask, Does the number sentence match the picture? How can you tell?

Write a number sentence for each picture.

1.

$$1 + 2 = 3$$

2.

$$2 + 1 = 3$$

Write a number sentence for each picture.

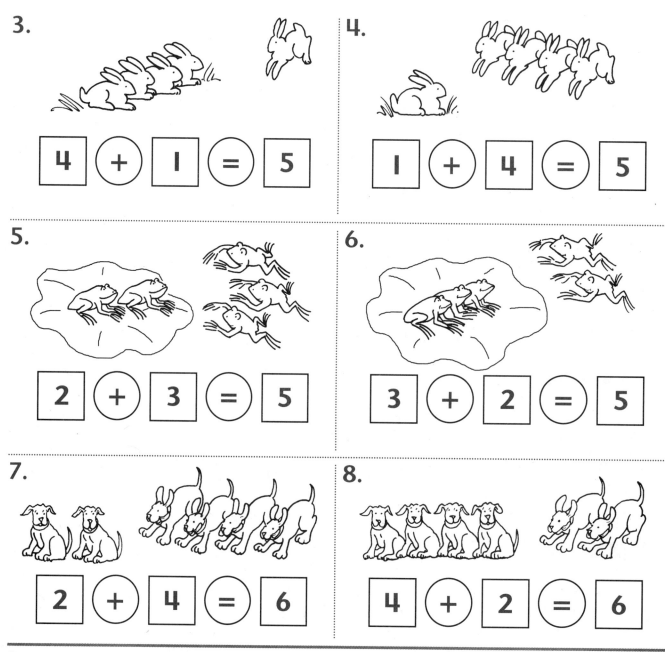

3.

$$4 + 1 = 5$$

4.

$$1 + 4 = 5$$

5.

$$2 + 3 = 5$$

6.

$$3 + 2 = 5$$

7.

$$2 + 4 = 6$$

8.

$$4 + 2 = 6$$

Draw a picture to match the number sentence.

9. $2 + 2 = 4$

Drawings will vary but should show addition and include the correct number of items.

Teacher Note: **Closing the Lesson** Ask, How does writing a number sentence help you solve problems?

Unit 3 • Lesson 3

Guided Practice: Model Exercise
Independent Practice: Exercises 1–10

Adding 1 More

Teacher Note: **Check Understanding** Ask, How can counting help you add 1 more?

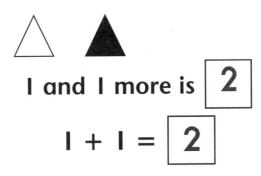

I and I more is $\boxed{2}$

$I + I = \boxed{2}$

Complete.

I.

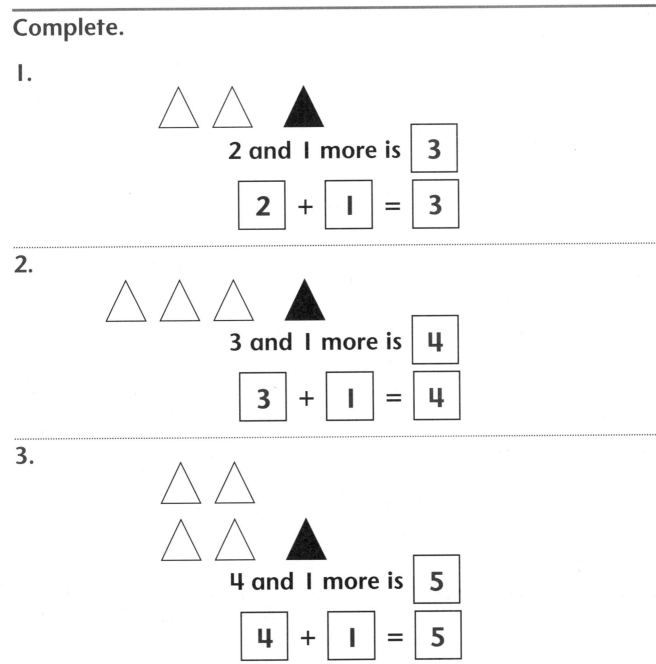

2 and I more is $\boxed{3}$

$\boxed{2} + \boxed{1} = \boxed{3}$

2.

3 and I more is $\boxed{4}$

$\boxed{3} + \boxed{1} = \boxed{4}$

3.

4 and I more is $\boxed{5}$

$\boxed{4} + \boxed{1} = \boxed{5}$

Unit 3 • Lesson 4

(seventy-three) 73

Complete.

4.

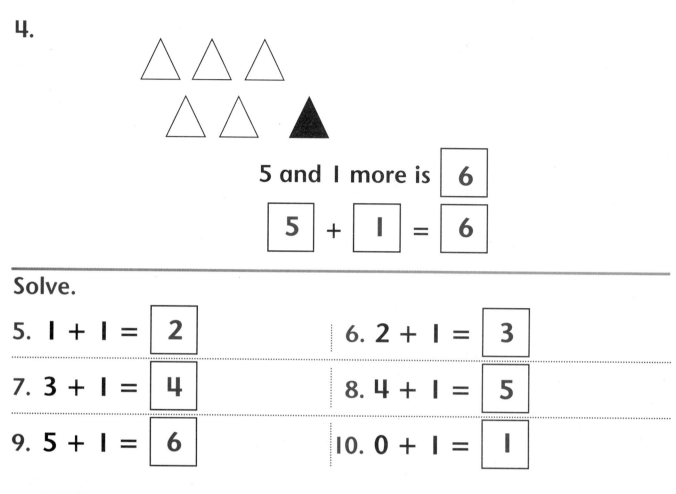

5 and 1 more is 6

5 + 1 = 6

Solve.

5. 1 + 1 = 2

6. 2 + 1 = 3

7. 3 + 1 = 4

8. 4 + 1 = 5

9. 5 + 1 = 6

10. 0 + 1 = 1

Problem Solving Reasoning

How do you find 1 more of a number?

Answers will vary. Possible answer: I count on 1 more.

Teacher Note: **Closing the Lesson** Ask, What happens when you add 1 more to a number?

✓ **Quick Check**

Complete.

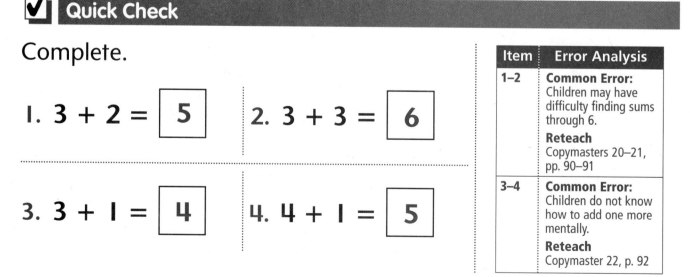

1. 3 + 2 = 5   2. 3 + 3 = 6

3. 3 + 1 = 4   4. 4 + 1 = 5

Item	Error Analysis
1–2	**Common Error:** Children may have difficulty finding sums through 6. **Reteach** Copymasters 20–21, pp. 90–91
3–4	**Common Error:** Children do not know how to add one more mentally. **Reteach** Copymaster 22, p. 92

Name _____

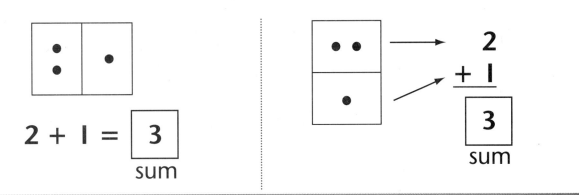

$2 + 1 = \boxed{3}$
sum

Write the sum.

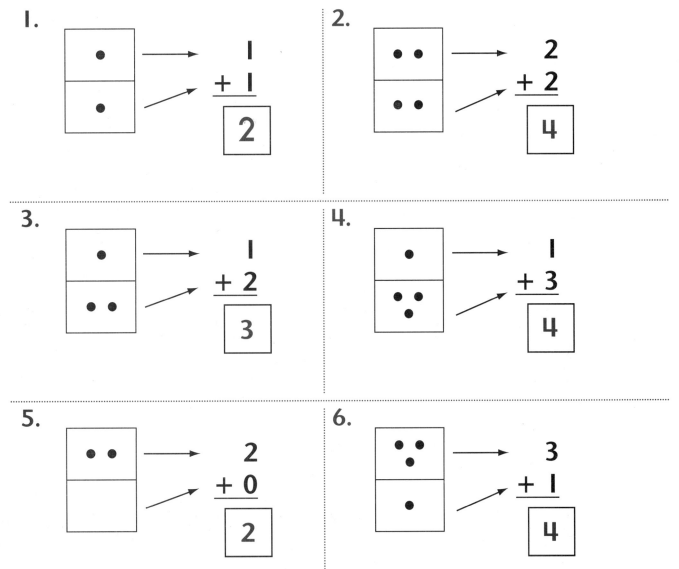

1.

$\begin{array}{r} 1 \\ + 1 \\ \hline \boxed{2} \end{array}$

2.

$\begin{array}{r} 2 \\ + 2 \\ \hline \boxed{4} \end{array}$

3.

$\begin{array}{r} 1 \\ + 2 \\ \hline \boxed{3} \end{array}$

4.

$\begin{array}{r} 1 \\ + 3 \\ \hline \boxed{4} \end{array}$

5.

$\begin{array}{r} 2 \\ + 0 \\ \hline \boxed{2} \end{array}$

6.

$\begin{array}{r} 3 \\ + 1 \\ \hline \boxed{4} \end{array}$

Write the sum.

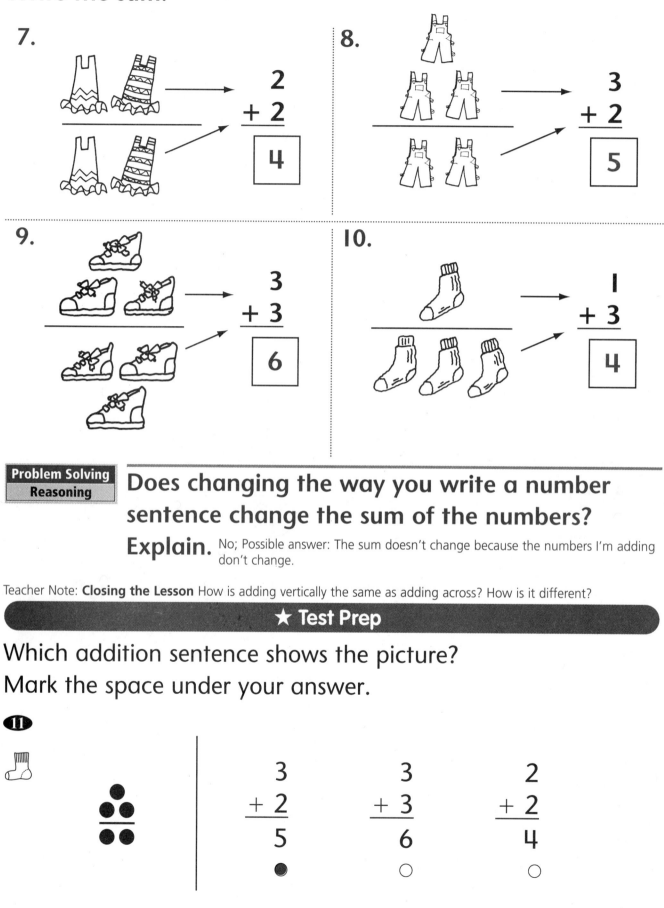

7.

$$\begin{array}{r} 2 \\ + 2 \\ \hline \boxed{4} \end{array}$$

8.

$$\begin{array}{r} 3 \\ + 2 \\ \hline \boxed{5} \end{array}$$

9.

$$\begin{array}{r} 3 \\ + 3 \\ \hline \boxed{6} \end{array}$$

10.

$$\begin{array}{r} 1 \\ + 3 \\ \hline \boxed{4} \end{array}$$

Problem Solving / Reasoning

Does changing the way you write a number sentence change the sum of the numbers?

Explain. No; Possible answer: The sum doesn't change because the numbers I'm adding don't change.

Teacher Note: **Closing the Lesson** How is adding vertically the same as adding across? How is it different?

★ Test Prep

Which addition sentence shows the picture?
Mark the space under your answer.

11

$$\begin{array}{r} 3 \\ + 2 \\ \hline 5 \end{array} \qquad \begin{array}{r} 3 \\ + 3 \\ \hline 6 \end{array} \qquad \begin{array}{r} 2 \\ + 2 \\ \hline 4 \end{array}$$

● ○ ○

Name _____ **Adding 0**

Teacher Note: **Check Understanding** Ask, What can you add to 6 to get a sum of 6?

Add.

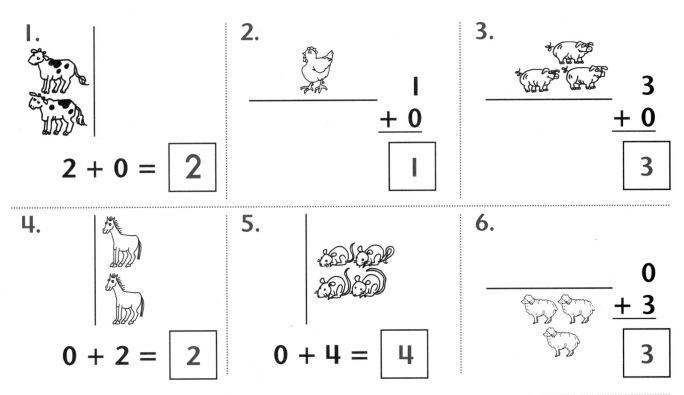

1.

$2 + 0 = \boxed{2}$

2.

$\begin{array}{r} 1 \\ + 0 \\ \hline \boxed{1} \end{array}$

3.

$\begin{array}{r} 3 \\ + 0 \\ \hline \boxed{3} \end{array}$

4.

$0 + 2 = \boxed{2}$

5.

$0 + 4 = \boxed{4}$

6.

$\begin{array}{r} 0 \\ + 3 \\ \hline \boxed{3} \end{array}$

Draw a picture. Complete.

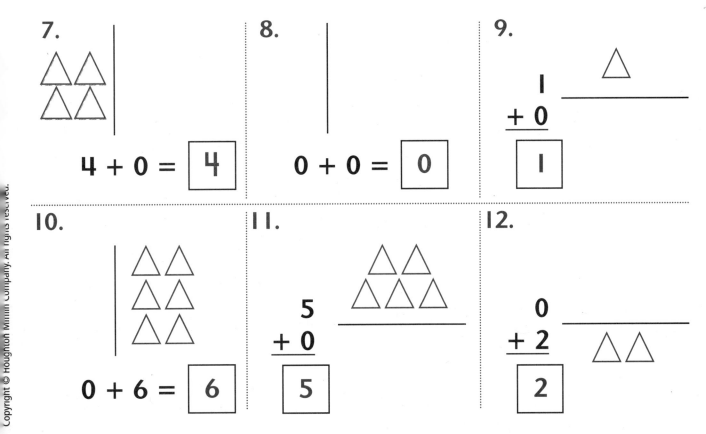

7.

$4 + 0 = \boxed{4}$

8.

$0 + 0 = \boxed{0}$

9.

$\begin{array}{r} 1 \\ + 0 \\ \hline \boxed{1} \end{array}$

10.

$0 + 6 = \boxed{6}$

11.

$\begin{array}{r} 5 \\ + 0 \\ \hline \boxed{5} \end{array}$

12.

$\begin{array}{r} 0 \\ + 2 \\ \hline \boxed{2} \end{array}$

Unit 3 • Lesson 6

(seventy-seven) 77

Write the number sentence.

13.

$$\boxed{4} + \boxed{0} = \boxed{4}$$

14.

$$\boxed{0} + \boxed{2} = \boxed{2}$$

15.

$$\boxed{4} + \boxed{2} = \boxed{6}$$

Complete.

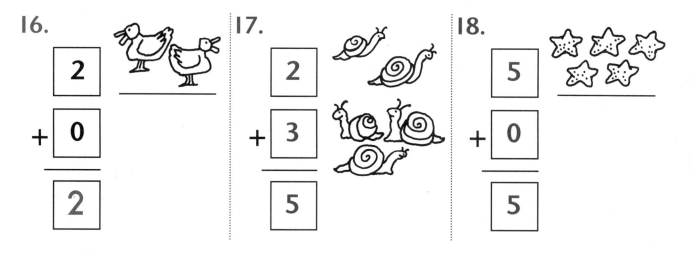

16.

$$\begin{array}{r} \boxed{2} \\ + \boxed{0} \\ \hline \boxed{2} \end{array}$$

17.

$$\begin{array}{r} \boxed{2} \\ + \boxed{3} \\ \hline \boxed{5} \end{array}$$

18.

$$\begin{array}{r} \boxed{5} \\ + \boxed{0} \\ \hline \boxed{5} \end{array}$$

Problem Solving Reasoning How many fingers would you hold up if you held up 0 on one hand and 0 on the other?

Teacher Note: **Closing the Lesson** Ask, What happens when you add zero to a number?

★ Test Prep

Which number correctly completes the number sentence? Mark the space under your answer.

19

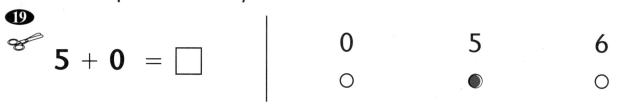

$$5 + 0 = \boxed{}$$

0	5	6
○	●	○

Unit 3 • Lesson 6

Guided Practice: Exercises 1, 7, 14, and 29
Name Independent Practice: Exercises 2–6, 8–13, 15–28, and 30–34

Order
Property

Teacher Note: **Check Understanding** Ask, What fact does 4 + 1 = 5 help you know?

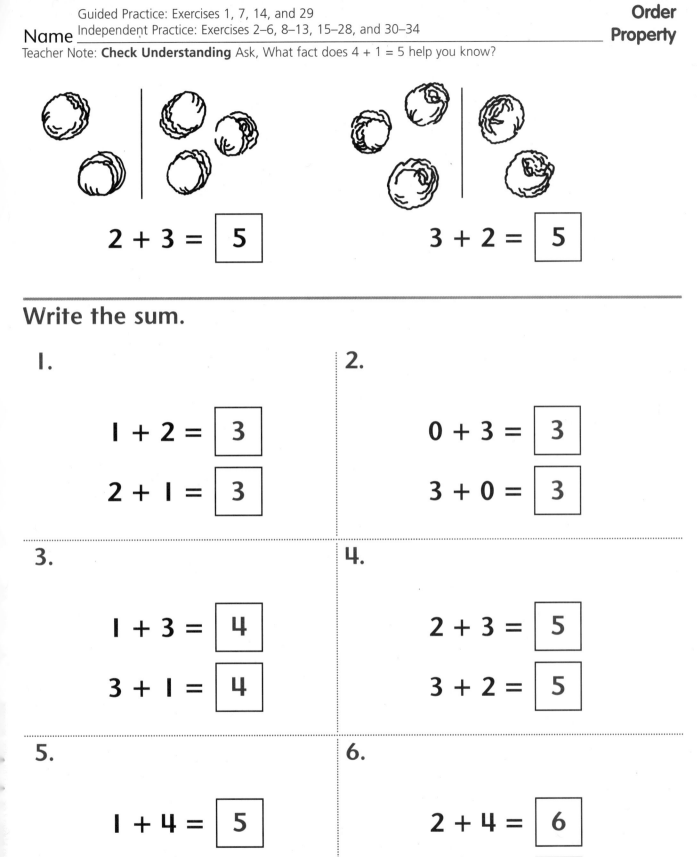

$2 + 3 =$ ⬚ 5

$3 + 2 =$ ⬚ 5

Write the sum.

1.

$1 + 2 =$ ⬚ 3

$2 + 1 =$ ⬚ 3

2.

$0 + 3 =$ ⬚ 3

$3 + 0 =$ ⬚ 3

3.

$1 + 3 =$ ⬚ 4

$3 + 1 =$ ⬚ 4

4.

$2 + 3 =$ ⬚ 5

$3 + 2 =$ ⬚ 5

5.

$1 + 4 =$ ⬚ 5

$4 + 1 =$ ⬚ 5

6.

$2 + 4 =$ ⬚ 6

$4 + 2 =$ ⬚ 6

$$\begin{array}{r} 2 \\ + 1 \\ \hline 3 \end{array} \qquad \begin{array}{r} 1 \\ + 2 \\ \hline 3 \end{array}$$

Add.

7.
$$\begin{array}{r} 4 \\ + 0 \\ \hline 4 \end{array} \qquad \begin{array}{r} 0 \\ + 4 \\ \hline 4 \end{array}$$

8.
$$\begin{array}{r} 5 \\ + 1 \\ \hline 6 \end{array} \qquad \begin{array}{r} 1 \\ + 5 \\ \hline 6 \end{array}$$

9.
$$\begin{array}{r} 3 \\ + 1 \\ \hline 4 \end{array} \qquad \begin{array}{r} 1 \\ + 3 \\ \hline 4 \end{array}$$

10.
$$\begin{array}{r} 3 \\ + 2 \\ \hline 5 \end{array} \qquad \begin{array}{r} 2 \\ + 3 \\ \hline 5 \end{array}$$

11.
$$\begin{array}{r} 6 \\ + 0 \\ \hline 6 \end{array} \qquad \begin{array}{r} 0 \\ + 6 \\ \hline 6 \end{array}$$

12.
$$\begin{array}{r} 4 \\ + 1 \\ \hline 5 \end{array} \qquad \begin{array}{r} 1 \\ + 4 \\ \hline 5 \end{array}$$

Problem Solving Reasoning

13. If you already know that **4 + 2 = 6**, what other number sentence for **6** do you know?

$$2 + 4 = 6$$

Unit 3 • Lesson 7

Name _____

Climb down the ladders.
Write the sums.

	Left ladder		Right ladder
14.	$1 + 5 = 6$	→	$5 + 1 = 6$
15.	$3 + 3 = 6$	→	$3 + 3 = 6$
16.	$5 + 0 = 5$	→	$0 + 5 = 5$
17.	$0 + 6 = 6$	→	$6 + 0 = 6$
18.	$2 + 4 = 6$	→	$4 + 2 = 6$
19.	$0 + 4 = 4$	→	$4 + 0 = 4$
20.	$2 + 0 = 2$	→	$0 + 2 = 2$
21.	$1 + 4 = 5$	→	$4 + 1 = 5$
22.	$3 + 2 = 5$	→	$2 + 3 = 5$
23.	$2 + 2 = 4$	→	$2 + 2 = 4$
24.	$3 + 0 = 3$	→	$0 + 3 = 3$
25.	$0 + 1 = 1$	→	$1 + 0 = 1$
26.	$1 + 3 = 4$	→	$3 + 1 = 4$
27.	$2 + 1 = 3$	→	$1 + 2 = 3$
28.	$0 + 0 = 0$	→	$0 + 0 = 0$

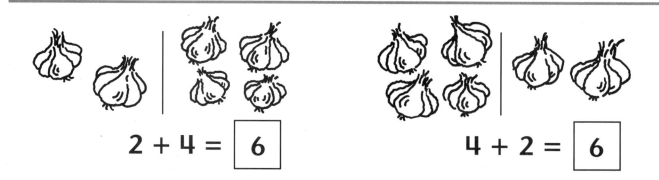

$2 + 4 = \boxed{6}$ $4 + 2 = \boxed{6}$

Add. Match the partners.

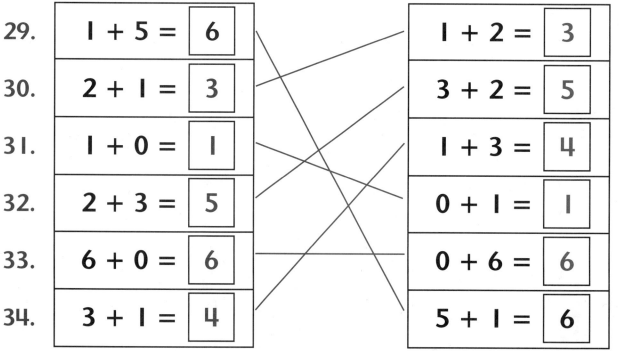

29. $1 + 5 = \boxed{6}$ $1 + 2 = \boxed{3}$

30. $2 + 1 = \boxed{3}$ $3 + 2 = \boxed{5}$

31. $1 + 0 = \boxed{1}$ $1 + 3 = \boxed{4}$

32. $2 + 3 = \boxed{5}$ $0 + 1 = \boxed{1}$

33. $6 + 0 = \boxed{6}$ $0 + 6 = \boxed{6}$

34. $3 + 1 = \boxed{4}$ $5 + 1 = \boxed{6}$

Teacher Note: **Closing the Lesson** Ask, What happens if you change the order of the two numbers you are adding?

✔ Quick Check

Complete.

1.   3
    $\underline{+\ 2}$
    $\boxed{5}$

2. $0 + 3 = \boxed{3}$

3. $5 + 1 = 6$

   $1 + 5 = \boxed{6}$

4. $3 + 1 = 4$

   $1 + 3 = \boxed{4}$

Item	Error Analysis
1	**Common Error:** Children copy a number rather than add. **Skills Tutorial** Strand P2, Skill 1
2	**Common Error:** Children write 0 for the answer when adding 0. **Reteach** Copymaster 23, p. 93
3, 4	**Common Error:** Children count rather than recognize the sum is the same as the related fact. **Reteach** Copymaster 24, p. 94

     Unit 3 • Lesson 7

Name _____
Guided Practice: Exercises 1 and 9
Independent Practice: Exercises 2–8 and 10–13

Penny, Nickel

Teacher Note: **Check Understanding** Ask, How many pennies have the same value as 1 nickel?

I penny	I penny	I nickel	I nickel
I cent	I cent	5 cents	5 cents
I¢	I¢	5¢	5¢

How much money?

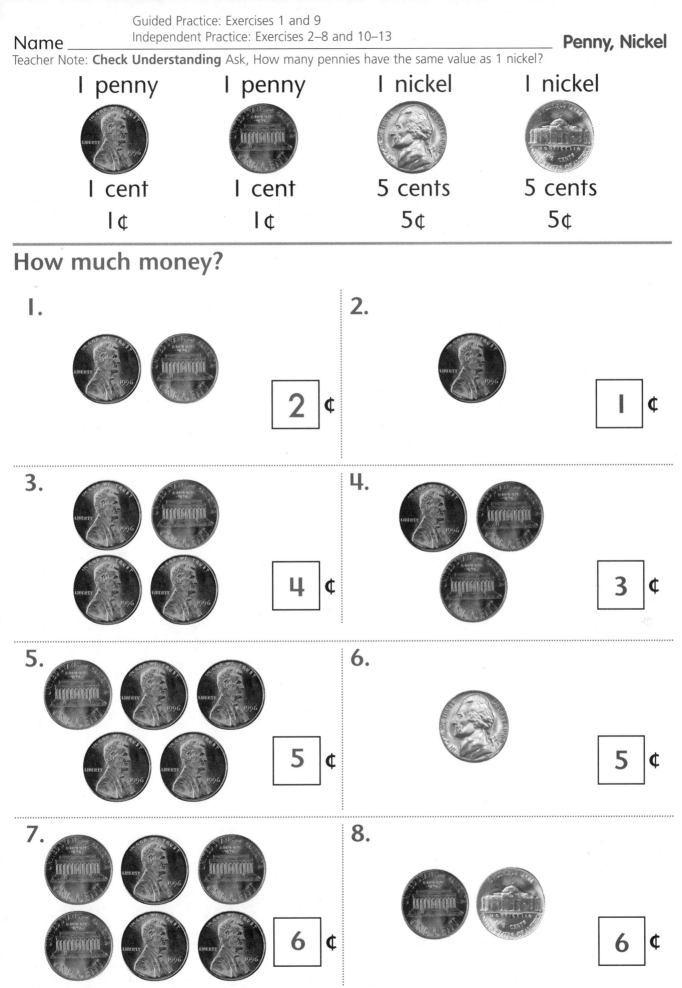

1. ☐ 2 | ¢

2. ☐ 1 | ¢

3. ☐ 4 | ¢

4. ☐ 3 | ¢

5. ☐ 5 | ¢

6. ☐ 5 | ¢

7. ☐ 6 | ¢

8. ☐ 6 | ¢

How much for both?
Ring the coins needed.

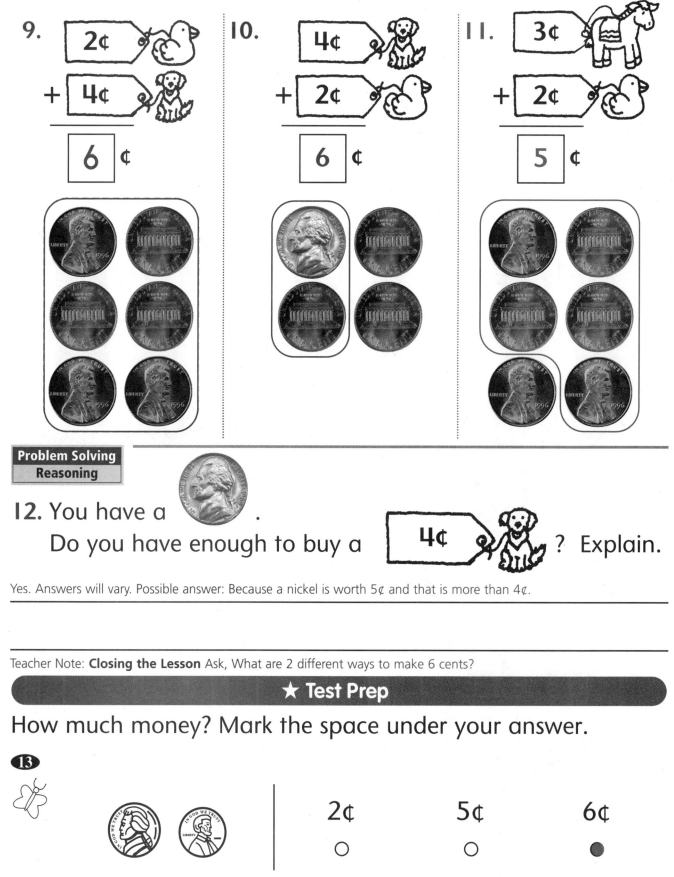

9.

2¢
+ 4¢
6 ¢

10.

4¢
+ 2¢
6 ¢

11.

3¢
+ 2¢
5 ¢

Problem Solving
Reasoning

12. You have a 🪙 .
Do you have enough to buy a | 4¢ 🐕 | ? Explain.

Yes. Answers will vary. Possible answer: Because a nickel is worth 5¢ and that is more than 4¢.

Teacher Note: **Closing the Lesson** Ask, What are 2 different ways to make 6 cents?

★ Test Prep

How much money? Mark the space under your answer.

13

2¢	5¢	6¢
○	○	●

Teacher Note: **Check Understanding** Ask, How can a picture show a number story?

Problem Solving Plan			
1. Understand	2. Decide	3. Solve	4. Look back

Can you tell a story for the picture?

$$\begin{array}{r} 4 \\ + \ 1 \\ \hline \boxed{5} \end{array}$$

Tell a story. Complete.

Think How do I use the pictures to tell a story?

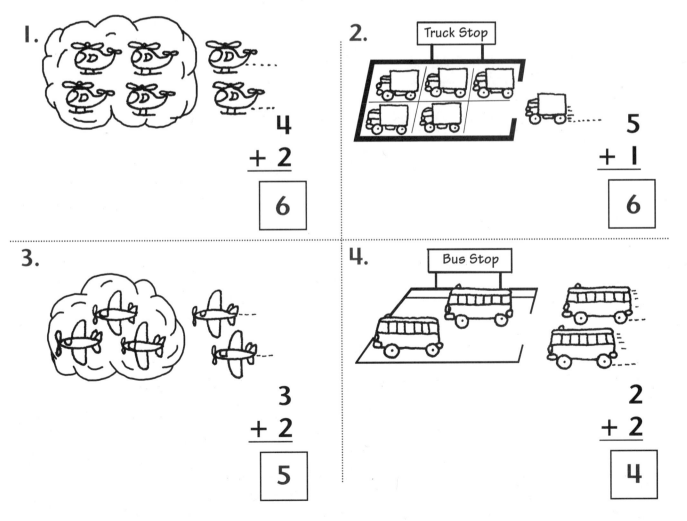

1.
$$\begin{array}{r} 4 \\ + \ 2 \\ \hline \boxed{6} \end{array}$$

2. Truck Stop
$$\begin{array}{r} 5 \\ + \ 1 \\ \hline \boxed{6} \end{array}$$

3.
$$\begin{array}{r} 3 \\ + \ 2 \\ \hline \boxed{5} \end{array}$$

4. Bus Stop
$$\begin{array}{r} 2 \\ + \ 2 \\ \hline \boxed{4} \end{array}$$

Unit 3 • Lesson 9

(eighty-five) 85

Tell a story. Ring the matching fact.

5.

$$\begin{array}{r} 2 \\ + 2 \\ \hline 4 \end{array}$$ (ringed) $$\begin{array}{r} 3 \\ + 1 \\ \hline 4 \end{array}$$

6.

$$\begin{array}{r} 3 \\ + 3 \\ \hline 6 \end{array}$$ $$\begin{array}{r} 2 \\ + 4 \\ \hline 6 \end{array}$$ (ringed)

Extend Your Thinking

Tell a story to match the fact. Draw a picture.

7. $$\begin{array}{r} 1 \\ + 5 \\ \hline 6 \end{array}$$

Stories and pictures will vary but should show addition
and include the correct number of items.

Teacher Note: **Closing the Lesson** Ask, How did you know which facts matched the pictures?

Teacher Note: **Check Understanding** Show 3 fingers. Ask, How many more fingers do I need to make 5?

Complete.

1.

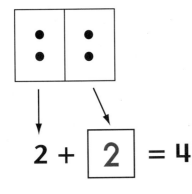

$2 + \boxed{2} = 4$ $1 + \boxed{3} = 4$ $2 + \boxed{1} = 3$

2.

$3 + \boxed{2} = 5$ $2 + \boxed{4} = 6$ $1 + \boxed{4} = 5$

3.

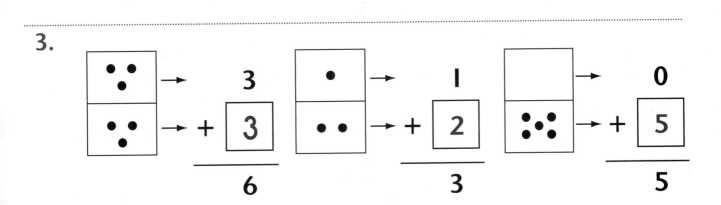

$\begin{array}{r} 3 \\ + \boxed{3} \\ \hline 6 \end{array}$ $\begin{array}{r} 1 \\ + \boxed{2} \\ \hline 3 \end{array}$ $\begin{array}{r} 0 \\ + \boxed{5} \\ \hline 5 \end{array}$

4.

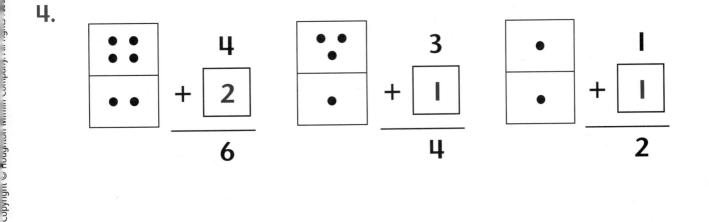

$\begin{array}{r} 4 \\ + \boxed{2} \\ \hline 6 \end{array}$ $\begin{array}{r} 3 \\ + \boxed{1} \\ \hline 4 \end{array}$ $\begin{array}{r} 1 \\ + \boxed{1} \\ \hline 2 \end{array}$

Complete.

5.

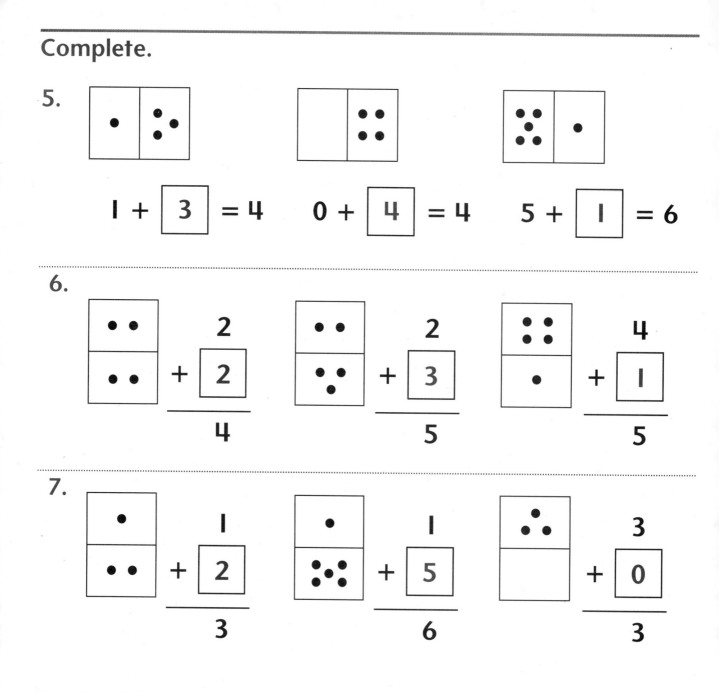

$1 + \boxed{3} = 4$ $0 + \boxed{4} = 4$ $5 + \boxed{1} = 6$

6.

$\begin{array}{r} 2 \\ + \boxed{2} \\ \hline 4 \end{array}$ $\begin{array}{r} 2 \\ + \boxed{3} \\ \hline 5 \end{array}$ $\begin{array}{r} 4 \\ + \boxed{1} \\ \hline 5 \end{array}$

7.

$\begin{array}{r} 1 \\ + \boxed{2} \\ \hline 3 \end{array}$ $\begin{array}{r} 1 \\ + \boxed{5} \\ \hline 6 \end{array}$ $\begin{array}{r} 3 \\ + \boxed{0} \\ \hline 3 \end{array}$

Teacher Note: **Closing the Lesson** Ask, How can you tell what number to add to 3 in order to make 5?

★ Test Prep

What number is missing in the number sentence?
Mark the space under your answer.

8

$3 + \square = 5$

2	3	5
●	○	○

Add. (3A)

1.	2.	3.	4.	5.
2	2	5	2	4
+ 1	+ 3	+ 1	+ 4	+ 0
3	5	6	6	4

6. 2 + 4 = __6__

7. 6 + 0 = __6__

8. 3 + 1 = __4__

9. 1 + 2 = __3__

How much money? (3B)

10. | 3 | ¢

11. | 6 | ¢

How much for both?
Ring the coins needed. (3B)

12.
| 1¢ | 🐤 |

+ | 3¢ | 🐕 |

| 4 | ¢

13.
| 3¢ | 🐕 |

+ | 2¢ | 🐟 |

| 5 | ¢

Write the number sentence. (3C)

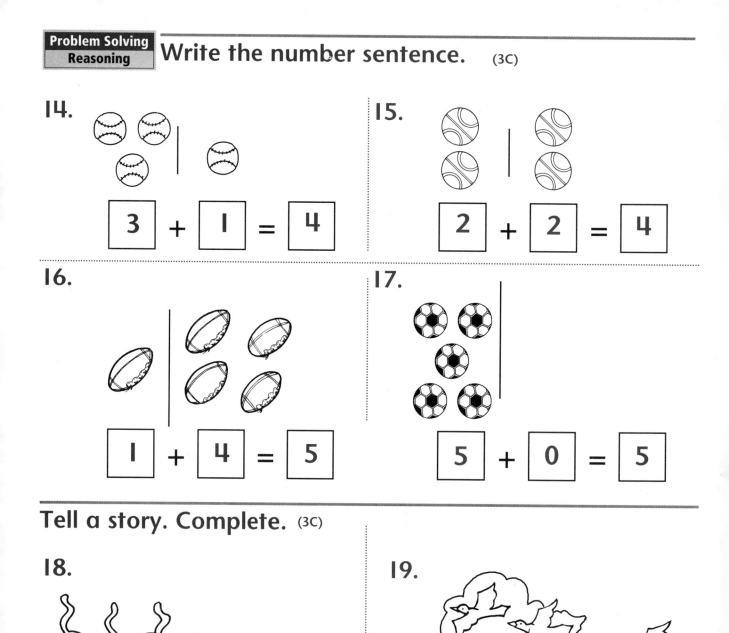

14.

$$3 + 1 = 4$$

15.

$$2 + 2 = 4$$

16.

$$1 + 4 = 5$$

17.

$$5 + 0 = 5$$

Tell a story. Complete. (3C)

18.

$$\begin{array}{r} 3 \\ + 2 \\ \hline 5 \end{array}$$

19.

$$\begin{array}{r} 4 \\ + 1 \\ \hline 5 \end{array}$$

Name _____

1 Which picture shows the triangle between the circles?
Mark the space under your answer. **(1B)**

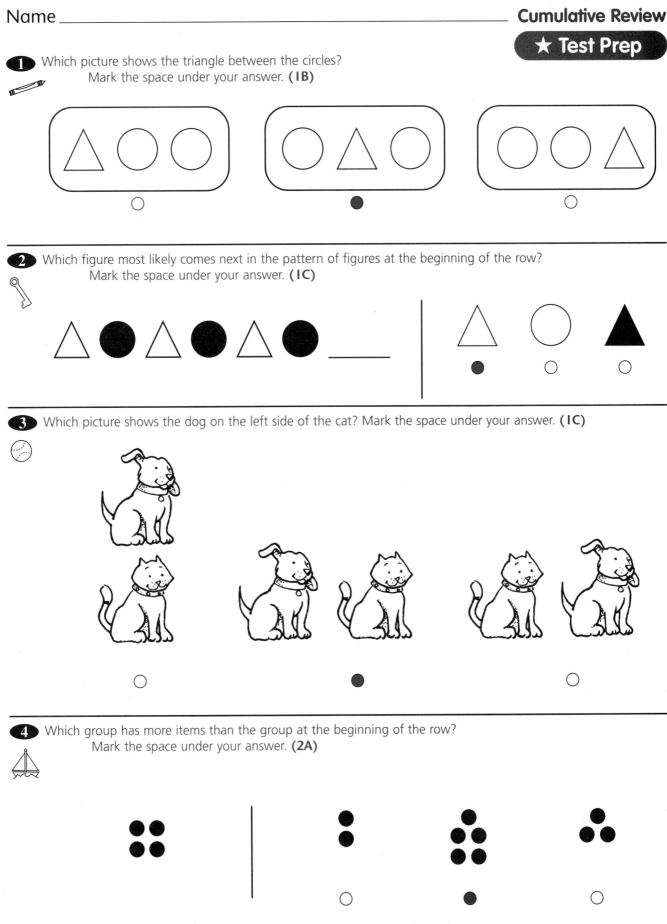

2 Which figure most likely comes next in the pattern of figures at the beginning of the row?
Mark the space under your answer. **(1C)**

3 Which picture shows the dog on the left side of the cat? Mark the space under your answer. **(1C)**

4 Which group has more items than the group at the beginning of the row?
Mark the space under your answer. **(2A)**

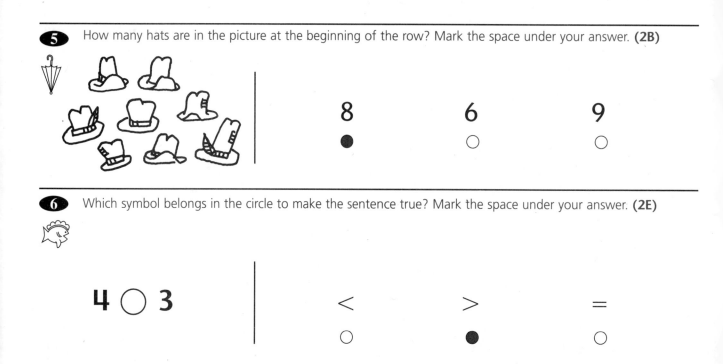

5 How many hats are in the picture at the beginning of the row? Mark the space under your answer. **(2B)**

8   6   9
●   ○   ○

6 Which symbol belongs in the circle to make the sentence true? Mark the space under your answer. **(2E)**

4 ○ 3

    <   >   =
    ○   ●   ○

Solve. Mark the space for your answer.

Tell the class that they will complete the rest of the test independently. **(3A)**

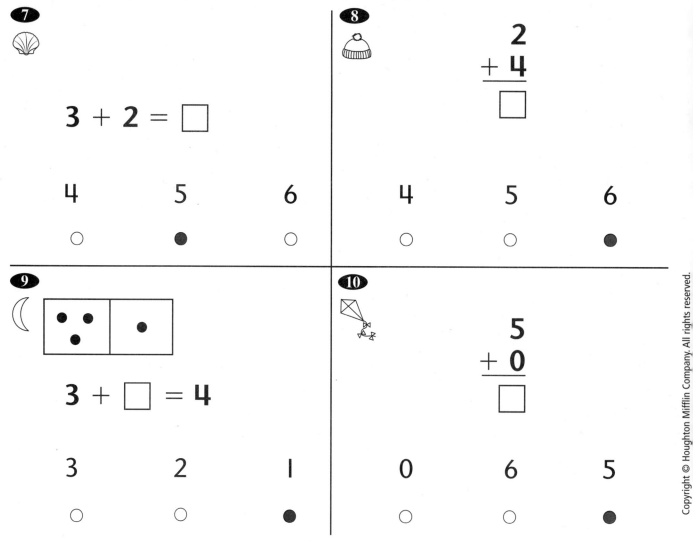

7

$$3 + 2 = \square$$

4   5   6
○   ●   ○

8

$$\begin{array}{r} 2 \\ + 4 \\ \hline \square \end{array}$$

4   5   6
○   ○   ●

9

$$3 + \square = 4$$

3   2   1
○   ○   ●

10

$$\begin{array}{r} 5 \\ + 0 \\ \hline \square \end{array}$$

0   6   5
○   ○   ●

Unit 3 • Cumulative Review

UNIT 4 • TABLE OF CONTENTS

Subtracting from 6 or Less

Dear Family,

During the next few weeks our math class will be learning when and how to subtract. We will be subtracting from 6 or less.

You can expect to see homework that provides practice with both take away and comparison subtraction situations.

As we learn about subtraction, you may wish to keep the following sample as a guide.

Take Away Subtraction

$$3 - 2 = \boxed{1}$$

Comparison Subtraction

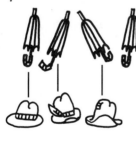

$$4 - 3 = \boxed{1}$$

$$\underline{1} \text{ more}$$

Knowing how and when to subtract is an important mathematics skill.

Sincerely,

Name _____

Teacher Note: **Check Understanding** Have 4 boys and 2 girls stand in front of the room. Ask, Who can tell a story that compares the number of boys to girls?

Listen.
Act out the story with your counters.
Write how many.

Read the following stories aloud as children act them out with counters:

1. 5 children play basketball. 3 of them go home. How many children are left?

2. Les scores 6 points. Jean scores 4 points. How many more points does Les score than Jean?

3. 4 players shoot the ball. 3 players make a basket. How many players do not make a basket?

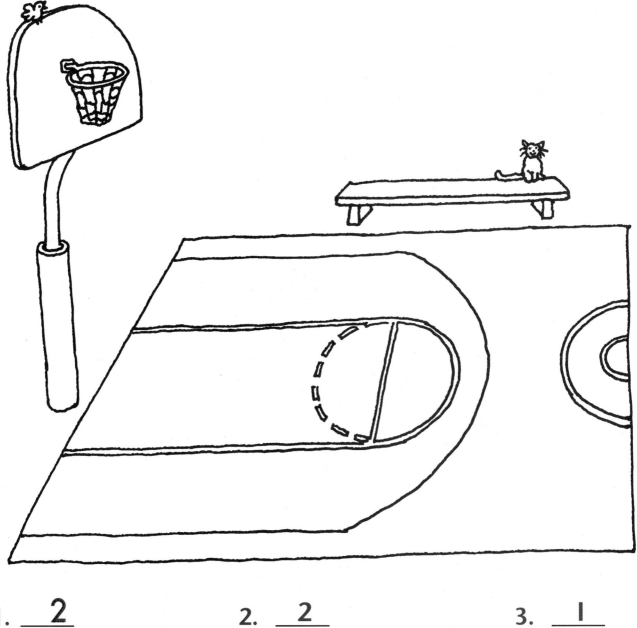

1. __2__   2. __2__   3. __1__

Unit 4 • Lesson 1

Listen.
Act out the story with counters.
Write how many.

Read the following stories aloud as children act them out with counters.

4. 4 children are at the board. Then 3 of them sit down. How many are left at the board?

5. 6 children stand in front of the room. 2 of them are wearing sneakers. The rest are not. How many are not wearing sneakers?

6. 2 children from another class walk into the room. Then the 2 of them walk out. How many children from the other class are left in the room?

4. __I__   5. __4__   6. __0__

Teacher Note: **Closing the Lesson** Have children tell a subtraction story about 5 birds in a tree.

★ Test Prep

Listen. Mark the space under your answer.

3 eggs were on a table. 2 rolled off. Which picture shows how many are left?

7

Teacher Note: **Check Understanding** Hold up 5 fingers on one hand.
Then put down 1. Ask, What number sentence tells how many are left up?

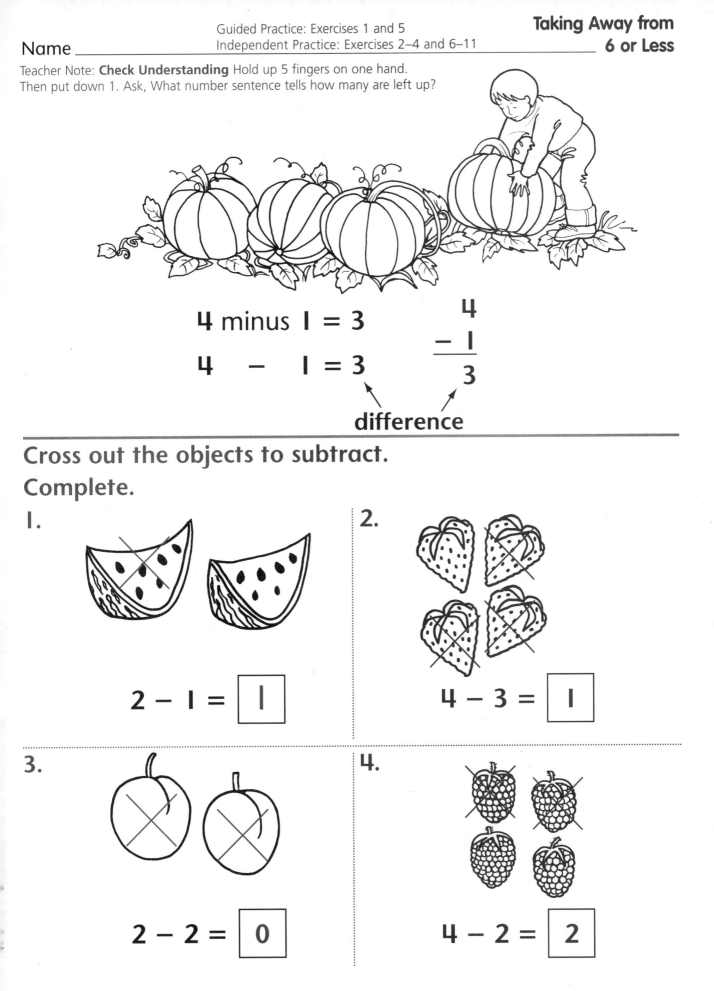

4 minus 1 = 3

4 – 1 = 3

$$\begin{array}{r} 4 \\ -\ 1 \\ \hline 3 \end{array}$$

difference

Cross out the objects to subtract.
Complete.

1.

2 – 1 = ☐ 1

2.

4 – 3 = ☐ 1

3.

2 – 2 = ☐ 0

4.

4 – 2 = ☐ 2

Cross out the objects to subtract.
Complete.

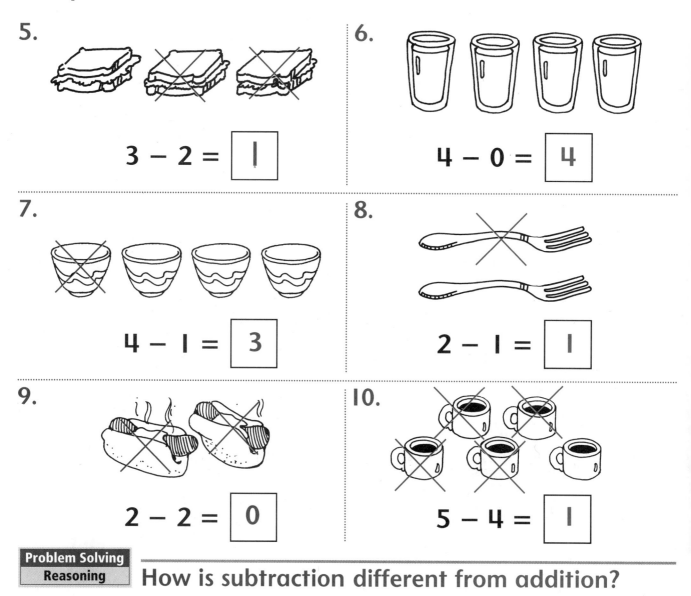

5.

$3 - 2 =$ | 1 |

6.

$4 - 0 =$ | 4 |

7.

$4 - 1 =$ | 3 |

8.

$2 - 1 =$ | 1 |

9.

$2 - 2 =$ | 0 |

10.

$5 - 4 =$ | 1 |

Problem Solving
Reasoning How is subtraction different from addition?

Answers will vary. Possible answer: In addition you put things together. In subtraction you take them away.

Teacher Note: **Closing the Lesson** Have children draw pictures that go with the number sentence $3 - 1 = 2$.

★ Test Prep

Which number belongs in the box?
Mark the space under your answer.

11.

$4 - 2 =$ ☐

| 4 | 3 | 2 |
| ○ | ○ | ● |

Name _____

Vertical Form

Teacher Note: **Check Understanding** Ask, How do you know how many turtles to cross out in exercise 1?

Cross out to subtract.
Complete.

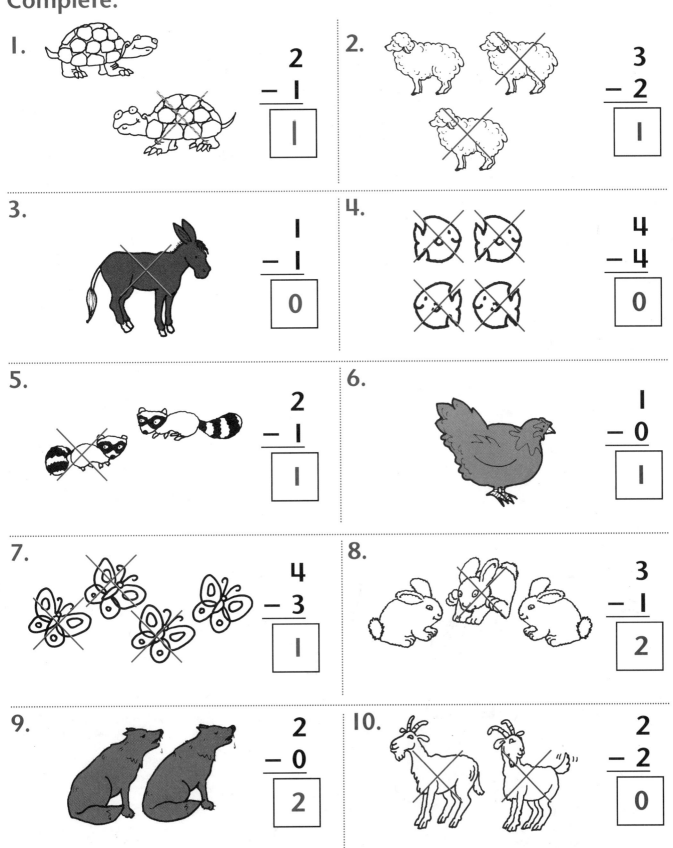

1.
$$\begin{array}{r} 2 \\ -\ 1 \\ \hline 1 \end{array}$$

2.
$$\begin{array}{r} 3 \\ -\ 2 \\ \hline 1 \end{array}$$

3.
$$\begin{array}{r} 1 \\ -\ 1 \\ \hline 0 \end{array}$$

4.
$$\begin{array}{r} 4 \\ -\ 4 \\ \hline 0 \end{array}$$

5.
$$\begin{array}{r} 2 \\ -\ 1 \\ \hline 1 \end{array}$$

6.
$$\begin{array}{r} 1 \\ -\ 0 \\ \hline 1 \end{array}$$

7.
$$\begin{array}{r} 4 \\ -\ 3 \\ \hline 1 \end{array}$$

8.
$$\begin{array}{r} 3 \\ -\ 1 \\ \hline 2 \end{array}$$

9.
$$\begin{array}{r} 2 \\ -\ 0 \\ \hline 2 \end{array}$$

10.
$$\begin{array}{r} 2 \\ -\ 2 \\ \hline 0 \end{array}$$

Cross out to subtract.
Complete.

11.

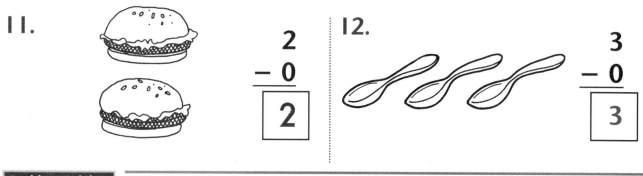

$$\begin{array}{r} 2 \\ -\ 0 \\ \hline \boxed{2} \end{array}$$

12.

$$\begin{array}{r} 3 \\ -\ 0 \\ \hline \boxed{3} \end{array}$$

Problem Solving Reasoning

Write the numbers 1, 4, and 5 in the boxes to make the problem true.

13.

$$\begin{array}{r} \boxed{5} \\ -\ \boxed{4} \\ \hline \boxed{1} \end{array}$$

or

$$\begin{array}{r} 5 \\ -\ 1 \\ \hline 4 \end{array}$$

Teacher Note: **Closing the Lesson** Ask, How is writing subtraction sentences vertically the same as writing them across? How is it different?

✓ Quick Check

Complete.

1.

$$3 - 1 = \boxed{2}$$

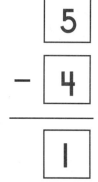

2.

$$4 - 0 = \boxed{4}$$

3.

$$\begin{array}{r} 5 \\ -\ 2 \\ \hline \boxed{3} \end{array}$$

Item	Error Analysis
1	**Common Error:** Children write the total number of people rather than the difference. **Reteach** Copymaster 27, p. 97
2	**Common Error:** Children think the difference is 0 when subtracting 0. **Reteach** Copymaster 28, p. 98
3	**Common Error:** Children add rather than subtract. **Skills Tutorial** Strand P3, Skill 1

Guided Practice: Exercises 1 and 7.
Independent Practice: Exercises 2–6 and 8–12.

How Many More?
How Many Fewer?

Teacher Note: **Check Understanding** Ask, How can we find out how many more (or fewer) boys there are than girls in our class?

Draw lines to match. Complete.

Tell how many more.

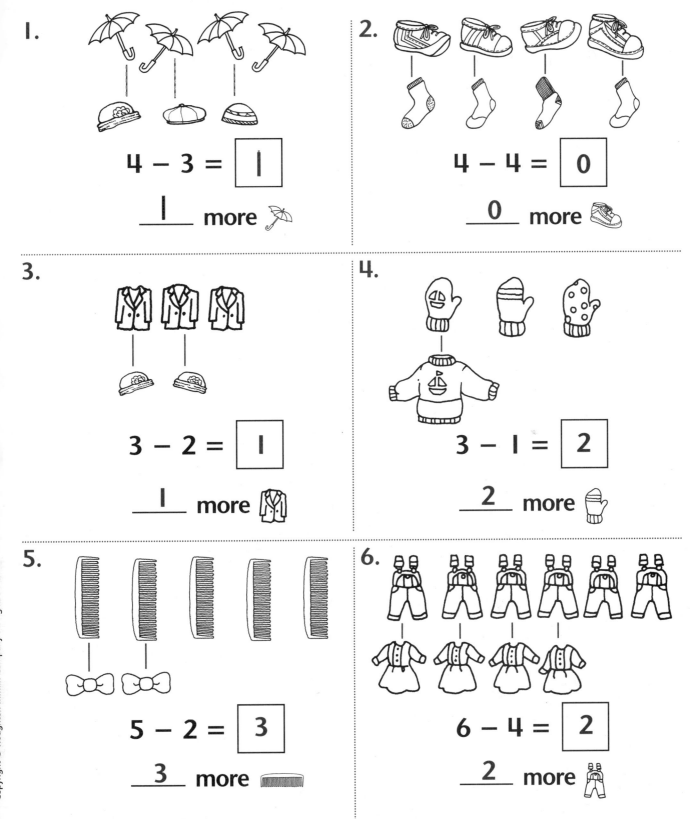

1.

$$4 - 3 = \boxed{1}$$

____1____ more

2.

$$4 - 4 = \boxed{0}$$

____0____ more

3.

$$3 - 2 = \boxed{1}$$

____1____ more

4.

$$3 - 1 = \boxed{2}$$

____2____ more

5.

$$5 - 2 = \boxed{3}$$

____3____ more

6.

$$6 - 4 = \boxed{2}$$

____2____ more

Draw lines to match. Complete.
Tell how many fewer.

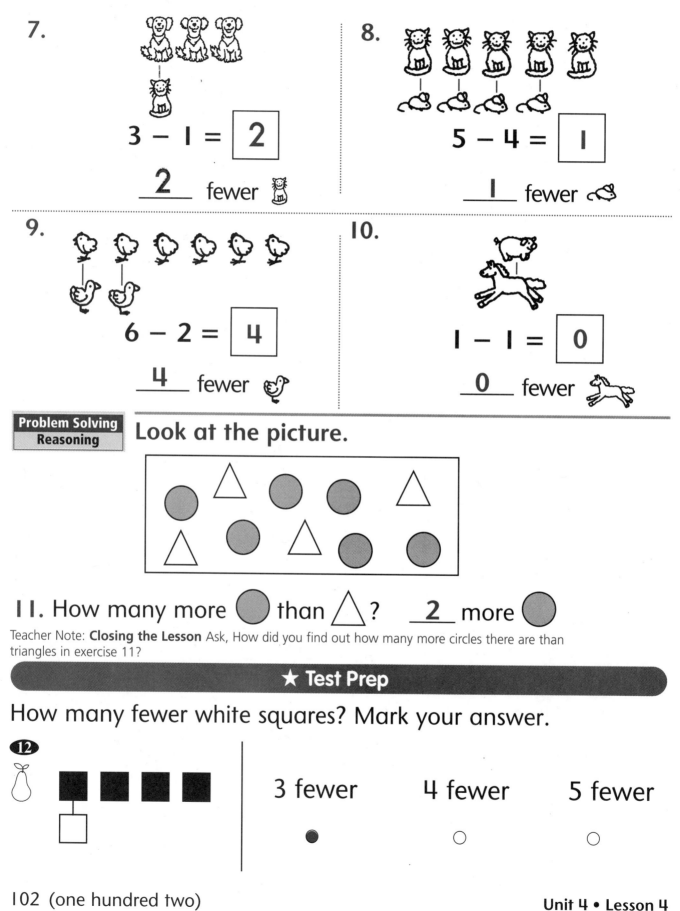

7.

$3 - 1 = \boxed{2}$

__2__ fewer

8.

$5 - 4 = \boxed{1}$

__1__ fewer

9.

$6 - 2 = \boxed{4}$

__4__ fewer

10.

$1 - 1 = \boxed{0}$

__0__ fewer

Problem Solving Reasoning

Look at the picture.

11. How many more ⬤ than △ ?   __2__ more ⬤

Teacher Note: **Closing the Lesson** Ask, How did you find out how many more circles there are than triangles in exercise 11?

★ Test Prep

How many fewer white squares? Mark your answer.

12.

3 fewer ●   4 fewer ○   5 fewer ○

Unit 4 • Lesson 4

Problem

What number sentence can you write for this picture?

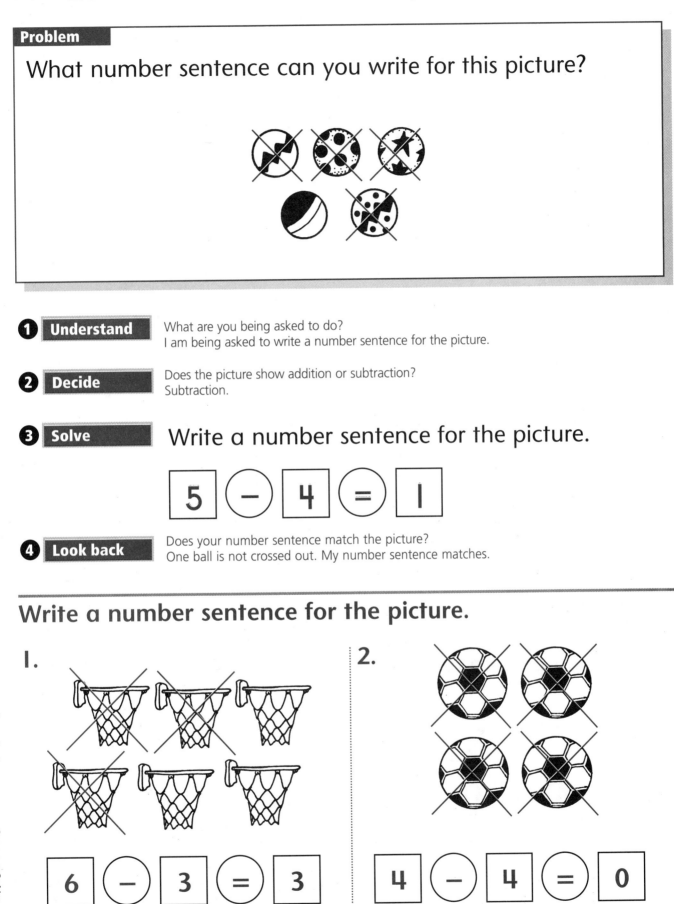

1 Understand   What are you being asked to do?
I am being asked to write a number sentence for the picture.

2 Decide   Does the picture show addition or subtraction?
Subtraction.

3 Solve   Write a number sentence for the picture.

$5 - 4 = 1$

4 Look back   Does your number sentence match the picture?
One ball is not crossed out. My number sentence matches.

Write a number sentence for the picture.

I.

$6 - 3 = 3$

2.

$4 - 4 = 0$

Unit 4 • Lesson 5

Write a number sentence for the picture.

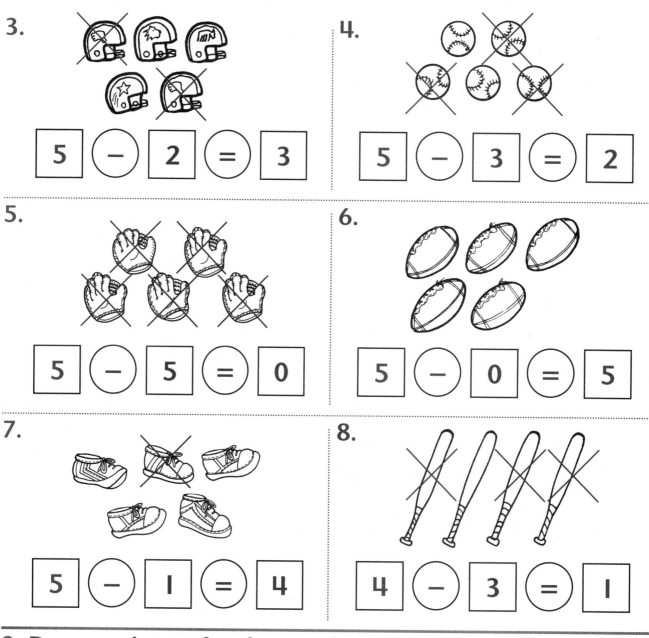

3.

$5 - 2 = 3$

4.

$5 - 3 = 2$

5.

$5 - 5 = 0$

6.

$5 - 0 = 5$

7.

$5 - 1 = 4$

8.

$4 - 3 = 1$

9. Draw a picture for the number sentence.

$$3 - 2 = 1$$

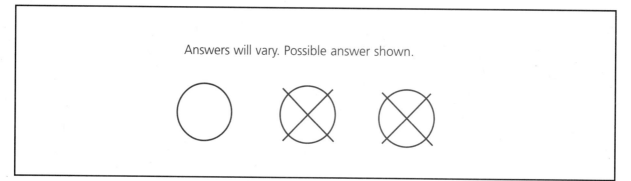

Answers will vary. Possible answer shown.

Teacher Note: **Closing the Lesson** Ask, How did you know how many pictures to cross out in exercise 9?

Name _____

Teacher Note: **Check Understanding** Ask, What number sentence can you write to show 5 take away 4?

Cross out to subtract.

Complete.

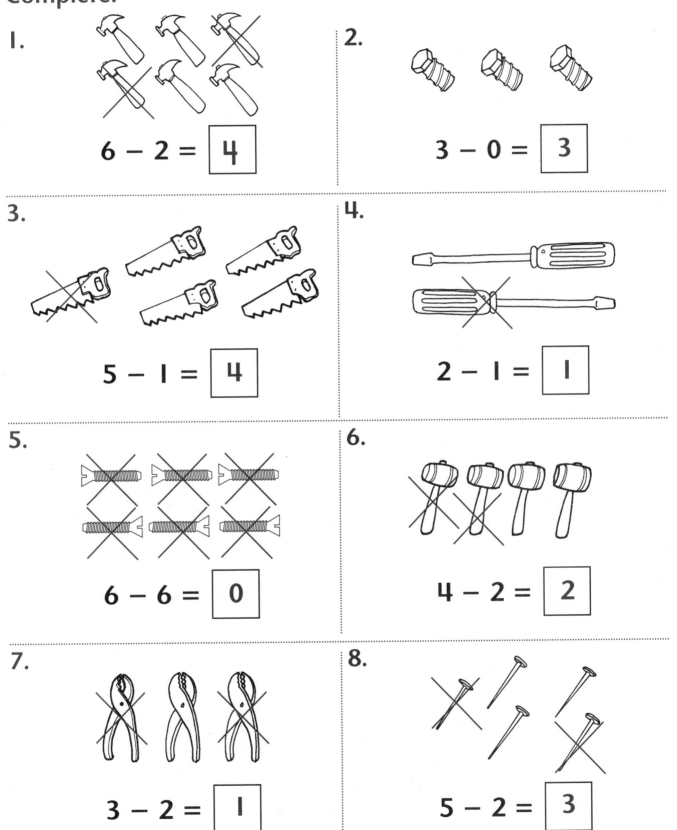

1.

6 – 2 = 4

2.

3 – 0 = 3

3.

5 – 1 = 4

4.

2 – 1 = 1

5.

6 – 6 = 0

6.

4 – 2 = 2

7.

3 – 2 = 1

8.

5 – 2 = 3

Unit 4 • Lesson 6

(one hundred five) 105

Draw a picture. Drawings will vary, but should match number sentences. Possible drawings shown.
Write the difference.

9.
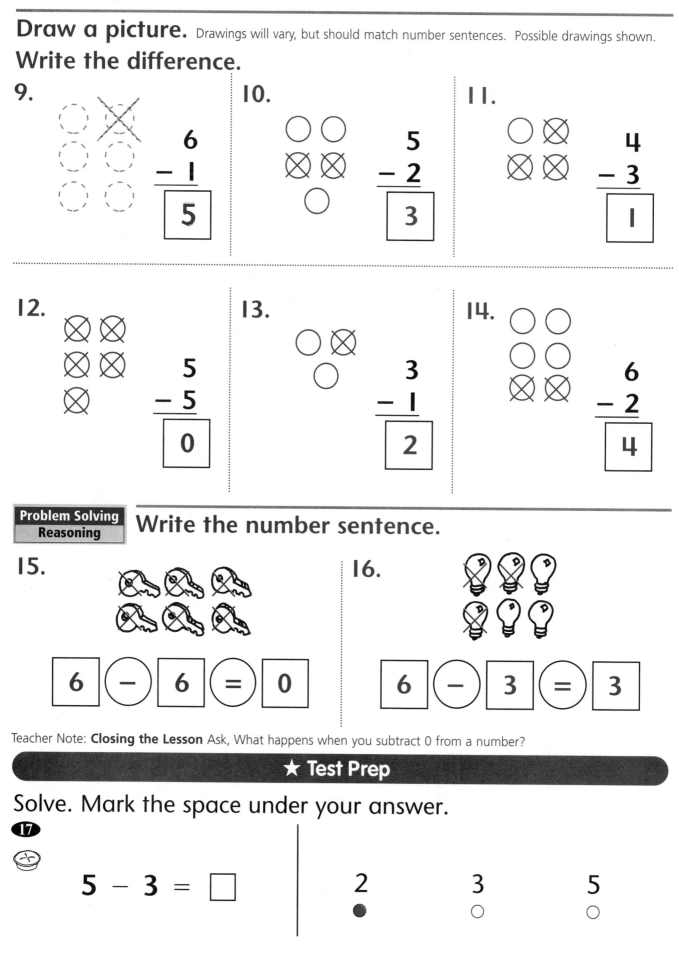

$$\begin{array}{r} 6 \\ -\ 1 \\ \hline \boxed{5} \end{array}$$

10.

$$\begin{array}{r} 5 \\ -\ 2 \\ \hline \boxed{3} \end{array}$$

11.

$$\begin{array}{r} 4 \\ -\ 3 \\ \hline \boxed{1} \end{array}$$

12.

$$\begin{array}{r} 5 \\ -\ 5 \\ \hline \boxed{0} \end{array}$$

13.

$$\begin{array}{r} 3 \\ -\ 1 \\ \hline \boxed{2} \end{array}$$

14.

$$\begin{array}{r} 6 \\ -\ 2 \\ \hline \boxed{4} \end{array}$$

Problem Solving Reasoning

Write the number sentence.

15.

$$\boxed{6} \ \bigcirc{-} \ \boxed{6} \ \bigcirc{=} \ \boxed{0}$$

16.

$$\boxed{6} \ \bigcirc{-} \ \boxed{3} \ \bigcirc{=} \ \boxed{3}$$

Teacher Note: **Closing the Lesson** Ask, What happens when you subtract 0 from a number?

★ Test Prep

Solve. Mark the space under your answer.

17

$$5 - 3 = \square$$

     2   3   5
     ●   ○   ○

Name _____

Problem Solving Application:
Use a Picture

Tell a story for the pictures.
Ring the matching number sentence.

Problem Solving Plan
1. Understand   2. Decide   3. Solve   4. Look back

Stories will vary, but should match pictures. Possible stories shown.

There are 6 tops. 3 tops spin away. 3 tops are left.

1.

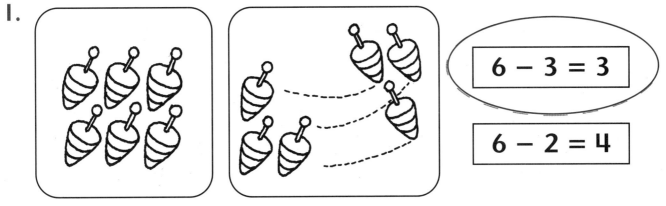

$6 - 3 = 3$

$6 - 2 = 4$

Think Does my answer match the pictures?

2. There are 6 balloons. 1 balloon flies away. 5 balloons are left.

$6 - 5 = 1$

$6 - 1 = 5$

3. There are 6 kites. 2 kites fly away. 4 kites are left.

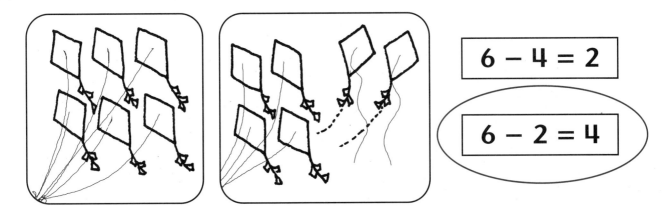

$6 - 4 = 2$

$6 - 2 = 4$

Unit 4 • Lesson 7

(one hundred seven) 107

Tell a story for the pictures.
Ring the matching number sentence.

5 balls are in a box. 4 balls roll out of the box. There is 1 ball left in the box.

4.

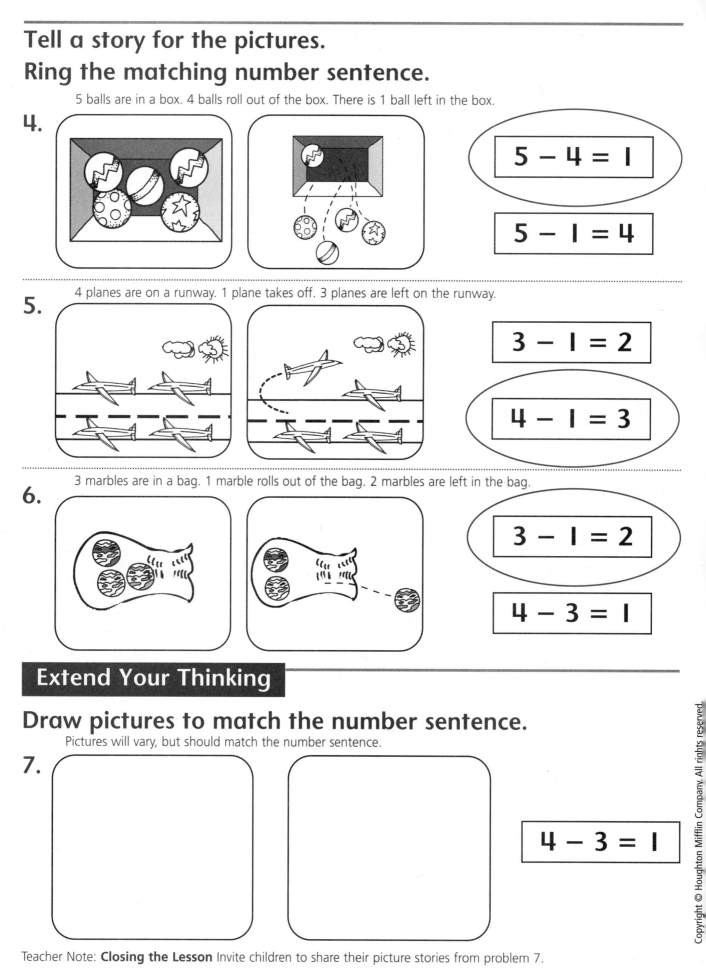

$$5 - 4 = 1$$

$$5 - 1 = 4$$

4 planes are on a runway. 1 plane takes off. 3 planes are left on the runway.

5.

$$3 - 1 = 2$$

$$4 - 1 = 3$$

3 marbles are in a bag. 1 marble rolls out of the bag. 2 marbles are left in the bag.

6.

$$3 - 1 = 2$$

$$4 - 3 = 1$$

Extend Your Thinking

Draw pictures to match the number sentence.

Pictures will vary, but should match the number sentence.

7.

$$4 - 3 = 1$$

Teacher Note: **Closing the Lesson** Invite children to share their picture stories from problem 7.

Subtracting Money

Teacher Note: **Check Understanding** Draw 3 pennies on the board. Cross out 2.
Ask, Who can tell a story to match the picture?

Cross out to subtract. Complete.

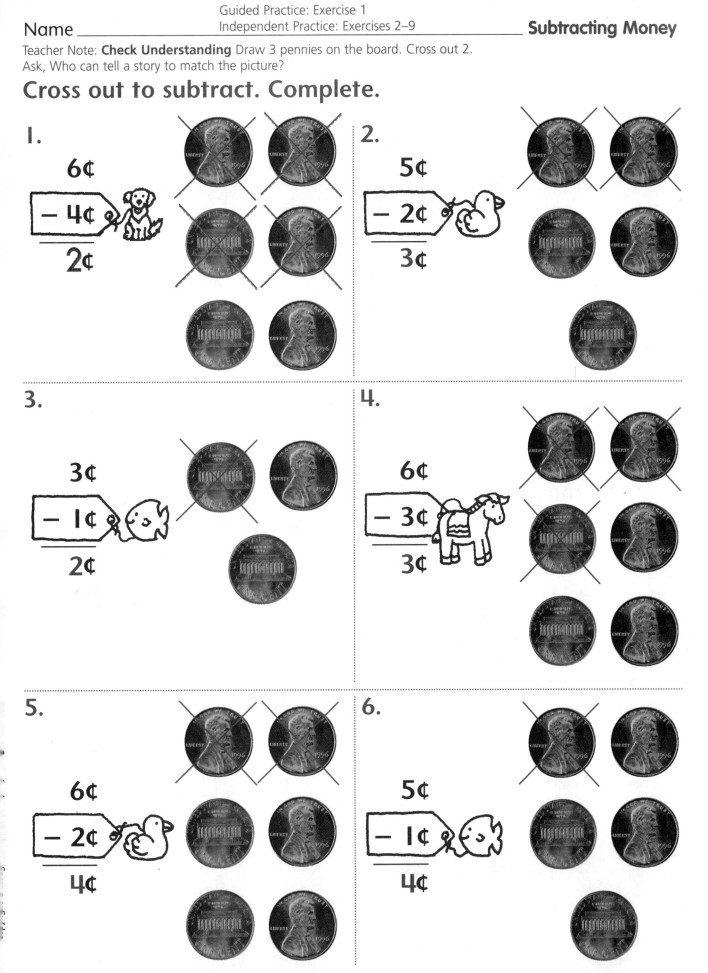

1.

6¢
− 4¢
2¢

2.

5¢
− 2¢
3¢

3.

3¢
− 1¢
2¢

4.

6¢
− 3¢
3¢

5.

6¢
− 2¢
4¢

6.

5¢
− 1¢
4¢

Cross out to subtract. Complete.

7.

6¢

− 1¢

5¢

8.

6¢

− 6¢

0¢

Solve.

9. You have **2** pennies.

How many more do you need to buy | 4¢ | ?

___2___ more pennies

Teacher Note: **Closing the Lesson** Draw 4 pennies with 1 crossed out. Ask, What number sentence goes with the picture?

✓ Quick Check

How many more ●?

1. ● ● ● ●
| | | |
○ ○ ○ | 1 | more

Cross out to subtract.
Complete.

3.

Solve.

2. 6
    − 4
    ┌───┐
    │ 2 │
    └───┘

    3
  − 1
  ┌───┐
  │ 2 │
  └───┘

Item	Error Analysis
1	**Common Error:** Children write the total number of black circles. **Reteach** Copymaster 29, p. 99
2	**Common Error:** Children make errors in subtracting from numbers through 6. **Reteach** Copymaster 30, p. 100
3	**Common Error:** Children do not cross out the correct number of pennies. **Reteach** Copymaster 31, p. 101

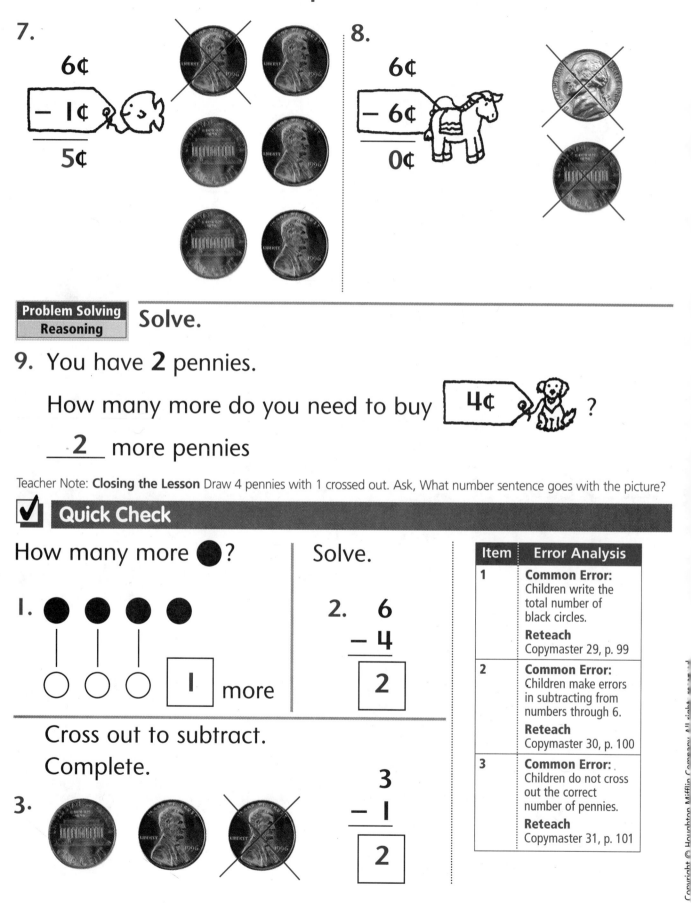

Name _____

Solve. (4A)

1.
```
    2
  - 1
  ___
    1
```

2.
```
    5
  - 2
  ___
    3
```

3.
```
    6
  - 4
  ___
    2
```

4.
```
    5
  - 0
  ___
    5
```

5. 4 – 4 = __0__

6. 6 – 2 = __4__

Cross out to subtract. Complete. (4B)

7.
```
    4¢
  - 1¢
  ____
    3¢
```

8.
```
    6¢
  - 5¢
  ____
    1¢
```

Problem Solving Reasoning

Ring the number sentence that matches the pictures. (4C)

9.

3 – 1 = 2

(4 – 1 = 3)

Write a number sentence for the picture. (4C)

10.

4 − 2 = 2

11.

6 − 6 = 0

Name _____

★ **Test Prep**

1 Which picture shows the car on the right side of the plane?
Mark the space under your answer. (1C)

●　　　　　　　○　　　　　　　○

2 Which figure most likely comes next? Mark the space under your answer. (1C)

○　　　　●　　　　○

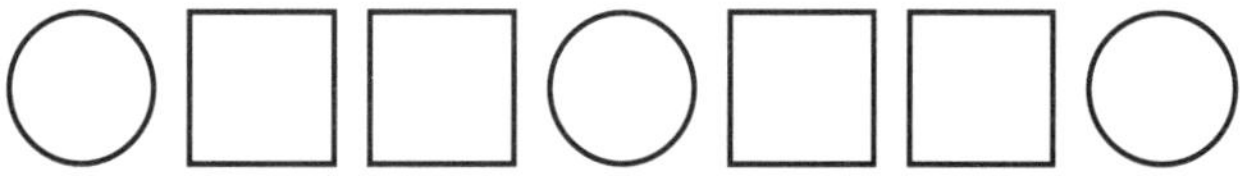

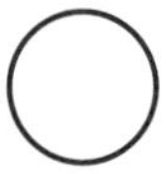

3 How many mittens are in the picture? Mark the space under your answer. (2B)

6　　　　8　　　　9
○　　　　○　　　　●

4 Which symbol belongs in the circle to make the sentence true? Mark the space under your answer. (2E)

6 ○ 9

<　　　　<　　　　=
●　　　　○　　　　○

5 How much is 4 + 2? Mark the space under your answer. (3A)

4 + 2 = □

2　　　　4　　　　6
○　　　　○　　　　●

6 How much is 5 minus 1? Mark the space under your answer. (4A)

5
− 1
□

4　　　　1　　　　3
●　　　　○　　　　○

112 (one hundred twelve)

Unit 4 • Cumulative Review

UNIT 5 • TABLE OF CONTENTS

Addition and Subtraction Facts through 6

UNIT 5 • TABLE OF CONTENTS

Dear Family,

During the next few weeks our math class will be learning and practicing addition and subtraction facts through 6.

You can expect to see homework that provides practice with addition and subtraction facts.

As we learn about related facts and fact families you may wish to keep the following sample as a guide.

Related Facts

$$3 + 1 = 4 \qquad 4 - 1 = 3$$

Fact Family

$$\begin{array}{r} 4 \\ + 2 \\ \hline 6 \end{array} \qquad \begin{array}{r} 2 \\ + 4 \\ \hline 6 \end{array} \qquad \begin{array}{r} 6 \\ - 2 \\ \hline 4 \end{array} \qquad \begin{array}{r} 6 \\ - 4 \\ \hline 2 \end{array}$$

Knowing addition facts can help children learn the related subtraction facts.

Sincerely,

Name _____

Teacher Note: **Check Understanding** Ask, How are addition and subtraction related?

Add or subtract.

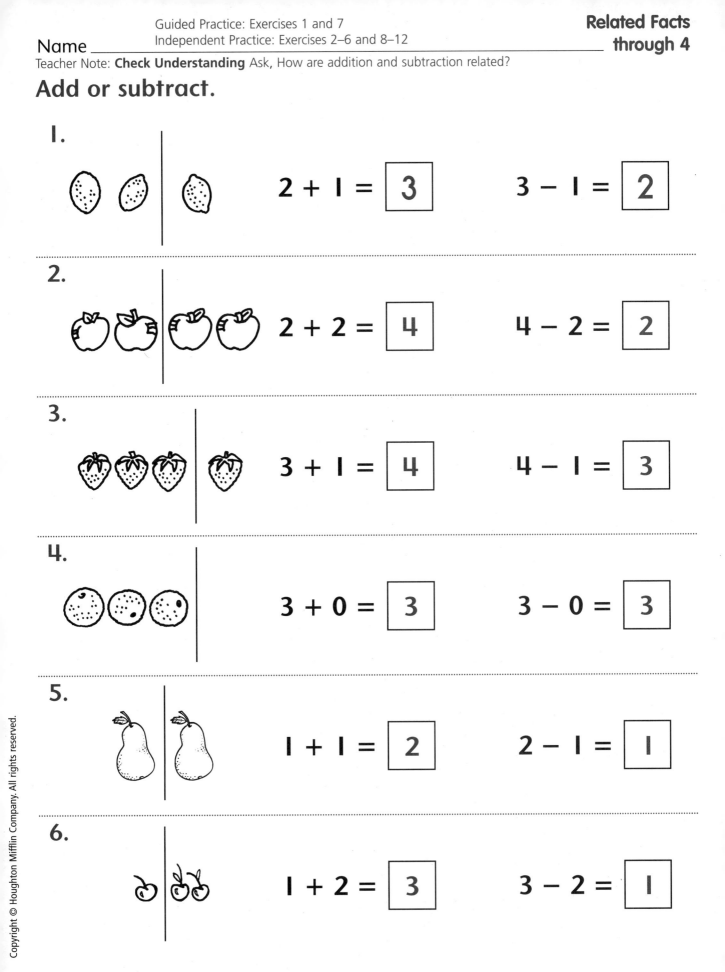

1.
$2 + 1 = \boxed{3}$ $3 - 1 = \boxed{2}$

2.
$2 + 2 = \boxed{4}$ $4 - 2 = \boxed{2}$

3.
$3 + 1 = \boxed{4}$ $4 - 1 = \boxed{3}$

4.
$3 + 0 = \boxed{3}$ $3 - 0 = \boxed{3}$

5.
$1 + 1 = \boxed{2}$ $2 - 1 = \boxed{1}$

6.
$1 + 2 = \boxed{3}$ $3 - 2 = \boxed{1}$

Unit 5 • Lesson 1

Add or subtract.

7.

3
+ 1
―――
4

4
− 1
―――
3

8.

3
+ 0
―――
3

3
− 0
―――
3

Practice your facts.

9.

1
+ 2
―――
3

3
− 1
―――
2

1
+ 3
―――
4

0
+ 4
―――
4

4
− 0
―――
4

10.

1
+ 1
―――
2

2
− 1
―――
1

1
+ 3
―――
4

4
− 3
―――
1

3
− 2
―――
1

**Problem Solving
Reasoning**

11. Which subtraction fact do you know if you know
2 + 1 = 3? <u>3 – 1 = 2 or 3 – 2 = 1</u>

Teacher Note: **Closing the Lesson** Say, 3 birds are in a tree. 1 more bird comes. Now there are 4.
Ask, Who can tell a related subtraction story?

★ **Test Prep**

Which number correctly completes the number sentence?
Mark the space under your answer.

12

3 − 1 = ☐

4
○

3
○

2
●

Unit 5 • Lesson 1

Name _____

Teacher Note: **Check Understanding** Ask, Is there any number sentence you can act out with just one counter?

Complete the fact family.

1.

$1 + 3 = \boxed{4}$

$3 + 1 = \boxed{4}$

$4 - 1 = \boxed{3}$

$4 - 3 = \boxed{1}$

2.

$4 + 0 = \boxed{4}$

$0 + 4 = \boxed{4}$

$4 - 0 = \boxed{4}$

$4 - 4 = \boxed{0}$

3.

$2 + 2 = \boxed{4}$

$4 - 2 = \boxed{2}$

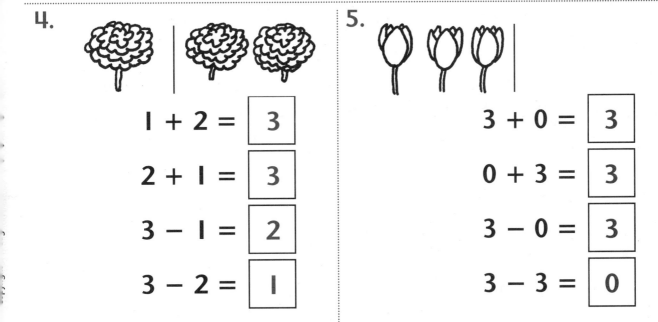

4.

$1 + 2 = \boxed{3}$

$2 + 1 = \boxed{3}$

$3 - 1 = \boxed{2}$

$3 - 2 = \boxed{1}$

5.

$3 + 0 = \boxed{3}$

$0 + 3 = \boxed{3}$

$3 - 0 = \boxed{3}$

$3 - 3 = \boxed{0}$

Complete the fact family.

6.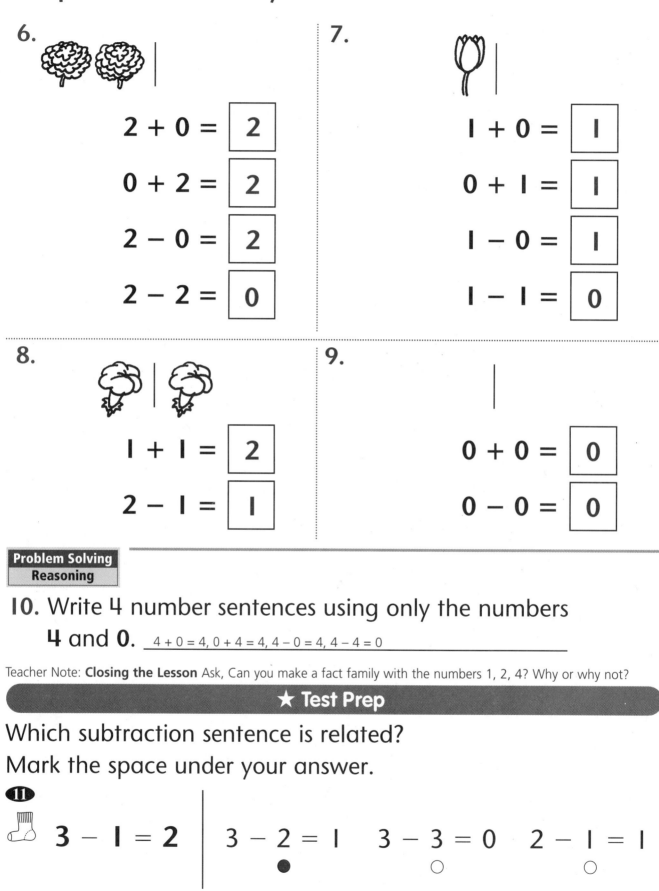

$2 + 0 = \boxed{2}$

$0 + 2 = \boxed{2}$

$2 - 0 = \boxed{2}$

$2 - 2 = \boxed{0}$

7.

$1 + 0 = \boxed{1}$

$0 + 1 = \boxed{1}$

$1 - 0 = \boxed{1}$

$1 - 1 = \boxed{0}$

8.

$1 + 1 = \boxed{2}$

$2 - 1 = \boxed{1}$

9.

$0 + 0 = \boxed{0}$

$0 - 0 = \boxed{0}$

Problem Solving Reasoning

10. Write 4 number sentences using only the numbers 4 and 0. $\underline{4 + 0 = 4, \ 0 + 4 = 4, \ 4 - 0 = 4, \ 4 - 4 = 0}$

Teacher Note: **Closing the Lesson** Ask, Can you make a fact family with the numbers 1, 2, 4? Why or why not?

★ Test Prep

Which subtraction sentence is related?

Mark the space under your answer.

11

$3 - 1 = 2$ | $3 - 2 = 1$ ● $3 - 3 = 0$ ○ $2 - 1 = 1$ ○

118 (one hundred eighteen)

Unit 5 • Lesson 2

Name _____

Teacher Note: **Check Understanding** Ask, How are 1, 3, and 4 related?

Look at the pictures.
Write the fact family.

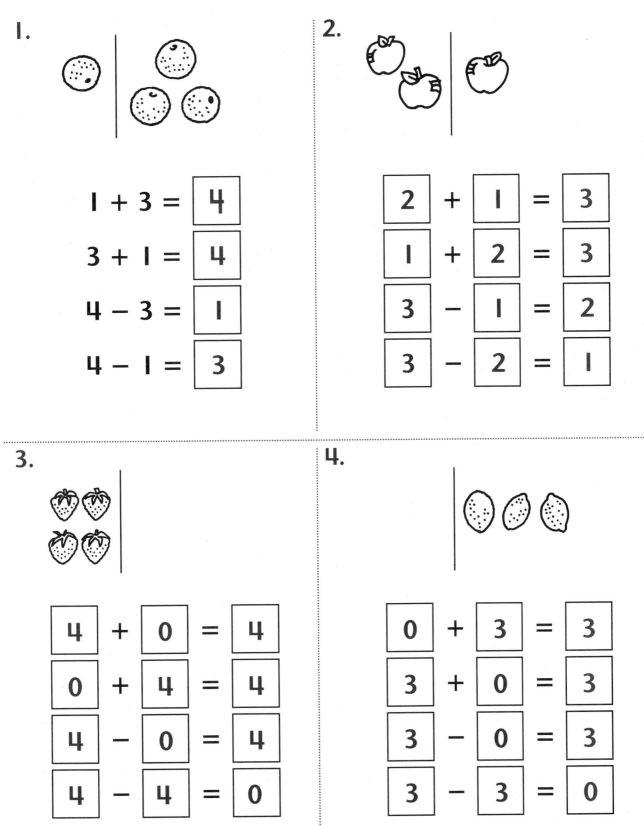

1.

$1 + 3 = \boxed{4}$

$3 + 1 = \boxed{4}$

$4 - 3 = \boxed{1}$

$4 - 1 = \boxed{3}$

2.

$\boxed{2} + \boxed{1} = \boxed{3}$

$\boxed{1} + \boxed{2} = \boxed{3}$

$\boxed{3} - \boxed{1} = \boxed{2}$

$\boxed{3} - \boxed{2} = \boxed{1}$

3.

$\boxed{4} + \boxed{0} = \boxed{4}$

$\boxed{0} + \boxed{4} = \boxed{4}$

$\boxed{4} - \boxed{0} = \boxed{4}$

$\boxed{4} - \boxed{4} = \boxed{0}$

4.

$\boxed{0} + \boxed{3} = \boxed{3}$

$\boxed{3} + \boxed{0} = \boxed{3}$

$\boxed{3} - \boxed{0} = \boxed{3}$

$\boxed{3} - \boxed{3} = \boxed{0}$

Complete.

5.

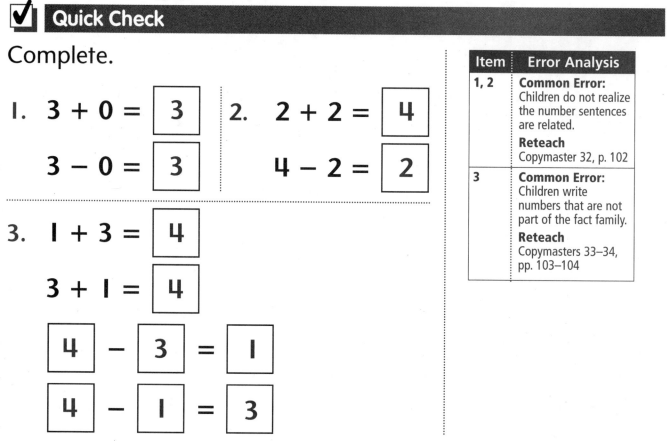

```
    1        2
  + 2      + 1
  ───      ───
    3        3

    3        3
  − 1      − 2
  ───      ───
    2        1
```

6.

```
    4        0
  + 0      + 4
  ───      ───
    4        4

    4        4
  − 0      − 4
  ───      ───
    4        0
```

Problem Solving
Reasoning

7. How are the fact families for **0 + 0**; **1 + 1**; and **2 + 2** alike? How are they different?

There are only 2 facts in each family. Their sums and differences are different.

Teacher Note: **Closing the Lesson** Ask, What is the family of facts for 3 and 0?

✓ Quick Check

Complete.

1. $3 + 0 = \boxed{3}$

   $3 - 0 = \boxed{3}$

2. $2 + 2 = \boxed{4}$

   $4 - 2 = \boxed{2}$

3. $1 + 3 = \boxed{4}$

   $3 + 1 = \boxed{4}$

   $\boxed{4} - \boxed{3} = \boxed{1}$

   $\boxed{4} - \boxed{1} = \boxed{3}$

Item	Error Analysis
1, 2	**Common Error:** Children do not realize the number sentences are related. **Reteach** Copymaster 32, p. 102
3	**Common Error:** Children write numbers that are not part of the fact family. **Reteach** Copymasters 33–34, pp. 103–104

120 (one hundred twenty)

Unit 5 • Lesson 3

Guided Practice: Model Problem
Independent Practice: Problems 1–3

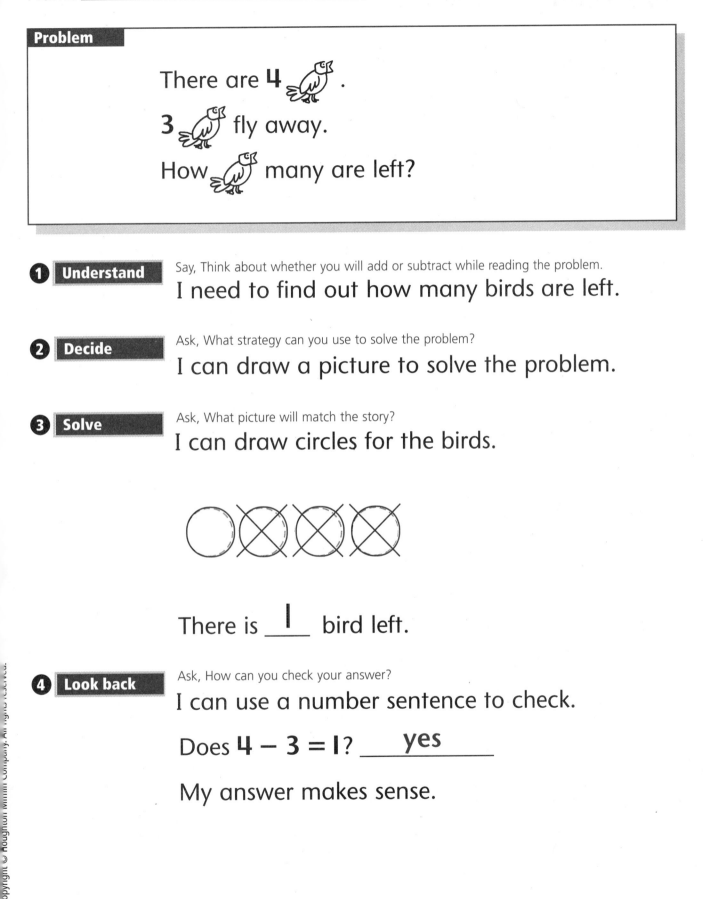

Problem

There are 4 🐦.

3 🐦 fly away.

How 🐦 many are left?

1 Understand

Say, Think about whether you will add or subtract while reading the problem.

I need to find out how many birds are left.

2 Decide

Ask, What strategy can you use to solve the problem?

I can draw a picture to solve the problem.

3 Solve

Ask, What picture will match the story?

I can draw circles for the birds.

There is __1__ bird left.

4 Look back

Ask, How can you check your answer?

I can use a number sentence to check.

Does 4 − 3 = 1? _____yes_____

My answer makes sense.

Draw a picture to solve.

1. There are 2 🐦 in a 🌲.

   3 more 🐦 fly onto the 🌲.

   How many 🐦 in all?

   __5__ 🐦

2. There are 3 🐦 in a 🌲.

   1 🐦 flies away.

   How many 🐦 are there now?

   __2__ 🐦

Tell a story to match the number sentence.
Draw a picture.

3. 2 + 4 = 6

○○ ○○○○

Teacher Note: **Closing the Lesson** Ask, How can you check that your answer to problem 3 is correct?

Unit 5 • Lesson 4

Guided Practice: Exercise 1
Independent Practice: Exercises 2–12

Teacher Note: **Check Understanding** Ask, How do you write a related subtraction sentence for 5 + 1 = 6?

Add or subtract.

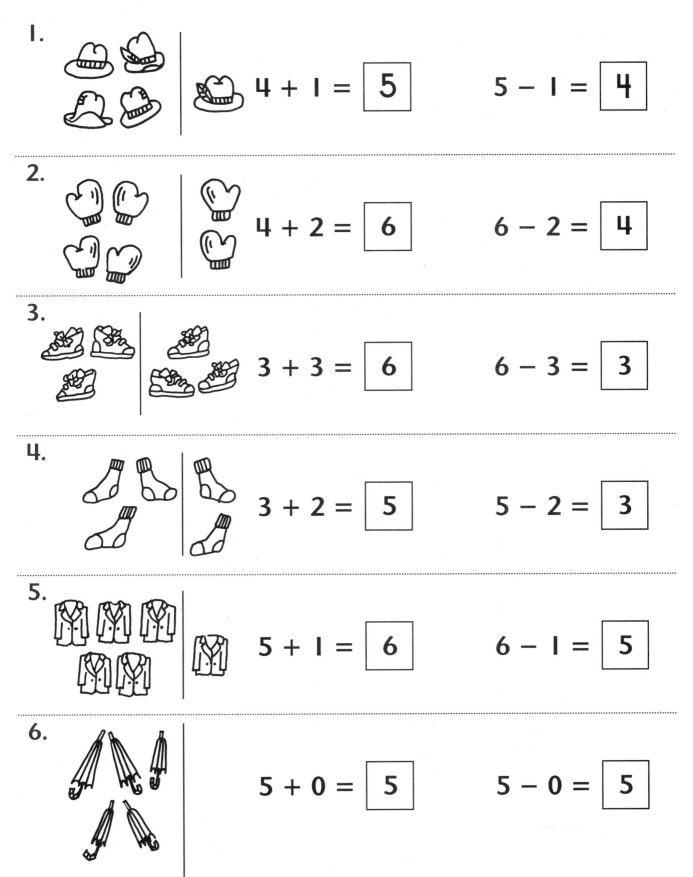

1.
$4 + 1 = \boxed{5}$ $5 - 1 = \boxed{4}$

2.
$4 + 2 = \boxed{6}$ $6 - 2 = \boxed{4}$

3.
$3 + 3 = \boxed{6}$ $6 - 3 = \boxed{3}$

4.
$3 + 2 = \boxed{5}$ $5 - 2 = \boxed{3}$

5.
$5 + 1 = \boxed{6}$ $6 - 1 = \boxed{5}$

6.
$5 + 0 = \boxed{5}$ $5 - 0 = \boxed{5}$

Unit 5 • Lesson 5   (one hundred twenty-three) 123

Add or subtract.

7.

$$\begin{array}{r} 2 \\ +\ 4 \\ \hline 6 \end{array} \quad \begin{array}{r} 6 \\ -\ 4 \\ \hline 2 \end{array}$$

8.

$$\begin{array}{r} 1 \\ +\ 5 \\ \hline 6 \end{array} \quad \begin{array}{r} 6 \\ -\ 5 \\ \hline 1 \end{array}$$

Practice your facts.

9.

$$\begin{array}{r} 4 \\ -\ 1 \\ \hline 3 \end{array} \quad \begin{array}{r} 3 \\ +\ 1 \\ \hline 4 \end{array} \quad \begin{array}{r} 6 \\ -\ 5 \\ \hline 1 \end{array} \quad \begin{array}{r} 5 \\ +\ 1 \\ \hline 6 \end{array} \quad \begin{array}{r} 5 \\ -\ 5 \\ \hline 0 \end{array}$$

10.

$$\begin{array}{r} 2 \\ +\ 1 \\ \hline 3 \end{array} \quad \begin{array}{r} 3 \\ -\ 1 \\ \hline 2 \end{array} \quad \begin{array}{r} 3 \\ +\ 2 \\ \hline 5 \end{array} \quad \begin{array}{r} 5 \\ -\ 2 \\ \hline 3 \end{array} \quad \begin{array}{r} 5 \\ -\ 0 \\ \hline 5 \end{array}$$

Problem Solving
Reasoning

11. Which addition fact do you know if you know
$$6 - 5 = 1 ? \quad \underline{5 + 1 = 6 \text{ or } 1 + 5 = 6}$$

Teacher Note: **Closing the Lesson** Say, 4 frogs are in a pond. 2 more frogs go into the pond. Now there are 6. Ask, Who can tell a related subtraction story?

★ Test Prep

Which number correctly completes the number sentence?
Mark the space under your answer.

12

$$5 - 3 = \square$$

1	2	3
○	●	○

Guided Practice: Exercise 1
Independent Practice: Exercises 2–10

**Fact Families
for 5 and 6**

Teacher Note: **Check Understanding** Ask, How are the numbers 1, 4, and 5 related?

Complete the fact family.

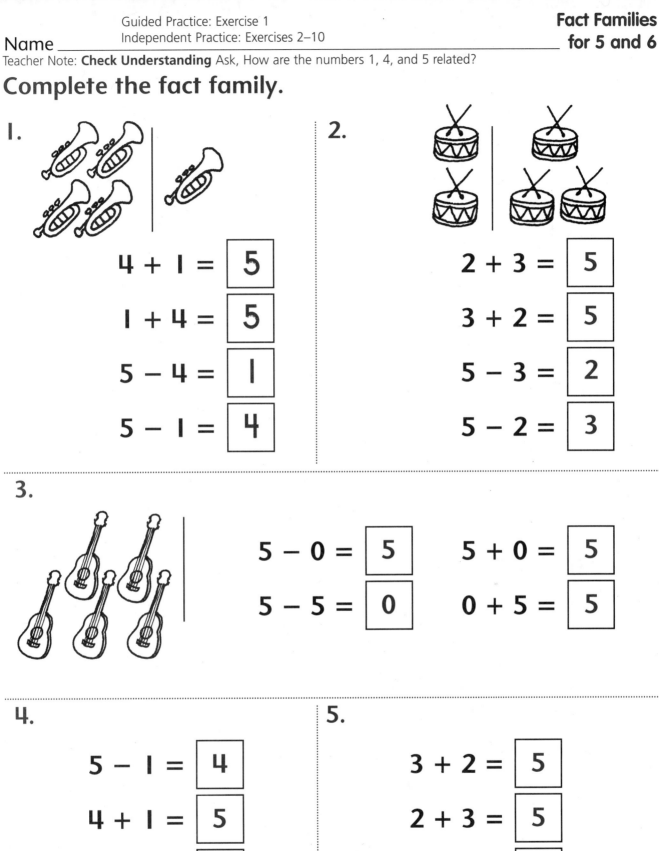

1.

4 + 1 = 5
1 + 4 = 5
5 − 4 = 1
5 − 1 = 4

2.

2 + 3 = 5
3 + 2 = 5
5 − 3 = 2
5 − 2 = 3

3.

5 − 0 = 5   5 + 0 = 5
5 − 5 = 0   0 + 5 = 5

4.

5 − 1 = 4
4 + 1 = 5
1 + 4 = 5
5 − 4 = 1

5.

3 + 2 = 5
2 + 3 = 5
5 − 3 = 2
5 − 2 = 3

Complete the fact family.

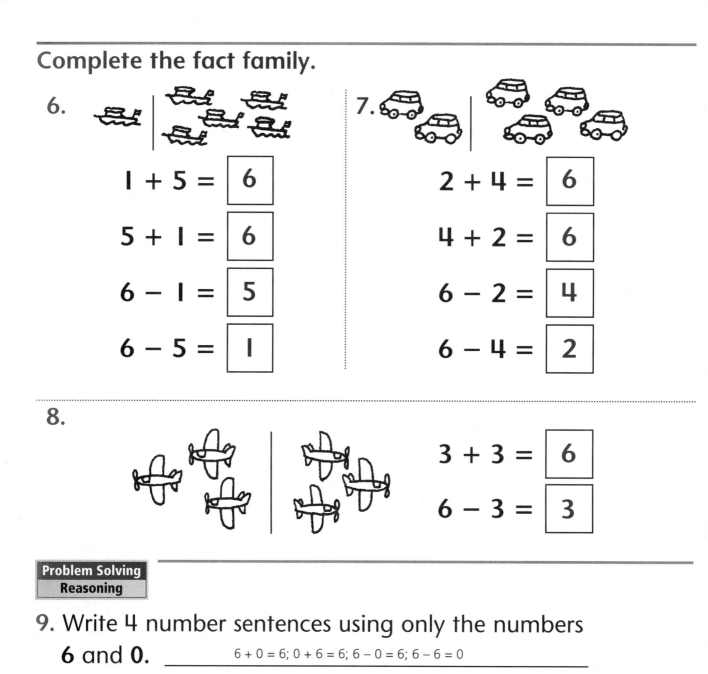

6.

$1 + 5 = \boxed{6}$

$5 + 1 = \boxed{6}$

$6 - 1 = \boxed{5}$

$6 - 5 = \boxed{1}$

7.

$2 + 4 = \boxed{6}$

$4 + 2 = \boxed{6}$

$6 - 2 = \boxed{4}$

$6 - 4 = \boxed{2}$

8.

$3 + 3 = \boxed{6}$

$6 - 3 = \boxed{3}$

Problem Solving Reasoning

9. Write 4 number sentences using only the numbers
6 and **0.** _____ $6 + 0 = 6; 0 + 6 = 6; 6 - 0 = 6; 6 - 6 = 0$ _____

_____

Teacher Note: **Closing the Lesson** Write the following on the chalkboard: 1, 2, 3, 5. Ask, Which 3 numbers can you use to make a fact family?

★ Test Prep

Which addition sentence is related?
Mark the space under your answer.

10

$4 + 2 = 6$ | $5 + 1 = 6$ $2 + 4 = 6$ $2 + 3 = 5$
○ ● ○

Teacher Note: **Check Understanding** Say, I had 4 counters. Now I have 2. Did I add or subtract?

$$3 \;(+)\; 1 = 4 \qquad\qquad 3 \;(-)\; 1 = 2$$

Make true sentences.
Write + or −.

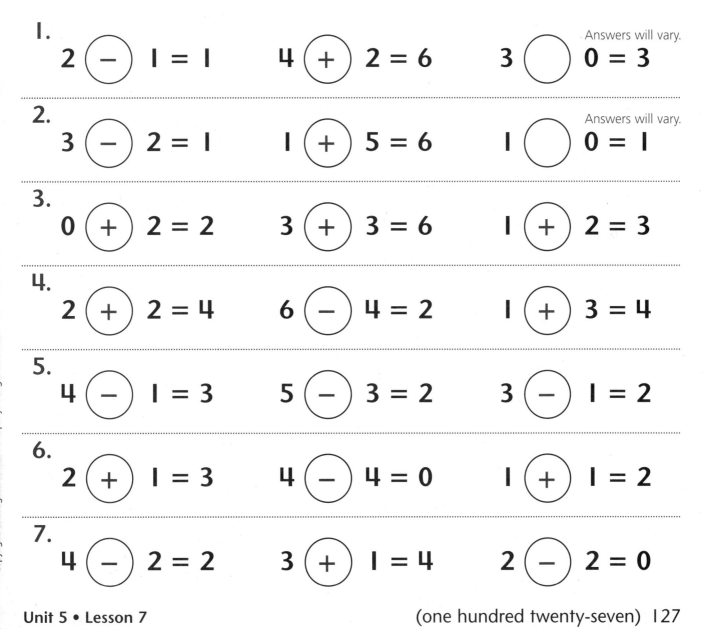

1.
$$2 \;(-)\; 1 = 1 \qquad 4 \;(+)\; 2 = 6 \qquad 3 \;()\; 0 = 3$$
Answers will vary.

2.
$$3 \;(-)\; 2 = 1 \qquad 1 \;(+)\; 5 = 6 \qquad 1 \;()\; 0 = 1$$
Answers will vary.

3.
$$0 \;(+)\; 2 = 2 \qquad 3 \;(+)\; 3 = 6 \qquad 1 \;(+)\; 2 = 3$$

4.
$$2 \;(+)\; 2 = 4 \qquad 6 \;(-)\; 4 = 2 \qquad 1 \;(+)\; 3 = 4$$

5.
$$4 \;(-)\; 1 = 3 \qquad 5 \;(-)\; 3 = 2 \qquad 3 \;(-)\; 1 = 2$$

6.
$$2 \;(+)\; 1 = 3 \qquad 4 \;(-)\; 4 = 0 \qquad 1 \;(+)\; 1 = 2$$

7.
$$4 \;(-)\; 2 = 2 \qquad 3 \;(+)\; 1 = 4 \qquad 2 \;(-)\; 2 = 0$$

Use the pictures to make the sentence true.
Write + or −.

8. $3 \ominus 2 = 1$

9. $2 \oplus 2 = 4$

10. How do you decide whether to put a + or − in a number sentence to make it true?_____

Answers will vary. Possible answer: I try both and see which one makes the sentence true.

Teacher Note: **Closing the Lesson** Have partners make up their own number sentence with a missing sign and exchange and solve them.

✓ Quick Check

Complete with related facts.

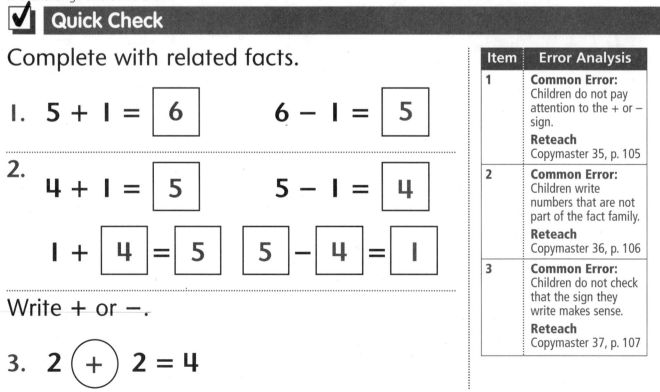

1. $5 + 1 = \boxed{6}$ $\qquad$ $6 - 1 = \boxed{5}$

2.
$4 + 1 = \boxed{5}$ $\qquad$ $5 - 1 = \boxed{4}$

$1 + \boxed{4} = 5$ $\qquad$ $5 - \boxed{4} = \boxed{1}$

Write + or −.

3. $2 \oplus 2 = 4$

Item	Error Analysis
1	**Common Error:** Children do not pay attention to the + or − sign. **Reteach** Copymaster 35, p. 105
2	**Common Error:** Children write numbers that are not part of the fact family. **Reteach** Copymaster 36, p. 106
3	**Common Error:** Children do not check that the sign they write makes sense. **Reteach** Copymaster 37, p. 107

Teacher Note: **Check Understanding** Ask, How do you know the other number sentence in problem 1 is not correct?

Ring the correct card.

Problem Solving Plan
1. Understand   2. Decide   3. Solve   4. Look back

Think Do you add or subtract?

1. There are 4  .

2  walk away.

How many are left?

4
+ 2
6

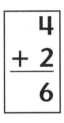

4
− 2
2

2. There are 4  .

1  joins them.

How many in all?

4
− 1
3

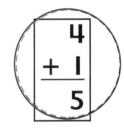

4
+ 1
5

3.

I have **3** 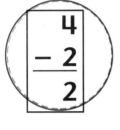 .

I find **2** 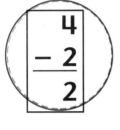 .

How many in all?

3
− 2
1

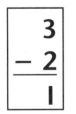

3
+ 2
5

4.

I have **3** 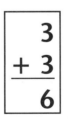 .

3 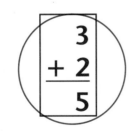 hop away.

How many are left?

3
+ 3
6

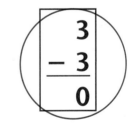

3
− 3
0

Solve.

Think Should I add or subtract?

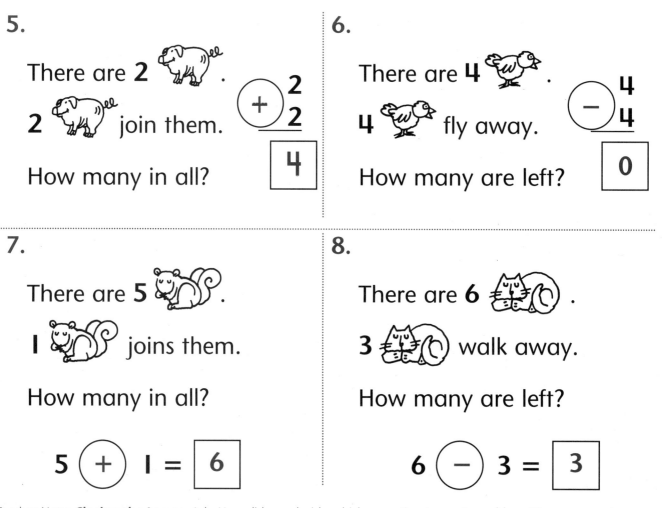

5.

There are 2 🐷.

2 🐷 join them.

How many in all?

$+\begin{matrix} 2 \\ 2 \end{matrix}$

4

6.

There are 4 🐦.

4 🐦 fly away.

How many are left?

$-\begin{matrix} 4 \\ 4 \end{matrix}$

0

7.

There are 5 🐿.

1 🐿 joins them.

How many in all?

5 (+) 1 = 6

8.

There are 6 🐱.

3 🐱 walk away.

How many are left?

6 (−) 3 = 3

Teacher Note: **Closing the Lesson** Ask, How did you decide which operation to use in problem 8?

Extend Your Thinking

Complete the problem and number sentence so that they match.   Answers will vary. Possible answer:

9.

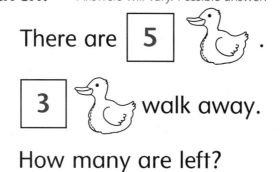

There are 5 🦆.

3 🦆 walk away.

How many are left?

5 (−) 3 = 2

Guided Practice: Exercises 1 and 7
Independent Practice: Exercises 2–6 and 8–11

Teacher Note: **Check Understanding** Ask, If I have money and spend some, do I add or subtract to find out how much I have left?

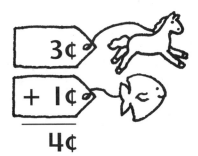

3¢
+ 1¢
___
4¢

How much for both?

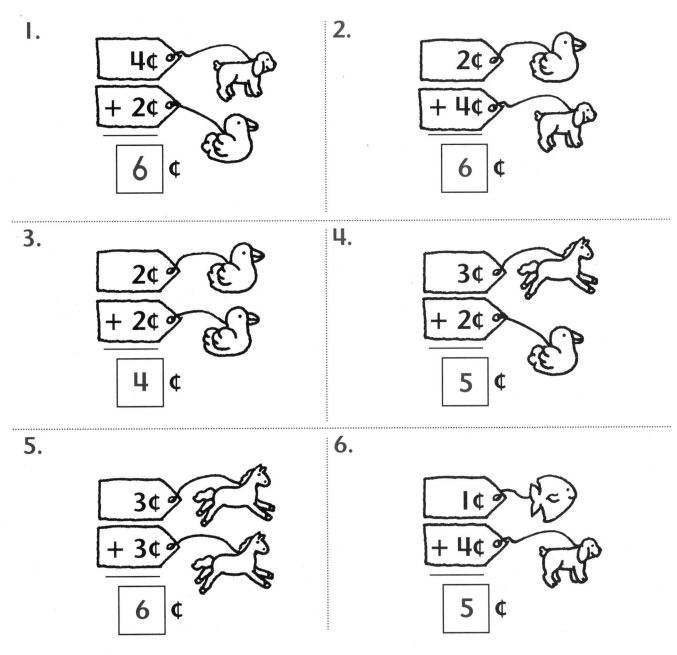

1.
4¢
+ 2¢
___
6 ¢

2.
2¢
+ 4¢
___
6 ¢

3.
2¢
+ 2¢
___
4 ¢

4.
3¢
+ 2¢
___
5 ¢

5.
3¢
+ 3¢
___
6 ¢

6.
1¢
+ 4¢
___
5 ¢

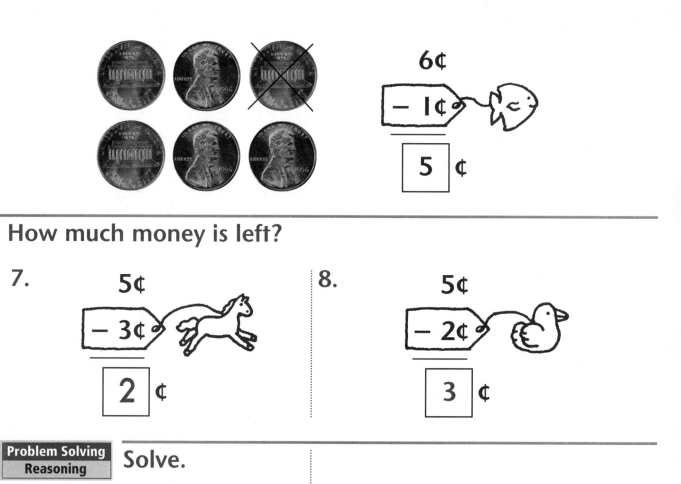

6¢

$- 1¢$

5 ¢

How much money is left?

7.

5¢

$- 3¢$

2 ¢

8.

5¢

$- 2¢$

3 ¢

Problem Solving Reasoning Solve.

9. You have **3¢.**
You find **2¢** more.
How much money
do you have?

3¢ ⊕ 2¢ = _5_ ¢

10. You have **5¢.**
You spend **1¢.**
How much money
do you have left?

5¢ ⊖ 1¢ = _4_ ¢

Teacher Note: **Closing the Lesson** Ask, How is adding and subtracting money like adding and subtracting numbers? How is it different?

★ Test Prep

Which amount shows how much money is left?
Mark the space under your answer.

11

$6¢ - 4¢ = \square$

1¢ ○

2¢ ●

3¢ ○

---

132 (one hundred thirty-two)

Unit 5 • Lesson 9

Solve. (5A)

1.	2.	3.	4.	5.
$\begin{array}{r} 6 \\ -\ 4 \\ \hline 2 \end{array}$	$\begin{array}{r} 3 \\ +\ 2 \\ \hline 5 \end{array}$	$\begin{array}{r} 4 \\ -\ 0 \\ \hline 4 \end{array}$	$\begin{array}{r} 2 \\ +\ 2 \\ \hline 4 \end{array}$	$\begin{array}{r} 4 \\ +\ 2 \\ \hline 6 \end{array}$

Complete the fact family. (5B)

6.

$5 + 1 = \boxed{6}$

$1 + \boxed{5} = \boxed{6}$

$\boxed{6} - \boxed{5} = \boxed{1}$

$\boxed{6} - \boxed{1} = \boxed{5}$

7.

$3 + 2 = \boxed{5}$

$2 + \boxed{3} = \boxed{5}$

$\boxed{5} - \boxed{3} = \boxed{2}$

$\boxed{5} - \boxed{2} = \boxed{3}$

Problem Solving Reasoning | ## Draw a picture. Solve. (5C)

8. $4 + 2 = \boxed{6}$

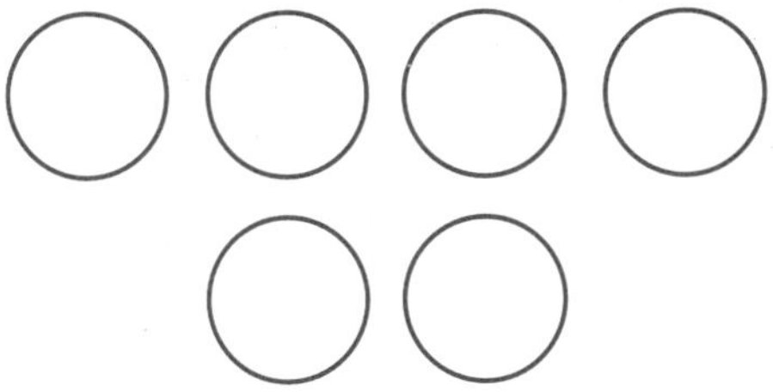

9. $4 - 1 = \boxed{3}$

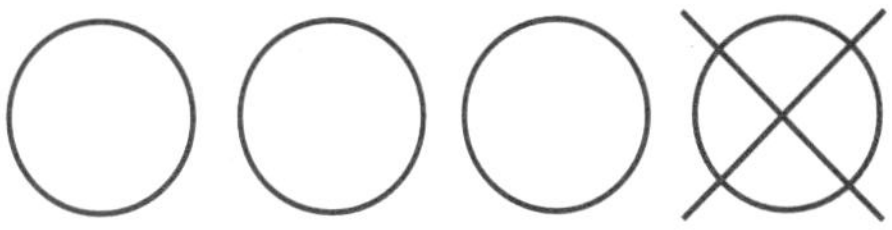

Add or subtract to solve. (5C)

10. There are **5** 🦓 .

2 🦓 walk away.

How many are left?

$5 \ominus 2 = \boxed{3}$

11. There are **3** 🐷 .

2 more 🐷 join them.

How many in all?

$3 \oplus 2 = \boxed{5}$

Name_____

1 How many crayons are in the picture? Mark the space under your answer. **(2B)**

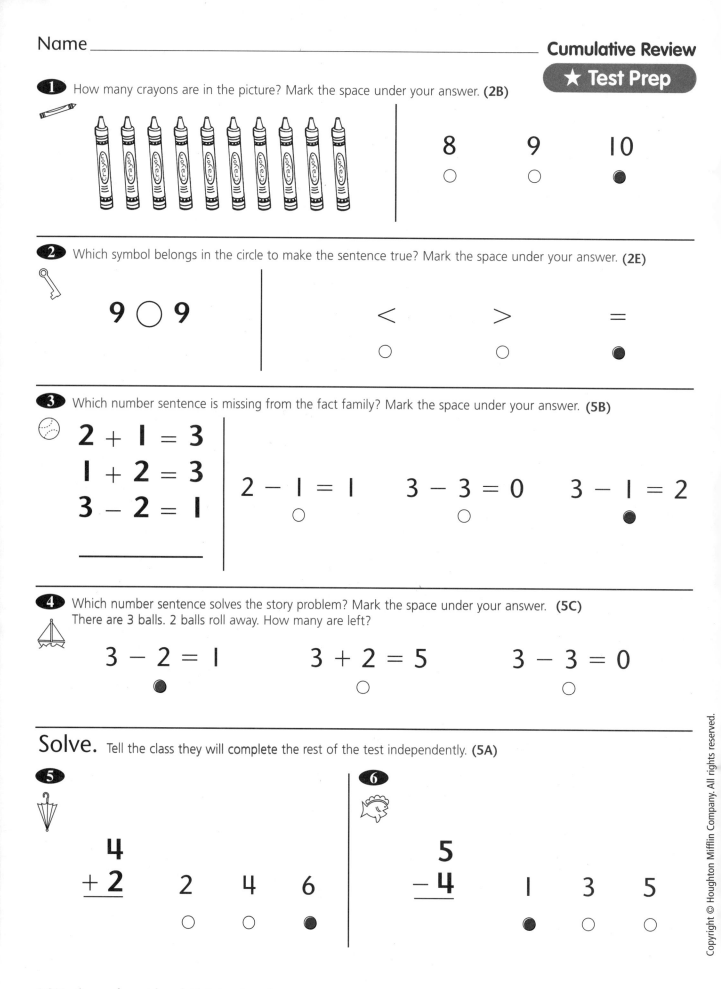

8   9   10
○   ○   ●

2 Which symbol belongs in the circle to make the sentence true? Mark the space under your answer. **(2E)**

9 ○ 9

<   >   =
○   ○   ●

3 Which number sentence is missing from the fact family? Mark the space under your answer. **(5B)**

$2 + 1 = 3$
$1 + 2 = 3$
$3 - 2 = 1$
_____

$2 - 1 = 1$ $3 - 3 = 0$ $3 - 1 = 2$
○   ○   ●

4 Which number sentence solves the story problem? Mark the space under your answer. **(5C)**
There are 3 balls. 2 balls roll away. How many are left?

$3 - 2 = 1$ $3 + 2 = 5$ $3 - 3 = 0$
●   ○   ○

Solve. Tell the class they will **complete** the rest of the test independently. **(5A)**

5

$\begin{array}{r} 4 \\ + 2 \\ \hline \end{array}$ 2   4   6
                    ○   ○   ●

6

$\begin{array}{r} 5 \\ - 4 \\ \hline \end{array}$ 1   3   5
                    ●   ○   ○

134 (one hundred thirty-four)

Unit 5 • Cumulative Review

UNIT 6 • TABLE OF CONTENTS

Addition and Subtraction Facts through 10

Dear Family,

During the next few weeks our math class will be learning and practicing addition and subtraction facts through 10.

You can expect to see homework that provides practice with addition and subtraction facts.

As we learn about related facts and fact families you may wish to keep the following sample as a guide.

We will be using this vocabulary:

fact family the related addition and subtraction facts

addend one of the numbers added in an addition problem

function tables A two-column chart of numbers in which the same number is added to or subtracted from each number in the first column resulting in the numbers in the second column

$$+3$$

1	4
2	5
3	6

Related Facts

$$7 + 3 = 10 \qquad 10 - 3 = 7$$

Fact Family

$$4 + 2 = 6 \qquad 6 - 4 = 2$$
$$2 + 4 = 6 \qquad 6 - 2 = 4$$

Knowing addition facts can help children learn the related subtraction facts.

Sincerely,

Teacher Note: **Check Understanding** Ask, How are 5 + 3 and 8 - 3 related?

$5 + 3 = \boxed{8}$ $8 - 3 = \boxed{5}$

Complete.

1. $6 + 1 = \boxed{7}$ $7 - 1 = \boxed{6}$

2. $5 + 2 = \boxed{7}$ $7 - 2 = \boxed{5}$

3. $4 + 4 = \boxed{8}$ $8 - 4 = \boxed{4}$

4. $2 + 6 = \boxed{8}$ $8 - 6 = \boxed{2}$

5. $7 + 0 = \boxed{7}$ $7 - 0 = \boxed{7}$

6. $0 + 8 = \boxed{8}$ $8 - 8 = \boxed{0}$

Solve.

7.
$$\begin{array}{r} 2 \\ + 6 \\ \hline 8 \end{array}$$

8.
$$\begin{array}{r} 8 \\ - 2 \\ \hline 6 \end{array}$$

9.
$$\begin{array}{r} 1 \\ + 3 \\ \hline 4 \end{array}$$

10.
$$\begin{array}{r} 4 \\ - 3 \\ \hline 1 \end{array}$$

11.
$$\begin{array}{r} 3 \\ + 3 \\ \hline 6 \end{array}$$

12.
$$\begin{array}{r} 6 \\ - 3 \\ \hline 3 \end{array}$$

13.
$$\begin{array}{r} 7 \\ - 5 \\ \hline 2 \end{array}$$

14.
$$\begin{array}{r} 5 \\ + 2 \\ \hline 7 \end{array}$$

Problem Solving Reasoning | **Draw a picture. Solve.** Pictures will vary.

15. There are **7** dishes on a table. **3** dishes fall. How many are left?

⎯⎯**4**⎯⎯ dishes

Teacher Note: **Closing the Lesson** Say, Five ducks are at the pond. Three more join them. Now there are eight. Ask, Who can tell a related subtraction story?

★ **Test Prep**

Which number correctly completes the number sentence? Mark the space under your answer.

16
☆ $3 + 5 = \square$ | 6 ○   2 ○   8 ●

Unit 6 • Lesson 1

Teacher Note: **Check Understanding** Ask, How are the addition facts in a fact family the same? How are they different?

Complete the fact family.

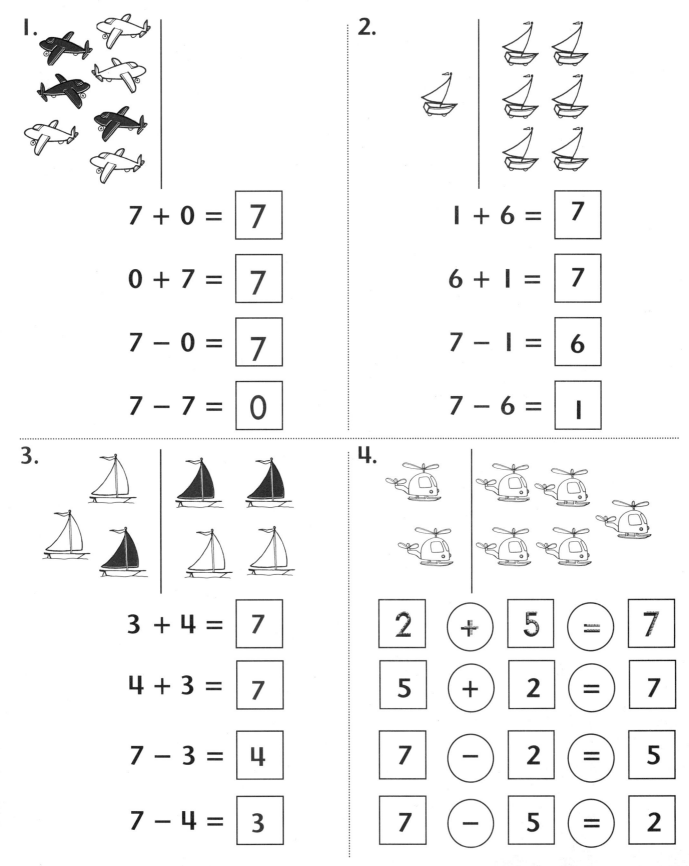

1.

7 + 0 = 7

0 + 7 = 7

7 − 0 = 7

7 − 7 = 0

2.

1 + 6 = 7

6 + 1 = 7

7 − 1 = 6

7 − 6 = 1

3.

3 + 4 = 7

4 + 3 = 7

7 − 3 = 4

7 − 4 = 3

4.

2 + 5 = 7

5 + 2 = 7

7 − 2 = 5

7 − 5 = 2

Unit 6 • Lesson 2

(one hundred thirty-nine) 139

Complete the fact family.

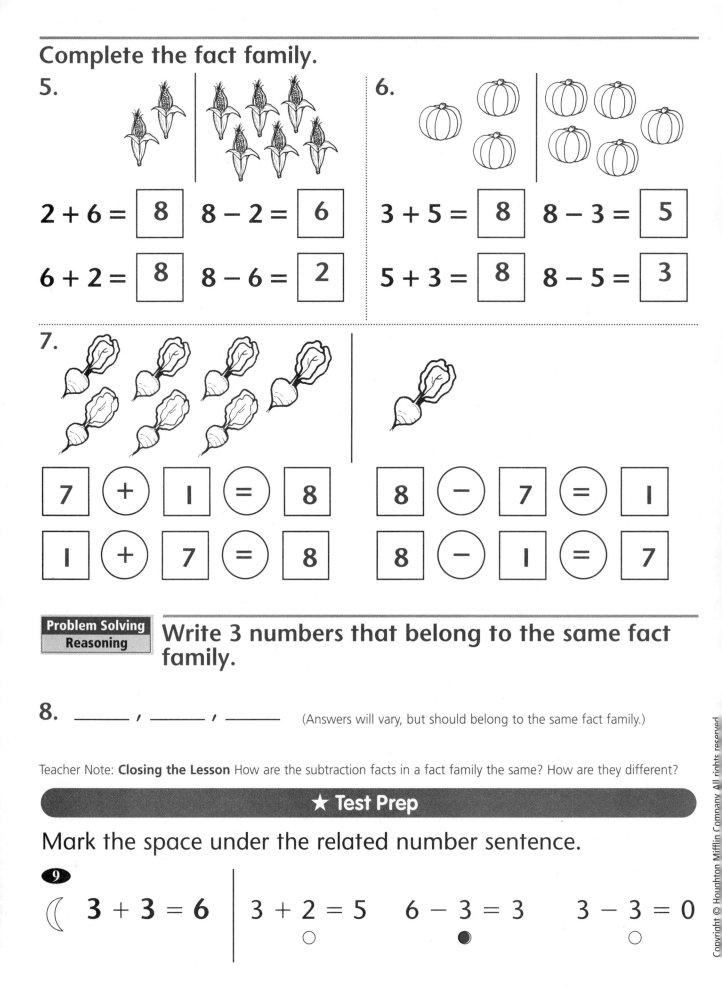

5.

$2 + 6 = \boxed{8}$ $8 - 2 = \boxed{6}$

$6 + 2 = \boxed{8}$ $8 - 6 = \boxed{2}$

6.

$3 + 5 = \boxed{8}$ $8 - 3 = \boxed{5}$

$5 + 3 = \boxed{8}$ $8 - 5 = \boxed{3}$

7.

$\boxed{7} \;(+)\; \boxed{1} \;(=)\; \boxed{8}$ $\boxed{8} \;(-)\; \boxed{7} \;(=)\; \boxed{1}$

$\boxed{1} \;(+)\; \boxed{7} \;(=)\; \boxed{8}$ $\boxed{8} \;(-)\; \boxed{1} \;(=)\; \boxed{7}$

Problem Solving / Reasoning Write 3 numbers that belong to the same fact family.

8. _____ , _____ , _____   (Answers will vary, but should belong to the same fact family.)

Teacher Note: **Closing the Lesson** How are the subtraction facts in a fact family the same? How are they different?

★ Test Prep

Mark the space under the related number sentence.

9

$3 + 3 = 6$ | $3 + 2 = 5$ $6 - 3 = 3$ $3 - 3 = 0$

○   ●   ○

Name _____

Guided Practice: Exercise 1, 6
Independent Practice: Exercises 2–5, 7

**Related Facts
through 10**

Teacher Note: **Check Understanding** Say, 3 + 4 = 7. What is a related subtraction fact?

Add or subtract.

1.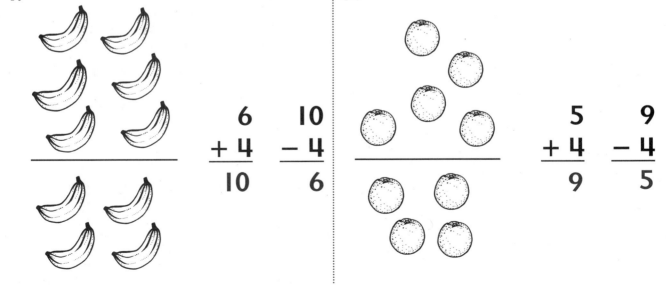

   $8 + 2 = \boxed{10}$ $10 - 2 = \boxed{8}$

2.

   $6 + 3 = \boxed{9}$ $9 - 3 = \boxed{6}$

3.

   $3 + 7 = \boxed{10}$ $10 - 7 = \boxed{3}$

4.

$$\begin{array}{r} 6 \\ +\ 4 \\ \hline 10 \end{array} \qquad \begin{array}{r} 10 \\ -\ 4 \\ \hline 6 \end{array}$$

5.

$$\begin{array}{r} 5 \\ +\ 4 \\ \hline 9 \end{array} \qquad \begin{array}{r} 9 \\ -\ 4 \\ \hline 5 \end{array}$$

Solve.

6. There are **8** dogs.
I dog joins them.
How many dogs
are there in all?

$$8 \; + \; 1 \; = \; 9$$

___9___ dogs

7. There are **9** frogs.
5 hop away.
How many frogs
are left?

$$9 \; - \; 5 \; = \; 4$$

___4___ frogs

Teacher Note: **Closing the Lesson** Ask volunteers to make up story problems for other children to solve.

✓ Quick Check

Write the fact family for the picture.

1.

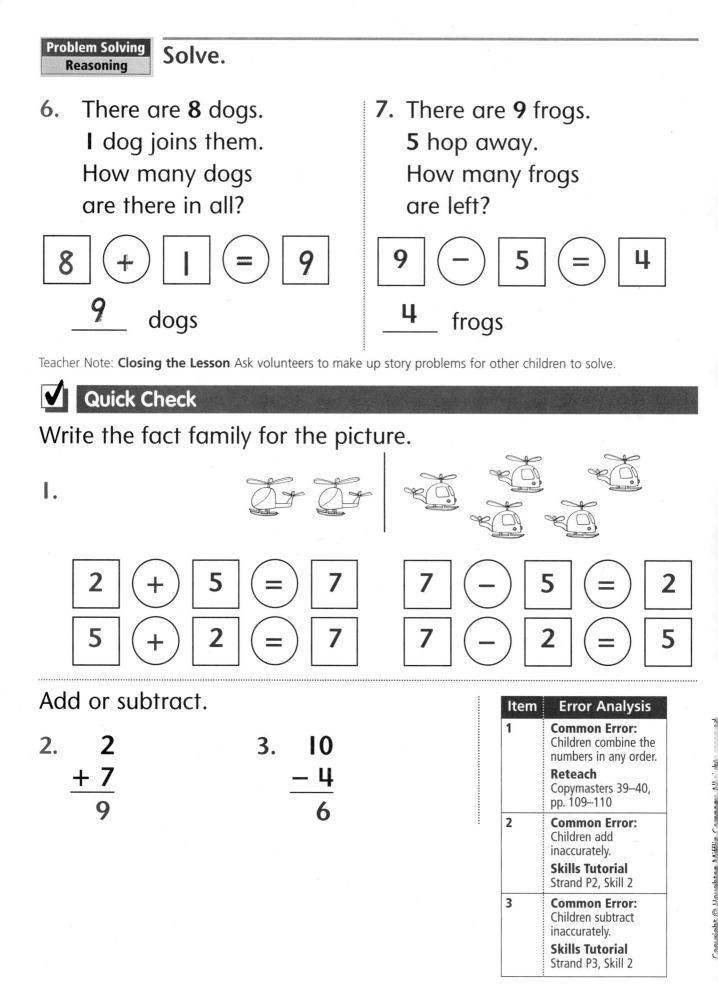

$$2 \; + \; 5 \; = \; 7$$

$$7 \; - \; 5 \; = \; 2$$

$$5 \; + \; 2 \; = \; 7$$

$$7 \; - \; 2 \; = \; 5$$

Add or subtract.

2.
$$\begin{array}{r} 2 \\ + \, 7 \\ \hline 9 \end{array}$$

3.
$$\begin{array}{r} 10 \\ - \, 4 \\ \hline 6 \end{array}$$

Item	Error Analysis
1	**Common Error:** Children combine the numbers in any order. **Reteach** Copymasters 39–40, pp. 109–110
2	**Common Error:** Children add inaccurately. **Skills Tutorial** Strand P2, Skill 2
3	**Common Error:** Children subtract inaccurately. **Skills Tutorial** Strand P3, Skill 2

Teacher Note: **Check Understanding** Ask, What fact family for 10 has only two related facts in the family?

Complete the fact family.

1.

$1 + 8 = \boxed{9}$

$8 + 1 = \boxed{9}$

$9 - 1 = \boxed{8}$

$9 - 8 = \boxed{1}$

2.

$2 + 7 = \boxed{9}$

$7 + 2 = \boxed{9}$

$9 - 2 = \boxed{7}$

$9 - 7 = \boxed{2}$

3.

$3 + 6 = \boxed{9}$

$6 + 3 = \boxed{9}$

$9 - 3 = \boxed{6}$

$9 - 6 = \boxed{3}$

4.

$\boxed{4} \ \bigcirc{+} \ \boxed{5} \ \bigcirc{=} \ \boxed{9}$

$\boxed{5} \ \bigcirc{+} \ \boxed{4} \ \bigcirc{=} \ \boxed{9}$

$\boxed{9} \ \bigcirc{-} \ \boxed{4} \ \bigcirc{=} \ \boxed{5}$

$\boxed{9} \ \bigcirc{-} \ \boxed{5} \ \bigcirc{=} \ \boxed{4}$

Complete the fact family.

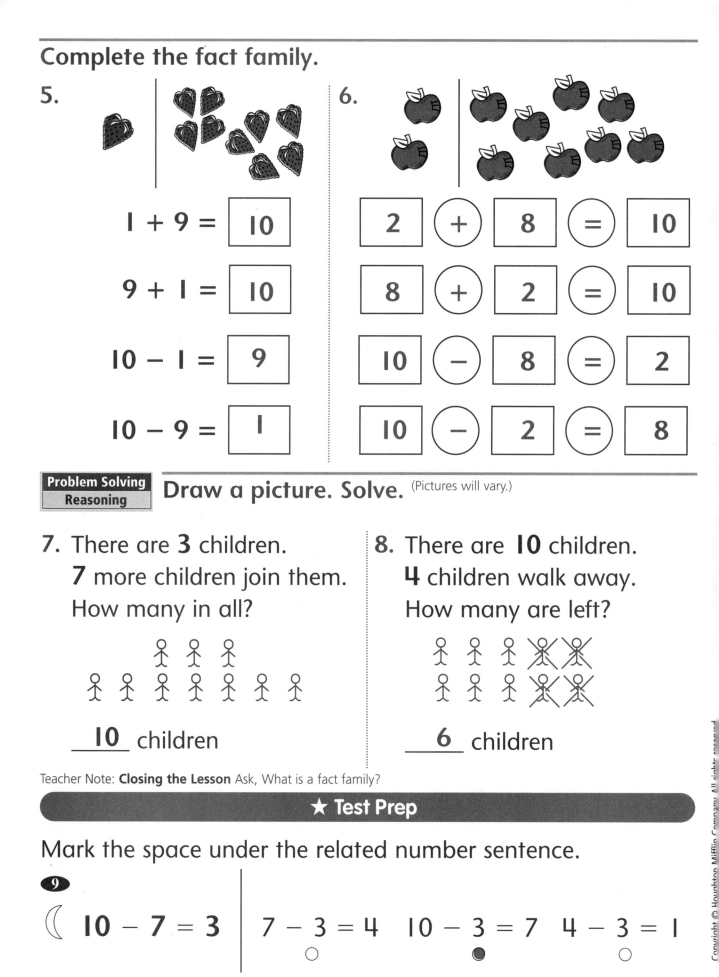

5.

$1 + 9 =$ | 10

$9 + 1 =$ | 10

$10 - 1 =$ | 9

$10 - 9 =$ | 1

6.

2 (+) 8 (=) 10

8 (+) 2 (=) 10

10 (−) 8 (=) 2

10 (−) 2 (=) 8

Draw a picture. Solve. (Pictures will vary.)

7. There are **3** children.
7 more children join them.
How many in all?

___10___ children

8. There are **10** children.
4 children walk away.
How many are left?

___6___ children

Teacher Note: **Closing the Lesson** Ask, What is a fact family?

★ Test Prep

Mark the space under the related number sentence.

9

$10 - 7 = 3$ | $7 - 3 = 4$ $\quad$ $10 - 3 = 7$ $\quad$ $4 - 3 = 1$
$\quad\quad\quad\quad\quad$ ○ $\quad\quad\quad\quad$ ● $\quad\quad\quad\quad$ ○

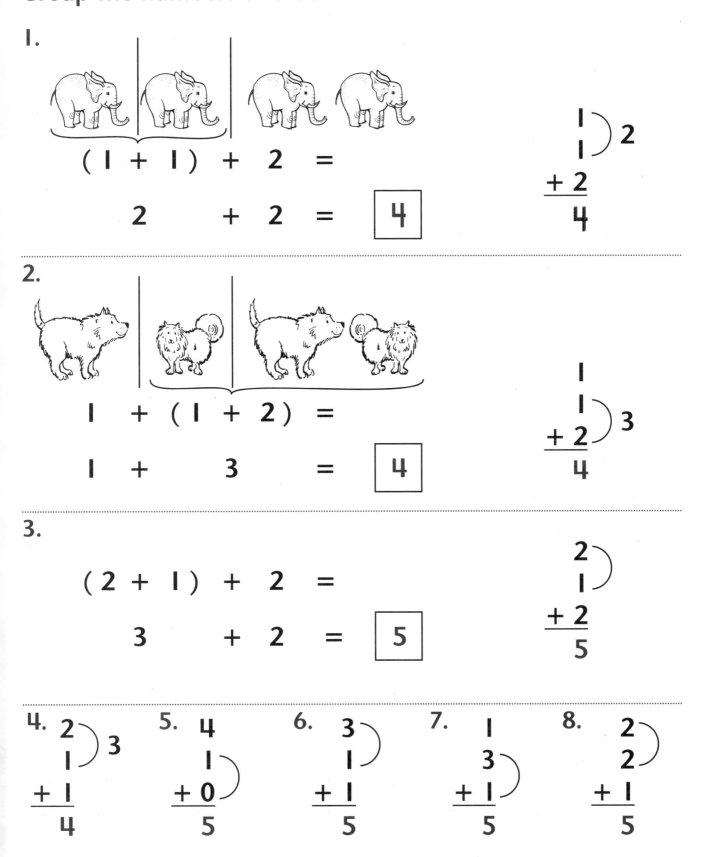

Name _____

Teacher Note: **Check Understanding** Ask, Does it matter which two numbers you add first?

Group the numbers and add.

1.

$(1 + 1) + 2 =$

$2 \quad + \quad 2 \quad = \quad \boxed{4}$

$$\begin{aligned} 1 \\ 1 \end{aligned} \Big) 2 \\ + 2 \\ \hline 4 \end{aligned}$$

2.

$1 + (1 + 2) =$

$1 \quad + \quad 3 \quad = \quad \boxed{4}$

$$\begin{aligned} 1 \\ 1 \\ + 2 \end{aligned} \Big) 3 \\ \hline 4 \end{aligned}$$

3.

$(2 + 1) + 2 =$

$3 \quad + \quad 2 \quad = \quad \boxed{5}$

$$\begin{aligned} 2 \\ 1 \end{aligned} \Big) \\ + 2 \\ \hline 5 \end{aligned}$$

4.
$$\begin{aligned} 2 \\ 1 \end{aligned} \Big) 3 \\ + 1 \\ \hline 4 \end{aligned}$$

5.
$$\begin{aligned} 4 \\ 1 \\ + 0 \end{aligned} \Big) \\ \hline 5 \end{aligned}$$

6.
$$\begin{aligned} 3 \\ 1 \end{aligned} \Big) \\ + 1 \\ \hline 5 \end{aligned}$$

7.
$$\begin{aligned} 1 \\ 3 \\ + 1 \end{aligned} \Big) \\ \hline 5 \end{aligned}$$

8.
$$\begin{aligned} 2 \\ 2 \end{aligned} \Big) \\ + 1 \\ \hline 5 \end{aligned}$$

Unit 6 • Lesson 5

(one hundred forty-five) 145

Find the sum.

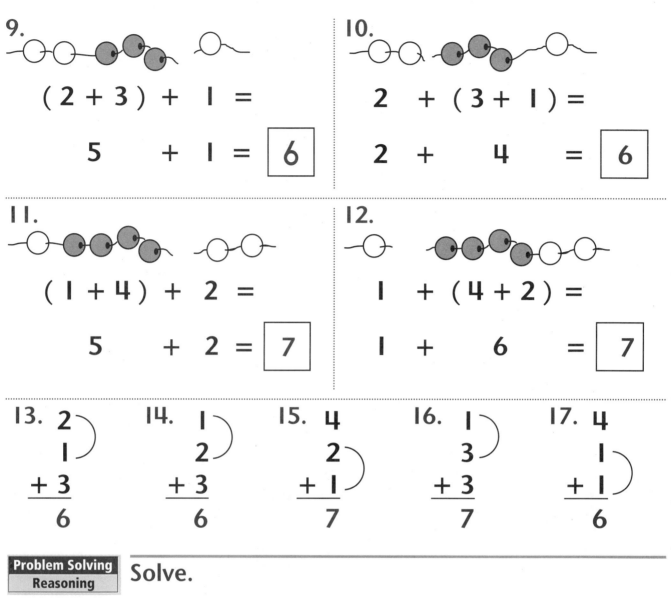

9.

$(2 + 3) + 1 =$

$5 + 1 = \boxed{6}$

10.

$2 + (3 + 1) =$

$2 + 4 = \boxed{6}$

11.

$(1 + 4) + 2 =$

$5 + 2 = \boxed{7}$

12.

$1 + (4 + 2) =$

$1 + 6 = \boxed{7}$

13.
$$\begin{array}{r} 2 \\ 1 \\ + 3 \\ \hline 6 \end{array}$$

14.
$$\begin{array}{r} 1 \\ 2 \\ + 3 \\ \hline 6 \end{array}$$

15.
$$\begin{array}{r} 4 \\ 2 \\ + 1 \\ \hline 7 \end{array}$$

16.
$$\begin{array}{r} 1 \\ 3 \\ + 3 \\ \hline 7 \end{array}$$

17.
$$\begin{array}{r} 4 \\ 1 \\ + 1 \\ \hline 6 \end{array}$$

Problem Solving
Reasoning Solve.

18. There are 2 red crayons, 3 blue crayons, and 2 black crayons. How many in all? __7__ crayons

Teacher Note: **Closing the Lesson** Ask, What are two different ways you can group the numbers to add 3 + 2 + 1?

★ Test Prep

Mark the space under the sum.

19

$2 + (2 + 2) = \square$

4	5	6
○	○	●

Teacher Note: **Check Understanding** Ask, How would you group to add 4 + 2 + 1? Why?

Group the numbers and add.

1.

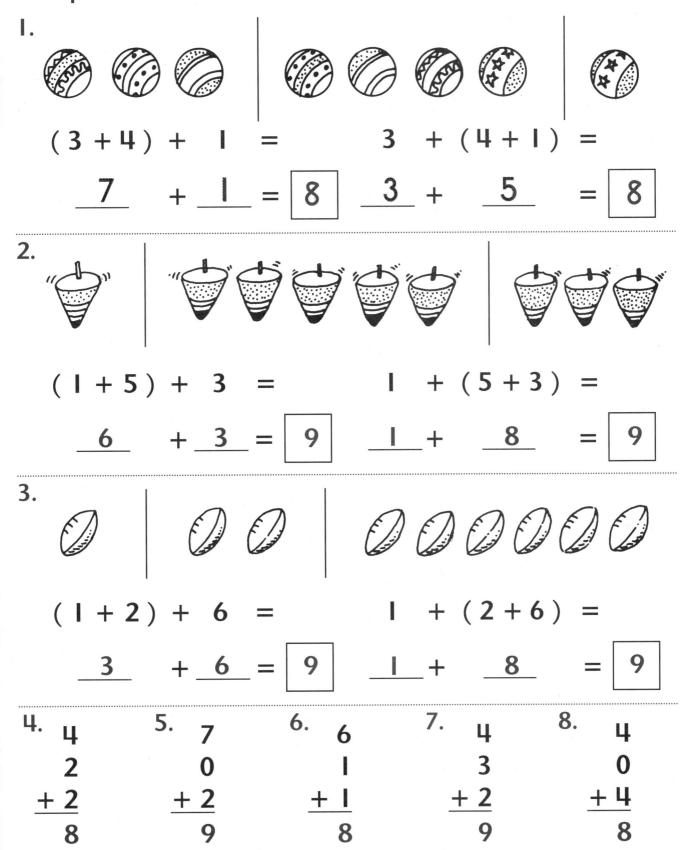

$(3 + 4) + 1 =$ $3 + (4 + 1) =$

__7__ + __1__ = $\boxed{8}$ __3__ + __5__ = $\boxed{8}$

2.

$(1 + 5) + 3 =$ $1 + (5 + 3) =$

__6__ + __3__ = $\boxed{9}$ __1__ + __8__ = $\boxed{9}$

3.

$(1 + 2) + 6 =$ $1 + (2 + 6) =$

__3__ + __6__ = $\boxed{9}$ __1__ + __8__ = $\boxed{9}$

4.
$$\begin{array}{r} 4 \\ 2 \\ +\,2 \\ \hline 8 \end{array}$$

5.
$$\begin{array}{r} 7 \\ 0 \\ +\,2 \\ \hline 9 \end{array}$$

6.
$$\begin{array}{r} 6 \\ 1 \\ +\,1 \\ \hline 8 \end{array}$$

7.
$$\begin{array}{r} 4 \\ 3 \\ +\,2 \\ \hline 9 \end{array}$$

8.
$$\begin{array}{r} 4 \\ 0 \\ +\,4 \\ \hline 8 \end{array}$$

Group the numbers and add.

9.

$(5 + 3) + 2 =$ $5 + (3 + 2) =$

$\underline{8} + \underline{2} = \boxed{10}$ $\underline{5} + \underline{5} = \boxed{10}$

10.

$(1 + 3) + 6 =$ $1 + (3 + 6) =$

$\underline{4} + \underline{6} = \boxed{10}$ $\underline{1} + \underline{9} = \boxed{10}$

11.	12.	13.	14.	15.	16.
4	3	4	1	0	1
4	4	4	4	4	3
+ 2	+ 2	+ 1	+ 5	+ 5	+ 5
10	9	9	10	9	9

Problem Solving Reasoning

(Answers will vary. Possible answer: 2, 3, 5)

17. What 3 numbers have a sum of 10? _____, _____, _____

Teacher Note: **Closing the Lesson** Ask, How can you change 5 + 4 = 9 to three addends with the same sum?

✓ Quick Check

Complete the fact family.

1. $6 + 4 = 10$ $10 - \boxed{6} = \boxed{4}$

$\boxed{4} + 6 = \boxed{10}$ $\boxed{10} - \boxed{4} = \boxed{6}$

Solve.

2. 1
    3
  + 2
    6

3. 3
    3
  + 2
    8

Item	Error Analysis
1	**Common Error:** Children do not associate inverse operations with fact families. **Reteach** Copymaster 41, p. 111
2, 3	**Common Error:** Children have difficulty remembering the first sum when grouping. **Reteach** Copymaster 42, p. 112 **Skills Tutorial** Strand P2, Skill 4

148 (one hundred forty-eight)

Unit 6 • Lesson 6

Name _____

Teacher Note: **Check Understanding** Show 7 fingers. Ask, How many more fingers do I need to make 10?

Fill in each ☐ .

1. Put in   Put in

3   + | 3 | =   6 in all

more

2. Put in   Put in

6   + | 4 | =   10 in all

more

3.

7   + | 2 | =   9 in all

4.

5   + | 3 | =   8 in all

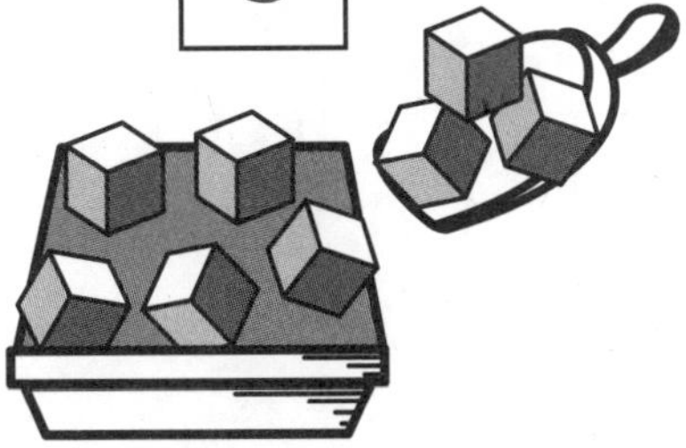

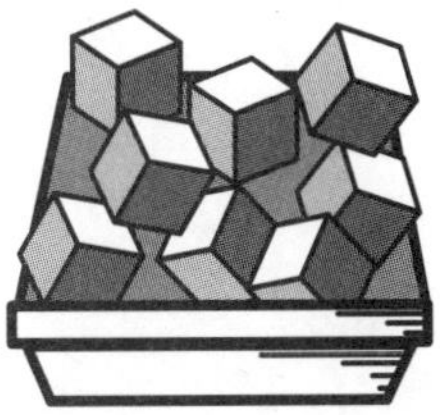

Write the missing number.

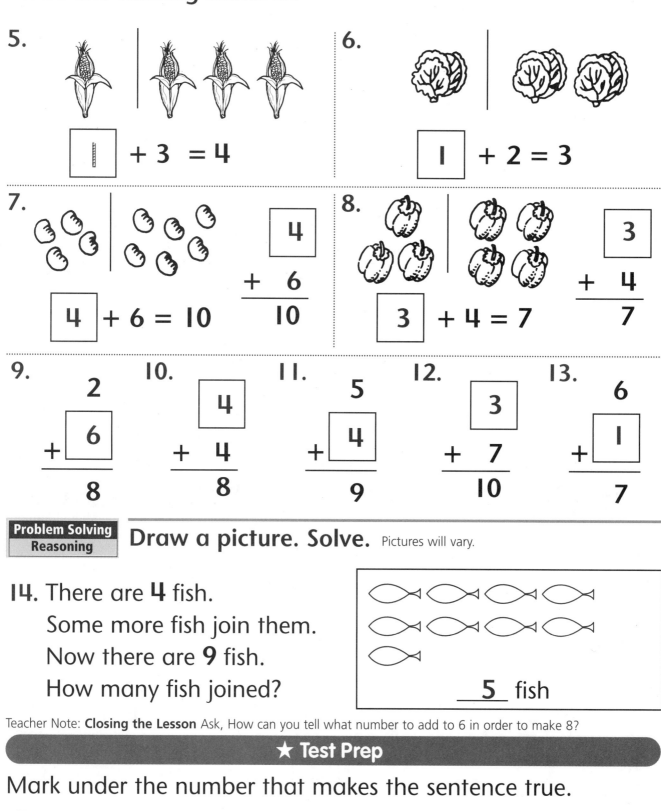

5.

$\boxed{1} + 3 = 4$

6.

$\boxed{1} + 2 = 3$

7.

$\boxed{4} + 6 = 10$

$\boxed{4}$
$+\ 6$
$\overline{\quad 10}$

8.

$\boxed{3} + 4 = 7$

$\boxed{3}$
$+\ 4$
$\overline{\quad 7}$

9.
2
$+\ \boxed{6}$
$\overline{\quad 8}$

10.
$\boxed{4}$
$+\ 4$
$\overline{\quad 8}$

11.
5
$+\ \boxed{4}$
$\overline{\quad 9}$

12.
$\boxed{3}$
$+\ 7$
$\overline{\quad 10}$

13.
6
$+\ \boxed{1}$
$\overline{\quad 7}$

| Problem Solving |
| Reasoning |

Draw a picture. Solve. Pictures will vary.

14. There are **4** fish.
Some more fish join them.
Now there are **9** fish.
How many fish joined?

_____5_____ fish

Teacher Note: **Closing the Lesson** Ask, How can you tell what number to add to 6 in order to make 8?

★ **Test Prep**

Mark under the number that makes the sentence true.

15

$\boxed{} + 3 = 8$

| 6 | 5 | 7 |
| ○ | ● | ○ |

Name _____

Teacher Note: **Check Understanding** Ask, What part of function table 1 stays the same? What part changes?

Complete the table.

1. **+2**

2	4
3	5
4	6
5	7

2. **+1**

8	9
7	8
6	7
5	6

3. **+3**

3	6
4	7
5	8
6	9

4. **−1**

7	6
6	5
5	4
4	3

5. **−3**

4	1
5	2
6	3
7	4

6. **−4**

7	3
6	2
5	1
4	0

7. **+2**

7	9
3	5
8	10
4	6
2	4
1	3
5	7

8. **−2**

9	7
3	1
7	5
10	8
5	3
8	6
4	2

9. **+4**

5	9
2	6
4	8
0	4
3	7
1	5
6	10

Unit 6 • Lesson 8

(one hundred fifty-one) 151

Complete the table.

10.

Rule + 4

In	3	1	2	4
Out	7	5	6	8

11.

Rule − 2

In	8	7	6	5
Out	6	5	4	3

12.

Rule − 3

In	6	5	7	8
Out	3	2	4	5

13.

Rule + 1

In	8	4	6	9
Out	9	5	7	10

Problem Solving Reasoning Write the rule.

14.

Rule +2

In	1	2	3	4	5	6	7	8
Out	3	4	5	6	7	8	9	10

How can you check if the rule is right? _____

(Answers will vary. Possible answer: I can add 2 to each number in the In row to see if I get the number in the Out row.)

_____

Teacher Note: **Closing the Lesson** Draw a function table with only the In row filled in with the numbers 1–4. Have children think of a rule, then fill in the Out row.

★ Test Prep

Mark the space under your answer to complete the table.

15.

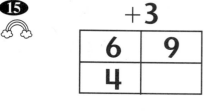

+3

6	9
4	

7   ●
8   ○
5   ○

Unit 6 • Lesson 8

Guided Practice: Problem 1
Independent Practice: Problems 2–10

**Problem Solving Application:
Use a Table**

Favorite Fruit	🍌	🍓	🍎	🍊	🍐
Number of Children	7	3	8	9	5

Use the table to answer the question.

Think Find the fruit in the table.
          Look at the number of children.

1. How many children like 🍊 ? __9__

2. How many children like 🍓 ? __3__

3. How many children like 🍐 ? __5__

Ring your answer.

4. Do more children like 🍎 than 🍌 ?   (yes)   no

5. Do fewer children like 🍐 than 🍓 ?   yes   (no)

Unit 6 • Lesson 9   (one hundred fifty-three) 153

Toy				
Cost	8¢	5¢	4¢	6¢

Look at the table. Write the cost of the toy.

Think Where is the object pictured?
How much does it cost?

6. _____ 8 ¢ | 7. _____ 4 ¢

Ring the coins needed to buy the toy.

8.

9.

Teacher Note: **Closing the Lesson** Ask, How did you decide which coins to ring in problem 9?

Extend Your Thinking

10. Can you pay for the dog another way?
What coins could you use? _____

(Answers may vary. Possible answer: I could use five pennies.)

Unit 6 • Lesson 9

Guided Practice: Exercise 1
Independent Practice: Exercises 2–6

Pennies, Nickels, and Dimes

Teacher Note: **Check Understanding** Ask, Which coin or coins could I use to buy a pencil for 5 cents?

I penny	I nickel	I dime	I dime
I cent	5 cents	10 cents	10 cents
I¢	5¢	10¢	10¢

How much money?

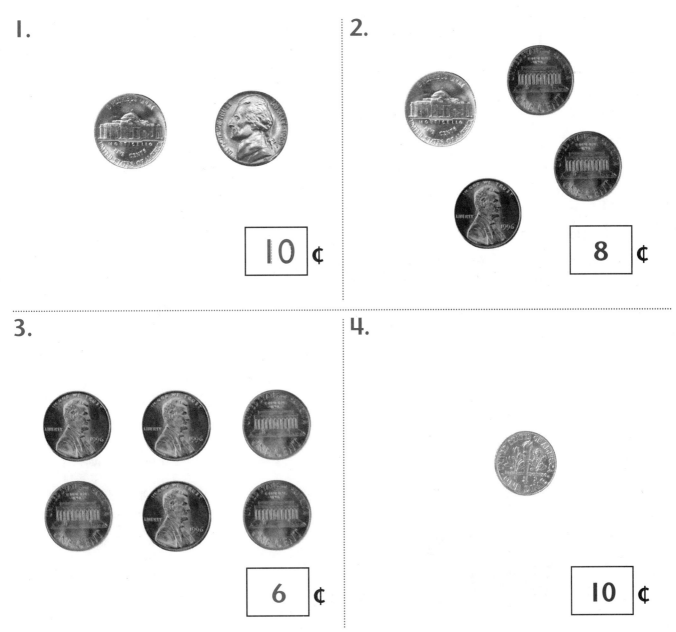

1.   10 ¢

2.   8 ¢

3.   6 ¢

4.   10 ¢

Unit 6 • Lesson 10

(one hundred fifty-five) 155

Ring the coins needed.

5.

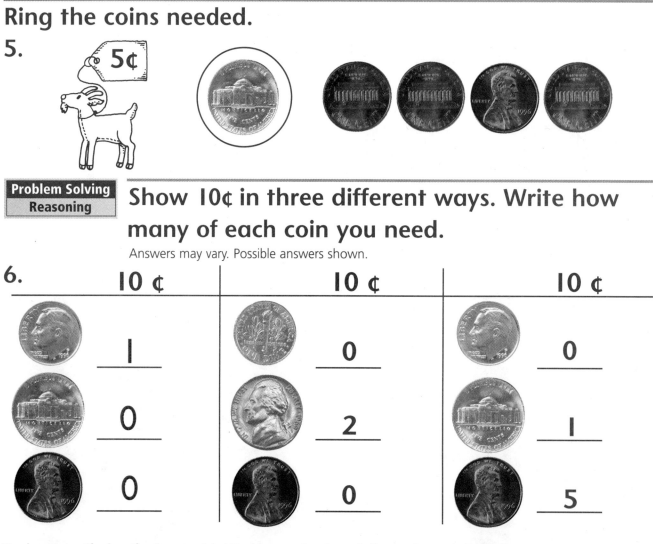

Problem Solving Reasoning

Show 10¢ in three different ways. Write how many of each coin you need.

Answers may vary. Possible answers shown.

6.

10 ¢	10 ¢	10 ¢
dime — 1	dime — 0	dime — 0
nickel — 0	nickel — 2	nickel — 1
penny — 0	penny — 0	penny — 5

Teacher Note: **Closing the Lesson** Ask, Would you rather have 1 dime or 8 pennies? Why?

☑ Quick Check

Complete.

1.

$$\begin{array}{r} \boxed{5} \\ +\ 2 \\ \hline 7 \end{array}$$

2.

−4

10	6
8	4
4	0

3. How much?

_7_ ¢

Item	Error Analysis
1	**Common Error:** Children add the two numbers rather than finding the missing addend. **Reteach** Copymaster 43, p. 113
2	**Common Error:** Children do not pay attention to the operation sign in the rule. **Reteach** Copymaster 44, p. 114
3	**Common Error:** Children may not know the value of the nickel. **Reteach** Copymaster 45, p. 115

Unit 6 • Lesson 10

Name _____

Guided Practice: Exercises 1, 7, and 12
Independent Practice: Exercises 2–6, 8–11, and 13–16

Adding and Subtracting Money

Teacher Note: **Check Understanding** Ask, If I have 3 pennies in one pocket and a nickel in the other, how can I find out how much money I have in all?

How much for both?

1.

5¢
+ 2¢
—————
[7] ¢

2.

2¢
+ 6¢
—————
[8] ¢

3.

4¢
+ 6¢
—————
[10] ¢

4.

6¢
+ 3¢
—————
[9] ¢

5.

3¢
+ 5¢
—————
[8] ¢

6.

4¢
+ 4¢
—————
[8] ¢

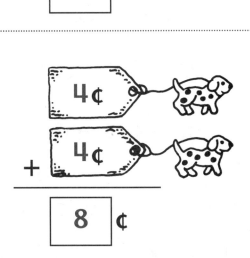
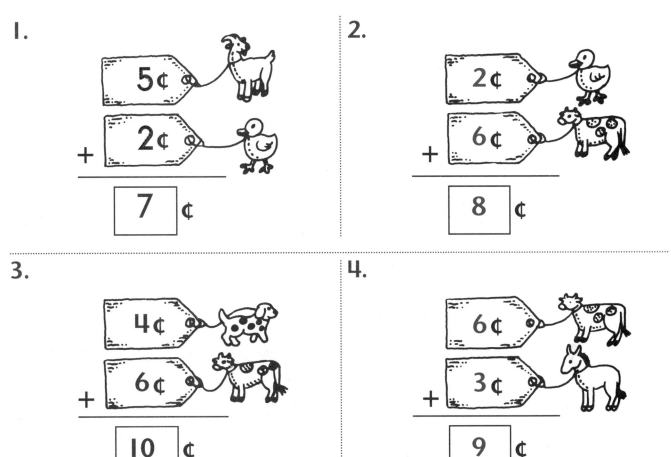

Unit 6 • Lesson 11

(one hundred fifty-seven) 157

Add.

7.
1¢
2¢
+ 6¢

9¢

8.
8¢
1¢
+ 1¢

10¢

9.
6¢
1¢
+ 2¢

9¢

10.
4¢
2¢
+ 3¢

9¢

11.
1¢
5¢
+ 2¢

8¢

How much money is left?

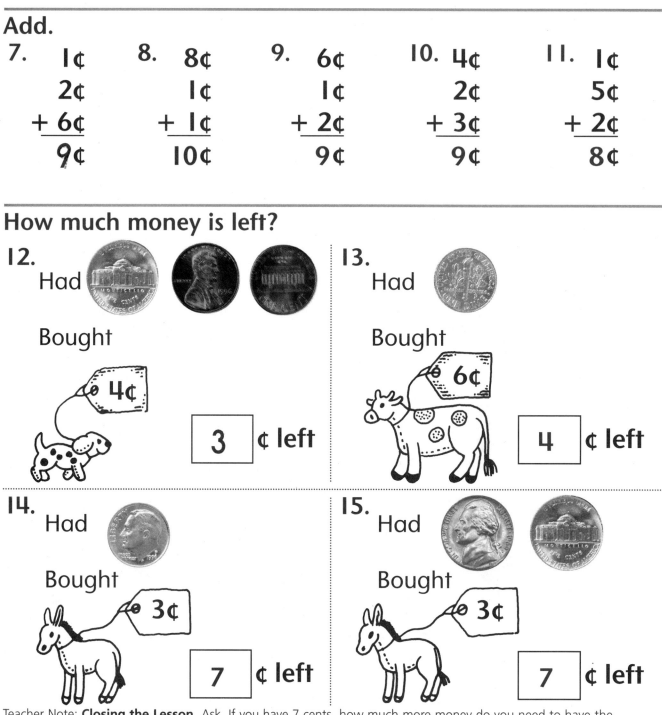

12. Had

Bought 4¢

3 ¢ left

13. Had

Bought 6¢

4 ¢ left

14. Had

Bought 3¢

7 ¢ left

15. Had

Bought 3¢

7 ¢ left

Teacher Note: **Closing the Lesson** Ask, If you have 7 cents, how much more money do you need to have the same value as a dime? How do you know?

★ Test Prep

How much do both cats cost in all?

Mark the space under your answer.

16
☆

6¢ 4¢

 ● ○   ○

Unit 6 • Lesson 11

Name _____

Guided Practice: Model Problem and Problem 1
Independent Practice: Problems 2–6

**Problem Solving Strategy:
Conjecture and Verify**

Problem

You have  .

Can you buy the ball?

1 Understand What do you need to find out?

I need to know if I have enough money.

2 Decide What strategy can you use?

I will guess then check.

3 Solve Invite children to look at the coins to guess if there is enough money. Have them count to check.

Can you buy the ball? _____**no**_____

4 Look back How much more money would you need to buy the ball?

Does my answer make sense?

Solve.

1. You have  . Can you buy the hat?

_____**yes**_____

Unit 6 • Lesson 12

(one hundred fifty-nine) 159

Guess and check. Solve.

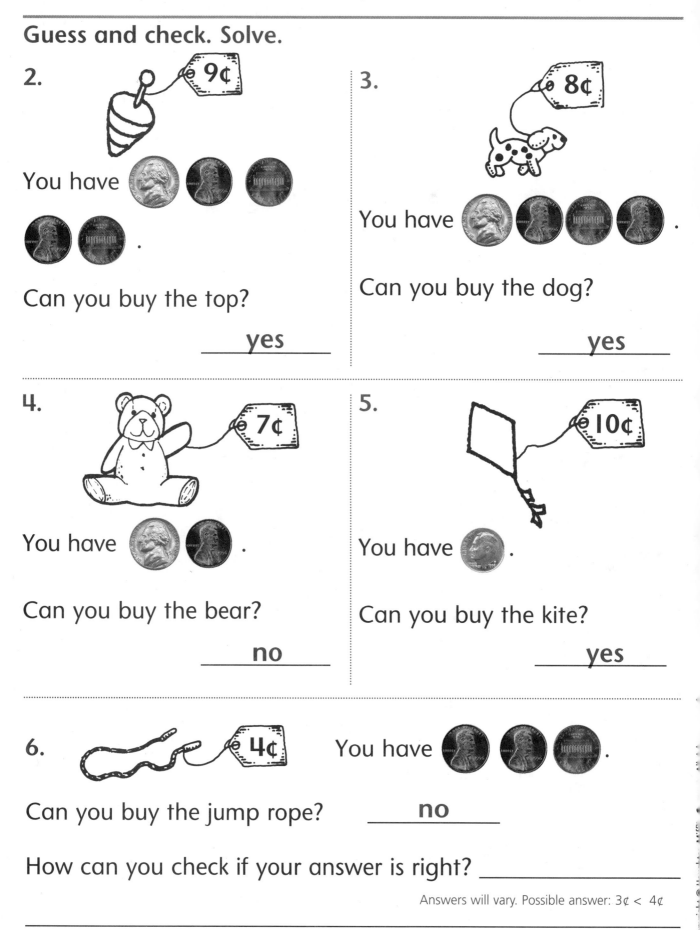

2. 9¢

You have ☉ ● ● ● ● .

Can you buy the top?

_____yes_____

3. 8¢

You have ☉ ● ● ● .

Can you buy the dog?

_____yes_____

4. 7¢

You have ☉ ● .

Can you buy the bear?

_____no_____

5. 10¢

You have ◐ .

Can you buy the kite?

_____yes_____

6. 4¢

You have ● ● ● .

Can you buy the jump rope? _____no_____

How can you check if your answer is right? _____

Answers will vary. Possible answer: 3¢ < 4¢

Teacher Note: **Closing the Lesson** Ask, If you have the same amount of money as the price of the item, do you have enough?

Unit 6 • Lesson 12

Complete the fact family. (6B)

1.

$9 + 1 = \boxed{10}$

$1 + \boxed{9} = 10$

$10 - \boxed{9} = 1$

$\boxed{10} - \boxed{1} = 9$

2.

$5 + 3 = \boxed{8}$

$3 + \boxed{5} = 8$

$8 - \boxed{5} = 3$

$\boxed{8} - \boxed{3} = 5$

Solve. (6A)

3.
$$\begin{array}{r} 10 \\ -\ 7 \\ \hline 3 \end{array}$$

4.
$$\begin{array}{r} 6 \\ +\ 4 \\ \hline 10 \end{array}$$

5.
$$\begin{array}{r} 4 \\ +\ 4 \\ \hline 8 \end{array}$$

6.
$$\begin{array}{r} 3 \\ +\ 2 \\ \hline 5 \end{array}$$

7.
$$\begin{array}{r} 1 \\ +\ 8 \\ \hline 9 \end{array}$$

8.
$$\begin{array}{r} 8 \\ -\ 5 \\ \hline 3 \end{array}$$

9.
$$\begin{array}{r} 3 \\ +\ 3 \\ \hline 6 \end{array}$$

10.
$$\begin{array}{r} 7 \\ -\ 6 \\ \hline 1 \end{array}$$

11.
$$\begin{array}{r} 9 \\ -\ 4 \\ \hline 5 \end{array}$$

12.
$$\begin{array}{r} 6 \\ -\ 0 \\ \hline 6 \end{array}$$

Add. (6C)

13.
$$\begin{array}{r} 5 \\ 2 \\ +\ 2 \\ \hline 9 \end{array}$$

14.
$$\begin{array}{r} 3 \\ 4 \\ +\ 1 \\ \hline 8 \end{array}$$

15.
$$\begin{array}{r} 6 \\ 0 \\ +\ 4 \\ \hline 10 \end{array}$$

16.
$$\begin{array}{r} 3 \\ 1 \\ +\ 3 \\ \hline 7 \end{array}$$

17.
$$\begin{array}{r} 4 \\ 2 \\ +\ 2 \\ \hline 8 \end{array}$$

Write the missing number. (6D)

18. $\boxed{3} + 6 = 9$

19. $4 + \boxed{0} = 4$

20. $2 + \boxed{6} = 8$

Ring the coins needed. (6E)

21.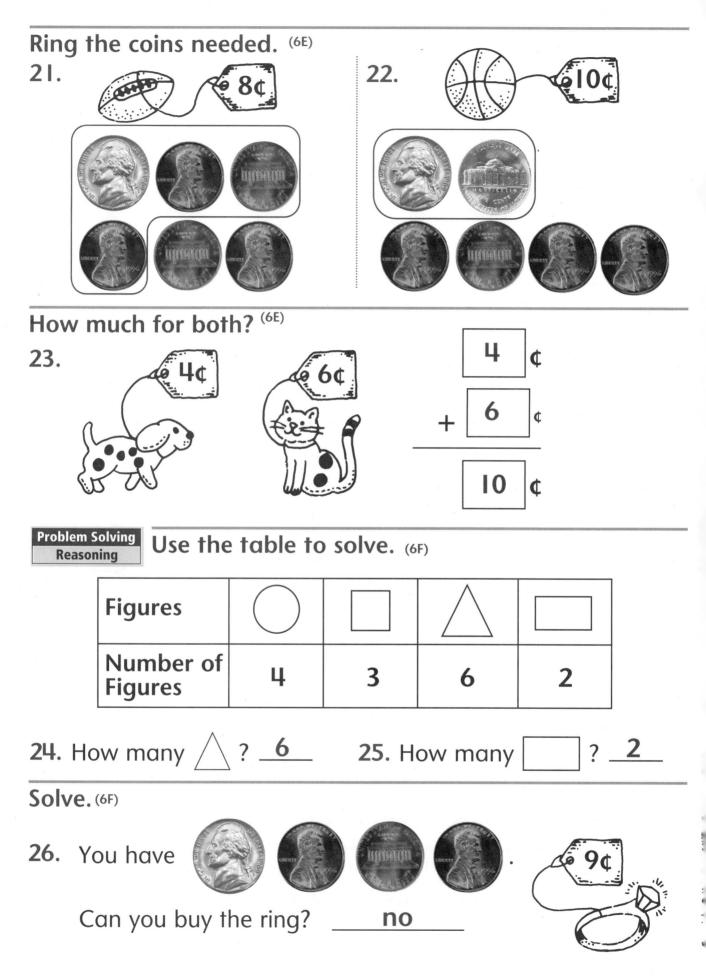

22.

How much for both? (6E)

23.

$$\begin{array}{r} 4\text{¢} \\ +\ 6\text{¢} \\ \hline 10\text{¢} \end{array}$$

Problem Solving / Reasoning

Use the table to solve. (6F)

Figures	○	□	△	▭
Number of Figures	4	3	6	2

24. How many △ ? __6__   **25.** How many ▭ ? __2__

Solve. (6F)

26. You have   .   9¢

Can you buy the ring? ____no____

Name_____

1 Which shape most likely comes next? Mark the space under your answer. **(1C)**

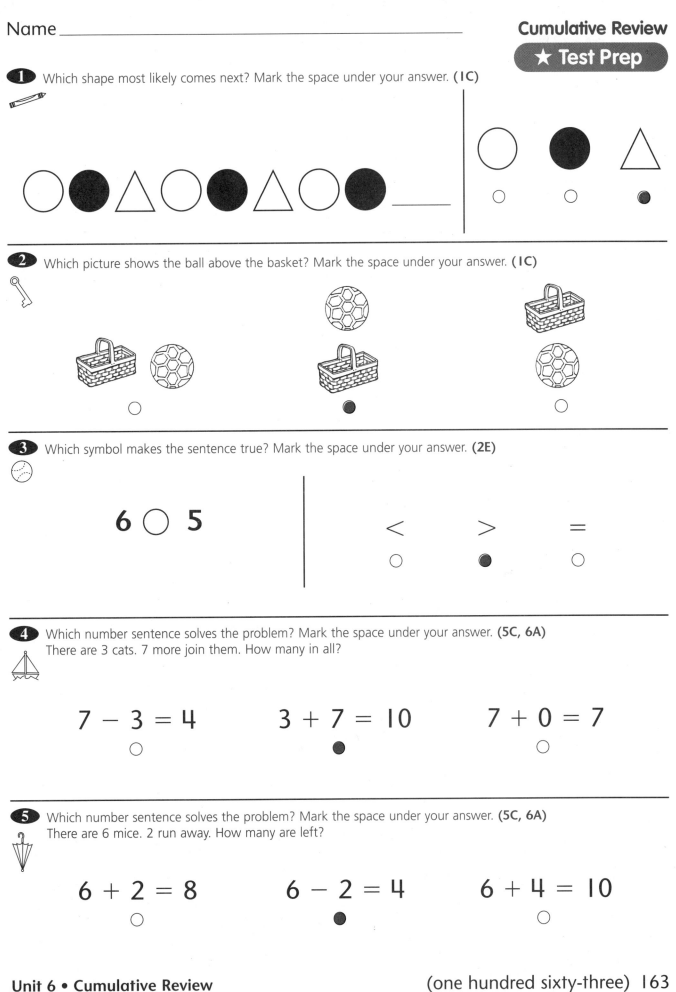

2 Which picture shows the ball above the basket? Mark the space under your answer. **(1C)**

3 Which symbol makes the sentence true? Mark the space under your answer. **(2E)**

$6 \bigcirc 5$

$<$ $>$ $=$

4 Which number sentence solves the problem? Mark the space under your answer. **(5C, 6A)**
There are 3 cats. 7 more join them. How many in all?

$7 - 3 = 4$ $3 + 7 = 10$ $7 + 0 = 7$

5 Which number sentence solves the problem? Mark the space under your answer. **(5C, 6A)**
There are 6 mice. 2 run away. How many are left?

$6 + 2 = 8$ $6 - 2 = 4$ $6 + 4 = 10$

Unit 6 • Cumulative Review

6 Which number sentence solves the problem? Mark the space under your answer. **(5C, 6A)**
There are 2 birds. 2 fly away. How many are left?

$2 + 2 = 4$ ○ $2 - 0 = 2$ ○ $2 - 2 = 0$ ●

7 Which fact is related to the fact in the beginning of the row? Mark the space under your answer. **(6B)**

$10 - 3 = 7$ | $7 - 3 = 4$ ○ $7 + 3 = 10$ ● $4 + 3 = 7$ ○

Solve. Tell children they will complete the rest of the test on their own. **(6A)**

8

$3 + 5 = \square$

8 ●   6 ○   9 ○

9

$5 + 3 = \square$

4 ○   8 ●   9 ○

10

$\begin{array}{r} 10 \\ -\ 7 \\ \hline \square \end{array}$

6 ○   3 ●   4 ○

11

$\begin{array}{r} 9 \\ -\ 7 \\ \hline \square \end{array}$

2 ●   5 ○   3 ○

12

$\begin{array}{r} 8 \\ -\ 4 \\ \hline \square \end{array}$

6 ○   2 ○   4 ●

13

$\begin{array}{r} 8 \\ -\ 8 \\ \hline \square \end{array}$

8 ○   6 ○   0 ●

164 (one hundred sixty-four)   **Unit 6 • Cumulative Review**

UNIT 7 • TABLE OF CONTENTS

Place Value through 99

UNIT 7 • TABLE OF CONTENTS

We will be using this vocabulary:

1 ten ten objects in a group, 10 ones

ordinal numbers numbers used to show
position or order:

1st	2nd	3rd	4th	5th
first	second	third	fourth	fifth

hundred chart a 10-by-10 grid that lists
the numbers 1–100 in rows of ten

Dear Family,

During the next few weeks our math
class will be learning and practicing
place value through 99.

You can expect to see homework
that provides practice with writing
and counting numbers from 1 through 99.

As we learn about place value you may wish to keep the following
sample as a guide.

The different forms of a number:
Word form: Fifteen

Standard form: 15

Place Value form:

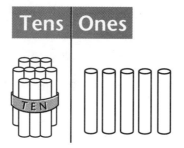

1 ten and 5 ones

Knowing place value can help children read, write, count, and
compare greater numbers and quantities.

Sincerely,

Guided Practice: Model Exercise and Exercise 1
Independent Practice: Exercises 2–7

**Place Value
through 15**

Teacher Note: **Check Understanding** Ask, How are the groups of ten we found alike?

10 objects in a group make 1 ten.

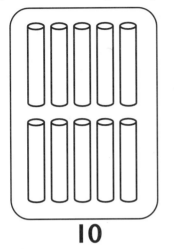

10

or

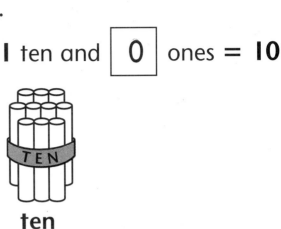

1 ten and $\boxed{0}$ ones = 10

ten

Ring a group of ten.
Write how many tens and ones.
Write the number.

1.

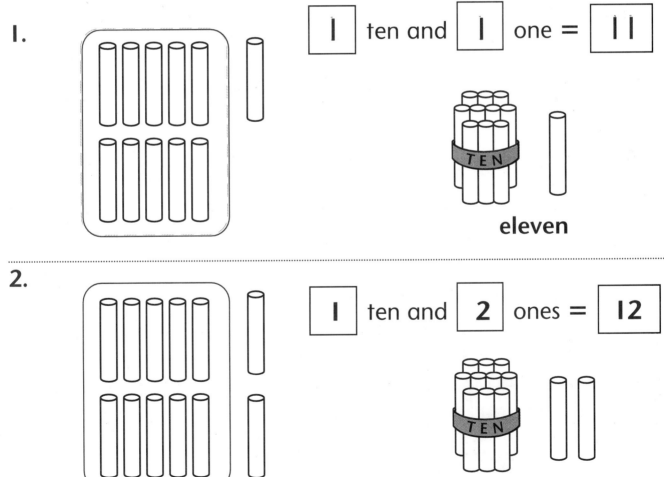

$\boxed{1}$ ten and $\boxed{1}$ one = $\boxed{11}$

eleven

2.

$\boxed{1}$ ten and $\boxed{2}$ ones = $\boxed{12}$

twelve

Ring a group of ten. Write how many tens and ones. Write the number.

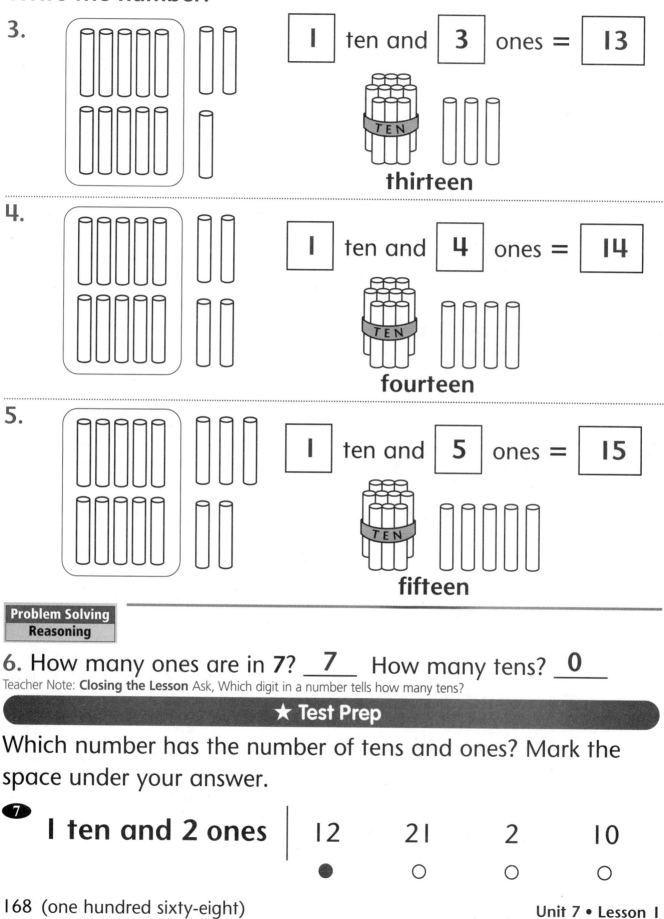

3. [1] ten and [3] ones = [13]

thirteen

4. [1] ten and [4] ones = [14]

fourteen

5. [1] ten and [5] ones = [15]

fifteen

Problem Solving Reasoning

6. How many ones are in 7? __7__ How many tens? __0__

Teacher Note: **Closing the Lesson** Ask, Which digit in a number tells how many tens?

★ Test Prep

Which number has the number of tens and ones? Mark the space under your answer.

7

1 ten and 2 ones | 12   21   2   10

● ○ ○ ○

Unit 7 • Lesson 1

Guided Practice: Exercise 1
Independent Practice: Exercises 2–14

**Place Value
through 19**

Teacher Note: **Check Understanding** Ask, How are the numbers 10–19 alike? Different?

Write how many tens and ones.
Complete the number sentence.

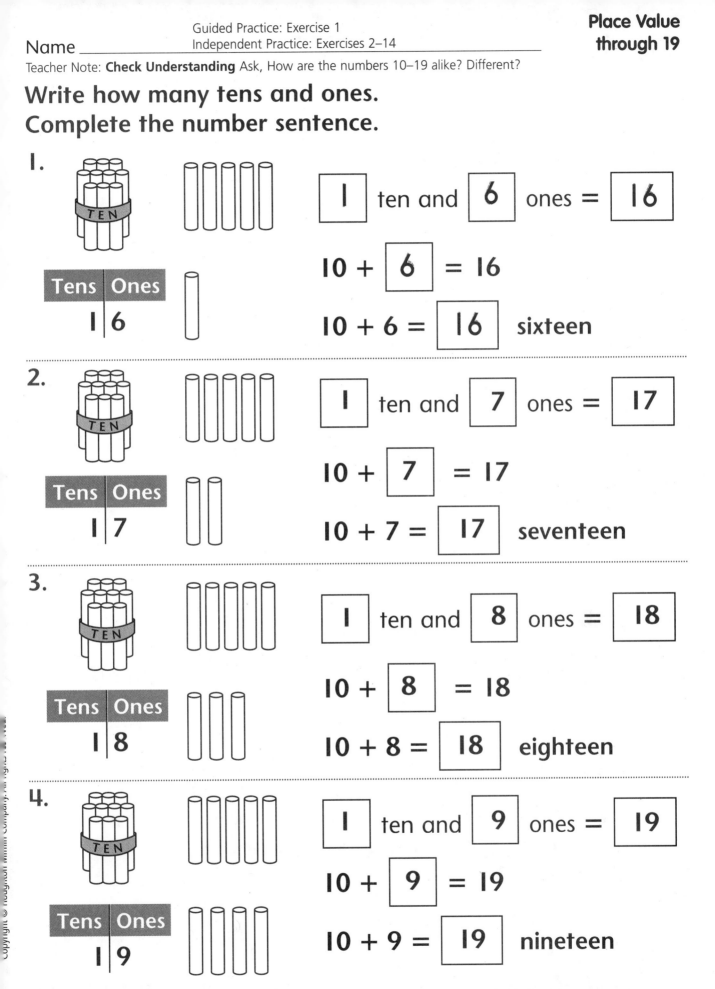

1.

Tens	Ones
1	6

☐ 1 ☐ ten and ☐ 6 ☐ ones = ☐ 16 ☐

10 + ☐ 6 ☐ = 16

10 + 6 = ☐ 16 ☐ sixteen

2.

Tens	Ones
1	7

☐ 1 ☐ ten and ☐ 7 ☐ ones = ☐ 17 ☐

10 + ☐ 7 ☐ = 17

10 + 7 = ☐ 17 ☐ seventeen

3.

Tens	Ones
1	8

☐ 1 ☐ ten and ☐ 8 ☐ ones = ☐ 18 ☐

10 + ☐ 8 ☐ = 18

10 + 8 = ☐ 18 ☐ eighteen

4.

Tens	Ones
1	9

☐ 1 ☐ ten and ☐ 9 ☐ ones = ☐ 19 ☐

10 + ☐ 9 ☐ = 19

10 + 9 = ☐ 19 ☐ nineteen

Complete.

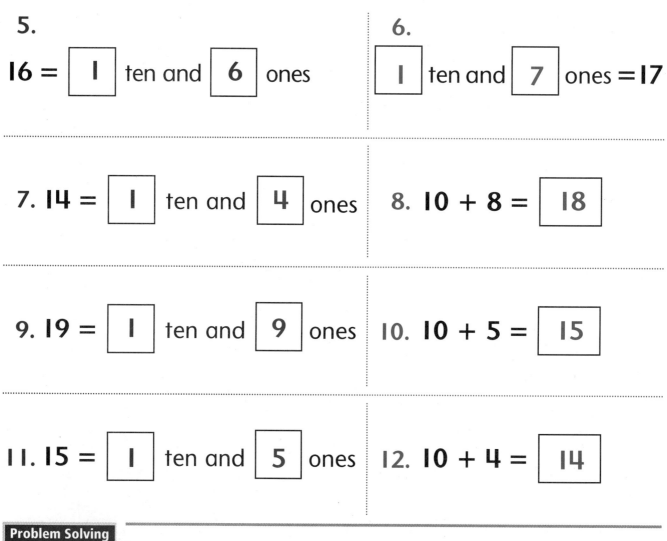

5.

$16 = \boxed{1}$ ten and $\boxed{6}$ ones

6.

$\boxed{1}$ ten and $\boxed{7}$ ones $= 17$

7. $14 = \boxed{1}$ ten and $\boxed{4}$ ones

8. $10 + 8 = \boxed{18}$

9. $19 = \boxed{1}$ ten and $\boxed{9}$ ones

10. $10 + 5 = \boxed{15}$

11. $15 = \boxed{1}$ ten and $\boxed{5}$ ones

12. $10 + 4 = \boxed{14}$

**Problem Solving
Reasoning**

13. What pattern do you see in the number word names?

Answers will vary. Possible answer: They all end in "teen."

Teacher Note: **Closing the Lesson** Ask, If you have a box of 10 crayons and 7 more crayons, how many do you have?

★ Test Prep

I have **18** sticks. How many bundles of ten sticks can I make?
Mark the space under your answer.

14

| 1 | 10 | 8 | 18 |

170 (one hundred seventy)

Unit 7 • Lesson 2

Guided Practice: Exercises 1 and 6
Independent Practice: Exercises 2–5 and 7–9

Teacher Note: **Check Understanding** Ask, If I have 40 sticks, how many bundles of ten do I have?

Complete.

1.

| ten |

| **1** | ten |

Tens	Ones
1	0

| **10** |

2.

twenty

| **2** | tens |

Tens	Ones
2	0

| **20** |

3.

thirty

| **3** | tens |

Tens	Ones
3	0

| **30** |

4.

forty

| **4** | tens |

Tens	Ones
4	0

| **40** |

5.

fifty

| **5** | tens |

Tens	Ones
5	0

| **50** |

Unit 7 • Lesson 3

(one hundred seventy-one) 171

Complete.

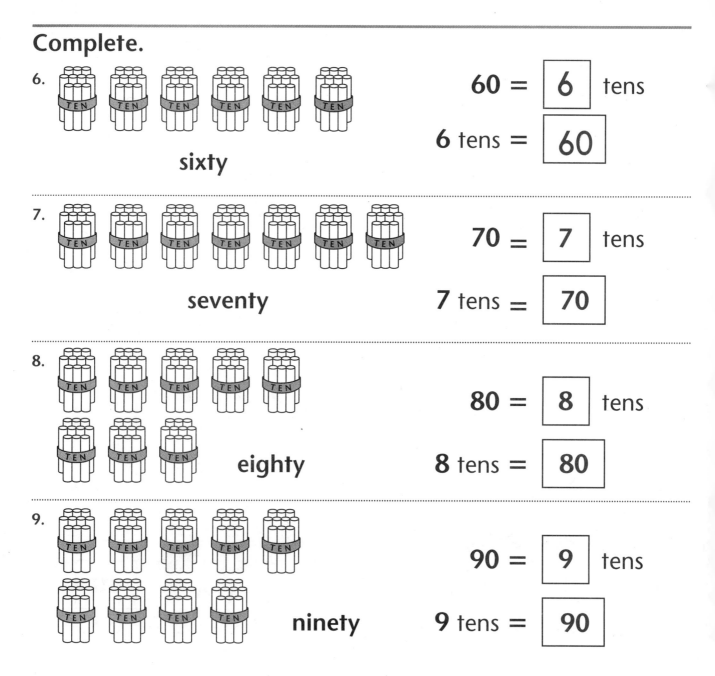

6.
sixty

$60 = \boxed{6}$ tens

6 tens $= \boxed{60}$

7.
seventy

$70 = \boxed{7}$ tens

7 tens $= \boxed{70}$

8.
eighty

$80 = \boxed{8}$ tens

8 tens $= \boxed{80}$

9.
ninety

$90 = \boxed{9}$ tens

9 tens $= \boxed{90}$

Teacher Note: **Closing the Lesson** Ask, What pattern do you see in the number words?

✔ Quick Check

Complete.

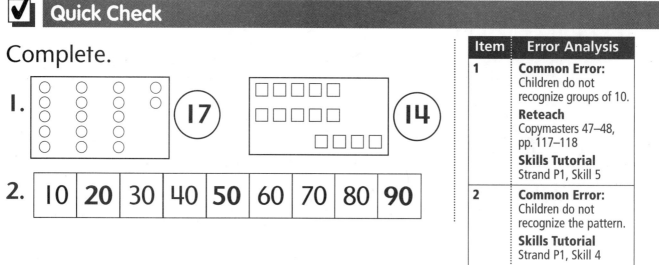

1. ⑰ ⑭

2.
10	20	30	40	50	60	70	80	90

Item	Error Analysis
1	**Common Error:** Children do not recognize groups of 10.
	Reteach Copymasters 47–48, pp. 117–118
	Skills Tutorial Strand P1, Skill 5
2	**Common Error:** Children do not recognize the pattern.
	Skills Tutorial Strand P1, Skill 4

Name _____

Teacher Note: **Check Understanding** Ask, Can you have a number that does not have any tens? If so, give an example. If not, tell why.

Complete.

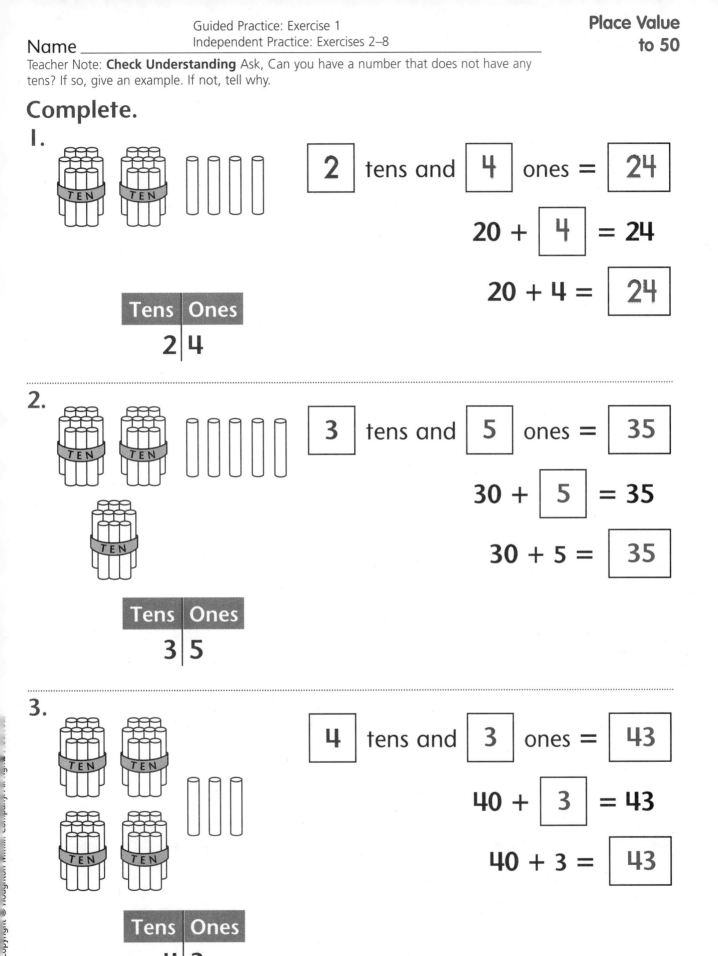

1.

$\boxed{2}$ tens and $\boxed{4}$ ones = $\boxed{24}$

$20 + \boxed{4} = 24$

$20 + 4 = \boxed{24}$

Tens	Ones
2	4

2.

$\boxed{3}$ tens and $\boxed{5}$ ones = $\boxed{35}$

$30 + \boxed{5} = 35$

$30 + 5 = \boxed{35}$

Tens	Ones
3	5

3.

$\boxed{4}$ tens and $\boxed{3}$ ones = $\boxed{43}$

$40 + \boxed{3} = 43$

$40 + 3 = \boxed{43}$

Tens	Ones
4	3

Unit 7 • Lesson 4

(one hundred seventy-three) 173

Complete.

4.

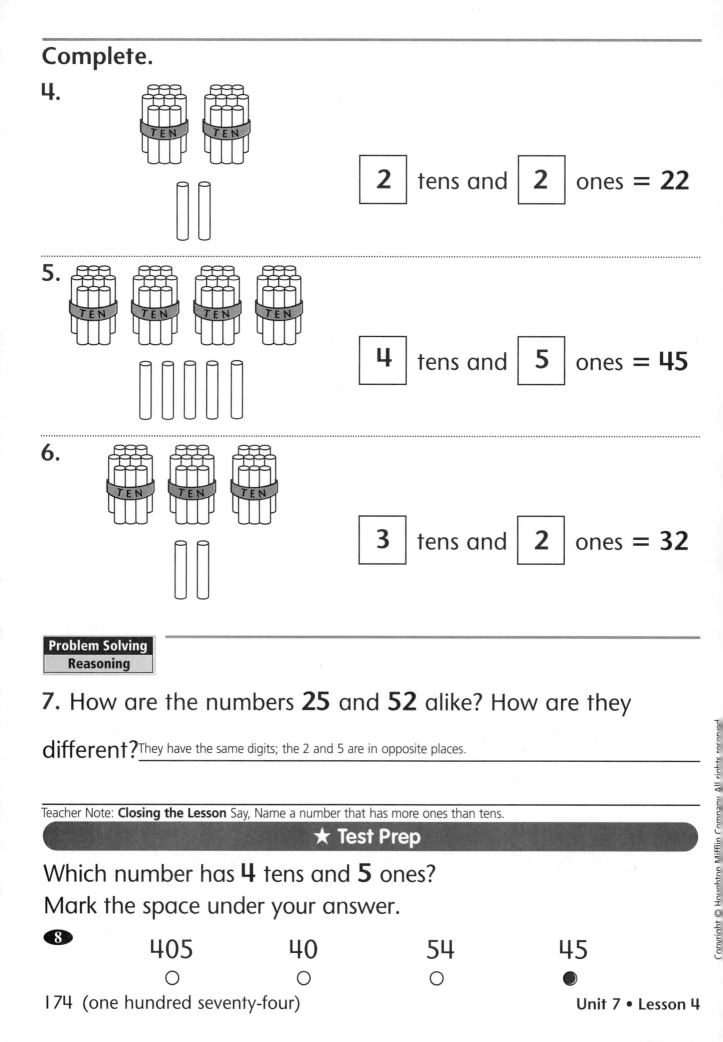

$\boxed{2}$ tens and $\boxed{2}$ ones = **22**

5.

$\boxed{4}$ tens and $\boxed{5}$ ones = **45**

6.

$\boxed{3}$ tens and $\boxed{2}$ ones = **32**

Problem Solving
Reasoning

7. How are the numbers **25** and **52** alike? How are they

different? They have the same digits; the 2 and 5 are in opposite places.

Teacher Note: **Closing the Lesson** Say, Name a number that has more ones than tens.

★ Test Prep

Which number has **4** tens and **5** ones?
Mark the space under your answer.

8
      405   40   54   45
      ○   ○   ○   ●

174 (one hundred seventy-four)　　　　　　　**Unit 7 • Lesson 4**

Teacher Note: **Check Understanding** Which has a greater value in the number 68, the 6 or 8? Why?

Complete.

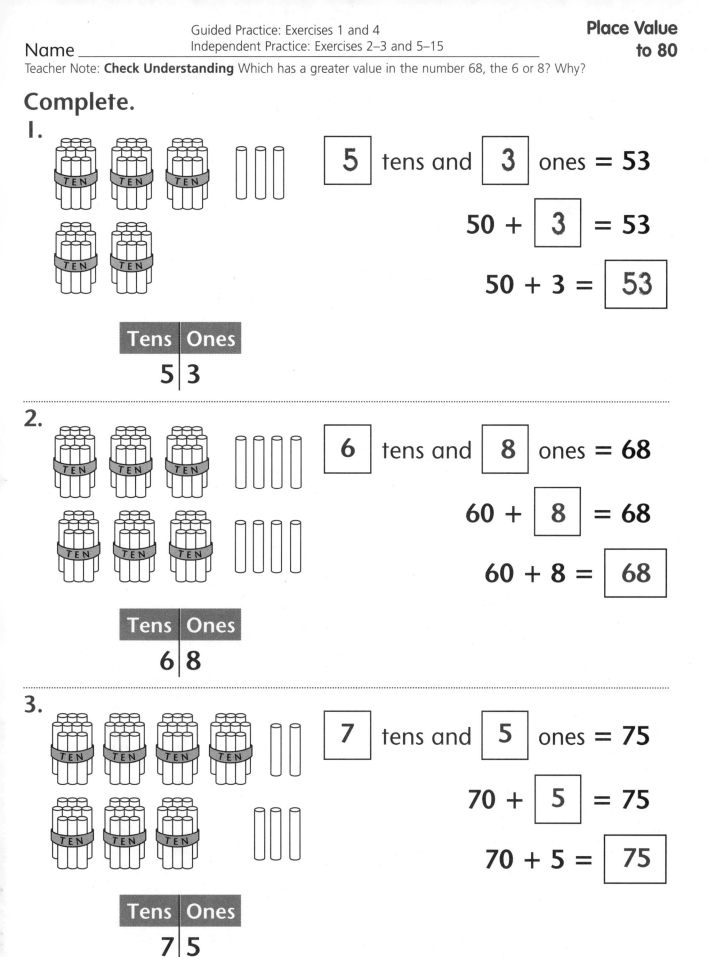

1.

$\boxed{5}$ tens and $\boxed{3}$ ones = **53**

$50 + \boxed{3} = 53$

$50 + 3 = \boxed{53}$

Tens	Ones
5	3

2.

$\boxed{6}$ tens and $\boxed{8}$ ones = **68**

$60 + \boxed{8} = 68$

$60 + 8 = \boxed{68}$

Tens	Ones
6	8

3.

$\boxed{7}$ tens and $\boxed{5}$ ones = **75**

$70 + \boxed{5} = 75$

$70 + 5 = \boxed{75}$

Tens	Ones
7	5

Complete.

4.

Tens	Ones
4	6

$\longrightarrow$ 46

5.

Tens	Ones
5	9

$\longrightarrow$ 59

6.

Tens	Ones
6	8

$\longrightarrow$ 68

7.

Tens	Ones
6	3

$\longrightarrow$ 63

8.

Tens	Ones
5	1

$\longrightarrow$ 51

9.

Tens	Ones
7	5

$\longrightarrow$ 75

10. **5** tens and **2** ones $\longrightarrow$ 50 + 2 = 52

11. **5** tens and **4** ones $\longrightarrow$ 50 + 4 = 54

12. **6** tens and **5** ones $\longrightarrow$ 60 + 5 = 65

13. **7** tens and **3** ones $\longrightarrow$ 70 + 3 = 73

**Problem Solving
Reasoning**

14. Write the value of the underlined digit in **5̲3**. ___50 or 5 tens___

Teacher Note: **Closing the Lesson** Ask, How many 2-digit numbers have a 7 in the tens place?

★ Test Prep

What is the value of the underlined digit?
Mark the space under your answer.

15 **4̲7**

7	4	40	47
○	○	●	○

176 (one hundred seventy-six)

Unit 7 • Lesson 5

Name _____

Teacher Note: **Check Understanding** Ask, Which numbers between 1 and 99 have the same number of tens as ones?

Complete.

1.

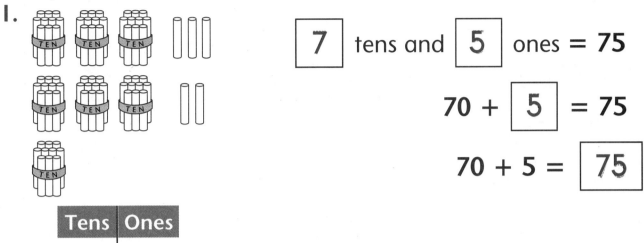

7 tens and 5 ones = 75

70 + 5 = 75

70 + 5 = 75

Tens	Ones
7	5

2.

8 tens and 2 ones = 82

80 + 2 = 82

80 + 2 = 82

Tens	Ones
8	2

3.

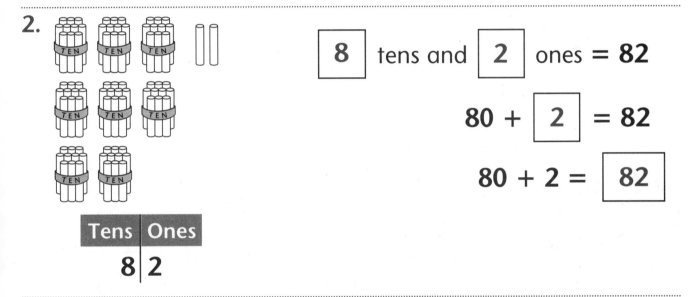

9 tens and 7 ones = 97

90 + 7 = 97

90 + 7 = 97

Tens	Ones
9	7

Unit 7 • Lesson 6

(one hundred seventy-seven) 177

Complete the tables.

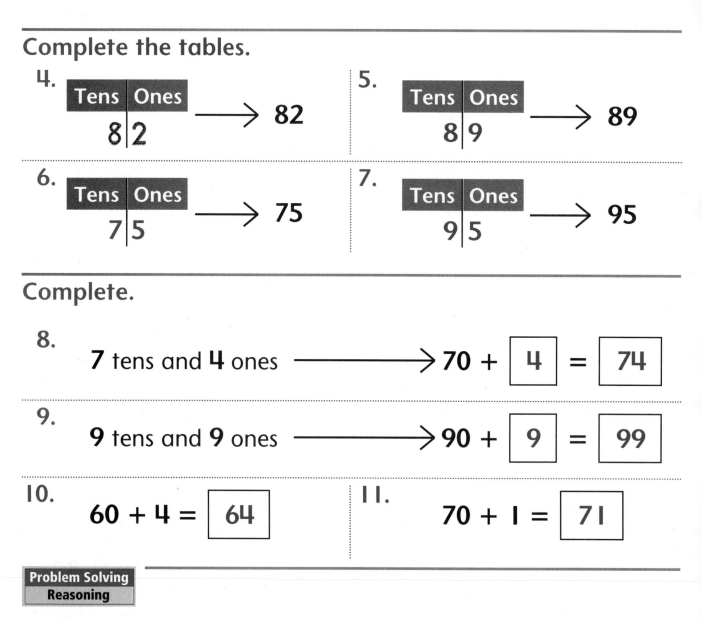

4.

Tens	Ones
8	2

$\longrightarrow$ **82**

5.

Tens	Ones
8	9

$\longrightarrow$ **89**

6.

Tens	Ones
7	5

$\longrightarrow$ **75**

7.

Tens	Ones
9	5

$\longrightarrow$ **95**

Complete.

8.

7 tens and **4** ones $\longrightarrow$ **70 +** $\boxed{4}$ **=** $\boxed{74}$

9.

9 tens and **9** ones $\longrightarrow$ **90 +** $\boxed{9}$ **=** $\boxed{99}$

10.

60 + 4 = $\boxed{64}$

11.

70 + 1 = $\boxed{71}$

Problem Solving
Reasoning

12. Write the value of the underlined digit in **<u>8</u>9**. <u>80 or 8 tens.</u>

Teacher Note: **Closing the Lesson** Ask, Which number has a 4 in the ones place and a 9 in the tens place?

✓ Quick Check

Complete.

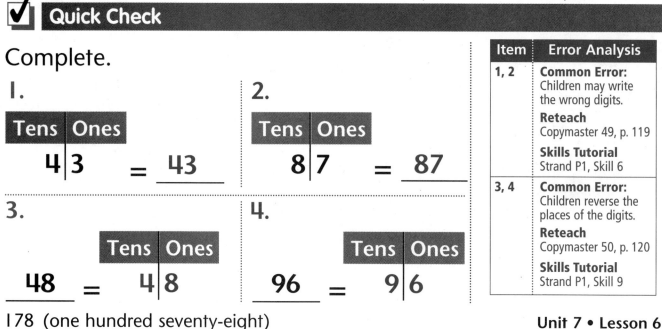

1.

Tens	Ones
4	3

= <u>43</u>

2.

Tens	Ones
8	7

= <u>87</u>

3.

<u>48</u> **=**

Tens	Ones
4	8

4.

<u>96</u> **=**

Tens	Ones
9	6

Item	Error Analysis
1, 2	**Common Error:** Children may write the wrong digits. **Reteach** Copymaster 49, p. 119 **Skills Tutorial** Strand P1, Skill 6
3, 4	**Common Error:** Children reverse the places of the digits. **Reteach** Copymaster 50, p. 120 **Skills Tutorial** Strand P1, Skill 9

Unit 7 • Lesson 6

Guided Practice: Exercises 1, 5, 9, 13, and 17

Name _____ Independent Practice: Exercises 2–4, 6–8, 10–12, 14–16, and 18–27

Comparing Numbers:
Using >,<, and =

Teacher Note: **Check Understanding** How can you use sticks to compare 12 and 17?

Compare the tens. The tens are the same.

Then compare the ones.

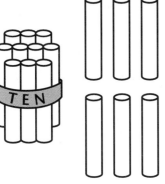 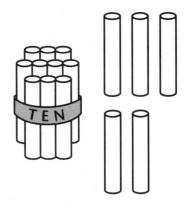

18 is greater than **15**.   **15** is less than **18**.

Ring the greater number.

1. | ⟨10⟩   7 | 2. | 4   ⟨11⟩ | 3. | ⟨13⟩   12 | 4. | 15   ⟨19⟩ |

Ring the number that is less.

5. | 18   ⟨12⟩ | 6. | ⟨5⟩   10 | 7. | ⟨13⟩   14 | 8. | ⟨11⟩   16 |

Ring the greatest.

9.   70   20   ⟨80⟩ | 10.   ⟨90⟩   10   30

11.   40   50   ⟨60⟩ | 12.   ⟨70⟩   50   20

Ring the least.

13. (70)   90   80 | 14. (20)   30   40

15. (50)   80   90 | 16. 40   (20)   60

Use >, <, or = .

17. $80 \,(>)\, 70$ 18. $40 \,(=)\, 40$ 19. $30 + 3 \,(<)\, 34$

20. $90 \,(>)\, 60$ 21. $50 \,(<)\, 70$ 22. $50 + 1 \,(<)\, 54$

23. $10 \,(<)\, 20$ 24. $30 \,(<)\, 60$ 25. $90 + 0 \,(=)\, 90$

Problem Solving
Reasoning

26. Jack says, "**29** is greater than **41**. I know because **9** is greater than **4** or **1**." Is Jack right? Why or why not? _____

No, because there are 4 tens in 41 and only 2 tens in 29. You have to compare tens before you compare ones.

_____

Teacher Note: **Closing the Lesson** Ask, If two 2-digit numbers do not have the same number of tens, should you compare the ones to see which is greater? Why or why not?

★ Test Prep

Which symbol belongs in the circle?
Mark the space under your answer.

27

    19 ◯ **17** | <   >   =   +
                                 ◯   ●   ◯   ◯

                    Unit 7 • Lesson 7

Name

Teacher Note: **Check Understanding** Ask, If you want to name a number greater than 6, will you go to the right or left of 6 on the number line?

Write the missing numbers.

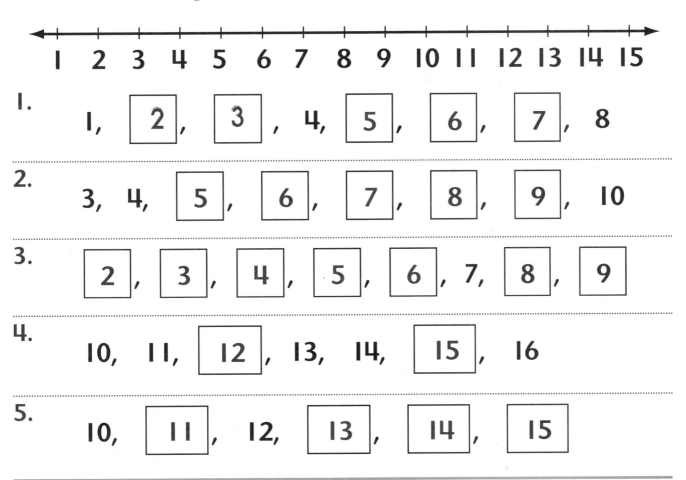

1. 1, 2, 3, 4, 5, 6, 7, 8

2. 3, 4, 5, 6, 7, 8, 9, 10

3. 2, 3, 4, 5, 6, 7, 8, 9

4. 10, 11, 12, 13, 14, 15, 16

5. 10, 11, 12, 13, 14, 15

Complete.

After	Between	Before
6. 9, 10	7. 7, 8, 9	8. 14, 15
9. 11, 12	10. 10, 11, 12	11. 10, 11
12. 8, 9	13. 4, 5, 6	14. 6, 7
15. 12, 13	16. 13, 14, 15	17. 12, 13

Write the missing numbers.

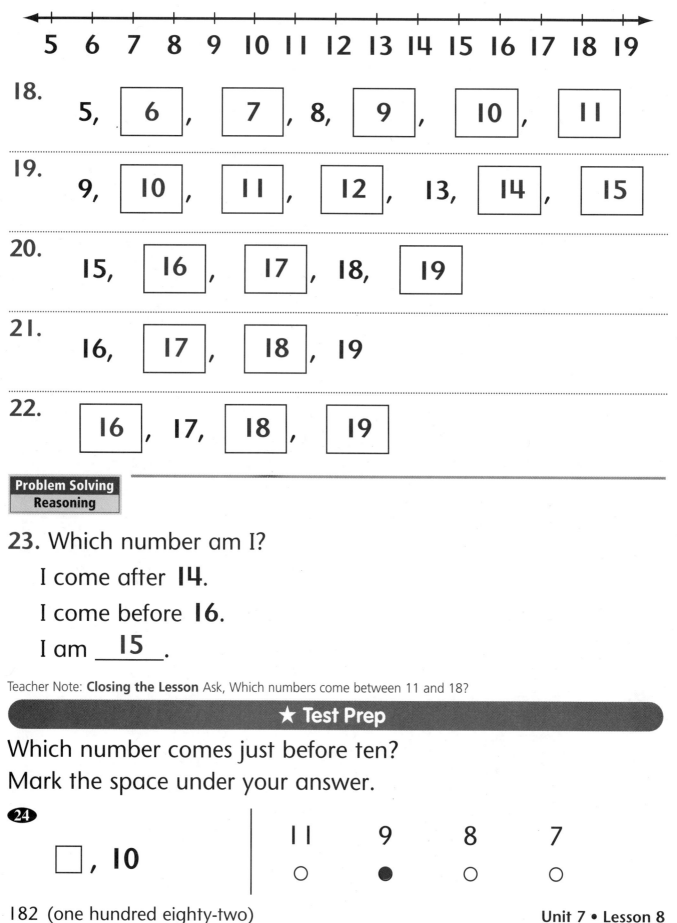

5 6 7 8 9 10 11 12 13 14 15 16 17 18 19

18. 5, [6], [7], 8, [9], [10], [11]

19. 9, [10], [11], [12], 13, [14], [15]

20. 15, [16], [17], 18, [19]

21. 16, [17], [18], 19

22. [16], 17, [18], [19]

Problem Solving
Reasoning

23. Which number am I?

I come after **14**.

I come before **16**.

I am __15__.

Teacher Note: **Closing the Lesson** Ask, Which numbers come between 11 and 18?

★ Test Prep

Which number comes just before ten?
Mark the space under your answer.

24

[ ], 10

11	9	8	7
○	●	○	○

Unit 7 • Lesson 8

Teacher Note: **Check Understanding** Ask, How does the number line help you find the numbers just before or just after a given number?

Write the missing numbers.

```
◄———┼———┼———┼———┼———┼———┼———┼———┼———┼———┼———►
   10   11   12   13   14   15   16   17   18   19   20
```

After	Between	Before
1. 11, [12]	2. 15, [16], 17	3. [19], 20
4. 16, [17]	5. 10, [11], 12	6. [11], 12
7. 19, [20]	8. 18, [19], 20	9. [15], 16
10. 14, [15]	11. 13, [14], 15	12. [17], 18

```
◄———┼———┼———┼———┼———┼———┼———┼———┼———┼———┼———►
   21   22   23   24   25   26   27   28   29   30
```

After	Between	Before
13. 22, [23]	14. 28, [29], 30	15. [29], 30
16. 27, [28]	17. 21, [22], 23	18. [22], 23
19. 25, [26]	20. 26, [27], 28	21. [26], 27
22. 29, [30]	23. 24, [25], 26	24. [28], 29

Unit 7 • Lesson 9

(one hundred eighty-three) 183

Write the missing numbers.

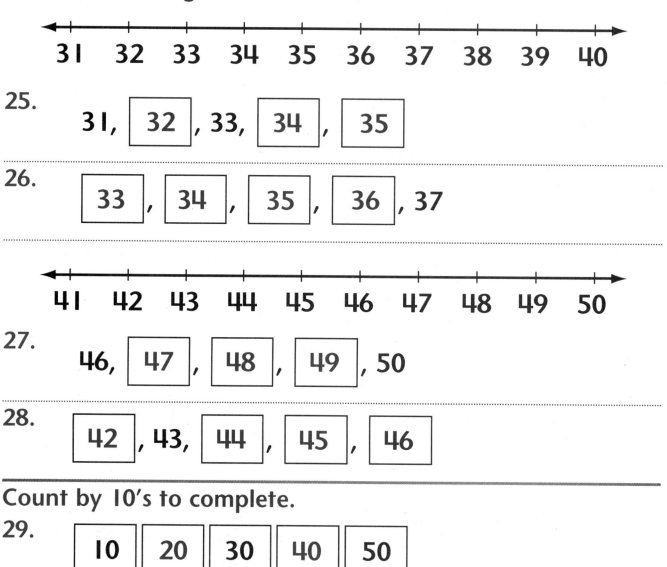

31 32 33 34 35 36 37 38 39 40

25.
31, ⬚32⬚, 33, ⬚34⬚, ⬚35⬚

26.
⬚33⬚, ⬚34⬚, ⬚35⬚, ⬚36⬚, 37

41 42 43 44 45 46 47 48 49 50

27.
46, ⬚47⬚, ⬚48⬚, ⬚49⬚, 50

28.
⬚42⬚, 43, ⬚44⬚, ⬚45⬚, ⬚46⬚

Count by 10's to complete.

29.
| 10 | 20 | 30 | 40 | 50 |

Teacher Note: **Closing the Lesson** Ask, Does the number 38 come after or before 40?

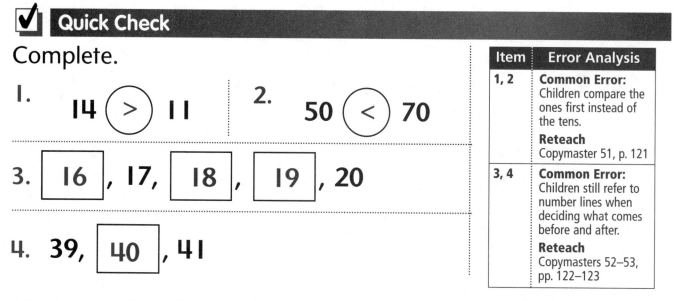

✓ Quick Check

Complete.

1. 14 ⬭>⬭ 11

2. 50 ⬭<⬭ 70

3. ⬚16⬚, 17, ⬚18⬚, ⬚19⬚, 20

4. 39, ⬚40⬚, 41

Item	Error Analysis
1, 2	**Common Error:** Children compare the ones first instead of the tens. **Reteach** Copymaster 51, p. 121
3, 4	**Common Error:** Children still refer to number lines when deciding what comes before and after. **Reteach** Copymasters 52–53, pp. 122–123

Unit 7 • Lesson 9

Name _____

Teacher Note: **Check Understanding** Ask, Do any 2-digit numbers with 8 tens come after 89? Before? If so, what are they?

Write the missing numbers.

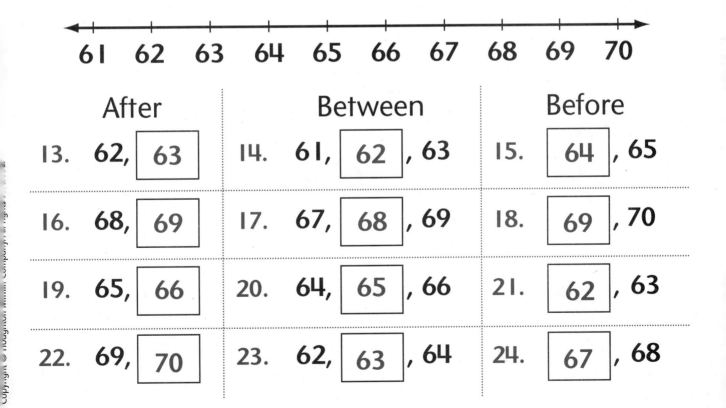

51 52 53 54 55 56 57 58 59 60

After	Between	Before
1. 55, **56**	2. 51, **52**, 53	3. **51**, 52
4. 59, **60**	5. 56, **57**, 58	6. **54**, 55
7. 52, **53**	8. 52, **53**, 54	9. **59**, 60
10. 57, **58**	11. 58, **59**, 60	12. **57**, 58

61 62 63 64 65 66 67 68 69 70

After	Between	Before
13. 62, **63**	14. 61, **62**, 63	15. **64**, 65
16. 68, **69**	17. 67, **68**, 69	18. **69**, 70
19. 65, **66**	20. 64, **65**, 66	21. **62**, 63
22. 69, **70**	23. 62, **63**, 64	24. **67**, 68

Write the missing numbers.

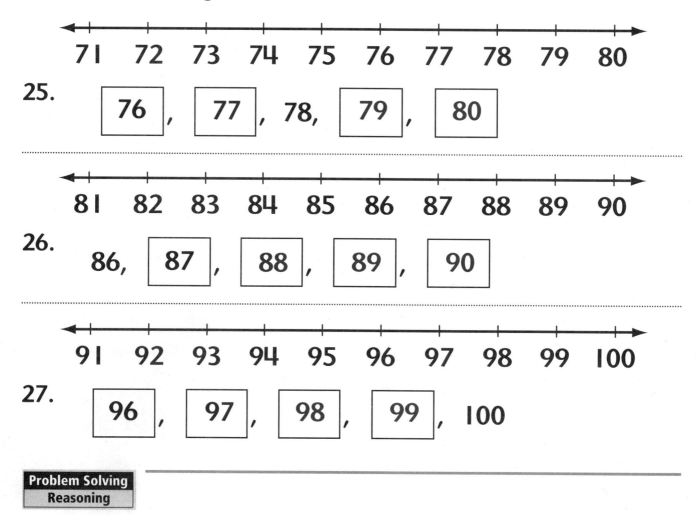

71   72   73   74   75   76   77   78   79   80

25. 76 , 77 , 78, 79 , 80

81   82   83   84   85   86   87   88   89   90

26. 86, 87 , 88 , 89 , 90

91   92   93   94   95   96   97   98   99   100

27. 96 , 97 , 98 , 99 , 100

Problem Solving
Reasoning

28. Which numbers are between **87** and **93**?

88, 89, 90, 91, 92

Teacher Note: **Closing the Lesson** Ask, If you can write the numbers 0 through 9, can you write the numbers 10 through 100? Why or why not?

★ Test Prep

Which number does not come after **71**? Mark the space under your answer.

29

74   80   69   92
○   ○   ●   ○

Unit 7 • Lesson 10

Teacher Note: **Check Understanding** Ask, How are the numbers alike? How are they different?

Count by 10's, forward and backward.

1.

🐰	🐰	🐰	🐰	🐰	🐰	🐰	🐰	🐰	🐰	**10**
🐰	🐰	🐰	🐰	🐰	🐰	🐰	🐰	🐰	🐰	**20**
🐰	🐰	🐰	🐰	🐰	🐰	🐰	🐰	🐰	🐰	**30**
🐰	🐰	🐰	🐰	🐰	🐰	🐰	🐰	🐰	🐰	**40**
🐰	🐰	🐰	🐰	🐰	🐰	🐰	🐰	🐰	🐰	**50**
🐰	🐰	🐰	🐰	🐰	🐰	🐰	🐰	🐰	🐰	**60**
🐰	🐰	🐰	🐰	🐰	🐰	🐰	🐰	🐰	🐰	**70**
🐰	🐰	🐰	🐰	🐰	🐰	🐰	🐰	🐰	🐰	**80**
🐰	🐰	🐰	🐰	🐰	🐰	🐰	🐰	🐰	🐰	**90**
🐰	🐰	🐰	🐰	🐰	🐰	🐰	🐰	🐰	🐰	**100**

2.

10	20	30	40	50	60	70	80	90	100

3.

100	90	80	70	60	50	40	30	20	10

Teacher Note: **Closing the Lesson** Ask, What pattern do you see in the numbers when you skip count by 10's?

★ Test Prep

Count by 10's. What number comes next? Mark the space for your answer.

4 40, 50, _____

30	60	90	100
○	●	○	○

Teacher Note: **Check Understanding** Ask, What pattern do you see in the ones place when you count by 5's?

Count by 2's.

1.

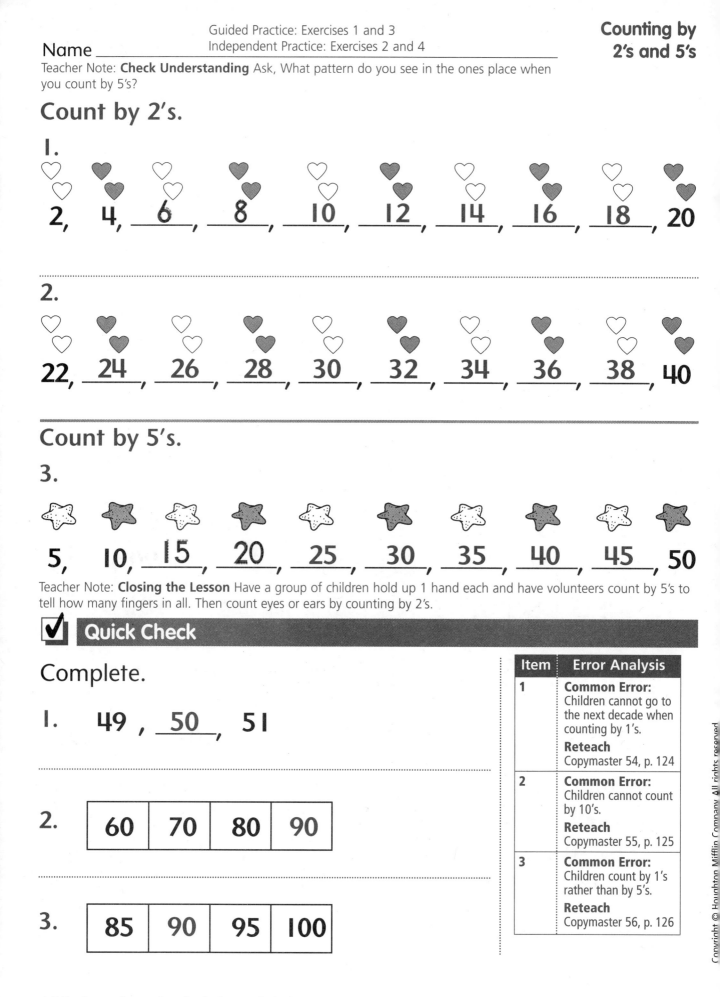

2, 4, 6 , 8 , 10 , 12 , 14 , 16 , 18 , 20

2.

22, 24 , 26 , 28 , 30 , 32 , 34 , 36 , 38 , 40

Count by 5's.

3.

5, 10, 15 , 20 , 25 , 30 , 35 , 40 , 45 , 50

Teacher Note: **Closing the Lesson** Have a group of children hold up 1 hand each and have volunteers count by 5's to tell how many fingers in all. Then count eyes or ears by counting by 2's.

✓ Quick Check

Complete.

1. 49 , 50 , 51

2.

| 60 | 70 | 80 | 90 |

3.

| 85 | 90 | 95 | 100 |

Item	Error Analysis
1	**Common Error:** Children cannot go to the next decade when counting by 1's. **Reteach** Copymaster 54, p. 124
2	**Common Error:** Children cannot count by 10's. **Reteach** Copymaster 55, p. 125
3	**Common Error:** Children count by 1's rather than by 5's. **Reteach** Copymaster 56, p. 126

Problem Solving Application:
Use a Picture

Problem Solving Plan
1. Understand   2. Decide   3. Solve   4. Look back

Use this picture to help solve the problem.

10 stars

Guess which box has 50 stars.   Answers may vary.

1.   red box   (gray box)

Think Does my answer make sense?
Ring groups of **10** to check.

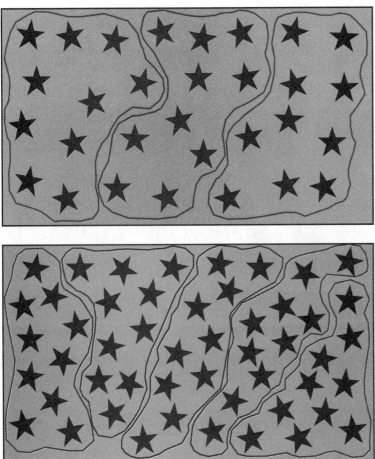

How many stars? | 30 |

How many stars? | 50 |

Use this picture to help solve the problem.

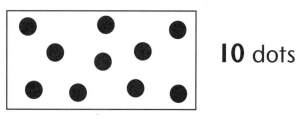 **10** dots

Guess which box has 63 dots. Answers may vary.

2. (red box)   gray box

Think Does my answer make sense?
Ring groups of **10** to check.

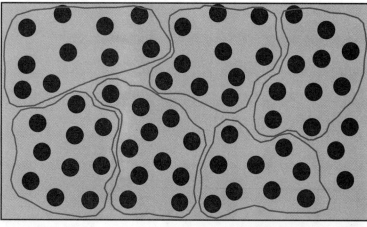 How many dots? 63

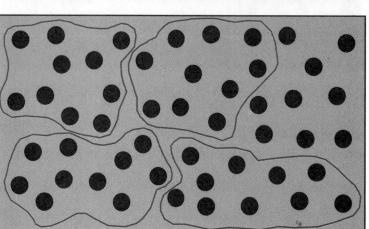 How many dots? 49

Teacher Note: **Closing the Lesson** Ask, Did you have to know the exact number of dots in each box to solve problem 2? Why or why not?

Extend Your Thinking

3. How did you use the picture to solve the problem? _____

Answers will vary. Possible answer: I saw how many ten dots were, then estimated how many sets of ten were in each box. Then I picked the box that looked like it had more than 60 dots.

190 (one hundred ninety)   Unit 7 • Lesson 13

Guided Practice: Exercises 1 and 8
Independent Practice: Exercises 2–7 and 9–13

Teacher Note: **Check Understanding** Ask, If you are seventh in line and you are last, how many people are in line?

1st	2nd	3rd	4th	5th	6th	7th
first	second	third	fourth	fifth	sixth	seventh

Look at the ordinal number.
Ring the object.

1. **5**th

2. **2**nd

3. **6**th

4. **1**st

5. **3**rd

6. **4**th

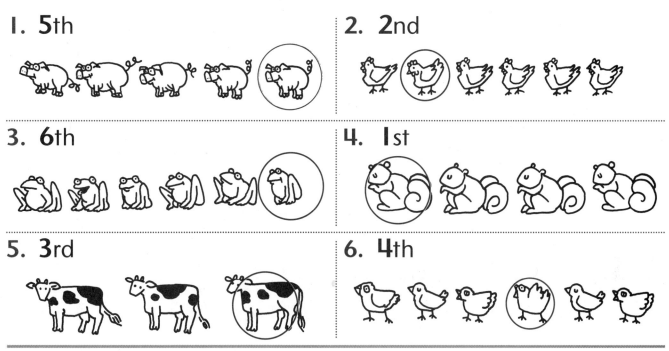

Complete the ordinal numbers.

7.

___1st ___2nd ___3rd ___4th ___5th ___6th ___7th

Read the ordinal numbers.
Match objects.

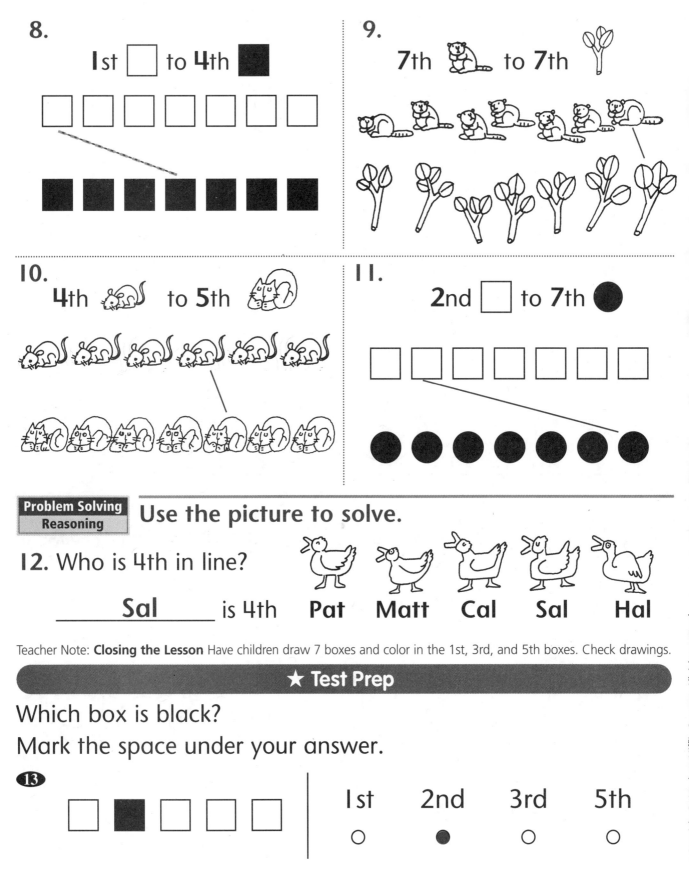

8.

1st ☐ to 4th ■

9.

7th 🦫 to 7th 🌿

10.

4th 🐭 to 5th 🐱

11.

2nd ☐ to 7th ●

Problem Solving Reasoning Use the picture to solve.

12. Who is 4th in line?

_____Sal_____ is 4th   Pat   Matt   Cal   Sal   Hal

Teacher Note: **Closing the Lesson** Have children draw 7 boxes and color in the 1st, 3rd, and 5th boxes. Check drawings.

★ Test Prep

Which box is black?
Mark the space under your answer.

13

	1st	2nd	3rd	5th
	○	●	○	○

Guided Practice: Model Problem
Independent Practice: Problems 1–8

Problem Solving Strategy:
Find a Pattern

Problem

15, 25, 35, 45, 55, __?__
What number comes next?

Say, As you read, ask yourself questions.

① **Understand**   I need to find the number that comes next.

Ask, How can you find the number? Can you see a pattern?

② **Decide**   I can shade the hundred chart to help.

③ **Solve**

1	2	3	4	5	6	7	8	9	10
11	12	13	14	15	16	17	18	19	20
21	22	23	24	25	26	27	28	29	30
31	32	33	34	35	36	37	38	39	40
41	42	43	44	45	46	47	48	49	50
51	52	53	54	55	56	57	58	59	60
61	62	63	64	65	66	67	68	69	70
71	72	73	74	75	76	77	78	79	80
81	82	83	84	85	86	87	88	89	90
91	92	93	94	95	96	97	98	99	100

What number comes next? __65__

④ **Look back**   Does my answer make sense?
Ask, What other strategy could you use to solve the problem?

Solve.

1. 4, 8, 12, 16, __?__

What number comes next? __20__

Use the hundred chart to help find patterns.

1	2	3	4	5	6	7	8	9	10
11	12	13	14	15	16	17	18	19	20
21	22	23	24	25	26	27	28	29	30
31	32	33	34	35	36	37	38	39	40
41	42	43	44	45	46	47	48	49	50
51	52	53	54	55	56	57	58	59	60
61	62	63	64	65	66	67	68	69	70
71	72	73	74	75	76	77	78	79	80
81	82	83	84	85	86	87	88	89	90
91	92	93	94	95	96	97	98	99	100

What numbers come next?
Continue the pattern.

2. **25, 26, 27, 28,** __29__ , __30__ , __31__ , __32__

3. **90, 80, 70, 60,** __50__ , __40__ , __30__ , __20__

4. **59, 58, 57, 56,** __55__ , __54__ , __53__ , __52__

Solve.

5. What number is **10** more than **19**? __29__

6. What number is **1** less than **75**? __74__

7. What number is **10** less than **41**? __31__

8. What number is **1** more than **81**? __82__

Teacher Note: **Closing the Lesson** What strategy did you use to solve exercises 5–8?
How might finding a pattern help?

Unit 7 • Lesson 15

Complete. (7A)

1. __35__ , __36__ , 37, 38, 39, __40__

2. 77, __78__ , __79__ , __80__ , __81__ , 82

Write the number. (7B)

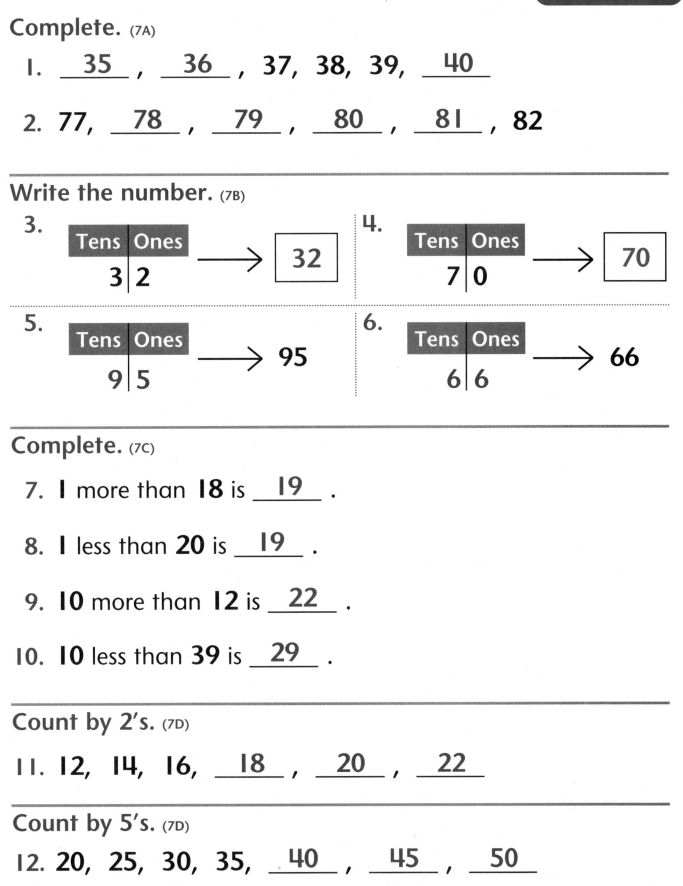

3.
Tens	Ones
3	2

→ 32

4.
Tens	Ones
7	0

→ 70

5.
Tens	Ones
9	5

→ 95

6.
Tens	Ones
6	6

→ 66

Complete. (7C)

7. I more than **18** is __19__ .

8. I less than **20** is __19__ .

9. **10** more than **12** is __22__ .

10. **10** less than **39** is __29__ .

Count by 2's. (7D)

11. **12, 14, 16,** __18__ , __20__ , __22__

Count by 5's. (7D)

12. **20, 25, 30, 35,** __40__ , __45__ , __50__

Count by 10's. (7D)

13. 40, 50, __60__ , __70__ , __80__ , 90

Write <, >, or = to make the sentence true. (7E)

14.   17 (=) 17   15. 23 (<) 32

Ring the 2nd figure. (7F)

16.

Use the hundred chart. Complete. (7G)

1	2	3	4	5	6	7	8	9	10
11	12	13	14	15	16	17	18	19	20
21	22	23	24	25	26	27	28	29	30
31	32	33	34	35	36	37	38	39	40
41	42	43	44	45	46	47	48	49	50
51	52	53	54	55	56	57	58	59	60
61	62	63	64	65	66	67	68	69	70
71	72	73	74	75	76	77	78	79	80
81	82	83	84	85	86	87	88	89	90
91	92	93	94	95	96	97	98	99	100

17. 1, 11, 21, 31, __41__ , __51__ , __61__

18. 80, 79, 78, 77, __76__ , __75__ , __74__

196 (one hundred ninety-six)   Unit 7 • Review

1 There are 6 ants. 4 ants run away. How many are left? Which number sentence will solve the problem? Mark the space next to your answer. **(5C)**

○ $4 - 0 = 4$ ○ $6 + 4 = 10$

● $6 - 4 = 2$ ○ $4 + 2 = 6$

---

2 Which number sentence is missing from the fact family? Mark the space next to your answer. **(6B)**

$7 + 3 = 10$

$3 + 7 = 10$

$10 - 7 = 3$

● $10 - 3 = 7$ ○ $10 - 10 = 0$

○ $4 + 3 = 7$ ○ $10 + 3 = 13$

---

3 Count by 1's. Which number comes next? Mark the space under your answer. **(7A)**

66, 67, 68, 69, ____

65	70	71	80
○	●	○	○

---

4 Which table shows how many tens and ones are in the 2-digit number? Mark the space under your answer. **(7B)**

97

Tens	Ones		Tens	Ones		Tens	Ones		Tens	Ones
7	7		7	9		9	7		0	9
○			○			●			○	

---

5 Count by 2's. Which number comes next? Mark the space under your answer. **(7D)**

16, 18, ____

19	17	20	18
○	○	●	○

---

6 Count by 5's. Which number comes next? Mark the space under your answer. **(7D)**

35, 40, 45, ____

46	48	47	50
○	○	○	●

7 Count by 10's. Which number is missing? Mark the space under your answer. **(7D)**

40, ____ , 60, 70

80	50	30	41
○	●	○	○

8 Which symbol belongs in the circle? Mark the space under your answer. **(7E)**

19 ◯ 16

>	<	=	+
●	○	○	○

9 Which is the third figure? Mark the space under your answer. **(7F)**

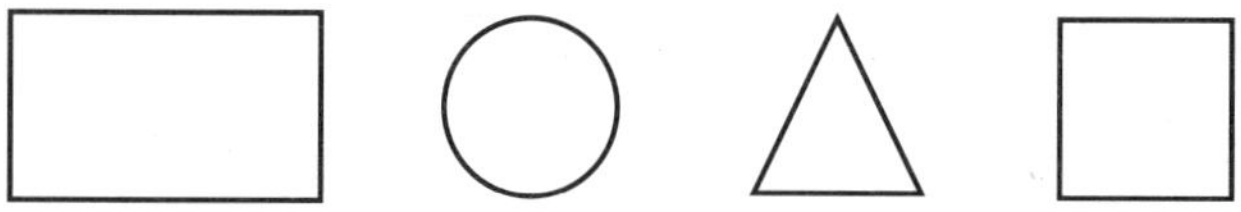

△ □ ◯ ▭ | ▭ ◯ △ □

| ○ | ● | ○ | ○ |

10 Which number is 10 more than 28? Mark the space under your answer. **(7C)**

18	27	38	29
○	○	●	○

31	32	33	34	35	36	37	38	39	40
41	42	43	44	45	46	47	48	49	50

11 Use the part of the hundred chart shown to help tell which number comes next in the pattern. Mark the space under your answer. **(7G)**

43, 42, 41, 40, ____

41	39	38	42
○	●	○	○

Decide on an answer. Mark the space for your answer. If the answer is **not here**, mark the space for **NH**. (6A)

Tell children they will complete the rest of the test independently.

12 10 − 6 = ☐

0	4	6	NH
○	●	○	○

13 10 − 4 = ☐

4	0	8	NH
○	○	○	●

198 (one hundred ninety-eight)

Unit 7 • Cumulative Review

UNIT 8 • TABLE OF CONTENTS

Time and Money

Lesson	Page

Dear Family,

During the next few weeks our math class will be learning about time and money.

You can expect to see homework that provides practice with telling time and counting money amounts using pennies, nickels, and dimes.

As we learn about time and money you may wish to keep the following samples as a guide.

Time

11 o'clock   or   11:00   half past 11   or   11:30

Money

I penny   I nickel   I dime
I¢   5¢   10¢

Knowing how to tell time and count money will help children with real life skills.

Sincerely,

Name _____

Guided Practice: Exercise 1
Independent Practice: Exercises 2–4

Ordering Events

Teacher Note: **Check Understanding** Ask, What is something you do before school? After school?

Write 1, 2, and 3 to show the correct order.

1.

2 _____   1 _____   3 _____

2.

2 _____   1 _____   3 _____

3.

2 _____   1 _____   3 _____

Teacher Note: **Closing the Lesson** Ask, Do you study before or after you take a spelling test?

★ Test Prep

Which picture shows what happened after the event at the beginning of the row? Mark your answer.

4    |

●   ○   ○

Unit 8 • Lesson 1

(two hundred one) 201

Teacher Note: **Check Understanding** Ask, Does it take longer to cook a pizza or eat a grape?

Watch a game.

hours

Eat a hot dog.

minutes

About how long? Ring minutes or hours.

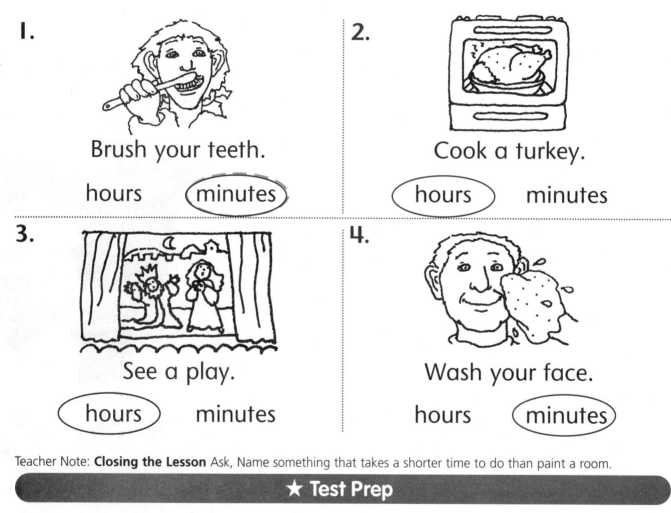

1. Brush your teeth.

hours (minutes)

2. Cook a turkey.

(hours) minutes

3. See a play.

(hours) minutes

4. Wash your face.

hours (minutes)

Teacher Note: **Closing the Lesson** Ask, Name something that takes a shorter time to do than paint a room.

★ Test Prep

About how long? Mark next to your answer.

5. Bake a cake.

● hours   ○ seconds

○ minutes   ○ days

Guided Practice: Exercise 1
Independent Practice: Exercises 2–12

Hour

Teacher Note: **Check Understanding** Say, Explain how to show four o'clock.

Write the correct time.

1. **7** o'clock

2. **9** o'clock

3. **12** o'clock

4. **3** o'clock

5. **4** o'clock

6. **6** o'clock

Write the time.

7.

_____3_____ o'clock

8.

_____6_____ :00

9.

_____12_____ o'clock

10.

_____9_____ o'clock

11.

_____11_____ :00

12.

_____10_____ o'clock

Teacher Note: **Closing the Lesson** Ask, How are the clocks on this page alike? How are they different?

✓ **Quick Check**

Write 1, 2, and 3 to show order.

1.

Water seeds. ___2___

Plant seeds. ___1___

Seeds sprout. ___3___

Ring the event that takes hours.

2.

Tie your shoes.

(Watch a movie)

Pour a drink.

Item	Error Analysis
1	**Common Error:** Children do not understand the concept of order. **Reteach** Copymaster 58, p. 128
2	**Common Error:** Children do not know the difference between hours and minutes. **Reteach** Copymaster 59, p. 129
3	**Common Error:** Children use the minute hand to identify the hour. **Reteach** Copymaster 60, p. 130

Complete.

3.

_____8_____ :00

Half Hour

Teacher Note: **Check Understanding** Ask, What two numbers will the hour hand be between at 9:30?

What time is it?

half past **12**   or   **12:30**

Write the correct time.

1.

___**7**___ :30

2.

half past ___**2**___

3.

___**4**___ :30

4.

___**6**___ :30

5.

half past ___**11**___

6.

___**10**___ :30

7.

half past ___**9**___

8.

___**8**___ :30

9.

half past ___**5**___

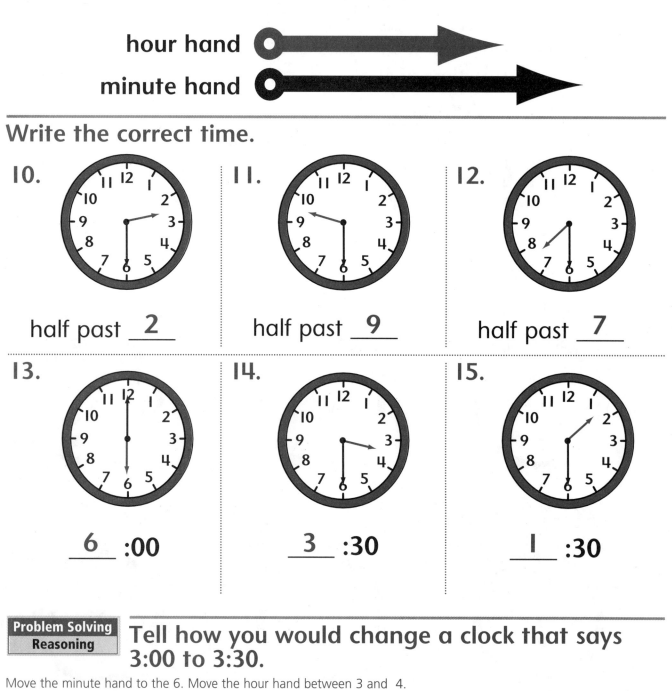

hour hand ➙

minute hand ➙

Write the correct time.

10.

half past __2__

11.

half past __9__

12.

half past __7__

13.

__6__ :00

14.

__3__ :30

15.

__l__ :30

**Problem Solving
Reasoning** Tell how you would change a clock that says 3:00 to 3:30.

Move the minute hand to the 6. Move the hour hand between 3 and 4.

Teacher Note: **Closing the Lesson** Say, Explain how to show 6:30 on a clock.

★ Test Prep

Which clock shows 5:30? Mark the space under your answer.

16

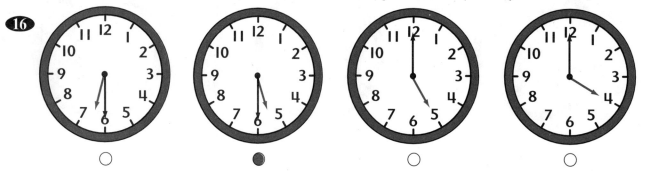

○   ●   ○   ○

Teacher Note: **Check Understanding** Say, What number is always on a digital clock when it is half past the hour?

Match.

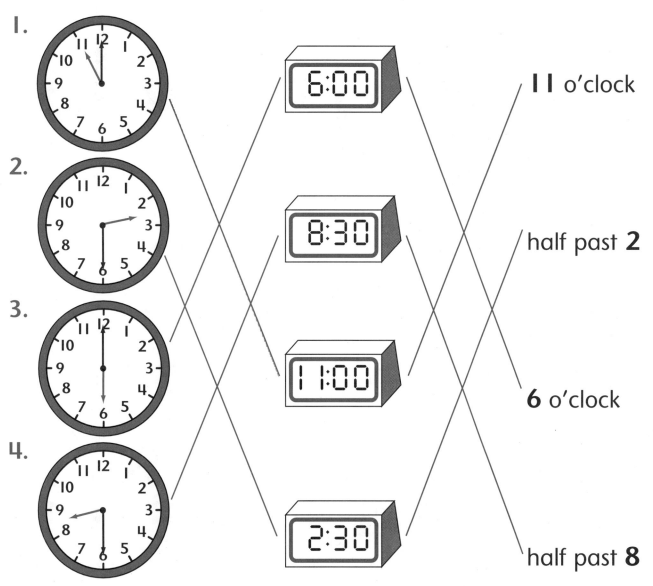

1.

2.

3.

4.

6:00   11 o'clock

8:30   half past **2**

11:00   **6** o'clock

2:30   half past **8**

Teacher Note: **Closing the Lesson** Ask, What do the numbers to the left of the colon on a digital clock tell? What do the numbers to the right tell?

★ Test Prep

Which digital clock shows the same time?
Mark next to your answer.

5

○ 10:30   ○ 9:00

● 9:30   ○ 6:30

Unit 8 • Lesson 5

Elapsed Time

Teacher Note: **Check Understanding** Say, Suppose it is 2:00. What time will it be in one hour?

Write the times. Answer the question.

1.

3:00   3:30   4:00

How long did the boys play? __I hour__

2.

2:00   2:30   3:00

How long did the girl rake? __I hour__

Teacher Note: **Closing the Lesson** Ask, How much time elapses from 6:00 to 7:00?

☑ **Quick Check**

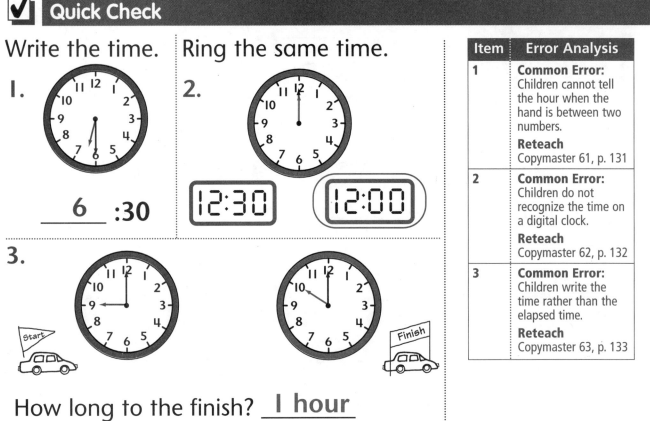

Write the time.   Ring the same time.

1. __6__ :30

2. | 12:30 | | 12:00 |

3. How long to the finish? __I hour__

Item	Error Analysis
1	**Common Error:** Children cannot tell the hour when the hand is between two numbers. **Reteach** Copymaster 61, p. 131
2	**Common Error:** Children do not recognize the time on a digital clock. **Reteach** Copymaster 62, p. 132
3	**Common Error:** Children write the time rather than the elapsed time. **Reteach** Copymaster 63, p. 133

Unit 8 • Lesson 6

**Problem Solving Application:
Use a Table**

Problem Solving Plan
1. Understand   2. Decide   3. Solve   4. Look back

Use the table to answer the question.

Morning Schedule

Time	Subject
9:00	Reading
10:00	Math
11:00	Science
11:30	Lunch
12:00	Recess

Think What does the question ask me to find out?

1. What time does math begin? __10:00__

2. What time does science begin? __11:00__

3. How long is reading? __1 hour__

Afternoon Schedule

Time	Subject
12:30	Music
1:00	Social Studies
2:00	Computers
3:00	Go home

4. Which subject begins at half past 12? __music__

5. When do the students go home? __3:00__

6. How long is social studies? __1 hour__

Use the table to answer the question.

Ticket Counter Lines

Number of People	Time
10	12:00
7	12:30
5	1:00
1	1:30

7. How many more people are in line at **1:00** than at **1:30**?
   __4__ more people

8. At what time were the most people in line? __12:00__

9. How many people were in line at **1** o'clock?
   __5__ people

Teacher Note: **Closing the Lesson** Ask, How did the tables help you solve the problems?

Extend Your Thinking

10. Make up your own problem about the table.
    Ask a friend to solve it.

Answers will vary. Possible answer: How many people are in line at 12:00?   (10)

_____

_____

_____

_____

Teacher Note: **Check Understanding** Ask, What date is two weeks after the 10th?

Look at the calendar. Answer the question.

January						
Sunday	Monday	Tuesday	Wednesday	Thursday	Friday	Saturday
		1	2	3	4	5
🍰 6	7	8	9	🍰 10	11	12
13	14	🍰 15	16	17	18	19
20	21	22	23	24	25	26
🍰 27	28	29	🍰 30	31		

1. How many

   Mondays? __4__   birthdays? __5__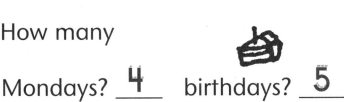

   days in this month? __31__   weekend days? __8__

2. What is the name of this month? __**January**__

3. How many days are in one week? __7__

4. What date of the month is

   the **fourth** Tuesday? __22__

   the **third** Sunday? __20__

Write in the name of this month.
Number the days like the calendar in your classroom.

5.

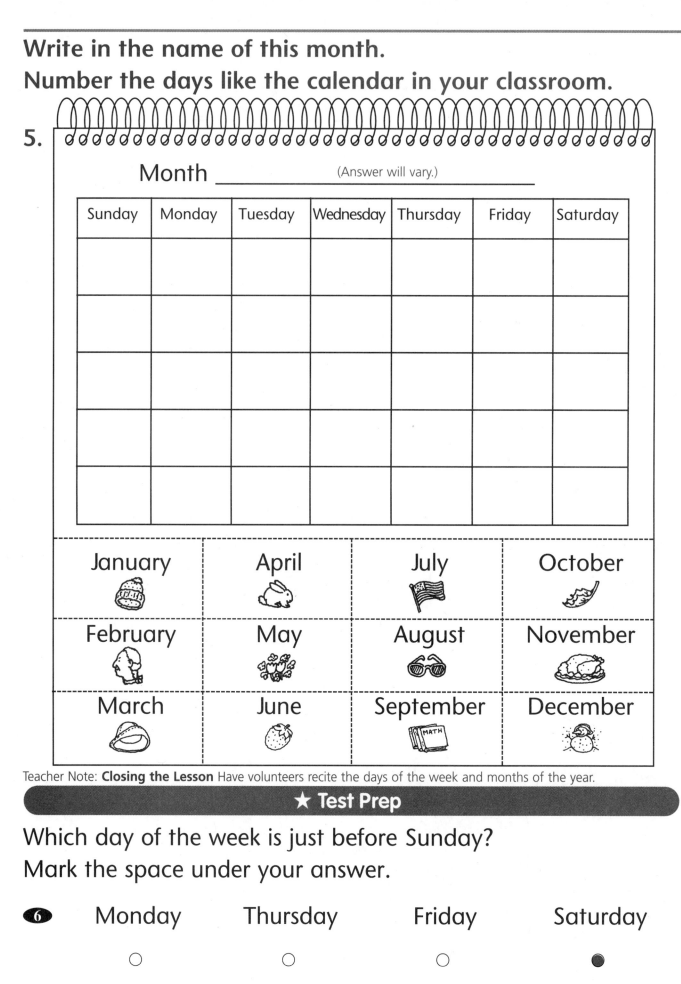

Month _____ (Answer will vary.)

Sunday	Monday	Tuesday	Wednesday	Thursday	Friday	Saturday

January	April	July	October
February	May	August	November
March	June	September	December

Teacher Note: **Closing the Lesson** Have volunteers recite the days of the week and months of the year.

★ Test Prep

Which day of the week is just before Sunday?
Mark the space under your answer.

6 Monday   Thursday   Friday   Saturday

          ○   ○   ○   ●

Teacher Note: **Check Understanding** Ask, Which coin do you count by 5's? Why?

Remember:

= 1¢ | or = 5¢

1 penny | **5 pennies** | **1 nickel**

Count by 5's. Write the amount.

1.

$\boxed{10}$ ¢

2.

$\boxed{15}$ ¢

3.

$\boxed{20}$ ¢

4.

$\boxed{25}$ ¢

5.

$\boxed{30}$ ¢

6.

$\boxed{35}$ ¢

Count by 5's.
Then count on by 1's. Write the amount.

7. 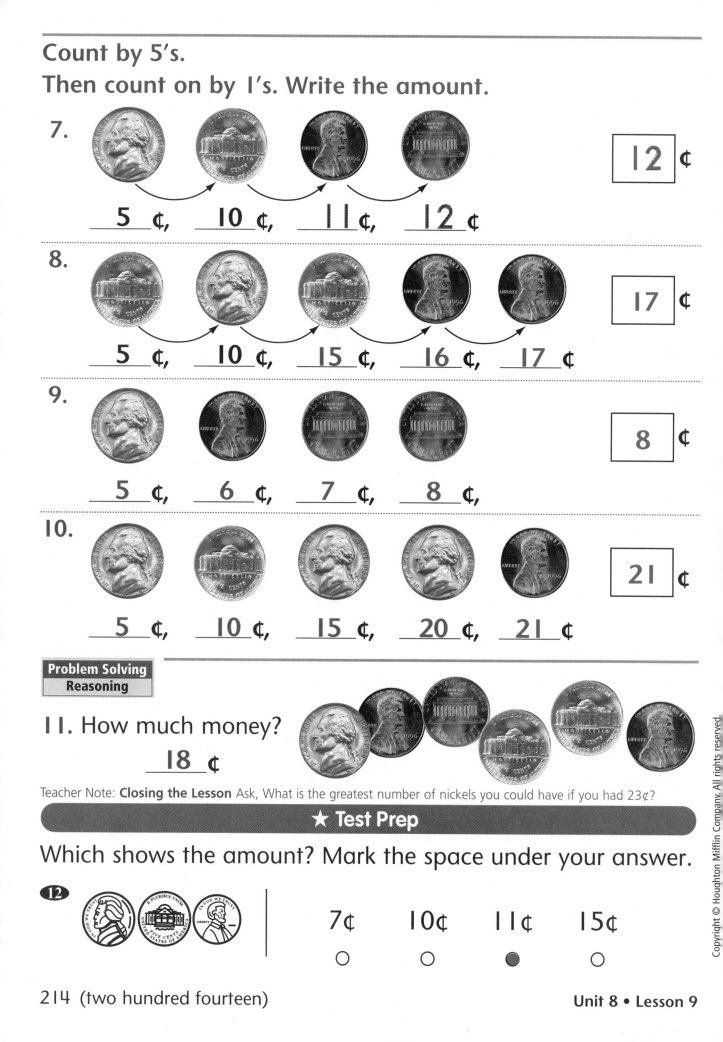   ___5___ ¢,   ___10___ ¢,   ___11___¢,   ___12___ ¢   [12] ¢

8.   ___5___ ¢,   ___10___ ¢,   ___15___ ¢,   ___16___ ¢,   ___17___ ¢   [17] ¢

9.   ___5___ ¢,   ___6___ ¢,   ___7___ ¢,   ___8___ ¢,   [8] ¢

10.   ___5___ ¢,   ___10___ ¢,   ___15___ ¢,   ___20___ ¢,   ___21___ ¢   [21] ¢

Problem Solving Reasoning

11. How much money?

___18___ ¢

Teacher Note: **Closing the Lesson** Ask, What is the greatest number of nickels you could have if you had 23¢?

★ **Test Prep**

Which shows the amount? Mark the space under your answer.

12.

| 7¢ | 10¢ | 11¢ | 15¢ |
| ○ | ○ | ● | ○ |

214 (two hundred fourteen)

Unit 8 • Lesson 9

Counting Dimes, Nickels, and Pennies

Name _____

Teacher Note: **Check Understanding** Ask, When I count amounts that have different coins, which coins do I count first? Why?

Remember:

10 pennies	**1 dime**
10¢	**10¢**

Count by 10's. Write the amount.

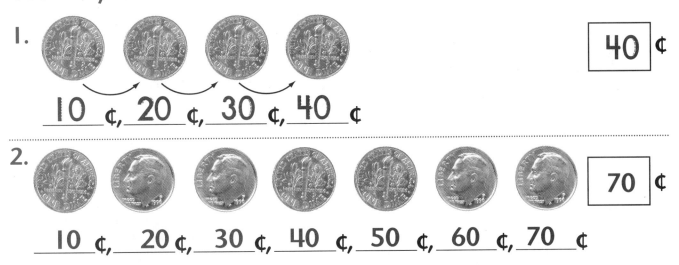

1. 40 ¢

__10__ ¢, __20__ ¢, __30__ ¢, __40__ ¢

2. 70 ¢

__10__ ¢, __20__ ¢, __30__ ¢, __40__ ¢, __50__ ¢, __60__ ¢, __70__ ¢

Count by 10's.
Then count on by 1's. Write the amount.

3. 23 ¢

__10__ ¢, __20__ ¢, __21__ ¢, __22__ ¢, __23__ ¢

4. 33 ¢

__10__ ¢, __20__ ¢, __30__ ¢, __31__ ¢, __32__ ¢, __33__ ¢

Ring the coins needed to buy each toy.

7.

10¢

8.

18¢

Solve.

9. I have some dimes, some nickels, and some pennies in my pocket. I take out **2** coins. How much money could I have? Write all the possible amounts. 20¢; 15¢; 10¢; 2¢; 11¢; 6¢.

_____ ¢, _____ ¢, _____ ¢, _____ ¢, _____ ¢, _____ ¢

Teacher Note: **Closing the Lesson** Ask, If you have 2 dimes, what coins do you need to make 23 cents?

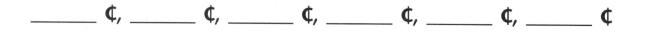

★ Test Prep

How much money?
Mark the space for your answer.

10

22¢ ○   26¢ ●   31¢ ○   30¢ ○

218 (two hundred eighteen)

Unit 8 • Lesson 11

Teacher Note: **Check Understanding** Ask, Could you buy a whistle that costs 30¢ with a quarter? Why or why not?

25¢

I quarter

25 cents

Use coins.

Find ways to make 25¢. Complete the chart.

Answer will vary. All possible answers shown.

I.

Ways to Make 25¢								
2	2	1	1	1	1	0	0	0
1	0	3	2	1	0	5	4	3
0	5	0	5	10	15	0	5	10

Solve.

2. Can you make **25¢** using only **I** coin? _____yes_____

If yes, write the name of the coin. _____quarter_____

Write the amount.

3. 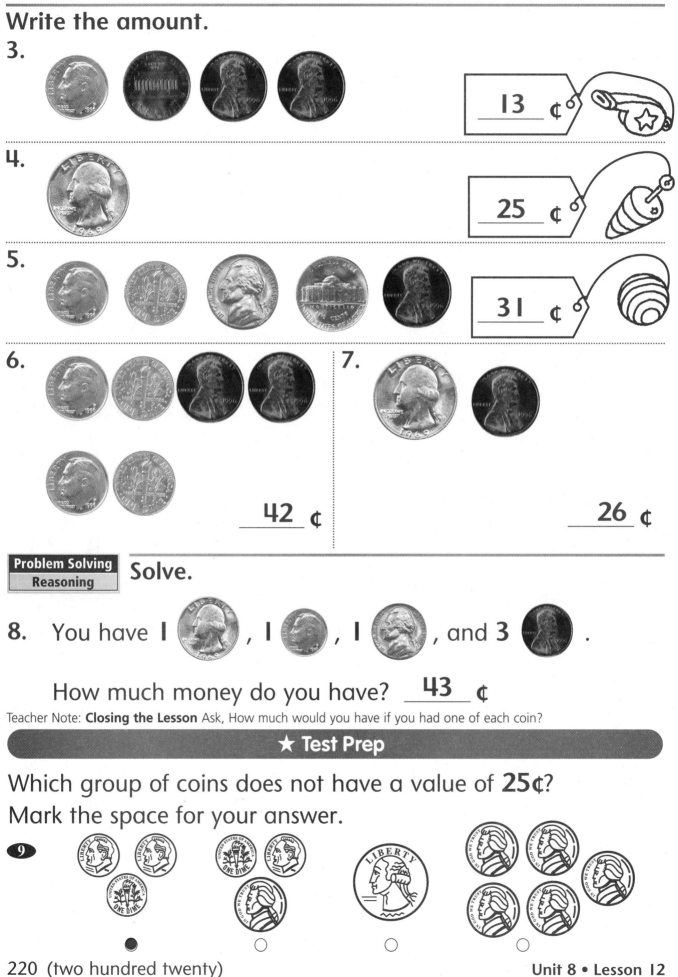 <u>13</u> ¢

4. <u>25</u> ¢

5. <u>31</u> ¢

6. <u>42</u> ¢

7. <u>26</u> ¢

Problem Solving Reasoning Solve.

8. You have **1** , **1** , **1** , and **3** .

How much money do you have? <u>43</u> ¢

Teacher Note: **Closing the Lesson** Ask, How much would you have if you had one of each coin?

★ Test Prep

Which group of coins does not have a value of **25¢**?
Mark the space for your answer.

9   ●   ○   ○   ○

Problem

Emily spends **5¢.**
Which stamps does she buy?

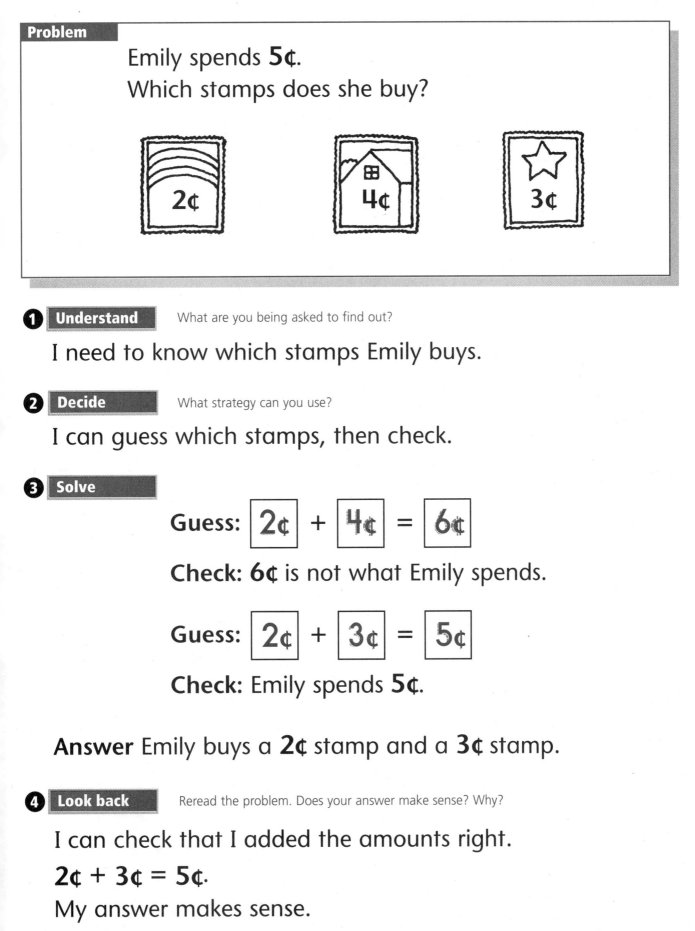

1 **Understand**   What are you being asked to find out?

I need to know which stamps Emily buys.

2 **Decide**   What strategy can you use?

I can guess which stamps, then check.

3 **Solve**

Guess: | 2¢ | + | 4¢ | = | 6¢ |

Check: **6¢** is not what Emily spends.

Guess: | 2¢ | + | 3¢ | = | 5¢ |

Check: Emily spends **5¢.**

Answer Emily buys a **2¢** stamp and a **3¢** stamp.

4 **Look back**   Reread the problem. Does your answer make sense? Why?

I can check that I added the amounts right.
2¢ + 3¢ = 5¢.
My answer makes sense.

Unit 8 • Lesson 13

Guess and check to solve.

1. Ellen spends **7¢**. Ring the stamps she buys.

2. Allan spends **8¢**. Ring the stamps he buys.

3. Marie spends **6¢**. Ring the stamps she buys.

4. Bill spends **9¢**. Ring the stamps he buys.

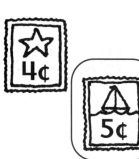

5. Mario spends **7¢**. Ring the stamps he buys.

6. Sylvia spends **10¢**. Ring the stamps she buys.

Teacher Note: **Closing the Lesson** Have children use the stamps in problem 6 to make up a new problem. Have them share and compare their problems and solutions.

Name _____

Match. (8A)

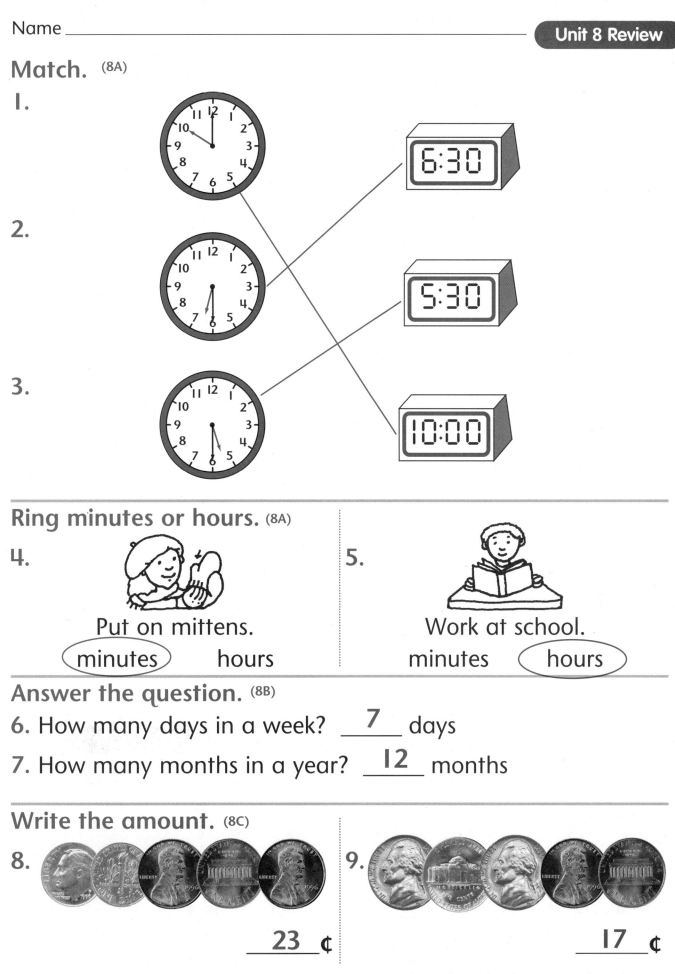

1.

2.

3.

6:30

5:30

10:00

Ring minutes or hours. (8A)

4.

Put on mittens.

(minutes)   hours

5.

Work at school.

minutes   (hours)

Answer the question. (8B)

6. How many days in a week? ___7___ days

7. How many months in a year? ___12___ months

Write the amount. (8C)

8.

___23___ ¢

9.

___17___ ¢

Unit 8 • Review

Ring the coins needed. (8C)

10.   **16¢**

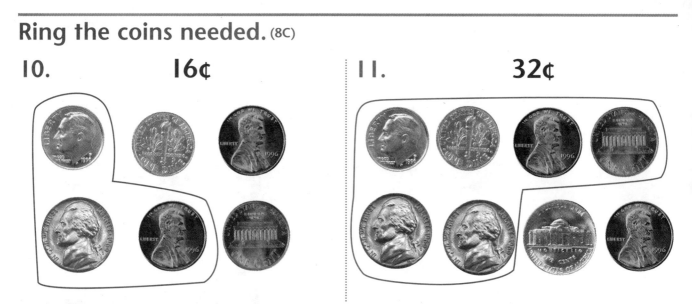

11.   **32¢**

Use the table to answer the question. (8D)

Bus Schedule

Leaves at	From
9:00	Bean Town
10:30	Greenvale
11:00	Middle Village
12:30	Mine City

12. What time does the bus leave Greenvale? __10:30__

13. Where will the bus leave from at **11** o'clock?
    Middle Village

Use guess and check to solve. (8D)

14.

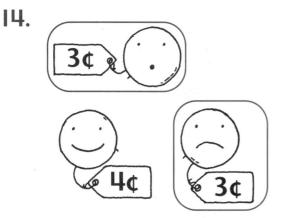

Bill spends **6¢.**
Ring the pins he buys.

15.

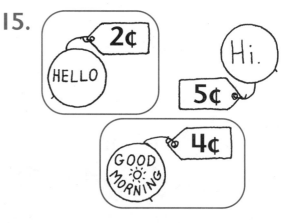

Ann spends **6¢.**
Ring the pins she buys.

       Unit 8 • Review

Name_____

1 Which number is missing? Mark the space under your answer. **(7A)**

72, 71, _____ , 69, 68

75	66	70	67
○	○	●	○

2 Which tells how many tens and ones are in the 2-digit number? Mark the space under your answer. **(7B)**

40

○ 4 tens, 4 ones   ● 4 tens, 0 ones

○ 0 tens, 4 ones   ○ 4 tens, 10 ones

3 Count by 5's. Which number is missing? Mark the space under your answer. **(7D)**

20, _____ , 30, 35

15	21	35	25
○	○	○	●

4 Which symbol belongs in the circle? Mark the space under your answer. **(7E)**

23 ○ 32

<	>	=	+
●	○	○	○

5 Which is the fifth letter? Mark the space under your answer. **(7F)**

A B C D E F G

B	E	F	G
○	●	○	○

6 Which number sentence solves the problem? Mark the space next to your answer. **(6A)**

There are 9 birds. 1 flies away. How many are left?

● $9 - 1 = 8$ ○ $9 + 1 = 10$

○ $8 - 1 = 7$ ○ $9 - 8 = 1$

7 Which number comes next in the pattern? Mark the space under your answer. **(7G)**

50, 48, 46, 44, _____

| 40 | 41 | 42 | 43 |
| ○ | ○ | ● | ○ |

8 Which time does the clock show? Mark the space under your answer. **(8A)**

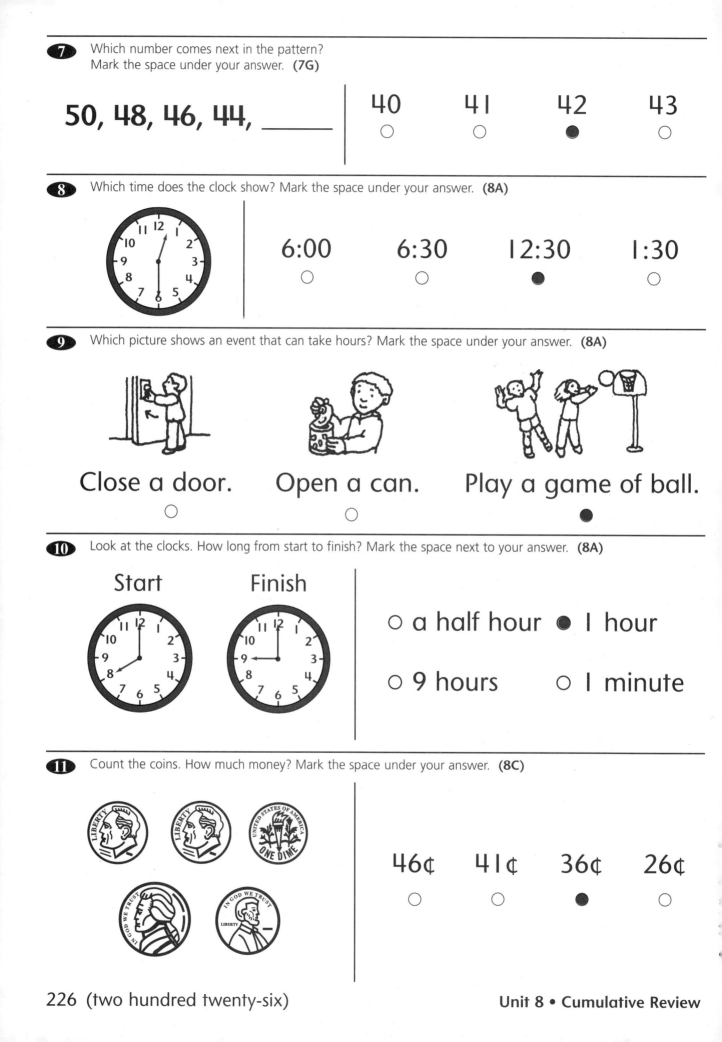

| 6:00 | 6:30 | 12:30 | 1:30 |
| ○ | ○ | ● | ○ |

9 Which picture shows an event that can take hours? Mark the space under your answer. **(8A)**

Close a door.   Open a can.   Play a game of ball.
        ○   ○   ●

10 Look at the clocks. How long from start to finish? Mark the space next to your answer. **(8A)**

Start   Finish

○ a half hour   ● 1 hour

○ 9 hours   ○ 1 minute

11 Count the coins. How much money? Mark the space under your answer. **(8C)**

| 46¢ | 41¢ | 36¢ | 26¢ |
| ○ | ○ | ● | ○ |

Unit 8 • Cumulative Review

UNIT 9 • TABLE OF CONTENTS

2-Digit Addition and Subtraction

Dear Family,

During the next few weeks our math class will be learning and practicing addition and subtraction of 2-digit numbers.

We will be using this vocabulary:

2-digit numbers from 10 through 99
table a chart that contains data in an organized way
addend one of the numbers added in an addition problem

You can expect to see homework that provides practice with addition and subtraction of numbers through 99.

As we learn about how to add and subtract 2-digit numbers, you may wish to keep the following sample as a guide.

Adding 2-Digit Numbers

Models

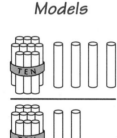

Place-Value Chart

Tens	Ones
1	4
+ 1	2
2	6

$$\begin{array}{r} 14 \\ + 12 \\ \hline 26 \end{array}$$

Subtracting 2-Digit Numbers

Models

Place-Value Chart

Tens	Ones
1	4
− 1	2
	2

$$\begin{array}{r} 14 \\ - 12 \\ \hline 2 \end{array}$$

Knowing how to add and subtract 2-digit numbers can help children learn how to solve more complex problems.

Sincerely,

Teacher Note: **Check Understanding** Have volunteers make up word problems to go with some of the addition problems.

Add.

1.

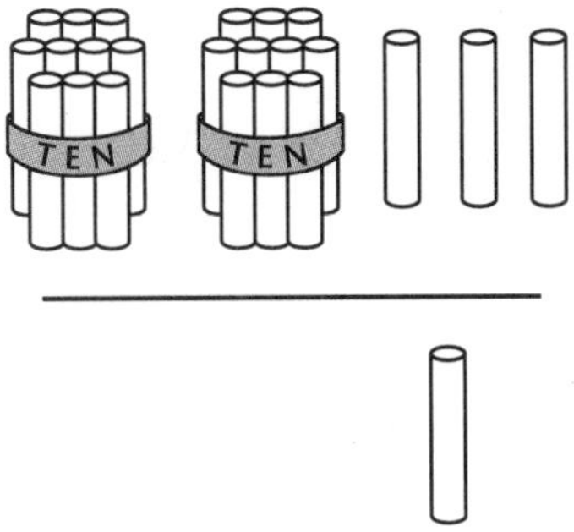

Tens	Ones
2	3
+	1
2	4

$$\begin{array}{r} 23 \\ + 1 \\ \hline 24 \end{array}$$

2.

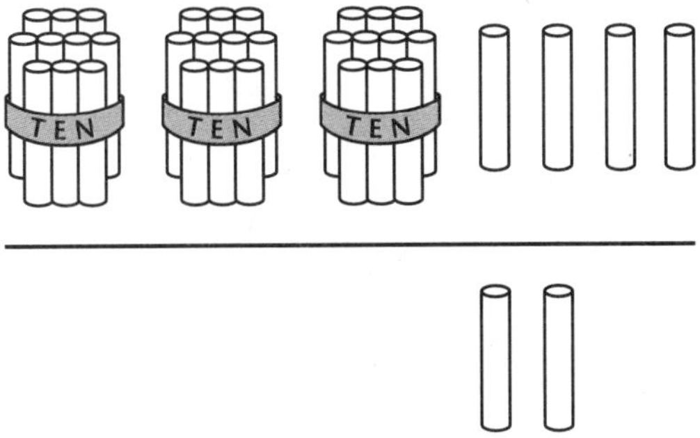

T	O
3	4
+	2
3	6

$$\begin{array}{r} 34 \\ + 2 \\ \hline 36 \end{array}$$

3.

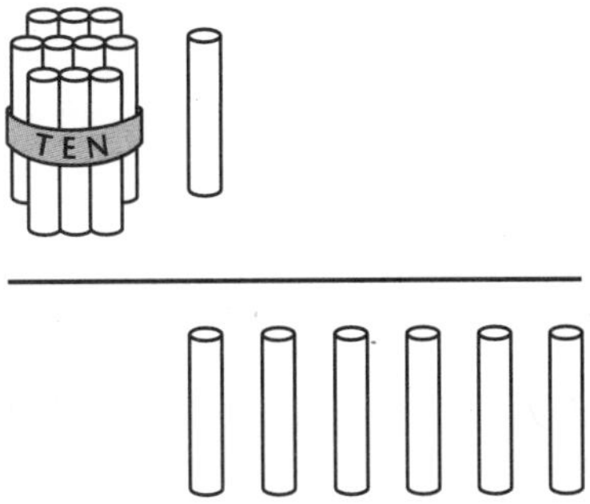

T	O
1	1
+	6
1	7

$$\begin{array}{r} 11 \\ + 6 \\ \hline 17 \end{array}$$

4.

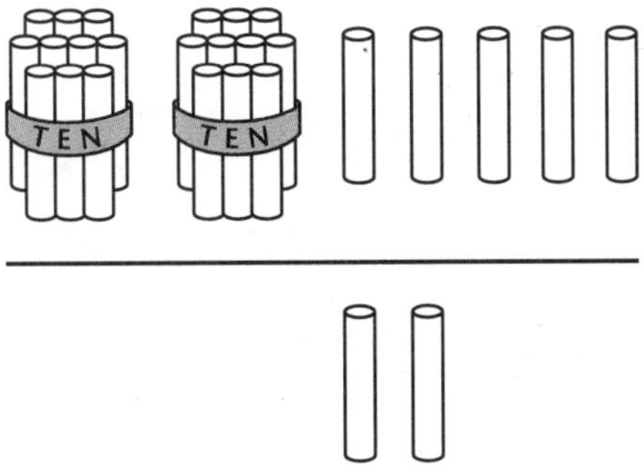

T	O
2	5
+	2
2	7

$$\begin{array}{r} 25 \\ + 2 \\ \hline 27 \end{array}$$

Unit 9 • Lesson 1

Add.

5.

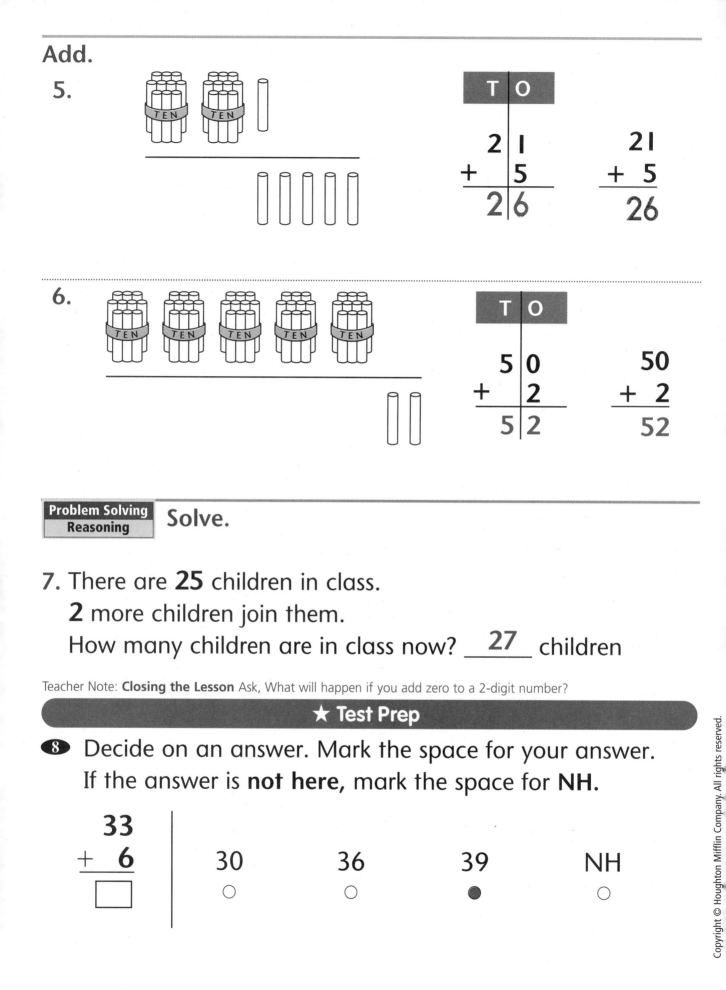

T	O
2	1
+	5
2	6

21
+ 5
26

6.

T	O
5	0
+	2
5	2

50
+ 2
52

Problem Solving Reasoning Solve.

7. There are **25** children in class.
   2 more children join them.
   How many children are in class now? ___27___ children

Teacher Note: **Closing the Lesson** Ask, What will happen if you add zero to a 2-digit number?

★ Test Prep

❽ Decide on an answer. Mark the space for your answer.
   If the answer is **not here**, mark the space for **NH.**

33
+ 6
☐

30 ○   36 ○   39 ●   NH ○

230 (two hundred thirty)   Unit 9 • Lesson 1

Name _____

Teacher Note: **Check Understanding** Have volunteers make up word problems to go with some of the addition problems.

Add.

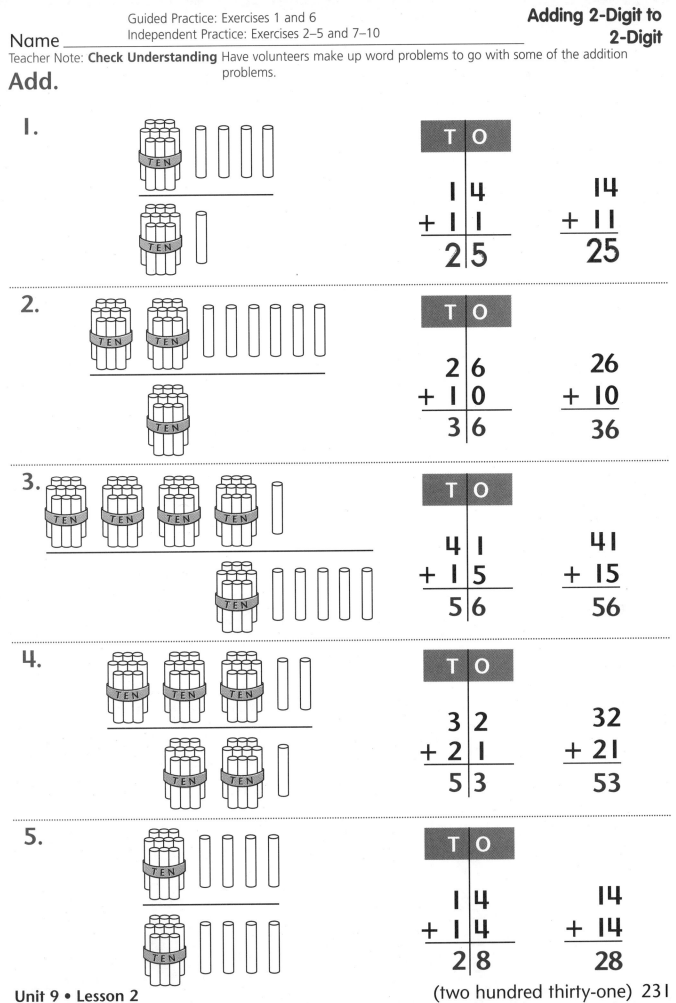

1.

T	O
1	4
+ 1	1
2	5

14
+ 11
25

2.

T	O
2	6
+ 1	0
3	6

26
+ 10
36

3.

T	O
4	1
+ 1	5
5	6

41
+ 15
56

4.

T	O
3	2
+ 2	1
5	3

32
+ 21
53

5.

T	O
1	4
+ 1	4
2	8

14
+ 14
28

Add.

6.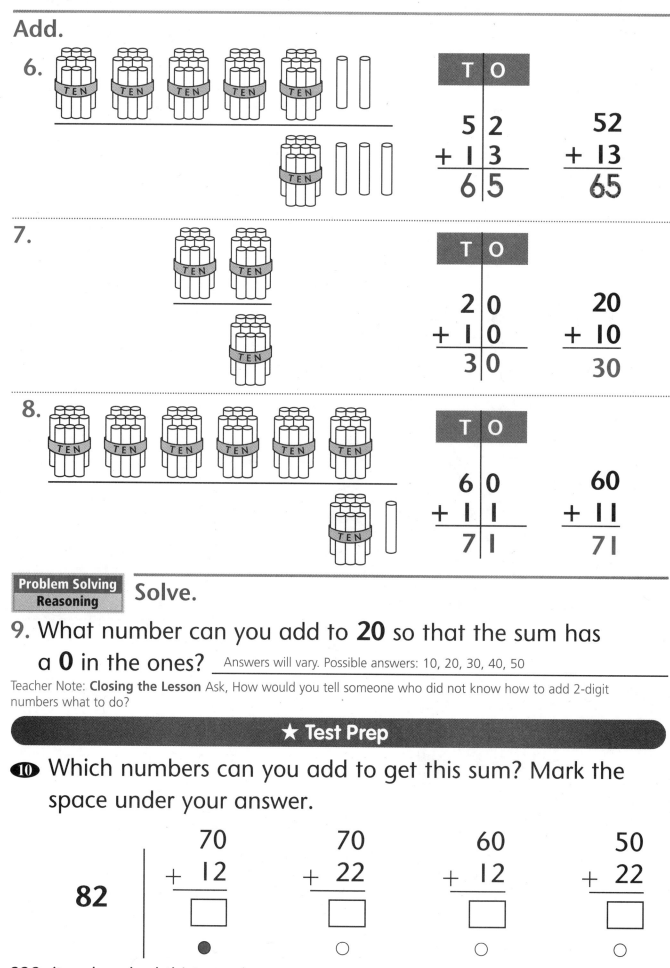

T	O
5	2
+ 1	3
6	5

$$\begin{array}{r} 52 \\ + 13 \\ \hline 65 \end{array}$$

7.

T	O
2	0
+ 1	0
3	0

$$\begin{array}{r} 20 \\ + 10 \\ \hline 30 \end{array}$$

8.

T	O
6	0
+ 1	1
7	1

$$\begin{array}{r} 60 \\ + 11 \\ \hline 71 \end{array}$$

Problem Solving Reasoning Solve.

9. What number can you add to **20** so that the sum has a **0** in the ones? _Answers will vary. Possible answers: 10, 20, 30, 40, 50_

Teacher Note: **Closing the Lesson** Ask, How would you tell someone who did not know how to add 2-digit numbers what to do?

★ Test Prep

10 Which numbers can you add to get this sum? Mark the space under your answer.

82

$\begin{array}{r} 70 \\ + 12 \\ \hline \square \end{array}$	$\begin{array}{r} 70 \\ + 22 \\ \hline \square \end{array}$	$\begin{array}{r} 60 \\ + 12 \\ \hline \square \end{array}$	$\begin{array}{r} 50 \\ + 22 \\ \hline \square \end{array}$
●	○	○	○

232 (two hundred thirty-two)   **Unit 9 • Lesson 2**

Name _____

Teacher Note: **Check Understanding** Check that all children know their addition facts to 10.

Add.

1.

T	O
2	1
+	1
2	**2**

2.

T	O
3	2
+	1
3	3

3.

T	O
1	2
+	2
1	4

4.

T	O
4	0
+	4
4	4

5.

T	O
4	1
+	3
4	**4**

6.

T	O
2	0
+	4
2	4

7.

T	O
1	3
+	5
1	8

8.

T	O
2	3
+	1
2	4

9.   42
       + 1
       ___
        43

10.   11
        + 3
        ___
         14

11.   10
        + 2
        ___
         12

12.   33
        + 1
        ___
         34

13.   32
        + 2
        ___
         34

14.   42
        + 7
        ___
         49

15.   30
        + 1
        ___
         31

16.   23
        + 1
        ___
         24

17.   41
        + 2
        ___
         43

18.   31
        + 6
        ___
         37

19.   22
        + 2
        ___
         24

20.   11
        + 3
        ___
         14

Unit 9 • Lesson 3

Now try these!

21.

T	O
1	2
+ 3	1
4	3

22.

T	O
3	0
+ 1	3
4	3

23.

T	O
2	0
+ 1	4
3	4

24.

T	O
7	3
+ 2	6
9	9

25.

T	O
3	4
+ 1	0
4	4

26.

T	O
4	6
+ 2	2
6	8

27.

T	O
1	1
+ 3	0
4	1

28.

T	O
2	2
+ 1	0
3	2

29.
```
  21
+ 13
  34
```

30.
```
  24
+ 10
  34
```

31.
```
  33
+ 10
  43
```

32.
```
  52
+ 27
  79
```

33.
```
  24
+ 20
  44
```

34.
```
  13
+ 11
  24
```

35.
```
  14
+ 30
  44
```

36.
```
  56
+ 33
  89
```

Teacher Note: **Closing the Lesson** Have volunteers draw pictures to show a few exercises from this page.

✓ Quick Check

Add.

1.
```
  41
+  7
  48
```

2.
```
  50
+ 37
  87
```

3.
```
  47
+ 22
  69
```

Item	Error Analysis
1	**Common Error:** Children have difficulty adding 1 digit to 2 digits. **Skills Tutorial** Strand P2, Skill 6
2	**Common Error:** Children write zero in the ones column when adding zero. **Skills Tutorial** Strand P2, Skill 7
3	**Common Error:** Children do not add columns correctly. **Reteach** Copymaster 69, p.139 **Skills Tutorial** Strand P2, Skill 8

Unit 9 • Lesson 3

Name _____

Teacher Note: **Check Understanding** Have volunteers make up word problems to go with some of the problems.

Subtract.

1.

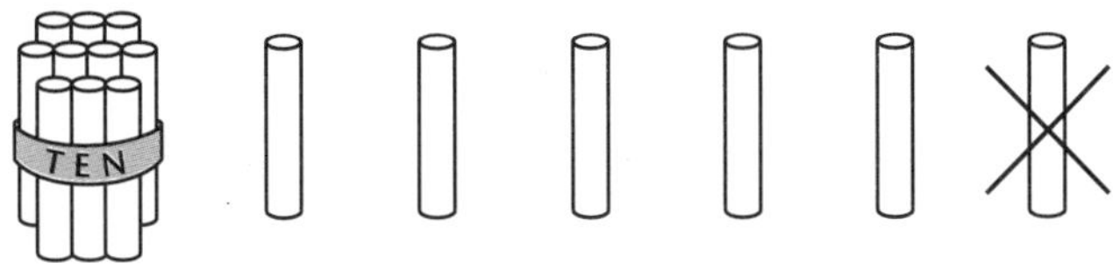

Tens	Ones
1	6
−	1
1	5

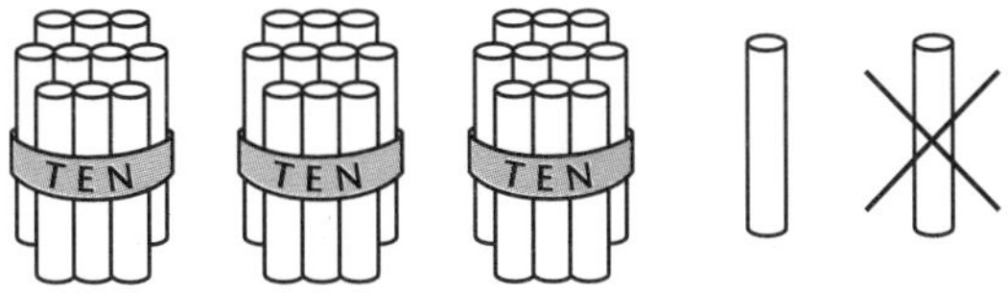

16
− 1
15

2.

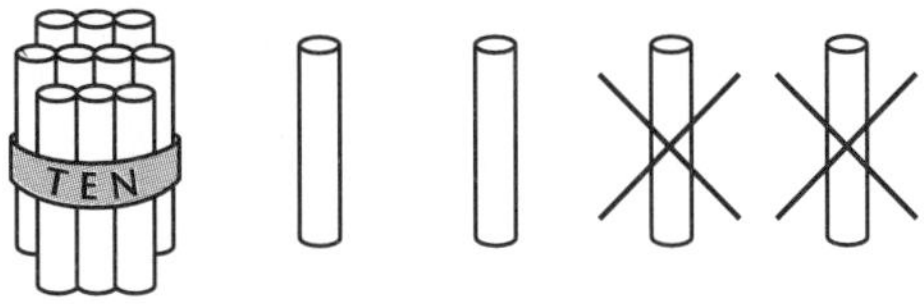

T	O
3	2
−	1
3	1

32
− 1
31

3.

T	O
1	4
−	2
1	2

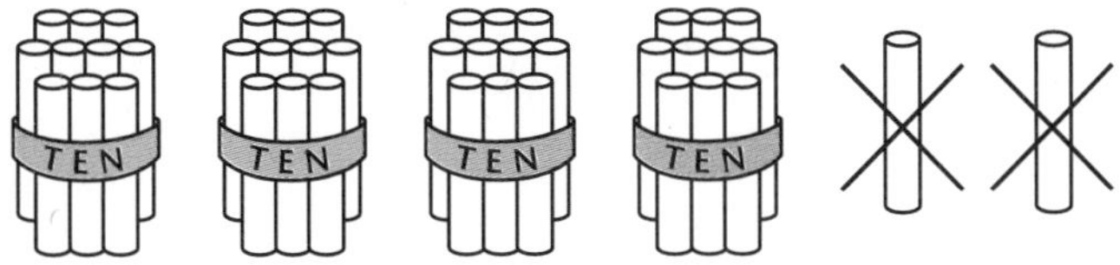

14
− 2
12

4.

T	O
4	2
−	2
4	0

42
− 2
40

Unit 9 • Lesson 4

(two hundred thirty-five) 235

Complete.

5.

	T	O
	1	4
−		3
	1	1

$$\begin{array}{r} 14 \\ -3 \\ \hline 11 \end{array}$$

6.

	T	O
	2	3
−		2
	2	1

$$\begin{array}{r} 23 \\ -2 \\ \hline 21 \end{array}$$

7.

	T	O
	4	5
−		5
	4	0

$$\begin{array}{r} 45 \\ -5 \\ \hline 40 \end{array}$$

Problem Solving Reasoning **Solve.**

8. There are **36** crayons in a box.

4 are broken.

How many are not broken? __**32**__ crayons

Teacher Note: **Closing the Lesson** Ask, What will happen if you subtract zero from a 2-digit number?

★ Test Prep

Decide on an answer. Mark the space for your answer.

If the answer is **not here**, mark the space for **NH**.

9

$$\begin{array}{r} 87 \\ -5 \\ \hline \square \end{array}$$

85	75	82	NH
○	○	●	○

Unit 9 • Lesson 4

Name _____

Subtracting 2-Digit from 2-Digit

Teacher Note: **Check Understanding** Have one partner give the other a subtraction problem to model and solve, then switch roles and repeat.

Subtract.

1.

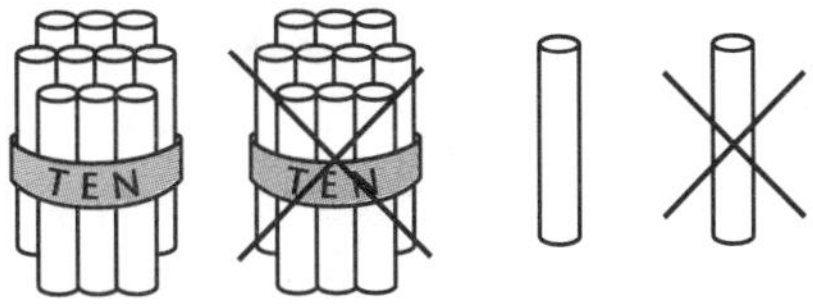

	T	O
	2	2
−	1	1
	1	1

22
− 11
11

2.

	T	O
	4	1
−	2	0
	2	1

41
− 20
21

3.

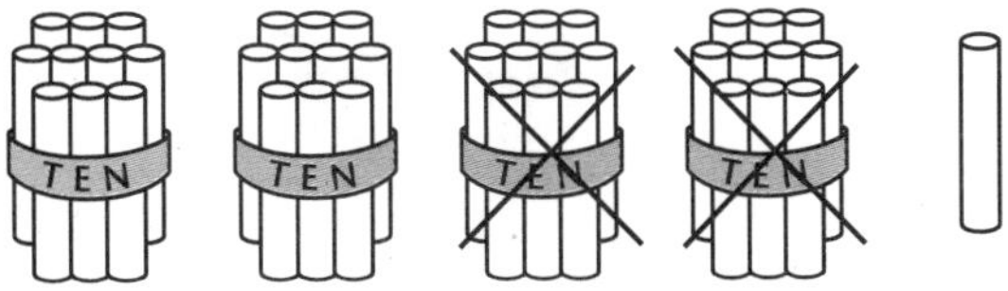

	T	O
	2	8
−	1	7
	1	1

28
− 17
11

4.

	T	O
	4	3
−	3	1
	1	2

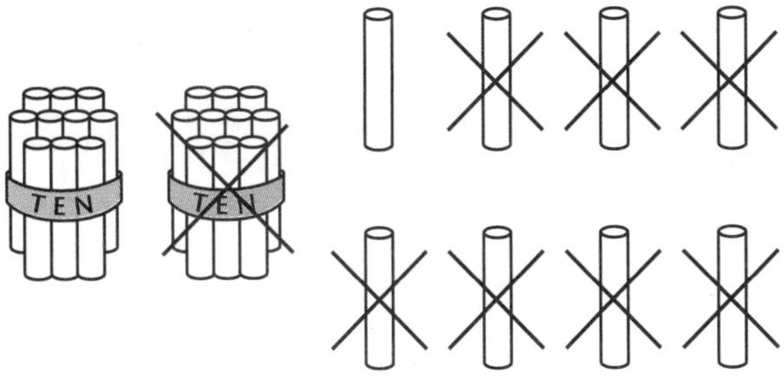

43
− 31
12

Unit 9 • Lesson 5

(two hundred thirty-seven) 237

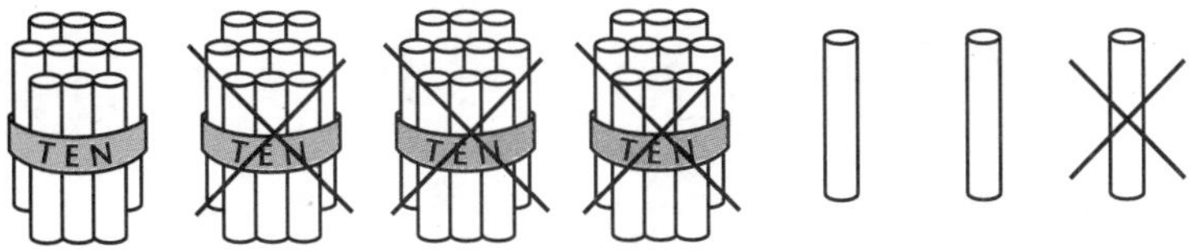

Complete.

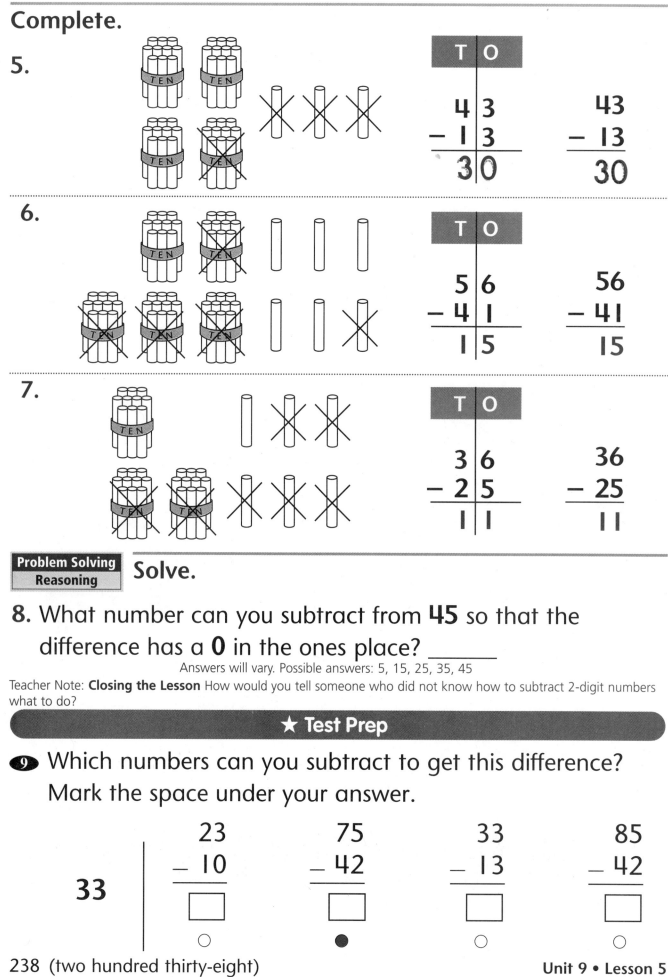

5.

T	O
4	3
− 1	3
3	0

$$43 - 13 \over 30$$

6.

T	O
5	6
− 4	1
1	5

$$56 - 41 \over 15$$

7.

T	O
3	6
− 2	5
1	1

$$36 - 25 \over 11$$

Problem Solving Reasoning Solve.

8. What number can you subtract from **45** so that the difference has a **0** in the ones place? _____

Answers will vary. Possible answers: 5, 15, 25, 35, 45

Teacher Note: **Closing the Lesson** How would you tell someone who did not know how to subtract 2-digit numbers what to do?

★ Test Prep

9 Which numbers can you subtract to get this difference? Mark the space under your answer.

33 | $$23 - 10 \over \Box$$ ○ $$75 - 42 \over \Box$$ ● $$33 - 13 \over \Box$$ ○ $$85 - 42 \over \Box$$ ○

238 (two hundred thirty-eight)

Unit 9 • Lesson 5

Guided Practice: Exercises 1, 9 and 17
Independent Practice: Exercises 2–8, 10–16, and 18–32

Subtracting 2-Digit Numbers

Teacher Note: **Check Understanding** Check that all children know their subtraction facts through 9.

Subtract.

1.

T	O
2	4
−	1
2	3

2.

T	O
3	4
−	2
3	2

3.

T	O
2	3
−	1
2	2

4.

T	O
1	4
−	3
1	1

5.

T	O
4	4
−	2
4	2

6.

T	O
3	4
−	1
3	3

7.

T	O
5	6
−	5
5	1

8.

T	O
2	4
−	4
2	0

9.
$$\begin{array}{r} 43 \\ -\ 2 \\ \hline 41 \end{array}$$

10.
$$\begin{array}{r} 23 \\ -\ 3 \\ \hline 20 \end{array}$$

11.
$$\begin{array}{r} 67 \\ -\ 4 \\ \hline 63 \end{array}$$

12.
$$\begin{array}{r} 22 \\ -\ 2 \\ \hline 20 \end{array}$$

13.
$$\begin{array}{r} 24 \\ -\ 3 \\ \hline 21 \end{array}$$

14.
$$\begin{array}{r} 88 \\ -\ 6 \\ \hline 82 \end{array}$$

15.
$$\begin{array}{r} 43 \\ -\ 1 \\ \hline 42 \end{array}$$

16.
$$\begin{array}{r} 95 \\ -\ 3 \\ \hline 92 \end{array}$$

Subtract the ones, then the tens.

17.

T	O
4	3
− 1	3
3	0

18.

T	O
2	4
− 1	4
1	0

19.

T	O
3	4
− 2	1
1	3

20.

T	O
2	4
− 1	0
1	4

21.

T	O
3	2
− 1	0
2	2

22.

T	O
8	5
− 5	1
3	4

23.

T	O
5	8
− 4	6
1	2

24.

T	O
3	4
− 1	4
2	0

25.
$$\begin{array}{r} 33 \\ -\ 12 \\ \hline 21 \end{array}$$

26.
$$\begin{array}{r} 76 \\ -\ 53 \\ \hline 23 \end{array}$$

27.
$$\begin{array}{r} 43 \\ -\ 20 \\ \hline 23 \end{array}$$

28.
$$\begin{array}{r} 34 \\ -\ 12 \\ \hline 22 \end{array}$$

29.
$$\begin{array}{r} 44 \\ -\ 31 \\ \hline 13 \end{array}$$

30.
$$\begin{array}{r} 34 \\ -\ 10 \\ \hline 24 \end{array}$$

31.
$$\begin{array}{r} 97 \\ -\ 65 \\ \hline 32 \end{array}$$

32.
$$\begin{array}{r} 43 \\ -\ 23 \\ \hline 20 \end{array}$$

Teacher Note: **Closing the Lesson** Have volunteers draw pictures to show several exercises on these pages.

✔ Quick Check

Subtract.

1.
$$\begin{array}{r} 89 \\ -\ 6 \\ \hline 83 \end{array}$$

2.
$$\begin{array}{r} 94 \\ -\ 60 \\ \hline 34 \end{array}$$

3.
$$\begin{array}{r} 79 \\ -\ 54 \\ \hline 25 \end{array}$$

Item	Error Analysis
1	**Common Error:** Children subtract the ones from the tens. **Skills Tutorial** Strand P3, Skill 4
2	**Common Error:** Children write zero in the ones column when subtracting zero. **Skills Tutorial** Strand P3, Skill 5
3	**Common Error:** Children do not subtract columns correctly. **Reteach** Copymaster 70, p.140 **Skills Tutorial** Strand P3, Skill 6

Teacher Note: **Check Understanding** Have volunteers make up and solve a word problem where they must add money amounts and one where they must subtract.

Count the dimes.
Add or subtract.

1.

	5	dimes	50¢
and	3	dimes	+ 30¢
	8	dimes	80¢

2.

	4	dimes	40¢
and	5	dimes	+ 50¢
	9	dimes	90¢

3.

	8	dimes	80¢
take away	6	dimes	− 60¢
	2	dimes	20¢

4.

	9	dimes	90¢
take away	5	dimes	− 50¢
	4	dimes	40¢

Add or subtract.

5. $\begin{array}{r} 35¢ \\ + 43¢ \\ \hline 78¢ \end{array}$

6. $\begin{array}{r} 26¢ \\ + 31¢ \\ \hline 57¢ \end{array}$

7. $\begin{array}{r} 42¢ \\ + 53¢ \\ \hline 95¢ \end{array}$

8. $\begin{array}{r} 40¢ \\ + 20¢ \\ \hline 60¢ \end{array}$

9. $\begin{array}{r} 84¢ \\ - 21¢ \\ \hline 63¢ \end{array}$

10. $\begin{array}{r} 67¢ \\ - 32¢ \\ \hline 35¢ \end{array}$

11. $\begin{array}{r} 58¢ \\ - 24¢ \\ \hline 34¢ \end{array}$

12. $\begin{array}{r} 73¢ \\ - 52¢ \\ \hline 21¢ \end{array}$

13. $\begin{array}{r} 57¢ \\ + 12¢ \\ \hline 69¢ \end{array}$

14. $\begin{array}{r} 41¢ \\ + 58¢ \\ \hline 99¢ \end{array}$

15. $\begin{array}{r} 32¢ \\ + 17¢ \\ \hline 49¢ \end{array}$

16. $\begin{array}{r} 65¢ \\ + 20¢ \\ \hline 85¢ \end{array}$

| Problem Solving | **Solve.**
| Reasoning |

17. Ann has **67¢**. Bob has **57¢**. How much more money does Ann have than Bob? __10¢__

18. Juan has **60¢**. Rita has **24¢**. How much money do they have in all? __84¢__

Teacher Note: **Closing the Lesson** Ask, How is adding and subtracting money like adding and subtracting numbers? How is it different?

★ Test Prep

Decide on an answer. Mark the space for your answer.
If the answer is **not here**, mark the space for **NH**.

19 $\begin{array}{r} 11¢ \\ + 52¢ \\ \hline \end{array}$

| 36¢ ○ | 64¢ ○ | 41¢ ○ | NH ● |

Write + or – in the ◯. Solve.

Problem Solving Plan
1. Understand 2. Decide 3. Solve 4. Look back

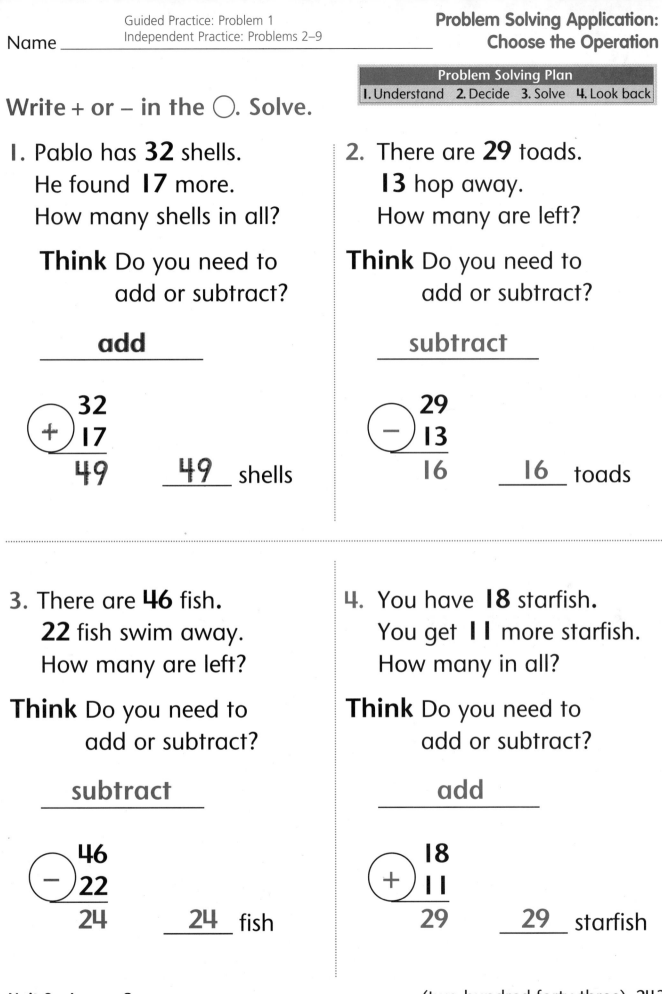

1. Pablo has **32** shells.
   He found **17** more.
   How many shells in all?

   Think Do you need to add or subtract?

   __**add**__

   ◯+ 32
   ◯   17
       49   __49__ shells

2. There are **29** toads.
   13 hop away.
   How many are left?

   Think Do you need to add or subtract?

   __subtract__

   ◯– 29
   ◯   13
       16   __16__ toads

3. There are **46** fish.
   22 fish swim away.
   How many are left?

   Think Do you need to add or subtract?

   __subtract__

   ◯– 46
   ◯   22
       24   __24__ fish

4. You have **18** starfish.
   You get **11** more starfish.
   How many in all?

   Think Do you need to add or subtract?

   __add__

   ◯+ 18
   ◯   11
       29   __29__ starfish

Solve.

5. You have **35** toy cars.
You buy **11** more.
How many toy cars in all?

$$\begin{array}{r}35\\ +11\\ \hline 46\end{array}$$

___46___ toy cars

6. There are **42** chicks.
12 fly away.
How many chicks are left?

$$\begin{array}{r}42\\ -12\\ \hline 30\end{array}$$

___30___ chicks

7. There are **64** rabbits.
13 rabbits join them.
How many in all?

$$\begin{array}{r}64\\ +13\\ \hline 77\end{array}$$

___77___ rabbits

8. There are **75** blue airplanes
and **31** red airplanes.
How many more airplanes
are blue?

$$\begin{array}{r}75\\ -31\\ \hline 44\end{array}$$

___44___ airplanes

Teacher Note: **Closing the Lesson** Say, Draw a picture to match one of the problems on this page.

Extend Your Thinking

9. Draw a picture to show one of the problems. Have a friend guess which problem.

> Pictures will vary but should match the problem chosen.

Guided Practice: Model Problem
Independent Practice: Problems 1–5

Problem Solving Strategy:
Make a Table

Problem

How many wheels are there on **4** bicycles?

1 **Understand**   Say, As you read the question, think about the math ideas.

I need to find out how many wheels are on
4 bicycles.

2 **Decide**   Ask, What strategy can you use to solve the problem?

I can make a table to count by **2**'s.
Then I can use the table to solve the problem.

3 **Solve**   Say, Fill the table to solve the problem.

Bicycles	1	2	3	4
Wheels	2	4	6	8

___8___ wheels

4 **Look back**   Ask, How can you check that your answer makes sense.

I can recheck the table to see if **4** bicycles
have **8** wheels. They do.
My answer makes sense.

Fill in the table.
Solve.

Hands	1	2	3	4	5
Fingers	5	10	15	20	25

1. How many fingers on **2** hands? __10__

2. How many fingers on **3** hands? __15__

3. How many hands if there are **20** fingers? __4__

4. How many fingers on **5** hands? __25__

5. What other strategy could you have used to solve problem **4**?

_____

Answers vary. Possible answer: I can draw a picture:
_____

Teacher Note: **Closing the Lesson** Ask, How did you know how to complete the table?

Add. (9A)

1.
$$\begin{array}{r} 16 \\ + 12 \\ \hline 28 \end{array}$$

2.
$$\begin{array}{r} 42 \\ + 13 \\ \hline 55 \end{array}$$

3.
$$\begin{array}{r} 34 \\ + 34 \\ \hline 68 \end{array}$$

4.
$$\begin{array}{r} 30 \\ + 40 \\ \hline 70 \end{array}$$

5.
$$\begin{array}{r} 41 \\ + 7 \\ \hline 48 \end{array}$$

6.
$$\begin{array}{r} 52 \\ + 46 \\ \hline 98 \end{array}$$

7.
$$\begin{array}{r} 35 \\ + 43 \\ \hline 78 \end{array}$$

8.
$$\begin{array}{r} 68 \\ + 30 \\ \hline 98 \end{array}$$

Subtract. (9B)

9.
$$\begin{array}{r} 38 \\ - 15 \\ \hline 23 \end{array}$$

10.
$$\begin{array}{r} 49 \\ - 23 \\ \hline 26 \end{array}$$

11.
$$\begin{array}{r} 80 \\ - 50 \\ \hline 30 \end{array}$$

12.
$$\begin{array}{r} 57 \\ - 47 \\ \hline 10 \end{array}$$

13.
$$\begin{array}{r} 96 \\ - 24 \\ \hline 72 \end{array}$$

14.
$$\begin{array}{r} 78 \\ - 5 \\ \hline 73 \end{array}$$

15.
$$\begin{array}{r} 98 \\ - 35 \\ \hline 63 \end{array}$$

16.
$$\begin{array}{r} 72 \\ - 40 \\ \hline 32 \end{array}$$

Add or subtract. (9C)

17.
$$\begin{array}{r} 25¢ \\ - 11¢ \\ \hline 14¢ \end{array}$$

18.
$$\begin{array}{r} 63¢ \\ + 2¢ \\ \hline 65¢ \end{array}$$

19.
$$\begin{array}{r} 34¢ \\ + 20¢ \\ \hline 54¢ \end{array}$$

20.
$$\begin{array}{r} 70¢ \\ - 30¢ \\ \hline 40¢ \end{array}$$

Solve. (9D)

21. There are **23** chicks.
    16 more chicks join them.
    How many in all?

    $+$ 23
         16
         ___
         39   ___39___ chicks

22. There are **48** ducks.
    15 fly away.
    How many are left?

    $-$ 48
         15
         ___
         33   ___33___ ducks

Fill in the table. Solve. (9D)

23.

Bicycles	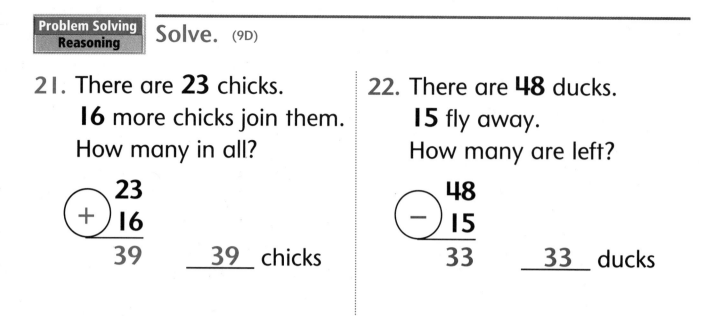 1	2	3	4	5	6
Wheels	2	4	6	8	10	12

24. How many wheels on **5** bicycles? ___10___

25. How many wheels on **6** bicycles? ___12___

26. How many bicycles if there are **6** wheels? ___3___

248 (two hundred forty-eight)

Unit 9 • Review

Name _____

1 Which fact belongs in the same fact family as the numbers shown at the beginning of the row? Mark the space next to your answer. **(6B)**

10, 2, 8

  ○ $10 - 3 = 6$ ● $10 - 8 = 2$

  ○ $6 + 2 = 8$ ○ $10 - 4 = 6$

2 Which number does the number word name? Mark the space under your answer. **(7A)**

twenty

12	2	20	02
○	○	●	○

3 Which shows the number? Mark the space under your answer. **(7B)**

3 tens and 7 ones

73	307	03	37
○	○	○	●

4 Count by 2's. Which number is missing? Mark the space under your answer. **(7D)**

4, 6, 8, _____, 12, 14

9	10	11	15
○	●	○	○

5 Which symbol belongs in the circle? Mark the space under your answer. **(7E)**

65 ◯ 56

<	>	=	+
○	●	○	○

6 Which picture shows what happens first? Mark the space under your answer. **(8A)**

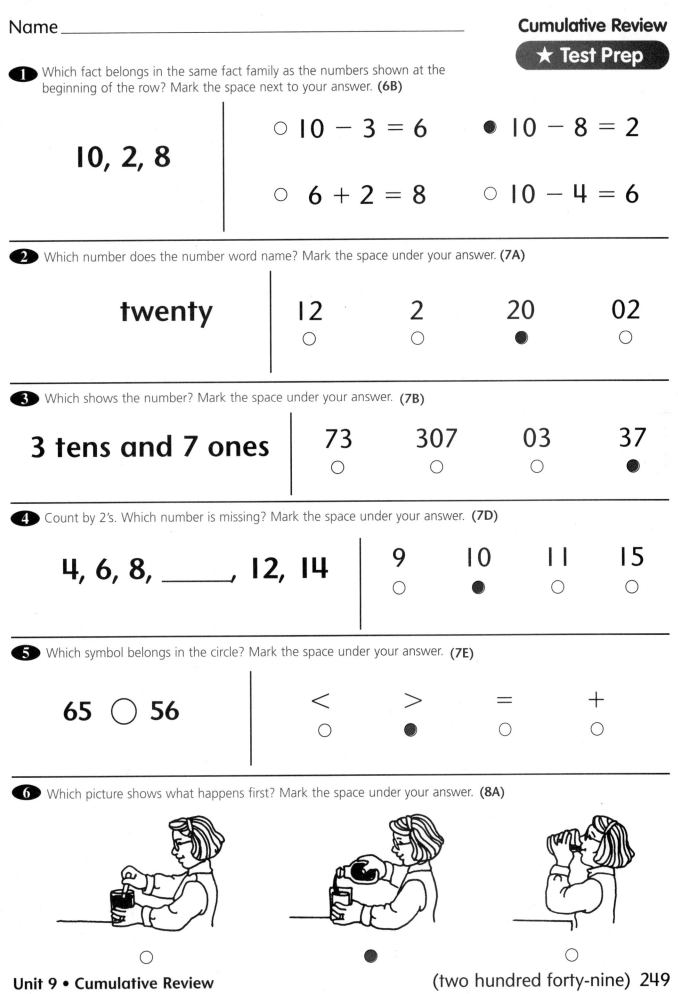

       ○   ●   ○

Unit 9 • Cumulative Review   (two hundred forty-nine) 249

7 How much money is shown? Mark the space under your answer. **(8C)**

52¢	37¢	32¢	17¢
○	●	○	○

Decide on an answer. Mark the space for your answer.
If the answer is **not here**, mark the space for **NH**.

Tell children they will complete the rest of the test independently.

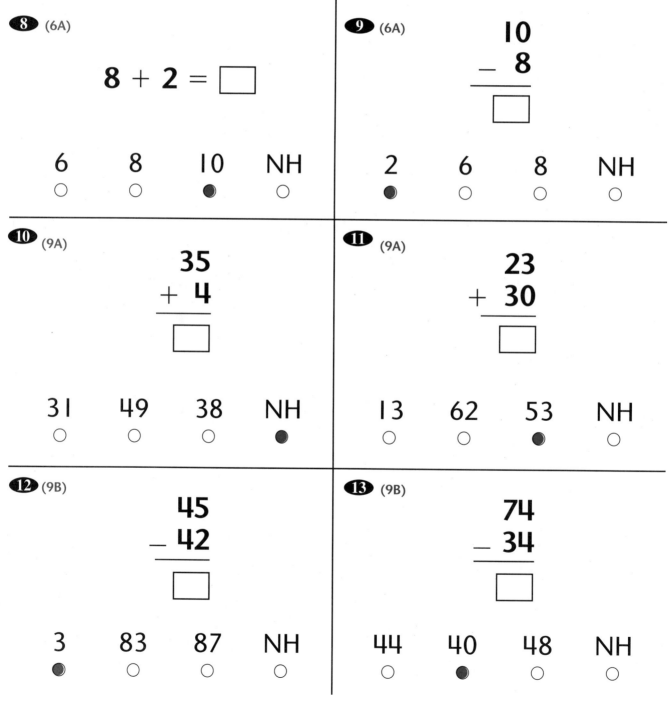

8 (6A)

$$8 + 2 = \square$$

6	8	10	NH
○	○	●	○

9 (6A)

$$\begin{array}{r} 10 \\ -\ 8 \\ \hline \square \end{array}$$

2	6	8	NH
●	○	○	○

10 (9A)

$$\begin{array}{r} 35 \\ +\ 4 \\ \hline \square \end{array}$$

31	49	38	NH
○	○	○	●

11 (9A)

$$\begin{array}{r} 23 \\ +\ 30 \\ \hline \square \end{array}$$

13	62	53	NH
○	○	●	○

12 (9B)

$$\begin{array}{r} 45 \\ -\ 42 \\ \hline \square \end{array}$$

3	83	87	NH
●	○	○	○

13 (9B)

$$\begin{array}{r} 74 \\ -\ 34 \\ \hline \square \end{array}$$

44	40	48	NH
○	●	○	○

250 (two hundred fifty)

Unit 9 • Cumulative Review

UNIT 10 • TABLE OF CONTENTS

Fractions and Measurement

Dear Family,

During the next few weeks our math class will be learning about fractions and measurement.

You can expect to see homework that provides practice with naming and recognizing fractions such as one half, one fourth, and one third as well as measuring length and comparing weight and capacity.

As we learn about fractions of a region you may wish to keep the following samples as a guide.

Fractions

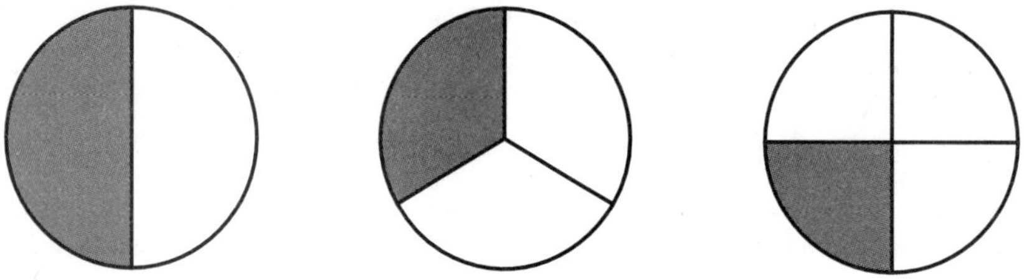

$$\frac{1}{2} \qquad \frac{1}{3} \qquad \frac{1}{4}$$

Knowing about fractions and measurement can help children find length, weight, and capacity in everyday life.

Sincerely,

Name _____

Guided Practice: Exercises 1 and 6
Independent Practice: Exercises 2–5 and 7–14

Equal Parts

Teacher Note: **Check Understanding** Ask, How many times must I fold a square to make 2 equal parts?

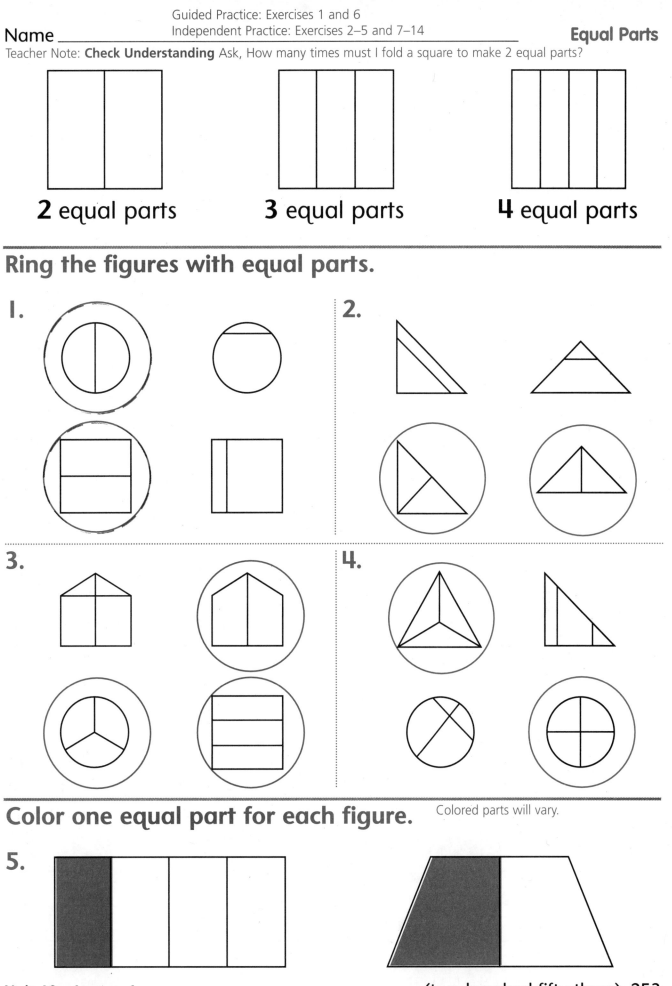

2 equal parts   **3** equal parts   **4** equal parts

Ring the figures with equal parts.

1.

2.

3.

4.

Color one equal part for each figure.   Colored parts will vary.

5.

Count the equal parts. Write how many.

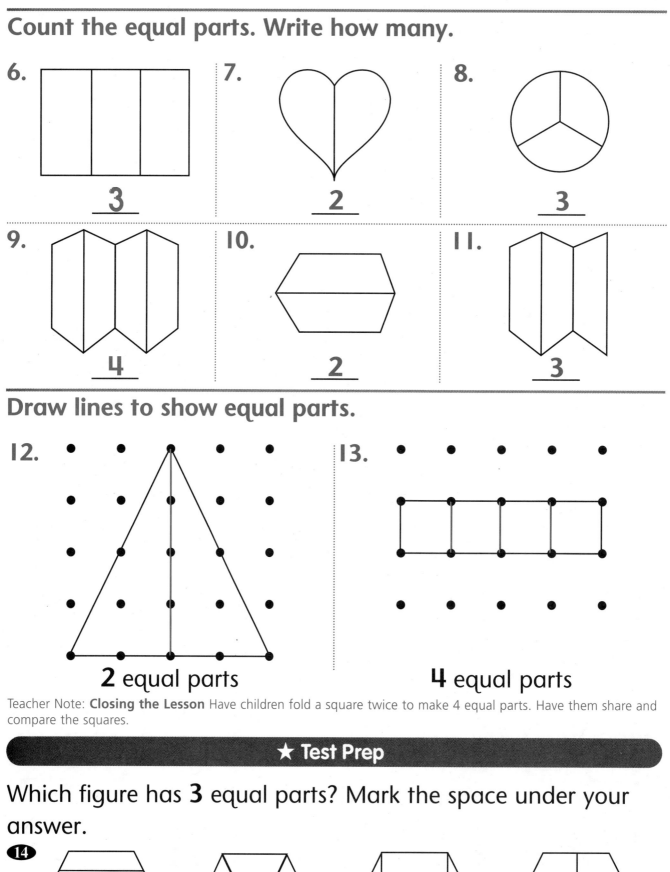

6. _3_

7. _2_

8. _3_

9. _4_

10. _2_

11. _3_

Draw lines to show equal parts.

12. **2** equal parts

13. **4** equal parts

Teacher Note: **Closing the Lesson** Have children fold a square twice to make 4 equal parts. Have them share and compare the squares.

★ Test Prep

Which figure has **3** equal parts? Mark the space under your answer.

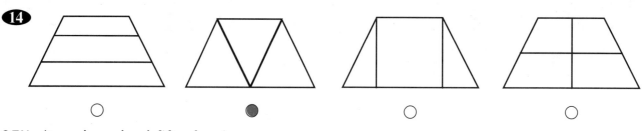

14 ○   ●   ○   ○

Guided Practice: Model Exercise and Exercise 1
Independent Practice: Exercises 2–16

One Half

Teacher Note: **Check Understanding** Ask, How can you show 2 parts of a figure and not show $\frac{1}{2}$?

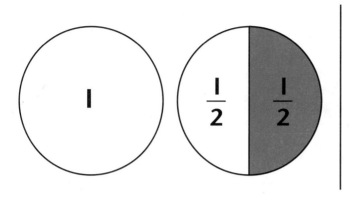

Color one half of the picture. Colored half will vary.

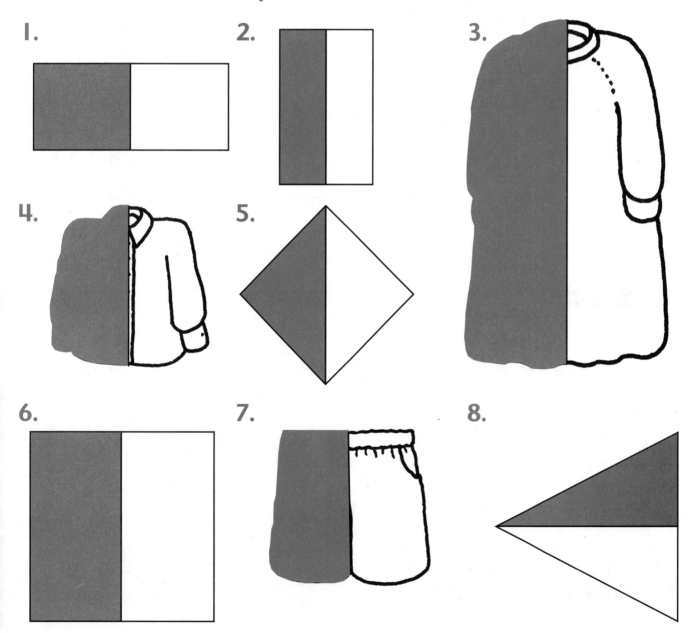

1.

2.

3.

4.

5.

6.

7.

8.

Color $\frac{1}{2}$ of the picture. Colored half will vary.

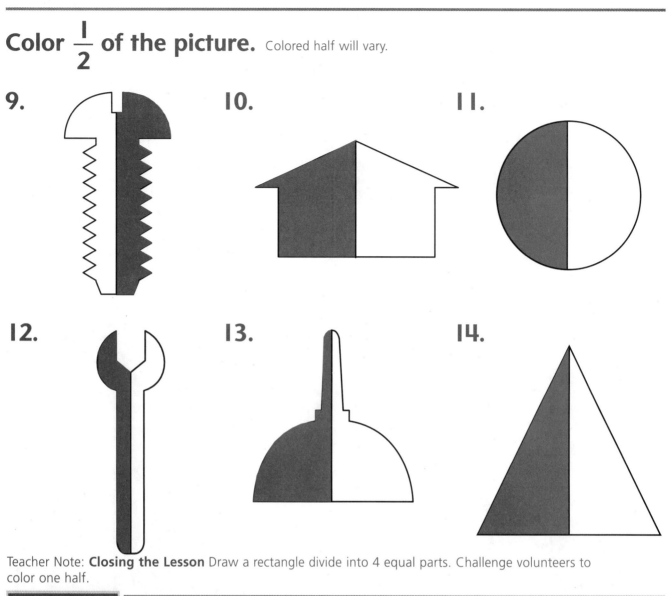

9.

10.

11.

12.

13.

14.

Teacher Note: **Closing the Lesson** Draw a rectangle divide into 4 equal parts. Challenge volunteers to color one half.

| Problem Solving |
| Reasoning |

Solve.

15. Maia broke a fruit bar in half. How many equal parts does she have? __2__

★ Test Prep

Which figure shows $\frac{1}{2}$ colored? Mark the space under your answer.

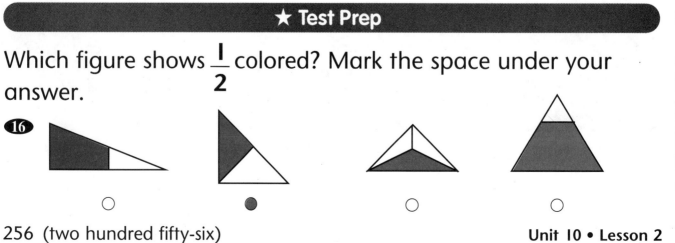

16

Guided Practice: Model Exercise and Exercise 1
Independent Practice: Exercises 2–13

One Fourth

Teacher Note: **Check Understanding** If you break a cracker into fourths, how many pieces will you have?

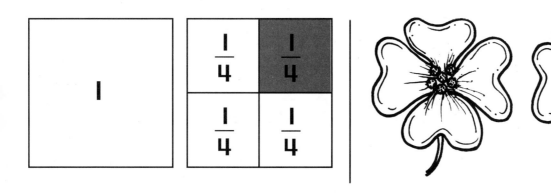

Color one fourth of the picture. Colored part will vary.

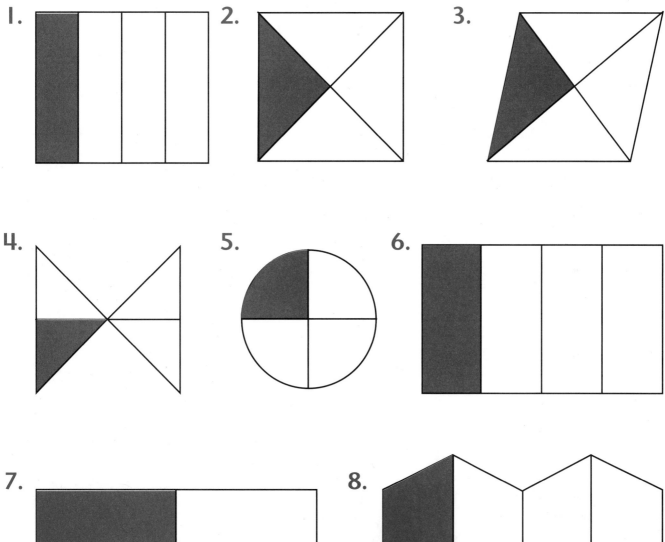

1.

2.

3.

4.

5.

6.

7.

8.

Unit 10 • Lesson 3

(two hundred fifty-seven) 257

Color $\frac{1}{4}$ of the picture. Colored part will vary.

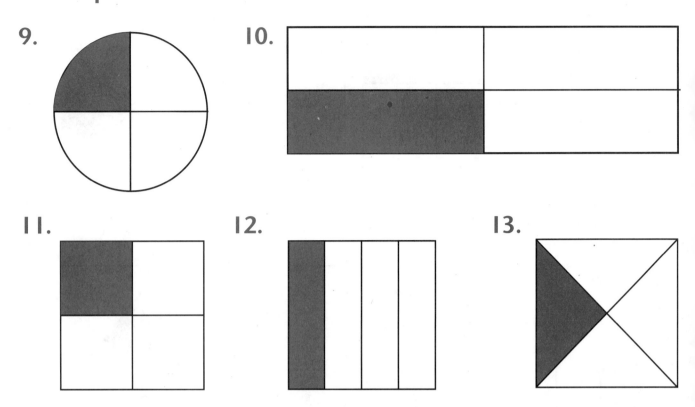

9. **10.** **11.** **12.** **13.**

Teacher Note: **Closing the Lesson** Have children fold different figures such as rectangles, squares, and circles to show fourths.

☑ Quick Check

Draw lines to show **3** equal parts.
Lines drawn may vary.

1.

Color to match the fraction.

2. $\frac{1}{2}$ **3.** $\frac{1}{4}$

Item	Error Analysis
1	**Common Error:** Children draw 3 unequal parts. **Reteach** Copymaster 72, p. 142
2	**Common Error:** Children do not realize $\frac{1}{2}$ means 1 of 2 equal parts, not just 1 of 2 parts. **Skills Tutorial** Copymaster 73, p. 143
3	**Common Error:** Children do not realize $\frac{1}{4}$ means 1 of 4 equal parts, not just 1 of 4 parts. **Skills Tutorial** Copymaster 74, p. 144

Unit 10 • Lesson 3

Teacher Note: **Check Understanding** Ask, If you color in $\frac{1}{3}$ of a circle, how many thirds are not colored in?

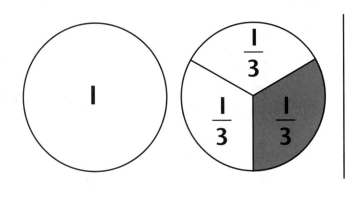 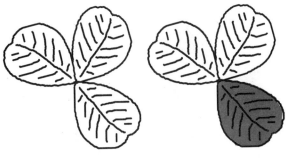

Color one third of the picture.

Colored part will vary.

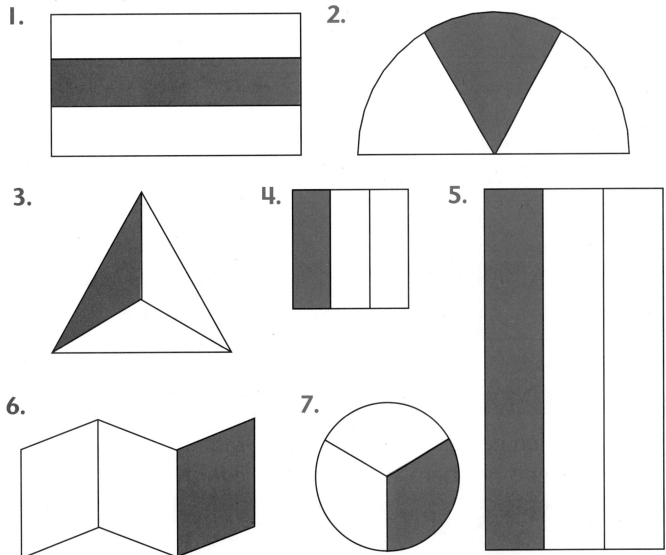

1.

2.

3.

4.

5.

6.

7.

Ring the fraction.

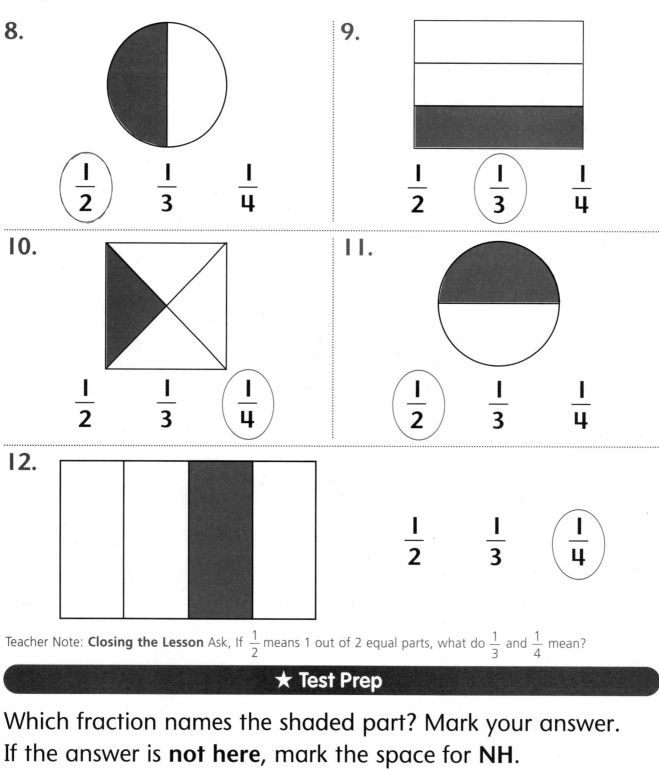

8.
$\frac{1}{2}$ (ringed) $\frac{1}{3}$ $\frac{1}{4}$

9.
$\frac{1}{2}$ $\frac{1}{3}$ (ringed) $\frac{1}{4}$

10.
$\frac{1}{2}$ $\frac{1}{3}$ $\frac{1}{4}$ (ringed)

11.
$\frac{1}{2}$ (ringed) $\frac{1}{3}$ $\frac{1}{4}$

12.
$\frac{1}{2}$ $\frac{1}{3}$ $\frac{1}{4}$ (ringed)

Teacher Note: **Closing the Lesson** Ask, If $\frac{1}{2}$ means 1 out of 2 equal parts, what do $\frac{1}{3}$ and $\frac{1}{4}$ mean?

★ Test Prep

Which fraction names the shaded part? Mark your answer.
If the answer is **not here**, mark the space for **NH**.

13
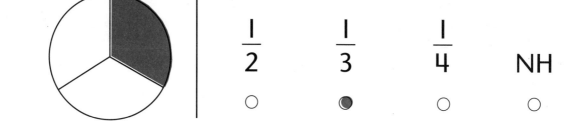

$\frac{1}{2}$ $\frac{1}{3}$ $\frac{1}{4}$ NH
○   ● (filled)   ○   ○

Unit 10 • Lesson 4

Teacher Note: **Check Understanding** Have volunteers show how to measure the length of a desk using chalkboard erasers.

This desk is about 6 erasers long.

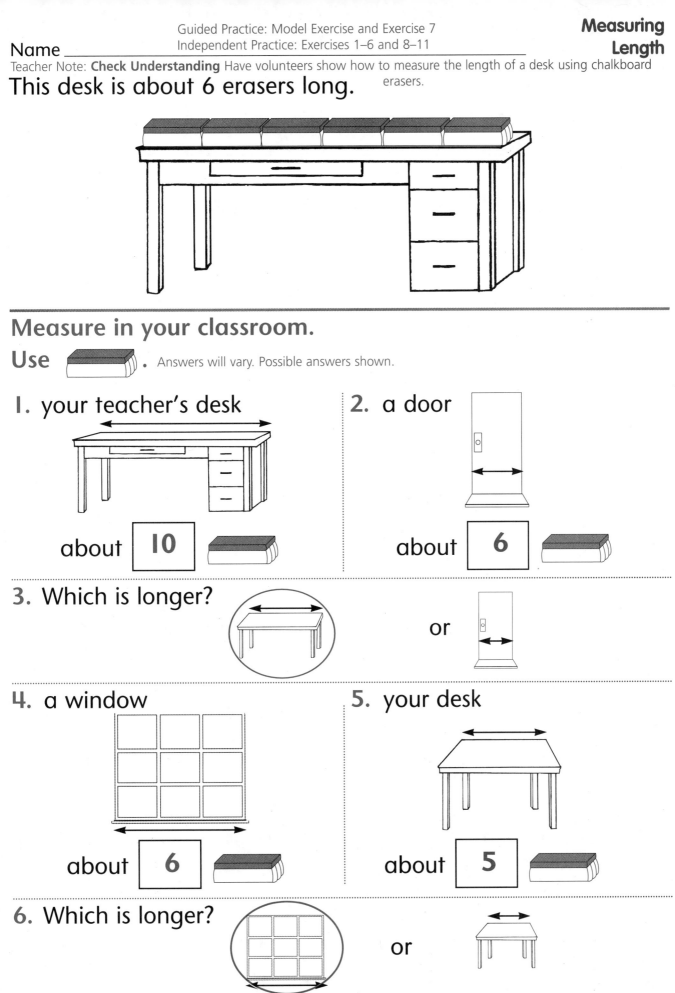

Measure in your classroom.

Use [image] . Answers will vary. Possible answers shown.

1. your teacher's desk

about **10** [eraser]

2. a door

about **6** [eraser]

3. Which is longer?

[table] or [door]

4. a window

about **6** [eraser]

5. your desk

about **5** [eraser]

6. Which is longer?

[window] or [table]

How long is this pencil?

7.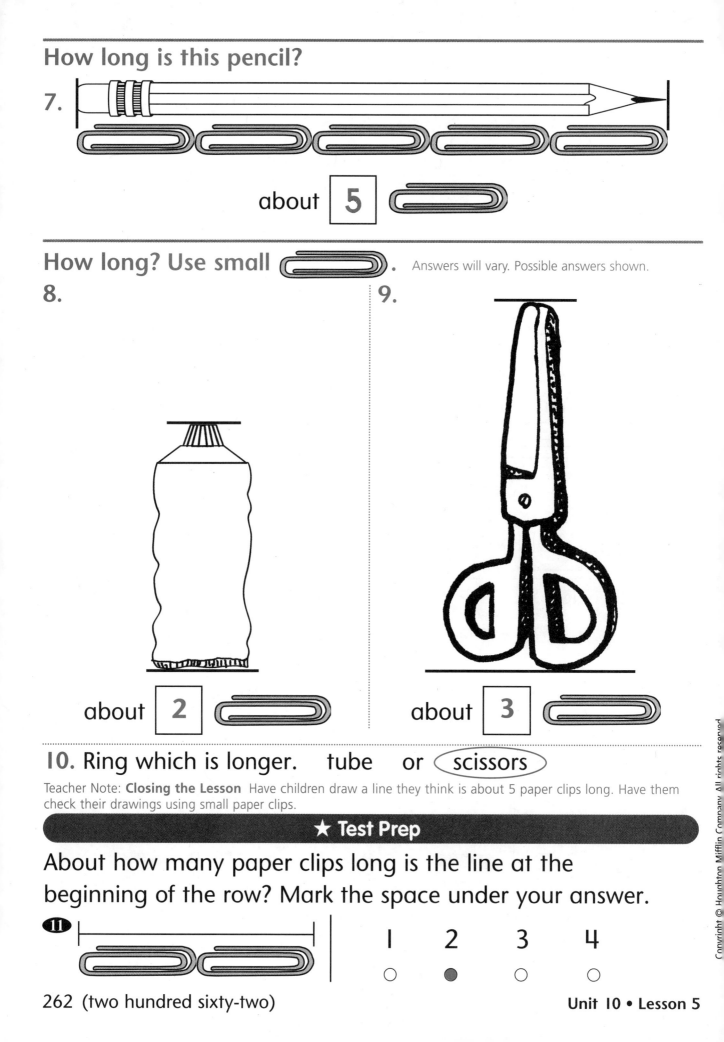

about $\boxed{5}$ ⬭

How long? Use small ⬭. Answers will vary. Possible answers shown.

8.

about $\boxed{2}$ ⬭

9.

about $\boxed{3}$ ⬭

10. Ring which is longer.   tube   or ⟨scissors⟩

Teacher Note: **Closing the Lesson** Have children draw a line they think is about 5 paper clips long. Have them check their drawings using small paper clips.

★ Test Prep

About how many paper clips long is the line at the beginning of the row? Mark the space under your answer.

⑪

1	2	3	4
○	●	○	○

262 (two hundred sixty-two)

Unit 10 • Lesson 5

Guided Practice: Problem 1
Independent Practice: Problems 2–8

**Problem Solving Application:
Use a Chart**

Problem Solving Plan
1. Understand   2. Decide   3. Solve   4. Look back

Object	Length in Paper Clips
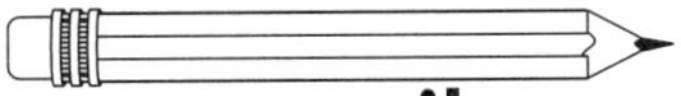 pencil	about 4
 crayon	about 3
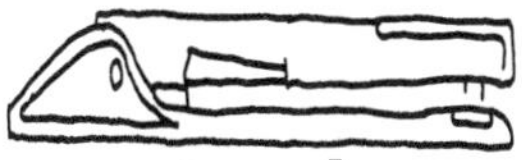 stapler	about 7
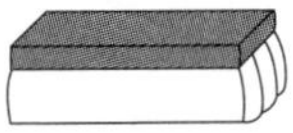 eraser	about 6

Use the chart to solve.

1. Which is the shortest object?

   <u>crayon</u>

2. Which is the longest object?

   <u>stapler</u>

3. Which is longer, the crayon or the pencil?

   <u>pencil</u>

4. Which object is about **6** paper clips long?

   <u>eraser</u>

Object	Length in Paper Clips	Length in Erasers
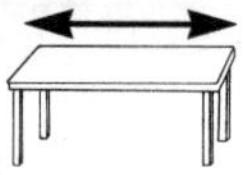 across a desk	about 36	about 6
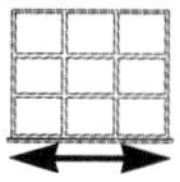 across a window	about 31	about 5
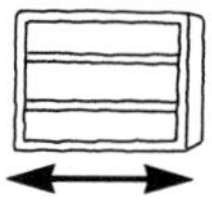 across a shelf	about 26	about 4

Use the chart to solve.

5. About how many paper clips long is the shelf?

   __26__ paper clips

6. Which is the shortest object?

   ____shelf____

7. Which object is about **6** erasers long?

   ____desk____

8. Which is longer, the window or desk?

   ____desk____

Teacher Note: **Closing the Lesson** Ask, Would you need more paper clips or more erasers to measure your height? Why?

Extend Your Thinking

Why are two different numbers used to tell how long the same object is?

Answers vary. Possible answer: Because the things used to measure are different sizes. The paper clip is smaller than the eraser, so it takes more paper clips to measure the same length that it takes erasers.

Teacher Note: **Check Understanding** Have children look at the inch blocks at the top of page 265. Ask, How many blocks long is your ruler?

These blocks are **I** inch long.

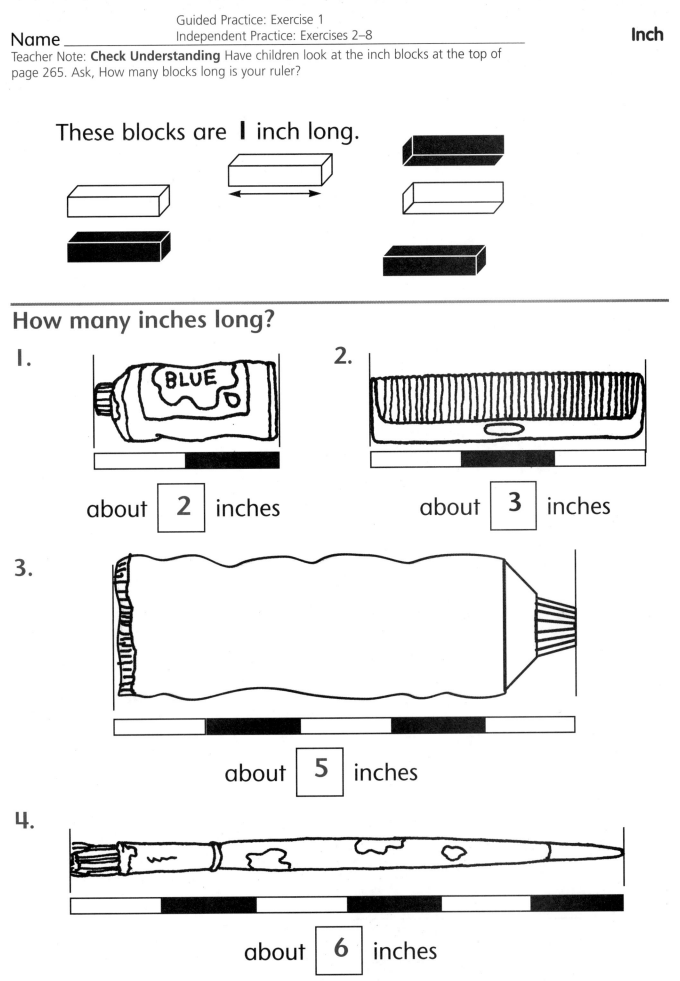

How many inches long?

1. about | 2 | inches

2. about | 3 | inches

3. about | 5 | inches

4. about | 6 | inches

Unit 10 • Lesson 7

(two hundred sixty-five) 265

About how long is the picture?

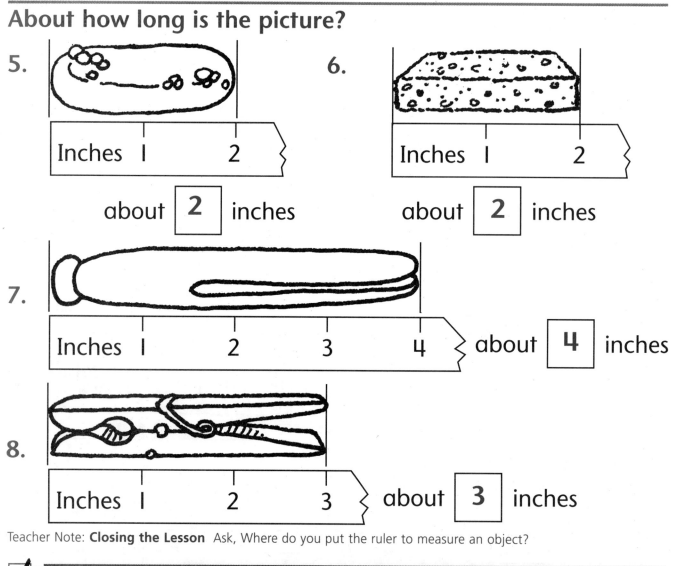

5. Inches | 1 | 2 >

about | **2** | inches

6. Inches | 1 | 2 >

about | **2** | inches

7. Inches | 1 | 2 | 3 | 4 > about | **4** | inches

8. Inches | 1 | 2 | 3 > about | **3** | inches

Teacher Note: **Closing the Lesson** Ask, Where do you put the ruler to measure an object?

✓ **Quick Check**

Ring the fraction.

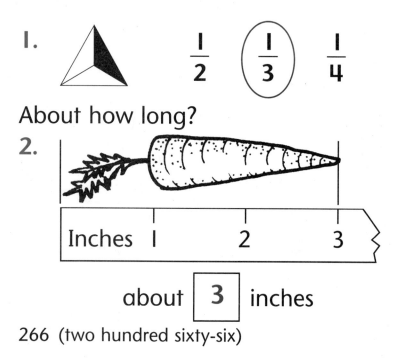

1. $\frac{1}{2}$ $\left(\frac{1}{3}\right)$ $\frac{1}{4}$

About how long?

2. Inches | 1 | 2 | 3 >

about | **3** | inches

Item	Error Analysis
1	**Common Error:** Children use unshaded part as denominator.
	Reteach Copymaster 75, p. 145
2	**Common Error:** Children do not read the ruler correctly.
	Reteach Copymasters 76–77, pp. 146–147

Unit 10 • Lesson 7

Name _____

Centimeter

Teacher Note: **Check Understanding** Have children look at the blocks at the top of page 267. Ask, How many blocks long is your centimeter ruler?

These blocks are **1** centimeter long.

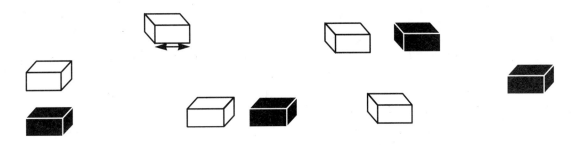

How many centimeters long?

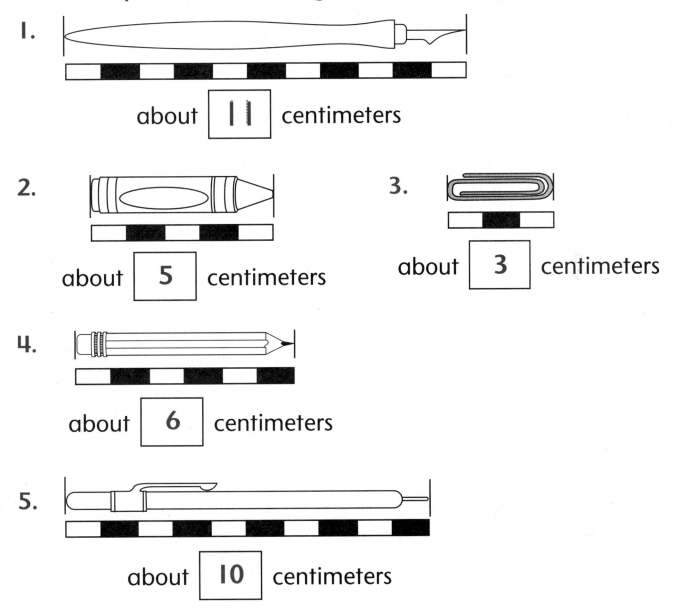

1. about | 11 | centimeters

2. about | 5 | centimeters

3. about | 3 | centimeters

4. about | 6 | centimeters

5. about | 10 | centimeters

About how long is the picture?

6.

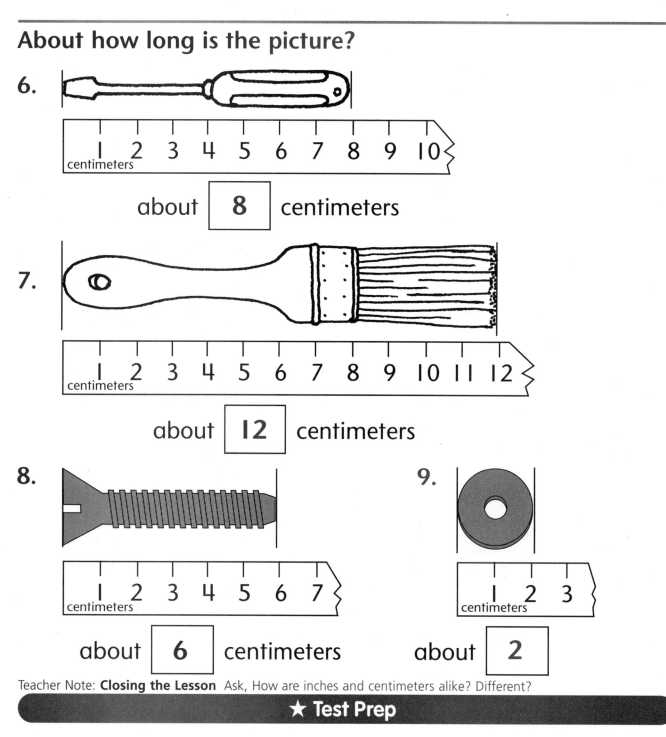

about | **8** | centimeters

7.

about | **12** | centimeters

8.

about | **6** | centimeters

9.

about | **2** |

Teacher Note: **Closing the Lesson** Ask, How are inches and centimeters alike? Different?

★ **Test Prep**

About how many centimeters long is the screwdriver? Mark the space under your answer.

10

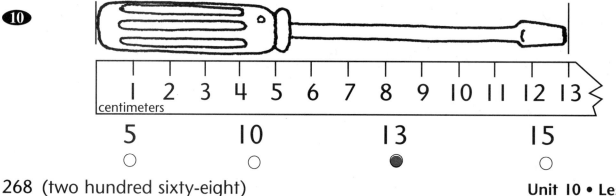

5   10   13   15
○   ○   ●   ○

268 (two hundred sixty-eight)

Problem

How tall are you?

1 Understand   What are you being asked to find out?

I need to find out how tall I am.

2 Decide   What strategy can you use?

I will use a tape measure and chalk to measure myself.

3 Solve

I stand against a wall.
I use chalk to mark the wall to show where the top of my head ends. I measure from the floor to the chalk mark.

My height is about ___Answer will vary.___ centimeters.

4 Look back   Does your measurement seem reasonable? Why or why not?

I can look back at the tape measure to see if my answer makes sense.

Work with a partner. Act it out.

Complete the chart. Answers will vary.

1.

	Partner 1	Partner 2
Height	about _____ centimeters	about _____ centimeters
Length of arm	about _____ centimeters	about _____ centimeters
Length of arm span	about _____ centimeters	about _____ centimeters

2. Who is taller? _____Partner 1 or 2_____

3. Whose arm is longer? _____Partner 1 or 2_____

4. Whose arm span is wider? _____Partner 1 or 2_____

Teacher Note: **Closing the Lesson** Ask, What other strategy could you use to solve these problems?

270 (two hundred seventy)   **Unit 10 • Lesson 9**

Teacher Note: **Check Understanding** Ask, Which is heavier, a brick or a pillow?

Lift each item.
The one that weighs more is **heavier.**

The one that weighs less is **lighter.**

The stapler is heavier than the pen.

Find objects like the ones shown. Lift each object.
Ring the one that is heavier.

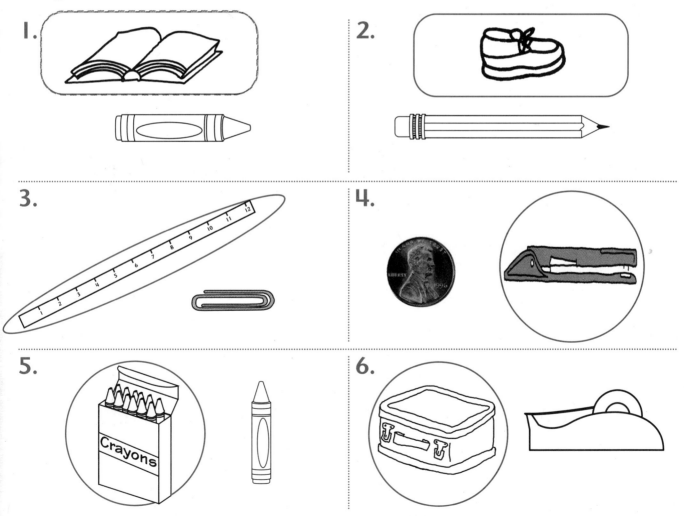

1.

2.

3.

4.

5.

6.

Use a balance.
Use cubes, paper clips, and pennies as units. Weigh each object using the different units.
Complete the chart.

Answers will vary. Possible answers shown.

	Object	Cubes	Paper clips	Pennies
7.	*pencil*	2	5	1
8.	*scissors*	8	10	5
9.	*crayons*	9	12	6
10.	**Draw your own.** Answers will vary.			

Teacher Note: **Closing the Lesson** Ask, Which measurement tool do you use to measure length? Weight?

★ Test Prep

Which item is most likely heavier than the shoe? Mark the space under your answer.

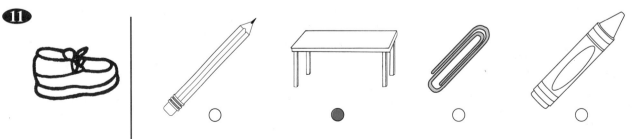

11.

Teacher Note: **Check Understanding** Say, Give an example of a container that holds about the same amount as a glass.

The pot **holds more** than the glass.

The glass **holds less** than the pot.

Ring which holds more.

1.

2.

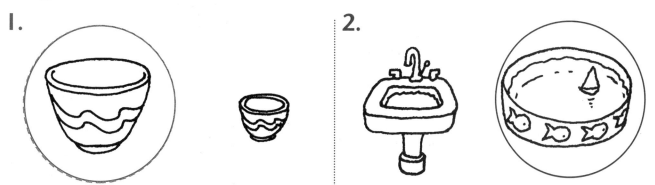

Ring which holds less.

3.

4.

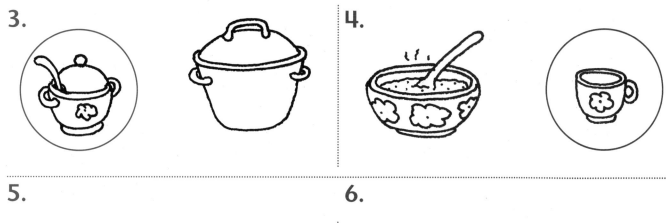

5.

6.

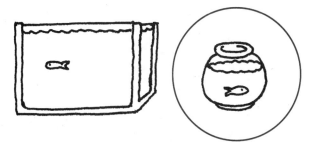

Ring which holds the most.
Cross out which holds the least.

7.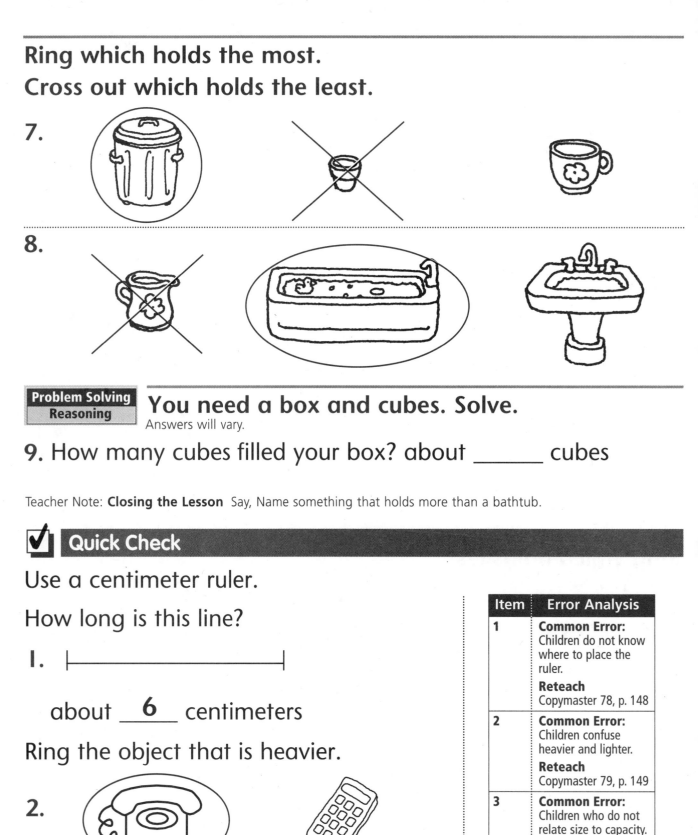

8.

Problem Solving Reasoning **You need a box and cubes. Solve.**
Answers will vary.

9. How many cubes filled your box? about _____ cubes

Teacher Note: **Closing the Lesson** Say, Name something that holds more than a bathtub.

✓ Quick Check

Use a centimeter ruler.

How long is this line?

1. |—————————————|

about __6__ centimeters

Ring the object that is heavier.

2.

Ring which holds more.

3.

Item	Error Analysis
1	**Common Error:** Children do not know where to place the ruler. **Reteach** Copymaster 78, p. 148
2	**Common Error:** Children confuse heavier and lighter. **Reteach** Copymaster 79, p. 149
3	**Common Error:** Children who do not relate size to capacity. **Reteach** Copymaster 80, p. 150

Ring the figure that shows equal parts. (10A)

1.

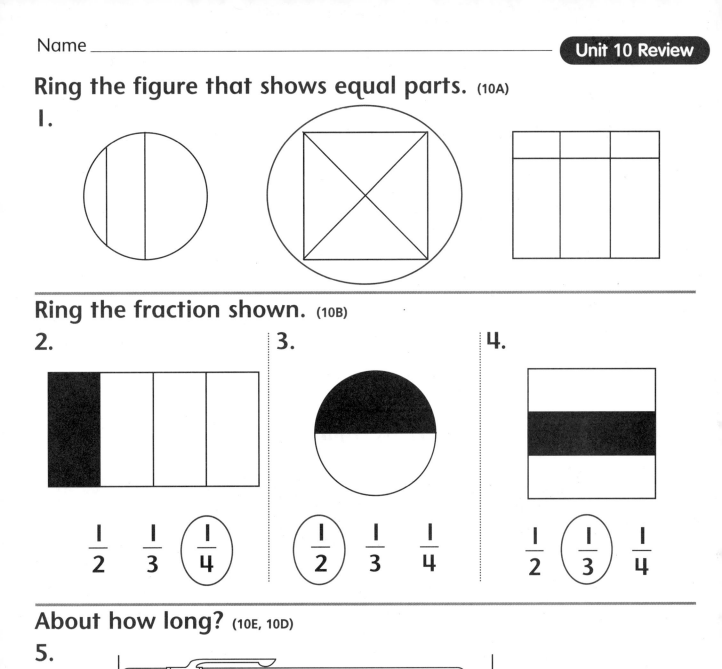

Ring the fraction shown. (10B)

2.

$\frac{1}{2}$ $\frac{1}{3}$ $\left(\frac{1}{4}\right)$

3.

$\left(\frac{1}{2}\right)$ $\frac{1}{3}$ $\frac{1}{4}$

4.

$\frac{1}{2}$ $\left(\frac{1}{3}\right)$ $\frac{1}{4}$

About how long? (10E, 10D)

5.

about $\boxed{4}$ inches

6.

about $\boxed{6}$ centimeters

Ring the longer carrot. (10C)

7.

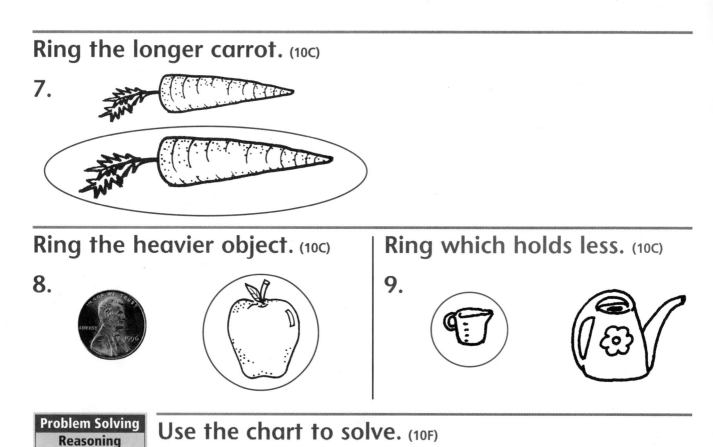

Ring the heavier object. (10C)

8.

Ring which holds less. (10C)

9.

Use the chart to solve. (10F)

Object	Length in Inches	Length in Centimeters
paper clip	about 2	about 5
crayon	about 3	about 7
tape	about 4	about 9

10. Which is longer, the crayon or the tape?

_____**tape**_____

11. How many centimeters long is the paper clip?
about __5__ centimeters

Unit 10 • Review

1 There are 9 eggs. 7 eggs break. How many eggs are left? What number sentence solves the problem? Mark the space next to your answer. **(6A)**

○ $6 + 3 = 9$ ○ $9 + 0 = 9$

● $9 - 7 = 2$ ○ $9 - 3 = 6$

2 Which fact is not in the same family as the fact in the beginning of the row? **(6B)**
Mark the space under your answer.

$2 + 5 = 7$

○ $5 + 2 = 7$ ○ $7 - 2 = 5$

● $7 + 2 = 9$ ○ $7 - 5 = 2$

3 Which number is shown in the table? Mark the space under your answer. **(7B)**

Tens	Ones
5	6

56   65   55   66
●   ○   ○   ○

4 Count by 10's. Which number is missing? Mark the space under your answer. **(7D)**

$40, \underline{\quad}, 60, 70, 80$

42   50   30   55
○   ●   ○   ○

5 Which fraction of the circle is shaded? Mark the space under your answer. **(10B)**

$\dfrac{1}{2}$ $\dfrac{1}{3}$ $\dfrac{1}{4}$ 4

○   ○   ●   ○

6 Which holds the most? Mark the space under your answer. **(10C)**

○   ○   ●   ○

Unit 10 • Cumulative Review   (two hundred seventy-seven) 277

7 How many centimeters long is the worm? Mark the space under your answer. **(10D)**

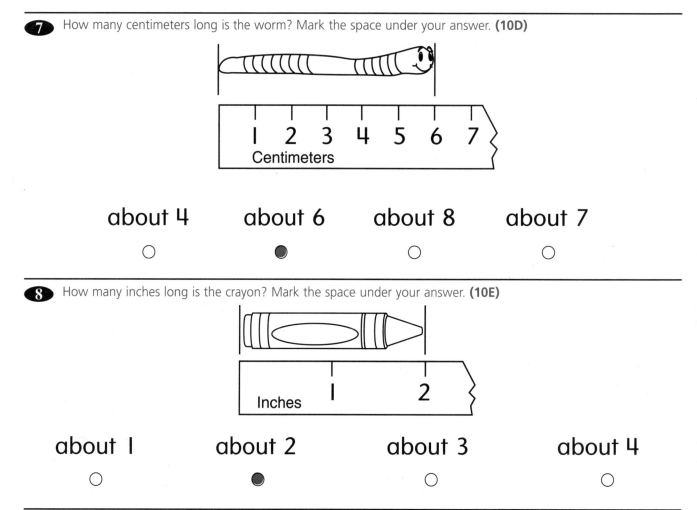

about 4	about 6	about 8	about 7
○	●	○	○

8 How many inches long is the crayon? Mark the space under your answer. **(10E)**

about 1	about 2	about 3	about 4
○	●	○	○

You will complete the rest of the test on your own.

Decide on an answer. Mark the space for your answer.

If the answer is **not here**, mark the space for **NH.** (9A, 9B)

9
$$65$$
$$+ \ 34$$

31	91	99	NH
○	○	●	○

10
$$22$$
$$+ \ 53$$

77	75	65	NH
○	●	○	○

11
$$33$$
$$+ \ 33$$

99	60	66	NH
○	○	●	○

12
$$75$$
$$- \ 30$$

40	45	50	NH
○	●	○	○

13
$$56$$
$$- \ 26$$

70	36	30	NH
○	○	●	○

14
$$98$$
$$- \ 63$$

30	33	38	NH
○	○	○	●

Unit 10 • Cumulative Review

UNIT 11 • TABLE OF CONTENTS

Addition and Subtraction Facts through 20

We will be using this vocabulary:

fact an addition or subtraction number sentence

fact family the related addition and subtraction facts

names for numbers the different expressions that are equivalent to the same number; for example: names for 12: 6 + 6; 7 + 5; 8 + 4; 9 + 3, etc.

Dear Family,

During the next few weeks our math class will be learning and practicing addition and subtraction facts through 20.

You can expect to see homework that provides practice with addition and subtraction facts.

As we learn about related facts and fact families you may wish to keep the following sample as a guide.

Related facts

$$7 + 5 = 12 \qquad 12 - 5 = 7$$

Fact Family

$$7 + 5 = 12 \qquad 12 - 7 = 5$$

$$5 + 7 = 12 \qquad 12 - 5 = 7$$

Knowing addition facts can help children learn the related subtraction facts.

Sincerely,

Name _____

Teacher Note: **Check Understanding** Have children use counters to show that 9 + 2 and 11 – 2 are related.

Add or subtract.

1. $9 + 2 = \boxed{11}$ $11 - 2 = \boxed{9}$

2. $8 + 3 = \boxed{11}$ $11 - 3 = \boxed{8}$

3. $7 + 4 = \boxed{11}$ $11 - 4 = \boxed{7}$

4. $9 + 3 = \boxed{12}$ $12 - 3 = \boxed{9}$

5. $8 + 4 = \boxed{12}$ $12 - 4 = \boxed{8}$

6. $7 + 5 = \boxed{12}$ $12 - 5 = \boxed{7}$

Add or subtract.

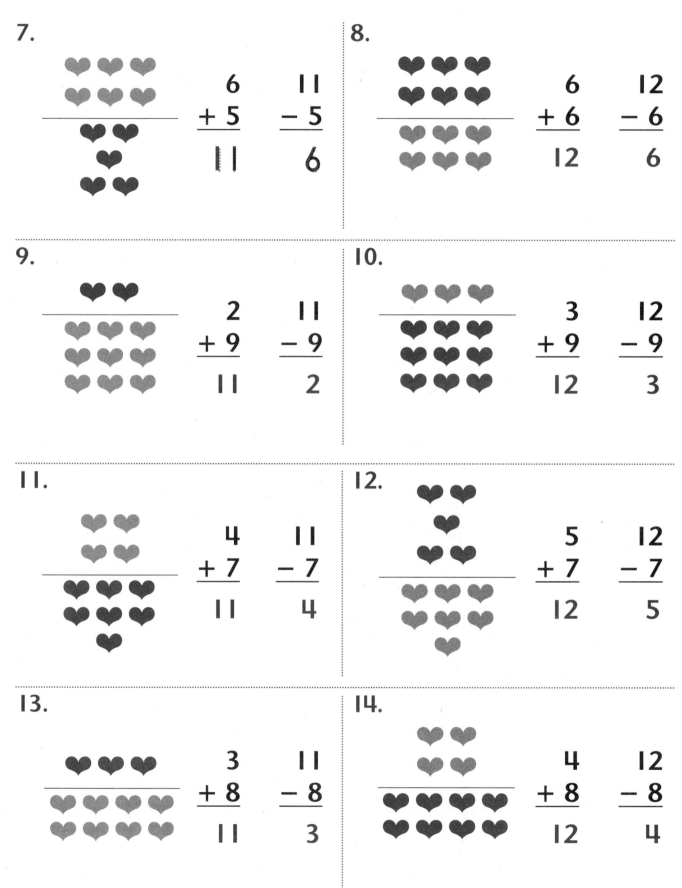

7.

$$6 + 5 = 11$$

$$11 - 5 = 6$$

8.

$$6 + 6 = 12$$

$$12 - 6 = 6$$

9.

$$2 + 9 = 11$$

$$11 - 9 = 2$$

10.

$$3 + 9 = 12$$

$$12 - 9 = 3$$

11.

$$4 + 7 = 11$$

$$11 - 7 = 4$$

12.

$$5 + 7 = 12$$

$$12 - 7 = 5$$

13.

$$3 + 8 = 11$$

$$11 - 8 = 3$$

14.

$$4 + 8 = 12$$

$$12 - 8 = 4$$

Unit 11 • Lesson 1

Add or subtract.

15.

$8 + 4 = \boxed{12}$ $12 - 4 = \boxed{8}$ $2 + 9 = \boxed{11}$

16.

$11 - 9 = \boxed{2}$ $6 + 6 = \boxed{12}$ $12 - 6 = \boxed{6}$

17.

$$\begin{array}{r} 11 \\ -\ 5 \\ \hline 6 \end{array} \qquad \begin{array}{r} 6 \\ +\ 5 \\ \hline 11 \end{array} \qquad \begin{array}{r} 12 \\ -\ 3 \\ \hline 9 \end{array} \qquad \begin{array}{r} 9 \\ +\ 3 \\ \hline 12 \end{array} \qquad \begin{array}{r} 7 \\ +\ 4 \\ \hline 11 \end{array}$$

18.

$$\begin{array}{r} 11 \\ -\ 4 \\ \hline 7 \end{array} \qquad \begin{array}{r} 11 \\ -\ 3 \\ \hline 8 \end{array} \qquad \begin{array}{r} 8 \\ +\ 3 \\ \hline 11 \end{array} \qquad \begin{array}{r} 5 \\ +\ 6 \\ \hline 11 \end{array} \qquad \begin{array}{r} 11 \\ -\ 6 \\ \hline 5 \end{array}$$

Practice your facts.

19.

$$\begin{array}{r} 7 \\ +\ 3 \\ \hline 10 \end{array} \qquad \begin{array}{r} 6 \\ +\ 4 \\ \hline 10 \end{array} \qquad \begin{array}{r} 6 \\ +\ 6 \\ \hline 12 \end{array} \qquad \begin{array}{r} 4 \\ +\ 5 \\ \hline 9 \end{array} \qquad \begin{array}{r} 3 \\ +\ 9 \\ \hline 12 \end{array}$$

20.

$$\begin{array}{r} 3 \\ +\ 4 \\ \hline 7 \end{array} \qquad \begin{array}{r} 5 \\ +\ 4 \\ \hline 9 \end{array} \qquad \begin{array}{r} 3 \\ +\ 7 \\ \hline 10 \end{array} \qquad \begin{array}{r} 4 \\ +\ 8 \\ \hline 12 \end{array} \qquad \begin{array}{r} 1 \\ +\ 9 \\ \hline 10 \end{array}$$

Practice your facts.

21.

12	10	9	12	8
$-\ 4$	$-\ 5$	$-\ 3$	$-\ 8$	$-\ 2$
8	5	6	4	6

22.

12	10	11	7	12
$-\ 6$	$-\ 4$	$-\ 9$	$-\ 6$	$-\ 9$
6	6	2	1	3

23.

8	11	9	10	11
$-\ 5$	$-\ 6$	$-\ 3$	$-\ 5$	$-\ 5$
3	5	6	5	6

Problem Solving Reasoning Solve.

24. There are **5** ducks.

6 ducks join them.

Now there are ⬚ 11 ⬚ ducks.

25. Paul sees **12** ducks.

8 ducks swim away.

Now Paul sees ⬚ 4 ⬚ ducks.

Teacher Note: **Closing the Lesson** Have volunteers make up story problems for related facts for 11 and 12.

★ Test Prep

Which is the related subtraction fact? Mark next to your answer.

26

$$9 + 2 = 11$$

- ○ $9 - 2 = 7$
- ● $11 - 2 = 9$
- ○ $11 - 3 = 8$
- ○ $12 - 3 = 9$

Guided Practice: Exercise 1
Independent Practice: Exercises 2–6

Teacher Note: **Check Understanding** Ask, How are all the facts in exercise 1 alike?

Complete the fact familiy.

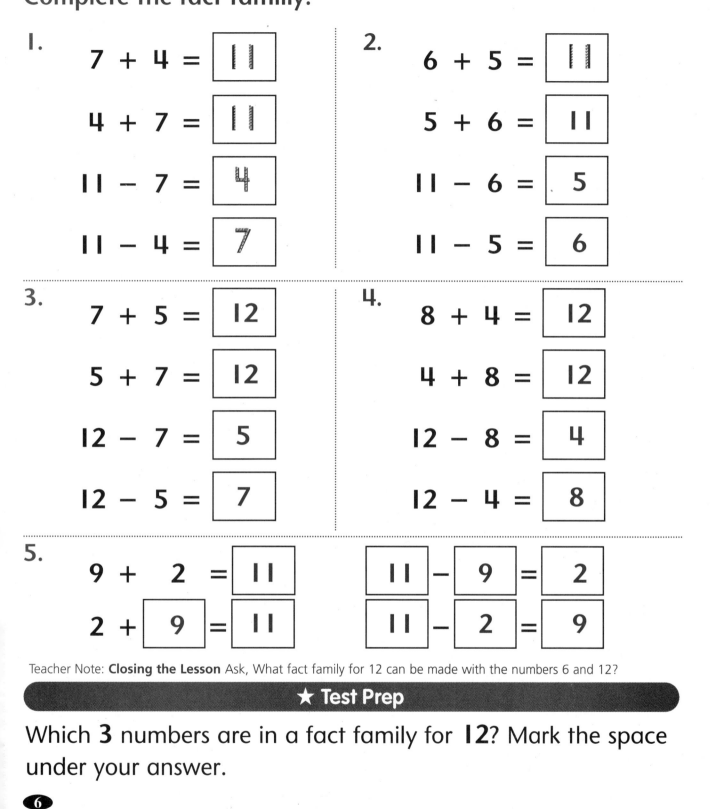

1.
$7 + 4 =$ 11
$4 + 7 =$ 11
$11 - 7 =$ 4
$11 - 4 =$ 7

2.
$6 + 5 =$ 11
$5 + 6 =$ 11
$11 - 6 =$ 5
$11 - 5 =$ 6

3.
$7 + 5 =$ 12
$5 + 7 =$ 12
$12 - 7 =$ 5
$12 - 5 =$ 7

4.
$8 + 4 =$ 12
$4 + 8 =$ 12
$12 - 8 =$ 4
$12 - 4 =$ 8

5.
$9 + 2 =$ 11
$2 + 9 =$ 11

$11 - 9 =$ 2
$11 - 2 =$ 9

Teacher Note: **Closing the Lesson** Ask, What fact family for 12 can be made with the numbers 6 and 12?

★ Test Prep

Which **3** numbers are in a fact family for **12**? Mark the space under your answer.

6

2, 9, 11   12, 10, 11   8, 4, 12   12, 8, 5
○   ○   ●   ○

Teacher Note: **Check Understanding** Have volunteers identify a variety of number sentences for 6; for example, 3 + 3 = 6; 7 - 1 = 6.

Ring the names for the number.

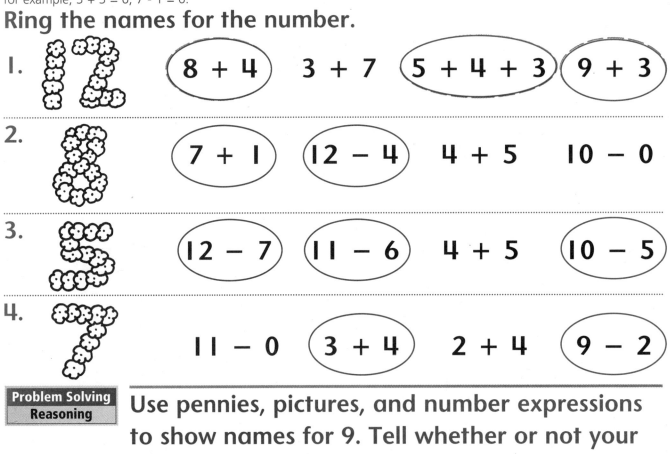

1. **12**   ⟨8 + 4⟩   3 + 7   ⟨5 + 4 + 3⟩ ⟨9 + 3⟩

2. **8**   ⟨7 + 1⟩   ⟨12 – 4⟩   4 + 5   10 – 0

3. **5**   ⟨12 – 7⟩   ⟨11 – 6⟩   4 + 5   ⟨10 – 5⟩

4. **7**   11 – 0   ⟨3 + 4⟩   2 + 4   ⟨9 – 2⟩

| **Problem Solving**
Reasoning | Use pennies, pictures, and number expressions to show names for 9. Tell whether or not your names for 9 match a friend's. (Answers will vary.) |

Teacher Note: **Closing the Lesson** Ask, Which number do 5 + 7, 8 + 4, and 6 + 6 all name?

✓ Quick Check

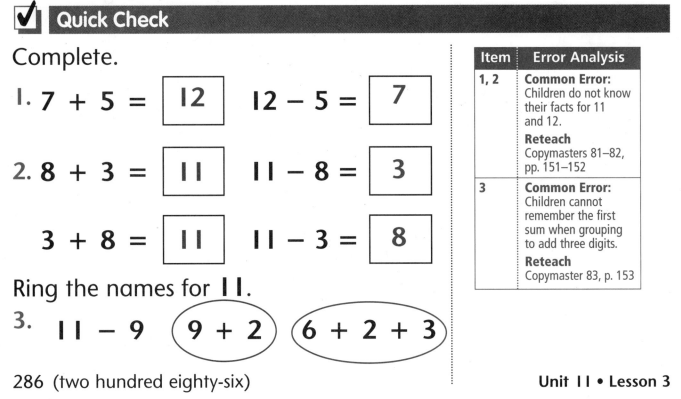

Complete.

1. $7 + 5 = \boxed{12}$ $12 - 5 = \boxed{7}$

2. $8 + 3 = \boxed{11}$ $11 - 8 = \boxed{3}$

   $3 + 8 = \boxed{11}$ $11 - 3 = \boxed{8}$

Item	Error Analysis
1, 2	**Common Error:** Children do not know their facts for 11 and 12. **Reteach** Copymasters 81–82, pp. 151–152
3	**Common Error:** Children cannot remember the first sum when grouping to add three digits. **Reteach** Copymaster 83, p. 153

Ring the names for **11**.

3. 11 – 9   ⟨9 + 2⟩   ⟨6 + 2 + 3⟩

Teacher Note: **Check Understanding** Have children use counters to show that 9 + 4 and 13 – 4 are related.

Add or subtract.

1. $9 + 4 = \boxed{13}$ $13 - 4 = \boxed{9}$

2. $9 + 5 = \boxed{14}$ $14 - 5 = \boxed{9}$

3. $8 + 7 = \boxed{15}$ $15 - 7 = \boxed{8}$

4. $9 + 7 = \boxed{16}$ $16 - 7 = \boxed{9}$

5. $8 + 5 = \boxed{13}$ $13 - 5 = \boxed{8}$

6. $8 + 6 = \boxed{14}$ $14 - 6 = \boxed{8}$

Add or subtract.

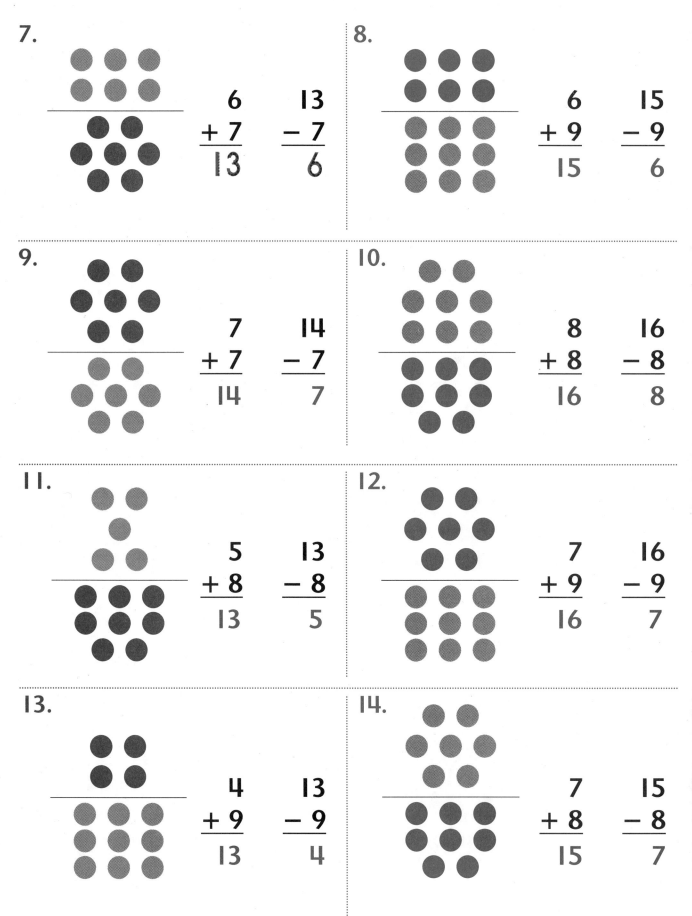

7.

$$\begin{array}{r} 6 \\ + 7 \\ \hline 13 \end{array}$$

$$\begin{array}{r} 13 \\ - 7 \\ \hline 6 \end{array}$$

8.

$$\begin{array}{r} 6 \\ + 9 \\ \hline 15 \end{array}$$

$$\begin{array}{r} 15 \\ - 9 \\ \hline 6 \end{array}$$

9.

$$\begin{array}{r} 7 \\ + 7 \\ \hline 14 \end{array}$$

$$\begin{array}{r} 14 \\ - 7 \\ \hline 7 \end{array}$$

10.

$$\begin{array}{r} 8 \\ + 8 \\ \hline 16 \end{array}$$

$$\begin{array}{r} 16 \\ - 8 \\ \hline 8 \end{array}$$

11.

$$\begin{array}{r} 5 \\ + 8 \\ \hline 13 \end{array}$$

$$\begin{array}{r} 13 \\ - 8 \\ \hline 5 \end{array}$$

12.

$$\begin{array}{r} 7 \\ + 9 \\ \hline 16 \end{array}$$

$$\begin{array}{r} 16 \\ - 9 \\ \hline 7 \end{array}$$

13.

$$\begin{array}{r} 4 \\ + 9 \\ \hline 13 \end{array}$$

$$\begin{array}{r} 13 \\ - 9 \\ \hline 4 \end{array}$$

14.

$$\begin{array}{r} 7 \\ + 8 \\ \hline 15 \end{array}$$

$$\begin{array}{r} 15 \\ - 8 \\ \hline 7 \end{array}$$

Unit 11 • Lesson 4

Add or subtract.

15.

$5 + 9 = \boxed{14}$ $14 - 9 = \boxed{5}$ $8 + 8 = \boxed{16}$

16.

$16 - 8 = \boxed{8}$ $7 + 8 = \boxed{15}$ $15 - 8 = \boxed{7}$

17.

$$\begin{array}{r} 5 \\ + 8 \\ \hline 13 \end{array} \qquad \begin{array}{r} 13 \\ - 8 \\ \hline 5 \end{array} \qquad \begin{array}{r} 9 \\ + 7 \\ \hline 16 \end{array} \qquad \begin{array}{r} 16 \\ - 7 \\ \hline 9 \end{array} \qquad \begin{array}{r} 9 \\ + 6 \\ \hline 15 \end{array}$$

18.

$$\begin{array}{r} 15 \\ - 6 \\ \hline 9 \end{array} \qquad \begin{array}{r} 7 \\ + 7 \\ \hline 14 \end{array} \qquad \begin{array}{r} 14 \\ - 7 \\ \hline 7 \end{array} \qquad \begin{array}{r} 9 \\ + 5 \\ \hline 14 \end{array} \qquad \begin{array}{r} 14 \\ - 5 \\ \hline 9 \end{array}$$

Practice your facts.

19.

$$\begin{array}{r} 6 \\ + 8 \\ \hline 14 \end{array} \qquad \begin{array}{r} 3 \\ + 9 \\ \hline 12 \end{array} \qquad \begin{array}{r} 6 \\ + 4 \\ \hline 10 \end{array} \qquad \begin{array}{r} 8 \\ + 3 \\ \hline 11 \end{array} \qquad \begin{array}{r} 7 \\ + 6 \\ \hline 13 \end{array}$$

20.

$$\begin{array}{r} 7 \\ + 7 \\ \hline 14 \end{array} \qquad \begin{array}{r} 4 \\ + 8 \\ \hline 12 \end{array} \qquad \begin{array}{r} 5 \\ + 5 \\ \hline 10 \end{array} \qquad \begin{array}{r} 7 \\ + 4 \\ \hline 11 \end{array} \qquad \begin{array}{r} 8 \\ + 7 \\ \hline 15 \end{array}$$

Practice your facts.

21.
$$\begin{array}{r} 15 \\ -\ 9 \\ \hline 6 \end{array}$$
$$\begin{array}{r} 14 \\ -\ 6 \\ \hline 8 \end{array}$$
$$\begin{array}{r} 15 \\ -\ 7 \\ \hline 8 \end{array}$$
$$\begin{array}{r} 16 \\ -\ 9 \\ \hline 7 \end{array}$$
$$\begin{array}{r} 10 \\ -\ 4 \\ \hline 6 \end{array}$$

22.
$$\begin{array}{r} 12 \\ -\ 4 \\ \hline 8 \end{array}$$
$$\begin{array}{r} 10 \\ -\ 7 \\ \hline 3 \end{array}$$
$$\begin{array}{r} 12 \\ -\ 5 \\ \hline 7 \end{array}$$
$$\begin{array}{r} 14 \\ -\ 7 \\ \hline 7 \end{array}$$
$$\begin{array}{r} 13 \\ -\ 4 \\ \hline 9 \end{array}$$

23.
$$\begin{array}{r} 13 \\ -\ 9 \\ \hline 4 \end{array}$$
$$\begin{array}{r} 14 \\ -\ 5 \\ \hline 9 \end{array}$$
$$\begin{array}{r} 16 \\ -\ 8 \\ \hline 8 \end{array}$$
$$\begin{array}{r} 12 \\ -\ 6 \\ \hline 6 \end{array}$$
$$\begin{array}{r} 11 \\ -\ 6 \\ \hline 5 \end{array}$$

Problem Solving Reasoning Solve.

24. Marina has **16** grapes.

She gives Pam **8** grapes.

Marina has ☐ **8** ☐ grapes left.

25. Tony has **7** kites.

He gets **8** more.

Tony has ☐ **15** ☐ kites.

Teacher Note: **Closing the Lesson** Write: There are ___ children. ____ more join them. How many children are there now? Have volunteers fill in the blanks so that the answers are 13, 14, 15, and 16.

★ Test Prep

26 Which is the related addition fact? Mark next to your answer.

$14 - 6 = 8$

○ $6 + 2 = 8$ ○ $9 + 5 = 14$

● $8 + 6 = 14$ ○ $8 + 4 = 12$

     Unit 11 • Lesson 4

Guided Practice: Exercise 1
Independent Practice: Exercises 2–6

**Fact Families
through 16**

Teacher Note: **Check Understanding** Ask, Which numbers from 13 to 16 will have doubles as addition facts?

Complete the fact family.

1.
$9 + 7 = \boxed{16}$

$7 + 9 = \boxed{16}$

$16 - 9 = \boxed{7}$

$16 - 7 = \boxed{9}$

2.
$8 + 5 = \boxed{13}$

$5 + 8 = \boxed{13}$

$13 - 8 = \boxed{5}$

$13 - 5 = \boxed{8}$

3.
$8 + 7 = \boxed{15}$

$7 + 8 = \boxed{15}$

$15 - 8 = \boxed{7}$

$15 - 7 = \boxed{8}$

4.
$9 + 4 = \boxed{13}$

$4 + 9 = \boxed{13}$

$13 - 9 = \boxed{4}$

$13 - 4 = \boxed{9}$

5.
$9 + 6 = \boxed{15}$

$6 + \boxed{9} = \boxed{15}$

$\boxed{15} - \boxed{6} = \boxed{9}$

$\boxed{15} - \boxed{9} = \boxed{6}$

Teacher Note: **Closing the Lesson** Ask, What fact family can you write with the numbers 5, 9, 14?

★ **Test Prep**

6 Which **3** numbers are in a fact family for **14**? Mark the space under your answer.

4, 9, 13   12, 13, 14   5, 9, 14   9, 13, 4
   ○   ○   ●   ○

Name _____

Teacher Note: **Check Understanding** How can you use a number expression to name your age?

Ring the names for the number.

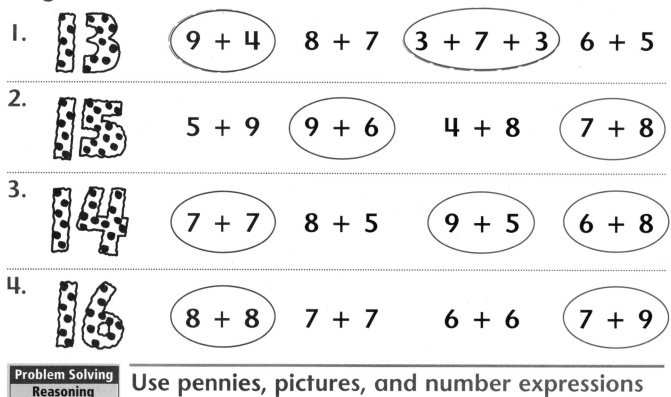

1. **13** $(9 + 4)$ 8 + 7 $(3 + 7 + 3)$ 6 + 5

2. **15** 5 + 9 $(9 + 6)$ 4 + 8 $(7 + 8)$

3. **14** $(7 + 7)$ 8 + 5 $(9 + 5)$ $(6 + 8)$

4. **16** $(8 + 8)$ 7 + 7 6 + 6 $(7 + 9)$

**Problem Solving
Reasoning**
Use pennies, pictures, and number expressions to show names for 12. Tell whether or not your names match a friend's. (Answers will vary.)

Teacher Note: **Closing the Lesson** Ask, How can you name the number 12 using a subtraction expression?

✓ Quick Check

Complete.

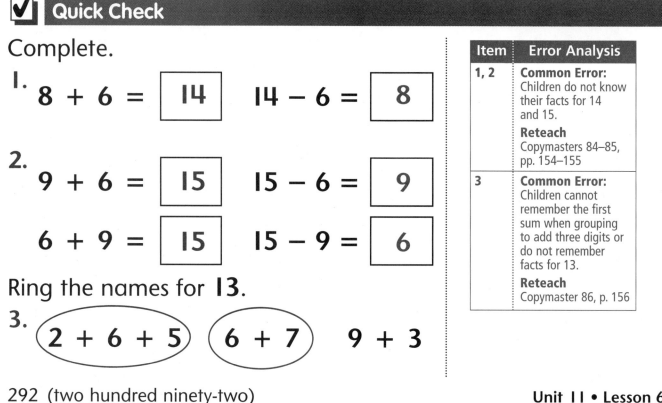

1. $8 + 6 = \boxed{14}$ $14 - 6 = \boxed{8}$

2. $9 + 6 = \boxed{15}$ $15 - 6 = \boxed{9}$

   $6 + 9 = \boxed{15}$ $15 - 9 = \boxed{6}$

Ring the names for **13**.

3. $(2 + 6 + 5)$ $(6 + 7)$ 9 + 3

Item	Error Analysis
1, 2	**Common Error:** Children do not know their facts for 14 and 15. **Reteach** Copymasters 84–85, pp. 154–155
3	**Common Error:** Children cannot remember the first sum when grouping to add three digits or do not remember facts for 13. **Reteach** Copymaster 86, p. 156

Unit 11 • Lesson 6

Guided Practice: Exercises 1 and 7
Independent Practice: Exercises 2–6 and 8–26

**Related Facts
through 18**

Teacher Note: **Check Understanding** Ask, Which subtraction facts do you know if you know 9 + 7 = 16?

Add or subtract.

1. $8 + 9 = \boxed{17}$ $17 - 9 = \boxed{8}$

2. $9 + 8 = \boxed{17}$ $17 - 8 = \boxed{9}$

3. $9 + 9 = \boxed{18}$ $18 - 9 = \boxed{9}$

4. $9 + 7 = \boxed{16}$ $16 - 7 = \boxed{9}$

5. $8 + 7 = \boxed{15}$ $15 - 7 = \boxed{8}$

6. $7 + 7 = \boxed{14}$ $14 - 7 = \boxed{7}$

Add or subtract.

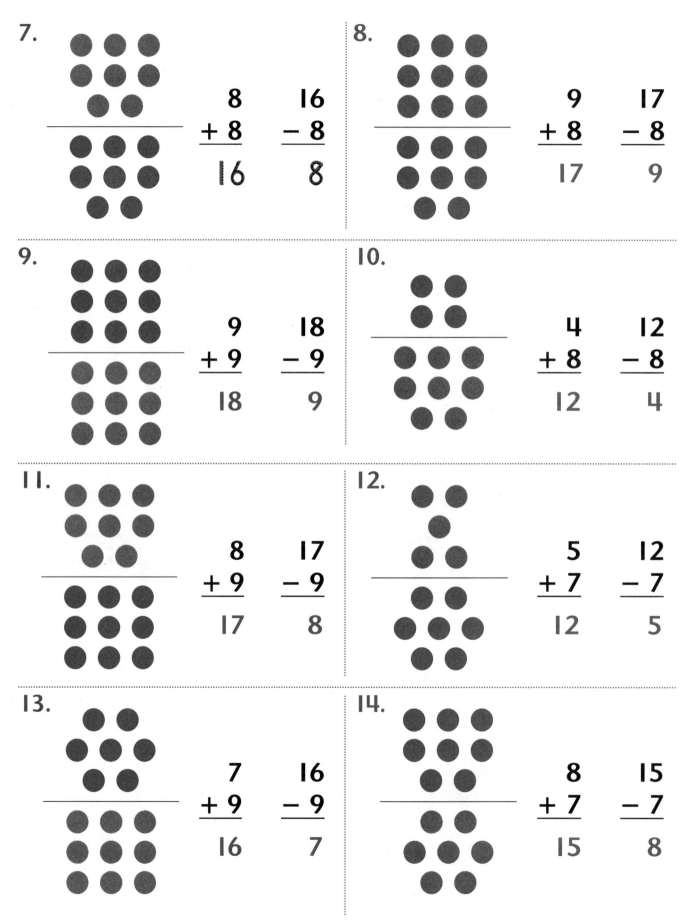

7.
$$\begin{array}{r} 8 \\ + 8 \\ \hline 16 \end{array}$$
$$\begin{array}{r} 16 \\ - 8 \\ \hline 8 \end{array}$$

8.
$$\begin{array}{r} 9 \\ + 8 \\ \hline 17 \end{array}$$
$$\begin{array}{r} 17 \\ - 8 \\ \hline 9 \end{array}$$

9.
$$\begin{array}{r} 9 \\ + 9 \\ \hline 18 \end{array}$$
$$\begin{array}{r} 18 \\ - 9 \\ \hline 9 \end{array}$$

10.
$$\begin{array}{r} 4 \\ + 8 \\ \hline 12 \end{array}$$
$$\begin{array}{r} 12 \\ - 8 \\ \hline 4 \end{array}$$

11.
$$\begin{array}{r} 8 \\ + 9 \\ \hline 17 \end{array}$$
$$\begin{array}{r} 17 \\ - 9 \\ \hline 8 \end{array}$$

12.
$$\begin{array}{r} 5 \\ + 7 \\ \hline 12 \end{array}$$
$$\begin{array}{r} 12 \\ - 7 \\ \hline 5 \end{array}$$

13.
$$\begin{array}{r} 7 \\ + 9 \\ \hline 16 \end{array}$$
$$\begin{array}{r} 16 \\ - 9 \\ \hline 7 \end{array}$$

14.
$$\begin{array}{r} 8 \\ + 7 \\ \hline 15 \end{array}$$
$$\begin{array}{r} 15 \\ - 7 \\ \hline 8 \end{array}$$

Practice your facts.

15.

$9 + 7 = \boxed{16}$ $8 + 9 = \boxed{17}$ $18 - 9 = \boxed{9}$

16.

$9 + 9 = \boxed{18}$ $17 - 8 = \boxed{9}$ $9 + 8 = \boxed{17}$

17.

$8 + 6 = \boxed{14}$ $13 - 8 = \boxed{5}$ $7 + 6 = \boxed{13}$

18.

13	8	9	12	16
− 4	+ 5	+ 6	− 6	− 7
9	13	15	6	9

19.

15	6	12	9	8
− 9	+ 4	− 3	+ 9	+ 7
6	10	9	18	15

20.

11	12	7	14	7
− 9	− 8	+ 8	− 9	+ 9
2	4	15	5	16

Practice your facts.

21.

$\begin{array}{r} 18 \\ -\ 9 \\ \hline 9 \end{array}$	$\begin{array}{r} 17 \\ -\ 9 \\ \hline 8 \end{array}$	$\begin{array}{r} 8 \\ +\ 8 \\ \hline 16 \end{array}$	$\begin{array}{r} 16 \\ -\ 7 \\ \hline 9 \end{array}$	$\begin{array}{r} 7 \\ +\ 7 \\ \hline 14 \end{array}$

22.

$\begin{array}{r} 6 \\ +\ 9 \\ \hline 15 \end{array}$	$\begin{array}{r} 13 \\ -\ 9 \\ \hline 4 \end{array}$	$\begin{array}{r} 16 \\ -\ 8 \\ \hline 8 \end{array}$	$\begin{array}{r} 5 \\ +\ 9 \\ \hline 14 \end{array}$	$\begin{array}{r} 9 \\ +\ 8 \\ \hline 17 \end{array}$

23.

$\begin{array}{r} 8 \\ +\ 5 \\ \hline 13 \end{array}$	$\begin{array}{r} 17 \\ -\ 8 \\ \hline 9 \end{array}$	$\begin{array}{r} 14 \\ -\ 5 \\ \hline 9 \end{array}$	$\begin{array}{r} 9 \\ +\ 6 \\ \hline 15 \end{array}$	$\begin{array}{r} 7 \\ +\ 9 \\ \hline 16 \end{array}$

Problem Solving Reasoning

24. Jean has **9** books.

Jonah gives her **8**

more books. Now

Jean has | **17** | books.

25. Tom has **18** tops.

He loses **9** tops. Now

Tom has | **9** | tops.

Teacher Note: **Closing the Lesson** Have children draw pictures to go with the number sentences $9 + 8 = 17$; $9 + 9 = 18$; $18 - 9 = 9$.

★ Test Prep

Mark next to the related fact.

26

$$9 + 9 = 18$$

○ $9 - 9 = 0$ ○ $17 - 9 = 8$

● $18 - 9 = 9$ ○ $18 - 10 = 8$

296 (two hundred ninety-six)

Unit 11 • Lesson 7

Teacher Note: **Check Understanding** Challenge volunteers to make up a word problem that can be solved using one of the facts in exercise 1.

Complete the fact family.

1. $9 + 8 = \boxed{17}$

   $8 + 9 = \boxed{17}$

   $17 - 9 = \boxed{8}$

   $17 - 8 = \boxed{9}$

2. $9 + 9 = \boxed{18}$

   $18 - 9 = \boxed{9}$

3. $6 + 5 = \boxed{11}$

   $5 + 6 = \boxed{11}$

   $11 - 6 = \boxed{5}$

   $11 - 5 = \boxed{6}$

4. $9 + 4 = \boxed{13}$

   $4 + 9 = \boxed{13}$

   $13 - 9 = \boxed{4}$

   $13 - 4 = \boxed{9}$

5. $8 + 4 = \boxed{12}$ $\boxed{12} - \boxed{4} = \boxed{8}$

   $4 + \boxed{8} = \boxed{12}$ $\boxed{12} - \boxed{8} = \boxed{4}$

Teacher Note: **Closing the Lesson** Ask, How many fact families did we learn for 17? 18?

★ Test Prep

Which **3** numbers are in a fact family for **17**?

Mark the space under your answer.

6   8, 9, 17   16, 17, 18   7, 8, 15   8, 8, 16

                ●   ○   ○   ○

Name _____

Teacher Note: **Check Understanding** Ask, How can you name 15 using an expression with 3 addends?

Ring the names for the number.

1. **17** $\enclose{circle}{9 + 8}$ $\enclose{circle}{4 + 5 + 6 + 2}$ 9 + 9

2. **18** 8 + 8 $\enclose{circle}{4 + 5 + 9}$ $\enclose{circle}{9 + 9}$ 7 + 9

| Problem Solving |
| Reasoning |

Solve.

3. I read **4** pages on Monday, **3** pages on Tuesday, none on Wednesday, and **8** pages on Thursday. How many pages did I read so far this week? _____ (15)

Teacher Note: **Closing the Lesson** Ask, How can you name the number 18 using an expression with 4 addends?

✓ **Quick Check**

Solve.

1. 9
  + 8
  —
  17

2. 14
  − 6
  —
  8

Complete the fact family.

3. 8 + 9 = | 17 | 17 − 9 = | 8 |

  9 + 8 = | 17 | 17 − 8 = | 9 |

Ring the names for **17**.

4. $\enclose{circle}{9 + 8}$ 5 + 6 $\enclose{circle}{9 + 4 + 4}$

Item	Error Analysis
1, 2	**Common Error:** Children do not know addition and subtraction facts for 18. **Skills Tutorial** Strand P2, Skill 3; Strand P3, Skill 3
3	**Common Error:** Children cannot complete a fact family. **Reteach** Copymaster 87, p. 157
4	**Common Error:** Children cannot group addends and add or do not know facts for 17. **Reteach** Copymaster 88, p. 158

**Problem Solving Application:
Choose the Operation**

Problem Solving Plan
1. Understand 2. Decide 3. Solve 4. Look back

Solve.

1. Anna has some erasers in her desk. She puts **6** more in her desk. Now she has **13**. How many erasers does she have in her desk to start with?

   Think Do you need to add or subtract?

   <u>**subtract**</u>

   13 ⊖ 6 = ___7___

   Answer ___7___ erasers

2. Sam has **18** balloons. **9** of them float away. How many does he have left?

   Think Do you need to add or subtract?

   <u>**subtract**</u>

   18 ⊖ 9 = ___9___

   Answer ___9___ balloons

3. Nina has **15** seashells. That is **9** more than Tae has. How many seashells does Tae have?

   Think Do you need to add or subtract?

   <u>**subtract**</u>

   15 ⊖ 9 = ___6___

   Answer ___6___ seashells

4. Ann has **16¢**. That is **8¢** more than Rita. How much money does Rita have?

   Think Do you need to add or subtract?

   <u>**subtract**</u>

   16¢ ⊖ 8¢ = ___8___

   Answer ___8___ ¢

Solve.

5. Anthony catches **6** fish from the lake. Sue catches **8** fish. How many fish do they catch in all?

8 (+) 6 = ___14___

Answer __14__ fish

6. Jason gives **6** cards to Lauren and **6** cards to Angela. How many cards does Jason give in all?

6 (+) 6 = ___12___

Answer __12__ cards

7. Mike found **15** shells. That was **6** more than Ellen found. How many shells did Ellen find?

15 (−) 6 = ___9___

Answer __9__ shells

8. Jim pays **8¢** for a tart. He pays **9¢** for a piece of pie. How much money does he spend?

8¢ (+) 9¢ = ___17___ ¢

Answer __17__ ¢

Teacher Note: **Closing the Lesson** Ask, Is there another way to solve exercise 4?

Extend Your Thinking

Draw a picture to show problem 7. (Answers will vary.)

9.

Teacher Note: **Check Understanding** Ask, What do you add to 10 to get 12?

Solve.

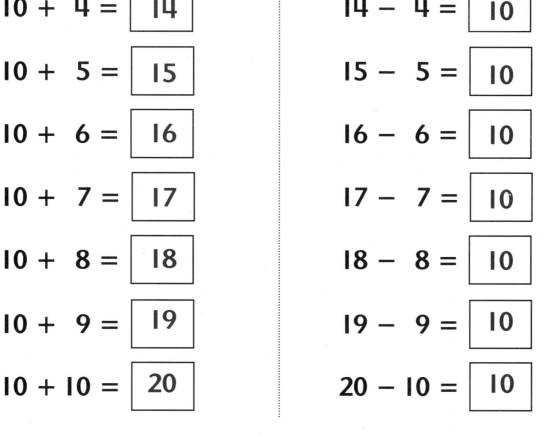

1. $10 + 1 = \boxed{11}$

    $10 + 2 = \boxed{12}$

    $10 + 3 = \boxed{13}$

    $10 + 4 = \boxed{14}$

    $10 + 5 = \boxed{15}$

    $10 + 6 = \boxed{16}$

    $10 + 7 = \boxed{17}$

    $10 + 8 = \boxed{18}$

    $10 + 9 = \boxed{19}$

    $10 + 10 = \boxed{20}$

2. $11 - 1 = \boxed{10}$

    $12 - 2 = \boxed{10}$

    $13 - 3 = \boxed{10}$

    $14 - 4 = \boxed{10}$

    $15 - 5 = \boxed{10}$

    $16 - 6 = \boxed{10}$

    $17 - 7 = \boxed{10}$

    $18 - 8 = \boxed{10}$

    $19 - 9 = \boxed{10}$

    $20 - 10 = \boxed{10}$

**Problem Solving
Reasoning** Solve.

3. What pattern do you see in the addition facts?_____

(Answers will vary. Possible answer: Each sum has 1 ten and increases by one until 10 + 10, which then has 2 tens and 0 ones.)

_____

_____

_____

Add or subtract.

4.
$$\begin{array}{r} 9 \\ + 6 \\ \hline 15 \end{array}$$

5.
$$\begin{array}{r} 10 \\ + 3 \\ \hline 13 \end{array}$$

6.
$$\begin{array}{r} 12 \\ - 8 \\ \hline 4 \end{array}$$

7.
$$\begin{array}{r} 17 \\ - 7 \\ \hline 10 \end{array}$$

8.
$$\begin{array}{r} 18 \\ - 9 \\ \hline 9 \end{array}$$

9.
$$\begin{array}{r} 9 \\ + 8 \\ \hline 17 \end{array}$$

10.
$$\begin{array}{r} 6 \\ + 5 \\ \hline 11 \end{array}$$

11.
$$\begin{array}{r} 10 \\ + 9 \\ \hline 19 \end{array}$$

12.
$$\begin{array}{r} 4 \\ + 6 \\ \hline 10 \end{array}$$

13.
$$\begin{array}{r} 10 \\ - 5 \\ \hline 5 \end{array}$$

14.
$$\begin{array}{r} 7 \\ + 7 \\ \hline 14 \end{array}$$

15.
$$\begin{array}{r} 8 \\ - 7 \\ \hline 1 \end{array}$$

16.
$$\begin{array}{r} 9 \\ - 9 \\ \hline 0 \end{array}$$

17.
$$\begin{array}{r} 8 \\ + 8 \\ \hline 16 \end{array}$$

18.
$$\begin{array}{r} 6 \\ + 8 \\ \hline 14 \end{array}$$

19.
$$\begin{array}{r} 20 \\ - 10 \\ \hline 10 \end{array}$$

Teacher Note: **Closing the Lesson** Have children look back at the subtraction exercises on page 301. Ask, What do you think 20 – 11 will be?

★ Test Prep

20 Listen. Mark the space next to your answer.

There are 10 people in line. 7 more get in line. How many are in line now? Which fact solves the problem?

○ $10 - 7 = 3$ ● $10 + 7 = 17$

○ $17 - 7 = 10$ ○ $10 + 0 = 10$

Unit 11 • Lesson 11

**Problem Solving Strategy:
Draw a Picture**

Problem

José is third in line.
There are **8** more children behind him.
How many children are in the line?

1 Understand

Ask, What are you being asked to do?

I need to find out how many children are
in the line.

2 Decide

Ask, What strategy can you use to solve the problem?

I can draw a picture to find out.

3 Solve

Ask, How many children does your picture show?

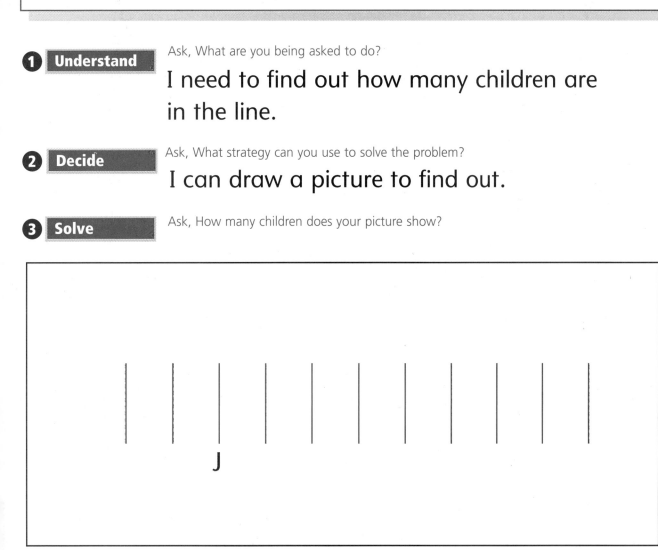

J

I can count __| |__ children in my picture.

There are __| |__ children in line.

4 Look back

Ask, How can you check that your answer is correct?

I can check my answer by adding.

3 + 8 = 11

My answer makes sense.

Draw a picture to solve.

1. There are **16** children in the classroom. **9** of them are girls. The rest are boys. How many are boys?

   _____**7**_____ are boys.

(Possible pictures are shown.)

```
X  X  X  X  X  X  X  X
G  G  G  G  G  G  G  G

X ( X  X  X  X  X  X  X )
G
        Boys
```

2. There are **12** eggs in a carton. **4** are broken. How many are not broken?

   _____**8**_____ eggs

```
o  o  o  o  o  o

o  o  ⊗  ⊗  ⊗  ⊗
```

3. There are **17** cups of milk. **5** are large, **6** are small. The rest are medium. How many are medium?

   _____**6**_____ cups

```
L  L  L  L  L  S  S  S

S  S  S  ☐ ☐ ☐ ☐ ☐
                medium
```

4. How can you check that your answer to problem **1** makes sense?_____

Answer will vary. Possible answer: Subtract 16 − 9 = 7. _____

_____

_____

Teacher Note: **Closing the Lesson** Ask, What other strategy could you use to solve problem 3?

304 (three hundred four)   Unit 11 • Lesson 12

Add. (11A)

1.
$$
\begin{array}{r}
8 \\
+\ 7 \\
\hline
15
\end{array}
$$

2.
$$
\begin{array}{r}
8 \\
+\ 8 \\
\hline
16
\end{array}
$$

3.
$$
\begin{array}{r}
9 \\
+\ 6 \\
\hline
15
\end{array}
$$

4.
$$
\begin{array}{r}
6 \\
+\ 7 \\
\hline
13
\end{array}
$$

5.
$$
\begin{array}{r}
9 \\
+\ 7 \\
\hline
16
\end{array}
$$

6.
$$
\begin{array}{r}
5 \\
+\ 8 \\
\hline
13
\end{array}
$$

7.
$$
\begin{array}{r}
10 \\
+\ 8 \\
\hline
18
\end{array}
$$

8.
$$
\begin{array}{r}
9 \\
+\ 9 \\
\hline
18
\end{array}
$$

9.
$$
\begin{array}{r}
7 \\
+\ 7 \\
\hline
14
\end{array}
$$

10.
$$
\begin{array}{r}
5 \\
+\ 9 \\
\hline
14
\end{array}
$$

Subtract. (11A)

11.
$$
\begin{array}{r}
14 \\
-\ 7 \\
\hline
7
\end{array}
$$

12.
$$
\begin{array}{r}
16 \\
-\ 8 \\
\hline
8
\end{array}
$$

13.
$$
\begin{array}{r}
15 \\
-\ 8 \\
\hline
7
\end{array}
$$

14.
$$
\begin{array}{r}
13 \\
-\ 6 \\
\hline
7
\end{array}
$$

15.
$$
\begin{array}{r}
15 \\
-\ 9 \\
\hline
6
\end{array}
$$

16.
$$
\begin{array}{r}
13 \\
-\ 4 \\
\hline
9
\end{array}
$$

17.
$$
\begin{array}{r}
17 \\
-\ 9 \\
\hline
8
\end{array}
$$

18.
$$
\begin{array}{r}
19 \\
-\ 9 \\
\hline
10
\end{array}
$$

19.
$$
\begin{array}{r}
13 \\
-\ 8 \\
\hline
5
\end{array}
$$

20.
$$
\begin{array}{r}
16 \\
-\ 9 \\
\hline
7
\end{array}
$$

Complete the fact family. (11C)

21.

$9 + 3 = \boxed{12}$

$3 + \boxed{9} = \boxed{12}$

$\boxed{12} - \boxed{9} = \boxed{3}$

$\boxed{12} - \boxed{3} = \boxed{9}$

22.

$7 + 5 = \boxed{12}$

$5 + \boxed{7} = \boxed{12}$

$\boxed{12} - \boxed{7} = \boxed{5}$

$\boxed{12} - \boxed{5} = \boxed{7}$

Ring the names for the number. (11B)

23. 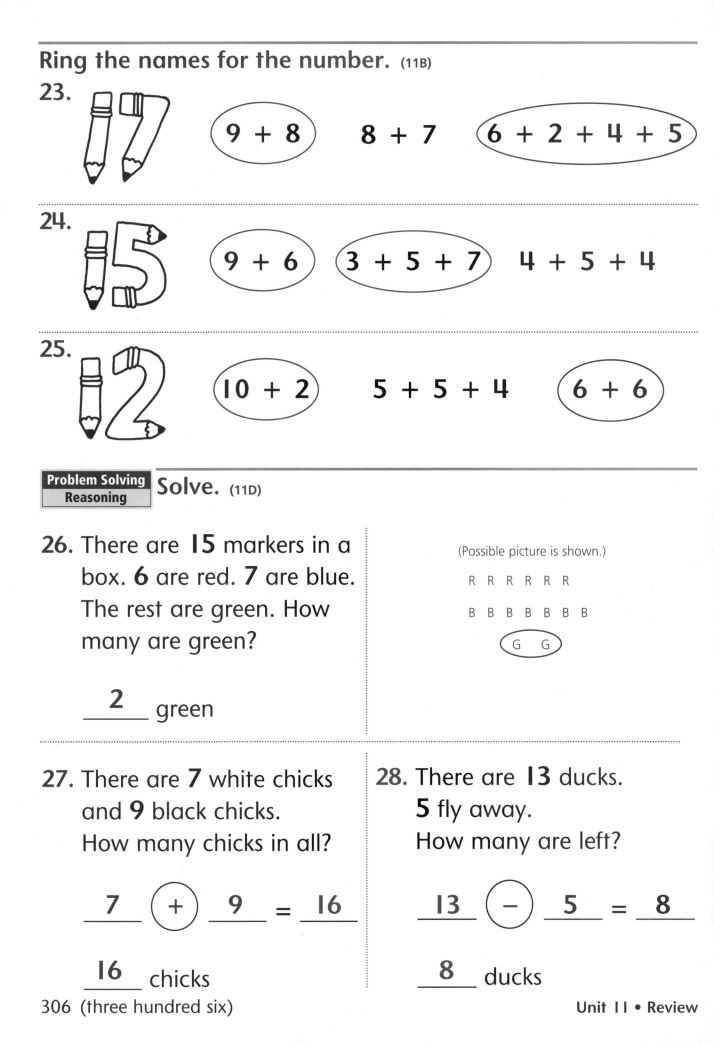 $9 + 8$ $8 + 7$ $6 + 2 + 4 + 5$

24. $9 + 6$ $3 + 5 + 7$ $4 + 5 + 4$

25. $10 + 2$ $5 + 5 + 4$ $6 + 6$

Problem Solving Reasoning Solve. (11D)

26. There are **15** markers in a box. **6** are red. **7** are blue. The rest are green. How many are green?

(Possible picture is shown.)

R R R R R R

B B B B B B B

G G

____2____ green

27. There are **7** white chicks and **9** black chicks. How many chicks in all?

___7___ $\left(+ \right)$ ___9___ $=$ ___16___

___16___ chicks

28. There are **13** ducks. **5** fly away. How many are left?

___13___ $\left(- \right)$ ___5___ $=$ ___8___

___8___ ducks

Name _____

1 Which fraction of the rectangle is shaded? Mark the space under your answer. **(10B)**

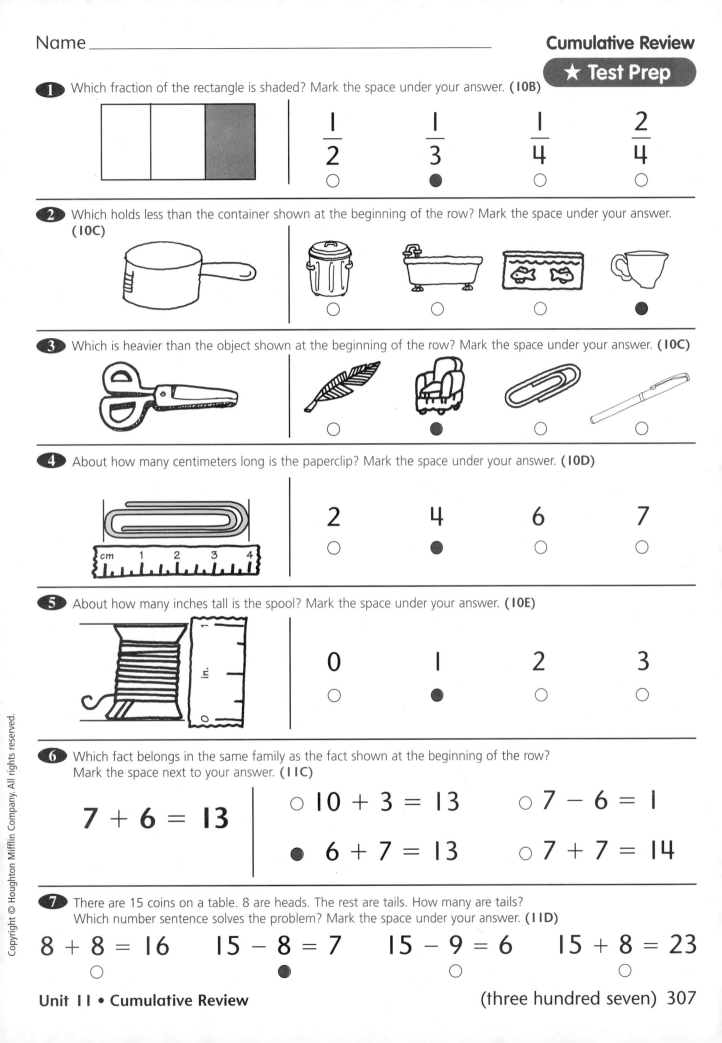

$\frac{1}{2}$ ○

$\frac{1}{3}$ ●

$\frac{1}{4}$ ○

$\frac{2}{4}$ ○

2 Which holds less than the container shown at the beginning of the row? Mark the space under your answer. **(10C)**

○   ○   ○   ●

3 Which is heavier than the object shown at the beginning of the row? Mark the space under your answer. **(10C)**

○   ●   ○   ○

4 About how many centimeters long is the paperclip? Mark the space under your answer. **(10D)**

2 ○

4 ●

6 ○

7 ○

5 About how many inches tall is the spool? Mark the space under your answer. **(10E)**

0 ○

1 ●

2 ○

3 ○

6 Which fact belongs in the same family as the fact shown at the beginning of the row? Mark the space next to your answer. **(11C)**

$7 + 6 = 13$

○ $10 + 3 = 13$ ○ $7 - 6 = 1$

● $6 + 7 = 13$ ○ $7 + 7 = 14$

7 There are 15 coins on a table. 8 are heads. The rest are tails. How many are tails? Which number sentence solves the problem? Mark the space under your answer. **(11D)**

$8 + 8 = 16$ ○

$15 - 8 = 7$ ●

$15 - 9 = 6$ ○

$15 + 8 = 23$ ○

Decide on an answer. Mark the space for your answer. If the answer is **not here**, mark the space for **NH**.

8 (9A)

$$54$$
$$+24$$

30　　70　　78　　NH
○　　○　　●　　○

9 (9A)

$$71$$
$$+18$$

67　　89　　99　　NH
○　　●　　○　　○

10 (9B)

$$63$$
$$-40$$

20　　23　　30　　NH
○　　●　　○　　○

11 (9B)

$$98$$
$$-28$$

60　　78　　76　　NH
○　　○　　○　　●

12 (11A)

$$9$$
$$+4$$

14　　13　　12　　NH
○　　●　　○　　○

13 (11A)

$$16$$
$$-7$$

9　　8　　6　　NH
●　　○　　○　　○

14 (11A)

$$10$$
$$+8$$

10　　8　　2　　NH
○　　○　　○　　●

15 (11A)

$$6$$
$$+8$$

12　　13　　14　　NH
○　　○　　●　　○

add

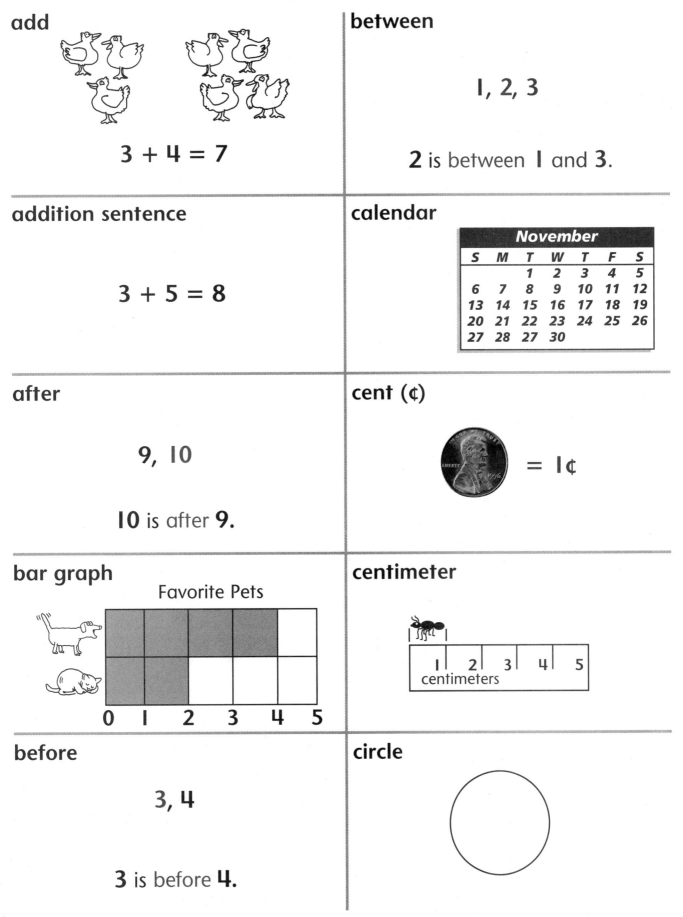

$$3 + 4 = 7$$

between

1, 2, 3

2 is between **1** and **3**.

addition sentence

$$3 + 5 = 8$$

calendar

November						
S	**M**	**T**	**W**	**T**	**F**	**S**
		1	*2*	*3*	*4*	*5*
6	*7*	*8*	*9*	*10*	*11*	*12*
13	*14*	*15*	*16*	*17*	*18*	*19*
20	*21*	*22*	*23*	*24*	*25*	*26*
27	*28*	*27*	*30*			

after

9, 10

10 is after **9**.

cent (¢)

= **1¢**

bar graph

Favorite Pets

0   1   2   3   4   5

centimeter

| 1 | 2 | 3 | 4 | 5 |
centimeters

before

3, 4

3 is before **4**.

circle

Picture Glossary

cone

dime

10¢   10 cents

corner

corner

equal parts

4 equal parts.

cube

equals

2 + 6 = 8

2 plus 6 equals 8.

cylinder

is equal to

4 = 4

4 is equal to 4.

difference

$8 - 4 = 4$

$$\begin{array}{r} 8 \\ -\ 4 \\ \hline 4 \end{array}$$

difference

face

face

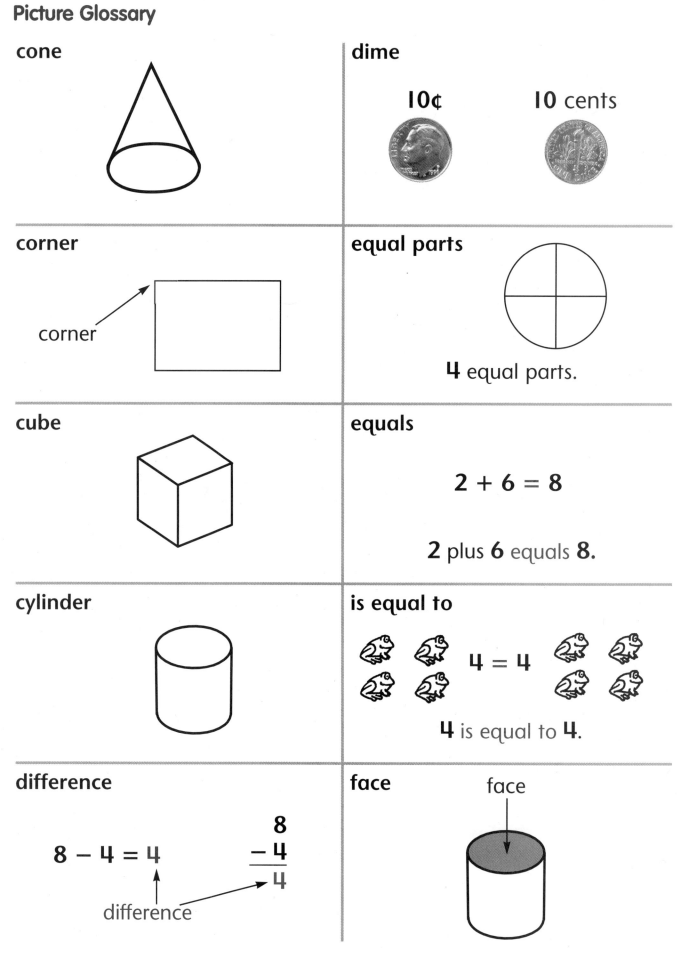

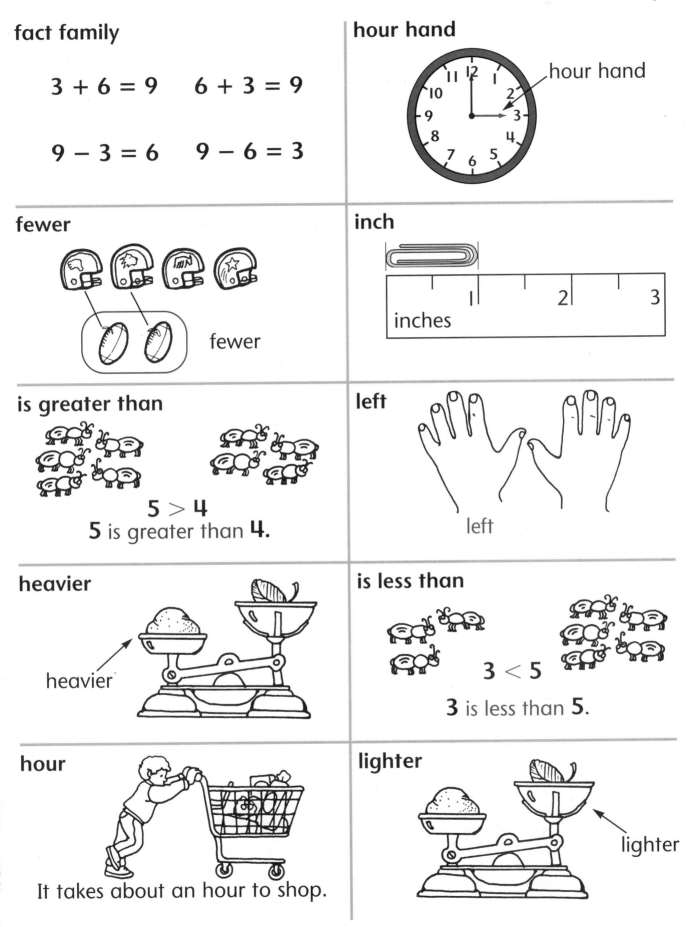

fact family

$$3 + 6 = 9 \qquad 6 + 3 = 9$$

$$9 - 3 = 6 \qquad 9 - 6 = 3$$

hour hand

hour hand

fewer

fewer

inch

inches

is greater than

$$5 > 4$$

5 is greater than 4.

left

left

heavier

heavier

is less than

$$3 < 5$$

3 is less than 5.

hour

It takes about an hour to shop.

lighter

lighter

Picture Glossary

longer

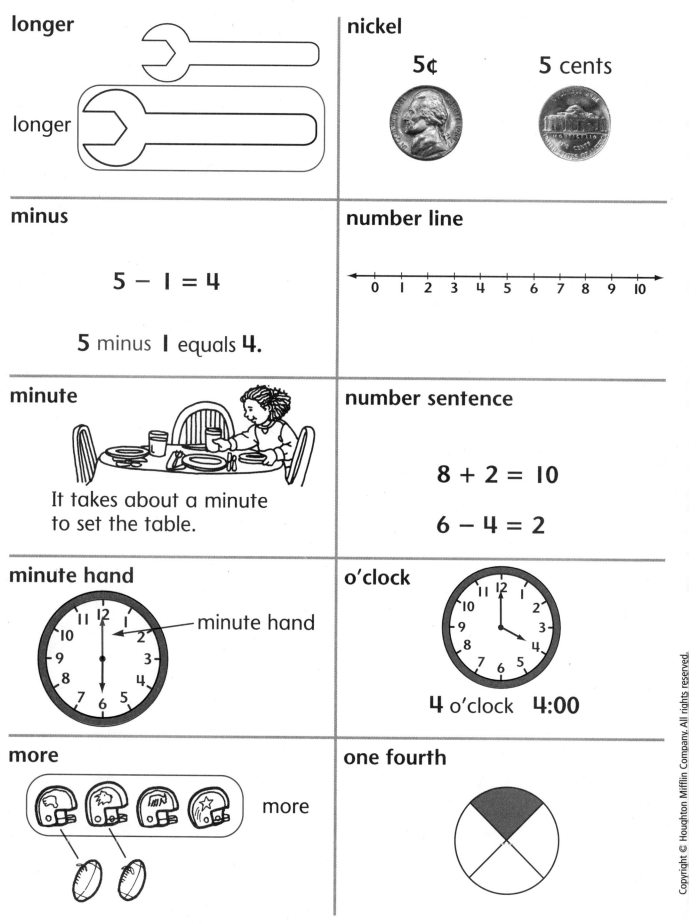

longer

nickel

5¢   5 cents

minus

$$5 - 1 = 4$$

5 minus 1 equals 4.

number line

0 1 2 3 4 5 6 7 8 9 10

minute

It takes about a minute
to set the table.

number sentence

$$8 + 2 = 10$$

$$6 - 4 = 2$$

minute hand

← minute hand

o'clock

4 o'clock   4:00

more

more

one fourth

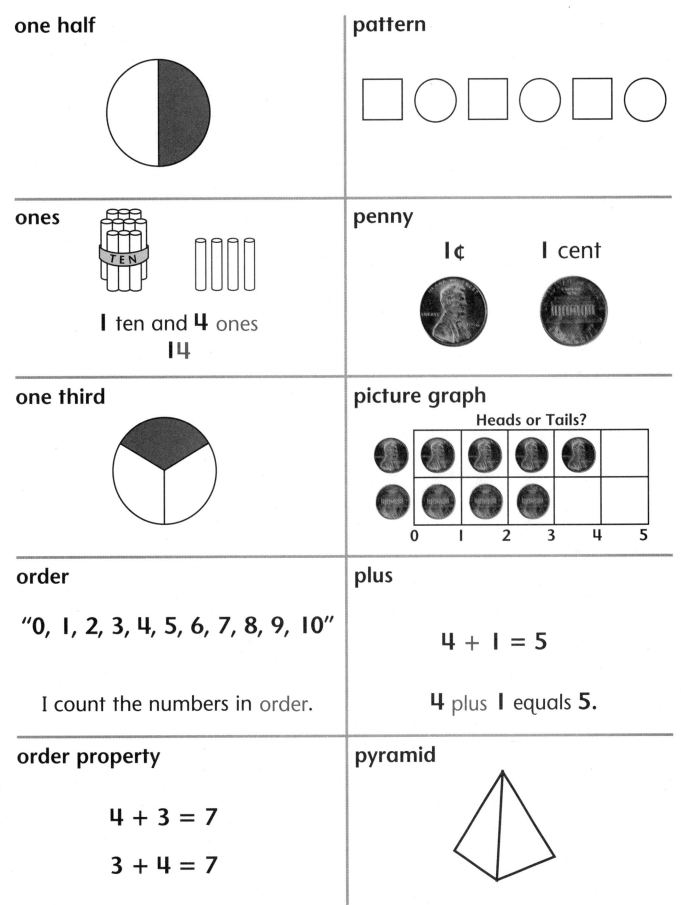

one half

pattern

ones

I ten and **4** ones
14

penny

I¢   I cent

one third

picture graph

Heads or Tails?

0   I   2   3   4   5

order

"0, I, 2, 3, 4, 5, 6, 7, 8, 9, 10"

I count the numbers in order.

plus

4 + I = 5

4 plus I equals **5**.

order property

4 + 3 = 7

3 + 4 = 7

pyramid

Picture Glossary

quarter

25¢   25 cents

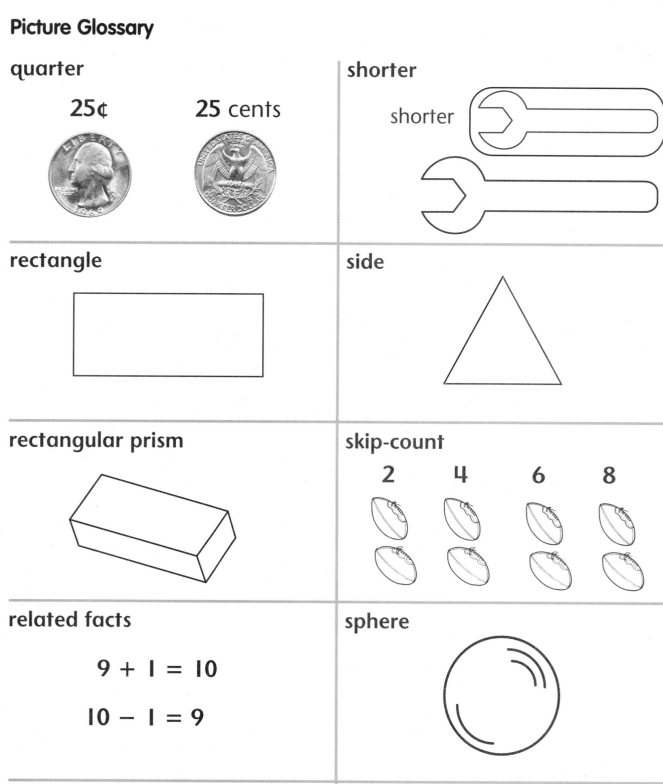

shorter

shorter

rectangle

side

rectangular prism

skip-count

2   4   6   8

related facts

$$9 + 1 = 10$$

$$10 - 1 = 9$$

sphere

right

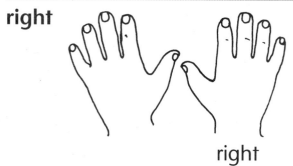

right

square

subtract

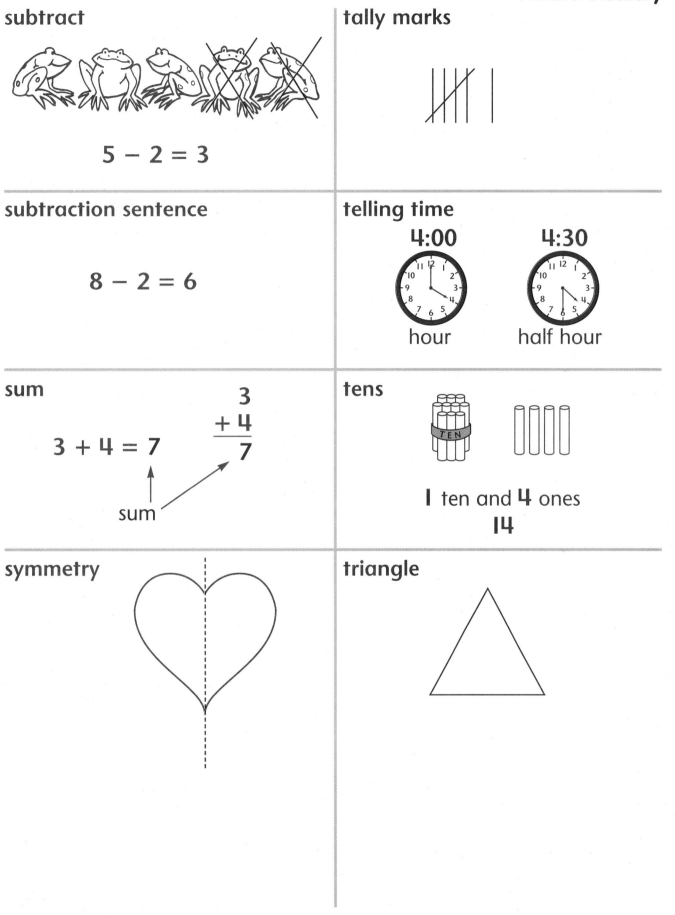

$$5 - 2 = 3$$

tally marks

subtraction sentence

$$8 - 2 = 6$$

telling time

4:00   **4:30**

hour   half hour

sum

$$3 + 4 = 7$$

$$\begin{array}{r} 3 \\ + 4 \\ \hline 7 \end{array}$$

sum

tens

TEN

I ten and **4** ones
14

symmetry

triangle

HOUGHTON MIFFLIN

Math
Steps

Scope and Sequence

Scope and Sequence

The following chart indicates the scope and sequence of the topics in *MathSteps*.
Type printed in bold denotes that a topic is being introduced. Although a topic might
appear at each level, the material will vary in place and depth. Use student page
references to see how the instruction varies.

Number Sense

K	1	2
Comparing	Comparing	Comparing
numbers	numbers to 10	**fractions** 103–104
numbers to 5 91–92, 95–96, 154, 156	**greater** 47–48, 179	whole numbers
numbers 6 to 10 119–120, 125–126, 160, 170	**greatest** 48, 179	greater 38
one more 162, 247	**least** 50, 180	greatest 38, 264
quantities	**lesser** 49, 179	least 38, 264
equal to 136	**using < and >** 51–52	using graphs to compare 51–54, 239–240
fewer 77–78, 95, 135, 138	**using <, > and =** 53–54, 180	**using =, ≠** 23–24, 75
fewest 80, 92, 170	**numbers to 99**	using <, > 25–26, 38, 67, 75, 250, 252, 254, 264
greater than 136	**using <, > and =** 179–180	Counting
greatest 170	quantities	quantities
less than 136	fewer 30, 32, 36, 102	quantities to 19 37–38
more than 75–76, 91–92, 95–96, 103, 119–120, 125–126, 135, 137, 138	more 29, 31, 38, 101	quantities to 100 41
most 79, 91	one fewer 30, 194	**quantities to 1,000** 249
one more 75–76, 162	one more 40, 73–74, 194	whole numbers
one-to-one correspondence 73–78, 83, 129–130	one-to-one correspondence 29–32	numbers through 19 37–38
same number 73–74	**using graphs to compare** 57–60	numbers through 100 39–42, 45, 249–263
some, all, none 81–82, 84	Counting	**numbers through 109** 251
Counting	numbers	**numbers through 200** 254
matching	numbers through 10 33–42	**numbers through 300** 255–256
numerals with quantities to 5 85–90, 93–94, 97–99, 101–102	numbers through 19 181–182	**numbers through 400** 257–258
numerals with quantities 6 to 10 113–116, 121–124, 127–128, 133	**numbers through 50** 183–184	**numbers through 500** 259–260
numerals with quantities 11 to 30 247–254, 259–262	**numbers through 100** 185–188	**numbers through 1,000** 249, 263–266
numbers	quantities	**Decimal notation in money** 267–274
numbers through 5 85–90, 93–94, 97–99, 151–155	quantities to 10 30, 34, 36–42	Estimating
numbers 6 to 10 113–116, 121–124, 127–128, 133, 151–164, 169–170	quantities to 19 167–169	for reasonableness of answers 47–48
numbers 11 to 30 247–254, 259–262	**quantities to 50** 173–174, 189	quantities 47–48, 68
quantities	**quantities to 80** 175, 189–190	using a referent 47–48, 68, 125–126, 128
quantities to 5 83–84, 85–90, 93–94, 97–99, 102	**quantities to 100** 177, 189	Fractions
quantities to 10 113–116, 121–124, 127–128, 133, 152–164, 169–170	Estimating	**comparing** 103–104, 106
quantities to 30 247–254, 259–262, 267–268	for reasonableness of answers 159–160, 189–190, 221–222	equal parts 253–254
money 221–226	quantities 159–160, 189–190	fractional parts of a region
	using a referent 189–190	**eighths** 105
	Fractions	**fifths** 105
	equal parts 253–254	fourths 103
	fractional parts of a region	halves 103
	one fourth 257–258, 260	**ninths** 105
	one half 255–256, 260	**sixths** 105
	one third 259–260	**tenths** 105
	meaning of fractions 255–260	thirds 103
	modeling fractions 255–260	
	Money	
	dime 155–156, 158, 159–160, 215–220, 241	

K

word names to ten 85–88, 93, 97, 113, 115, 121, 123, 127

Estimating
   for reasonableness of answers 105–106, 267–268
   quantities 105–106, 137–138, 267–268

Fraction concepts
   equal parts 237–240
   halves 239–240

Money
   dime 225–226
   nickel 223–224
   penny 221–222

Number line 113, 115, 117–118, 121, 123, 127, 131–132, 136, 257

Number meanings 85–90, 93–94, 97–99, 101–102, 113–116, 121–124, 127–128, 133, 247–254, 259–262

Number relationships 100, 117–118, 131–132, 134, 152, 257–258

Ordering whole numbers
   numbers to 5 100
   numbers 6 to 10 117–118, 131–132, 134
   numbers 11 to 30 257–258

Place value
   expanded form 247, 249, 251, 253
   making groups of ten 259–262
   pictorial models
      tens and ones 247–254, 259–262
   standard form 247, 249, 251, 253, 259–262
   2-digit numbers
      through 12 247–248
      through 16 249–250
      through 20 251–252
      through 30 253–254

Reading whole numbers
   numbers through 5 85–102
   numbers 6 to 10 113–127, 131–132, 135–136
   numbers 11 to 30 247–254, 259–262

Writing whole numbers
   numbers to 10 151–162, 169–170
   numbers 11 to 30 247, 249, 251, 253, 259–262, 265–266

1

nickel 83–84, 110, 155–156, 158, 159–160, 213–220
penny 43–44, 83–84, 109–110, 155–156, 158–160, 213–220
quarter 219–220

Hundred chart 193–194

Names for numbers
   using diagrams 169, 171, 173, 175, 177
   using expressions 70, 169–170, 173, 175, 177, 286, 292, 298
   using models 167–169, 171–175, 177, 286

Number line 45–50, 52, 181–186

Number meanings 33–42, 167–170

Number relationships 45–46, 181–186

Ordering whole numbers
   numbers to 10
      after 45–46
      before 45–46
      between 45–46
   numbers to 19
      after 181–182
      before 181–182
      between 181–182
   numbers to 50
      after 183–184
      before 183–184
      between 183–184
   numbers to 100
      after 185–186
      before 185–186
      between 185–186

Ordinal numbers 191–192

Place value
   in addition
      tens and ones without regrouping
         chart 229–234
         picture models 229–232
   expanded form 169–170, 173, 175–178
   making groups of tens 171–172
   making groups of tens and ones 167–170, 173–178, 179
   pictorial models 167–175, 177, 179, 229–232
   place value chart 169, 171, 173, 175–178
   standard form 167–178, 229–234
   in subtraction
      tens and ones without regrouping
         chart 235–240
         picture models 235–238
   2-digit numbers
      through 19 167–170
      to 50 173–174
      to 80 175–176

2

fraction of a number 107–108
fractional parts of a set 107–108
meaning of fractions 103, 105
modeling 103–107
non-unit fractions 105–106, 108
recognizing fractional equivalent of one whole 105
unit fractions 103–104, 107

Hundred chart 45–46, 255–259

Money
   dime 55–58, 215–218, 269–270
   dollar 269–270, 272
   half–dollar 271–272
   nickel 215–218
   penny 57–58, 217–218
   quarter 219–220

Names for numbers
   using diagrams 21, 37–42, 251, 253, 257, 259, 262
   using expressions 21–22, 251, 253, 255, 257, 259, 261–262
   using models 37–39, 41, 249, 251, 253, 259, 261–262

Number line 49

Number meanings 37–44, 249–262

Number relationships 38–39, 45–46, 49–50, 249, 251, 254, 256, 258, 260, 263

Ordering whole numbers
   numbers to 19 (before, after, between) 38
   numbers to 100 39, 45–46, 49–50
      after 46
      before 46
      between 46
   numbers to 1,000 249, 251, 254, 256, 258, 260, 263
      after 254, 256, 260, 263
      before 254, 256, 260, 263
      between 254, 256, 258, 260

Ordinal numbers 213–214

Place value
   and addition
      tens and ones without regrouping
         chart 139–140
         picture models 139–140
      tens and ones with regrouping
         chart 143, 145–147, 149–151, 153, 157–158
         picture models 143, 145–147, 149, 157
      hundreds, tens, and ones with regrouping
         chart 283–284
      hundreds, tens, and ones without regrouping
         chart 279–281

Number Sense *continued*

K

1

through 99 177–178
whole numbers
 tens and ones 167–170, 173–178
 tens 171–172
Reading numbers
 fractions
  symbols 255–260
  words 255, 257, 259
 whole numbers
  through 10 33–42
  through 19 167–170
  to 50 173–174
  to 80 175–176
  through 99 177–178
  word names
   through nineteen 167–169
   through ninety 171–172
   through ten 33–40
Skip-counting
 by 2's 188, 245
 by 5's 188, 213–214, 216, 246
 by 10's 171–172, 184, 187, 215–216
Writing
 whole numbers
  through 10 33–42
  through 19 167–170
  to 50 173–174
  to 80 175–176
  through 99 177–178

2

expanded form 43–44, 251–253, 255, 257, 259, 261–262
groups of hundreds 249
groups of hundreds, tens, and ones 251, 253
groups of tens 39–40
groups of tens and ones 37–38, 41–44, 143, 145–147, 149
pictorial models 37–39, 41, 143, 145–147, 149, 169–171, 173, 175, 179, 181, 185, 249–251, 253, 261–262
place-value chart 37–42, 249, 251, 253, 255, 257, 259, 261–262
and subtraction
 hundreds, tens, and ones with regrouping
  chart 283–286
 hundreds, tens, and ones without regrouping
  chart 279–281
 tens and ones with regrouping
  chart 171–175, 179–181, 185, 187
  picture models 171, 173, 175, 179, 181, 185
 tens and ones without regrouping
  chart 167, 169–170
  picture models 167, 169–170
standard form 37–44, 249–263
3-digit numbers
  through 109 251–252
  through 200 253–254
  through 300 255–256
  through 400 257–258
  through 500 259–260
  through 1,000 249–250, 261–263
2-digit numbers
  through 19 37–38
  through 99 39–44
 whole numbers
  hundreds 249–263
  ones 37–38, 41–44, 251–263
  tens 37–44, 251–263
Reading numbers
 fractions
  words 103, 105
  symbols 103, 105–108
 whole numbers
  through 99 39–40, 42–44
  through 109 251–252
  through 200 253–254
  through 300 255–256
  through 400 257–258
  through 500 259–260
  through 1,000 261–263
  word names through ninety 39
Skip-counting
 by 2's 49, 297–300

Number Sense *continued*

K	1	2

		by **3's** 49, 301
		by **5's** 50, 303
		by **10's** 50, 311
		by 100's 249
		Writing
		  fractions 104–105
		  whole numbers
		    through 19 37–38
		    through 99 39–46, 49–50
		    through 109 251–252
		    through 200 253–254
		    through 300 255–256
		    through 400 257–258
		    through 500 259–260
		    through 1,000 261–263

Computation and Operations

K	1	2

Addition
  adding whole numbers 179–188
  concrete/pictorial representations 177–188, 199–202, 247, 249, 251, 253–254
  horizontal form 181–188
  meaning of addition
    as joining 177–188
    as increasing 247, 249, 251, 253
    as part, part, whole 179–188, 200
  number sentences 181–188
  readiness for addition
    adding 1 181–187, 247, 253
    adding 2 179, 181, 183, 185–188, 247
    adding 3 179–188, 249
  story problems 177–178, 199–202
  strategies for adding
    counting on 247, 249, 251, 253
  symbols
    equals sign (=) 181
    plus sign (+) 181
Mental Math
  counting on 247, 249
  using patterns 251, 253
Subtraction
  concrete/pictorial representations 189–202
  horizontal form 193–198
  meaning of subtraction
    as take away 191–200, 202
  number sentences 193–198
  readiness for subtraction
    subtracting 1 191–197
    subtracting 2 191, 193–196
	Addition
	  adding 0 77–78
	  adding 1 more 73–74
	  adding two-digit and one-digit numbers
	    without regrouping 229–230, 233
	  adding two-digit and two-digit numbers
	    multiples of ten 232, 241
	    without regrouping 231–232, 234, 241–244
	  adding whole numbers 69–82, 115–126, 137–150, 281–284, 287–302
	  basic addition facts
	    through 6 67–82, 115–130
	    through 10 137–144
	    through 12 281–286
	    through 16 287–292
	    through 18 293–298
	    through 20 301–302
	  concrete/pictorial representations 69–78, 85–88, 115–120, 123–128, 137, 139–141, 143–150, 229–232, 281–282, 287–288 293–294
	  fact families
	    through 6 117–120, 125–126
	    through 10 139–140, 143–144
	    through 12 285
	    through 16 291
	    through 18 297
	  horizontal form 69–74, 79, 81–82, 117–119, 123, 125–126, 137, 139–150, 281, 285–287, 291–293, 297–298, 301
	  meaning of addition
	    as increasing 73–74, 149–150, 299–300
		Addition
		  adding whole numbers 3–9, 13–20, 27–28, 53–54, 65–70, 73–84, 137–141, 143–154, 189–192, 252, 279–284
		  basic addition facts
		    to 10 3–8
		    to 14 13–16
		    to 16 65–70
		    to 18 73–78
		    to 20 83–84
		  concrete/pictorial representations 7–8, 13, 17–18, 65–66, 67, 69, 73, 77, 83, 137, 139–140, 143, 145–147, 149, 157
		  fact families
		    through 10 7–8
		    through 14 15–16
		    through 16 69–70
		    through 18 77–78
		    through 20 83–84
		  horizontal form 4–5, 7, 9, 13–15, 17–18, 27–28, 53–54, 65, 67–69, 73–74, 77, 79, 83–84, 137–138, 153, 191–192, 252
		  meaning of addition
		    as increasing 13–14, 81
		    as joining 27–28, 53–54
		  part, part, whole 11–12, 14, 67
		  missing addends 9–10, 15–16, 20, 67, 69–70, 74–75, 77–78, 80, 82, 153
		  money 155–156, 287–292
		  number sentences 4–5, 7, 9, 13–15, 17–18, 27–28, 53–54, 65, 67–69, 73–74, 77, 79, 83–84, 137–138, 153, 191–192, 252

Computation and Operations *continued*

K

subtracting 3 191, 194–196, 198–199
story problems 189–190, 199–202
subtracting whole numbers 193–200, 202
symbols
   equals sign (=) 181–182, 193
   minus sign (−) 193

1

as joining 67–69, 71–72, 85–86, 128–130, 142, 144, 230, 244
as part-part-whole 67–70, 75–78, 137–141, 143–144
missing addends 87–88, 149–150
money 84, 131–132, 157–158, 241–242
number sentences 69–74, 79, 81–82, 115, 117–119, 123, 125–126, 130, 137, 139–150, 281, 285–287, 291–293, 297–298, 301
properties
   grouping property 145–148
   order property 79–82
   zero property 77–78
related facts
   through 4 115–116
   through 6 123–124
   through 8 137–138
   through 10 141–142
   through 12 281–284
   through 16 287–290
   through 18 293–296
story problems 67–68, 71–72, 85–86, 122, 129–130, 142, 144, 146, 150, 230, 242–244, 284, 290, 296, 299–300, 303–304
strategies for adding
   counting on 73–74, 230
   using properties 77–82, 145–148
symbols
   equals sign (=) 69–70
   plus sign (+) 69–70, 129–130, 243–244, 299–300
three addends
   through 7 145–146
   through 10 147–148
   through 18 286, 292, 298
using place value concepts
   tens and ones without regrouping
      chart 229–234
      picture models 229–232
vertical form 75–78, 80, 85–86, 116, 120, 124, 129, 138, 145–148, 229–234, 243–244, 282–284, 288–289, 294–296
Mental Math
   counting on 73–74, 194, 230
   using patterns 193–194, 301
   one less 193–194
   one more 40, 73–74, 193–194
   ten less 193–194
   ten more 193–194
   using properties 77–82, 145–148
Multiplication readiness
   skip-counting
      by 2's 188, 245
      by 5's 188, 213–214, 216, 246
      by 10's 171–172, 184, 187, 215–216

2

properties
   grouping property 17–18, 79–80
   order property 3–4, 79–80, 284
related facts
   through 10 5–6
   through 14 13–14
   through 16 65–66
   through 18 73–74, 153
repeated addition and multiplication 298
story problems 11–12, 27–28, 53–54, 71–72, 75–76, 85–86, 119–120, 142, 150, 152, 154, 159–160, 161–162, 183–184, 239–240, 286, 292, 307–308
strategies for adding
   adding tens and fives 137–138
   counting on 144, 148
   mental math 3–5, 137–138, 144, 148, 282
   using patterns 81, 83–84, 138
   using properties 3–4, 17–20, 79–80, 284
three addends 17–20, 79–80, 157–158
   1-digit addends 17–20, 79–80
   2-digit addends 157–158
   2-digit numbers with regrouping 145–146, 149–150, 152, 154, 189–190, 191–192
   2-digit numbers without regrouping 83–84, 167–170, 176, 191–192
   2-digit and 1-digit numbers with regrouping 143–144, 147–148, 151, 153, 157–158, 191–192
   2-digit and 1-digit numbers without regrouping 141, 279
   3-digit and 2-digit numbers without regrouping 280
   3-digit numbers with regrouping 283–284
   3-digit numbers without regrouping 281–282
   multiples of ten 137–138
using place value concepts
   hundreds, tens, and ones with regrouping
      chart 283–284
   hundreds, tens, and ones without regrouping
      chart 279–281
   tens and ones with regrouping
      chart 143, 145–147, 149–151, 157–158
      picture models 143, 145–147, 149, 157
   tens and ones without regrouping
      chart 139–140
      picture models 139–140

K	1	2

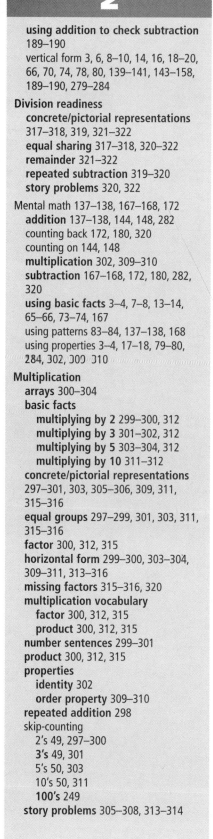

Computations and Operations *continued*

K	1	2
	subtracting whole numbers 97–108, 115–126, 129–130, 137–144, 281–297, 299–302	**symbol**, times (×) 299
	symbols	**vertical form** 301–304
	equals sign (=) 69–70	**whole numbers** 299–304, 309–312, 315–316
	minus sign (−) 97–98, 243–244, 299–300	One less 46
	using place value concepts	One more 46
	tens and ones without regrouping	Subtraction
	chart 235–240	basic subtraction facts
	picture models 235–238	through 10 5–8
	vertical form 99–100, 106, 116, 120, 124, 129, 138, 235–240, 243–244, 282–284, 288–290, 294–296	through 14 13–16
	Ten less 193–194	through 16 65–70
	Ten more 187, 193–194	through 18 73–78

K	1	2
		2-digit and 1-digit numbers without regrouping 169–170, 179–180, 185–186, 191–192
		2-digit numbers with regrouping 173–176, 181–182, 187–192
		2-digit numbers without regrouping 83–84, 167–170, 176, 191–192
		3-digit and 1-digit numbers without regrouping 279
		3-digit and 2-digit numbers without regrouping 280
		3-digit numbers with regrouping 285–286
		using place-value concepts
		hundreds, tens, and ones with regrouping chart 283–286
		hundreds, tens, and ones without regrouping chart 279–281
		tens and ones with regrouping chart 171–175, 179–181, 185, 187 **picture models** 171, 173, 175, 179, 181, 185
		tens and ones without regrouping chart 167, 169–170 picture models 167, 169–170
		vertical form 6, 8, 10, 14, 16, 20, 66, 70, 74, 78, 169–176, 179–182, 185–190, 279–282, 285–286
		Ten less 46
		Ten more 46

Algebra and Functions

K

Meaning of + 181

Meaning of − 193

Meaning of = 181, 193

Number sentences
- addition number sentences 181–188
- completing number sentences 181–188, 193–198
- subtraction number sentences 193–198
- writing number sentences 187–188

Patterns
- describing patterns
  - color patterns 65–66
  - geometric patterns 63–64, 66
  - number patterns 167–168
  - shape patterns 61–62, 167–168
  - size patterns 65–66
- extending patterns
  - color patterns 63, 65–66
  - geometric patterns 63–64
  - number patterns 167–168
  - shape patterns 61–62, 66, 167–168
  - size patterns 65–66
- finding patterns to solve problems 167–168
- identifying patterns 61–66
  - color patterns 63, 65–66
  - geometric patterns 63–64
  - number patterns 167–168
  - shape patterns 61–62, 66, 167–168
  - size patterns 65–66
- using patterns
  - to make predictions 61–66
  - to solve problems 167–168

1

Expressions as names for numbers 70, 171–178, 286, 292, 298

Functions
- **find a function rule** 152
- **follow a function rule** 152–153
- **tables** 152–153

Grouping property 145–148

Inverse operations 115–120, 123–126, 137–144, 281–285, 287–291, 293–297

Location on a grid 21–22

Making true sentences 100, 127–128

Meaning of + 69–70, 85–86, 127–130, 243–244, 299–300

Meaning of − 97–98, 127–130, 243–244, 299–300

Meaning of = 69–70

Missing addends 87–88, 149–150

Missing numbers 46, 54, 100, 181–182, 184, 186–188

Names for numbers 70, 171–178, 286, 292, 298

Number sentences
- addition number sentences 69–74, 79, 81–82, 115, 117–119, 123, 125–126, 130, 137, 139–150, 281, 285–287, 291–293, 297–298, 301
- completing number sentences 69–74, 79–82, 97–98, 101–106, 115, 117–119, 123, 125–126, 130, 137, 139–144, 146–150, 281, 285–287, 291–293, 297, 301
- **formulating and solving a problem with a number sentence**
  - **addition sentence** 71–72, 85–86, 122, 129–130, 243–244, 299–300
  - **subtraction sentence** 103–104, 107–108, 121–122, 129–130, 243–244, 299–300
- subtraction number sentences 97–98, 101–108, 115, 117–119, 123, 125–126, 130, 137, 139–144, 281, 285–287, 291–293, 297, 301
- writing number sentences
  - **to solve addition problems** 71–74, 78, 119, 139–140, 142–144
  - **to solve subtraction problems** 100, 103–104, 119, 126, 130, 142–144

Order property 79–82

Patterns
- describing patterns
  - color patterns 16
  - geometric patterns 15–16
  - number patterns 46, 193–194, 301
  - shape patterns 15–16

2

Coordinate grid 101–102

Expressions as names for numbers 21–22, 251, 253, 255, 257, 259, 261–262

Functions
- find a function rule 29–30, 81
- follow a function rule 29, 81, 312
- tables 29–30, 81, 312

Grouping property of addition 17–18, 79–80

Identity property of multiplication 302

Inequalities 23–26, 38, 67, 75, 250, 252, 254, 264

Inverse operations 5–6, 13–14, 65–66, 73–74, 153, 189–190

Meaning of + 27–28, 53–54, 279

Meaning of − 27–28, 53–54, 279

Meaning of = 23–24

Meaning of ≠ 23–24

Meaning of × 299

Missing addends 9–10, 15–16, 20, 67, 69–70, 74, 77–78, 80, 82, 153

Missing factors 315–316, 320

Missing numbers 29–30, 38, 45–46, 49–50, 67, 249, 251, 254, 256, 258, 260, 263, 265–266

Number sentences
- addition number sentences 4–5, 7, 9, 13–15, 17–18, 27–28, 53–54, 65, 67–69, 73–74, 77, 79, 83–84, 137–138, 153, 191–192, 252
- completing number sentences 4–5, 7, 9, 13–15, 17–18, 27–28, 53–54, 65, 67–69, 73–75, 77, 79, 83–84, 137–138, 153, 167–168, 183–184, 191–192, 239–240, 252, 299–300, 305–306, 313–314, 319
- Making true sentences 23–26, 75
- **multiplication number sentences** 299–300, 303–306, 309–311, 313–316
- subtraction number sentences 5, 7, 13–15, 27–28, 53–54, 65, 69, 73, 75, 77, 83–84, 167–168, 191–192, 319
- writing number sentences
  - to solve addition problems 27–28, 53–54, 68, 71–72, 75–76, 85–86, 119–120, 161–162, 183–184, 239–240
  - **to solve multiplication problems** 305–306, 313–314
  - to solve subtraction problems 27–28, 53–54, 68, 71–72, 75–76, 85–86, 119–120, 161–162, 183–184, 239–240

K	1	2

	size patterns 15–16
	extending patterns 15–16, 193–194, 301
	   color patterns 16
	   geometric patterns 15–16
	   number patterns 46, 181–182, 184, 186–188, 193–194
	   shape patterns 15–16
	   size patterns 15–16
	finding patterns to solve problems 15–16, 46, 193–194
	identifying patterns
	   color 16
	   geometric 15–16
	   number 46, 181–182, 184, 186–188, 193–194, 301
	   size 15–16
	   shape 15–16
	in a hundred chart 193–194
	in tables 245–246
	using patterns
	   in addition and subtraction 115–120, 123–126, 137–144, 281–285, 287–291, 293–297, 301
	   to make predictions 15–16
	   to solve problems 46, 193–194, 301
	
	Symbols showing relations
	   equal (=) 53–54
	   greater than (>), less than, (<) 51–54
	
	Zero property 77–78
		Order property
		   of addition 3–4, 79–80, 284
		   of multiplication 309–310
		Patterns
		   describing patterns
		     number 29–30, 83, 265–266
		   extending patterns
		     number 29, 38, 45, 49–50, 83–84, 138, 249, 251, 254, 256, 258, 260, 263, 265–266, 312
		   finding patterns to solve problems 84, 265–266
		   identifying patterns
		     number 29–30, 45–46, 49–50, 83, 138, 168, 249, 251, 249, 251, 254, 256, 258, 260, 263, 265–266
		   in tables 29–30
		   in a hundred chart 45–46, 255–259, 265–266
		   using patterns
		     in addition and subtraction 29–30, 83–84, 137–138, 167–168
		     in multiplication 312
		     to make predictions 45–46, 49–50, 265–266
		     to solve problems 84, 255–259
		Symbols showing relations
		   equal (=), **not equal (≠)** 23–24, 75
		   greater than (>), less than(<) 25–26, 38, 67, 75, 250, 252, 254, 264

Measurement

K	1	2

Capacity
   holds more 235
   holds less 236
Comparing measurements
   capacity 235–236
   length, height 25–32, 228
   weight 233–234
Estimating measurements
   area 105–106
   length 227–232
Length
   nonstandard units 227–232
	Capacity
	   holds more, holds less 273
	   holds the most, holds the least 274
	   measuring with nonstandard units 274
	Comparing measurements
	   capacity 273–274
	   length, height 261–264, 270
	   weight 271–272
	Customary measurement
	   length 265–266
	Estimating measurement
	   length 261–264
	Length
	   centimeter 267–270, 269–270
		Area readiness 123–124
		Capacity
		   cup, pint, quart, gallon 127
		   liter 128
		   nonstandard units 128
		Comparing measurements
		   capacity 127–128
		   length, height 118
		   weight 125
		Customary measurement
		   capacity 127
		   length 117–118
		   weight 125
		Estimating measurement
		   area 123–124

Scope and Sequence Algebra and Functions

Measurement *continued*

K	1	2
	use a calendar 211–212	modeling amounts 58, 221, 223–224, 268, 270–271

Geometry

K

Identifying equal parts 237–240

Plane figures
  classifying by attributes 11–20
  drawing or constructing 20, 149–150
  identifying 11–20
    circles 11–12
    rectangles 17–18
    squares 13–14
    triangles 15–16
  related to solid shapes 9–10
  same shape 9–10, 41
  same size and shape 43–44

Positional words
  above 49
  after 55, 58
  before 55–58
  below 50
  between 57–58
  first 51–54
  last 52, 54
  left 59–60
  middle 53
  right 59–60

Solid figures
  classifying by attributes 3–8, 19–20
  identifying solid figures
    cones 7–8
    cubes 3–4
    spheres 5–6
  relating to plane figures 9–10
  relating to real-world objects 4, 6, 8

Spatial sense 10, 26, 41, 43–44

1

Identifying equal parts 17–18, 253–254, 256

Location on a grid 21–22

Plane figures
  classifying by attributes 7–8, 11–14
  drawing or constructing 6, 12
  identifying plane figures
    circle 7–8
    rectangle 7–8
    square 7–8
    triangle 7–8
  relating to solid figures 5–6
  same shape 8
  same size and shape 13–14
  sides and corners 11–12

Positional words
  above 20
  after 9–10
  before 9
  behind 20
  below 20
  between 9–10
  far 19
  left 19
  near 19
  next to 19, 20
  right 20

Solid figures
  classifying by attributes 3–4
  identifying solid figures
    cone 3–4
    cube 3–4
    cylinder 3–4
    pyramid 3–4
    rectangular prism 3–4
    sphere 3–4
  relating to plane figures 5–6
  relating to real-world objects 3, 6

Spatial sense 6, 17–18

Symmetry
  in geometric figures 18
  in real-world objects 17–18

2

Combining and subdividing figures 99–100

Congruent figures 97

Identifying equal parts 253–254

Location on a grid 101–102

Plane figures
  classifying by attributes 95–96, 97
  drawing or constructing 95, 99–100, 102
  identifying plane figures
    circle 95
    rectangle 95
    square 95
    triangle 95
  relating to solids figures 95–96
  same figure 95, 101
  same size and shape 97
  sides and corners 96

Solid figures
  classifying by attributes 93–94
  comparing solid figures 94
  faces, edges, corners 93
  identifying solid figures
    cone 93–94
    cube 93–94
    cylinder 93–94
    pyramid 93–94
    rectangular prism 93–94
    sphere 93–94
  relating to plane figures 95–96
  same figure 102

Spatial sense 99–100

Symmetry 98

Statistics, Data Analysis, and Probability

Scope and Sequence Data Analysis, Statistics, and Probability

Mathematical Reasoning

K

Classifying and sorting
  by coin 221–226
  by differences 41–46
  by function 45–48
  by pattern 41–48, 61–66, 143
  by position (above, after, before, below, between, bottom, first, last, top) 49–60
  by shape 3–8, 11–20, 41–44, 46, 103–104, 163–166
  by similarities 41–46
  by size 21–30, 41–44

Determining the effect of operations 177–202

Discussing 10, 18, 26, 42, 46–48, 178, 188, 229, 234, 236, 250, 267, 268

Drawing conclusions 211–214, 234, 236

Explaining reasoning 33–34, 46–48, 55–56, 62, 66, 105–106, 129–130, 167–168, 201–202, 250

Identifying relationships
  magnitude of numbers 91–92, 95–96, 119–120, 125–126, 154, 156, 160, 170
  position 49–60

Justifying thinking 33, 46, 56, 130, 170, 228, 229, 234, 236

Listening 177–178, 189–190

Logical reasoning 42, 47–48, 56, 178, 188, 190, 228, 250, 265

Making decisions
  choosing an operation 202
  choosing a strategy 170
  deciding which belongs 46, 48
  deciding which does not belong 45–46, 48
  deciding what information is known 33–34, 47–48, 105–106, 129–130, 163–164, 167–168, 199–200, 201–202, 213–214, 229–230, 255–256, 267–268
  deciding what information is needed 105–106, 129–130, 167–168, 199–200, 201–202, 229–230, 255–256, 267–268
  deciding what materials are needed 19–20, 33–34, 60, 199–200, 229–230

Making predictions 105–106, 212, 218, 229–230, 265, 267–268

Number meanings 85–90, 93–94, 97–99, 101–102, 113–116, 121–124, 127–128, 133, 247–254, 259–262

Number relationships 91–92, 95–96, 100, 117–118, 125–126, 131–132, 134, 152, 257–258

Reasonableness of method and solution 33–34, 105–106, 129–130, 167–168, 229–230, 267–268

Relative magnitude of numbers 91–92,

1

Classifying and sorting
  by position (before, after, between) 9–10
  by shape 3–4, 7–8, 12–14, 102
  by size 13–14

Comparing and contrasting 8, 98, 120, 174

Determining the effect of operations 67–74, 77–78, 85–86, 95–96, 101–102, 127–130, 142, 151–152, 299–300

Discussing 8, 10, 74, 76, 98, 206, 264, 286, 292

Drawing Conclusions 76, 180, 221, 264

Explaining reasoning 10, 15, 31–32, 52, 71, 74, 121–122, 128, 193, 206

Formulating and solving problems
  with a subtraction sentence 104, 107–108, 122, 210
  with an addition sentence 71–72, 85–86, 122

Identifying relationships
  basic facts 79–82, 115–120, 123–126, 137–144, 148, 281–298
  direction 21–22, 191–192
  location 22
  magnitude of numbers 47–54, 179–180
  measurement 264
  position 9–10, 19–20, 191–192

Justifying thinking 31–32, 103, 107, 189–190

Listening 67–68, 95–96

Logical reasoning 8, 152, 180, 182, 218–220, 232, 238, 264

Making connections among similar problems 15–16, 31–32, 71–72, 80, 85–86, 103–104, 107–108, 116, 118, 121–122, 130, 159–160, 189–190, 193–194, 243–246, 264, 303–304

Making decisions
  choosing a strategy 46, 48, 50, 70, 80, 84, 102, 110, 116, 118, 124, 126, 130, 140, 152, 154, 156, 180, 218, 238, 298
  choosing an operation 103, 127–130, 243–244, 299–300
  deciding what information is known 31, 71, 103, 138, 144, 159–160, 221–222
  deciding what information is needed 31–32, 121, 193, 221–222
  deciding which belongs 12, 140, 148
  deciding which does not belong 12, 140

Making predictions 15–16, 159–160, 189–190, 221–222

Naming attributes used to sort and classify 4

2

Classifying and sorting
  by position or location 101–102
  by shape 93–95, 97, 101–102

Comparing and contrasting 8, 16, 38, 44, 51–52, 54, 56, 65, 94, 104, 106, 130, 183–184, 236, 273–274, 310

Determining the effects of operations 5–6, 13–14, 24, 27–30, 53–54, 68, 71–72, 76, 86, 119–120, 190, 239–240, 291–292, 299, 302, 307–308

Discussing 52, 65, 144

Drawing conclusions 10, 30, 38, 56, 70, 104, 116, 124, 161–162, 206, 234, 236, 243–244, 274, 302, 307

Explaining reasoning 11, 26, 30, 38, 47, 52, 54, 56, 71–72, 80, 85, 99, 104, 118, 120, 124, 144, 159, 168, 190, 193, 212, 216, 223, 234, 240, 265, 274, 291, 302, 305, 307–308

Formulating and solving problems
  with a subtraction sentence 162, 184
  with an addition sentence 86, 158, 162, 184

Generalizing 4, 8, 16, 18, 65, 116, 118, 130, 138, 168, 190, 208, 236, 243–244, 282, 302, 310

Identifying relationships
  basic facts 3–8, 10, 13–16, 23–24, 65–66, 78
  direction, location, position 101–102
  magnitude of numbers 25–26, 38, 51, 67, 75, 250, 252, 254, 264
  measurement 116, 118

Identifying relevant information 71–72, 76, 161–162, 183–184

Justifying thinking 11, 18, 26, 47, 56, 72, 80, 85, 104, 106, 116, 118, 124, 190, 193, 206, 211, 216, 234, 236, 265, 274, 289, 302, 308

Logical reasoning 4, 11–12, 18, 30, 65, 70–72, 116, 142, 190, 216, 223–224, 234, 240, 243–244, 274, 292

Making connections among similar problems 10, 11–12, 16, 21–22, 84, 138, 168, 193–194, 289–290

Making decisions
  choosing a strategy 22, 27–28, 56, 68, 72, 82, 100, 104, 106, 118, 119–120, 142, 150, 152, 154, 156, 174, 176, 178, 182, 188, 286, 322
  choosing an operation 24, 27–28, 53–54, 68, 71–72, 75–76, 85–86, 119–120, 183–184, 193, 239–240, 291–292, 307–308

Mathematical Reasoning *continued*

K

95–96, 119–120, 125–126, 154, 156, 160, 170

Sequencing 100, 117–118, 131–132, 134, 152, 211–212, 257–258

Using strategies to find solutions 33–34, 47–48, 105–106, 129–130, 167–168, 199–200, 229–230, 267–268

Vocabulary development 3–8, 11–18, 21–32, 49, 73–82, 85–88, 93–94, 97–98, 113–116, 121–124, 127–128, 135–136, 181, 193, 209–210, 215, 221, 223, 225, 239–240

Writing 266

1

Number meanings 33–42, 167–178

Number relationships 45–46, 181–186

Prove or disprove 180, 189–190, 219, 221–222

Reasonableness of method and solution 15–16, 31–32, 71–72, 103–104, 121–122, 159–160, 193–194, 221–222, 245–246, 303–304

Recognizing more than one solution to a problem 31–32, 34, 48, 50, 70, 154, 156, 218–219

Relative magnitude of numbers 47–52, 179–180

Sequencing 171–172, 181–188, 193–194, 201

Using strategies to find solutions 15–16, 31–32, 67–68, 71–72, 95–96, 103–104, 121–122, 159–160, 189–190, 193–194, 221–222, 245–246, 269–270, 303–304

Visual Thinking 9–10, 13–14, 21–22, 189–190

Vocabulary development 3, 5, 7, 9–10, 19–20, 29–30, 33–39, 43, 45, 47–50, 69, 97, 155, 167–169, 171–172, 191, 206, 219, 255–259, 271–274

Writing 16, 84, 120, 128, 152, 154, 160, 170, 174, 180, 210, 246, 301, 304

2

deciding what information is known 11, 47, 161–162, 291–292

deciding what information is needed 11, 47, 53–54, 71–72, 85, 99, 123, 161–162, 183–184, 211, 273–274, 289

Making predictions 47–48, 123–124, 159–160, 234, 241–244, 265–266

Naming attributes used to sort and classify 29–30, 94

Number meanings 37–44, 249–262

Number relationships 38–39, 45–46, 49–50, 249, 251, 254, 256, 258, 260, 263

Prove or disprove 26, 30, 52, 56, 99, 190, 206, 216, 274, 292, 308, 310

Reasonableness of method and solution 11–12, 27, 47–48, 72, 85–86, 99–100, 120, 123–124, 159–160, 193–194, 223–224, 239–240, 243–244, 265–266, 289–290, 305–306

Recognizing more than one solution to a problem 22, 80, 162, 223–224

Relative magnitude of numbers 25–26, 38, 67, 75, 104, 250, 252, 254, 264

Sequencing 38–39, 45–46, 49–50, 249, 251, 254, 256, 258, 260, 263, 265–266

Solving a simpler problem 193–194, 289–290

Using strategies to find solutions 11–12, 47–48, 85–86, 99–100, 123–124, 159–160, 193–194, 223–224, 243–244, 265–266, 289–290, 305–306

Visual Thinking 11–12, 47–48, 97–98, 99–100, 123–124

Vocabulary development 17–18, 39–40, 45–46, 79–80, 93, 95, 97–98, 103, 117–118, 121–122, 126–130, 215–220, 237–238, 241–242, 269, 299, 312

Writing 4, 8, 12, 16, 18, 38, 54, 56, 70, 72, 80, 83, 86, 94, 104, 116, 118, 120, 124, 130, 138, 158, 162, 168, 184, 190, 206, 208, 211, 216, 234, 236, 240, 274, 282, 292, 302, 310, 314

Problem Solving

K

Applications
  Addition Applications 177–180, 199–202
  Calendar Applications 265–266
  Choosing an Operation 202
  Statistics Applications 103–104, 139–140, 165–166, 255–256
  Subtraction Applications 189–192, 199–202
  Using a Bar Graph 103–104, 139–140, 255–256
  Using Manipulatives 33–34, 104, 105–106, 165, 199–200, 227–228, 229–230
  Using a Picture 19–20, 59–60, 101–102, 163–164, 201–202, 213–214

Skills
  looking back 33, 47, 105, 129, 167, 199, 229, 267
  representing problems 33–34, 46, 60, 124, 129–130, 165–166, 199–200, 240
  using a four-step process 33–34, 47–48, 105–106, 129–130, 167–168, 199–200, 229–230, 267–268

Strategies
  Act It Out 33–34, 47–48, 199–200
  Choose an Operation 202
  Conjecture and Verify 105–106, 229–230, 267–268
  Draw a Picture 129–130
  Find a Pattern 167–168

1

Applications
  Addition Applications 67–68, 71–72, 85–86, 122, 129–130, 142, 144, 146, 243–244, 284, 290, 296, 299–300, 303–304
  Calendar Applications 211–212
  Choosing an Operation 129–130, 142, 243–244, 299–300
  Geometry Applications 102
  Measurement Applications 261, 269–272, 274
  Money Applications 44, 84, 110, 132, 154, 158–160, 218, 221–222, 242, 299–300
  Place-Value Applications 168, 174, 176
  Probability Applications 55–57
  Statistics Applications 57–60, 153
  Subtraction Applications 95–96, 107–108, 121–122, 129–130, 138, 142, 144, 243–244, 284, 290, 296, 299–300, 303–304
  Time Applications 201–202, 209–210
  Use a Graph 59–60
  Use a Chart 263–264
  Use a Picture 19–20, 85–86, 103–104, 107–108, 157–158, 189–190, 191–192
  Use a Table 153–154, 209–210, 245–246
  Using Manipulatives 67–68, 95–96, 269–270

Skills
  formulating problems 72, 85–86, 104, 107–108, 121–122, 210
  looking back 15, 31, 71, 103, 121, 159, 193, 221, 245, 269, 303
  reading for understanding 15, 21, 71, 103, 121, 159, 193, 221, 245, 269, 303
  representing problems 4, 12, 19–20, 29–32, 72, 67–68, 97–100, 104–110, 122, 138, 144, 150, 303–304
  using a four-step process 15–16, 31–32, 71–72, 103–104, 121–122, 159–160, 193–194, 221–222, 245–246, 269–270, 303–304

Strategies
  Act It Out 67–68, 95–96, 269–270
  Choose an Operation 127–130, 243–244, 299–300
  Conjecture and Verify 159–160, 189–190, 221–222
  Draw a Picture 31–32, 104, 121–122, 138, 144, 150, 303–304
  Find a Pattern 15–16, 193–194
  Make a Table 245–246
  Write a Number Sentence 71–72, 103–104, 142

2

Applications
  Addition Applications 11–12, 27–28, 53–54, 68, 71–72, 75–76, 85–86, 119–120, 142, 150, 152, 154, 159–160, 161–162, 183–184, 239–240, 286, 292, 307–308
  Calendar Applications 214, 308
  Choosing an Operation 24, 27–28, 53–54, 68, 71–72, 75–76, 85–86, 119–120, 183–184, 193, 239–240, 291–292, 307–308
  Division Readiness Applications 320, 322
  Geometry Applications 94, 99–100
  Measurement Applications 116, 118, 119–120, 121–122, 123–124, 193–194
  Money Applications 56, 156, 178–179, 216, 223–224, 273–274, 288–290
  Multiplication Applications 305–308, 313–314
  Not Enough Information 161–162
  Place Value Applications 265–266
  Probability Applications 241–244
  Statistics Applications 51–54, 183–184, 231–240, 313
  Subtraction Applications 11–12, 27–28, 53–54, 68, 71–72, 75–76, 82, 85–86, 119–120, 161–162, 174, 176, 182, 183–184, 188, 193–194, 239–240, 286, 292, 307–308
  Time Applications 208, 211–212
  Too Much Information 71–72, 76
  Using a Bar Graph 51–54, 235, 239–240
  Using a Picture 47–48, 99–100, 101–102, 117, 123–124, 231–232, 273–274
  Using a Schedule 211–212
  Using a Table or Chart 29–30, 81, 183–184, 233–234, 237, 244, 265–266
  Using Manipulatives 95, 99–100, 115–116, 123–124, 243–244, 305–306

Skills
  formulating problems 86, 158, 162, 184, 212
  looking back 11, 47–48, 85, 99, 123, 159, 193, 223, 243, 265, 274, 289, 305
  reading for understanding 11, 47–48, 85, 99, 123, 159, 193, 223, 289, 291, 305
  representing problems 11–12, 14, 28, 40, 72, 86, 99–100, 106, 208, 303, 305–306
  using a four–step process 11, 47, 85, 99, 123, 159, 193, 223, 243, 265, 289, 305

Strategies
  Act it Out 305–306

Problem Solving *continued*

K	**1**	**2**
		Choose an Operation 24, 27–28, 53–54, 68, 71–72, 75–76, 85–86, 119–120, 183–184, 193, 239–240, 291–292, 307–308
		Conjecture and Verify 47–48, 68, 99–100, 115–116, 123–124, 159–160
		Draw a Picture 11–12, 14, 28, 95, 99–100, 208
		Find a Pattern 138, 168, 265–266
		Make a List 223–224
		Make a Table 243–244
		Solve a Simpler Problem 193–194, 289–290
		Write a Number Sentence 68, 71–72, 75–76, 85–86, 119–120, 239–240, 305–308

Index

Index

Index